NOV 2 2 2005

W9-ABZ-409

Camden House History of German Literature

Volume 7

The Literature of Weimar Classicism

The Camden House History of German Literature

Volume 7

The Camden House History of German Literature

Edited by James Hardin

Vol. 1: Early Germanic Literature and Culture
Edited by Brian Murdoch and Malcolm Read,
University of Stirling, UK

Vol. 2: German Literature of the Early Middle Ages
Edited by Brian Murdoch, University of Stirling, UK

Vol. 3: German Literature of the High Middle Ages
Edited by Will Hasty, University of Florida

Vol. 4: Early Modern German Literature
Edited by Max Reinhart, University of Georgia

Vol. 5: German Literature of the Eighteenth Century:
The Enlightenment and Sensibility
Edited by Barbara Becker-Cantarino, Ohio State University

Vol. 6: Literature of the Sturm und Drang
Edited by David Hill, University of Birmingham, UK

Vol. 7: The Literature of Weimar Classicism
Edited by Simon Richter, University of Pennsylvania

Vol. 8: The Literature of German Romanticism
Edited by Dennis F. Mahoney, University of Vermont

Vol. 9: German Literature of the Nineteenth Century, 1832–1899
Edited by Clayton Koelb and Eric Downing,
University of North Carolina

Vol. 10: German Literature of the Twentieth Century:
From Aestheticism to Postmodernism
Ingo R. Stoehr, Kilgore College, Texas

The Literature of
Weimar Classicism

Edited by
Simon Richter

CAMDEN HOUSE

PT
311
.L58
2005

Copyright © 2005 by the Editor and Contributors

All Rights Reserved. Except as permitted under current legislation, no part of this work may be photocopied, stored in a retrieval system, published, performed in public, adapted, broadcast, transmitted, recorded, or reproduced in any form or by any means, without the prior permission of the copyright owner.

First published 2005
by Camden House

Camden House is an imprint of Boydell & Brewer Inc.
668 Mt. Hope Avenue, Rochester, NY 14620, USA
www.camden-house.com
and of Boydell & Brewer Limited
PO Box 9, Woodbridge, Suffolk IP12 3DF, UK
www.boydellandbrewer.com

ISBN: 1–57113–249–X

Library of Congress Cataloging-in-Publication Data

The literature of Weimar classicism / edited by Simon J. Richter.
    p. cm. — (Camden House history of German literature; v. 7)
Includes bibliographical references and index.
ISBN 1–57113–249–X (hardcover : alk. paper)
    1. German literature—18th century—History and criticism. 2. Classicism
—Germany—Weimar (Thuringia)—History—18th century. I. Richter,
Simon. II. Title. III. Series.

PT311.L58 2005
830.9'145—dc22

                                                                2005007642

  A catalogue record for this title is available from the British Library.

This publication is printed on acid-free paper.
Printed in the United States of America.

58546257

Contents

Illustrations

Preface and Acknowledgments

WEIMAR CLASSICISM (roughly the period from Johann Wolfgang von Goethe's return to Germany from Italy in 1788 to the death of his friend and collaborator Friedrich Schiller in 1805) is widely regarded as an apogee of literary art, the brief historical moment when a handful of German writers seemed to rival Homer, Virgil, and Dante, and a small duchy in Germany vied with the glory of Athens, Rome, and Florence. Although many scholars dispute the legitimacy of regarding Weimar Classicism as a distinct period, arguing that it is a species of European Romanticism, there is no disputing the significance of many works produced during this time. The present volume offers readers a major reference work characterized by new approaches to the key figures, literary works, and cultural contexts of Weimar. Contributions from leading German, British, and North American scholars open up multiple interdisciplinary perspectives on the period. Major essays on drama, poetry, and the novel are joined by accounts of the role of antiquity, politics, philosophy, aesthetics, visual culture, women writers, and science. Readers are introduced to the full panoply of cultural life in Weimar, its groundbreaking accomplishments as well as its excesses and follies. Sympathetic and critical at the same time, this volume identifies in Weimar Classicism an aspiration to wholeness of life that, however problematic, still warrants the attention of the educated world.

Many have participated in bringing this volume to life. First and foremost I would like to thank the distinguished contributors who rose to the challenge of surpassing previous accounts of Weimar Classicism (and there are many!) with new approaches and fresh insights. Cumulatively, they have succeeded in producing a distinctly new vision of Weimar Classicism that will stand for many years. For their assistance in helping me clarify my own thinking on Weimar Classicism now reflected in the introduction to this volume, I am grateful to the students who participated in a graduate seminar on Classicism in 2002 at the University of Pennsylvania. Many ideas and positions were first formulated in interaction with them. My thanks to the editor of the Camden House History of German Literature, James Hardin, for his intellectual engagement with the project, his willingness to give and take, and his prodding and patience. It has been a pleasure to work with Jim Walker, the Camden House editor, whose assistance in the editing process has been swift and judicious. I gratefully acknowledge that without the generous support of Dean Rebecca Bushnell and

Dean Joseph Farrell at the University of Pennsylvania the juggling act that was necessary to complete this volume would have been a disaster. I owe a huge debt of gratitude to Matt Kalamar, my research assistant for two years, who tirelessly hunted down quotations, found English translations for German passages, brought the essays into conformity with house guidelines, and assembled the bibliography. Finally, I would like to mention the forbearance and understanding of my family, Tina, Toby, and Sam, who too often did without Papa in the hope that soon this project would be done.

Simon Richter
Philadelphia, Pennsylvania, 2005

Conventions, Editions, and Abbreviations

Conventions of This Volume

THE LIFE DATES OF INDIVIDUALS are given in parentheses at the first mention. Titles of works are given in German throughout, with an English translation and date of first publication also at first mention. Readers who consult essays out of sequence will therefore find the index helpful. All quotations from the German are followed by a translation in English by the author of the respective article unless it is explicitly indicated that an existing translation has been used.

Goethe and Schiller Editions and Abbreviations

Contributing authors cite from a number of Goethe and Schiller editions. The abbreviations and editions are listed here rather than in the individual endnotes.

BA   Johann Wolfgang von Goethe. *Werke*. Berliner Ausgabe (Berlin edition). Ed. Deutsche Akademie der Wissenschaften zu Berlin. 24 vols. Berlin: Akademie, 1952–73.

FA   Johann Wolfgang von Goethe. *Sämtliche Werke, Briefe, Tagebücher und Gespräche*. Frankfurter Ausgabe (Frankfurt edition). Ed. Dieter Borchmeyer et al. 40 vols in 2 secs. Frankfurt am Main: Deutscher Klassiker Verlag, 1985–.

HA   Johann Wolfgang von Goethe. *Werke*. Hamburger Ausgabe (Hamburg edition). Ed. Erich Trunz. 14 vols. Hamburg: Wegner, 1948–60.

MA   Johann Wolfgang von Goethe. *Sämtliche Werke nach Epochen seines Schaffens*. Münchner Ausgabe (Munich edition). Ed. Karl Richter et al. 20 vols. Munich: C. Hanser, 1985–98.

NA   Friedrich von Schiller. *Schillers Werke*. Nationalausgabe (national edition). Ed. Julius Petersen et al. 42 vols. Weimar: Hermann Böhlaus Nachfolger, 1943–.

SW Friedrich von Schiller. *Sämtliche Werke*. Ed. Gerhard Fricke and Herbert G. Göpfert. 5 vols. Munich: C. Hanser, 1958–59.

WA Johann Wolfgang von Goethe. *Goethes Werke*. Weimarer Ausgabe (Weimar edition; aka Sophienausgabe). Weimar: Hermann Böhlaus Nachfolger, 1887–1919.

WuB Friedrich von Schiller. *Werke und Briefe*. Ed. Klaus Harro Hilzinger et al. 12 vols. Frankfurt am Main: Deutscher Klassiker Verlag, 1988–2004.

Other References

For ease of reference, poems and plays by Goethe and Schiller that are typically numbered by line in almost all editions are cited by line number only.

In the case of letters, many of which come from the Schiller-Goethe correspondence, references are often confined to the author, date, and recipient of the letter. Readers will easily locate relevant letters in editions of the correspondence and in the FA, NA, and WA.

References to Johann Peter Eckermann's *Gespräche mit Goethe* (Conversations with Goethe, 1835) and Kanzler Friedrich von Müller's *Unterhaltungen mit Goethe* (Conversations with Goethe, 1870) are indicated by the date of the conversation.

Goethe in the Italian Campagna
by Johann Heinrich Wilhelm Tischbein, oil on canvas, 1786.
Courtesy of Städelsches Kunstinstitut,
Frankfurt am Main. Photograph © Ursula Edelmann.

Introduction

Simon Richter

IF LITERARY HISTORIANS agree on anything, it is that Weimar Classicism as a distinct literary period ought not to exist. And of course they are right. Literary periodization is heuristic and even arbitrary under the best of circumstances. But to assert that the efforts of two men, Johann Wolfgang von Goethe (1749–1832) and Friedrich Schiller (1759–1805), from the time of the former's eye-opening journey to Italy in 1786 to the death of the latter in 1805, constitute a literary period in its own right seems excessive. Not only is the membership of the putative period so small (we could and will add lesser known names to the list) and so local (confined to those residing or sojourning in the small duchy of Saxe-Weimar, or wishing they did), the major problem, as many critics have shown, is that the characteristics of Weimar Classicism are perfectly consistent with those of European Romanticism, a bona fide literary period that easily embraces the phenomenon under discussion.[1] Indeed, as twentieth-century scholars have never tired of pointing out, from the perspective of English and French literary history, Goethe and Schiller are among Germany's premiere Romantic writers. Only nineteenth-century German nationalism thought to exalt them to the level of the classical.[2] Even Goethe himself can readily be enlisted in the effort to debunk the myth of Weimar Classicism. In an essay written at the height of Weimar Classicism and published in *Die Horen*, Schiller's journal for the propagation of classical aesthetics and literature, Goethe categorically dismisses the possibility of a German classicism on the grounds that the requisite political and cultural conditions for the *Bildung* (formation or education) of classical authors simply were not given.[3] Whether he leaves the door open for individual writers to achieve a status comparable to the classical is another question. Nor should we ignore the fact that Schiller often and flatteringly stylized Goethe as a classic in modern times.

Nonetheless, Weimar Classicism is here to stay. Unwittingly, the detractors and doubters of Weimar Classicism have themselves increasingly become responsible for the term's continued durability. Every conference, every article, anthology, and monograph that calls into question the legitimacy of Weimar Classicism — and there have been many — further entrenches the concept.[4] Because of this sustained and considerable critical attention, Weimar Classicism has become an enduring cliché, an indestructible straw man for tireless ideology critique, an irresolvable myth in constant need of demythologizing. In the end, no one is happy: neither the person who is invested in a notion of Goethe and Schiller's unique literary accomplishments, who may feel assailed and offended by the interminable barrages leveled at the authors, nor the person who views literature from a cultural perspective and favors a model of complexity to one of monumentality or derision. Both are ill served with the image of Weimar Classicism evoked through dismissive critique. No wonder that some scholars, in a laudable effort to break with the constraints and petty politics of periodization, avoid the designation altogether and speak of the time "around 1800" instead.

When all is said and done — and this is the cumulative contention of this volume, despite the differences in outlook of the individual contributors — there is and was a Weimar Classicism. I will not maintain that it constituted a discreet literary period, although I will accept the slightly less arbitrary dates of 1786 and 1805 as the beginning and terminus of a local cultural phenomenon that attracted European, even world attention and set itself apart.[5] In terms of period, this volume in the Camden House History of German Literature will assume that the texts that Goethe, Schiller, and others wrote during this time necessarily participate in the traditions and conventions of both the Enlightenment and Romanticism, in addition to bearing affinities to the Sturm and Drang, that other problematic period of German literary history. Readers are therefore advised to consult the other relevant volumes in the set, where they will find additional, complementary accounts of Goethe, Schiller, and their contemporaries.

What sets Weimar Classicism apart, while allowing it to participate in and even initiate broader literary trends, is what might best be termed its "project." That project, eventually under the joint aesthetic and philosophical leadership of Goethe and Schiller, involved nothing less than an ambitious attempt not only to imagine but also to achieve a new quality of wholeness in human life and culture at a time when fragmentation, division, and alienation appeared to be the norm. That sense of wholeness or totality (*Ganzheit*) was based on a vision of classical Greece that had been enthusiastically conveyed by the Enlightenment art historian Johann Joachim Winckelmann (1717–68) as early as 1755. His descriptions of the Laocoön and other Hellenistic sculptures were in Goethe's mind as he studied the Vatican art collections and developed his own complex notion of the classical. Because this project was to be more than a mental exercise, the material reality of a locus, a place, was instrumental. Two would prove crucial: Rome (and more generally Italy) for the schooling of the senses and artistic taste, and Weimar, an otherwise insignificant little town that would allow for all manner of literary, cultural, social, and erotic experimentation. Participants in the project involved friends and acquaintances from Goethe's Italian journey or others who had schooled themselves in Italy in correspondence with Goethe, as well as select members of the Weimar community, all orbiting in varying degrees of proximity to Goethe, Schiller, and the heart of the project. The supporting players will be introduced in due course.

In both this introduction and the essays that follow, Weimar Classicism is understood as explicitly offering an aesthetic solution to troubled times. Numerous political, social, and cultural factors and events coincide to make up the fragmented, stultifying, and occasionally terrifying world in which Goethe and Schiller lived, while others enabled their aesthetic response. Many of them are obvious: the ongoing French Revolution, the splintered nature of Germany, vexed relations between the nobility and rising middle class, the contrast of modern European culture with that of the ancient Greeks, advances in aesthetics beginning with Alexander Baumgarten (1714–62) and culminating in Immanuel Kant (1724–1804) and the beginnings of idealist philosophy. Others are less so: for example, new conceptions of the physiology of the human body, a new morality and pedagogy founded on the notion of controlling sexual drives, new developments in the field of classical philology, a new concept of education and specialized knowledge that would result in the founding of the Friedrich Wilhelm University in Berlin in 1810, new business ventures of an international scope involving the commodification of art. In other words, Weimar Classicism arises at a time of great complexity, ferment, and even violence. As a project with utopian tendencies, it necessarily overreaches itself, strains under its own impossibility, collides and colludes with the dominant discourses of its times. No account of Weimar Classicism should be satisfied with a survey of the project's successes, its literary triumphs uncritically rendered. We must be prepared to confront its internal contradictions, its excesses and follies, its moments both sublime and — readers will forgive me — ridiculous. Emancipatory and doctrinaire by turns, the project of Weimar Classicism is best approached as a complex whole, a *cultural*, and not only a literary phenomenon. We may best remember Goethe's novel *Wilhelm Meisters Lehrjahre* (Wilhelm Meister's Apprenticeship, 1795–96) and *Faust* (1808), Schiller's plays *Maria Stuart* (1800) and *Wilhelm Tell* (1804), not to mention his essays *Über die ästhetische Erziehung des Menschen* (On the Aesthetic Education of Man, 1795) and *Über naive und sentimentalische Dichtung* (On Naive and Sentimental Poetry, 1795/96) — the key aesthetic treatises of the project. These works and many others (for example, Goethe's *Römische Elegien* [Roman Elegies, 1795] and *Hermann und Dorothea* [1797], Schiller's "Die Götter Griechenlands" [The Gods of Greece; 1788] and "Die Künstler" [The Artists,"1789]) must be seen in proximity to other lesser known, blithely ignored, even happily forgotten efforts in literature, the visual arts, architecture, art history, classical philology, theater, politics, cultural critique, science, and medicine. What we aim to capture is the unique cultural imprint of Weimar Classicism that distinguishes it from the overarching literary trends in which it participated.

Faustian Classicism

One thing should be stated from the outset: the desire that lurks behind the Classical project is gargantuan, excessive, and, as such, thoroughly unclassical. The sharpest indicator of this is Goethe's *Faust* as Goethe was working on it around 1800. Reluctantly returning to the fragments he had written in his Sturm und Drang days, the so-called *Urfaust*, Goethe completed *Faust I* in response to Schiller's prodding and his own reading of the philosophy and aesthetics of Immanuel Kant.[6] On the face of it there is nothing classical about Faust: he is, after all, based on an actual historical figure, a shady, Reformation-era teacher and magician who reputedly made a pact with the devil. Certainly no one would be tempted to include the chapbook containing the *Damnable Adventures of Doctor Johann Faust* in the same breath with Homer or Sophocles. Nor does Goethe's *Faust, Part the First* with its *Knittelvers* (rhyming couplets), the Walpurgis Night scene, Witch's Kitchen, and other demonic shenanigans strike one as the least bit classical. Of course, *Wilhelm Meisters Lehrjahre*, the other major publication of the Classical period, set in eighteenth-century Germany, does not at first glance seem classical either. But as Schiller's effusive response to the latter indicates, what is classical about *Meister* is the author's sovereign touch, his ability to construct a self-contained world with deft, restrained strokes of language. In other words, the serenity of Goethe's masterful prose as it renders the plot satisfies the requirements of aesthetic autonomy and thus is comparable in a broad sense to the works of Greek antiquity — in a word, classical. But we would be hard-pressed to make the same argument about the rather amorphous *Faust*, Part One. Part Two, completed decades later, would prove even more ungainly. Yet, it is precisely in that huge work that we find the Helena act and the phantasmagorical classical Walpurgisnacht. Among the sections Goethe composed for Part One around 1800 is the pact scene portraying the protracted negotiation between Faust and Mephistopheles that finally, as if by accident (*Irrtum*), leads to the wager. And it is here, in the formulation of the wager, in this apparently most unclassical of literary texts, that classical desire achieves one of its signature formulations:

> Werd ich zum Augenblicke sagen:
> Verweile doch! Du bist so schön!
> Dann magst Du mich in Fesseln schlagen,
> Dann will ich gern zugrunde gehn! (1699–1702)

[If to the moment I should say:
Abide, you are so beautiful —
Put me in fetters on that day,
I *wish* to perish then, I swear.[7]]

What has brought Goethe's Faust to such a point of crisis and desperation that he is prepared to strike a wager with the devil is his overwhelming desire to reconcile all the structuring oppositions of human life. His famous Two Souls speech depicts a man who desires access to the spiritual realm (characterized by terms such as eternal, infinite, absolute, and ideal) while cleaving to the material realm (temporal, finite, contingent, and real):

> Zwei Seelen wohnen, ach, in meiner Brust,
> Die eine will sich von der andern trennen:
> Die eine hält in derber Liebeslust,
> Sich an die Welt mit klammernden Organen;
> Die andre hebt gewaltsam sich vom Dunst
> Zu den Gefilden hoher Ahnen. (1112–17)

[Two souls, alas, are dwelling in my breast,
And one is striving to forsake its brother.
Unto the world in grossly loving zest,
With clinging tendrils, one adheres;
The other rises forcibly in quest
Of rarefied ancestral spheres.[8]]

We recognize the basic opposition in the language of the wager: Faust challenges Mephistopheles to assist him in encountering a moment (an "Augenblick") that is of such a nature that he would wish its eternal perpetuation. One of the remarkable things about the wager with Mephistopheles is that Faust wants to lose! His desperate confidence that Mephistopheles will fail comes from his recognition that every moment is contingent, dependent, and incomplete. What he desires is a moment in time that is absolute, self-contained, and complete in itself. Such a moment would be beautiful — notice that the fitness of the moment is adjudged in aesthetic terms — and would indeed have achieved the eternity expressed in the wish "Abide" so that Faust would willingly depart this life for the condition of non-existence he is certain follows death. To lose the wager would be Faust's gain, to win his loss.

Faust's project, for all the unclassical trappings, for all its Sturm und Drang beginnings, for all its melancholy and megalomania, is essentially a version of the project of Weimar Classicism. Goethe tips his hand when he transforms the traditional pact into a wager regarding a single moment and introduces the concept of beauty as the measure of its perfection. Both of these — the moment or *Augenblick* and beauty — are key terms in Weimar Classicism. Indeed, Faust's fundamental and unreasonable desire — the reconciliation of all life-structuring oppositions — is precisely what Weimar Classicism seeks to accomplish, if in apparently more restrained fashion. Turn to any page of the programmatic treatises and poems of Weimar Classicism (primarily authored by Schiller, but also on occasion by Goethe and others) and one finds signs of strenuous dialectical efforts to overcome the obstacles standing in the way of a perfected human existence, often mapped out along the fault lines of historical difference. How was it possible for the ancient Greeks to achieve such harmony among forces that now rip modernity apart? How might the social, cultural, and aesthetic achievement of the Greeks be duplicated in Weimar and Germany?

Winckelmann, Goethe, and Classical Antiquity

Schiller was convinced that the answer, if there was one, lay in his companion and their mutual friendship and alliance. From the beginning of their acquaintance in the late 1780s, both had been keenly aware of the fundamental difference in their characters. A retrospective memoir of their first substantial encounter written by Goethe laid the groundwork for the mythologization of their friendship.[9] A dispute over Goethe's notion of the *Urpflanze* (archetypal plant) was the occasion for laying bare the apparently insurmountable difference between them: Schiller maintained it was an idea, Goethe insisted it was a matter of empirical experience. Against the odds, certainly counter to Goethe's expectation, a mutually beneficial and respectful friendship flourished between them. In this friendship between the philosophical idealist and the intuitive realist one of the major oppositions appeared to be bridged for all to see. As the project's theorist, it fell to Schiller to stylize Goethe as a genius who in accordance with inner laws gave renewed birth to Greece in modern times and northern climes. He did so in flattering letters early in their correspondence (in particular, in the famous birthday letter of 23 August 1794), as well as in barely veiled portraits of Goethe in his aesthetic treatises as the exemplar of the artist and man who succeeds in overcoming the fragmentation of modern life. "Sie werden," Schiller writes in a letter of 20 October 1794 about the *Aesthetische Briefe*, "in diesen Briefen Ihr Porträt finden" (In these letters you will find your portrait). And on 2 July 1796, as he enthusiastically responds to Goethe's *Meister*, he writes: "Wie rührt es mich, wenn ich denke, [daß,] was wir sonst nur in der weiten Ferne eines begünstigten Altertums suchen und kaum finden, mir in Ihnen so nahe ist" (How it moves me, when I contemplate that I can discover in you what we otherwise seek and barely find in the far distance of blessed antiquity).

Even as a local phenomenon, confined to the efforts of two writers and several others around them, Weimar Classicism — however we choose to think about it — has a unique ability to draw us in, to absorb us in its depths, and blind us to the world around. We easily lose a comparative perspective. The nineteenth-century adjective "German" still silently underlies the "Weimar" that replaced it. We forget to ask if there are similar fixations on antiquity in other European countries at that time. Expanding our gaze to include phenomena in England, France, Denmark, and Italy, we have to concede: yes, sporadically. In fact, we could argue that Weimar Classicism is a piece with a transnational, if dispersed neo-Hellenic or neoclassical movement with its occasional headquarters in Rome. Antiquarians, scholars, sculptors, art historians, and sexual adventurers from various European countries participated in an alternately real and virtual multi-national community with an enthusiastic reverence for the grandeur that was Greece. The founding member of the community, and of European neo-Hellenism, was Johann Joachim Winckelmann, a self-taught German antiquarian, whose powerful vision of an enchanted antiquity captured the attention of many.[10] Born in Stendahl in northern Germany, Winckelmann was initially drawn by the Greek textual corpus, by Homer and the tragic poets, but perhaps even more by the accounts and descriptions of Greek artists and works of art. He made his way to Dresden as a librarian under the patronage of nobility where he for the first time encountered plaster casts of famed sculptures, among them the Laocoön group, the original of which dated from around 40–20 B.C. He conjured an artistic and cultural universe in radical contrast with his own baroque times and uttered a challenge in what would become the manifesto of eighteenth-century neo-Hellenism. In his *Gedanken über die Nachahmung der griechischen Werke in der Malerei und Bildhauerkunst* (Reflections on the Imitation of Greek Works of Art in Painting and Sculpture, 1755) he programmatically states: "Der einzige Weg für uns, groß, ja, wenn es möglich ist, unnachahmlich zu werden ist Nachahmung der Alten"[11] (The only way for us to become great, indeed, if possible, to become inimitable, is through imitation of the ancients). Soon after, he converted to Catholicism and gratefully left Germany for Rome, where he joined his friend the neoclassical artist Anton Rafael Mengs (1728–1779).

The Emblem of Classicism: Laocoön and the Aesthetics of Containment

The importance of the Laocoön statue for Weimar Classicism cannot be overestimated.[12] Already in Winckelmann's manifesto, the statue holds pride of place as the exemplar of what he called "edle Einfalt" (noble simplicity) and "stille Größe" (quiet grandeur). The famous statue, still standing in a courtyard in the Vatican museum where Winckelmann and Goethe saw it too, represents the Trojan priest Laocoön and his two sons as they are being attacked by two serpents — the story is familiar to readers of Virgil's *Aeneid*. What particularly appealed to Winckelmann about the statue was the balance the artist struck between the pain inflicted on Laocoön's body and the hero's ability to withstand the pain, almost entirely to contain it: "Dieser Schmerz, sage ich, äußert sich dennoch mit keiner Wut in dem Gesicht und in der ganzen Stellung. Er erhebet kein schreckliches Geschrei" (*Gedanken*, 20; This pain, I maintain, expresses itself with no sign of rage in his face or in his entire bearing. He emits no terrible screams). This image of the containment of pain would become the predominant figure of much of the literary and aesthetic production of Weimar Classicism.[13] We will encounter versions of the Laocoön statue in numerous and unlikely places.

When Goethe saw the Laocoön statue in Rome some thirty years later, he had the words of Winckelmann in mind. In 1798, as he launched the *Propyläen*, his own short-lived journal that sought to foster neo-classical values in the arts, he published his reflections on the statue in an essay entitled "Über Laokoon" (On the Laocoön, 1798). Goethe takes Winckelmann's analysis and that of others who had written authoritatively on the statue in the meantime (Gotthold Ephraim Lessing [1729–1781] and Johann Gottfried Herder [1744–1803], for example) and focuses intently on the moment of containment, essentially rewriting eighteenth-century aesthetics in the direction of an extreme form of aesthetic autonomy. Because this essay contains key concepts of Weimar Classicism and locates them in the Laocoön statue, it will be worth our while to engage in a more detailed analysis.

For Goethe, the Laocoön is constituted by the same dynamic Winckelmann had identified: pain and its containment. But Goethe is more rigorous in regarding the statue as a work of art. The key question for Goethe is how the containment is accomplished. He begins his analysis by abstracting the "story" or narrative of the statue from its context. Putting Virgil aside, he calls the statue a tragic idyll, even suppressing the hero's name in the anonymity of a role: "Ein Vater schlief neben seinen beiden Söhnen, sie wurden von Schlangen umwunden und streben nun, erwachend, sich aus dem lebendigen Netze loszureissen" (MA 4.2:81; a father was sleeping next to his two sons; they were attacked by two snakes, and, now awake, they are trying to extricate themselves from this reptilian net). One way of understanding Goethe's first move is to associate it with what is often called aesthetic autonomy: on a basic level, aesthetic autonomy means that a work of art is sufficient in itself. By reducing the plot to a structural minimum and stripping it of narrative and mythological context, Goethe asserts that it stands on its own legs. A total stranger to western culture could approach the Laocoön and understand the statue. Of course, as we shall see, aesthetic autonomy implies a great deal more than that.

In a second move, Goethe isolates the moment of pain and relates it to Lessing's concept of the pregnant or fertile moment (*der fruchtbare Moment*) as the ideal moment for visual representation. It should be a moment of transition. Goethe provides several examples: a child happily skipping along is suddenly struck hard by a playmate; Eurydice strolls through the woods with freshly picked flowers and a snake bites her heel. He compares such moments to an electric shock that suddenly runs through the whole body. Happiness is abruptly disturbed by pain. Both conditions of the body are still evident as one gives way to the other. We readily see how these two examples are variations of the rudimentary Laocoön narrative. Goethe subjects the statue to an almost medical analysis: "Der Punkt des Bisses, ich wiederhole es, bestimmt die gegenwärtigen Bewegungen der Glieder: das Fliehen des Unterkörpers, das Einziehen des Leibes, das Hervorstreben der Brust, das Niederzücken der Ächsel und des Hauptes, ja alle Züge des Angesichts seh ich durch diesen augenblicklichen, schmerzlichen, unerwarteten Reiz entschieden" (MA 4.2:82; The location of the bite determines the present movements of the body: the evading motion of its lower part, the contraction of the abdominal muscles, the outward thrust of the chest, the lowering of the shoulder and the head. Even the facial expression is determined by this momentary, painful, unexpected stimulus). One can imagine that Winckelmann would not have been pleased with this elaboration of his description of the statue. Where is the great-souled hero in all of this? Is his body merely a medium for the detailed expression of physical pain? Perhaps the effort to contain the pain will restore Laocoön's dignity and set humanists at ease.

Remarkably, this is not the case. Having established the moment of pain as the statue's center, a perfect instance of impact and violent change, Goethe proceeds to a discussion of "containment," but once again his interest is deflected from the hero. What contains the pain, what makes it presentable to the human eye, is the aesthetic composition of the artwork. In words that resonate with many similar passages in Goethe, Schiller, and Karl Philipp Moritz (1756–93), Goethe offers a programmatic statement concerning aesthetic autonomy:

> Jedes Kunstwerk muß sich als ein solches anzeigen, und das kann es allein durch das, was wir sinnliche Schönheit oder Anmut nennen. Die Alten, weit entfernt von dem modernen Wahne, daß ein Kunstwerk dem Scheine nach wieder ein Naturwerk werden müsse, bezeichneten ihre Kunstwerke als solche durch gewählte Ordnung der Teile, sie erleichterten dem Auge die Einsicht in die Verhältnisse durch Symmetrie und so ward ein verwickeltes Werk faßlich. Durch ebendiese Symmetrie und durch Gegenstellungen wurden in leisen Abweichungen die höchsten Kontraste möglich. Die Sorgfalt der Künstler, mannigfältige Massen gegeneinander in eine regelmäßige Lage zu bringen, war äußerst überlegt und glücklich, so daß ein jedes Kunstwerk, wenn man auch von dem Inhalt abstrahiert,

wenn man in der Entfernung auch nur die allgemeinsten Umrisse sieht, noch immer dem Auge als ein Zierat erscheint. (MA 4.2:77)

[Every work of art must be identifiable as such; this is only possible if it exhibits what we call physical beauty, or grace. The artists of antiquity were not laboring under our present-day misconception that a work of art must appear to be a work of nature; rather, they identified their works of art as such by a conscious arrangement of components, employed symmetry to clarify the relationship among these components, and thus made a work of art comprehensible. Through slight variations in symmetry and position-ing the most effective contrasts became possible, and their careful efforts to juxtapose diverse subjects and particularly to achieve harmonious posi-tioning of the extremities in groups were most judicious and successful, with the result that, even if one abstracts from the content, even if one were to see only the most general outlines from a distance, it would still appear to the eye as an ornament.]

The statue as a work of art does not require its narrative context, nor even the diminished content Goethe had summed up in the phrase "tragic idyll." It stands alone and appeals to the eye as an ornament. I hope that readers fully register the momentousness of this pronouncement.[14] On the face of it, the notion of ornament is fully incompatible with conventional understandings of classicism. The latter idealizes and privileges the human being — body and soul. Ornament, by contrast, is superficial, devoid of content and depth. Nonetheless, there is something in the idea of aesthetic autonomy that occasionally pushes Weimar Classicism into this extreme and virtually anti-humanist position. As we stated at the outset, Weimar Classicism is a project with numerous irresolvable contradictions.

In the case of the Laocoön in particular, it is not the great-souled hero who contains the pain — it is the snakes. Even as the one snake bites the hero's side and creates the pain at the center of the statue, the two snakes together through their extension, looping and coiling around the figures, render the hero and his sons immobile. "Durch dieses Mittel der Lähmung wird, bei der großen Bewegung, über das Ganze schon eine gewisse Ruhe und Einheit verbreitet" (MA 4.2:84; Through this medium of paralysis, a certain sense of tranquility and unity pervades the group despite all move-ment). The snakes are the means through which the artist transforms the pain into a work of art. "Es ist," writes Goethe, "ein grosser Vorteil für ein Kunstwerk, wenn es selbständig, wenn es geschlossen ist" (MA 4.2:78; it is a great advantage for a work of art to be autonomous, closed in itself).

Following Goethe's example, we may push his abstraction one step further and state hypothetically that according to the classicism instantiated in his essay on the Laocoön, a work of art achieves self-sufficiency and closure — its aesthetic autonomy — if it involves both inflicting pain and containing it through artistic means. Suddenly, Weimar Classicism assumes another aspect. We imagine a Goethe, a Schiller, drawn to a tragic theme precisely because it affords them an opportunity, indeed a challenge, to attempt to fashion an aesthetic containment. Once one begins to read the works of Weimar Classicism through the lens of the Laocoön, one begins to encounter snakes everywhere, often as metaphorical insertions that nonetheless refer self-reflexively to the Laocoön-based aesthetics of their setting. In *Wallensteins Tod* (Wallenstein's Death, 1799), the concluding play of Schiller's *Wallenstein* trilogy, for example, Max Piccolomini laments his tragic situation: "Warum muß / Der Väter Doppelschuld und Freveltat / Uns gräßlich wie ein Schlangenpaar umwinden?" (2137–39; Why must the double fault and blasphemy of our fathers encircle us horribly like a pair of snakes?). Even in such an unlikely place as the *Roman Elegies*, Goethe's poems of classical and erotic contentment, the snakes rear their ugly heads:

> Eines ist mir verdrießlich vor allen Dingen, ein andres
> Bleibt mir abscheulich, empört jegliche Faser in mir,
> Nur der bloße Gedanke. Ich will es euch, Freunde, gestehen:
> Gar verdrießlich ist mir einsam das Lager zu Nacht.
> Aber ganze abscheulich ist's, auf dem Wege der Liebe
> Schlangen zu fürchten und Gift unter den Rosen der Lust,
> Wenn im schönsten Moment der hin sich gebenden Freude
> Deinem sinkenden Haupt lispelnde Sorge sich naht. (FA 1.1:429)

> [One thing I find more irksome than anything else, and another / Thing I supremely abhor — it really curdles my blood, / Even the thought of it does. Let me tell you, my friends, what these two are: / First, to sleep by myself irks me, I truly confess. / But what I utterly loathe is the fear that on pathways of pleasure, / Under the roses of love, serpents and poison may lurk.[15]]

In this case, the snakes that threaten to destroy the most beautiful moment, the moment of classical fulfillment (we must recall Faust's wager), stand for venereal disease. Pain comes in many guises.

Perhaps the most explicit formulation of aesthetic containment as a motivating factor in artistic production in Classical Weimar comes in the foreword of one of Schiller's last plays, *Die Braut von Messina* (The Bride of Messina, 1803). Entitled "Über den Gebrauch des Chors in der Tragödie" (On the Use of the Chorus in Tragedy), here Schiller famously defends his seemingly anachronistic reintroduction of the ancient chorus in an early nineteenth-century play. The chorus, he argues, heightens the artificiality of the play so that no one might mistake it for nature — in other words, it has been placed in the service of aesthetic autonomy: "So sollte er [the chorus] uns eine lebendige Mauer sein, die die Tragödie um sich herumzieht, um sich von der wirklichen Welt rein abzuschließen, und sich ihren idealen Boden, ihre poetische Freiheit zu bewahren" (NA 10:11; the chorus should be a living wall that the tragedy draws around itself in order to cut itself off completely from the real world and to preserve its ideal ground, its ideal freedom). The chorus, like the snakes in the statue, encircles and contains the tragic plot and the passions it arouses: "So wie der Chor in die Sprache Leben bringt, so bringt er Ruhe in die Handlung — aber die schöne und hohe Ruhe, die der Charakter eines edeln Kunstwerkes sein muß" (NA 10:14; Just as the chorus brings life to the language, it also brings tranquility to the plot — but the beautiful and grand tranquility, which must be the character of a noble artwork). There is no question that the plot of Schiller's play cries out for aesthetic containment. Although Schiller preferred to render historical material in aesthetic form (hence his *Wilhelm Tell, Maria Stuart, Wallenstein,* and *Die Jungfrau von Orleans* [The Maid of Orleans, 1801]), for *Die Braut von Messina* he contrived a brutally tragic plot of Oedipal proportions containing scenes of fratricide and incest. Repeating the very word Goethe had used to identify the moment of pain (*Schlag*), Schiller associates the chorus with the idea of catharsis: "Der Chor reinigt also das tragische Gedicht" (NA 10:13; The chorus thus purifies the tragic poem). It makes pain bearable for the viewer, even as it abstracts the play and the viewer from the real world.

Readers will undoubtedly have noticed that Schiller introduces a third sense of containment and abstraction. For Goethe it is a matter of the containment of pain and establishment of the difference between the work of art and nature. For Schiller, retreat from the real world means more than aesthetic abstraction. It is also a matter of flight and escape from oppressive circumstances. Although one searches in vain for similar expressions in Goethe's classical corpus (duly mindful of the fact that it is present in earlier works right up to his precipitous "flight" to Italy), in Schiller's work it is a frequent and distinctive refrain. A number of programmatic poems written during the Classical period counsel flight from the dross and pain of sensate life into the pure realm of the ideal. In "Das Ideal und das Leben," we read: "Wollt ihr hoch auf ihren Flügeln schweben, / Werft die Angst des Irdischen von euch, / Fliehet aus dem engen, dumpfen Leben / In des Ideales Reich!" (27–30; If you want to fly high on the wings of form / Cast off the anxiety of earthly existence, / Flee from narrow, stifling life / Into the realm of the ideal!). Such moments deny the Faustian wager as well as the enabling role of pain that Schiller recognizes in other places (for example, in the foreword to *Die Braut von Messina*). In this poem, the Laocoön statue becomes an allegory of the suffering that is human life (111–13; "Wenn der Menschheit Leiden euch umfangen, / Wenn dort Priams Sohn der Schlangen / Sich erwehrt mit namenlosem Schmerz" [When human suffering encircles you, / When the son of Priam defends himself, / Against the snakes with unspeakable pain]), a stark contrast to a higher region of pure forms: "Hier darf Schmerz die Seele nicht durchschneiden, / Keine Träne fließt hier mehr dem Leiden" (124–25; Here no pain may cut through the soul, / Here no tears of suffering flow).

One may offer several explanations for Schiller's favoring the idea of flight, ranging from the personal to the political and philosophical. For one thing, we must keep in mind that Schiller continually suffered from ill health. His sober reports in letters to Goethe about the multiple accommodations required to make the daily racking pain of his body bearable are quite moving. We soon realize that almost everything Schiller wrote during the Classical period was wrested from great physical suffering. Small wonder that Schiller regarded the human body with ambivalence. A second explanation for the anti-corporeal thrust in Schiller's work is that he was by disposition a philosopher, an idealist, with little patience for reality — this, of course, was the crux of his first encounter with Goethe. Schiller struggled with this, like Faust with his two souls. It was obvious to him that a philosophical life of abstraction was fundamentally incomplete — hence his attraction to Goethe. The realist poet struck him as healthy, vibrant, alive. In a letter to Goethe from 16 October 1795 he describes how he strives to hold the two impulses in balance: "Wenn der Philosoph seine Einbildungskraft und der Dichter seine Abstraktionskraft ruhen lassen darf, so muß ich [. . .] diese beiden Kräfte immer in gleicher Anspannung erhalten, und nur durch eine ewige Bewegung in mir kann ich die 2 heterogenen Elemente in einer Art von Solution erhalten" (If the philosopher may allow his imagination to rest and the poet his power of abstraction, I must hold both these powers constantly in equal tension, and only through an eternal motion in myself am I able to maintain these two heterogeneous elements in a sort of solution). To accomplish what Goethe appeared to do off-handedly required the greatest effort on Schiller's part.

The third explanation we may offer is far more specific historically. As scholars and readers of works of the Classical period, we must never forget that their production coincided with the greatest European cataclysm of the eighteenth century — the French Revolution. To all appearances (and without regard for social and economic factors), Enlightenment principles pronounced in the texts of Rousseau (1712–78), Voltaire (1694–1778), and other thinkers had been seized and put into action with unforeseen and horrifying consequences. A king, a queen, members of the nobility, and even opposing participants in the Revolution in increasing numbers had been executed. The bloodletting of the terror shocked the world. During the course of the 1790s it became evident that the Revolution could not be contained, but would have effects elsewhere. Prussia, and with it the Duchy of Saxe-Weimar led by Duke Carl-August (1757–1828) with Goethe in tow, advanced unsuccessfully on France. Later Napoleon would invade Germany, French troops would be quartered in Goethe's home, and Goethe would barely escape with his life. Philosophically and politically opposed to the French Revolution, Goethe and Schiller turned to the aesthetic as a necessary antidote. To some extent this movement too can be regarded as flight. Consider, for instance the announcement of Schiller's important new journal, *Die Horen* (The Horae) in 1794: "Mitten in diesem politischen Tumult soll sie [the journal] für Musen und Charitinnen einen engen vertraulichen Zirkel schließen, aus welchem alles verbannt seyn wird, was mit einem unreinen Partheygeist gestempelt ist"[16] (In the midst of this political tumult, the journal shall enclose muses and charities in a narrow, intimate circle from which everything shall be banned that bears the stamp of impure partisanship). We notice the by-now familiar aesthetic enclosure of the circle and realize that Schiller's journal assumes the same position vis-à-vis the French Revolution as does the chorus vis-à-vis the tragic action and the world in the *Braut von Messina*.

Die Horen and Aesthetic Education

Schiller's journal embodies the Classical project. In the brief letter dated 13 June 1794 that initiated the famous correspondence between them, Schiller approached Goethe with a humble request for his participation in an effort that had already won the assent of several Jena luminaries, among them the philosopher Johann Gottlieb Fichte (1762–1814) and linguist Wilhelm von Humboldt (1767–1835). The letter was accompanied by the announcement from which we quoted above. Goethe obliged: "Ich werde mit Freuden und von ganzem Herzen von der Gesellschaft sein" (24 June 1794; I will participate with pleasure and my whole heart). Not only would Goethe provide essays, poems, and stories, he essentially became Schiller's co-editor, evaluating manuscripts and discussing editorial policy. Although the journal was relatively short-lived (twelve issues in three years from 1795 to 1797), their congenial cooperation set the pattern for many subsequent projects. Schiller and Goethe both understood that *Die Horen* was not meant to be just another literary journal. On the contrary, the ambition of the journal, like that of Classicism itself, was gargantuan, nothing less than the transformation of German culture through aesthetic means. Thus, the appearance of flight and escape from intolerable political circumstances that might be awakened by Schiller's announcement of the new journal is deceiving. Certainly in his mind and to some extent in Goethe's, *Die Horen* was conceived as a necessary and essential political intervention, possibly the only salvation for Germans and humanity from the extreme violence of the Revolution, on the one hand, and extreme repression of arbitrary forms of government on the other. A Weimar old-timer and peripheral Classicist, Christoph Martin Wieland (1733–1813), duly registered the investment, even if he did not share it: "Anfänglich sei es [*Die Horen*] eine Bundeslade geweßen, die niemand habe anrühren dürfen, ohne das Feuer daraus hervorgegangen sei, und die Frevler zu verzehren gedroht habe"[17] (In the beginning it was a holy ark that no one could touch without fire proceeding from it, threatening to consume the blasphemers). It undoubtedly had not escaped Wieland that Schiller's enterprise was also meant to eclipse an array of other journals, not least among them Wieland's own *Teutscher Merkur* (German Mercury).

Of the many significant articles and prose pieces that appeared in *Die Horen*, Schiller's *Über die ästhetische Erziehung des Menschen* stands out. In a series of letters (often called the *Aesthetische Briefe* [Aesthetic Letters]) published over the course of several issues, Schiller attempts to address the fundamental dilemma of his times: As tyrannies and monarchies are threatened and collapse under the violent pressure of democratic insurgency, how do we reconcile law and desire? The clean moral lines of a government rationally conceived will not win the acclamation and consent of a long repressed mob suddenly able to act on its desires. What could possibly mediate between the two? The answer, writes Schiller, is art. Humanity is in need of aesthetic education, of training and acculturation, as it were, in a parallel and virtual realm, freed of the constraints and violence of the real world. Grounded psychologically and anthropologically in something Schiller notably called the "Spieltrieb" (play drive), the beautiful in art is offered as the only possible means to school humanity in the virtues of balance, harmony, and the greater good. In art one could encounter an apprehensible vision of what it might mean to be human and to live in a human society. In theory, a spillover effect should result in the un-coerced transfer of civil virtue from the aesthetic realm to the political. As Schiller's conclusion after prodigious dialectical efforts to marshal all the pieces indicates, success is far from assured. The "aesthetic state" exists primarily as a need in every sensitive individual. In reality, however, one finds it only in "einigen wenigen auserlesenen Zirkeln"[18] (very few select circles) — hardly a state in other words, and probably not a city, but perhaps a few select intellectuals in a small town in Thuringia known as Weimar.

Weimar: "Athens on the Ilm"[19]

In a poem written in 1782, Goethe compares Weimar to Bethlehem: "klein und gros!" (small and great).[20] There is no question that Weimar was small. With a population hovering around 6,000 inhabitants, at a remove from important travel corridors, void of significant industry, its economy totally focused on the life of the ducal court that ruled the double principality of Saxe-Weimar-Eisenach with a total population of approximately 100,000, Weimar seemed as unlikely as Bethlehem for the birth of anything of world significance. The transformation began in 1758 when the young and recently widowed Duchess Anna Amalia (1739–1807) suddenly found herself in power until the eldest of her two sons, Carl August, came of age. Having received a fine education with Enlightenment accents in Braunschweig, she combined a restrained economic policy with the cultivation of the arts. A series of illustrious tutors looked after the education of her sons, most famously Christoph Martin Wieland, who came to Weimar in 1772 and remained there and nearby in Ossmannstedt under ducal patronage until his death. If Wieland had been a coup, one of Carl August's first acts was a national sensation. Shortly after assuming power, the young duke called Goethe to Weimar and appointed him to his privy council. In Goethe's train came numerous others, among them Johann Gottfried Herder in 1776, for whom Goethe had engineered a position as general superintendent of Saxe-Weimar responsible for schools and religion. Increasingly Weimar became a magnet for writers, artists, scientists, actors, musicians, composers, and architects. If in 1782 the comparison to Bethlehem seemed apt, by 1800 the more appropriate, even if still somewhat incongruous association was with Athens in all its classical brilliance. Between Weimar and the neighboring university town of Jena, some twenty kilometers distant and also part of the duchy, an unprecedented accumulation of talent had been assembled. In 1787 Schiller moved first to Weimar and two years later to Jena where he became professor of history. Goethe's lifelong friend Wilhelm von Humboldt resided in Jena from 1794–97. As a member of the Privy Council, Goethe had a hand in making a series of high-profile appointments to the University of Jena, among them Fichte in 1794, Schelling (1775–1854) in 1798, and Hegel (1770–1831) in 1801.[21] The two Schlegel brothers, August (1767–1845) and Friedrich (1772–1829), also made their way to Jena in 1796 — early Romanticism went to school with Schiller and Goethe and produced its manifestos and other cultural manifestations in Jena. Although I have mentioned only those who are readily recognizable to contemporary readers, we must bear in mind that many other noteworthy individuals lived or sojourned in Weimar and Jena during this period. If the essence of classical Athens was the vision of Socrates in conversation with Aristophanes as Sophocles, Pericles, and Phidias pass by, Weimar in its own way duplicated this. Rarely has a city seen such a concentration of first- and second-rate artists, writers, and thinkers. That they were collected in the unlikely towns of Weimar and Jena makes it all the more remarkable.

Of course, this is the stuff of legends, and legends soon gained the upper hand. At the same time that we objectively recognize the remarkable cultural circumstances of Weimar around 1800 and involuntarily register a feeling of awe, we must not lose sight of political, social, and material reality. The structuring binaries of the Faustian wager can be traced right into the fabric of the city. Coarse quotidian aspects of life were never far away. Numerous farms housed animals within the city walls. Even Goethe's long-time common-law wife Christiane Vulpius (1765–1816) kept pigs, much to Goethe's disgust. The streets were largely unpaved and in poor condition. After eleven o'clock at night chamber pots could be emptied out of windows into gutters that theoretically washed their contents out of the city. Aesthetic autonomies and circles of containment of all kinds may have been strenuously aspired to within its precincts, but only through complex negotiations and at a cost. We must observe the culture of Weimar minutely, and thus gain an additional perspective on the classical project to which Weimar lent its name.[22]

Remarkably, one of the enabling factors of the sort of cultural sociability enjoyed by nobility and the cultivated middle class in Weimar was a catastrophic fire that gutted the residential palace in 1774. Bereft of spaces for theatrical and musical performance, Weimar could not sensibly sustain a professional theater troupe. In its place, a tradition of amateur performance was established involving Goethe and other members of the ducal family, nobility, and cultural community. Performances took place in a variety of venues, among them the *Redoutenhaus* (ballroom) in the town, the duchess's summer palace in Ettersburg, and the park at Tiefurt, a small village and castle down the river Ilm where Anna Amalia liked to summer. Most famous of these performances is the premiere of the prose version of Goethe's *Iphigenie* in 1779, well before he left for Italy, in which Goethe played Orestes, Corona Schröter (1751–1802), a remarkable singer and actress whom Goethe had brought to Weimar, the title role, and, in successive performances, both Carl August and his brother Constantin (1758–1793) played Pylades. The legends are never far away. What is important to recognize is that the amateur theater had the effect of modestly suspending a small range of class difference, not in such a way as to cast courtly culture into question but to offer cultivated and artistic individuals an aesthetic space for truly human interaction. This is what Schiller was talking about in the *Aesthetische Erziehung*. There were consequences and possibilities here for women as well. Not only Schröter, whose poems and songs were published, but many others as well were involved in the aesthetic projects of the court. For the longest time, scholarship neglected or trivialized their accomplishments and productions, but the last twenty-five years have seen considerable rectification of the situation. As the classical project took shape, the ambition of women writers in Weimar and Jena also expanded, contributing to, challenging, and even confounding the male guardians of the arts. Three of these female players will be discussed individually when we come to the "who's who" of Weimar Classicism.

Another venue for the practice of aesthetic living was the newly designed park on the Ilm river. Soon after Goethe arrived in Weimar, Carl August presented him with the legendary *Gartenhaus*, which was directly in the park, as his primary residence. By 1778, Goethe was already busy with plans to refashion the park as an English garden in the manner of Wörlitz near Dessau. In the early stages, efforts focused on the creation of sentimental locations (ruins, an abandoned cloister, a hermit's hut, and so on) — stages for aesthetic performance — but during the 1790s the grounds themselves were modeled into a sequence of picturesque scenes according to the best principles of landscape gardening. Even though Goethe officially moved into the considerably roomier and more stately *Haus am Frauenplan* in 1782, he continued to seek out the garden house for refuge and refreshment. His precipitous and, for the time in Weimar, scandalous affair with Christiane Vulpius when he returned from Italy was played out in the garden house. In 1803 he was once again spending the summer in the garden house as he read Winckelmann's correspondence and contemplated his memorial essay on the art historian. At Carl August's bidding, Goethe erected the most classically styled building in Weimar, the *Römisches Haus* (Roman house), Carl August's summer residence, overlooking the park and in plain view of the garden house. Begun in 1792, the structure was complete in 1794, although it was 1797 before the duke could move in.

Other circles of edifying and playful convivial encounter proliferated in Weimar. The *Freitagsgesellschaft* convened once a month at Goethe's house or Anna Amalia's city palace from 1791 to 1797 and featured presentations of works in progress by resident scientists, writers, artists, and intellectuals. Guests from Jena and elsewhere often attended, as did the ducal couple and Anna Amalia. The *Naturforschende Gesellschaft* (Society for Nature Research) met monthly in Jena from 1793–1805 with Goethe often in attendance. This is where Goethe and Schiller had their historic first meeting. The *Mittwochskränzchen* (Wednesday Circle) met every two weeks at Goethe's house for a brief period from 1801–1802 and was intended to replicate the *cour d'amour* of medieval *Minnesang* culture. Eroticism and play should have held sway; instead, Goethe took pains to regulate every aspect and members rebelled at the lifeless formality once spring weather set in. A regular ball season and concerts in the park called *Vauxhalls* provided additional venues for socializing between nobility and the upper middle class. Strict regulations assured that participants remained masked during the ball and that no servant or attendant appeared in disguise. Once the newly constructed Hoftheater (court theater) opened in 1791 under Goethe's and eventually Goethe and Schiller's joint direction, Weimar was treated to first-rate performances by the resident theater troupe of a variety of challenging dramas and operas as well as light entertainments and melodramas. The tradition of amateur theater came to an end.

Other organizations also instanced or envisioned new forms of society, but less playfully and aesthetically than Goethe and Schiller advised. A Masonic lodge bearing the name of its protectress, Anna Amalia, had been in existence in Weimar since 1764. Goethe sought and received membership in 1780 and advanced to the level of master. Eighteenth-century Freemasonry throughout Germany professed to be apolitical, and almost allegorically, if ineffectually, represented the promise of a classless society. Other secret societies, including student organizations, were in existence before the beginning of the French Revolution, but Carl August, Goethe and other members of the Privy Council clamped down illiberally on these associations.[23] Peasants who organized protests and fought for their rights were subject to similarly illiberal measures. Insofar as Weimar Classicism responded to the French Revolution, it would be legitimate to see Goethe's assent to and participation in forms of political repression as another variety of containment. The political spirit that Schiller had meant to keep at bay through the charmed circle of the *Horen* and aesthetic education manifested itself insistently in relation to bread and butter issues on Weimar's doorstep.

Who's Who in Weimar Classicism

At this point it makes sense to introduce the major and minor players involved in Goethe and Schiller's project individually. It belongs to the anomalous nature of Weimar Classicism that comparatively many of their collaborators are virtually unknown and neglected. This may be a function of their relative artistic value in the marketplace of canon formation, but if we are to do justice to Weimar Classicism as a noteworthy project — and not as a distinct literary period — we must certainly take them into account. It has already become clear that Weimar and Jena during the 1790s and first half of the first decade of the nineteenth century were the locations of a great deal of cultural ferment. Weimar Classicism, Jena Romanticism, and Idealist philosophy (not counting Kant) all have their origin in the duchy, and at roughly the same time. And although Friedrich Schlegel began his career with an essay more "classical" than Schiller's contemporaneous *Ueber naive und sentimentalische Dichtung* (I am referring to Schlegel's *Ueber das Studium der Griechischen Poesey* [On the Study of Greek Poetry, 1795]), I will not include the Romantics in this discussion; they are treated in volume eight of the Camden House History of German Literature. I have, however, included another group of writers who did make their way to Weimar, even if only briefly, and shared an affinity with the project, although a sense of mutual rejection and incompatibility mixed with regret and/or disdain was the final upshot. I refer to the classical "unclassical" trio of Jean Paul Richter (1763–1825), Heinrich von Kleist (1777–1811), and Friedrich Hölderlin (1770–1843). In fact, all three writers find their way into the essays that follow. To this threesome, I have added Sophie Mereau (1770–1806). One other writer worthy of mention, though usually neglected — he is discussed in the essay on drama and theater in the present volume — is the dramatist and theater director August Kotzebue (1761–1819).

We should begin with Christoph Martin Wieland. We have already referred to him in connection with Anna Amalia's first efforts to improve the cultural climate in Weimar. In terms of age, Wieland falls precisely between Winckelmann and Goethe. Wieland was sixteen years older than Goethe, and sixteen years can make a difference. Wieland imbibed the Enlightenment in full measure, and encountered the Greek and Roman classics on different terms. (For that reason, Wieland and his important *Bildungsroman, Die Geschichte des Agathon* [The History of Agathon, 1766–67], are treated in the volume on the Enlightenment.) His earliest "classicistic" works are in the mode of the rococo, playful erotic entertainments, what T. J. Reed calls "a lightweight classicism" (75). Many of his works are set in antiquity (the novel *Agathon*, the verse narration *Musarion* [1768], the novel *Die Abderiten* [1774/80], and the musical drama *Alkeste* [1773]), but in ways that allowed him to explore Enlightenment issues in a foreign setting. As early as 1774 Goethe took Wieland to task for his inauthentic representation of the Greeks in a short farce entitled *Götter, Helden und Wieland* (Gods, Heroes and Wieland). Little did Goethe know that Wieland would graciously receive him a year later when he too moved to Weimar. By the time the project of Weimar Classicism really got underway, Wieland was in his sixties, responded to the French Revolution with less aversion than Goethe and Schiller, and was not interested in claiming aesthetic autonomy for the arts. In 1799, Goethe's sometime friend, the archeologist and philologist Karl August Böttiger (1760–1835), reported that Goethe called Wieland "die zierliche Jungfrau von Weimar"[24] (the dainty virgin of Weimar). For his part, Wieland regarded Goethe and particularly Schiller's project with a large dose of cynicism. Not to appear unbalanced, Böttiger reports a conversation with Wieland in which the latter attacked Schiller's aesthetic journal with cloacal humor: "Da wäre in den Horen ein Cloacinentempel errichtet worden, in welchen die großen Männer ihre Nothdurft verrichteten, u. sich für ihr cacatum non pictum 4 Louisd'or bezahlen ließen"[25] (A sewer temple had been erected in the form of the *Horen*, in which the illustrious gentlemen relieved themselves, and charged 4 Louisd'or for their *cacatum non pictum*). Even if Wieland remained a peripheral Weimar Classicist, his presence was important, and Goethe honored him with respect until his death. The Jena Romantics, on the other hand, mocked him and his literary efforts unmercifully. Although no single essay is devoted to Wieland in this volume, he receives his due in the essay on the politics of Weimar.

Another peripheral Classicist, though closer to Goethe in age and mentality than Wieland, is Johann Gottfried Herder. Their friendship dates to the early 1770s and the period of the Sturm und Drang. Pleased to be called to Weimar, Herder and his wife Caroline (1750–1809) had a mixed experience there until his death. Although Herder was the addressee of many of the letters that Goethe wrote from Italy and was involved in some of the early Classicist projects (the verse version of *Iphigenie*, for example), during the 1790s he was at variance with Goethe in crucial respects: Italy, which he visited in 1788–89, left him cold; he disagreed fundamentally with Kant and elaborated an anti-Kantian aesthetics; like Wieland, he was sympathetic to aspects of the French Revolution; he clashed with Goethe when the duke — for political reasons — reneged on his promise to pay for Herder's children's education; and he criticized some of Goethe's classicistic writings on moral, even prudish grounds. When the *Roman Elegies* were published in the *Horen*, Herder snidely remarked that the journal should from now on be known as the *Huren* (whores). Nonetheless, we must recognize that Herder's contributions during the 1770s and 1780s toward notions of humanity and *Bildung* were taken up by Goethe and Schiller and became components of the classical project. Like Wieland, Herder could cast a jaundiced eye on the goings-on in Weimar. Our shady informant Böttiger recalls a conversation in which Herder stated: "Zwei Dinge sind schändlich hier in Weimar. Der falsch erborgte Schimmer, mit dem wir auswärts Gleisnerei treiben, u. die jämmerliche Geistes- und Bücherarmuth, in der wir hier schmachten"[26] (Two things are scandalous here in Weimar. The falsely borrowed shimmer with which we hypocritically represent ourselves to the external world, and the miserable poverty of spirit and books in which we languish). These are bitter and corrective tones that we should not fail to note.

To Weimar (and later Jena) resident Carl Wilhelm von Knebel (1744–1834), royal tutor to both Weimar princes, fell the honor of introducing Goethe to the two princes in 1774 in Frankfurt and thus initiating an era. Goethe and he soon became close friends. Although Knebel failed to produce much of literary substance, he was Goethe's intellectual companion in a variety of literary and scientific efforts. His peculiar contribution to the Classicism project was a translation of the elegies of Propertius in 1788–89. The translation was important for Goethe as he crafted his *Roman Elegies*. In the aftermath, Knebel published eighteen elegies of his own in Schiller's *Horen*. However, Knebel, like his friend Herder, fell afoul of the duke and Goethe because of his outspoken support of the French Revolution.

Another Weimar resident of note is Friedrich Justin Bertuch (1747–1822).[27] If Weimar ever had a chance to find a firm financial footing based not on a feudal agrarian economy but on Adam-Smith-style capitalist principles, it was through the indefatigable efforts of Bertuch, who from 1775–96 served as the duke's financial manager. A self-made man, Bertuch was drawn to literature and the arts early on. A first-ever complete German translation of *Don Quixote* brought him needed capital. Wieland relied on him as a co-editor of his journal *Der teutsche Merkur*. Indeed, Bertuch would go on to build a publishing empire featuring several very successful journals, among them the *Allgemeine Literatur-Zeitung*, closely linked to the academic life of the university in Jena, and the *Journal des Luxus und der Moden*, the first women's magazine devoted to matters of fashion and taste in Germany. Carrying reports from Paris and abroad, with advice for German women, the *Journal* had a remarkable run from 1786–1827. If Schiller proposed aesthetic education as a condition for a civilized state, Bertuch argued for the necessity of modernizing fabrication, distribution, and marketing in order to establish the material conditions needed to escape the feudal situation of a fragmented Germany. In 1791 he consolidated his empire in what was called the Landes-Industrie-Comptoir.

Bertuch's relation to the luminaries of Weimar and the project of Weimar Classicism was sticky. Although many of those associated with Goethe and Schiller felt queasy about Bertuch's capitalistic impulses and his advocacy of commercial fashion, the reason for their nervousness may have been an awareness of a considerable overlap between their aesthetic principles and those advocated by Bertuch. Perhaps the most visible manifestation of the interpenetration of commodity culture and Classicism is Bertuch's canny marketing of the latter through the advertising and sale of mass-produced plaster casts of sculptural busts of Weimar's icons and of other celebrities and classical sculptures. If all the world (think of Madame de Staël [1766–1817]) and certainly all of Germany looked to Weimar in imitative appreciation of its mode of aesthetic living, to what extent was that the accomplishment first and foremost of Bertuch and the *Journal*? In other words, who put Weimar on the map?

The friends and associates mentioned so far all either lived in or came to Weimar long before the Classical project got underway. This is not true of those who follow. The writer Karl Philipp Moritz,[28] for instance, met Goethe in Rome, and the latter put him up as a houseguest for nine months after their staggered returns from Italy. Goethe profited from Moritz's *Versuch einer deutschen Prosodie* (1786) and his personal advice as he converted *Iphigenie* from prose to verse. Although neglected by scholars for many years, Moritz — and not Schiller — is the initial theorist of classical aesthetic autonomy. His 1785 essay, based on prior work in that direction by Moses Mendelssohn (1729–86), beats Kant to the punch by several years. Once in Italy and in almost eerily close relationship with Goethe, Moritz registers and works out the theory of what would become the autonomy aesthetics of Weimar Classicism in an essay called *Über die bildende Nachahmung des Schönen* (On the Creative Imitation of the Beautiful).[29] In ways disturbing to later scholars, Goethe would make this essay his own to the point of almost negating Moritz's authorship.[30] At the beginning of the correspondence between Goethe and Schiller, the essay appears as Goethe lends it to Schiller — his first gift, as it were — who read it with interest. Schiller then passed it on to Wilhelm von Humboldt (of whom more shortly). The essay glorifies the sovereign autonomy of art and the creative artist in provocative ways that lead, as we have seen, to strong assertions about the relation of beauty, the inutility of art, and ornament. The essay also calls attention to an almost masochistic awareness of the relationship between beauty and pain. It is Moritz, not Schiller, who stands directly behind Goethe's radical observations about pain in the Laocoön.

The Swiss artist and art historian Johann Heinrich Meyer (1760–1832) is someone else Goethe met in Rome and invited back to Weimar as houseguest. Meyer remained in Goethe's home from 1791 until he married in 1802. Regarded by scholarship as something of a Dr. Watson to Goethe's Holmes — if remarked at all — Meyer initially attracted Goethe's attention as an expert on art by making a confident attribution when everyone else was stumped. Now, of course, we know that Meyer was mistaken — the painting of "St. George and the Dragon" was by Bordone, not Pordenone as Meyer asserted — but it was enough for Goethe to be convinced that Meyer possessed the knowledge he desired. During four decades of close friendship, Meyer played a supporting — most would say epigonal — role in Goethe's projects. Among his many and varied activities during Weimar Classicism, he redesigned portions of Goethe's house including the impressive front staircase while Goethe accompanied Carl August on the Prussian military campaign into France in 1792. He was Goethe's consultant for art purchases and on the editorial board of the *Horen* and the *Propyläen*, to both of which he also contributed articles. His essay on eighteenth-century art was taken up in Goethe's commemorative *Winckelmann und sein Jahrhundert* (Winckelmann and His Century, 1805). Meyer and Goethe were the key "Weimarer Kunstfreunde" (friends of art), who in the mid 1790s held art contests in a vain and ill-conceived effort to jump-start a German classicism of art at a time when Caspar David Friedrich (1774–1840) and Philipp Otto Runge (1777–1810) were already forging the visual vocabulary of Romanticism. After the death of the initial editor, Carl Ludwig Fernow (1763–1808), Meyer assumed the editorship of the collected works of Winckelmann. Evidently, Goethe's "Kunscht-Meyer" as he was known — (because of the frequency of the last name Meyer an adjective is often added locally to avoid confusion; "Kunscht" approximates the pronunciation of the word *Kunst* or art in dialect) — is the best representative of the dogmatic side of Weimar Classicism. One marvels at his uninspired and loyal pedantry and Goethe's inability to assess it correctly. Residing in the same house over many years, there was no occasion for a monumental correspondence on the order of the Goethe-Schiller correspondence, and we are therefore wont to forget him. As scholars interested in a balanced sense of the nature of the project of Weimar Classicism, however, we must keep Meyer and his pedantry in mind.

We have already had occasion to cite passages from Karl August Böttiger's posthumously published *Literarische Zustände und Zeitgenossen*

(1838). Böttiger came to Weimar in 1791 and remained until 1804. He was a classical philologist and archaeologist by training, director of the Weimar *Gymnasium*, and an active participant in many of the projects and circles of Weimar Classicism, including the *Horen* and the *Propyläen*, as well as Wieland's *Merkur* and Bertuch's *Journal*. He earned the ire of Goethe and Schiller through numerous indiscretions[31] and scandal mongering. Given the bitterness of their parting and his weakness for gossip, his recollections of life in Classical Weimar are at the same time entertaining and of uncertain reliability.

Wilhelm von Humboldt is known to most as a linguist and founder of the university in Berlin in 1810 that is now called the Humboldt University. Humboldt did not meet Goethe in Italy, nor did he reside in Weimar, but he did live in Jena for long stretches, first as a friend of Schiller and soon thereafter as Goethe's during the height of classical aesthetic theorizing. Along with Fichte, Humboldt was one of the first people Schiller engaged for the *Horen*. In 1794, he met with Schiller and Goethe for a protracted aesthetic summit, as it were, and all sides found themselves in agreement. Humboldt translated Aeschylus and Pindar, wrote an essay on Homer and two other essays that were published in the *Propyläen*. Just as Moritz had advised Goethe on transposing *Iphigenie* into verse, Humboldt proofed Goethe's efforts to compose a Homeric epic in dactylic hexameter. The poem in question is *Herrmann und Dorothea* (1797).[32] Because of Humboldt's involvement in the poem and its centrality to past conceptions of Weimar Classicism and the Classical project, a digression is in order.

Set against the background of the flight of French citizens across the Rhine and into Germany, *Herrmann und Dorothea* strikes early twenty-first-century readers as an almost trivial boy-meets-girl story rendered in heroic and Homeric mode. The juxtaposition of exalted verse and a Winckelmannian sculptural ideal with the small-town circumstances of the shy innkeeper's son may seem more than faintly ludicrous to us now, but almost from its inception and throughout the nineteenth century *Herrmann und Dorothea* was among Goethe's most popular and beloved works.[33] If we are prepared to accept the self-aware poetic and erotic stylings of the *Roman Elegies* — also a juxtaposition of a classical mode with modern content — we draw the line at the representation of a German middle-class milieu as though it were as naive and simple as an old Homeric goat herder, and with good reason: not even Homer — especially not Homer — was that naive. Most of Goethe's contemporaries, however, were smitten by the piece. Wieland wrote that the characters in the poem "sind Figuren in Marmor gehauen" (figures carved in marble).[34] Even the rumor-mongering Böttiger has only praise for the piece. It is, he writes, "die *einzige Odyssee*, die in unsern Tagen noch möglich schien" (84; the *only Odyssey* still possible in our times). Wilhelm von Humboldt offered the most lavish, even excessive response to the epic poem. In the manner of a latter-day idealist Aristotle he derived a classical poetics solely on the basis of *Herrmann und Dorothea*. Entitled *Ueber Goethe's Hermann und Dorothea* (1799), this sizable work is, incidentally, the first-ever monograph on a Goethe text. Although we are even less likely to read Humboldt's book than the epic itself, it behooves us to take it seriously as a crucial manifestation of Weimar Classicism. According to Humboldt's lights, *Herrmann und Dorothea* was the classical work par excellence, totally embodying the aspirations of Weimar Classicism: eighteenth-century Germany transformed. Jane Brown argues that *Herrmann und Dorothea* is the one work of Goethe's that most perfectly conforms to the challenge Schiller sets in the *Aesthetic Letters*. She points in particular to a passage in book eight where the two young people are transformed into what Schiller calls "lebende Gestalt"[35] (living form). This happens at a point where Dorothea stubs her toe and Herrmann catches her:

> So stand er,
> Starr wie ein Marmorbild, vom ernsten Willen gebändigt,
> Drückte nicht fester sie an, er stemmte sich gegen die Schwere.
> Und so fühlt' er die herrliche Last, die Wärme des Herzens,
> Und den Balsam des Atems, an seinen Lippen verhauchet,
> Trug mit Mannesgefühl die Heldengröße des Weibes.
> Doch sie verhehlte den Schmerz. . . . (MA 4.1:617)

[Thus he stood, as immobile as a marble sculpture, bound by serious will, did not hold her closer, he planted himself against her weight. And thus he felt the splendid burden, the warmth of her heart, and the balsam of her breath as it transpired on his lips, bore with manly feeling the heroic grandeur of the woman. Yet she concealed her pain.]

No question, this is another instantiation of the Laocoön, a moment of pain aesthetically contained and rendered for eternity. And precisely for this reason, *Herrmann und Dorothea* is a crux for current scholarship. On the one hand, how can we take this heroic, sculptural transformation of small-town eighteenth-century Germany and an anecdote about a stubbed toe seriously? And, on the other, as Brown convincingly argues, how can we not? To point to Goethe's irony as some have done[36] helps up to a point, but does not absolve us from taking the poem and its aspiration seriously. In any case, the uncritical resonance the poem enjoyed may have gone to Goethe's head. One of his next projects was the ill-starred *Achilleis*, a wooden attempt to insert an epic poem accounting for Achilles' death between the *Iliad* and the *Odyssey*. This project was never completed.

Goethe might never have undertaken to write *Herrmann und Dorothea* had it not been for Johann Heinrich Voss (1751–1826) who first visited Goethe in 1794 and moved to Jena in 1802. In 1781, Voss had translated Homer's *Odyssey* and would go on to translate the *Iliad* in 1793. Voss's idyllic epic (or epic idyll) *Luise* (1783–84) was an acknowledged and admired forerunner of Goethe's efforts, as were Voss's accomplishments in producing the classical long line, the hexameter. The substance of their friendship and the basis for Goethe's respect for Voss consisted in his knowledge of and facility in the adaptation of classical meter to the German language.

The final male participant in Weimar Classicism is Carl Ludwig Fernow, who came to Jena in 1791 to study with Schiller and the Kantian philosopher Carl Leonhard Reinhold (1758–1823), one of Wieland's sons-in-law, and a co-editor of Wieland's *Merkur*. Fernow left for Rome in 1794 to study art, but determined he was better suited for philosophy and aesthetics. A series of lectures on art and aesthetics informed by Kantian principles delivered in Rome in 1795–96 earned him a reputation, and in 1802 he was appointed to the faculty of the University of Jena, although it was 1803 before he left Rome to assume the position. Despite some initial hesitation on Goethe's part, he became a key player in the latter years of Weimar Classicism. Like Meyer, Fernow was involved in the commemorative Winckelmann project and was appointed the editor of the collected works of Winckelmann. He died in 1808 after completing two volumes.

Beginning with Anna Amalia (she remained a vital cultural force in Weimar until her death in 1807, that is, throughout the period in question), women played an important role in the cultural and aesthetic life of Weimar. The *Liebhabertheater* in particular enabled performative, literary, and musical contributions from women and men alike, though most often under the sign of the ephemeral. More than a few turned their hands to the pen. At the point when Goethe and Schiller aspired to something like the classical, however, the stakes changed. Schiller did publish poems and prose by women writers in the *Horen*, but also and more often in his less prestigious *Musenalmanach*. The submissions of women writers were the occasion for a lively discussion about dilettantism, with predictable results. The turn to Greece and the imitation of its homosocial, if not homoerotic culture made it difficult for women to ally themselves with the project. Nonetheless, several women tried. Three of them will be introduced, all resident in Weimar, all challenging Goethe in the field of the drama, the novel, and the epic poem respectively. A more substantial discussion of women writers and their relation to Weimar Classicism can be found in Elisabeth Krimmer's essay in this volume.[37]

We usually think of Charlotte von Stein (1742–1827) as Goethe's longtime platonic lover from the early, pre-Italian days. Even though many of the letters that are taken up in the *Italienische Reise* are addressed to her, his abrupt and unannounced departure for Italy, his affair with Christiane Vulpius, and the publication of the *Roman Elegies* exacerbated the rupture between them and would seem to have precluded her participation in the Classicism project. Nonetheless, she remained an informed observer. Taking a critical position on the periphery, she wrote *Dido: Ein Trauerspiel in Fünf Akten* (A Tragedy in Five Acts, 1794–95, although not published in her lifetime) in which she confronted Goethe and the phenomenon of classicism.[38] Often seen in relation to Goethe's *Iphigenie* — some have called it an "anti-Iphigenie" — her play and her perspective on the consequences of Goethe's Classicism allow for no happy ending. A Goethe-like poet colludes with others in order to force the widowed Queen Dido to marry a Barbarian king in hopes of bringing an end to female rule. Seeing no way out, the heroine commits suicide, but not before exposing the issues that bring her to this point.

Caroline von Wolzogen (1763–1847, born Lengefeld) was Schiller's sister-in-law. After divorcing her first husband she married Schiller's old friend Wilhelm von Wolzogen, joining him in Weimar. She led a lively salon in her home at which Goethe was a frequent guest. Delightful for our purposes is the fact that her novel *Agnes von Lilien*, a sort of female counterpart to *Wilhelm Meister*, published anonymously in installments in the *Horen*, was almost universally assumed to have been written by Goethe. Once her authorship was revealed, the putative female flaws became apparent and it was evident to everyone that it could not have been written by Goethe after all. Wieland took his own line: "Agnes von Lilien könnte ein klassisches Buch der Nation geworden seyn, wenn nicht die Verfasserin im Verfolg des Buches auf einmal in Schillers mystischer Metaphysik zu sprechen gelüstet hätte"[39] (Agnes von Lilien could have become a classical book of the nation, had the author, in continuing the book, not suddenly developed a taste for speaking in Schiller's metaphysical manner). Goethe acknowledged her talent, but found her prose lacking classical tranquility.

Goethe made a similar if harsher judgment with respect to a third woman writer of Weimar, Anna Amalia von Imhoff (1776–1831). Born in Weimar, she became acquainted with Goethe as a child and grew up in the milieu of Duchess Anna Amalia's *Musenhof.* Meyer gave her lessons in drawing and composing poetry and Goethe recommended some of her poems to Schiller for his *Musenalmanach*, certainly a less prestigious venue than the *Horen*. Goethe taught her the craft of composing in hexameter, and she undertook to write an epic poem *Die Schwestern von Lesbos* (The Sisters of Lesbos, 1800). For Goethe and Schiller she was a study in unfortunate dilettantism. For our purposes, she stands as a sign of female participation in the Classical project, however importunate to its guardians. We also realize that Goethe's judgments can by no means be trusted implicitly. When Goethe renders a judgment on a work of literature or art from the doctrinaire position we associate with Meyer, we may safely conclude something about Goethe, but must reserve judgment about the work in question until we have read or seen it ourselves.

If these three women stood on the periphery, in part prevented from full participation by gender obstacles erected by Goethe and Schiller, three other writers, in this instance three men, also occupied places on the periphery and encountered obstacles of a different kind. Jean Paul Richter, Friedrich Hölderlin, and Heinrich von Kleist have generally been lumped together as anomalies — not belonging to Classicism proper or to Romanticism narrowly understood. In the larger picture, there is no question that they have their place in European Romanticism, but when it comes to Weimar and Jena, they find no home. At different points, each of them was strongly attracted to Classical Weimar, to Goethe or Schiller or both. From our perspective, we can identify aspects of the Classicism project to which their work bore unmistakable affinities: an orientation to the Greeks and classical notions of form, for example, or an aspiration to a classical fullness of life. A tendency toward excess in contrast to classical restraint, however, or a desire to probe pain and other emotions and conditions of life in ways that compromised aesthetic containment made it clear to all parties that they should go separate ways.

Johann Paul Friedrich Richter, or Jean Paul as he wanted to be known, first attracted attention with his best-selling novel *Hesperus* (1795) and his remarkable talent for mixing satire and humor with sentimentalism. Soon thereafter, Goethe and Schiller invited him to Weimar in order to gauge his abilities and possibly to win him for their project. Jean Paul obliged but declined Schiller's offer to join the editorial board of the *Horen*; what is worse, he found Goethe's company and classical aura repulsive. The only alliance that made sense to him was with Herder and Wieland, two other peripheral classicists who shared his pro-Republican outlook, and with several of the women of Weimar. Jean Paul rejected both Weimar's return to Greece and the Jena Romantics turn to the Christian middle ages.[40] In his novel *Titan* (1800–1803), Jean Paul confronts Weimar Classicism head on, even conferring features of Goethe and Schiller on two of his characters. The novel rejects the Classical project outright.

As a young man, Heinrich von Kleist also came to Weimar, though not on anyone's invitation. After three ineffectual months in Weimar in late 1802, Wieland invited him to stay at his home in Ossmannstedt, encouraging him as a writer, convinced of the powerful talent Kleist possessed. Goethe would later recognize Kleist's talent repeatedly, but could not accept the profoundly tragic and fragmented world represented in his plays. Pain on the one hand and relentless bitter comedy on the other overwhelmed any notion of classical restraint. Nonetheless, Goethe and Kleist remained in somewhat prickly contact over a period of years from 1802 to 1808. Although he was unconvinced that Kleist's *Der zerbrochene Krug* (The Broken Jug, 1808) could be successfully staged, Goethe went ahead and produced the play in Weimar. Essentially a comical and sophisticated retelling of Sophocles' *Oedipus*, the play suffered in Goethe's hands. The classical style of acting and several directorial interventions (breaking the play into three distinct acts, for example) assured its disaster. The play that brought about Goethe's final rupture with Kleist was *Penthesilea*, an alternative account of the death of Achilles (remember that Goethe had unsuccessfully attempted to write an *Achilleis*) at the hands of an Amazon queen. In this play of wild and exuberant excess with a tragic conclusion loosely modeled on Euripides' *Bacchae*, Kleist literally takes the classical body (Achilles) and classical diction and form and tears them to shreds in cannibalistic fury. In the face of such a tragic vision, no containment is possible. Language itself attains dangerous physical qualities. Recognizing what she has done to her hotly pursued lover, Penthesilea slays herself with a metaphor. In 1811, Kleist killed himself and the cancer-ridden Frau Vogel in a double suicide on the shore of Wannsee outside Berlin. It would be a century and more before Kleist gained the recognition he deserved.

As a young man Friedrich Hölderlin had studied theology in Tübingen together with Hegel and Schelling. The philosophical appeal of Jena may have brought him to Saxe-Weimar in any event, but in fact it was Schiller who was able to secure a position as tutor for the struggling writer in the Weimar home of his longtime friend Charlotte von Kalb (1761–1843) in 1793. After a few months he moved to Jena, where he remained until 1795. Schiller recognized Hölderlin's poetic talent and urged him on a dismissive Goethe. Confronted with two of Hölderlin's poems that Schiller sent him in 1797, Goethe famously and obtusely recommended that the poet confine himself to short, simple idylls with maximum human interest. Schiller unsuccessfully championed his novel *Hyperion* (1797–1799; *Fragment von Hyperion* appeared in Schiller's *Thalia* in 1794). Set in contemporary Greece in the midst of war against the occupying Turks, the novel is informed by a strongly elegiac mood. Less sensationally than Kleist, but more incisively, Hölderlin explored the limits of Classicism. He probed tragic depths in translations of Sophocles, his own tragedy *Empedokles* (1797) and accompanying philosophical essays, and explored classical mythology and poetic form in a series of odes modeled on those of the Greek poet Pindar. Since the twentieth century, it has been apparent that Hölderlin is the poet's poet, possessed of an infallible instinct for the possibilities and burden of poetic language and form. There are no fragmented, blood-bespattered corpses in his work — although plenty of thought-provoking fragments in his poetic corpus. Even as he succeeded in occupying classical forms (ode, elegy, and hymn) in unprecedented ways, Hölderlin became convinced that the grandeur of Greece was forever lost. His rejection of Classicism involved a turn to *Vaterlandsdichtung* (poetry of the fatherland), remarkable hymns that celebrated and allegorized the German landscape. In 1806 Hölderlin became mentally ill and his former poetic production all but ceased. In 1807 he was moved into a tower residence on the river Neckar in Tübingen until his death in 1843.[41]

To this unclassical trio, I have added Sophie Mereau (born Schubart; 1770–1806), another writer best situated between Classicism and Romanticism.[42] At age twenty-one she had already published a poem in Schiller's *Thalia*. Two years later, in 1793, she married Karl Mereau, a Jena university librarian (later a professor of law), who had lured her into a loveless marriage with promises of friendship to Schiller and literary fame. She shocked society with her self-assured independence, auditing Fichte's lectures and departing publicly for Berlin in the company of her lover. A letter from Schiller to Goethe in response to his curiosity about "die kleine Schönheit" (the little beauty) indicates that Mereau had discussed her marital difficulties with Schiller, hoping for his advice (15 October 1796). In 1798 she met the significantly younger Romantic writer Clemens Brentano (1778–1842), with whom she carried on a stormy affair and eventually married after she became pregnant. She published poems and prose in Schiller's *Horen* and *Musenalmanach*. The two texts that stand out in relation to Weimar Classicism are *Amanda und Eduard* (1803), an epistolary novel that responds to *Wilhelm Meister*, and most particularly her biographical essay "Ninon de Lenclos" (1802), essentially a philosophical recuperation of a seventeenth-century Frenchwoman famed for her great sexual liberty, published in *Kalathiskos*, a journal she founded and edited. This may be Mereau's most classical text and the most classical text written by a woman of Weimar. The concept of erotic freedom developed here is in tune with Winckelmannian notions, while the sovereign ease of her prose and her unapologetic defense of Ninon's lifestyle is equal to that of Goethe's own essay on Winckelmann written about the same time. In 1805 she followed Brentano to Heidelberg. She died of complications from giving birth to their third child. None of her children by Brentano survived more than a few days.

The final outsider to Goethe and Schiller's Classicism to be introduced is August Friedrich Ferdinand Kotzebue (1761–1819). Born in Weimar, Kotzebue was a prolific playwright of comedies and melodramas. Goethe refused to recognize his plays as art, but in recognition of their popularity made them a staple of the Weimar theater's productions. In 1802 Kotzebue set out on a campaign to penetrate Goethe's inner circle and to claim the recognition he was convinced he deserved. Rebuffed by both Goethe and Schiller, on the one hand, and lampooned by the Romantics, on the other, he took on the entire literary establishment in Weimar, provoking a feud of public proportions. He assailed a production by Goethe of a piece by Friedrich Schlegel and succeeded in alienating large segments of the Weimar theater audience from Goethe's project. In hopes of driving a wedge between Goethe and Schiller, he planned a large *Schiller-Fest*, but the Weimar authorities refused him access to public buildings. In 1803, Kotzebue left for Berlin, but his invective did not diminish. He established a journal with Böttiger and another disaffected writer called *Der Freimüthige* (The Honest One) in which he vented his critical spleen. In 1819 Kotzebue was assassinated in Mannheim by a student from Jena in a bizarre case of misunderstood international intrigue. Obviously, Kotzebue does not belong to Weimar Classicism proper. But perhaps it makes sense to think of him as Goethe's doppelganger, Weimar Classicism's ghost, a legitimate and annoying haunting, as it were, of Classicism's noblest aspirations.

Gender and Sexuality in Weimar Classicism

Common wisdom holds that the figures in Henry James's novels resemble people wading waist deep through water at the beach — the reader sees only the upper half. Not so in Weimar Classicism. The human being who corresponds to the utopian aspirations of the classical project is known as "der ganze Mensch" (the complete person) which we can read in the double sense of un-fragmented (the usual interpretation), on the one hand, and including *all* the body parts, on the other. This is important, for in many ways the times did not favor such a conception of the body. A revolution in the conception of the body and how it — and especially youthful bodies — should be disciplined had taken place over the last decades of the eighteenth century, principally through the efforts of Joachim Campe (1746–1818) and his fellow Philanthropinists as they were called. An intense campaign to combat supposedly epidemic levels of masturbation and encourage maternal breast-feeding as opposed to the use of wet nurses had gripped Germany and everywhere left its mark.[43] Open-minded in the sense of admitting these regions of the body and their desires into language, this movement was clearly a product of the Enlightenment. Nonetheless, its general thrust was repressive, with consequences for culture in the widest sense. An insistent linkage of the propensity to masturbate with the availability of literature and a corresponding outbreak of *Lesewut* (addiction to reading) assured that the authors in our who's who, especially Wieland, but also Goethe, Schiller, and others, were aware of the stakes.

From the beginning, eighteenth-century neo-classicism throughout Europe had been associated with eroticism and alternative sexual practice. Its most famous and original proponent, Johann Joachim Winckelmann, had left for Italy also because of the erotic liberties it afforded. There is substantial documentary evidence, both of a private and a public nature, that Winckelmann cultivated a form of male-male friendship — known as Greek or Socratic friendship — that concerned the whole man (*der ganze Mensch*). The descriptions of sculptures and paintings of specific heroes and gods (for example, Ganymede and Apollo) in his compendious *Geschichte der Kunst des Altertums* (History of the Art of Antiquity, 1764) are often erotically charged. In particular, his predilection for the androgynous body of eunuchs or castrati (as they were known in his own opera-obsessed times) finds its way into his theorizing about classical beauty. For his part, Goethe did not shy from addressing Winckelmann's sexuality. He honored Winckelmann's practice of friendship in a section of his commemorative biographical essay on Winckelmann simply entitled "Freundschaft" (Friendship). "Zu einer Freundschaft dieser Art fühlte Winckelmann sich geboren, derselben nicht allein sich fähig, sondern im höchsten Grad bedürftig" (MA 6.2:354; Winckelmann felt himself to be born for friendship of this kind, not only capable of it, but in extreme need of it).

What sexual significance Italy might have had for Goethe has been a matter of considerable conjecture and dispute. Some have argued that Rome is where Goethe enjoyed his first and decidedly belated sexual experience. Certainly, some of his private letters to the duke from the time are characterized by sexual bravado. Likewise, *The Roman Elegies*, originally entitled *Erotica Romana*, hint broadly at pleasurable sexual encounters of a more than literary kind. Already in his lifetime speculation was rife. A favored interpretation of the elegies is to suggest that they really concern the splendid sexual ease he shared with Christiane Vulpius in the beginning of their affair upon his return from Italy. Others have gone to great lengths to unearth the historical "Faustina."[44] One or two late twentieth-century scholars have argued that Goethe also experimented with homosexuality in Rome, although this is a difficult case to make empirically.[45] They can point to his great interest in the public display in Italy of what we would call homosexual behavior, a line of verse in the Venetian epigrams,[46] and his too registering the omnipresence of castrati.

Sexual affairs were nothing new to courtly life, and did not require Italy for inspiration. French and German prototypes reaching back into the seventeenth century (for example Ninon de Lenclos [1620–1705], the woman whose sovereign sexuality was celebrated by Sophie Mereau) were sufficient. Duke Carl August maintained an official mistress, Caroline Jagemann (1777–1848), openly visiting her and their children with the tacit consent of his wife. Other young residents of Weimar could also point to him or his brother as father. Goethe's affair with Vulpius would have been acceptable on this model, if only he had not had the effrontery to actually live with this woman of a lower social station.[47] Any other resident of Weimar would certainly have been called before the Consistory (and therefore Herder) and possibly punished. Affairs, divorces, and remarriage were not infrequent occurrences — although divorce did require a special dispensation from the duke — and not worthy of any attention more serious than gossip.

Indeed, marriage has an ambiguous status in Weimar Classicism. Celebrated in *Herrmann und Dorothea*, long deferred in Goethe's relationship with Vulpius, marriage is the subject of critical reflection in a number of classical Goethean texts. If the Sturm und Drang and Classical versions of the play *Stella* toyed comically (1776) and tragically (1803) with the idea of a formal ménage-a-trois, Goethe's *Natürliche Tochter* (Natural/Bastard Daughter, 1803) allegorized cross-class marriage as the only way to safeguard classical aesthetics in Revolutionary times. Driven to the brink by the machinations of courtly intrigue, the noble Eugenie at first rejects a proposal of marriage from an upright middle-class town councilor. A protracted rhetorical skirmish over the meaning of marriage ensues. The councilor asserts: "Im Hause, wo der Gatte sicher waltet, / Da wohnt allein der Friede, den vergebens du, da draußen, suchen magst. / Unruh'ge Mißgunst, grimmige Verleumdung, / Verhallendes, parteiisches Bestreben, / Nicht wirken sie auf diesen heil'gen Kreis" (2179–84; In the home, where the husband rules securely, that is the only place where peace resides, for which you may search outside in vain. Restless resentment, bitter slander, passing biased efforts, they have no effect on this holy circle). Eugenie recognizes new patterns of male dominance instead: "Der Gatte zieht sein Weib unwiderstehlich / In seines Kreises abgeschloßne Bahn. / Dorthin ist sie gebannt, sie kann sich nicht / Aus eigner Kraft besondre Wege wählen" (2295–98; The husband draws his wife irresistibly into the enclosure of his circled path. There she is banished, she is powerless to choose paths of her own). Choosing finally between certain death and marriage, she opts for the latter: "Im Verborgnen / Verwahr' er mich, als reinen Talisman" (2852–53; Let him hide me as innocent talisman). The mesalliance of the *Natürliche Tochter* is the precise inverse of Goethe's eventual marriage to Christiane Vulpius. In both cases, however, the alliance turns on preserving the possibility of aesthetic life in its fullest sense for the future. At the same time, we are reminded not to forget the concept of class in Classicism.

There was, however, something different and new about the intersection of Weimar Classicism with courtly sexual practice. Classicism celebrated the body. It focused public attention on the contours and rhythms of nude Greek sculpture. It imagined sexual encounter not as conquest in the spirit say of Casanova (1725–1798) or *Les Liaisons dangereuses* (1782) by Choderlos de Laclos (1741–1803). At a time when expressions of sexual desire were under fire from Campe and his fellow reformers, Weimar Classicism generally and Goethe specifically ventured to imagine sexuality differently. After considerable back and forth as to the seemliness of doing so, Schiller published a mildly censored version of Goethe's *Roman Elegies*, in an issue that contained a concluding installment of his own *Aesthetische Briefe*, prompting Goethe to call the joint product a centaur: a philosophical head joined to a randy body. Modeled on the playful erotic elegies of Catallus, Propertius, Tibullus, and Ovid, Goethe's elegies combined classical erudition with frank eroticism. For all their classical styling, distinctly modern tones sound through. By publishing these poems, Goethe offered his readers nothing less than an opportunity to re-mythologize their sex lives, to conceive themselves as gods in resplendent sexual ease.

Nehme dann Jupiter mehr von seiner Juno, es lasse
  Wohler sich, wenn er es kann, irgend ein Sterblicher sein.
Uns ergötzen die Freuden des echten nacketen Amors
  Und des geschaukelten Betts lieblicher knarrender Ton.[48] (FA 1.1:394)

[Now not Jupiter's pleasure in Juno's embraces is greater,
  And no mortal's content vies, I will wager, with mine!
Ours is the true, the authentic, the naked Love; and beneath us,
  Rocking in rhythm, the bed creaks the dear song of our joy.[49]]

For all their differences, the two component parts of the centaur, the *Aesthetische Briefe* and the *Roman Elegies*, pursue a common goal: the creation of complete people, complete in themselves, of aesthetic lives, aesthetically lived. The sexual politics of Weimar are as continuous with the Enlightenment as their moral opponent, Campe's determined effort at disciplining the body. Both strive for containment, yet what a difference between the moral and aesthetic varieties! What Weimar Classicism aimed at was nothing less than an emancipation of the body.[50]

Of course, the fact that certain elegies were not published gives the lie to the success of the enterprise. Those that were published provoked scandal enough, even in Weimar. Literary efforts of this kind were deemed inappropriate for publication; such fare was more aptly passed from hand to hand in manuscript form and not disclosed to the hoi polloi. Goethe did not retreat, however, nor did he voice regret over the publication. Even so, it would be more than a century, even two, before numbers of scholars were fully aware of the dimensions of Goethe's ambitions for sexual reform. Two additional poems long suppressed, written at the same time and in similar form, inspired by the same Latin elegies, were not published for decades, and then only discreetly, hidden away in an appendix of a late volume of the Weimar edition of Goethe's works, dissociated from their companion elegies. Known as the priapic poems, named after the god Priapus, a Latin garden god with an erect and oversize penis, these poems are now considered by many scholars to be the initial and concluding poems of the *Roman Elegies* cycle. In the second of these, Priapus addresses the poet directly and thanks him for restoring his dignity.

Nun, durch deine Bemühung, o! redlicher Künstler, gewinn ich
  Unter Göttern den Platz, der mir und andern gebührt. (FA 1.1:441)

[Now, thanks to your good work, honest craftsman, I have been granted
  My due place among gods, fitting for me and for all.[51]]

That place among the gods is explicitly addressed in the central poem of the cycle, though, tellingly, only the mythologically informed reader will realize this. The poem imagines a pantheon of gods in an artist's studio. Last to be mentioned is Cythere, who appears to be asking her lover Bacchus: "Sollte der herrliche Sohn uns an der Seite nicht stehn?" (FA 1.1:415; Should not our splendid son stand by our side?). The son in question is none other than Priapus.

These Priapic poems are no anomaly for Weimar Classicism. Other texts and drawings by Goethe, as well as Priapic items in his collections of art works and other objects picked up while in Italy and after, testify to a more than passing interest. In fact, as one pursues this submerged discursive strand, one discovers a widespread interest in Priapic matters among the male participants of Weimar Classicism. Most seem to be aware of an essay by William Hamilton (1730–1803), an acquaintance from Goethe's Italian days, "On the Worship of Priapus in the Kingdom of Naples" as well as *Discourse on the Worship of Priapus* (1786) of Richard Payne Knight (1751–1824) in which Hamilton's essay found its home. Böttiger was known for having an extensive collection of classical Priapea. Even Wieland, looking back on passages and texts in his own corpus that caused moral indignation, is reported to have said:

> Ich habe besondere Vorstellungen von den sacris phallicis des grauen Alterthums. Es waren die ehrwürdigsten Naturfeierlichkeiten. So bald der Mensch nur ein Glied an seinem Leibe hat, dessen er sich schämen muß, hat er seine Unschuld verloren. Man tadelt es, daß nackte Figuren da aufgestellt werden, wo Mädchen im Hause sind. Hätte ich nur recht viel, ich wollte all meine Zimmer davon anfüllen. Warum ziehn wir denn den Hunden und Ochsen nicht auch Hosen an? Der heiligste Naturtrieb ist durch Pfafferei entadelt und verschrien worden.[52]

> [I have my own ideas about the sacris phallicis of hoary antiquity. They were the most honorable celebrations of nature. As soon as man has a single member of his body of which he feels ashamed, he has lost his innocence. People criticize those who display naked figures where girls are at home. If only I had many such figures, I'd fill all the rooms in my house with them. Why don't we put pants on dogs and oxen? The most holy natural drive has been denigrated and impugned by hypocrisy.]

If Laocoön and the role of pain in the production of classical beauty form one of the secret poles of Weimar Classicism, perhaps Priapus and the cult of the erect penis (one might almost say, the sculptural penis) constitute another. Between them and arcing through the manifestations of Classicism discussed in our "who's who" (Moritz's masochism, Bertuch's marketing strategies, Meyer's pedantry, Humboldt's extravagant investment in *Herrmann und Dorothea*, and the proto-feminist interventions of von Stein and von Wolzogen), our understanding of the project of Weimar Classicism is in the process of being fleshed out.

Since we have once again mentioned the women of Weimar Classicism, we should conclude this section on gender and sexuality with a question about the assigned place of femininity and women in the project. An anthology of pertinent texts published in 1992 by Sigrid Lange is aptly entitled *Ob die Weiber Menschen sind: Geschlechterdebatten um 1800* (Whether Women are Human: Gender Debates Around 1800).[53] Enlightenment, Romantic, Classicist, and Idealist texts are here assembled, and for all their differences speak almost with one voice regarding the subordinate role of women. Despite the poems and prose by women published in the *Horen*, their participation in the aestheticization of life in Weimar, their roles in the affairs and marriages of the project's principals and supporting cast, Goethe and Schiller and their male comrades found ways to keep women at a distance from the heart of the project. Femininity, "adequately" theorized, as in Humboldt's essay "Über den Geschlechtsunterschied und dessen Einfluß auf die organische Natur" (On Sexual Difference and Its Influence On Organic Nature, 1795) published in the *Horen*, could certainly be admitted, as could representations of women in poems, plays, and novels. But writerly women remained dilettantes in Goethe and Schiller's view, incapable of aspiring individually to the human completeness in principle available to men.

Weimar Classicism's Legacy

The concept of the classical fell out of favor during the course of the twentieth century. From mid-century on, reverence for Goethe and Schiller increasingly and variously gave way to scorn, skepticism, ideological critique, and neglect. If the nineteenth century favored Schiller as a national poet, the twentieth century found Goethe more to its liking. The fortunes of individual works rose and fell on the stock market of literary criticism. The reputation of *Herrmann und Dorothea* plummeted, while stockholders in *Die Wahlverwandschaften* saw unexpected returns. *Faust* and *Wilhelm Meister* held their ground. Schiller's *Aesthetische Erziehung* proved a lightening rod for criticism. Scholars and critics schooled in poststructuralist and postmodern thought roundly rejected many of the values and concepts of Weimar Classicism. The very suggestion of aesthetic norms, the preposterousness of aesthetic autonomy, and the political impropriety of visions of totality were enough to cast the project of Weimar Classicism and its adherents in an unsavory light. We have rejected the Faustian wager. A single soul — or, perhaps, a single *multiple* soul — dwells in our breast. No longer clamoring for the absolute, we cleave to the earth and practice cultural studies.

The nadir of the popular reception of Goethe and Schiller occurred in the 1970s and 80s in the wake of the 1968 student movement. While the German education system worked hard to liberate its curriculum from mandatory readings of *Faust* and memorization of Schiller's "Das Lied von der Glocke" (The Song of the Bell — a poem about bourgeois values that was greeted by shrieks of laughter and derision from the Romantics), at American universities the literary canon was assailed and in the assault Goethe and Schiller necessarily suffered. Efforts on both continents seemed bent on producing the cultural conditions for which the question "who is that?" would be the most common response to the names Goethe and Schiller. Yet one virtuoso reader of canonical literary texts remembered particularly Schiller in a different way. I am referring to the deconstructionist critic Paul de Man. In two important essays, Schiller served de Man as a punching bag for a critique of aesthetic ideology.[54] In a series of deft if dubious rhetorical moves, de Man associated the aesthetics of Schiller's *Aesthetische Erziehung* with Hitler, Goebbels, and National Socialism. Suddenly it appeared that the *Ganzheit* (totality) of Goethe and Schiller's vision — the basic aspiration of the Classical project — was linked to the totalitarianism of the Nazi regime. A single (causal?) strand ran from Weimar to Auschwitz. Who, in good conscience, could cherish the writings of Schiller and Goethe now?

Of course, after his death in 1983, it was revealed that de Man himself had been complicit with Nazi ideology in articles and reviews written during the Nazi occupation of his native Belgium. The true object of his scathing critique may have been his earlier self. In any event, Goethe and Schiller survived. Since then, they have continued to receive critical — and politically critical — attention. Several waves of justified feminist critique resulted in the recuperation of women writers whom they both hindered and enabled. The myth of the friendship of poet and statesman, Goethe and Carl August, and the liberal, humane government that they achieved for their blessed subjects has been debunked by the dogged revisionist work of Daniel Wilson. But this is a scholarship Goethe and Schiller deserve in both senses of the word. Our understanding of Weimar Classicism is challenged and sharpened as a result. Such critique is not inconsistent with what we can happily call a return to Goethe and Schiller, a flourishing of scholarship and interpretation during the 1990s partially due to the festivities associated with the 250th birthday of Goethe in 1999, and preceded by the fall of the Berlin Wall in 1989,[55] but also because their texts speak to us once again.

We may and should approach Weimar Classicism and its many manifestations with due caution, but also with pleasure and delight, marvel and melancholy. One of the salutary effects of cultural studies is that it reveals the hybridity in monolithic institutions. Weimar Classicism has always seemed monolithic. The approach taken in this volume, however, is designed to display Weimar Classicism's variety, its contradictions and inconsistencies, its strengths and weaknesses, its multiple voices and contrary ends. The fact that we cannot say precisely what a Classical text might be — *Faust, Iphigenie auf Tauris, Wilhelm Meister*, the *Roman Elegies, Herrmann und Dorothea*, or the

Achilleis — is not a cause for concern, but rather recognition and acknowledgement of the striving ambition of the Classical project. "Es irrt der Mensch, solang er strebt" (317; man errs as long as he strives) — the Lord's forgiving pronouncement regarding Faust seems a fitting judgment on the culture of Weimar Classicism. The errors, as Goethe well knew, are more than half the fun. To which Schiller might add: "[Der Mensch] ist nur da ganz Mensch, wo er spielt" (62; A human being is only entirely human where he plays). This volume is your ticket to play.

Notes

[1] René Wellek, "The Term and Concept of Classicism in Literary History," *Discriminations: Further Concepts of Criticism* (New Haven and London: Yale UP, 1970), 55–89; and "The Concept of Romanticism in Literary History," *Concepts of Criticism* (New Haven and London: Yale UP, 1963), 128–98. See also Klaus Berghahn's important intervention, "Weimarer Klassik + Jenaer Romantik = Europäische Romantik?," *Monatshefte* 88 (1996), 480–88.

[2] See Klaus L. Berghahn, "Von Weimar nach Versailles: Zur Entstehung der Klassik-Legende im 19. Jahrhundert," *Die Klassik-Legende*, ed. by Reinhold Grimm and Jost Hermand (Frankfurt a.M.: Athenäum, 1970), 50–78.

[3] "Literarischer Sansculottismus," MA 4.2:15–20.

[4] Some of the more important contributions to the debate about Weimar Classicism are: *Die Klassik-Legende*, ed. by Reinhold Grimm and Jost Hermand; Elizabeth M. Wilkinson and L. A. Willoughby, "Missing Links or Whatever Happened to Weimar Classicism?," in *"Erfahrung und Überlieferung" Festschrift for C. P. Magill*, ed. by Hinrich Siefkin and Alan Robinson (Cardiff: U of Wales P, 1974), 57–74; *Klassik und Moderne: Die Weimarer Klassik als historisches Ereignis und Herausforderung im kulturgeschichtlichen Prozeß*, ed. by Karl Richter and Jörg Schönert (Stuttgart: Metzler, 1983); *Verlorene Klassik? Ein Symposium*, ed. by Wolfgang Wittkowski (Tübingen, Max Niemeyer, 1986); Hans Robert Jauß, "Deutsche Klassik — Eine Pseudo-Epoche?," in *Epochenschwelle und Epochenbewußtsein* (= *Poetik und Hermeneutik* 11), ed. by Reinhart Herzog and Reinhart Koselleck (Munich: Wilhelm Fink, 1987), 581–85; three essays by Victor Lange, Hans-Georg Werner, and Terence James Reed, solicited by Wilfried Barner, for the *Jahrbuch der deutschen Schillergesellschaft* 32 (1988), 347–74; *Klassik im Vergleich: Normativität und Historizität europäischer Klassiken. DFG Symposion 1990* (Stuttgart: Metzler, 1993); *A Reassessment of Weimar Classicism*, ed. by Gerhart Hoffmeister (Lewiston, Queenstown, Lampeter: Edwin Mellen, 1996); and *Klassik und Anti-Klassik: Goethe und seine Epoche*, ed. by Ortrud Gutjahr and Harro Segeberg (Würzburg: Königshaus und Neumann, 2001). The two standard accounts of Weimar Classicism are T. J. Reed, *The Classical Center: Goethe and Weimar 1775–1832* (London and New York: Croom Helm and Barnes & Noble, 1980) and Dieter Borchmeyer, *Weimarer Klassik*, 2nd revised edition (Weinheim: Beltz Athenäum, 1994).

[5] Only slightly less arbitrary: A case could be made that Goethe and Schiller independently begin work on what would become their mutual project well before Goethe left for Italy (the first version of *Iphigenie*, for instance, is from 1779 and work began on a version in blank verse at Wieland's suggestion in 1780). Alternatively, if Weimar Classicism is fundamentally bound with their alliance, then it shouldn't begin before 1794, when their friendship began. It is also possible to raise questions about Schiller's death in 1805 as the period's conclusion, given Goethe's continued preoccupation with things classical and pronouncements he made regarding the Romantics vis-à-vis the Classics. Still, I would argue that the textual evidence strongly suggests that with and at the time of Schiller's death Goethe was deeply aware that their mutual project had come to an end and that Goethe's later work might best be understood as "post-classical." This volume for the most part confines itself to works from 1786–1805, although occasionally it makes sense for single contributions to deal with works that fall outside these parameters (e.g., *Faust II* and *Wilhelm Meisters Wanderjahre*).

[6] For a helpful model for understanding the stages of composition over Goethe's lifetime and the consequences for interpretation see Jane Brown, "*Faust*" in *The Cambridge Companion to Goethe*, ed. by Lesley Sharpe (Cambridge: Cambridge UP, 2002), 84–100. On the importance of Kant's *Critique of Pure Reason* for *Faust*, see Géza von Molnár, "Hidden in Plain View: Another Look at Goethe's *Faust*," *Goethe Yearbook* 11 (2002), 33–76.

[7] The English translation is from *Goethe's Faust*, trans. by Walter Kaufmann (New York: Anchor, 1961), 185. I have substituted the word beautiful for fair, sacrificing the rhyme for accuracy.

[8] Goethe, *Goethe's Faust*, trans. Kaufmann, 145.

[9] "Glückliches Ereignis" (1817, FA 24:437). See Erich Heller, "Goethe and the Idea of Scientific Truth," *The Disinherited Mind: Essays in Modern German Literature and Thought* (New York: Farrar, Straus and Cudahy, 1957), 3–9.

[10] On Winckelmann, see Alex Potts, *Flesh and the Ideal: Winckelmann and the Origins of Art History* (New Haven and London: Yale UP, 1994).

[11] Johann Joachim Winckelmann, *Gedanken über die Nachahmung der griechischen Werke in der Malerei und Bildhauerkunst* (Stuttgart: Philipp Reclam, 1969), 4. Hereafter cited as *Gedanken*.

[12] For an account of the importance of the statue for eighteenth-century German aesthetics see Simon Richter, *Laocoon's Body and the Aesthetics of Pain: Winckelmann, Lessing, Herder, Moritz, Goethe* (Detroit: Wayne State UP, 1992).

[13] Readers familiar with Weimar Classicism will realize that the concept of aesthetic containment, especially in Goethe and Schiller's hands, entails the stock attributes of classicism: harmony, moderation, and balance. The emphasis on pain and its containment, however, underscores the sense in which these values are not easily achieved and shifts the interest from the harmonious result to the difficult process.

[14] I am indebted to Helmut Pfotenhauer's discussion of ornament in his essay in this volume.

[15] Johann Wolfgang von Goethe, *Erotic Poems*, trans. by David Luke (Oxford and New York: Oxford UP, 1999), 53.

[16] Friedrich Schiller, "Ankündigung," *Über die Aesthetische Erziehung des Menschen*, ed. Klaus L. Berghahn (Stuttgart: Reclam, 2000), 195–96.

[17] This quotation is from the entertaining and occasionally scandalous Karl August Böttiger, *Literarische Zustände und Zeitgenossen: Begegnungen und Gespräche im klassischen Weimar*, ed. by Klaus Gerlach and René Sternke (Berlin: Aufbau, 1998), 165. Of course, Böttiger is not completely reliable as a source.

[18] Schiller, *Aesthetische Erziehung*, 123.

[19] For background information on Goethe and Weimar the following works are invaluable: Effi Biederzynski, *Goethes Weimar: Das Lexikon der Personen und Schauplätze* (Zurich: Artemis & Winkler, 1993), *Goethe Handbuch* (4 volumes), ed. by Bernd Witte et al. (Stuttgart and Weimar: Metzler, 1996–98); Gero von Wilpert, *Goethe-Lexikon* (Stuttgart: Alfred Kröner, 1998); and *Metzler Goethe Lexikon*, ed. by Benedikt Jessing et al. (Stuttgart and Weimar: Metzler, 1999). See also Helmut Brandt, "Weimar: Wie die Deutschen zu ihrer literarischen Hauptstadt kamen," *Stätten deutscher Literatur: Studien zur literarischen Zentrenbildung. 1750–1815* (Frankfurt am Main and New York: Peter Lang, 1998), 351–91.

[20] "Auf Miedings Tod," lines 1–2.

[21] For a treatment of Goethe's relation to the Jena philosophers see Liliane Weissberg, "Weimar and Jena: Goethe and the New Philosophy," *Goethe und das Zeitalter der Romantik*, ed. by Walter Hinderer (Würzburg: Königshaus & Neumann, 2002), 163–74.

[22] For more on the town of Weimar in Goethe's time, see Jochen Klauss, *Weimar. Stadt der Dichter, Denker und Mäzene: Von den Anfängen bis zu Goethes Tod* (Düsseldorf: Artemis & Winkler, 1999), and Walter Horace Bruford, *Culture and Society in Classical Weimar* 1775–1806 (London: Cambridge UP, 1962).

[23] W. Daniel Wilson, *Das Goethe-Tabu: Protest und Menschenrechte im klassischen Weimar* (Munich: Deutscher Taschenbuch Verlag, 1999). For a summary of some of his findings in English see "Skeletons in Goethe's Closet: Human Rights, Protest, and the Myth of Political Liberality," *Unwrapping Goethe's Weimar*, 295–309.

[24] Böttiger, *Literarische Zustände und Zeitgenossen*, 255.

[25] Böttiger, *Literarische Zustände und Zeitgenossen*, 165.

[26] Böttiger, *Literarische Zustände und Zeitgenossen*, 107.

[27] Bertuch has received a great deal of attention of late. I recommend Daniel Purdy, "Weimar Classicism and the Origins of Consumer Culture," in *Unwrapping Goethe's Weimar*, 36–62, or, for a more extensive treatment: Purdy, *The Tyranny of Elegance: Consumer Cosmopolitanism in the Era of Goethe* (Baltimore: Johns Hopkins UP, 1998).

[28] For Moritz see Mark Boulby, *Karl Philipp Moritz: At the Fringe of Genius* (Toronto, Buffalo, and London: U of Toronto P, 1979); and Richter, *Laocoon's Body*, 131–62.

[29] On this essay see Jonathan Hess, *Reconstituting the Body Politic: Enlightenment, Public Culture and the Invention of Aesthetic Autonomy* (Detroit: Wayne State UP, 1999), 163–65. The classic treatment of Moritz's aesthetics is Thomas P. Saine, *Die ästhetische Theodizee: Karl Philipp Moritz und die Philosophie des 18. Jahrhunderts* (Munich: Wilhelm Fink, 1971).

[30] See Tzvetan Todorov, *Theories of the Symbol*, trans. by Catherine Porter (Ithaca: Cornell UP, 1982), 148–64.

[31] Among them, the unauthorized release of Schiller's play, *Wallensteins Lager*, which was promptly performed in Copenhagen. Schiller first learned of it when he read a review.

[32] In the first edition "Herrmann" is written with two Rs, presumably in order to stress the character's manliness (Herr equals master). In subsequent editions the name is regularized, although the Munich edition reverts to Herrmann.

[33] A good part of that appeal had to do with the poem's apparent nationalistic jingoism at the conclusion.

[34] Böttiger, *Literarische Zustände und Zeitgenossen*, 260.

[35] Jane K. Brown, "Schiller und die Ironie von *Hermann und Dorothea*," in *Ironie und Objektivität: Aufsätze zu Goethe* (Würzburg: Königshausen & Neumann, 1999), 164–79, here 177.

[36] Frank G. Ryder and Benjamin Bennett, "The Irony of Goethe's *Hermann und Dorothea*: Its Form and Function," *PMLA* 90 (1975), 433–46.

[37] For important additional feminist contributions regarding women and Weimar Classicism, see Susan Cocalis and Kay Goodman, eds., *Beyond the Eternal Feminine: Critical Essays on Women and Literature*, Stuttgarter Arbeiten zur Germanistik, vol. 98 (Stuttgart: H. D. Heinz, 1982); Christa Bürger, *Leben Schreiben: Die Klassik, die Romantik und der Ort der Frauen* (Stuttgart: Metzler, 1990); Kay Goodman and Edith Waldstein, eds., *In the Shadow of Olympus: German Women Writers Around 1800* (Albany: State U of New York P, 1992); Susanne Kord, *Ein Blick hinter die Kulissen: Deutschsprachige Dramatikerinnen im 18. und 19. Jahrhundert* (Stuttgart: Metzler, 1992); Susan L. Cocalis and Ferrel Rose, eds., *Thalia's Daughters: German Women Dramatists from the Eighteenth Century to the Present* (Tübingen: Francke, 1996); Anthony J. Harper and Margaret C. Ives, eds., *Sappho in the Shadows: Essays on the Work of German Women Poets of the Age of Goethe* (New York and Oxford: Peter Lang, 2000); and Linda Dietrick, "Women Writers and the Authorization of Literary Practice," in *Unwrapping Goethe's Weimar: Essays in Cultural Studies and Local Knowledge*, ed. by Burkhard Henke, Susanne Kord, and Simon Richter (Rochester: Camden House, 2000), 213–32.

[38] On von Stein's *Dido* see Arnd Bohm, "Charlotte von Stein's *Dido, Ein Trauerspiel*," *Colloquia Germanica* 22 (1989), 38–52; and Linda Dietrick, "Woman's State: Charlotte von Stein's *Dido, Ein Trauerspiel* and the Aesthetics of Weimar Classicism," in *Verleiblichungen: Literatur- und kulturgeschichtliche Studien über Strategien, Formen und Funktionen der Verleiblichung in Texten von der Frühzeit bis zum Cyberspace*, ed. by Burkhardt Krause and Ulrich Scheck (St. Ingbert: Röhrig Universitätsverlag, 1996), 111–31.

[39] Böttiger, *Literarische Zustände und Zeitgenossen*, 235.

[40] See Kurt Wölfel, "Antiklassizismus und Empfindsamkeit: Der Romancier Jean Paul und die Weimarer Kunstdoktrin," *Deutsche Literatur zur Zeit der Klassik*, ed. by Karl Otto Conrady (Stuttgart: Reclam, 1977), 362–79.

[41] I am very grateful to Cyrus Hamlin for his thoughtful account of Hölderlin in the context of classical elegy in his essay in this volume.

[42] For Sophie Mereau see Simon Richter, "Sophie Mereau (1770–1806)," in *Women Writers in German-Speaking Countries: A Bio-Bibliographical Critical Sourcebook*, ed. by Elke P. Frederiksen and Elizabeth G. Ametsbichler (Westport, CT and London: Greenwood, 1998), 333–40; and Christa Bürger, " 'Die mittlere Sphäre.' Sophie Mereau — Schriftstellerin im klassischen Weimar," in *Deutsche Literatur von Frauen*, ed. by Gisela Brinker-Gabler (Munich: Beck, 1988), 366–88.

[43] On the relationship between Campe's project and Weimar Classicism, see Simon Richter, "Priapean Fantasies: The Sexual Politics of Weimar Classicism," in *Sexualität und Imagination: Pathologien der Einbildungskraft im medizinischen Diskurs der frühen Neuzeit*, ed. by Daniela Watzke, Stefanie Zaun, and Jörn Steigerwald (Frankfurt am Main: Vittorio Klostermann, 2003), 193–208.

[44] Most recently Roberto Zapperi, *Das Inkognito: Goethes ganz andere Existenz in Rom*, trans. from the Italian by Ingeborg Walter (Munich: C. H. Beck, 1999).

[45] Sander Gilman makes the strongest case in "Goethe's Touch: Touching, Seeing, and Sexuality" in *Inscribing the Other* (Lincoln, NE and London: U of Nebraska P, 1991), 29–49.

[46] "Knaben liebt ich wohl auch . . .," FA 1.1:472.

[47] On Christiane Vulpius in general see Sigrid Damm, *Christiane und Goethe* (Frankfurt a.M and Leipzig: Insel, 1998). Damm discusses the social and legal complexity of Christiane and Goethe's relationship, 122–57.

[48] In fairness it should be noted that these verses were never published in the *Horen*, and remained virtually unknown until the twentieth century.

[49] Goethe, *Erotic Poems*, trans. Luke, 7.

[50] For the *Roman Elegies* I recommend Hans Vaget's introduction to Johann Wolfgang von Goethe, *Erotic Poems*, trans. by David Luke (Oxford and New York: Oxford UP, 1997), ix–xlvi; and Wolfgang Riedl, "Eros und Ethos: Goethes *Römische Elegien* und *Das Tagebuch*," *Jahrbuch der deutschen Schillergesellschaft* 40 (1996), 147–80.

[51] Goethe, *Erotic Poems*, trans. Luke, 63.

[52] Böttiger, *Literarische Zustände und Zeitgenossen*, 172–73.

[53] Sigrid Lange, *Ob die Weiber Menschen sind: Geschlechterdebatten um 1800* (Leipzig: Reclam, 1992).

[54] The essays in question are "Aesthetic Formalization: Kleist's *Über das Marionettentheater*," *The Rhetoric of Romanticism* (New York: Columbia UP, 1984); and "Kant and Schiller" in *Aesthetic Ideology*, ed. by Andrzej Warminski (Minneapolis: U of Minnesota P, 1996). Michael Jones has ably come to Schiller's defense against de Man and Marc Redfield, who has continued the ideological critique of Schiller. See Michael T. Jones, "Schiller, Goebbels, and Paul de Man: The Dangers of Comparative Literature" in *Mosaic* 32 (1999), 53–72; and "Schiller Trouble: The Tottering Legacy of German Aesthetic Humanism" in *Goethe Yearbook* 10 (2001), 222–45.

[55] Since Weimar was in East Germany, Western scholars had limited access to the Goethe/Schiller archives.

What is Classicism?

Dieter Borchmeyer

A RE THERE GERMAN CLASSICS?" Nietzsche poses this question in the
second volume of *Human, All Too Human*.[1] He cites Charles
Augustin Sainte-Beuves's (1804–69) essay "Qu'est-ce qu'un classique?"
(What Is a Classic?) in the *Causeries du lundi* (Monday Lectures, 1851),
where we read that "the word 'classic' does not suit the genius of certain
literatures. For instance, nobody could talk seriously of 'German classics.' "[2] But that is precisely what happened with increasing frequency in
Germany in the course of the nineteenth century. The concept of the classical was used in an inflationary manner. In *Einen Jux will er sich machen*
(He Wants to Play a Joke, 1842), a comedy by Johannes Nepomuk
Nestroy (1802–62), we find satirical confirmation of this observation. The
dimwitted house servant Melchior finds everything "classical." "Was hat er
denn immer mit dem dummen Wort klassisch?" asks the principal Zangler
brusquely (Why are you so obsessed with that dumb word classical?).

Melchior: Ah, das Wort is nit dumm, es wird oft dumm angewend't.
Zangler: Ja das hör' ich, das muß er ablegen, ich begreif nicht, wie
           man in zwei Minuten 50mal dasselbe Wort repetieren kann.
Melchior: Ja, das ist klassisch.[3]

[Melchior: Ah, the word is not dumb, but its application often is.
Zangler: Yes, I hear you, but you must stop, I just don't understand
           how one can repeat the same word fifty times in two
           minutes.
Melchior: Yes, that is classic.]

In the course of the nineteenth and twentieth centuries three distinct
epochs in German literature came to be dubbed *Klassik*. The Middle High
German cultural highpoint around 1200 is known as "Staufische [for
Hohenstauffen] Klassik"; the literary works of Goethe and Schiller during
their Weimar years (or rather a portion thereof) are known as "Weimarer
Klassik"; and Viennese Classicism designates the pinnacle of European and
German music: the epoch of Haydn, Mozart, and Beethoven. In the
meantime, the concept of the classical and the classic is more debated now
than ever before. This is certainly true for Weimar Classicism, an epochal
designation that never succeeded in gaining recognition or acceptance in

the world of English or French literary criticism: for critics from other European countries the German classicists are lumped together with the Romantics. The concept of Viennese Classicism, on the other hand, has proven to be durable, and not only in German-speaking countries. Yet this designation is a later construction, based on even less textual support than so-called Weimar Classicism, whose authors reflected on the concept of the classical in detail. Moreover, Weimar Classicism is indisputably a locally circumscribed group phenomenon whose representatives made up a distinct comprehensible entity, one based on common aesthetic principles, even aspiring at times to "classicalness."

In the nineteenth century the concept of German Classicism became more and more involved in nationalistic identity formation. This also holds true for the elaboration of the epochal designation of *classicisme* in France. The doctrine of classicism is an aesthetic construction that parallels the discourse of the national state, along with its nationalistic side effects. These are manifest in the circumstance that, on the one hand, theoreticians of French *classicisme* have denied the existence of any modern classicism outside France; as André Gide wrote in 1924: "I know of no other classicism since antiquity than that of France. In its classical art, the genius of France is fully realized."[4] On the other hand, the inauguration of German Classicism is accompanied by a feeling of superiority vis-à-vis French *classicisme* (especially the "haute tragédie" of Corneille and Racine) that has been smugly disparaged by Germans ever since Lessing.

Precisely because of the national implications of the doctrine of classicism, the construction of a musical Viennese Classicism on the pattern of literary Weimar Classicism is arbitrary in an instructive sense, because late eighteenth-century Viennese musical culture, as a result of the dominance of Italian music, did not fit any brand of classicism in the sense of a nineteenth-century nationalism that bore increasingly ethnic characteristics. It was the doctrine of classicism of the German educated classes (the *Bildungsbürgertum*) that severed the connections between German and Italian music by placing Haydn and Mozart — although they composed Italian operas — on the classical pedestal, but not Salieri, even though he served for four decades as the royal Kapellmeister in Vienna, taught both Beethoven and Schubert, and even wrote a German *Singspiel* (drama with music). Such problems never arose in the case of Weimar Classicism, since it was essentially shaped by national-literary considerations. Still, the exclusively nationalistic tenor of the nineteenth-century doctrine of classicism necessarily cut off the cosmopolitan connections of Weimar Classicism, particularly to the tradition of European Enlightenment. For that reason, Wieland, a sort of Salieri of Weimar Classicism, was never seriously considered a part of it.

The literary concept of classicism or the classical should be seen in close proximity to that of Romanticism. The "Classicists" as well as the

"Romantics" defined both terms around 1800 as polar opposites. In a letter written 9 January 1938 to the literary historian Fritz Strich, Thomas Mann posed the following question in reference to the typological opposition between Classicism and Romanticism: "Did the 'Classics' call themselves classics or are 'Classicism' and 'Classic' later, historical designations? In other words: Was German Classicism a conscious and programmatic school, which expressly named itself such, in the way that Romanticism and later naturalism and expressionism bore their respective names?"[5] The answer to this question should be "no." Every classicism is basically a result, a "legend." As a category of literary historical canon formation and epochal designation, the concept is necessarily retrospective, the product of a process of reception. This is true not only for German Classicism, but also for French "classicisme," especially in view of the fact that the term was only really established once the assault on the system of "romantisme" had begun.

The dispute between Classicists and Romantics appears as a new version of the "Querelle des anciens et modernes" in France at the end of the seventeenth century, that secular conflict between authoritative antiquity and progressive modernity, whose apologists attempted to liberate themselves from the canon of Greco-Roman antiquity as a normative past, while the *Anciens* held to the exemplariness of the ancient model. The conflict found a solution in the recognition that the works of the ancients as well as the moderns could no longer be judged according to an absolute norm of perfection, but rather according to historically determined criteria. That the conflict had not found a satisfactory and final theoretical solution is apparent from the circumstance that it did not end with the end of the "Querelle," but was revived in the late eighteenth century. The young Herder already finds the word "classical" one of the most annoying *paroles* of the *Anciens*. In his *Fragmente über die neuere deutsche Literatur* (Fragments about Recent German Literature, 1767), he polemicizes against the tendency "daß man alles *Unklassische* vermied, um nicht von den Alten abzuweichen" (that one avoided everything unclassical in order not to stray from the ancients) and thus renounced one's individuality (Eigenheit): "man opferte alles auf, das uns den Namen *klassisch* streitig machen könnte; und ward ein *klassischer* Nachahmer! — O das verwünschte Wort: *klassisch!*"[6] (one sacrificed everything that might call into question the name classical and thus became a classical imitator! — Oh, the accursed word classical!).

Epochs and periods are heuristic and consensus-based attempts at bringing order to literary and cultural production. For the artistic tendencies of modernity it is characteristic that participants delude themselves into believing their period can be defined. And modern cultural histories have often accepted such self-denominations by the authors as legitimate period designations. This is true, as Thomas Mann correctly mentioned, of the "conscious and programmatic schools" of naturalism and expressionism — but not, however, as he incorrectly supposes, without further ado for Romanticism. It has recently been convincingly demonstrated that the early Romantic authors did not use the words "romantisch, Romantik, Romantiker" in the sense of a self-designation. When they spoke of themselves, they referred to "unsere Schule" (our school), "Partei" (party), or "Faktion" (faction). It is the anti-Romantic critique of Johann Heinrich Voss and others that brings about their identification as Romantics — as we still call them — but in a decidedly negative sense.

If Romanticism therefore did not identify itself with this term, to what extent did German Classicism think of itself in terms of the classic? Even less, because "Classicism," as we stated above, is a category of canon formation over which the authors themselves have no power. Goethe and Schiller never saw themselves as classics, even though, or perhaps precisely because the concept in all its historical variation was very much on their minds. "Wer mit den Worten, deren er sich im Sprechen oder Schreiben bedient, bestimmte Begriffe zu verbinden für eine unerläßliche Pflicht hält, wird die Ausdrücke 'klassischer Autor, klassisches Werk' höchst selten gebrauchen" (Whoever regards it as an imperative duty to combine a definite concept with the words he uses in speaking or writing will use the terms "classical author, classical work" very infrequently) writes Goethe in his 1795 essay "Literarischer Sansculottismus" (MA 4.2:16). Goethe's caution about use of this concept, that is, the danger of prematurely idolizing works and authors, finds its counterpart in a letter Schiller wrote to Gottfried Körner on 21 January 1802: It is "im Charakter der Deutschen, daß ihnen alles gleich fest wird, und daß sie die unendliche Kunst, so wie sie es bei der Reformation mit der Theologie gemacht, gleich in ein Symbolum hineinbannen müssen. Deshalb gereichen ihnen selbst treffliche Werke zum Verderben, weil sie gleich für heilig und ewig erklärt werden, und der strebende Künstler immer darauf zurückgewiesen wird. An diese Werke nicht religiös glauben, heißt Ketzerei, da doch die Kunst über allen Werken ist" (It is in the German character that they fix everything, and that they immediately channel eternal art into a symbol, as they did with theology in the Reformation. That is why even good works of art are damaging to them, because they immediately declare them to be holy and eternal, and the striving artist is constantly referred back to this. Not to believe religiously in these works amounts to heresy since art, after all, is superior to all other human activities). Such statements did not of course prevent posterity from crowning Goethe and Schiller with wreathes of classical fame soon after the latter's death: "Und du und Schiller ihr seid hernach Classische Schrieftsteller — wie Horaz Lifius — Ovid u wie sie alle heißen. . . . was werden alsdann die Professoren Euch zergliedern — auslegen — und der Jugend einpleuen" (And you and Schiller will hereafter be classical authors — like Horace Livius — Ovid and the rest of them.

And won't the professors one day analyze you — interpret you — and beat you into the heads of the youth) writes Catharina Elisabeth Goethe in a letter to her son Johann Wolfgang dated 25 December 1807.

The concept of the classical has been with us for almost two thousand years. Romanticism, by contrast, with its three-hundred-year-long history, is a terminological parvenu. What connects both concepts, however, is their high degree of polysemy and the constant overlapping of their various applications. Around 1800 the history of the meaning of the classical is essentially concluded — assuming we ignore the ideological implications on the German as well as the French side in the nineteenth century. The Weimar litterateurs and their Jena counterparts at the turn of the century knew as well as we do now what classic means. (The concept of the Romantic, on the other hand, assumes its specific meanings around this time.)

In Roman times "classicus" originally meant "belonging to the highest class of taxpayers (classis prima)." In the second century A.D. Gellius makes of the civis classicus a scriptor classicus. This transition signals the circumstance that what is materially first class is also first class in a mental sense; the model author, "id est classicus assiduusque aliquis scriptor, non proletarius" — a first class, taxpaying author, not a proletarian (who doesn't belong to a taxpaying class). In his aforementioned 1851 essay "Qu'est-ce qu'un classique?" Sainte-Beuve still alluded to the materially advantaged status of a "classic": A "classique" is "un écrivain de valeur et de marque, un écrivain qui compte, qui a du bien au soleil, et qui n'est pas confondu dans la foule des prolétaires"[7] (a writer of value and distinction, a writer who counts, who owns a piece of property, and who does not mingle with the masses of the proletariat).

In modern times the normative and value-laden concept of the classical (as the exemplary and masterful) has become identical with that of the ancient — as the quintessentially exemplary. Since the eighteenth century the classic has above all been the ancient author. The synonymy of the classical and the ancient has persisted to the present in relation to the name of the discipline that deals with the literature of antiquity, namely classical philology, and its subject, the classical languages and literatures. The combination of the normative with the historical term leads to the absolutization of the model of form derived from antiquity; the normative concept becomes a stylistic one for the designation of the harmony and measure of the ancient art form (cf. Schiller, Humboldt, and others). This concept of style persists even when the valuation once associated with it can no longer be maintained and the Romantic takes its place next to the classical as a polar opposite. Both stylistic concepts continue to have a historical reference: just as the classical is associated with antiquity, Romanticism looks back to the Middle Ages as the cradle of modernity. The normative (classical = exemplary), historical (= ancient), and style-typological (= harmoniously proportioned, self-contained) concepts of classical are joined by the epochal usage of the concept, which is legitimated either through an alleged stylistic affinity with the epoch of antiquity, as in the case of French *classicisme* (here the stylistic and normative concepts are blended), or simply by characterizing a flourishing culture, such as the Periclean or Augustan age in antiquity.

We can find countless instances of usage of these four variants of the classical — the normative, historical, stylistic, and epochal — in the discourse of the Classical-Romantic literary period. The concepts of the "classical," the "classic," and "classicism" are most comprehensively used by Goethe (the German term "Klassik" as a period designation was unfamiliar to both Goethe and Schiller). We encounter the epochal concept, for example, in his essay "Literarischer Sansculottismus," in which, on the basis of comparison between the cultural circumstances in the German realm and the periods of cultural flourishing among other peoples, he rejects the possibility that anything approaching a classical literary period might take place in Germany. We find the historical concept in the frequently used metaphor of "klassischem Boden" (classical soil), especially in *Italienische Reise* and the *Roman Elegies*, and the stylistic concept in the opposition between the classical and the Romantic. The original normative sense is almost always admixed to the other three, but it can also be absent, in which case characteristic fluctuations of judgment about non-classical formal traditions occur.

When Goethe plays out the classical as "das Gesunde" (healthy) against the Romantic as "das Kranke" (pathological) in his conversation with Eckermann on 2 April 1829 — probably more with respect to French Romanticism than German — his value judgment eclipses the stylistic difference. However, a half year later, once again in conversation on 16 December 1829, Goethe believes himself to be in agreement with the French in an objective comparison of both artistic tendencies: " 'Es its alles gut und gleich,' sagen sie, 'Klassisches wie Romantisches, es kommt nur darauf an, daß man sich dieser Formen mit Verstand zu bedienen und darin vortrefflich zu sein vermöge. So kann man auch in beiden absurd sein, und dann taugt das eine so wenig wie das andere!' " ("Everything is good and equal," they say, "Classical as well as Romantic, it just depends on whether one understands how to use the forms in an excellent way. One can also be absurd in both and then neither of them is worth anything!"). It is therefore a matter of two partners of equal birth, equal value; excellence in this case is not a monopoly of the classical, but far more a concept of value that transcends style and can be attributed to every artistic form as long as it is achieves perfection according to the measure of its own possibilities.

Goethe likes to play with the polysemy of the term, for example when (again in conversation with Eckermann on 2 April 1829) he says of the *Nibelungenlied* that it is "klassisch wie der Homer." In a historical sense the *Nibelungenlied* could only be called Romantic, but Goethe's pleasure in the paradoxical formulation allows him to select the predicate "classical" in its normative sense. Following this logic, the Romantic (in its historical and stylistic meaning) can also be classical, that is, excellent.

As early as the notations to his translation of *Rameaus Neffe* (Rameau's Nephew, 1805), Goethe had emphasized that the canon of classical forms is no longer sufficient for the modern poet, that he will not be able to dispense with the "barbarischen Avantagen" (barbarian advantages) which had been developed "durch die romantische Wendung ungebildeter Jahrhunderte" (MA 7:666; through the Romantic turn of uncivilized centuries [that is, the Middle Ages]). Here we have a paradoxical situation: on the one hand, the classical standard remains valid and unchanged, while, on the other, the Romantic art forms — still lambasted with pejorative attributes (barbarian, uncivilized) — are considered indispensable advantages for the modern artist.

It never entered Goethe's mind to endeavor to be a "classic" even if this entailed a departure from the ideal of art from the perspective of an absolute aesthetic standard. Years earlier, in a letter of 27 June 1797, he had confessed to Schiller in connection with his *Faust* that he would not bother to satisfy the "höchsten Forderungen" (highest demands) nor be irritated by the "barbarische Komposition" (barbaric composition) of this poem that fluctuates between the genres (epic and drama, tragedy and comedy). In more advanced years and as a result of his attentive observation of the confrontations between the Classicists, who were oriented to antiquity, and the Romantics, who derived their aesthetic norms from their modernity, Goethe's ambivalent valuation of unclassical traditions of form gave way to value-free opposition of both artistic tendencies (even if the "classical" prejudice frequently appears in emotional eruptions against the contemporary Romantics).

In his essay "Klassiker und Romantiker in Italien, sich heftig bekämpfend" (Classicists and Romantics in Italy, Engaged in Violent Battle, 1820), Goethe objects with regard to the former — as the representatives of the ancients — that their dependence on the "unnachahmlichen Werke" (inimitable works) of antiquity runs the risk of leading to a kind of "Starrsinn und Pedanterie" (stubbornness and pedantry): "Wer bloß mit dem Vergangenen sich beschäftigt, kommt zuletzt in Gefahr, das Entschlafene, für uns Mumienhafte, vertrocknet an sein Herz zu schließen. Eben dieses Festhalten aber am Abgeschiedenen bringt jederzeit einen revolutionären Übergang hervor, wie das vorstrebende Neue nicht länger zurückzudrängen, nicht zu bändigen ist, so daß es sich vom Alten losreißt, dessen Vorzüge nicht anerkennen, dessen Vorteile nicht mehr benutzen will" (MA 11.2:259; Whoever busies himself only with the past runs the risk of dryly embracing something deceased and mummy-like. It is precisely this fixation on the past that every time summons forth a revolutionary transition, just as the innovation can no longer be repressed nor contained, so that it tears away from the model of antiquity, and no longer wants to recognize or make use of its advantages). And that is what "Romanticism" is! Although the concept of the revolutionary is used here only in a metaphorical sense, in his *Maximen und Reflexionen* Goethe draws a direct comparison between the political and economic goals of the French Revolution and Romanticism: Every "Ordnung" (order) based on the ancients eventually gives way to "Pedanterie"; "um diese [Pedanterie] los zu werden, zerstört man jene [Ordnung], und es geht eine Zeit hin, bis man gewahr wird, daß man wieder Ordnung machen müsse" (to get rid of the pedantry one destroys order and a time passes before one becomes aware that order has to be restored again). Examples for the conflict between the preservation of the tried and true and innovation are for Goethe the struggle between "Classizismus und Romanticismus, Innungszwang und Gewerbsfreiheit, Festhalten und Zersplittern des Grundbodens" (MA 17:779; Classicism and Romanticism, guild coercion and free trade, the preservation and destruction of tradition).

In the strife between the classics and the Romantics, Goethe has no desire to join one side, but rather "diesen Kampf so mäßigen, daß er ohne Untergang der einen Seite sich ins Gleiche stelle" (to moderate the battle in such a manner that an equilibrium is achieved without the destruction of any side), as he puts it in the aforementioned aphorism in *Maximen und Reflexionen*. In the Helena act of *Faust II*, known as the "klassisch-romantische Phantasmagorie" (classical-Romantic phantasmagoria), Goethe undertook the poetic attempt of mediating between the classical and the Romantic. Here, as he stated to Eckermann on 16 December 1829, "[sollten] beide Dichtungsformen entschieden hervortreten und eine Art von Ausgleichung finden" (both poetic forms should emphatically appear and find a sort of balance).

Goethe liked to call the synthesis of the classical and the Romantic "classic" in a higher, re-valued sense. On an occasion of his passionate reading of the *Globe*, a journal of French Romanticism, and its customary defense of the "Freiheiten der romantischen Schule" (liberties of the Romantic school), that is, the "Befreiung von den Fesseln nichtssagender Regeln" (emancipation from the chains of meaningless rules — such as those of the three unities of classicistic tragedy), Goethe calls out in conversation with Eckermann on 17 October 1828: "Was will der ganze Plunder gewisser Regeln einer steifen veralteten Zeit, und was will all der Lärm über klassisch und romantisch! Es kommt darauf an, daß ein Werk durch und durch gut und tüchtig sei, und es wird auch wohl klassisch sein" (What is all this rubbish about certain rules from a stiff and antiquated time and what is all this racket about classical and Romantic! It all comes down to whether a work is thoroughly good and competent and then it will also certainly be classic) — that is, will set itself apart through a consistency and vitality of form that is characteristic of all great art: "Denn alles, was vortrefflich sei, sei eo ipso klassisch, zu welcher Gattung es auch gehöre" (for everything that is excellent is *eo ipso* classic regardless of the genre to which it belongs), as Goethe stated in a letter to Johann Heinrich Voss as early as 26 January 1804.

The word "classic" also played a dominant role as the complement to "romantic" in early Romantic discourse — and in precisely the same variations as for Goethe. When August Wilhelm Schlegel, for instance, speaks about the "klassischen und wahrhaft exemplarischen Hauptwerken"[8] (classical and truly exemplary main works) of literature in his *Vorlesungen über Enzyklopädie der Wissenschaften* (Lectures on the Encyclopedia of Knowledge, 1803–4), he uses the concept of the classical in a normative sense. When in the third part of the *Vorlesungen über schöne Kunst und Literatur* (Lectures on the Beautiful Arts and Literature, 1803–4), he comments: "Übrigens liegt unserm Geist und Gemüt unstreitig die romantische Poesie näher als die klassische"[9] (Moreover, Romantic poetry is indisputably closer to our spirit and disposition than classical poetry), he is naturally speaking in the historical sense, opposing ancient poetry to medieval-modern poetry. Schlegel applies the style-typological variant in his discussion in the *Vorlesungen* about older and newer music, where he maintains: "daß das Vorwaltende in der alten Musik eben das war, was in den übrigen Künsten das Plastische, rein Klassische, streng Begrenzende; in der neueren hingegen das Pittoreske, Romantische oder wie man es nennen will"[10] (what prevails in older music is what we call plastic, purely classical, starkly containing in the other arts; in newer music by contrast it is the picturesque, the Romantic, or whatever one is pleased to call it). It is this "starkly containing" aspect that can — from a "Romantic" perspective — be declared obsolete: "Alle klassischen Dichtarten in ihrer strengen Reinheit sind jetzt lächerlich"[11] (All classical poetic varieties in their rigorous purity are now laughable) writes Friedrich Schlegel in one of his fragments (1797).

The idea of the total self-containment of the individual work of art can be transferred to all of antiquity, thus combining the stylistic with the normative and epochal variants, since the overlapping of the variants is no less characteristic for Romantic discourse than it is, as we have described, for Goethe. "Es dürften aber auch alle einzelnen Klassiker in den verschiedenen Fächern unübertrefflich sein," writes August Wilhelm Schlegel in the third part of the *Vorlesungen über schöne Kunst und Literatur*,

> so könnte dennoch das gesamte klassische Altertum unübertrefflich bleiben: denn es ist ein Ganzes, und zwar nicht als bloßes Aggregat gleichartiger Teile, sondern dem eine innere Einheit und Harmonie beiwohnt. Eben diese vermissen wir bei unsrer modernen, aus sehr ungleichartigen Bestandteilen zusammengeschlossenen, oft in sich widersprechenden und unverhältnismäßigen Bildung [. . .]. In diesem Chaos zum Teil großer Bestrebungen, in dem wir uns noch befinden, ist das klassische Altertum mit seiner einfachen Vollendung gleichsam . . . ein Typus gesetzmäßiger

organischer Geistesbildung: das Vorbild der Alten dient den neuen Erweiterern auf dem noch unbekannten Ozean, welchen sie befahren, als Leitstern und Kompaß. (KAV 3:57)

[Even if the classics in their various disciplines may have been individually unsurpassable, nonetheless classical antiquity in its entirety could equally remain unsurpassable: for it is a whole, and not merely the aggregate of similar parts, but rather something in which an inner unity and harmony resides. And it is precisely this that we are missing in our modern context, which consists of very dissimilar components that often stand in contradictory and disproportionate relation to each other. In this chaos of, to some extent, large aspirations in which we find ourselves, classical antiquity with its simple completeness is as it were a type of orderly, organic spiritual formation; the example of the ancients serves those who expand our horizons as they sail on yet unfamiliar waters, as a guiding star and compass.]

Or Friedrich Schlegel in *Ideen* (Ideas, 1800): "Alle klassischen Gedichte der Alten hängen zusammen, unzertrennlich, bilden ein organisches Ganzes, sind richtig angesehen nur *ein* Gedicht, das einzige in welchem die Dichtkunst selbst vollkommen erscheint"[12] (All classical poems of the ancients cohere, inseparably, forming an organic whole; properly viewed they are *one* poem, the only one in which the art of poetry itself comes into perfect appearance).

Thus we see that the use of the classical norm in opposing ancient and modern is by no means exhausted for the Romantics, as these references from the Schlegel brothers in the first decade of the nineteenth century amply show. In the light of the classical norm, the aesthetic appearances of modernity continually fall into a problematic shadow, from which they can only re-emerge when the classical and romantic are fused. Their synthesis was one of the goals of the Romantics — as it was for the late Goethe — and they saw it achieved in Goethe's literary works.

Wilhelm Meister, according to Friedrich Schlegel in his *Gespräch über Poesie* (Conversation about Poetry, 1800), initiates "eine ganz neue endlose Aussicht auf das, was die höchste Aufgabe aller Dichtkunst zu sein scheint, die Harmonie des Klassischen und Romantischen"[13] (an entirely new and unlimited perspective on what seems to be the highest goal of all literature: the harmony of the classical with the romantic[14]). Schlegel recognizes only Cervantes and Shakespeare as poets with whom Goethe's universality might be compared. "Nur ist Goethes Kunst durchaus progressiv" (But only Goethe's art is thoroughly progressive). That Schlegel honors Goethe with this important trademark concept of Romanticism — "Die romantische Poesie ist ein progressive Universalpoesie" (Romantic poetry is a progressive universal poetry), as he famously formulated in *Athenäumsfragment* 116 (1798) — shows that the synthesis of the classical and romantic is not accomplished, as is the case with Goethe, in the spirit of Classicism, but rather in the spirit of Romanticism. The overarching, integrative concept for a poetry that reconciles ancient and modern artistic tendencies is for Goethe that of the classical, for the Romantics that of the romantic.

Between these two artistic tendencies there lies no absolute border; rather, they are to be understood as dialectical opposites. In the third part of August Wilhelm Schlegel's *Vorlesungen über schöne Kunst und Literatur* we read once again:

> Wir haben zwar klassische und romantische Poesie einander von jeher in diesen Vorträgen entgegengesetzt, aber keine Trennung ist so absolut, daß nicht Elemente des Getrennten sich auf beiden Seiten finden sollten, nur daß sie in verschiedener Rangordnung hervortreten oder zurückstehen. Wir haben schon mehrmals bemerkt, daß einzelne Dichter, ja ganze Gattungen der antiken Poesie, welche nach den klassischen Gesetzen beurteilt, nicht bestehen können, ein dem unsrigen sich annäherndes Streben verraten, nur freilich unreif und nicht mit gehöriger Reife entfaltet.[15]

> [We have, it is true, continually opposed classical and Romantic poetry against each other in these lectures, but no separation is absolute such that elements of the separated entities are not found on both sides, just that they are prominent or recede in varying degrees. We have several times already observed that individual poets, indeed entire genres of ancient poetry, which when judged according to the laws of classicism would fail, reveal a striving that approaches our own, but they are immature and underdeveloped.]

Even the ancients were not always — in the normative and stylistic sense — classical, totally resting in themselves, but rather "striving" as do the moderns; in other words, sometimes the ancients were already Romantics — just underdeveloped.

Statements from the early Romantics about the concept of the romantic show that they almost always develop its variants of meaning in connection with the concept of the "classical": Middle Ages including modernity vs. antiquity, irregularity vs. classical regularity, briccolage vs. completeness, endlessness vs. self-containment, and so on. We may cite a passage from the second part of August Wilhelm Schlegel's lectures *Über dramatische Kunst und Literatur* (On Dramatic Art and Literature, 1808), a work in which these oppositions are particularly pronounced:

> Die antike Kunst und Poesie geht auf strenge Sonderung des Ungleichartigen, die romantische gefällt sich in unauflöslichen Mischungen; alle Entgegengesetzten, Natur und Kunst, Poesie und Prosa, Ernst und Scherz, Erinnerung und Ahndung, Geistigkeit und Sinnlichkeit, das Irdische und Göttliche, Leben und Tod verschmilzt sie auf das innigste miteinander. [. . .] Die gesamte alte Poesie und Kunst [ist] gleichsam ein rhythmischer Nomos, eine harmonische Verkündigung der auf immer festgestellten Gesetzgebung einer schön geordneten und die ewigen

Urbilder der Dinge in sich abspiegelnden Welt. Die romantische hingegen ist der Ausdruck des geheimen Zuges zu dem immerfort nach neuen und wundervollen Geburten ringenden Chaos, welches unter der geordneten Schöpfung, ja in ihrem Schoße sich verbirgt [. . .]. Jene ist einfacher, klarer und der Natur in der selbständigen Vollendung ihrer einzelnen Werke ähnlicher; diese, ungeachtet ihres fragmentarischen Ansehens, ist dem Geheimnis des Weltalls näher.[16]

[Ancient art and poetry tend toward rigorous separation of dissimilar things, while Romantic art and poetry prefer inseparable mixtures; all oppositions, nature and art, poetry and prose, seriousness and silliness, memory and prophecy, spirituality and sensuousness, earthly and divine, life and death are melded together most intimately. . . . Ancient poetry and art in its entirety is, as it were, a rhythmic *nomos*, a harmonious pronouncement of the eternal legislation of a beautifully ordered world that mirrors in itself the eternal forms of things. Romantic art and poetry, by contrast, is the expression of a secret impulse toward a chaos in which new and amazing creations are formed, which conceals itself in the orderliness of nature, indeed in its very lap. . . . The former is simpler, clearer, and more resembles nature in the independent completion of its individual creations; the latter, despite its fragmentary appearance, is closer to the secret of the world.]

In a conversation with Eckermann on 21 March 1830, Goethe maintained: "Der Begriff von klassischer und romantischer Poesie, der jetzt über die ganze Welt geht und so viel Streit und Spaltungen verursacht, ist ursprünglich von mir und Schiller ausgegangen" (The concept of classical and Romantic poetry that is now on everyone's tongue and causes so much strife and stratification originally came from me and Schiller). The polarity had already been developed in Schiller's *Über naive und sentimentalische Dichtung*. Goethe continued: "Die Schlegel ergriffen die Idee und trieben sie weiter, so daß sie sich denn jetzt über die ganze Welt ausgedehnt hat und jedermann von Klassizismus und Romantizismus redet, woran vor fünfzig Jahren niemand dachte" (The Schlegels took up the idea and developed it further so that it has now spread over the entire world and everyone speaks of classicism and Romanticism, whereas fifty years ago it never occurred to anyone to do so).

Goethe aligns the concept of the naïve, understood as "objektives Verfahren" (objective procedure), with the classical, and that of the sentimental, understood as "subjektives Wirken" (subjective effect), with the Romantic. With these concepts Schiller had wanted to distinguish Goethe's artistic nature from his own, but had simultaneously also made clear that Goethe's creativity was not confined to the limits of the naive (= classical, objective) form of poetry. "Er bewies mir, daß ich selber, wider Willen, romantisch sei, und meine *Iphigenie*, durch das Vorwalten der Empfindung, keineswegs so klassisch und im antiken Sinne sei, als man vielleicht glauben möchte"[17] (He proved to me that I am, against my will, romantic and that my *Iphigenie*, because of the prevalence of sentiment, is not as classical in the ancient sense as one would perhaps like to believe).

Goethe's assertion that the Schlegel brothers owed their typology of the classical and Romantic to Schiller is not entirely off the mark. With his theory of the naive and sentimental, Schiller had established the ground for an entirely new aesthetics, as Goethe notes in another place: "Denn *hellenisch* und *romantisch* und was sonst noch für Synonymen mochten aufgefunden werden, lassen sich alle dorthin zurückführen, wo vom Übergewicht reeller [= objektiver] oder ideeller [= subjektiver] Behandlung die Rede war"[18] (For *hellenic* and *romantic* and all the other synonyms one might invent can all be referred back to the notion of whether real [= objective] or ideal [= subjective] treatment dominates). Friedrich Schlegel wrote his treatise *Über das Studium der griechischen Poesie* (On the Study of Greek Poetry) at almost exactly the same time as Schiller's investigation of poetic typologies. Like Schiller, Schlegel attempted to determine the unique nature of ancient and modern poetry. While Schiller, however, more or less proceeding from the solution of the "Querelle des anciens et des modernes," strives to interpret both ancient-naive and modern-sentimental poetry according to their own standards, Schlegel still appears to fall back into what Schiller would later mock as the "Gräkomanie" (graecomania) of the *ancien*, since his representation of ancient ("objective") poetry decidedly places modern ("interesting") poetry at a disadvantage, although occasional judgments contrary to the main tendency can also be found.

After reading Schiller's treatise, Schlegel realized his aesthetic error and, in a foreword added later, attempted a half-hearted justification of his own treatise in reference to Schiller's indubitably more convincing opposition of ancient and modern. Schlegel must have found a remark in Schiller's treatise such as the following to be an embarrassing refutation of his own investigation: "Denn freilich, wenn man den Gattungsbegriff der Poesie zuvor einseitig aus den alten Poeten abstrahiert hat, so ist nichts leichter, aber auch nichts trivialer, als die modernen gegen sie herabzusetzen"[19] (For indeed if one first abstracts the genre concept on the basis of the ancient poets, then nothing is easier, but also nothing more trivial, than to disparage the modern poets by contrast).

In order to prevent the application of this verdict to his own essay, Schlegel formulates the very argument — clearly borrowed from Schiller — that he himself must fear most, and thus creates the impression that he is not affected by it. If one takes the "reine Gesetze der Schönheit und der Kunst [. . .] ohne nähere Bestimmung und Richtschnur der Anwendung zum Maßstab der Würdigung der modernen Poesie: so kann das Urteil nicht anders ausfallen, als daß die moderne Poesie, die jenen Gesetzen fast durchgängig widerspricht, gar keinen Wert hat"[20] (the pure laws of beauty and art as the standard for evaluation of modern poetry without closer determination and guidelines for application, the verdict is inevitable: modern poetry, which is in almost total contradiction to those rules, has no value). This diplomatic chess move did not help Schlegel with Schiller in the slightest. In a letter to Goethe dated 19 July 1799 Schiller still mocks Schlegels "Rodomontaden von Griechheit" (rodomontades of Greekness).

Schlegel admits in his retrospective foreword that Schiller's treatise had thrown new light "über die Grenzen des Gebiets der klassischen Poesie"[21] (on the borders of the region of classical poetry). Schiller's influence had finally helped him cut loose from the perspective of the absolutization of Greek poetry, and cleared the way for a positive valuation of modern poetry, indeed for the foundation of the Romantic theory of art. The relation of the latter to Schiller's conception of the sentimental is unmistakable. Sentimental and Romantic poetry are both poetries of reflection, which allow the unbroken unity of art and nature, spirituality and sensuousness to separate and transcend the closed nature of the world of appearances in a process that can never be contained.

Schiller's theory of sentimental poetry is in the final analysis an anti-classical theory of literature. The fact that he anchors Goethe's and his own poetry in the dialectic of the naive and sentimental mirrors their vacillation between classical and anti-classical formal models, even though the latter really only dominates in a temporally discrete period of their literary productivity. Goethe's first hesitant involvement with the anti-classical occurred during his first decade in Weimar (1775–86), during which time his aesthetic production was overshadowed by his governmental duties in the duchy of Saxony-Weimar. His Italian journey by contrast signals a decided turn to classicism, as the revision and completion of the dramatic works begun during his first decade in Weimar, especially the second version of *Iphigenie auf Tauris*, clearly indicate. Ever since, this "gräzisierende[s] Schauspiel" (Graecizing play, Goethe to Schiller, 19 January 1802) has counted in Germany as the work that best embodies Weimar Classicism, even if Schiller and the later Goethe himself did not find it to be particularly classical because of its sentimental emotionalism. The gesture back to Euripidean tragedy, the affinity with Winckelmann's interpretation of ancient sculpture in terms of its putative emotional calmness and balanced composition, but also the formal proximity to *tragédie classique* with its unities of place, time, and plot — conceded by Goethe — and its deference to the law of decorum reflected in its elevated declamatory style — all these factors have contributed to the repeated application of the term classical to this play. In connection with this work, as with other works of Goethe and Schiller, such a judgment implies a conjunction of formal criteria (rejection of the eruptive style of the Sturm and Drang), thematic aspects (humanizing of ancient myth), and ethical goals (renunciation).

In such classical "virtues" one may recognize a breathing of life into values belonging to a late- or post-courtly culture that had been most rigidly developed by the absolutistic courtly civilization in France and with which seventeenth-century tragedy, especially in its Racinian guise, is in tune. What is classical about *tragédie classique* is its mirroring of the courtly disciplining of emotion.[22] Of course, this suppression of emotion in the ceremonial declamatory posture of Racine is frequently counterpoised by raging passion (*amour-passion*) of the tragic personnel that can often only be constrained by outward measures, while in Goethe's "classical" dramas (*Iphigenie, Tasso, Die natürliche Tochter*), the containment of uncontrolled outbreaks is more often accomplished inwardly, that is, the purification of the characters into a condition of self-discipline and balance is either asserted from the beginning or achieved in the finale — as for example Orestes, who is healed from his madness; Thoas, who finally renounces his claim to Iphigenie; and Iphigenie herself, who transforms all barbarism into "pure humanity."

The *Italienische Reise* (1816–17), Goethe's autobiographical report from a temporal distance of thirty years, in a certain sense unconsciously contributes toward establishing the foundational myth of Weimar Classicism — despite its skepticism with respect to the possibility of a German classicism. If, almost fifteen years after the *Italienische Reise*, in *Zweiter Römischer Aufenthalt* (Second Roman Sojourn, 1829), Goethe speaks of the "Gegenwart des klassischen Bodens" (the presence of classical soil), of the certainty "daß hier das Große war, ist und sein wird" (MA 15:542; that "here the magnificent was, is and ever will be) — an utterance to be found in the autobiographical report which therefore does *not* come from the time of the Italian journey itself — then we are dealing with a deliberate glorification of the Italian experience that aims at the "renaissance" of the ancient as an eternally valid aesthetic paradigm. In other words, it aims at the "classical," which was at the time being played out, decidedly even if in unspoken terms, against the Romantic movement.

Schiller also participated in the creation of the myth of classicism. In his 23 August 1794 letter to Goethe on the latter's birthday five days later — a letter, incidentally, that initiates the friendly alliance between them — he describes a Goethe who, unlike the Greek or the Italian, for whom a beautiful nature and idealizing art were always at hand, was born into a northern world of "mangelhaften Gestalten" (inadequate forms) and who had to find the grand style within himself "und so gleichsam von innen heraus [. . .] ein Griechenland [. . .] gebären" (and so as it were give birth to a Greece from within). Schiller himself, who had with interruptions been in Weimar since 1787, had programmatically set himself the goal of a simplicity and a type of classicism oriented around Greek art as well as a grand style as he undertook to approach Goethe. In this way the path was prepared for their epoch-making friendship, whose aesthetic premises were determined in equal measure by the events of the French Revolution.

In the face of the form-dissolving tendencies of the revolutionary period, the Weimar Classicism of this friendly alliance represents the attempt to establish an artistic form that was oriented around antiquity and the tradition of humanistic poetics. In this joint effort Goethe and Schiller strove to combine the dusty aesthetic values of pre-revolutionary courtly culture with middle-class Enlightenment thought and the aesthetics of Karl Philipp Moritz and Kant — maintaining an equal distance from the Revolution and the ancien régime. This synthesizing experiment could only be successful for a small creative elite living in the small duchy of the "Musenhof" (Court of Muses) of Sachsen-Weimar — where bourgeois and Enlightenment values had in large measure already been accepted. Under these limited conditions and in this circumscribed location it was possible for the appearance of a common style to flicker in pre-revolutionary festive splendor one last time.

The classicism of this alleged common style, however, was also compromised by Goethe and Schiller through opposing individualistic concepts and, after Schiller's death, by Goethe's efforts to integrate the "Avantagen" of the Romantic formal tradition. It has become clear that it is not possible to speak of a classicism around 1800 in the full semantic breadth of the concept. A classical style shared by many was no longer possible. Weimar Classicism is a conditional classicism, a classicism that is constantly called into question through its own self-relativization.

— Translated by Simon Richter

Notes

[1] Friedrich Nietzsche, *Human, All Too Human: A Book for Freespirits*, trans. by Paul V. Cohn (New York: Russell and Russell, 1964), 258.

[2] Quoted in Nietzsche, *Human, All Too Human*, 258.

[3] Johann Nepomuk Nestroy, *Komödien*, 3 vols., ed. Franz H. Mautner (Frankfurt am Main: Insel, 1987), 2:442–43.

[4] Quoted from Dieter Borchmeyer, *Weimarer Klassik: Portrait einer Epoche* (Weinheim: Beltz Athenäum, 1994), 14.

[5] Thomas Mann, *Briefe 1937–1947*, ed. Erika Mann (Kempten: Allgäuer Heimatverlag, 1963), 43–44.

[6] Johann Gottfried Herder, *Über die neuere deutsche Literatur: Fragmente, als Beilagen zu den Briefen, die neueste Literatur betreffend. Dritte Sammlung* (1767), *Werke*, 10 vols., ed. Martin Bollacher et al. (Frankfurt am Main: Deutscher Klassiker Verlag, 1985), 1:418.

[7] Quoted in Borchmeyer, 25.

[8] August Wilhelm Schlegel, *Vorlesungen über Enzyklopädie der Wissenschaften* (1803–4), *Kritische Ausgabe der Vorlesungen*, 3 vols., ed. Ernst Behler (Paderborn, Munich, Vienna, Zurich: F. Schöningh, 1989), 1:356. This edition hereafter cited as KAV.

[9] KAV 2:8.

[10] KAV 1:367.

[11] Friedrich Schlegel, *Kritische Fragmente* (1797), *Kritische Friedrich-Schlegel-Ausgabe*, 24 vols., ed. Ernst Behler et al. (Paderborn, Munich, Vienna, Zurich: F. Schöningh, 1958–1991), 2:154. This edition hereafter cited as KA.

[12] KA 2:265.

[13] KA 2:179.

[14] English translation from Friedrich Schlegel, *Dialogue on Poetry and Literary Aphorisms*, trans. Ernst Behler and Roman Struc (University Park, London: Pennsylvania State UP, 1968), 112.

[15] KAV 2:184.

[16] *August Wilhelm Schlegel's sämmtliche Werke*, 12 vols., 3rd edition, ed. Eduard Böcking (Leipzig: Weidmann, 1846) 6:161.

[17] Goethe to Eckermann, 21 March 1830, quoted in Woldemar Freiherr von Biedermann, ed., *Anhang an Goethes Werke. Goethes Gespräche*, 10 vols. (Leipzig: F. W. von Biedermann, 1889–96), 7:277.

[18] *Einwirkung der neueren Philosophie*, 1820; MA 12:97.

[19] Schiller, SW 5:718.

[20] Friedrich Schlegel, *Kritische Schriften*, ed. Wolfdietrich Rasch (Munich: Hanser, 1964), 115.

[21] Schlegel, *Kritische Schriften*, 116.

[22] Cf. especially Norbert Elias, *The Court Society*, trans. by Edmund Jephcott (New York: Pantheon, 1983).

The Laocoön group. Roman copy, perhaps after Agesander, Athenodorus, and Polydorus of Rhodes. Marble, 1st century A.D. *Courtesy of Alinari / Art Resource, NY. Vatican Museums, Vatican State.*

Antiquity and Weimar Classicism

Charles A. Grair

WEIMAR CLASSICISM can be said to begin in 1786 when Goethe places his Iphigenie on the rocky shores of Tauris, longing for home, "das Land der Griechen mit der Seele suchend" (HA 5:7; seeking the land of the Greeks with her soul). The search for Greece, for a distant poetic homeland where one could find the beauty, harmony, and fulfillment lacking in the modern world, captivated an entire generation. Not only Goethe and Schiller, but their contemporaries from Lessing, Klopstock (1724–1803), and Wieland to the younger Jena Romantics shared the search for Iphigenie's Greece. Although the term "Weimar Classicism" correctly reflects a debt to the styles and traditions of antiquity, neither Goethe nor Schiller, nor any of their contemporaries, considered themselves classical. The term itself is a relatively recent coinage, designed to replace the misleading "deutsche Klassik," which was a product of nineteenth century nationalistic literary hagiography.[1] *Weimar* classicism is also potentially misleading, for it suggests an exclusive or dominant form of classicism and sets a select group of authors — often only Goethe and Schiller — apart from their German and European contemporaries.[2] In fact, the works of the Weimar writers represent only one current of Romantic Hellenism, one vision of classical revival among many. For writers at the close of the eighteenth century, "antiquity" did not signify a coherent historical or philosophical system; it was, rather, like Iphigenie's faraway home, an absent ideal that reflected the dreams and ambitions of artists and their frustrations with their own imperfect age. The following discussion examines the fascination of German authors in this period with the legacy of classical antiquity and describes some of their responses to the challenges it posed.

Iphigenie's passionate longing for Greece was new to the cultural landscape of Germany, but Goethe's drama was by no means the first attempt to reclaim the classical tradition. Indeed, neoclassicism had never been entirely out of style. German writers from the Renaissance through the early eighteenth century saw themselves as descendants of a tradition that had begun in Greece and Rome. They followed models such as Virgil, Anacreon, and Pindar, based their poetics on authorities such as Aristotle and Seneca, and set many of their works in a classical landscape. Before the revival of classical studies in the mid-eighteenth century, however, acquaintance with original Greek texts was often quite superficial. Roman material was usually given preference because Latin authors were more accessible than the Greeks, but most authors did not differentiate carefully between ancient cultures. These earlier images of antiquity were strongly influenced by foreign writers and generally followed European trends; the French *querelle des anciens et des modernes*, for example, shaped critical debate in Germany through the first half of the eighteenth century. The defenders of the ancients, even among such relatively late writers as Lessing and Wieland, often found it difficult to accept the heathen views, barbaric practices, and rough language of Homer. What separates Weimar Classicism at the end of the century from these previous "classicisms" is not only a greater knowledge of antiquity in general, but a new image of ancient Greece in particular to which the writers felt an intense personal affinity.

The "rediscovery" of Greece in the late eighteenth century influenced German and European taste and thought over a broad continuum, from neoclassical art, literature, and fashion, to aesthetics and criticism, even pedagogy and politics. Antiquity in this period denoted not just the discovery of antiques or the fashion for Greek and Roman styles, but a world of the imagination and a collection of beliefs based on the artistic remnants of the past. The core belief was that Greek culture reflected humankind in a simpler, less corrupted time, when nature, the gods, man, and art existed together in freedom and harmony. Greek art and literature were granted exemplary status because they portrayed "complete" men and women in their natural state, living free and contented lives in an environment permeated by the divine. These elements reappear in individual variations among all the writers of the period. The myth of a Greek golden age represented a dynamic social model because it contained the tensions of the historically *real* and the aesthetically *ideal*, as well as chiliastic images of an irretrievable past, an arduous present, and a hopeful future. The associated stylistic ideals of clarity, proportion, and restraint or containment served as a corrective to the superficiality of courtly culture and, on a deeper level, to the unnatural fragmentation and alienation experienced in modernity.

The first to heed the cry to Greece was Johann Joachim Winckelmann (1717–68), who discovered, in the words of Goethe, "als ein neuer Kolumbus, ein lange geahndetes, gedeutetes und besprochenes, ja man kann sagen ein früher schon gekanntes und wieder verlorenes Land" (HA 12:110; as a new Columbus a long suspected, interpreted and discussed, yes, one can even say a previously known and then forgotten land). Winckelmann's meteoric rise from cobbler's son to Prefect of Papal Antiquities in Rome is one of the astounding success stories of the century. His passionate interest in Greece is especially remarkable because it was shared by so few scholars at the time. His isolation ended in 1755 with the publication of his popular treatise, *Gedanken über die Nachahmung der griechischen Werke in der Malerei und in der Bildhauerkunst.* Inspired by his visits to the Dresden gallery — where he saw casts and copies, but not a single original work — this essay exerted a profound influence on his contemporaries and changed not only their image of Greece, but the way in which works of art were viewed and understood. In collaboration with Adam Friedrich Oeser (1717–1799), his friend in Dresden and later Goethe's drawing instructor in Leipzig, Winckelmann argued that the pinnacle of artistic perfection was to be found in Greek antiquity; therefore, in order to create true beauty, modern artists have little choice but to imitate the Greek masters: "Der einzige Weg für uns, groß, ja, wenn es möglich ist, unnachahmlich zu werden, ist die Nachahmung der Alten. . . ."[3] (The only way for us to become great, yes, if it is possible, incomparable, lies in the imitation of the ancients.) The superiority of the Greeks, Winckelmann reasons, can be traced to the immediacy and harmony of their contact with nature. The influence of a mild climate and clear sky, a society devoted to art, athleticism, and the free expression of nudity combined to produce images of beauty that were both true to nature and ideal. Modern societies, Winckelmann implies, suffer from a Rousseauistic separation of nature and culture; they have suppressed natural instincts and thus alienated themselves from the source of art and life. Without the advantages enjoyed by the Greeks, a German artist would toil in vain to discover beauty through the study of nature alone. For one seeking aesthetic inspiration, there can be no more direct route than through antiquity:

> Folget nicht daraus, daß die Schönheit der griechischen Statuen eher zu entdecken ist, als die Schönheit in der Natur . . . ? Das Studium der Natur muß also wenigstens ein längerer und mühsamerer Weg zur Kenntnis des vollkommenen Schönen seyn, als es das Studium der Antiquen ist. . . . (*Gedanken*, 17)

> [Does it not follow that the beauty of Greek statues can be more readily discovered than the beauty of nature . . . ? The study of nature must be at least a longer and more toilsome path to knowledge of perfect beauty than the study of the ancients. . . .]

Winckelmann's belief in the superiority of Greek culture was the foundation of his teaching. From the Renaissance on, Rome had been seen as the center of antiquity, but Winckelmann denied flatly that Roman artists had much originality at all. To find the true spirit of culture and humanity in the ancient world, he sorted through two millennia of false copies to locate the Greek original. His famous characterization of Greek art as "edle Einfalt und stille Größe" (noble simplicity and serene grandeur) reflected his belief that classical art expresses not only the physical beauty of the Greeks, but their moral and civil nobility as well. By portraying the noble character of its citizens, Greek art revealed to Winckelmann an *ethical* ideal of humanity: the beautiful man, free and purposeful, able to develop all his faculties and interests without hindrance in harmonious balance with the natural and the divine. The greatness of Greek character for Winckelmann can be seen in his description of Laocoön, whose stoic calm dynamically reflects his control over inner turmoil, restraint over pain and passion: "So wie die Tiefe des Meeres allezeit ruhig bleibt, die Oberfläche mag noch so wüten, ebenso zeigt der Ausdruck in den Figuren der Griechen bei allen Leidenschaften eine große und gesetzte Seele" (Just as the depths of the sea always remain calm, even though the surface may rage, so the expressions in the figures of the Greeks reveal amidst all passions a great and reposed soul; *Gedanken*, 24).[4]

Winckelmann's obsession with antiquity led him, like many to follow, to Italy. Rome was the repository for art of the classical world, and the latter half of the eighteenth century was an exciting time for scholars. The excavations at Herculaneum (begun 1737) and Pompeii (1748) brought about immediate and drastic revisions to previous notions of Roman life and art; new discoveries appeared almost weekly in the area around Rome. Winckelmann launched himself into archaeological and historical research for his monumental work, *Geschichte der Kunst des Altertums* (History of the Art of the Ancient World, 1764–67). His primary insight was that art developed in antiquity in the context of changing cultural and historical conditions, following an organic model of rise and decline. Unlike previous art histories based on the biographies of artists, Winckelmann based his investigations on the changing moral and political ethos of the Greek states. Although his study was limited by the paucity of available works and by his frequent confusion of Roman copies with Greek originals, his framework laid the foundation for virtually all subsequent histories of art. Works were no longer viewed simply as individual creations, but as cultural expressions unique to a specific time and place. This historical view of Greece essentially repudiates the timeless, normative understanding of Greek art that he had advanced in his earlier essay. "Imitation" for Winckelmann signified the decadence and sterile eclecticism characteristic of cultural decline. Despite his insistence that Greek art represents a unique and irreproducible combination of the human and the divine, the sensuous and the ideal, the allure of this image was difficult for artists and poets to resist.[5] The paradox of Winckelmann's classical revival can thus be described as the imitation of the inimitable, the search for a lost ideal that cannot be recovered.

As late as 1767, Johann Hermann Riedesel made a generous offer to take Winckelmann on a voyage to Greece so that his friend could see the monuments of antiquity for himself. His decision to forego the voyage, a curiosity in itself, is characteristic of the period. Not a single member of the Weimar circle ever set foot in Greece. Although Goethe traveled as far as Sicily, others saw the land of Homer only through the veil of Winckelmann and Rome. Travel descriptions of Greece began appearing regularly only in the latter third of the century, and most of these adventurers and tourists were interested only in describing or recovering previously known artistic ruins and did little to revise preconceived notions of antiquity.

Accurate information from academic sources was also scanty. The humanistic tradition in Germany, which produced such scholars as Conrad Celtis (1459–1508), Johannes Reuchlin (1455–1522), and Ulrich von Hutten (1488–1523), had died out by the mid-seventeenth century. Latin continued to be taught as the language of scholarship, but the study of Greek declined into a backwater of theology, and classical literature was neglected as a serious academic pursuit. The most notable of the early "new humanists" in the eighteenth century was Johann Matthias Gesner (1691–1761), who resurrected the study of the classics at Göttingen. After his death, his position at the university was taken by Christian Gottlob Heyne (1729–1812), who lectured for nearly fifty years, inspiring most of the following generation of classical scholars in Germany. His influence extended over nearly all aspects of ancient life; he lectured and wrote on the Greek and Latin poets, mythology, archaeology, antiquities, and history. Like Gesner before him, he was convinced that the study of the ancients should encompass not only their language and wisdom, but their way of life and thought, their spirit and character.

Under the influence of Winckelmann and Heyne, classical studies began to blossom. A milestone was reached when Friedrich August Wolf (1759–1824) entered Göttingen in 1777, signing his matriculation book as *Studiosus Philologiae* — a field that did not yet exist. If only symbolically, this anecdote records the changing attitudes that led to the liberation of classical philology from the bonds of theology in the eighteenth century. Wolf's appointment at Halle initiated a revival of classical scholarship unparalleled since the sixteenth century. He viewed classical humanistic education as the study of humankind at the time of its highest cultural achievement, a study that elevates the powers of the mind and soul as could no other field. Among Wolf's supporters was Wilhelm von Humboldt, a confidant of the Weimar circle and later educational reformer in Prussia, who helped to inscribe this view of antiquity into the pedagogical canon of the nineteenth century. After Wolf, classical philology quickly developed a self-assured professionalism. The generation of Barthold Georg Niebuhr (1776–1831), Gottfried Hermann (1772–1848), and August Boeckh (1785–1867) in the early nineteenth century produced outstanding scholarship, but although their historicization of classical authors revealed a more accurate image of antiquity, they lost Winckelmann's ability to inspire readers with ideal images of human perfection and natural harmony.

Winckelmann's early cry for the imitation of the ancients, despite his later misgivings, found a receptive audience. Although artists recognized that narrow imitation would produce sterile works, the *emulation* of classical models posed difficulties that were no less daunting. What were the true principles of Greek art? How was one to recover them from a distorted classical tradition? And, more important, how was one to transform those principles into pleasing, meaningful works for a contemporary audience? Although Weimar Classicism is typically regarded as a mature, self-confident period in Goethe's and Schiller's lives, their solutions to the neoclassicist dilemma are often experimental and improvisational, and their failures as notable as their successes. Their images of antiquity reflect less an appropriation of conventional elements than a process of individual search and discovery. For Goethe, this meant a long and difficult journey south.

If Goethe's flight from Carlsbad in September 1786 bore all the outward signs of unpremeditated desperation, it was also the culmination of a long-cherished plan. Inspired by his father's travels, the dream of an Italian journey had occupied his thoughts since childhood and had resurfaced with increasing urgency in later years. Italy represented not only freedom from personal and professional constraints in Weimar, but the continuation of an interrupted humanistic education according to the conventions of the age. Venice, Florence, Rome, and Naples had long been stations on the Grand Tour, the expected journey for any young man of means who hoped to acquire knowledge of the world.[6] The magnificent prose of the *Italienische Reise* obscures the fact that much of the journey was quite ordinary.[7] He carried Volkmann's guidebook with him, the standard text for travelers in Italy, and at times adhered closely to the recommendations and opinions offered therein.[8] On the other hand, Goethe's work is not just a travel report, but an artist's autobiography of discovery and self-cultivation; he was simultaneously the narrating subject and the historical object of poetic treatment. The composition history explains some of the complexities of the work. He began revising his letters and diaries only in 1813, finished the first volume in 1816 and the second a year later. The "Zweiter römischer Aufenthalt" (Second Roman Sojourn) was not completed until 1829, more than forty years after the journey itself. Goethe destroyed many of the primary sources for the second volume, so that it is difficult to separate the *truth* from the *poetry* in his account. Furthermore, the late publication date placed his views in opposition to the prevailing enthusiasm for medieval religious art — the Nazarenes, for example, had supplanted the neoclassical artists in Rome — forcing Goethe into a defensive stance in his preference for the art of antiquity.

The *Italienische Reise* as a whole narrates Goethe's rebirth as an artist, but the subjective moments of revelation are embedded within a more encompassing attempt to understand the objective world around him. Of the four areas of greatest interest, Goethe's foremost passion was the art of classical antiquity and that of its emulators from the Renaissance to the present. His own (rather mediocre) attempts in the pictorial arts can be seen as a practical exercise in learning to view nature and antiquity through the eyes of an artist. The second area concerns his scientific interests in botany, geology, mineralogy, and meteorology, all of which opened his eyes to the climate and natural history of Italy. The third area includes the high-spirited, "carefree" people of Naples and Sicily, in whose vibrant outdoor life Goethe sensed vestiges of the public character of Athenian tragedy. Above all, he claimed, it was the beautiful landscapes of Italy, especially that of Sicily, with its clear blue sky, remnants of Greek architecture, and paradisiacal vegetation, that inspired him with the living presence of antiquity.

The transfigured landscape of the *Italian Journey* helped create the myth of Italy as a land of heightened experience and rebirth that has influenced and overwhelmed readers ever since. But it was not an easy image for Goethe to claim. He had always seen Italy as a land of fulfillment — "das Land, wo die Zitronen blühn" (the land where the lemon trees bloom) — as he had written in Mignon's song from *Wilhelm Meister* a few years earlier. Winckelmann had strengthened his belief that the fulfillment he desired — educational, artistic, erotic — was not only possible, but had been achieved by the ancients and recorded in their monuments. He thus arrived in Rome with expectations of immediate access to and inspiration from the works of antiquity. His first impressions reveal an anticipation of rebirth:

> Nun bin ich hier und ruhig und, wie es scheint, auf mein ganzes Leben beruhigt. Denn es geht, man darf wohl sagen, ein neues Leben an, wenn man das Ganze mit Augen sieht, das man teilweise in- und auswendig kennt. Alle Träume meiner Jugend seh' ich nun lebendig. . . . (HA 11:126)

> [Now I am here and restful and, as it appears, content for my entire life. For a new life begins, one might well say, when one has seen with one's own eyes the whole, which one in part knows so well and intimately. All the dreams of my youth I now see alive. . . .]

Despite such optimism, the "Golgotha" of Rome did not yield her secrets readily to the untrained eye, and Goethe found to his astonishment that he had much to learn and unlearn. Completely fulfilled sensual enjoyment of art required laborious mental reconstruction to perceive an intact work from the ruins. He therefore began an intense study of Winckelmann and the treasures of the eternal city. He spent most of his time with German painters, a large group among the cosmopolitan art scene in Rome. Through J. H. W. Tischbein (1751–1829), with whom he shared lodgings, Goethe was introduced to Johann Georg Schütz (1755–1815), Friedrich Bury (1763–1823), Alexander Tippel (1744–93), Angelica Kaufmann (1741–1807) — the most successful of the group — and Johann Heinrich Meyer, who would later follow Goethe to Weimar as the director of the art academy there. In Naples, he met Phillip Hackert (1737–1807), who was his drawing instructor for a time, and C. H. Kniep (1748–1825), who accompanied him on his travels through Sicily. These neoclassical artists catered mostly to the tourists who wished to purchase landscapes and portraits in the Italian style as souvenirs of their travels. The most famous of these works is Tischbein's portrait of Goethe in the Roman *campagna*. Tischbein posed Goethe as a typical gentleman on the Grand Tour, resting in contemplation amid the ruins of three great classical civilizations. He sits on a toppled obelisk reminiscent of Egypt; the circular Roman tomb of Caecilia Metalla is visible in the background, and the fragment of a Greek pediment relief lies behind him. The scene depicted on the relief is Tischbein's invention, the moment in Goethe's *Iphigenie* when Orestes and Pylades are presented to their sister as condemned captives. The historical allusions are meant to suggest that Goethe himself is the latest incarnation of a timeless classical ideal. By using antique styles to represent a continuity of cultures, the painting embodies the symbolic language of neoclassicism.

Following Winckelmann's belief that the art of antiquity and that of its greatest imitators, Raphael (1483–1520) and Michelangelo (1475–1564), approached moral and physical perfection, the neoclassical ideal came to form a normative basis for all aesthetic judgments. The principles of purity, refinement, clarity, elegance, and restraint opposed the "frivolous" rococo style associated with the extravagance of absolutist courts and reflected a new nobility and solemn austerity that was supposed to delight the mind as well as the heart. The new style appealed to the aesthetic sensibilities of the late Enlightenment, and by the mid 1780s was the accepted standard across much of the continent. In fact, because the styles of antiquity were seen to embody good taste, neoclassical designs dominated nearly every facet of living at the turn of the nineteenth century, from private and public architecture, landscaping and garden design to interior decoration, furniture, porcelain, and even women's fashion.[9] The most enduring neoclassical forms, however, were created in architecture. Thomas Jefferson (1743–1826) chose neoclassical designs for his public works as much for their political associations as their beauty; Monticello and the University of Virginia express the virtues of economy, elegance, and dignity that characterized the ideals of the new republic. For many of the same reasons, but without the democratic associations, neoclassical works were built throughout the German territories in the late eighteenth and early nineteenth centuries. The best known example is Karl Langhans's (1733–1808) Brandenburg Gate (1788–91); shortly thereafter, Leo von Klenze (1784–1864) and Karl Friedrich Schinkel (1781–1841) dramatically redesigned Munich and Berlin along neoclassical lines. Weimar participated in the fashion for neoclassical buildings, too. Goethe himself remodeled his house on the *Frauenplan* (aided by Heinrich Meyer) in the Italian style, so that even today it resembles a small museum dedicated to neoclassical sculpture.

Goethe's interest in the neoclassicists, like his fascination with Raphael and Palladio, stems from the shared aesthetic challenges they faced in the adaptation of classical models to the demands of a later age. Palladio (1508–80), in particular, represented for Goethe the successful synthesis of the ancient and the modern, a noble architectural style that neither succumbed to sterile antiquarianism nor sacrificed the ideal to the petty demands of church or court.[10] Goethe's attempt at a Palladian solution in his own writing can be found in his verse revisions of *Iphigenie,* which were completed during his first months in Rome. The new version represents, in form and content, the triumph of classical restraint over the monstrous threat of the Tantalid curse. Although the result appeared to his contemporaries as a magnificent recreation of authentic Greek character, it was still, as Nicholas Boyle describes it, a poetry of desire rather than classical fulfillment.[11] It reflected Goethe's expectant longing for Italy rather than his actual experiences in Rome. After four months of disappointed study, he left the city and its ghosts to seek inspiration farther south.

While most travelers on the Grand Tour came to see ruins and dwell in the "pleasurable melancholy" of the past, Goethe had a profound distaste for lifeless artifacts. During his visits to Pompeii and Herculaneum, for example, he was impressed by the wall paintings, but disturbed by the ruins. The two epiphanies Goethe records in the *Italienische Reise* take place in Magna Graecia, the region of Italy that was settled by Greeks in ancient times and which was later on less affected by Roman influences. At Paestum, Goethe found his first encounter with Greek originals deeply unsettling. Accustomed to the slender proportions of Palladio, he was shocked by the "lästig, ja furchtbar" (oppressive, even terrible) fifth century Doric temples:

> [D]er erste Eindruck konnte nur Erstaunen erregen. Ich befand mich in einer völlig fremden Welt. . . . Doch nahm ich mich bald zusammen, erinnerte mich der Kunstgeschichte, gedachte der Zeit, deren Geist solche Bauart gemäß fand, vergegenwärtigte mir den strengen Stil der Plastik, und in weniger als einer Stunde fühlte ich mich befreundet. . . . (HA 11:219–20)

> [The first impression could only arouse astonishment. I found myself in an utterly alien world. . . . Yet I soon took hold of myself, remembered the history of art, considered the age whose spirit found such construction appropriate, recalled to mind the severe style of their sculpture, and in less than an hour I felt as if we had become good friends. . . .]

Confronted with the true spirit of the Greeks, Goethe adjusted his thinking to conform to a new image and soon found himself on better terms with it. When he later returned through Paestum, he found his views confirmed: "Es ist die letzte und, fast möcht' ich sagen, herrlichste Idee, die ich nun nordwärts vollständig mitnehme" (HA 11:323; It is the final, and I would like to say, most splendid idea that I will now take, complete and whole, with me back to the north).

The second epiphany took place in the gardens of Palermo, in Sicily. The exotic vegetation, clear sky, and warm sea breeze reminded Goethe of the world of Homer, of the enduring presence of antiquity in the classical landscape: "Aber der Eindruck jenes Wundergartens . . . rief mir die Insel der seligen Phäaken in die Sinne sowie ins Gedächtnis. Ich eilte sogleich, einen Homer zu kaufen . . ." (HA 11:241; The impression of the miraculous garden called the island of the blessed Phaeacians to the senses and to mind. I hurried at once to buy a copy of Homer). Classical fulfillment was finally at hand; Goethe felt he had found the symbolic destination of his journey: "Italien ohne Sizilien macht gar kein Bild in die Seele: hier ist erst der Schlüssel zu allem" (252; Italy without Sicily leaves absolutely no image in our soul; only here is the key to everything). Reading the scene from the island of the Phaeacians, he felt inspired to write a drama about Nausikaa and her tragic love affair with Odysseus.[12] The few lines that he finished breathe the spirit of Sicily — as Goethe claimed, "es war in dieser Komposition nichts, was ich nicht aus eigner Erfahrung nach der Natur hätte ausmalen können" (300; There was nothing in the composition I could not have described from nature according to my own experience). Like the wanderer Goethe in Palermo, Odysseus awakens to find himself on an island paradise, unsure if he is waking or dreaming. The following couplet from the *Nausikaa* fragment beautifully expresses the immediacy of nature in his Sicilian experience: "Ein weißer Glanz ruht über Land und Meer / Und duftend schwebt der Äther ohne Wolken" (HA 5:72; A white sheen rests over land and sea/ And the ether floats hazily without a cloud).

Goethe's final ten months in Rome (*Zweiter Römischer Aufenthalt*) are narrated in a different compositional pattern, his correspondence juxtaposed with reports taken from memory and his diaries. The tone changes as well. The exciting images of discovery and self-discovery fade as Goethe attempts to transform the insights gained in Sicily into principles for his art and life. He abandons his incognito and joins in the social life of the city, even allowing himself the luxury of a Roman mistress. Humphry Trevelyan's claim that Goethe became a pagan in Rome might be an exaggeration, but he did cultivate a lifestyle influenced by the sensuous vitality of the ancients as he understood them.[13]

Goethe's views on Greek mythology can be surmised through his friend Karl Phillip Moritz, whose *Götterlehre* (Mythology, 1791) arose from their daily conversations on the topic in the summer of 1787. Moritz intended to write an account of classical mythology "in rein menschlichem Sinne" (from a purely human perspective) to reveal the aesthetic potential of the myths to a new generation of artists and poets (HA 11:391). He denied any theological considerations; abstract concepts such as eternity and omnipotence are entirely foreign to the myths, he claims, as are later concepts of morality. Nor should myths be understood as history or allegory, though they share aspects of both. Rather, in one of the earliest formulations of aesthetic autonomy, Moritz states that a myth is "die Sprache der Phantasie" (the language of the imagination), and as a true work of art, it is "etwas in sich Fertiges und Vollendetes, das um sein selbst willen da ist, dessen Wert in ihm selber und in dem wohlgeordneten Verhältnis seiner Teile liegt"[14] (A true work of art, a beautiful poem is something complete and perfect in itself, existing only for its own sake and whose value lies in itself and in the harmonious proportion of its parts). In Moritz's aesthetic reading of the myths, the gods serve no higher purpose, but exist only as poetic images of the natural forces in the world. The humane divinities that Iphigenie sought so desperately to believe in have given way to beings whose chief attribute is power and whose quarrels — "Macht gegen Macht" (force against force) — reflect the inevitable destruction that is part of nature. This view of myth allowed Moritz — and with him Goethe — to see the greatness of classical art and poetry as pure expressions of the human imagination, beyond good and evil, and beyond all notions of convention or utility.

Goethe's *Italienische Reise* closes with a sense of fulfillment in his quest for self-cultivation, with growing confidence in his views on art and antiquity and in his calling as a poet. Although critics have rightly questioned the biographical veracity of such self-stylization, it is significant that the terms chosen for his poetic rebirth reflect a belief in the supremacy of classical art and in the regenerative power of classical soil — beliefs expressed later in Faust's own journey through antiquity.

The first fruit of Goethe's Italian experience was the poetic cycle *Erotica Romana*, conventionally referred to as the *Römische Elegien* (Roman Elegies, composed 1789–90, published 1795).[15] Ancient Rome and the antique spirit still present in the city form the central images of the work. In the poetic consciousness of the narrator, a wanderer from the North, the art and mythology of the past unite with the sensual pleasures and eroticism of the present to form a poetic image that echoes the elegies of the Latin writers Catullus, Propertius, and Tibullus. The wanderer comes to Rome seeking a personal understanding of the classical world, and in a delicate balance of reflection and experience finds the fulfillment of his desire in the arms of a Roman mistress. The ideal of antique wholeness appears realized in an erotic union, which reveals the fundamental unity of nature and classical art. Dreaming of marble goddesses, the wanderer taps hexameters on his sleeping lover's back, and the rhythm of his fingers becomes the poetry of the present. The opening lines of the famous fifth elegy express the wanderer's growing insight into the heathen spirit of antiquity:

Froh empfind' ich mich nun auf klassischem Boden begeistert,
    Vor- und Mitwelt spricht lauter und reizender mir.
Hier befolg' ich den Rat, durchblättre die Werke der Alten

Mit geschäftiger Hand, täglich mit neuem Genuß.
Aber die Nächte hindurch hält Amor mich anders beschäftigt;
    Werd' ich auch halb nur gelehrt, bin ich doch doppelt beglückt.
Und belehr ich mich nicht, indem ich des lieblichen Busens
    Formen spähe, die Hand leite die Hüften hinab?
Dann versteh' ich den Marmor erst recht: ich denk' und vergleiche,
    Sehe mit fühlendem Aug', fühle mit sehender Hand.

(HA 1:160)

[Gladly I tread upon classical soil, enthused with its spirit,
    Present and past, Rome speaks more clearly, more warmly to me.
Here I follow advice, page through the works of the ancients
    With industrious hands, daily with newfound delight.
Nightly, however, Amor provides me with different diversions,
    If I'm only half beginning to learn, I'm doubly blessed.
And am I not teaching myself, observing the shape of her body,
    Guiding my hand down her hips and over her delicate breast?
That's when I understand marble: I think and compare,
    See with eyes that can feel, feel with a hand that can see.]

The moment of fulfillment is genuine, a sensuous eroticism refreshingly free of moral conventions and social limitations, but it is not the spontaneous experience of antique wholeness. For the wanderer, fulfillment is always mediated by reflection and by the guiding hand of classical art. The Romantic tension between the *perfection* of the past and the *longing* of the present (like the tensions between the North and South, between classical repose and modern restlessness) defines the boundaries of the poems. Only in the timeless city of Rome can the gulf separating antiquity and modernity be bridged, poetically suspended in a consciousness that embraces the fleeting possibility of recapturing the heathen spirit of the past. The ironic playfulness of such a re-enactment of a classical lifestyle does not diminish the power of Goethe's poetry, but it does underscore the distance between the two worlds. The classical past cannot be recovered directly; the wanderer sustains the illusion of presence only through constant and ironic reference to the remnants of a vanished civilization.

The eroticism of the *Römische Elegien* reflects the conventions of the classical genre. Even though Goethe suppressed the four most outrageous poems, the work occasioned a scandal as contemporaries read the elegies as an autobiographical account of the author's own illicit affairs. The classical setting clearly heightened their suspicions. Roma — Amor: in the erotic fantasies of the age, Rome was associated with exotic beauty and a permissiveness reminiscent of the antique world. In Johann J. W. Heinse's (1746–1803) notorious novel, *Ardinghello und die glückseligen Inseln* (Ardinghello and the Blissful Isles, 1787), set in Renaissance Italy and Greece, Rome figures as the scene of unbridled pagan eroticism. The protagonist's visit to classical sites leads to discussions of antiquity and art, and finally to the desire to experience firsthand the physical beauty and passion enjoyed by the ancients. The artists strip their models down to their shirts and have them perform a Spartan dance in which the girls willingly abandon their clothing and inhibitions. The climax of the *Götterfest* (divine festival) comes as the narrator is seized by a "raging Penthesilea" in the thunderous cataracts of a Bacchantic storm. Like Goethe's elegies, Heinse's work reveals the sexual energy that lay beneath the marble surface of antiquity. Few German writers besides Kleist explored this theme so explicitly, but it was well represented in the pictorial arts, where the classical tradition permitted free expression of the human body.

The *Römische Elegien*, with their alternating moments of reflection and fulfillment, illustrate the poetological distinction between modern and antique that Schiller formulated in his *Horen* essays of the mid 1790s. The modern "sentimental" poet, living in a fragmented social world and alienated from nature, can only strive to create within himself the lost classical harmony, and thus *through reflection* give expression to an ideal which no longer exists as a tangible reality. As Schiller explains in a letter to Herder, neoclassical poetry in the modern age reflects the positive, "sentimental" striving for an absent ideal: "Daher scheint es mir gerade ein Gewinn für ihn [den poetischen Geist] zu seyn, daß er seine eigne Welt formiert und durch die Griechischen Mythen der Verwandte eines fernen, fremden und idealischen Zeitalters bleibt da ihn die Wirklichkeit nur beschmutzen würde"[16] (Thus it seems to me a great triumph for the poet that he creates his own world and, through the agency of the Greek myths, remains the kinsman of a distant, foreign and ideal age, since reality could do nothing but befoul him).

Schiller reached this view of antiquity largely through isolated study. His first direct encounter with classical plastic art had come in 1785, when he described a visit to the Mannheim Collection of Antiquities in the essay "Brief eines reisenden Dänen" (Letter of a Traveling Dane). Influenced by Winckelmann and Lessing, his account of the sacred "temple of art" is hardly original, but it anticipates the poem "Die Götter Griechenlands" (The Gods of Greece, 1788), a landmark in Schiller's aesthetic view of antiquity. Several lines reappear almost verbatim in the poem: "Da die Götter menschlicher noch waren, / waren Menschen göttlicher" (when the gods were still more human, / men were more godlike).[17] The union of the human and the divine expressed here is the defining characteristic of the golden age of Greece evoked in the opening stanzas. The gods are everywhere, animating the entire landscape with a mythical presence that gives beauty and meaning to art and poetry. The natural harmony of gods and men, depicted in example upon example, engenders a fullness of life and feeling that even death cannot threaten. Schiller is not interested in an historical depiction of antiquity; his Greece is an ideal world of myth and legend, a fictional land of fable that stands in stark contrast to the disenchanted world of modernity.

Schiller's rhetorical celebration of the golden age heightens the sense of loss expressed in the latter half of the poem. The gods have vanished, and with them the power of myth to sustain life and poetry:

> Schöne Welt, wo bist du? — Kehre wieder,
> Holdes Blütenalter der Natur!
> Ach, nur in dem Feenland der Lieder
> Lebt noch deine goldne Spur.[18]

> [Beautiful world, where are you? Return again,
> Sweet blossom age of nature!
> Oh, only in the fairy land of song
> Still lives your golden trace.]

The artistic remnants of the past are all that remind the poet of the ideal that is absent in his "entgötterte Natur" (nature bereft of the divine). His cries and the empty echoes in the forest poignantly express the pain of loss and isolation felt by the poet. In place of mythic harmony, sterile rationalism and a distant Christian god rule over the soulless mechanism of the universe. Elsewhere Schiller embraces these aspects of modernity as manifestations of progress, but the lament in "Die Götter Griechenlands" contains no hint of reconciliation. In the final stanza, the poet rejects the modern goddess of truth and her fruitless, overpowering precepts, and pleads instead for the return of her gentler sister, the goddess of beauty.

Schiller's attack on enlightened rationalism, modern science, and religion provoked many of his contemporaries. The poet Count Friedrich Leopold von Stolberg (1750–1819) denounced the poem from an orthodox perspective and unleashed a controversy over the place of heathen mythology in a Christian age. Although the criticism was based on a misunderstanding of the spiritual predicament of the artist, Schiller felt compelled to revise the poem in 1800. In the new and shorter version, he deleted the most "objectionable" verses and added a note of consolation in the conclusion. Although the gods have departed, the ideal has not vanished entirely from the earth; the beauty and harmony of the golden age have been rescued, transformed through art into an eternal beacon for the future: "Was unsterblich im Gesang soll leben / Muß im Leben untergehen"[19] (what should live immortally in song / must perish in life).

The dense mythological references in "Die Götter Griechenlands" reveal Schiller's intense study of the classical world during his first stay in Weimar. He considered the literature of antiquity a kind of finishing school in his study of aesthetics. In a letter to Christian Gottfried Körner (1756–1831) dated 20 August 1788, he wrote: "In den nächsten 2

Jahren . . . lese ich keine modernen Schriftsteller mehr. . . . die Alten geben mir jetzt wahre Genüsse. Zugleich bedarf ich ihrer im höchsten Grade, um meinen eigenen Geschmack zu reinigen. . . . Du wirst finden, daß mir ein vertrauter Umgang mit den Alten äußerst wohltun, — vielleicht Klassizität geben wird" (I plan to read no more modern authors for the next two years. . . . And the ancients provide me now with true pleasure. I also need them in the highest degree to purify my taste. . . . You will find that an intimate acquaintance with the ancients will serve me well, perhaps even grant me classicality). Although Schiller's extreme Hellenism diminished with his historical studies and his reading of Kant, his understanding of the classical world and its significance for modern poetry would remain essentially unaltered. For Schiller, the Greek ideal of simplicity and harmony directed the poet not back to an irretrievable Arcadia, but ahead to a future Elysium. The aesthetic challenge of expressing this ideal through a modern poetic consciousness gained particular urgency as political tensions fragmented the German cultural landscape.

The outbreak of the French Revolution confronted Goethe and Schiller with the challenge of reconciling their Greek vision to the demands of contemporary politics in an age of discord and conflict. Their individual and later collaborative efforts to create a classical literary program bore fruit in a series of theoretical works in the 1790s, in which they attempted to elucidate the defining characteristics of art forms appropriate for their time. As different as their methods and interests were, the conclusions of both authors bore the unmistakable stamp of Greek influences.

"Welche neuere Nation verdankt nicht den Griechen ihre Kunstbildung? Und, in gewissen Fächern, welche mehr als die deutsche?" (HA 12:38; Which modern nation does not owe its education in art to the Greeks? And, in certain fields, which more than the German?) Goethe's rhetorical question in the introduction to his *Propyläen* is in effect a commandment not to stray from classical soil. Many contemporaries and later critics have with some justification construed Goethe's interest in the art of antiquity and in representations of an idealized humanity as a flight from the real issues of the age; Goethe himself certainly did not.[20] He saw social conflict rooted not in political inequality, but in the barbarous level of cultivation in the population at large. Here Goethe shared Schiller's conviction that social progress lay in the cultivation of humanity through a higher form of art. The program of their journals *Horen* and *Propyläen* was based on the conviction that human fulfillment was to be realized through aesthetic means and that the art of antiquity, with its images of ethical perfection in man, would provide the model for cultural and social renewal. Their mission was threefold: first, they wanted to assimilate and adapt classical principles for their own time, thus distinguishing true art and beauty from the mediocrity and dilettantism that seemed to dominate the German cultural landscape; second, the aesthetic principles derived from this endeavor would form the ideological basis for an intellectual community, a fellowship of scholars and artists devoted to the propagation of a new humanity; and third, the works of this community would reveal the possibilities of holistic, harmonious existence in all its aesthetic, moral, and social dimensions, and thus exert a civilizing influence on a receptive public and foster social development without the danger of violent political convulsions.

Of course, the program was a failure. Their cry for a community of like-minded artists fell on deaf ears, and neither journal survived more than a few years. Only the first stage can be considered a success. In works such as Moritz's "Über die bildende Nachahmung des Schönen" (On the Plastic Imitation of the Beautiful) and Goethe's "Einfache Nachahmung der Natur, Manier, Stil" (Simple Imitation of Nature, Manner, Style, 1789), his essay on Laocoön and·his introduction to the *Propyläen*, proper appreciation of art is described as a Winckelmannian gaze: only an objective, selfless and disinterested (*uneigennutzig*) perspective will allow the highest enjoyment of the beautiful. Schiller carries the idea of aesthetic autonomy further in *Briefe über die ästhetische Erziehung des Menschen*. In his terms, beauty as a "living form" connotes "freedom in appearance," the apparent self-determination of a work of art which allows it to transcend any subjugation to external forces. In this way, true art represents a realm of freedom or play, a holistic experience that harmonizes the sensual and intellectual desires. The classical ideal of human wholeness is thus realized as an aesthetic experience.

The moral and political dimensions of the Greek ideal are explored in the opening letters (one to five), where Schiller describes how an ideal state depends not on institutions, but on the moral character of its citizens. The developments of the French Revolution, however, reveal that his contemporaries are not yet capable of transforming the state of necessity into the state of reason. To illustrate the alienation and artificiality of modern society, Schiller presents an idealized comparison with ancient Greece in letter six. The Greeks experienced a harmony of sensualism and rationalism that permitted the first flowering of humankind, an unparalleled combination of "die Jugend der Phantasie mit der Männlichkeit der Vernunft in einer herrlichen Menschheit"[21] (the youth of fantasy with the manliness of reason in a splendid humanity). Unlike modern states in which the individual is treated only as a fragment (*Bruchstück*), the Greeks knew no discord in their character, it is argued, but lived as complete, independent beings in a free society. The Greek state, which fostered such a maximum of humanity, thus serves as the model for a future state in which the mythic wholeness of man will be realized on a higher moral level.

Conspicuous by its absence in these essays is the association of ancient Greece with political freedom, democracy, or equality. Although German Jacobins, like their counterparts abroad, appealed openly to the virtues of

Greek democracies and the Roman Republic in order to justify the abolition of tyranny, the Weimar artists avoided any reference to such political concepts as the basis or the manifestation of antique spirit. They were well aware that the Greek city states were poor models of political stability and peace, and they clearly preferred a mythical past which suggested a political ideal only through its supposed cultivation of individual humanity. Freedom for Goethe and Schiller was not a pragmatic political objective, but a cultural goal that lay at the end of the aesthetic education of man — "weil es die Schönheit ist, durch welche man zu der Freiheit wandert"[22] (because it is beauty, through which one progresses to freedom).

Johann Gottfried Herder's *Briefe zu Beförderung der Humanität* (Letters for the Advancement of Humanity, 1793–97) echo his Weimar compatriots' belief in the ethical perfection of antiquity. For him too, the Greeks revealed the possibilities of an ideal human existence; their art "kannte, ehrte, und liebte die Menschheit im Menschen" and their artists "läuterten alles Schöne, Vortrefliche, Würdige im Menschen . . . zur Gottheit hinauf"[23] (recognized, honored and loved the humanity in man . . . [and their artists] purified and elevated what was beautiful, great and worthy in man . . . to their images of gods). In their culture of humanity, he wrote, "müssen wir alle Griechen werden, oder wir bleiben Barbaren" (354; In this we must all become Greeks, or we will remain barbarians). Herder's historical relativism, however, led him to condemn the attempt to recreate classical art as a betrayal of German artistic integrity: "In Sprache und Sitten werden wir nie Griechen und Römer werden; wir wollen es auch nicht seyn"[24] (In language and customs we will never become Greeks and Romans; nor would we wish to). Despite his admiration for Winckelmann, he rejected the imitation of the ancients as a path toward artistic achievement. The art of Greece was "eine Schule der Humanität; unglücklich ist, wer sie anders betrachtet" (343; Greek art is a school of humanity; unlucky is he who views it otherwise).

Herder's warning would go unheeded. For Wilhelm von Humboldt, the Greeks represent an ideal whose very unattainability spurs imitation. In fact, he considered a feeling for Greek antiquity the "touchstone" (*Prüfstein*) of modern nations. Although the Weimar writers viewed the classical world as the heritage of all nations, with Humboldt the relationship to antiquity begins to assume distinctly nationalistic contours. In his "Geschichte des Verfalls und Unterganges der griechischen Freistaaten" (History of the Decline and Fall of the Greek States, 1807), he claims that the Germans have "das unstreitige Verdienst" (indisputable merit) of being the first to develop a deep comprehension and true feeling for Greek culture, and that "ein ungleich festeres und engeres Band" (a tighter and more secure bond) now unites the Greeks to the Germans than to any other nation.[25] The reason for this special affinity lies in the "unläugbare Aehnlichkeit" (undeniable similarity) of the two nations in language and character as well as in their feudalism and political fortunes. Friedrich Schlegel extended the idea of affinity further. At the conclusion of his essay "Über das Studium der griechischen Poesie" (On the Study of Greek Poetry, 1797), he claims that the spirit of antiquity has been reborn in Germany, identifying the entire eighteenth-century canon of German writers with their classical counterparts. While other nations, notably France, lack a true appreciation of Greek poetry, a unique and incomparably higher level of classical studies has been achieved in Germany and will probably remain the "ausschließliches Eigentum" (exclusive property) of the Germans for some time.[26] Schlegel's explicit comparison with the French reveals an attempt to assert German cultural superiority at a time of political impotence. The affinity to Greece provided a patent of legitimacy for a German identity distinct from, and in many respects superior to the leading European powers. The inconsequential German states could thus be compared favorably with the Greek *poli*, with Weimar figuring as the modern Athens! Although such patriotic self-fashioning was perhaps understandable at the time, the myth of German Hellenism later became an established article of faith in German scholarly circles: Walter Rehm's monumental *Griechentum und Goethezeit* (Hellenism and the Age of Goethe, 1936) serves as a prime example.

The fashion for Hellenic works reached its zenith at the turn of the nineteenth century and was marked by increasingly ambitious and experimental attempts to discover the original spirit of Greek culture and to transform that vision into modern works of literature. The most influential scholarly work was F. A. Wolf's *Prolegomena ad Homerum* (1795), in which he argued that an original Homer had completed a greater part of the songs attributed to him, but that succeeding generations of rhapsodes (*Homeriden*) increased and altered the songs to form the unity of the *Iliad* and *Odyssey* when finally put into writing. Although Heyne and Herder later claimed to have discovered the rhapsodic origin of the poems independently, most contemporaries saw Wolf's theory as a literary impiety. The "Homeric question" continued to occupy scholars for generations, but Goethe quickly warmed to the idea that he, like the ancient *Homerides*, could also compose Homeric verses. In the poem "Hermann und Dorothea," he toasts the health of the man who had boldly freed him from the severe genius of Homer:

> Denn wer wagte mit Göttern den Kampf? und wer mit dem Einen?
> Doch Homeride zu sein, auch nur als letzter, ist schön.
>
> (HA 1:198)

> [For who dared to war with the gods, and who with Homer?
> Yet to be a Homeride, if only the last, is beautiful.]

German *Homerides* flourished in these years. The generation inspired by Heyne and Wolf sought to reveal the originality of antique works through new translations, undistorted by previous views. Nearly all the notable writers and critics in this period — Goethe, Herder, Humboldt, Hölderlin — translated the ancients, even Schiller in his Hellenic period translated Euripides with the aid of Latin and French editions. Their purpose was not only to refine their taste and broaden their knowledge, but to develop a personal understanding of antiquity and to expand the expressive possibilities of the German language. The task of the translator was to lead the reader to an authentic appreciation of the original, even if this meant exploding the usual syntax and rhythm of German. The novelty of this approach can be seen in a comparison with Wieland, who strove by all faithfulness to the original to produce a work of elegance and clarity; the "improvement" of difficult or unclear passages was a pardonable sin, if not an outright virtue. The younger generation, on the other hand, sought to retain absolute fidelity to the original, so that the translation, in the words of Humboldt, "den Geist des Lesers gleichsam zum Geist des Schriftstellers stimmt"[27] (attunes the spirit of the reader to the spirit of the writer). The foremost challenge was Homer. The enthusiastic students of Heyne in Göttingen, the *Hainbrüder* Gottfried August Bürger (1747–1794), Friedrich Leopold Stolberg, and Johann Heinrich Voss, all set out to render Homer's works in German. Bürger's iambic, balladesque sections appeared in 1771 and 1776, Stolberg's hexameter version in 1778, only to be overshadowed by Voss's masterful *Odyssey* of 1781. His *Iliad* appeared in 1793, together with a revised version of the *Odyssey*, and immediately became the standard for the next century. His translations brought Homer to a wider audience and, although not the first to use the verse form, Voss popularized hexameters in Germany, influencing Goethe and others in their own epics. While Voss revised his translations in an increasingly strange and archaic manner, he also composed creative works that attempted to modernize the epic form for a contemporary readership. His *Luise* (1795) retains the simplicity and harmony of Homer in the idyllic portrait of a rural parsonage family in Germany.

Voss's successful combination of folk poetry and classical form found a strong resonance among readers and artists. Goethe in particular felt inspired to try his hand at classical epic. His *Hermann und Dorothea* (1797) narrates in Homeric language and form the simple story of a young man finding a bride among refugees fleeing the French Revolution. The idyllic character of bourgeois life in Germany is contrasted with political conflict abroad, and the ensuing tension is harmonized in the marriage of the protagonists. The Homeric epithets and veiled allusions to the *Iliad* reveal with gentle humor what Goethe in a 5 December 1796 letter to Heinrich Meyer called "das rein Menschliche der Existenz einer kleinen deutschen Stadt" (the purely human in the existence of a small German town). The work further illustrates the faith of the Weimar circle in the ability of art to transform destructive forces into beauty with the power to reconcile and heal. *Hermann and Dorothea* was an astounding critical and popular success, hailed by contemporaries as a profound union of the classical and the contemporary. Despite the Homeric structure, however, the limitations of *Hermann and Dorothea* as a classical epic are evident: the narrow scope avoids any direct confrontation with the political issues of the age, and the playful mock heroism and bourgeois worldview are entirely modern. If Goethe wanted to be a serious *Homeride*, he would have to confront Homer on his own territory.

In 1798 he began study for a continuation of the *Iliad*, an epic of eight cantos that would recreate in language and spirit the epics of antiquity and reflect on a grand stage the conflicts of the French Revolution. Goethe's *Achilleis* would have depicted the passion of Achilles for the Trojan princess Polyxena against the political intrigues of both sides during negotiations to end the war. The assassination of Achilles during the wedding destroys the fragile peace, and the action descends into chaos, with the madness of Ajax symbolizing the brutal inevitability of continued bloodshed. The one canto that Goethe finished (1799) contains all the familiar Homeric elements — the austere, objective perspective, the inexorable hand of fate, the gods intervening in human affairs — but the continuation would have included modern elements as well, sentimental love and political intrigue foreign to Homer. Despite moments of beauty, it is not a completely successful poem, and the remaining cantos would have posed difficulties even for Goethe. Was he unable or unwilling to finish the work? One can only speculate that he had reached the limits of Winckelmannian imitation, that the disparity of the antique and the modern could not be reconciled in a work that attempted to be wholly classical.

The spirit of experimentation also led Schiller to engage in, as he put it in a letter to the actor August Wilhelm Iffland (1759–1814), "einen kleinen Wettstreit mit den alten Tragikern" (a small contest with the ancient dramatists) in his *Braut von Messina* (22 April 1803). The family curse and the prophesies of doom are reminiscent of *Oedipus rex*, as is the analytic structure leading to the recognition of Beatrice, a lost sister fated to destroy the dynasty. The most obvious classical borrowing, however, was Schiller's use of a chorus, which he defended as necessary to sustain the poetic atmosphere of the play — "weil er die moderne gemeine Welt in die alte poetische verwandelt"[28] (because it transforms the modern vulgar world into the old poetic one). By creating a moment of reflection, the chorus also establishes a calming detachment from the emotional turbulence of the action and thus ensures the aesthetic freedom of the audience. Although Schiller was convinced that his ambitious classical drama was a success — boasting in a letter to Humboldt (17 February 1803) that he might have beaten Sophocles for a dramatic prize — his adaptations of the chorus and his concept of fate both vary considerably from classical models. Fate is revealed to be guilt — the final word in the drama — and the choral odes, despite their beautiful poetry, fail to provide objective reflection on the action.

More shocking still was Heinrich von Kleist's foray into classical drama with his *Penthesilea* (1808). Despite his reliance on the Hellenic tradition and his use of Vossian language, Kleist made no concessions to contemporary taste in a work that reads like a deliberate repudiation of Winckelmann's Greek ideal. Adam Müller (1779–1829), his close friend, describes the classical imagery as a facade: "Sie werden in der Penthesilea wahrnehmen, wie er die Äußerlichkeiten herbeizieht, um . . . doch nicht darin verkannt zu werden, daß von keiner Nachahmung, von keinem Affektieren der Griechheit die Rede sei. Demnach ist Kleist sehr mit Ihnen zufrieden, wenn Sie von der Penthesilea sagen, daß sie *nicht* antik sei"[29] (You will note in the Penthesilea how he casts away all similarities with antiquity, using anachronisms . . . in order to show that there is no imitation, no affectation with Hellenism. Thus Kleist would be very content with you if you would say of Penthesilea that it is *not* antique). Müller's comments, however, more accurately reflect his rejection of the Weimar image of wholeness and harmony in antiquity. For Kleist, the classical world is a "Dionysian" setting for tragic sublimity, for monumental suffering, beauty, and death.[30] Penthesilea, the Amazon queen, is herself a figure of extreme disharmony; she is conflicted in her desire as a woman for Achilles and in her heroic pride as a warrior and queen. Following the law that Amazon women can only mate with men they have subdued in battle, she seeks out Achilles only to be rendered unconscious and captured. Realizing her shameful failure, her wounded pride transforms into mad fury and, in a final duel, she slays the now willingly submissive Achilles. Resembling her patron goddess Diana in pursuit of Actaeon, she joins her ravenous dogs biting and tearing the flesh of her fallen lover. Kleist's intentional reversal of Achilles' fate parallels his reversal of the classical aesthetic; unlike Laocoön's containment of passion or Iphigenie's humane triumph over barbarism, the terrible beauty of Penthesilea's desire itself drives her descent into bestial, cannibalistic behavior. The concluding *Liebestod* demonstrates the hopelessness of Penthesilea's fate in Kleist's Romantic vision of antiquity; her death cannot restore harmony and balance to a fractured world.

The tragic yearning for the recovery of a lost classical ideal lies at the heart of Friedrich Hölderlin's poetry. Inspired as no poet before or since by his own vision of Greece, "the last of the Winckelmannites" represents the climax of Romantic Hellenism in Germany.[31] In the works of his mature period before his mental dissolution in 1806, he uses familiar images of Greece to create "a personal mythology, or a coherent poetic world" that expresses his longing for a classical rebirth.[32] "Der Archipelagus" (1800) narrates in sweeping hexameters a story of loss and recovery that provides hope for the anguished speaker in the poem. He begins with images of springtime in Greece — nature has survived, as have the gods, only the Greeks themselves have vanished. In the fifth stanza, the poet's imaginary journey takes him back to a moment in history when the unity of nature, the gods, and the Greeks was most profoundly revealed. He narrates the Battle of Salamis in epic grandeur, emphasizing both the destruction of Greece and the unified action of the people in defense of their liberty. Unlike the Weimar artists, whose image of antiquity was an ahistorical age of myth, Hölderlin sees Greek greatness in their (idealized) political history. The communal ethos that brought victory over Xerxes also ensures their triumph over the loss and devastation wrought by the Persians. The recovery of their culture, enacted poetically in the rebuilding of Athens in the tenth stanza, reveals Hölderlin's interest in the democratic ideal of a community in harmony with itself and its universe. The happiness of that age of light stands in bitter contrast to the poet's own time: "Aber weh! Es wandelt in Nacht, es wohnt, wie im Orkus / Ohne Göttliches unser Geschlecht"[33] (But alas, our race wanders in night, we live, as in Hades / Without the divine). And yet, the poet hears from afar the songs of celebration. The memory of past recovery promises cultural and spiritual rebirth in the future — an autumn that will bring the Greek spring to fruition. The poem closes with the solace that Greece still survives, if only in memory — "Aber blühet indes, bis unsere Früchte beginnen" (But bloom in the meantime, until our own fruits begin) — a hope that will guide the poet in his age of darkness.

As with any outgoing fashion, the rarefied ideal of Hellenism soon inspired parody such as Julian von Voss's (1768–1832) comedy, *Die Griechheit* (Greekness, 1807), in which a German baron is so taken by the fantasy world of ancient Greece that he decides to "Hellenize" himself and his entire estate. He plants olive trees, renames objects and people, clothes his servants in Greek dress, and even goes so far as to speak only in classical verse. The humorous exaggeration of contemporary taste reveals the obvious incongruity between Schiller's "fairy land of song" and the provincial German territories. In a deeper sense, Voss also points out how artificial the transplantation of classical ideals was for most Germans; Greece could be cultivated perhaps in the hothouse of Weimar, but not propagated in the open air of the dark northern climate.

The productive potential of Winckelmann's cry for the imitation of the ancients exhausted itself in the disappointments of the age. Herder's faith in Greece as a school of humanity, like Goethe and Schiller's belief in aesthetic education and Hölderlin's longing for the rebirth of the democratic spirit of antiquity were all frustrated by a reality that seemed to distance itself ever more from the ideal. The rise of nationalism led the Romantics to abandon their "Grecomania" in favor of a glorified medievalism, and even Goethe turned to other cultures for inspiration. The Greek world continued to exert a strong influence in other areas, architecture above all, and politically engaged philhellenic poetry celebrating Byron (1788–1824) and the Greek War for Independence experienced great popularity in the 1820s, but the Weimar project of fostering an ideal of classical humanity was out of step with the times. One notes, for example, the defensive tone in Goethe's *Italienische Reise* when he describes aesthetic revelations lying thirty or forty years in the past.

Schiller's death in 1805 marked the end of Hellenism as a dominant cultural influence in Weimar. Goethe's biographical sketch of the same year, published in the collection *Winckelmann und sein Jahrhundert* (Winckelmann and his Century) portrays their shared image of Greece as something already historical in nature. "Barock und wunderlich" (HA 12:107; baroque and strange) is his description of Winckelmann's essay on imitation. The admonition of his conclusion, to draw inspiration from Winckelmann's grave and to continue "mit Eifer und Liebe" (129; with zeal and love) what the master had started, cannot have been very persuasive, since Goethe had earlier remarked how sad it is to find something finished and complete, like a dusty museum that imparts only feelings of ghosts and graves. In this context, continued allegiance to Winckelmann reminds one of Hölderlin's fears of reviving the dead, the inevitable sterility of any attempt to return a lifeless ideal to the land of the living.

Goethe's final resurrection of the dead in *Faust II* (1832) avoids such dangers by situating Helena's return in the aesthetic realm to which she rightly belongs. The first lines of the Helena act were composed in 1800, but unlike the poetic hubris of his *Achilleis* of 1799, Goethe summons the Homeric world only as a self-consciously artificial landscape in his most Romantic and modern work. Like the *Roman Elegies*, Faust's union with Helena is presented as the confrontation of a northern wanderer with the ideal beauty and eroticism of antiquity. Faust also searches for fulfillment, for the wholeness of classical experience that might satisfy his unquenchable desire. With Helena's appearance in act 3, the frantic pace and incessant striving of the modern world are suspended in the illusion of serene grandeur of Winckelmann's Greece. In the moment of their union, through a dialogue of distant cultures, Goethe presents a poetic image of the eternally fulfilled presence of classical art:

> Faust: Nun schaut der Geist nicht vorwärts, nicht zurück,
>   Die Gegenwart allein —
> Helena: Ist unser Glück.
>
> (9381–82)
>
> [Faust: Desiring neither future nor the past,
>   The present alone —
> Helena: Is our happiness.]

Faust's ensuing monologue poetically transforms the scenery into a neo-classical painting of Arcadia whose idyllic beauty evokes the natural wholeness and harmony of classical existence. The illusion is shattered, poetically and historically, by their child Euphorion, who embodies the Byronic spirit of the Romantic age, the glorious and tragically short-lived union of the classical and the Faustian. With his death, Helena vanishes, and her chorus dissolves into the landscape as pantheistic spirits. Faust's final vision of Helena summarizes the classical experience not only for himself, but for the generation of artists inspired by Winckelmann's Greece. Standing atop German mountains, he sees Helena's image in the clouds:

> Ich seh's! Junonen ähnlich, Leda'n, Helenen,
> Wie majestätisch lieblich mir's im Auge schwankt.
> Ach, schon verrückt sich's! Formlos breit und aufgetürmt
> Ruht es in Osten, fernen Eisgebirgen gleich,
> Und spiegelt blendend flücht'ger Tage großen Sinn. (10050–54)

> [I see it now! Like Juno, Leda, Helena;
> With what majestic loveliness it glimmers there.
> Alas, already drifting off! Its formless, broad,
> And towering peaks lie in the distant east, reflect
> With blinding light the brilliance of those fleeting days.]

Although Faust (and his readers) must return to the contentious realm of modernity, his brief contact with the classical world was a cultivating and enriching experience of deep significance. The bright light in the east, ethereal and unattainable, endures as a memory and an inspiration for those who, like Faust, would seek the ideal.

Notes

[1] Klaus L. Berghahn presents an overview of the discussions of the "Klassik-Legende" in "Das andere der Klassik: Von der 'Klassik-Legende' zur jüngsten Klassik-Diskussionen," *Goethe Yearbook* 6: 1992: 1–27. See also Gerhart Hoffmeister, Introduction, *A Reassessment of Weimar Classicism*, ed. Gerhart Hoffmeister (Lewiston, Queenston, Lampeter: Edwin Mellon, 1996), 1–10; and Dieter Borchmeyer, *Weimarer Klassik: Portrait einer Epoche* (Weinheim: Beltz Athenäum, 1994), 13–43.

[2] See Klaus L. Berghahn, "Weimarer Klassik + Jenaer Romantik = Europäische Romantik?," *Monatshefte* 88 (1996): 480–88.

[3] Johann Joachim Winckelmann, *Gedanken über die Nachahmung der griechischen Werke in der Malerei und Bildhauerkunst*, first edition of 1755 (Nendeln: Kraus Reprint, 1968), 8. Henceforth *Gedanken*.

[4] For a discussion of Laocoön and its role in the aesthetic discussions of eighteenth-century Germany, see Simon Richter, *Laocoön's Body and the Aesthetics of Pain* (Detroit: Wayne State UP, 1992).

[5] For the literary reception of Winckelmann, see Max L. Baeumer, "Simplicity and Grandeur: Winckelmann, French Classicism, and Jefferson," *Studies in Eighteenth-Century Culture* 7 (1978): 63–78; and Jochen Schmidt, "Griechenland als Ideal und Utopie bei Winckelmann, Goethe und Hölderlin," *Hölderlin Jahrbuch* 28 (1992/93): 94–110.

[6] For an account of Goethe's *Italian Journey* and its subsequent reception, see Gretchen L. Hachmeister, *Italy in the German Imagination: Goethe's "Italian Journey" and Its Reception by Eichendorff, Platen, and Heine* (Rochester: Camden House, 2002).

[7] See Hans-Wolf Jäger, "Goethe reist auch traditionell: Ein Vortrag," *Goethe Yearbook* 5 (1990): 65–84.

[8] Johann Jakob Volkmann (1732–1809), *Historisch-kritische Nachrichten von Italien*, 3 vols. (1770–71). Goethe valued "der gute und so brauchbare Volkmann" (HA 11:332; the good and so useful Volkmann), though he did point out inconsistencies whenever he found them.

[9] See David Irwin, *Neoclassicism* (London: Phaidon, 1997), who illustrates the astounding commercial success of the neoclassical style through the first half of the nineteenth century.

[10] See William J. Lillyman, "Andrea Palladio and Goethe's Classicism," *Goethe Yearbook* 5 (1990): 85–102.

[11] Nicholas Boyle, *Goethe: The Poet and the Age* (Oxford: Clarendon, 1991), 1:447–56.

[12] For Goethe's "Homeric" works and the role of Sicily in their composition, see David Constantine, "*Achilleis* and *Nausikaa:* Goethe in Homer's World," *Oxford German Studies* 15: (1984): 95–111.

[13] Humphry Trevelyan, *Goethe and the Greeks* (Cambridge: Cambridge UP, 1941), 148.

[14] Karl Philipp Moritz, *Götterlehre oder mythologische Dichtungen der Alten* (Berlin, Munich, Vienna: Herbig, n.d., orig. 1791), 9.

[15] The term "elegy" refers here to the elegiac distichon, a classical verse form of alternating hexameters and pentameters.

[16] Schiller, letter to Wilhelm von Humboldt, 4 November 1795.

[17] Schiller, "Die Götter Griechenlands," SW, 3:133.

[18] Schiller, "Die Götter Griechenlands," 132.

[19] Schiller, "Die Götter Griechenlands," 137.

[20] Anthony Stevens presents a balanced view of the complexities of the Weimar authors' response to the revolution in "Weimar Classicism as a Response to History," *Papers from the Annual Symposium of the Australian Academy of the Humanities*, ed. John Hardy and Andrew McCredie (Melbourne: Oxford UP, 1983), 86–102.

[21] Schiller, *Briefe über die ästhetische Erziehung*, SW, 5:323.

[22] Schiller, *Aesthetische Erziehung*, 314.

[23] Johann Gottfried Herder, *Sämtliche Werke*, ed. Bernhard Suphan, 33 vols. (Hildesheim: Georg Olms, 1967), reprint of the Berlin edition of 1887–1913, 17:352–54.

[24] Herder, "Beförderung der Humanität," Suphan 18:140.

[25] Wilhelm von Humboldt, "Geschichte des Verfalls und Unterganges der griechischen Freistaaten," *Werke in fünf Bänden*, ed. Andreas Flitner and Klaus Giel (Stuttgart: Cotta, 1961), 2:87.

[26] Friedrich Schlegel, "Über das Studium der griechischen Poesie," *Schriften zur Literatur* (Munich: Deutscher Taschenbuch Verlag, 1985), 190.

[27] Humboldt, "Über das Studium des Altertums," *Werke* 2:23.

[28] Schiller, "Über den Gebrauch des Chors in der Tragödie," *Werke* 2:249.

[29] Adam Müller, letter to Friedrich Gentz, 6 February 1808.

[30] See Hilda Meldrum Brown, *Heinrich von Kleist: The Ambiguity of Art and the Necessity of Form* (Oxford: Clarendon, 1998), 290–320.

[31] E. M. Butler, *The Tyranny of Greece over Germany* (Boston: Beacon, 1958, orig. 1935), 239.

[32] David Constantine, *Hölderlin* (Oxford: Clarendon, 1988), 152–81, argues that Hölderlin's poetry from 1800–1802, the most productive period in his life, represents a personal mythology or coherent poetic world, constructed largely, but not exclusively, from Greek imagery. He cites "Der Archipelagus" as "eminently a poem of Hölderlin's coherent world" (175).

[33] Friedrich Hölderlin, "Der Archipelagus," *Werke Briefe Dokumente* (Munich: Winkler, 1969), 135.

Goethe's house on the Frauenplan, Weimar.
Engraving by O. Wagner and L. Schütze,
with a saying of Goethe's from 1828. Courtesy of
Stiftung Weimarer Klassik, Kunstsammlungen.

The Correspondents' Noncorrespondence: Goethe, Schiller, and the *Briefwechsel*

Gail Hart

I

THE GOETHE-SCHILLER correspondence is a monument of Weimar Classicism and a banquet for the student of Weimar culture inasmuch as it records the literary, aesthetic, scientific, editorial, and personal exchanges of the two central figures of the tradition. Beginning in 1794, when Schiller invited Goethe to contribute to a new literary journal, and continuing with frequent, often daily, communications until Schiller's death in 1805, the epistolary collaboration comprises over 1,000 letters that provide a wide range of data, opinions, and ideas not available in any other documentation of the period. Indeed, literary historians have often expressed regret that the two authors occasionally spent time together since these personal encounters resulted in gaps in their thorough and illuminating correspondence that no existing sources can fill. Particularly important and engaging in the collection are the first-hand accounts of writing some of the great works of German literature and also of revising these texts in response or resistance to criticism from the other correspondent. One has, as it were, a glimpse into the poetic workshop of the Weimar Classicists and can follow the genesis of major texts from idea to completion, while witnessing and scrutinizing the process; this is particularly true of *Wilhelm Meisters Lehrjahre* (Wilhelm Meister's Apprenticeship, 1795/96), which took final shape over roughly eighteen months of epistolary praise, criticism, and haggling.

One can also follow technical discussions of poetic material and its assignment to appropriate genres, as well as some of the foundational thinking on (German) genre itself. There are lengthy commentaries on public taste and how to improve it; on contemporary literature and its purveyors; on philosophy and aesthetic theory; and insights into the nuts and bolts of late eighteenth-century publishing, as well as its financial aspects. Politics and world affairs register on the margins of this long conversation, as the movements of the French armies affect acquaintances and travel plans, but only on the margins, since absolutist subjects had little say in territorial — and even less in continental — politics. There is also a wealth of personal information on topics such as health, family, recreation, and living habits, and a good deal of social negotiation, such as Goethe's solicitousness toward Schiller's wife and Schiller's near absolute refusal to acknowledge Goethe's companion, Christiane Vulpius, whom he did not marry until 1807.[1] All in all, this rich and sustained correspondence offers a significant and unique entry into the intellectual and material worlds of Weimar Classicism.

The English word "correspondence" fails in many ways to capture the essence of the enterprise and can even be misleading because this exchange of letters, thoughts, pleasantries, and information is based on a fundamental *noncorrespondence* between two great literary minds and also on a power differential between corresponding but noncorresponding friends. To begin with the latter noncorrespondence, it should be pointed out that, despite Goethe's effusive accounts of the collaboration and of his various debts to Schiller, the friendship was asymmetrical from start to finish — and even beyond, when Goethe both edited the correspondence and, not incidentally, secured what he thought to be Schiller's skull for his library. Given Goethe's enormous stature in Weimar, the fact that he was ten years older, and that Schiller was a "fan" from his youth, some measure of inequality is to be expected, but I emphasize the point because of a strong tendency in the secondary literature to celebrate a perceived parity. The statue of the two poets standing before the Weimar theater, holding hands and grasping the same laurel crown, is evidence of the popular invention of equality and fraternity. They were indeed friends, but theirs was a professional friendship, and they never ceased to address each other with the formal "Sie."

Goethe and Schiller might have met during Schiller's school days, when Duke Karl Eugen of Württemberg hosted Goethe and his duke, Carl August, at a prize ceremony at the Hohe Karlsschule in Stuttgart in 1779. The school was the duke's invention, and he compelled the best students in his realm to enroll in it for training as future servants of the state. He also tried to engage the best teachers available and delighted in exhibiting his staff and scholars to visiting dignitaries. Schiller received several prizes that evening for his excellence in medical studies, but there is no indication that Goethe even noticed him. Years later, in 1788, they had a brief conversation after Goethe returned from Italy to find Schiller residing in Weimar, but this did not lead to further communication. Goethe, who acknowledged being offended by the youthful excess of Schiller's wildly successful play, *Die Räuber* (The Robbers, 1781), pretty much ignored his colleague from 1788 until 1794, when the two finally spoke pleasurably and productively after a meeting of a scientific society in Jena. Thus the two poets finally achieved a rapport through their mutual interest in natural science, a topic that led them to remark and accept the stark differences in their basic thinking, the noncorrespondence that had until then prevented any meaningful intellectual alliance, namely Goethe's devotion to experience and "empirical realities" versus Schiller's involvement in speculation and "mental structures."[2]

Schiller had long chafed at Goethe's indifference and had complained to his close friend and confidante, Christian Gottfried Körner, of a love-hate relationship with the older poet. Nonetheless, emboldened by the success of their conversation in Jena, he wrote Goethe on behalf of *Die Horen*, a literary magazine that he was in the process of founding (13 June 1794). Schiller included an announcement that outlined the project in great detail (NA 22:103–5), noting persuasively that the success of a literary journal depends on the quality of its contributions and that the quality of the contributions often depends on the success of the journal, since only success attracts good writers to a particular venue. It was Schiller's announced purpose to reach a broad reading public, indeed to "unite" the German reading public, by drawing readers from the disparate journals already in circulation with the work of Germany's foremost writers. High on his agenda was the matter of taste formation and education of the public to finer forms of thought and creativity. Indeed, the project of the *Horen* appears in part to be an extension of Schiller's epistolary essay, *Über die ästhetische Erziehung des Menschen in einer Reihe von Briefen* (On the Aesthetic Education of Man in a Series of Letters, 1795), which itself came out in the first issues of *Die Horen*. Goethe's response to the project was swift and encouraging since he shared many of Schiller's concerns about the state of public taste and German literature.

The letters that follow, numerous and various as they are, tend disproportionately toward the fostering of Goethe's literary projects, though Schiller's work comes up frequently in the later years, and the two even seem to merge for a time during the production of the collaborative *Xenien* (1797), prompting Goethe's comment,

> Daß man uns in unsern Arbeiten verwechselt, ist mir angenehm; es zeigt, daß wir immer mehr die Manier loswerden und ins allgemeine Gute übergehen. Und dann ist zu bedenken, daß wir eine schöne Breite einnehmen können, wenn wir mit einer Hand zusammenhalten und mit der andern so weit ausreichen, als die Natur uns erlaubt hat. (26 December 1795)

> [I am pleased that readers confuse us in our work; it shows that we are moving away from mannerism and toward the general good. And then it should be considered that we can cover a lot of ground if we hold on to each other with one hand and stretch the other one out as far as nature will allow.]

It was the hands outstretched in opposite directions that were most characteristic of their friendship, and from the very beginning the two poets engaged in a self-conscious construction of a productive union of opposites, achieving a rapid codification of the relationship based firmly on "die Verschiedenheit unserer Naturen" (10 August 1796; the difference in our natures).

It is this latter noncorrespondence of "natures" that made for a productive partnership and profoundly affected German letters because it enabled each (non)correspondent to supplement and problematize the other by arguing for — or merely remarking on — the missing elements in the other's conceptual schemes, be they experiential or theoretical. Goethe provided a grounding in nature and experience, whereas Schiller contributed an analytical and theoretical dimension to the wide variety of problems they endeavored to develop or solve. Thus, they worked from a productive friction that caused each to re-examine his own premises. In July of 1796, while commenting on the manuscript of *Wilhelm Meisters Lehrjahre*, Schiller asked his friend, "Aber im Ernste — woher mag es kommen, daß Sie einen Menschen haben erziehen und fertig machen können, ohne auf Bedürfnisse zu stoßen, denen die Philosophie nur begegnen kann?" (But seriously, how does it happen that you have been able to educate and complete a human being without encountering the needs that only philosophy can meet?). The answer, also supplied by Schiller, is that Wilhelm, like his creator, exists in an aesthetic dimension, a zone where sensuality and morality do not conflict and where the need for speculative thinking or pure reason is alien. This is not Schiller's zone, but he was driven to contemplate and to theorize about it, and had by this point in 1796 already written the essay that defined the two natures, *Über naïve und sentimentalische Dichtung* (On Naïve and Sentimental Poetry, 1795), which posited the naïve poet's closeness to and harmony with nature as opposed to the sentimental poet's need to work his way back to nature from a position of reflection and speculative thought. The key word for the sentimental poet in this process was "work." Whereas the naïve poet seemed merely to pluck the fruit of his poetic spirit, his sentimental counterpart had to labor to achieve poetry (and prose and drama), expending a great deal of effort to produce what was a natural expression for the naïve poet. Just as post-lapsarian salvation entails perhaps greater rewards than prelapsarian existence, so the sentimental poet gains a fuller intellectual reward from his exertions, but remains generally excluded from the immediacy and spontaneity experienced by the naïve poet.

In addition to this spiritual or intellectual divergence, the correspondence records a noncorrespondence in the physical world, namely Goethe's relative good health and Schiller's premature fragility. Even as a young man, Schiller had suffered from fevers, deep coughs, headaches, and respiratory ailments that eventually weakened his system, compromised his work routines, and led to his early death at the age of forty-six. Prior to the correspondence, he had suffered a serious crisis in 1791, with a near-fatal lung infection, from which he never fully recovered. Many found it miraculous that Schiller lived another fourteen years after the breakdown, and it is quite astonishing that he was able to produce so much of the German classical theatrical repertoire, in addition to poetry and his widely-read philosophical and aesthetic essays, in spite of his physical deterioration. He also had a strong sensitivity to bad weather, which was plentiful in Jena, and grew to expect seasonal exacerbations of his condition. These physical considerations of a highly metaphysical thinker are often reflected in the letters, as when he explains to Goethe, who had invited him to Weimar:

> Mit Freuden nehme ich Ihre gütige Einladung nach W an, doch mit der ernstlichen Bitte, daß Sie in keinem einzigen Stück Ihrer häuslichen Ordnung auf mich rechnen mögen, denn leider nötigen mich meine Krämpfe gewöhnlich, den ganzen Morgen den Schlaf zu widmen, weil sie mir des Nachts keine Ruhe lassen, und überhaupt wird es mir nie so gut, auch den Tag über auf eine *bestimmte* Stunde sicher zählen zu dürfen. . . . Die Ordnung, die jedem anderen Menschen wohl macht, ist mein gefährlichster Feind. . . . Ich bitte bloß um die leidige Freiheit, bei Ihnen krank sein zu dürfen.

> [I happily accept your kind invitation to W, but with the earnest request that you do not let any part of your domestic routine depend on me, because unfortunately my cramps usually oblige me to dedicate the entire morning to sleep since they leave me no peace during the night and I am never well enough that one may depend on my being available at any *specific* hour during the rest of the day. . . . The daily routine that is so good for others is my most dangerous enemy. . . . I ask only for the miserable freedom to be permitted to be sick in your home.]

The ailing Schiller was most welcome in Goethe's house after 1794, and illness remained a substantial element of their discourse as Schiller's mind far outpaced the fragile body that caused him so much pain and severely restricted his work time.

Schiller's chronic illness also restricted his mobility and prevented him from traveling, so that Goethe, the passionate natural and cultural tourist, functioned to an extent as his eyes on the world. The idea of Schiller as fixed point, *reading* about foreign lands and their natural and man-made splendors, and Goethe, the traveler, hiker, mountain climber, as active live witness to these phenomena, crops up repeatedly in the letters. Schiller's letter of 6 October 1797 expresses the poet's delight that his description of a whirlpool in "Der Taucher" (The Diver, 1797) struck Goethe as being true to nature. Schiller had never seen a whirlpool and had consulted Homer's description of Charybdis for details. He adds, "Vielleicht führt Ihre Reise Sie an einem Eisenhammer vorbei, und Sie können mir sagen, ob ich dieses kleinere Phänomen richtig dargestellt habe" (Perhaps your trip will take you past a forge and you can tell me whether I have portrayed this phenomenon properly). This poignant request underscores the naïve-sentimental dichotomy — the Goethean experiential and the Schillerian abstract intellectual — and their two very different routes to poetic description. Schiller rarely wrote from experience and enjoys the distinction of having written the Swiss national drama, *Wilhelm Tell* (1804), replete with paeans to the landscape and local customs, without ever having set foot in Switzerland.

Only in 1823, seventeen years after Schiller's death, did Goethe begin the work of collecting the letters. Over the next few years he edited them and arranged them for publication. As the surviving partner, he took control of the correspondence[3] and its legacy and provided the context for presentation in autobiographical accounts of the events that led up to the correspondence and of the benefits that he drew from his consultations with Schiller, notably "Glückliches Ereignis" (Happy Event, 1817), which also appeared under the title "Erste Bekanntschaft mit Schiller" (First Acquaintanceship with Schiller). In these accounts, we hear of the initial coldness between the two and of the massive benefit that Goethe drew from Schiller's advice and criticism. Already in 1798, he had written to his friend, "Sie haben mir eine zweite Jugend verschafft und mich wieder zum Dichter gemacht" (6 January 1798; You have given me a second youth and made me a poet again). In Goethe's controlling reading, which was adopted by subsequent generations, it is this service that is the central and notable achievement of the correspondence and of the friendship it represents.

As for Goethe's appropriation of the skull, Schiller's remains were placed in a coffin at his death, and this was piled with other coffins in the Kassengewölbe in Weimar. In 1818, his wife began the bureaucratic process of having him removed from the crowded mausoleum and buried in his own grave. Finally, in 1826, officials actually entered the Kassengewölbe to retrieve him and found that the stacked coffins had rotted and burst, mingling the bones of almost two dozen people. From a field of 23 skulls, the largest was selected, compared with a bust made from Schiller's death mask, and declared to be Schiller's skull.[4] It was this trophy that Goethe claimed for his library, thus bringing home what he thought to be the vessel of the powerful mind that had assisted him in writing, revising, and, as he indicated, understanding so many of his great poetic works. It was an unusual talisman, and its private display did not reflect established practice. One cannot help but sense the collector's drive to possess and contextualize an object, something Goethe did with the correspondence, which was in many ways the counterpart to Schiller's skull. The rest of Schiller's remains were not resurrected from the pile, and over the years several scientists have declared on the basis of various criteria that the skull Goethe had was not Schiller's. It now lies in the sealed coffin marked "Schiller" in the Weimar Fürstengruft, and the Stiftung Weimarer Klassik has not allowed DNA testing.

II

Goethe was most explicit and detailed on the benefits he drew from his (non)correspondence with Schiller in a long letter to Councilor Christoph Friedrich Ludwig Schultz (1781–1834) dated 10 January 1829, as the edited correspondence was appearing. In this document, Goethe indicates very plainly that we have Schiller to thank for some of his best-known works:

> Hätt es ihm nicht an Manuskript zu den 'Horen' und 'Musenalmanachen' gefehlt, ich hätte die 'Unterhaltungen der Ausgewanderten' nicht geschrieben, den 'Cellini' nicht übersetzt, ich hätte die sämtlichen Balladen und Lieder, wie sie die 'Musenalmanache' geben, nicht verfaßt, die 'Élegién' wären, wenigstens damals, nicht gedruckt worden, die Xenien hätten nicht gesummt, und im Allgemeinen wie im Besonderen wäre manches anders geblieben. Die sechs Bändchen Briefe lassen hievon gar vieles durchblicken.

> [If (Schiller) had not needed manuscripts for the 'Horen' and the 'Musenalmanacs' I would never have written the 'Conversations of German Émigrés,' nor would I have translated 'Cellini;' I would not have written all of those ballads and songs as they appear in the 'Musenalmanacs,' the '[Roman] Elegies' would not have been published — at least not then — the Xenien would never have buzzed, and much would have been different, both generally and specifically. These six little volumes of letters show how a great deal of this happened.]

We will now turn to some of the specific matters in which Schiller helped Goethe realize his poetic goals and conclude with attention to Schiller's activity during the period of the correspondence and how it was affected by Goethe's less frequent, but sustained and focused, interventions.

In the announcement for the *Horen*, Schiller enumerated certain types of material and opinions that would not be represented in the journal, noting that anything that was only of narrow interest would be excluded. He added:

> Vorzüglich aber und unbedingt wird sie sich alles verbieten, was sich auf Staatsreligion und politische Verfassung bezieht. Man widmet sie der schönen Welt zum Unterricht und zur Bildung, und der gelehrten zu einer freien Forschung der Wahrheit und zu einem fruchtbaren Umtausch der Ideen. (NA 22:103)

> [Most important — and unconditionally — the journal will forbid itself anything that relates to state religion and political opinion. We will devote it to the world of beauty for instruction and education, and to the world of scholarship for the free exploration of truth and the productive exchange of ideas.]

The exclusion and containment of politics are major themes of one of Goethe's contributions to the first issues, *Unterhaltungen deutscher*

Ausgewanderten (Conversations of German Emigres, 1795). This is a frame narrative that positions a small number of German aristocrats as refugees fleeing the advancing French armies, though they pursue their conversations or entertainments in comfortable circumstances on an estate that is relatively far from the conflict — a Boccaccian setting for narrative invention. Rather than dwelling on the political circumstances that have caused their displacement, the émigrés pass their time telling stories, seven of them, according to — and sometimes not according to — rules imposed by their hostess, and thus reconstruct an orderly alternative society in the wake of the French Revolution, whose ongoing violence had disturbed and alienated both Goethe and Schiller. The series of stories was developed and refined in epistolary dialogue as Goethe sought Schiller's opinion of the themes he had chosen. Schiller made suggestions and even invoked *Die Horen*'s rules of political neutrality, when he thought that the figures' sentiments might be attributed to their author, but these remarks resulted in only small changes to the manuscript. As on many occasions, Schiller functioned as a sounding board, an appreciative reader, whose objections did not move Goethe to change his work in major ways. Most of their discussion of the collection focused on the enigmatic, yet potentially highly symbolic final piece, "Das Märchen" (The Fairy Tale), as has most of the reception of *Unterhaltungen* from 1795 until the present day. Goethe's tale of the lovely lily and her magical adventures carries the generic title and stands as an exemplary text in the German *Kunstmärchen* (artistic fairytale) tradition.

Another, lesser known project mentioned by Goethe in the quotation above was his translation from the Italian of the marvelous autobiography of the Italian artist Benvenuto Cellini (1500–71). Cellini, who exaggerated the events of his unquestionably extraordinary life, was a noted goldsmith, silversmith, coin and medal maker, and author of treatises on the technical aspects of art. He was also a soldier, a brawler, a multiple murderer, statutory rapist, and a talented historian and storyteller. His account of casting the famous statue of Perseus (1555) that stands in the Loggia in Piazza Signoria in Florence is one of the most exciting and suspenseful pieces of prose from any era, especially when one considers the relative blandness of its subject. As Schiller put it, "Die Belagerung von Troja oder Mantua kann keine größere Begebenheit sein und nicht pathetischer erzählt werden als diese Geschichte" (7 February 1797; The siege of Troy or Mantua cannot have been more significant events, nor can they have been described in a more stirring fashion than this story). Goethe's interest in the translation grew out of his engagement with Cellini's artistic treatises. Schiller was eager to have more copy for his journal and also found Cellini to be an amusing and endearing mixture of gallantry and crudeness (20 June 1796), almost an element of comic relief, as he indicates in his letter of 10 October 1796: "Unterdessen erinnern Sie sich doch auch wieder des *Cellini*. Wie froh wäre ich, wenn wir noch etwas Neues und Lustiges zu lesen zum Schluss des IIten *Horen*-Jahrgangs auftreiben könnten!" (And please remember [to send the next installment of] Cellini. I would be so happy if we were able to provide something new and humorous to read for the close of the second year of the *Horen*). The *Horen* was often in need of lighter fare, and Schiller's contribution in this case was steady encouragement and appreciation. Most references to the translation, which was published in successive excerpts, are merely technical: Goethe notes that he is sending more material and Schiller acknowledges receipt or prods for another segment. On 16 October 1796, Schiller acknowledged an anonymous review of the translated fragments of Cellini in Johann Friedrich Reichardt's (1752–1814) journal *Deutschland*. The reviewer, thought to have been either Romantic poet and essayist Friedrich Schlegel or the influential Romantic writer, critic, and editor Ludwig Tieck (1773–1855),[5] criticized Cellini's character and also complained that some of the better portions of the autobiography had been skipped. Goethe indicated in his letter of 19 October 1796 that he feared a competitor in the reviewer, and he resolved to finish the translation soon and publish it as a whole, though his complete translation was not to appear until 1803. With this exception, contemporary reception of the translation was good, filled with high praise for Goethe's fidelity to the spirit of Italian culture and to the voice of Cellini. Later critics found fault with various aspects of the translation, and even with the text Goethe used as the basis for his original translation. Cellini never published the *vita* and, although written in the mid-sixteenth century, it did not appear in print until the early eighteenth, and then from a copy that had been heavily altered by the publisher. That Cellini philology was a nightmare did not figure in Goethe's treatment of the autobiography, and he was frequently congratulated in print for having brought this extraordinary text to the German reading public in such a clear and lively translation.

In the letter to Schultz cited above, Goethe also credits Schiller with inspiring him to finish *Wilhelm Meisters Lehrjahre*, widely considered the inaugural *Bildungsroman*, which he had begun in the 1770s as *Wilhelm Meisters theatralische Sendung* (Wilhelm Meister's Theatrical Calling). After registering his public's lack of enthusiasm for the artist-drama *Torquato Tasso* (1790), Goethe told Schultz:

> Mit 'Wilhelm Meister' ging es mir noch schlimmer. Die Puppen waren den Gebildeten zu gering, die Komödianten den Gentlemen zu schlechte Gesellschaft, die Mädchen zu lose; hauptsächlich aber hieß es, *es sei kein 'Werther.'* Und ich weiss wirklich nicht, was ohne die Schillersche Anregung aus mir geworden ware.[6]

> [It was even worse for me with 'Wilhelm Meister.' The light figures were too limited for educated readers, the actors were bad company for gentlemen, and the girls were too loose; but mainly everyone was saying,

it's no Werther. And I really do not know what would have become of
me without Schiller's support.]

Schiller's support began with his very first letter, in which he asked
Goethe to contribute *Wilhelm Meister* to the *Horen*. Goethe had already
made arrangements for serial publication, but most books of the novel
remained unfinished. The following one and a half years of correspondence
saw the development and completion of the *Lehrjahre* in dialogue with
Schiller, though the latter's commentary was mainly monological, unan-
swered by Goethe except in the most general terms. The discussion of
Wilhelm Meister proceeded mostly in segments, as Goethe sent manuscripts
for the various books and later the published books themselves, and Schiller
reacted with his own commentary on the immediate drafts and the whole
as it was taking shape. He also reported the critical reactions of several
friends, notably the Berlin writer and educator Wilhelm von Humboldt,
and once included a very astute and practical review of the eighth book
written by his wife, Charlotte (1766–1826). Unlike the brief encouraging
acknowledgments of Goethe's translation of Cellini segments, Schiller's
response to *Wilhelm Meister* was enthusiastic to the point of obsession. He
spoke of "hunger" for more pieces of the manuscript and wrote euphoric
descriptions of his pleasure in reading them: "Mit wahrer Herzenslust habe
ich das erste Buch *W Meisters* durchlesen und verschlungen, und ich danke
demselben einen Genuß, wie ich lange nicht und nie als durch Sie gehabt
habe" (9 December 1794; I read through and devoured the first book of
Wilhelm Meister with truly heart-felt joy and I owe to it a pleasure that I
have not known for a long time and then only through you). Beyond the
euphoria and dithyrambic remarks that comprise the bulk of his writing on
Wilhelm Meister, Schiller also applied his analytical arsenal to the novel,
especially in a series of long letters in July 1796. In these letters, Schiller
spoke on behalf of the readership he imagined for the novel and asked
Goethe to reconsider a number of elements. He found Marianne's death to
be inappropriate and Mignon's to be both inappropriate and without its
necessary resonance; he thought that the novel became at times too the-
atrically technical and too involved in theater in general; he found central
ideas to be subordinated to chance or to amazing and surprising elements;
and he made Goethe aware of minor errors and chronological infelicities.

Goethe reacted to these lengthy and detailed letters with strong
expressions of gratitude, and he invited more comment: "Fahren Sie fort,
mich mit meinem eigenen Werke bekannt zu machen, schon habe ich in
Gedanken Ihren Erinnerungen entgegen gearbeitet" (7 July 1796;
Continue to acquaint me with my own work; I have already started working toward your suggestions in my thoughts). He made small changes,
especially where he found outright errors or awkward phrases, but he

rarely incorporated any of Schiller's more invasive suggestions, explaining in his oft-cited letter of 10 August 1796:

> Ich habe zu Ihren Ideen Körper nach meiner Art gefunden, ob Sie jene geistigen Wesen in ihrer irdischen Gestalt wiedererkennen werden, weiß ich nicht. . . . Es liegt in der Verschiedenheit unserer Naturen, daß es Ihrer Forderungen niemals ganz befriedigen kann. . . .

> [I have realized your ideas in my own way and I don't know whether you will recognize these intellectual creatures in their material form. . . . It is a consequence of the difference in our natures that it [the novel] will never fully satisfy your requirements.]

As noted above, the difference in their natures was more or less neutralized for a time by a project suggested by Goethe in a letter of 23 December 1795. *Die Horen* had not been as enthusiastically received as they had hoped, and this was likely due to an unrecognized or unreflected elitism that guided the composition and selection of prose, poetry, dramatic scenes, and philosophical essays. Schiller, for example, believed that he was writing in a popular style in some of his famously vexed essays, including *Über naïve und sentimentalische Dichtung*, and both usually proceeded in a manner designed to bring the public up to their standards, rather than being actively attentive to existing taste — an idealistic wager and an entrepreneurial error. *Die Horen* was not selling well, and intellectuals and critics were lambasting it or parts of it in learned journals all over the German territories. Goethe proposed to Schiller that they write anonymous epigrams aimed at the many competing literary and intellectual journals on the German market and publish these in another of Schiller's journals, the *Musenalmanach*. The brief epigrams were to be written in large quantities as distichs (couplets consisting of one line in hexameter and one in pentameter) in the classical manner of Martial, a Latin poet of the first century A.D., who was known for his ribald epigrams. Martial had titled a collection of his short poetic commentaries *Xenia*, or gifts for guests. Goethe proposed the *Xenien* as witty and pointed judgments of the competing and critical journals, their values, and their content. Schiller liked the idea, but proposed that they extend their critical range to include individual works and authors, and wrote up an entire catalogue of contemporaries to be targeted, including jurist and writer Friedrich Wilhelm Ramdohr (1752–1822); the Stolberg brothers, Friedrich Leopold and Christian (1748–1821), poets who were highly critical of Goethe's later work; Berlin author and bookseller Friedrich Nicolai (1733–1811); and the philosopher Johann Gottlieb Fichte (1762–1814), whom Schiller evoked as "die metaphysische Welt mit ihren Ichs und Nicht-Ichs" (29 December 1795; the metaphysical world with its I's and Not-I's,).

Both Goethe and Schiller began to produce large numbers of *Xenien*, which they exchanged and from which they chose the best for publication. While Schiller's proposal for the *Horen* as a journal that would unite the readership and replace all others in its class was aggressive, the *Xenien* represented, despite some efforts at moderation, a full-scale attack on the Weimar-era cultural scene, a scandal in the opinion of many critics. Both authors knew contemporary literature and philosophy intimately, and they rendered their many criticisms, objections, saucy observations, and naked peeves as light poetry. The rapid and copious generation of *Xenien* attests to the authors' genuine enjoyment of the form, and the content reveals two German literary giants exploiting their superiority and reveling in the fun of teasing and even insulting their lesser colleagues. The *Xenien* address a wide variety of topics; they come with both classical and contemporary allusions; and they generally feature titles that interact with the distichs in both amusing and explanatory ways. Some examples:

Jamben
Jambe nennt man das Tier mit einem kurzen und langen
    Fuß, und so nennst du mit Recht Jamben das hinkende Werk
                                                    (FA 18:528)

[Iambs: Iamb is what we call the beast with one short and one long / Foot, and thus you are right to call iambs (iambic meter) the limping work]

Das Desideratum
Hättest Du Phantasie und Witz und Empfinden und Urteil
    Wahrlich dir fehlte nicht viel, Wieland und Lessing zu sein
                                                    (FA 18:592)

[The Desideratum: If you had imagination, and wit, and sensitivity, and judgment, / Really you would not lack much for being (like) Wieland and Lessing]

Reception was swift and carried an even sharper point. The stricken struck back, and a number of "anti-Xenien" appeared in journals and collections. Critic Caspar Friedrich Manso (1759–1826) and publisher Johann Gottfried Dyck (1750–1813) replied with "Gegengeschenke an die Sudelköche in Jena und Weimar von einigen dankbaren Gästen" (Reciprocal Gifts for the Swill Cooks in Jena and Weimar from some Grateful Guests, 1797), in which they called Schiller "Kant's Affen in Jena" (Kant's ape/imitator in Jena) and Goethe a "stößigen Bock" (an offensive goat).[7] Goethe and Schiller maintained that this was graceful fun and were surprised that their targets became so irritated. Charlotte Schiller reflected this attitude in a letter of 3 March 1797:

Alles, was noch dagegen [against the Xenien] gesagt wurde, gibt einen neuen Beweis, daß sie [Goethe and Schiller] manches Wahre gesagt haben, nämlich über die Fähigkeit and Art, die Dinge aufzunehmen, des gelehrten Publikums. Manche haben platte Deutungen gemacht, die sie erst selbst hineingelegt haben; manche haben es moralisch zu ernstlich genommen; keiner hat aber den Reichtum von Witz aufweisen können, den die beiden verschwendet haben, und es ist noch nichts erschienen, was dagegen aufkommen könne.[8]

[Everything that has been said against them serves only to prove that they have said a number of true things, namely about the educated public's ability to accept things and the manner in which they do it. Some have crass interpretations that they themselves have read into the epigrams, some have taken it much too seriously in a moral sense; no one has been able to match the wealth of wit that the two have expended on these, and nothing has appeared to date that can compare with them.]

Schiller wrote Körner that the educated public did not have a sense of humor adequate to the comic *Xenien*, and that they lacked the depth required for the more profound or serious observations in the distichs (28 October 1796).[9] Whether the public was "right" or not regarding the interest value or quality or propriety of the *Xenien* can neither be determined nor ventured with much authority as opinion. Many of the distichs address men and matters long forgotten and have thus, for the most part, lost their punch. The "punch" can often be reconstructed with recourse to ample annotation, but this kind of close scholarly scrutiny both depends on the interpretation of the annotator and undermines the immediacy of the points. The *Xenien*, not all of which are dated or inaccessible, occupy an honored place in literary history and in Goethe and Schiller editions, but they are generally less frequently read and discussed than the longer works, and one can say of many of them — more so than of other products of Weimar Classicism — that "you had to be there." Nonetheless, "being there" must have been a rare pleasure for those who were not easily offended.

Goethe and his readers drew enormous benefit from his long and lively (non)correspondence with Schiller. In addition to the texts mentioned above and the collaborative *Xenien*, Schiller encouraged and occasionally published a long list of familiar Goethe productions. These include the *Römische Elegien* (1795) and the *Venetianische Epigramme* (Venetian Epigrams, 1795), the stunning epic *Herrmann und Dorothea*, the exemplary short prose piece *Novelle* (1828), scientific works like the *Farbenlehre* (Theory of Colors, 1808–10), and, most important, *Faust*. Although Goethe worked on *Faust* until the end of his life, it was during his correspondence with Schiller and under Schiller's enthusiastic prodding that he picked up the long-neglected manuscript and began once again to work on it. On 29 November 1794, Schiller requested the unpublished parts of the manuscript, telling Goethe in good classical manner that the fragments he had read struck him like the Torso of Hercules. This is an ambiguous figure, to be sure, since the Torso of Hercules is one of the most famous

and beautiful pieces of ancient Greek sculpture, but *in its incomplete state*.
Schiller was both hinting at sufficiency and asking for more. He continued:
"Es herrscht in diesen Szenen eine Kraft und eine Fülle des Genies, die den
besten Meister unverkennbar zeigt, und ich möchte diese große und
kühne Natur, die darin atmet, so weit als möglich verfolgen" (These scenes
are governed by a power and fullness of genius, that unmistakably reveal
the greatest master, and I want to follow this great and bold nature that
breathes within them as far as possible). Schiller seems to have viewed
Faust as a showcase for Goethe's mind, and asked in these lines not so
much for more *Faust* as for more Goethe. He had to wait, because Goethe
did not announce the resumption of work on the manuscript until 22 June
1797, and then shortly thereafter laid it aside again. Goethe worked in fits
and starts on *Faust* for the rest of Schiller's life and barely finished Part II
before his own death in 1832, but the *Faust* exchanges — sometimes at
long intervals — like the *Wilhelm Meister* discussions, show the power of
Schiller's commitment to the texts that fascinated him and confirm his
enormous value to Goethe as critic and supporter.

III

Before turning to Goethe's value to Schiller in *his* poetic production,
I want to evoke briefly the climate for women's writing in classical Weimar
and Goethe's and Schiller's interaction with the women they published, a
group they generally referred to as "unsere Dichterinnen" (our poetesses).
The correspondence records attitudes as well as ideas and information, and
it conveys a distinct sense of the ways in which women's literary work was
approached, experienced, and received. Aggregating terms such as
"women's writing" are often more likely to obfuscate than designate, but
they are entirely appropriate here, since Goethe and Schiller considered
Dichterinnen to be a category distinct from the various other kinds of writers whose work they evaluated for publication. The aggregation of women
they published during the run of the correspondence included Louise
Brachmann (1777–1822), Friederike Brun (1765–1835), Amalie von
Imhoff, Sophie Mereau, Elise von der Recke (1754–1833), and Caroline
von Wolzogen, who was a talented writer and Schiller's sister-in-law. They
also met and worked with a number of other educated women of the
upper-middle class or minor aristocracy, who wrote privately and for publication, notably Sophie von la Roche (1730–1807) and Charlotte von
Stein.[10] They drew distinctions among the group members, found some to
be far stronger writers than others, and noted promise and improvement
as well, but they subjected the literary production to a uniform discourse
that set these women apart from other contributors.

As the letters show, Goethe and Schiller were generally receptive to the work of their *Dichterinnen*, but consistently approached it with unquestioned assumptions of its limitations. At least they regularly found the shortcomings they expected in works by women, and their vocabulary was fairly consistent in describing these limitations. They expressed cautious admiration for the prose and poetry they discussed, but would then designate the best of it to be some sort of near-miss at art, an "almost-art," something that looked like it from a distance, but turned out to be less than appearances suggested. These pieces were found rather to be pleasant (*angenehm*), naturalistic, sentimental, and dilettantish. As Schiller put it: "Ich muß mich doch wirklich drüber wundern, wie unsere Weiber jetzt, auf bloß dilettantischem Wege, eine gewisse Schreibgeschicklichkeit sich zu verschaffen wissen, die der Kunst nahekommt" (30 June 1797; It really surprises me how our women, in a purely dilettantish way, have been able to acquire a certain skill in writing that is nearly artistic). Schiller also picked up the theme of closeness to art in the letters and had already made his position on art and the feminine very clear in *Über das Pathetische* (1793), where, in a note to the original publication, he discoursed on the difference between Angelika Kaufmann's drawings and art, declaring her work to be "bloß angenehm" (merely pleasant) and thus without beauty. They were to be classified among the objects that pander to the senses and that are therefore excluded from that art that is characterized "durch einen edeln und männlichen Geschmack" (NA 21:188; by [the exercise of] a noble and masculine taste). Both Goethe and Schiller appear to have been guided by a sense of art or even excellence in literature as masculine, something that can be approximated, but never achieved by the anatomically female, an attitude that distinguishes them from many of the Romantic poets, who were their younger contemporaries.

Although Schiller and Goethe found the women's contributions to the *Horen* and the *Musenalmanache* to be useful as a popularizing element, pieces that could entice a larger audience and thus position it for more serious instruction in matters of taste, the repeated artistic failures of talented women writers appear to have puzzled them. At least they discussed the matter in some detail. Goethe theorizes on 1 July 1797 that the reasons for the collective shortfall have to do with women sharing the lot of any new group of artists, namely that they need to educate themselves through a great deal of observation and practice because they have no models of their own:

> Keine Theorie gibt's, wenigstens keine allgemein verständliche, keine entschiedene Muster sind da, welche ganze Genres repräsentierten, und so muß denn jeder durch Teilnahme und Anähnlichung und viele Übung sein armes Subjekt ausbilden.

[They have no theory, at least no generally comprehensible one, no definite models are there that represent entire genres; so each one has to educate herself through participation, approximation, and a lot of practice.]

Goethe's observations regarding the obstacles that face women writers are
interestingly similar to those of Virginia Woolf in "A Room of One's Own"
(1929). Although Goethe believed that women need to adapt with whatever difficulty to male writers' models in the absence of their own tradition,
and Woolf sees a tradition developing or to be developed, both identify the
lack of direct and coherent models as the reason for the perceived otherness
or inferiority of women's work. For Woolf, it was an argument, among others, for the slow emergence of women writers, but for Schiller and Goethe,
it explained their usual findings. The differences in men's and women's
natures, whatever they were, made it difficult or impossible for women to
draw the same benefit from the available models, much less to proceed
without them.

As has been suggested, there was a circularity to Schiller and Goethe's
reasoning about women and aesthetics. They found the usual flaws in
women's writing, that is, when they knew or suspected that it was women's
writing they were reading. Several incidents of misperception might have
caused them to question their criteria. In his letter of 25 June 1798,
Schiller wrote Goethe that part of a drama he read anonymously was
indeed rather interesting, though it was a dilettantish product and not
worthy of an artistic judgment. He noted,

Es zeugt von einer sittlich gebildeten Seele, einem schönen und gemäßigten
Sinn und von einer Vertrautheit mit guten Mustern. Wenn es nicht von
weiblicher Hand ist, so erinnert es doch an eine gewisse Weiblichkeit der
Empfindung, auch insofern ein Mann diese haben kann.

[It evinces a morally educated soul, a beautiful and moderate mind and
an intimate acquaintance with good models. If it does not come from a
feminine hand, it does at least recall a certain femininity of sensation, to
the extent that a man can have this.]

Schiller used all the catch words of literary femininity, and then hedged his
bets, possibly because he was unaware of authorship, but strongly suggesting that he detected a woman behind *Elpenor*. Goethe wrote back on
28 June 1798 that he had written the drama fragment — he thought
Schiller had understood that — something he did not much care for and
had written sixteen years earlier, and congratulated Schiller for describing
so well the condition he had been in at the time and the reasons why it was
unacceptable.

Goethe was mistaken for a woman — or a woman was mistaken for
Goethe — once before, when Friedrich and Dorothea Schlegel
(1763–1839) reacted to the anonymous publication of the beginning of

Caroline von Wolzogen's popular "Agnes von Lilien" (1798) in the *Horen*. Schiller reports on 6 December 1796 that Friedrich Schlegel had no doubts that it was Goethe's work, and that Dorothea Schlegel thought that he had never created such an excellent female character, and that her opinion of Goethe had risen considerably. The reader's access to the anonymous writer's gender has long been debated, along with the question of whether there is such a thing as an identifiably female (ethnic or generational) form of writing, or even a reliably consistent set of gender conventions that would qualify a text as feminine. As citizens of their culture, both Goethe and Schiller were apparently "hard-wired" to detect tender sentiment, naturalistic or straightforward mimetic tendencies, and pleasantness instead of beauty in writing they knew to be women's, and perhaps even to detect women writers behind texts they found to be naturalistic, proper, and pleasant. They were not willing to receive these texts as art, but they did encourage, assist, and publish some of the best women writers of their circle, and they did so in journals that were designed to improve public taste. That the works they published may have been intended as the frosting on the cake of serious aesthetic endeavor does not completely diminish the quality of the enabling gesture.

IV

We have thus far followed Goethe's assessment of the epistolary exchange as the encounter that sustained, assisted, and encouraged his poetic activity, and it is important to focus, however briefly, on the value of the correspondence for Schiller. What specific benefits did Schiller derive from the *Briefwechsel* that did so much for Goethe's poetic progress and that bears witness to the literary sponsorship of so many talented women? In other words, what was in it for him? Not surprisingly, Schiller also profited tremendously from the correspondence and the friendship. First, he had the opportunity to commune with Goethe, something he had wanted to do long before 1794 and which proved even more intellectually rewarding than he had initially expected. He had almost daily access to one of the greatest contemporary minds on record and functioned often as the first witness to many of the most highly regarded texts of German literature. Schiller also obtained a number of excellent contributions and crucial editorial assistance from Goethe for the journals he needed to fill, both in order to advance his goal of aesthetic education and to maintain a reasonable income. And, finally, Schiller received inspired advice and stalwart encouragement as he tried to realize his literary goals in spite of the massive obstacles presented by his poor health and other practical concerns, such as the aforementioned need for income.

One aspect of the difference in their natures was Goethe's relative reticence on the poetic process and Schiller's careful schematic analyses of his own and Goethe's writing. Goethe's commentary on Schiller's works in progress is rarely as thorough, as deeply analytical, or as lengthy as the commentaries he received from Schiller. His remarks on Schiller's poetic production are usually confined to a few lines in which he acknowledges Schiller's efforts and offers encouragement. However, there were several cases in which Goethe did offer detailed advice to Schiller on the composition of poetry and plays, indicating an awareness of his debt and a restricted willingness to repay in kind. On 12 December 1798, in response to Schiller's expressions of gratitude for poetic assistance, Goethe wrote: "Es freut mich, daß ich Ihnen etwas habe wiedererstatten können von der Art, in der ich Ihnen so manches schuldig geworden bin" (I am pleased to have been able to repay you in the way in which I have become so indebted to you). Two instances of this repayment of an enormous debt, examples of a deeper involvement on Goethe's part in Schiller's composition process, are the poem "Die Kraniche des Ibykus" (1797) and the *Wallenstein* trilogy (1800).

"Kraniche," a ballad that begins with the murder of the singer Ibykus on his way to a bardic competition, is famous for making a court of law of the ancient Greek theater and for delivering justice through the appearance of cranes who are present at the murder and then fly over the theater. The murderers, struck with holy fear by the spectacle of the Eumenides on stage and the appearance of the birds, cry out and thus identify themselves to the rest of the audience, who initiate the prosecution. Much depends on the constitution of the moment of the murderers' cry, the elements that lead up to their conclusion that nature and the gods have conspired to avenge Ibykus, and on the drama of the utterance. Goethe literally seized this moment and counseled Schiller on the best ways to enhance and ground it. Cranes, he noted, travel in flocks and there should be a flock of cranes, rather than just a few birds, present at the murder scene and over the theater, a more realistic depiction of natural behavior that integrates well into the symbolic level of the poem, creating at least three multitudes (Eumenides, crowd, cranes) in the theater scene that appear to confront the pair of guilty men. He asked for a more interesting Ibykus and for another verse, describing the mood of the crowd as the chorus withdraws, to set the scene for the murderers' sudden outcry (22 August 1797), and also here contributed his strong sense for the empirical, natural, and psychological to the symbolic movement of Schiller's poem. Schiller incorporated most of Goethe's numerous suggestions, but resisted the latter's sense that only those sitting near the murderers should hear their cry and that the tumult begun in the murderers' vicinity should slowly spread to the entire theater as too cumbersome (7 September 1797). Goethe responded with the maxim according to which he himself lived and wrote: "Der Künstler muß selbst am besten wissen, inwiefern er sich fremder Vorschläge bedienen kann" (The artist himself has to decide the extent to which he can profit from the suggestions of others, 25/26 September 1797). Neither Goethe nor Schiller seemed to have been entirely comfortable rejecting the other's suggestions, and this is one of the greatest occasions for social awkwardness in the letters, but each weighed, evaluated, and selected what he needed from the available store of advice. That Goethe ignored more advice than Schiller may stem from the fact that he got more of it.

The *Wallenstein* trilogy (1800) was an immense undertaking for a number of reasons, including the massive complexity of the historical background, namely the Thirty Years' War and the figure of Wallenstein; the size of the manuscript that grew from a prologue into three individual plays; the ambitions Schiller had for this historical tragedy; the theoretical problems he had making Wallenstein's downfall tragic; and the seriousness of the sickness that he fought for work time. The composition process itself was dramatic, as Goethe began preparing the theatrical productions of each segment while Schiller was still writing. Goethe prodded Schiller for more scenes and more text, and Schiller, driven, responded to Goethe's stimulus and wrote (literally) feverishly to complete this gigantic task. Although Schiller first conceived the Wallenstein tragedy in the early 1790s, as he was working with his *Geschichte des Dreißigjährigen Krieges*, he first mentioned it in a letter to Goethe in 1796, writing that he was waiting for "eine mächtige Hand, die mich hineinwirft" (a powerful hand that will throw me into [the work on *Wallenstein*], 23 October 1796). Goethe obliged, recommending that Schiller read Aristotle's *Poetics* to aid his thinking on the tragic motif. Schiller found Aristotle to be too empirical and regulative, but he was in full agreement with Aristotle's emphasis on the particular concatenation of events as the essence of a tragic plot (5 May 1797), and working from this classically endorsed insight, he built his tragedy.

Schiller's major problem with the figure of Wallenstein was that his ruin was more or less his own doing, and it was in the addition of outside forces, including the astrological motif, that the potentially untragic Wallenstein of history became Schiller's greatest tragic figure. Goethe's assistance during these deliberations and his encouragement during Schiller's times of extreme physical weakness are best rendered through the metaphor of athletic "coaching," a process in which a flagging player is ruthlessly challenged and inspired by a more experienced athlete to employ every bit of his or her strength to reach a goal. No other image available accounts for the sheer physical effort that one partner produced and the other elicited. Goethe showed extreme dedication and vigilance in supervising Schiller's training program and performance. He suggested the partition of the material (28 May 1797; 2 December 1797); he reported regularly on the preparations for the premiere of each play and the enthusiasm of the actors (9 December 1797 and passim); he presented the plays in the Weimar court theater (premieres on 24 December 1798 [*Wallensteins Lager*]; 17 March 1799 [*Die Piccolomini*]; 20 April 1799 [*Wallensteins Tod*]) and told Schiller of the reactions of the audiences and critics. Given his physical limitations Schiller responded to Goethe's coaching with superhuman prowess and delivered an astonishing volume of strong dramatic material to his cheering fans.

The language of Schiller's acknowledgements also fits with the metaphor of assisted physical exertion because he describes a process of exceeding personal limits:

> Ich finde augenscheinlich, daß ich über mich selbst hinausgegangen bin, welches die Frucht unsres Umgangs ist; denn nur der vielmalige kontinuierliche Verkehr mit einer so objektiv mir entgegenstehenden Natur, mein lebhaftes Hinstreben darnach und die vereinigte Bemühung, sie anzuschauen und zu denken, konnte mich fähig machen, meine subjektiven Grenzen so weit auseinanderzurücken. (5 January 1798)

> [I think it is clear that I have outdone myself and that this is the fruit of our association; because only the frequent and continued interaction with a nature so objectively opposite to mine, my lively striving toward this nature, and the unified effort to achieve this, have made me capable of exceeding my personal limitations to such a degree.]

The *Wallenstein* exchange, as an account of artistic creation, does not lack any of the excitement of Cellini's account of the casting of Perseus. Goethe was intensely involved because of his immediate interest in producing the plays for the Weimar stage, and this intensity drove Schiller to what was perhaps the greatest accomplishment of his career. Although Goethe and other commentators repeat the refrain that "without Schiller" certain Goethe texts would never have been realized, the case of *Wallenstein* makes it clear that "without Goethe" we would have had significantly less from Schiller.

The correspondents' noncorrespondence generated the principles of Weimar Classicism as we know it; their interactions as friends, colleagues, publishers, and epistolary partners produced the bulk of the "content" to which these principles applied. That the published correspondence issues from Goethe's editorial perspective has consequences for general considerations of the entire collection. But this is also a collection of individual letters, individual volleys and discussions involving multiple letters, individual exchanges of ideas and information, and individual disagreements. The full *Briefwechsel* exists within the ponderous context of Weimar Classicism, and generalizations must somehow answer to this context. But the units and segments that make up this long conversation have a life apart from the laurel wreath and from this independent position, and they invite more and closer scrutiny.

Notes

[1] Schiller was highly critical of the cohabitation in letters to others and Goethe's regular sign-off, "Leben Sie recht wohl und grüssen Sie Ihre liebe Frau" (Farewell and give my regards to your dear wife), was never reciprocated.

[2] T. J. Reed, "Weimar Classicism: Goethe's Alliance With Schiller," in *The Cambridge Companion to Goethe*, ed. Lesley Sharpe (Cambridge: Cambridge UP, 2002), 102; see especially Schiller's letter of 23 August 1794 for an account of the differences.

[3] Most of the 1013 letters that were located by Goethe and subsequent editors are housed in the Goethe-Schiller-Archiv in Weimar and a few dozen are in other libraries and private collections.

[4] See Albrecht Schöne, *Schillers Schädel* (Munich: C. H. Beck, 2000), 14–24.

[5] *Der Briefwechsel zwischen Schiller und Goethe in drei Bänden*, ed. Siegfried Seidel (Leipzig: Insel Verlag, 1984), 3:165.

[6] Seidel 3:165.

[7] In Franz Schwarzbauer, *Die Xenien: Studien zur Vorgeschichte der Weimarer Klassik* (Stuttgart: Metzler, 1992), 340.

[8] Schwarzbauer, *Die Xenien*, 344.

[9] Quoted in Schwarzbauer, *Die Xenien*, 355.

[10] See Janet Besserer Holmgren, "'Die Horen haben jetzo wie es scheint ihr weibliches Zeitalter. . .': The Women Writers in Schiller's *Horen*," diss. UC Irvine, 2000.

Johann Gottfried Herder: The Weimar Classic Back of the (City)Church

Thomas P. Saine

A NYONE WHO HAS BECOME familiar with the *loci* of Classical Weimar can place Herder on the city map: the Herderplatz is on the open, visible side of the Stadtkirche of Saints Peter and Paul — long since, of course, renamed the Herderkirche — just off the city center, where Herder preached and is buried. The plaza is adorned with a statue of the famous man. Overshadowed by the church, on the other side, "back of" it, as Herder often said, is the street where the parsonage is located, where Herder and his growing family lived from his arrival in Weimar in 1776 until his death in 1803. A parsonage is of course a "Dienstwohnung" — the Herders never owned any real property in Weimar, and in spite of his exalted official titles Herder was too often regarded and treated as just one of the help. After all, keeping the people properly religious was (and of course still is) often regarded as a function of the state, not just a personal vocation.

In identifying himself or talking about himself, Herder was likely to place himself "hinter der Kirche" (back of the church) or "hinter der Stadtkirche." This was not simply a geographical location; it was above all an expression of the Herders' resignation to their meager and often uninfluential circumstances (poor and meek of spirit, like the church mice "hinter der Kirche"), but it described their place professionally and socially as well. The irony of the post at the Stadtkirche (instead of a Hofkirche [court church]) is not to be overlooked: Herder was the official court preacher (*Hofprediger*) at a court that rarely took communion or heard him preach (especially not Duke Carl August),[1] so that he mostly preached to the *Stadt*, or at least the more privileged part of the city population. Such service to the bourgeois stratum moreover points to Herder's true socio-economic and political sympathies,[2] which were often in conflict with the needs of his master and had to be toned down, out of loyalty and in order to avoid frictions in his job. His social place was between court and city; he moved in court circles at times, but only officially, and not by right (in contrast to Goethe, who enjoyed free access and could participate fully, especially after his ennoblement in 1782). And finally his position "back of" the church determined both his profile (obscured, hidden by the church) and in many respects his intellectual attitudes: he was first and foremost a churchman and theologian, with a relatively restricted sphere of free self-expression.

Although Herder was hired for Saxe-Weimar on the strong recommendation of Goethe, who had a high opinion of his friend's talents and great expectations for his contributions both to official life and to making his (Goethe's) own social and intellectual life more interesting, the appointment was handled in the end not so much as a gracious exercise of ducal patronage, but rather more like the tailor's seven flies at one blow. Herder was appointed in the main to be church superintendent for Saxe-Weimar, which also entailed supervision of the schools;[3] he had some responsibilities for theological education at the university in Jena and for examining and certifying newly fledged preachers before they could be put into service; he was a member of the Weimar consistory with the title *Oberconsistorialrat* (over-consistorial councilor; after 1788 vice-president and in his last years even president thereof) and court preacher entrusted with the Stadtkirche (and thus also the parsonage). He was to be paid the sum of the budgeted allocations for the different parts of his duties, so that, especially taking account of the free use of the parsonage, he should have been assured of a comfortable living in exchange for the burdens of his many offices. Because, however, Carl August generally assigned church and school affairs a low priority to begin with — probably a good thing as far as tolerance and liberal thinking were concerned[4] — it was a constant struggle for Herder to avoid budget cuts and downsizings (leaving positions unfilled) right and left as Carl August's political ambitions and military play-acting cost ever more in the 1780s, the *Fürstenbund* (League of Princes) period (not to speak of the costs and strains of the French Revolutionary period after 1789). Significant reforms and improvements in pay scales so as to attract more qualified preachers and teachers were out of the question.[5] Furthermore, Herder was faced with significant conservative opposition in both Church and school affairs and had to be careful not to antagonize all his colleagues and underlings. Goethe supported him manfully and long mediated between Herder, Carl August, and the rest of the government where he could, but eventually dropped Herder (and especially Caroline [1750–1809], as is well known) like hot potatoes in 1795 over Caroline's demands that Carl August fulfill his promises to provide for the education of the Herder sons.[6]

Herder was a bargain for the Saxe-Weimar government, especially since at least until 1788 he was not even paid all that he had been promised when he moved to Weimar.[7] It is well known that the family was in constant financial difficulties, though it is not clear that the Herders were spendthrifts or whether an inability to handle money complicated their situation. In any case, like many other eighteenth-century intellectuals unable to survive on official bread alone and forced to sell himself in print, Herder had a busy agenda governed by the symbiotic relationship with his old friend and publisher Johann Friedrich Hartknoch in Riga: continuing advances and loans from Hartknoch kept Herder writing and in debt to Hartknoch's company store. In March 1788, not long before Herder's departure for Italy, he received a gift of 2000 *Gulden* from an anonymous admirer and a *Gehaltszulage* (bonus) of 300 *Reichstaler* from Carl August, which, according to Christoph Fasel, sufficed to pay the family's most pressing debts.[8] Yet by the time Herder (then in Italy) received a letter from Christian Gottlob Heyne (dated March 15, 1789), officially offering him a position as professor of theology and consistorial councilor in Göttingen and inviting him to name his own salary and terms,[9] the Herders were back in debt by some 2000 talers. Much of the deliberating in the correspondence between Herder and Caroline before Herder's return to Weimar revolved around the question of whether it was more realistic to try to get Göttingen to help pay off the debts in exchange for his accepting the position, or to pressure Carl August to help out in order to keep him in Weimar.[10] In the end, Goethe mediated between Carl August and the church superintendent (who in reality, when push came to shove, did not want to become a professor of theology after all[11]), and Herder stayed in Weimar. But in spite of all the promises and a temporary improvement in his situation, in the long run he was no better off, for he was still in debt, swamped with official duties, and chained to his writing desk. The churchman had made one attempt to break out of his confinement back of the church and live the life of a Goethe when he traveled to Italy in 1788–89. In this regard, and in most others, the trip was a failure; in addition, it was a great strain on his marriage and the family finances. Returning to his space after the journey, he soon found a lot in Weimar culture, personal politics, government attitudes, and other shenanigans to be unhappy with. And in the course of the 1790s he became more and more isolated from Goethe and the court, and from the newest trends in contemporary culture.[12]

Was Herder Classical?

Obviously it would not do to claim that Herder was always classical, just as Goethe, Schiller, and other writers of the age went through various stages or phases in their development before reaching a "classical" stage; Schiller died a Classic (final stage) because he died prematurely, while in Goethe's case, Classicism was superseded by other and possibly better phases during the rest of his long life. Particularly in the case of major authors such as Herder, Goethe, and Schiller, rethinking periodization is always in order. In fact these three writers all began in similar enthusiastic and elevated fashion in the mode known as *Sturm und Drang* (Storm and Stress), of which

Herder unfortunately has been tagged by literary historians as having been the initiator without quite knowing what he was doing (since the *Stürmer und Dränger* were a gaggle of younger literati with no better ideas of their own, and whom, with the exception of Goethe, Herder hardly even knew).[13]

A main tenet of *Sturm und Drang* has been alleged to be antipathy to the Enlightenment, which it is claimed was shallow and worn-out by the time Herder and the *Stürmer und Dränger* received it, and consequently the urge to overthrow and transcend it. This entailed as much verbal violence as sharp-eyed critique. While Goethe and others are allowed to have fulfilled the goal of getting beyond Enlightenment, Herder is often alleged to have struggled to overcome it only to relapse into Enlightenment modes of thought again at some unspecified point instead of going on to become a "classic" like some of his contemporaries. Clearly, Herder was not thinking "classic" or "classicism" in much of his early work; he promoted the indigenous Northern or "German" culture of the English (Shakespeare) and the Norse, while being highly critical of contemporary French classical models such as Voltaire.[14] He damaged his eventual influence and reputation severely with the oracular, often elliptical, and rhetorical effusions that made up so much of his early oeuvre and were so breathlessly imitated by the youngsters of the 1770s. Part of his enthusiasm and exuberance manifested itself in the urge to devour books and express his opinions and ideas about them (for example, the earliest published work, the three-volume *Kritische Wälder* [Critical Sylvae, 1769], with which he threw himself upon the literary landscape, aiming to change it instantaneously). An ambitious scholar, he hungered to get close to the sources, as in his *Volkslied* (folk song) collecting and his interpretation of Genesis, the *Älteste Urkunde des Menschengeschlechts* (Oldest Document of the Human Race, 1774; followed later by much more favorably received studies such as *Vom Geist der ebräischen Poesie* [On the Spirit of Hebrew Poetry, 1782–83]). In much of his early work, for example on the Old Testament, Herder was not "anti" anything and he made grateful use of older and contemporary scholarship, enlightened or otherwise.

To be sure, in his early major treatise on the philosophy of history, *Auch eine Philosophie der Geschichte zur Bildung der Menschheit* (Also a Philosophy of History for the Education of Mankind) of 1774, Herder became shrilly polemical and critical of the presumption of so-called enlightenment (not actually of the Enlightenment itself, but of the "enlightened age"). The end of the work features a critique of colonialism that is actually comparable to twenty-first-century anti-globalism:

> Was warens für elende *Spartaner*, die ihre *Heloten* zum Ackerbau brauchten,[15] und für barbarische *Römer*, die ihre Sklaven in die Erdgefängnisse einschlossen! In Europa ist die Sklaverei abgeschafft, weil berechnet ist, wie viel diese Sklaven mehr kosteten und weniger

brächten, als freie Leute: Nur Eins haben wir uns noch erlaubt, *drei Weltteile als Sklaven* zu *brauchen*, zu *verhandeln*, in Silbergruben und Zuckermühlen zu *verbannen* — aber das sind nicht *Europäer*, nicht *Christen*, und dafür bekommen wir Silber und Edelgesteine, Gewürze, Zucker und — heimliche Krankheit: also des *Handels* wegen und zur *wechselseitigen Bruderhülfe* und *Gemeinschaft* der Länder . . . *Drei Weltteile* durch uns *verwüstet* und *polizieret*, und wir durch sie *entvölkert*, *entmannet*, in Üppigkeit, Schinderei und Tod versenkt: das ist reich gehandelt und glücklich . . . Der alte Name, Hirt der Völker, ist in Monopolisten verwandelt — und wenn die ganze Wolke mit hundert Sturmwinden denn bricht — großer Gott Mammon, — dem wir *alle jetzt dienen*, hilf uns! —[16]

[What kind of miserable people were the *Spartans*, who used their *helots* for tilling the fields, and the barbarian *Romans*, who locked their slaves in dungeons! In Europe slavery is abolished, because it was calculated how much more slaves cost and how much less they bring in than free men: Yet we have permitted ourselves one new thing, namely to *use three whole parts of the world* as our *slaves*, to *deal* in them, and to *put them away* in silver mines and sugar mills — but those aren't *Europeans*, not *Christians*, and by using them we get silver and precious stones, spices, sugar and — a secret illness: so for the sake of *trade* and for the sake of *fraternal assistance* and *community* of the nations . . . *Three quarters of the world laid waste* and *governed* by us, and we are *depopulated, emasculated* by them, debauched in luxury, villainy and death: that is acting richly and happily . . . The old name, shepherd of the peoples, has been turned into monopolist — and if then the whole huge cloud bursts with a hundred storm winds — great God Mammon — whom *we all serve now*, help us! —]

Such passages of historical and social critical engagement could be multiplied from the works of the young Herder almost at will, but he was not yet "classical" and of course could not simply repeat the anger later in classical dress, although he retained most of his critical views.

To raise the question why Herder should be regarded as Classical or as a Classic is not really much different than posing the same question in the case of Goethe, Schiller, and assorted lesser figures of the period; it is essentially a matter of choosing and agreeing on definitions (and readers can agree that "X" is a Classic without agreeing entirely on the reasons). Definitions can begin at the bottom with the narrow "classical Weimar" of the Goethe-Schiller collaboration and friendship. Such a specification of course disregards the fact that Schiller had been in Weimar and Jena for seven years before he managed to focus Goethe's interest on himself and also poses the question whether Goethe's *Iphigenie auf Tauris* and *Torquato Tasso* can really be regarded as classical if Schiller was not involved in their production, while *Egmont*, a decidedly un-classical and Romantic piece, was completed at the same time. One should conclude that Goethe's classicism was post-Italian, but that not all his post-Italian production was classical. From the Goethe-Schiller parameter one can then proceed to the philosophical movement to resurrect the "classical" atmosphere of ancient Greece and Rome by resurrecting the artist as a genius and the work of art as a piece of perfection in itself without reference to externals, along the lines of Karl Philipp Moritz's doctrine of "das in sich selbst Vollendete" (that which is complete in itself) and Immanuel Kant's "interesseloses Wohlgefallen" (disinterested pleasure) which, by way of Schillerian theorizing, also contributed to the rise of Romantic theory. One problematic aspect of this train of thought is that the definitions and prescriptions are much more easily applicable to the visual arts, possibly also to mythology, than to poetry. Another problem is the status of Schiller himself and his Kant-based aesthetic theory within that context, regarding Goethe as the true naïve classic and trying to justify his own existence as a sentimentalist. Under one pretext or another, this involved much imitation of the ancients, à la Laocoön and Winckelmann, and admiration of "edle Einfalt und stille Größe" (noble simplicity and quiet grandeur).[17] Finally, we can choose between the narrow world of Goethe/Schiller and their epigones, or the wide world of a "Classical Age" that takes in major first-rate writers (another dictionary definition of classical, of course, based on the Roman "classicus" tax category), from Lessing and Wieland to young Grillparzer and Heine at the end of the Age of Goethe or, to use Heine's term, the *Kunstperiode* [age of art]).

Under the circumstances, and not least of all because he definitely belongs in a volume that treats Goethe and Schiller, it should not be a large stretch to get Herder under the classical tent. Herder journeyed to Italy shortly after Goethe had returned from there, but found he could not enjoy the milieu and ambience of Italy like Goethe had, because he was not an artist himself, and he was also very much a Christian and not able to let himself go like a sensual pagan, à la Winckelmann. He was not able to finish his course of study in Roman antiquities with Aloys Hirt (1759–1837), the hired *cicerone*, because of the disruptive lack of interest of his traveling companions in such antiquities,[18] and as far as hands-on experience of classical landmarks and remains, it is unlikely that he advanced far beyond the level of Volkmann's tourist guide, the major resource and Bible of most German visitors of the period.

Goethe while in Italy had discovered definitively and gratefully that he was a poet. There was nothing comparable for Herder to discover. He reaped some fond memories and much disillusionment and brought home a diary of sorts.[19] Most of the high-ranking acquaintances he made were thanks to Duchess Anna Amalia and thanks to the fact that he represented Saxe-Weimar as the equivalent of a Lutheran bishop, and while he felt honored to meet Italian nobles and princes of the Church, they were surely of little consequence for his later life. When he invested himself in art and art appreciation, he got into trouble: he praised Angelika Kaufmann and wrote so touchingly of his sentimental appreciation of her that Caroline became quite jealous, and some apologizing had to be done. But Angelika remained safely in Rome when Herder returned to Weimar; what did eventually make the trip to Weimar was Alexander Trippel's (1744–93) bust of Herder, commissioned by Carl August as a counterpart to Trippel's bust of Goethe, to which, however, Herder unfavorably compared his own.[20] Another highly interesting and revealing Roman acquaintanceship was that with the writer Karl Philipp Moritz, which was mediated by Goethe. Herder met Moritz in Rome shortly before Moritz's own return to Germany and was impressed with his person and with his aesthetic views. In turn, he recommended Moritz to Caroline because Moritz was passing through Weimar on his way back to Berlin. In Weimar, Moritz stayed several weeks with Goethe; he also visited Caroline a number of times and impressed her favorably. Goethe, too, was solicitous of Caroline, all of which Caroline reported back to Herder in her letters (which unfortunately were always two to three weeks in transit, leaving him to nurse his feelings of jealousy). Finally, all this was too much for poor Herder, and he exploded in a fit of pique directed at both Moritz and Goethe:

> So ists auch mit Moriz Philosophie u. Abhandlung [*Über die bildende Nachahmung des Schönen*]. Sie ist ganz Göthisch, aus seiner u. in seine Seele; er ist der Gott von allen Gedanken des guten Moritz . . . mir ist diese ganze Philosophie im feinsten Organ zuwider: sie ist selbstisch, abgöttisch, unteilnehmend u. für mein Herz desolierend. Ich mag die Öde nicht, in der auch ein Gott um sein selbst willen allein existieret.[21]

> [It's the same with Moritz's philosophy and his treatise (On the Creative Imitation of the Beautiful). It is completely Goethean, written from his soul and for his soul; he is the God of all of good Moritz's thoughts . . . I find this whole philosophy abhorrent to the depths of my soul: it is selfish, idolatrous, uncaring and desolating for my heart. I can't stand the desert in which a god too could exist for his own sake.]

It was important for Herder that art had to speak to the heart. He was never engaged in culture abstractly or only from a theoretical point of view, but always from a personal-moral perspective. He was not a deep thinker addicted to systematic philosophical and aesthetic thought, but his was a fertile and suggestive mind. From the 1780s on, as he shed the *Sturm und Drang* mannerisms of his beginnings, he can be regarded as a serious, popular writer in the Lessing-Mendelssohn mold, with an audience for his works: a publisher could count on selling his books. He was genuinely interested in the history and culture of antiquity, and, one might assume, more broadly so than Goethe, Schiller, and others in the Weimar sphere of influence, who had a more limited interest, namely in the imitation and re-creation of ancient art. Herder, for his part, as he began to demonstrate in his *Ideen zur Philosophie der Geschichte der Menschheit* (Ideas towards the Philosophy of the History of Mankind), wanted to fit all human endeavor and development, including art and culture, into the grand scheme of universal history.

It is naturally not possible to deal in the space available with all of Herder's works of the 1780s and 1790s; in any case, there is enough redundancy among them that some can be left out without detriment to the whole, including, for example, the *Zerstreute Blätter* (Scattered Leaves) of the 1780s, which paralleled his work on the *Ideen*, and the *Christliche Schriften* (Christian Writings), which Herder wrote in the 1790s at the same time as the *Briefe zu Beförderung der Humanität* (Letters for the Furthering of Humanity, 1793–97).[22] It is, however, essential to keep in mind that Herder was a thoroughly religious and Christian person from start to finish, a fact that distinguished him from other Weimar luminaries. He began his career as a preacher and teacher in Riga with a strong sense of his vocation, and throughout his life he held responsible Church positions.[23] From the late 1770s on he was in mental dialogue with Gotthold Ephraim Lessing: with the posthumous fragments of Hermann Samuel Reimarus's deistic critique of the Bible and Gospel history that had been published by Lessing; with the positions argued in the ensuing controversy between Lessing and pastor Johann Melchior Goeze (1717–86), an orthodox cleric who considered drama immoral; and with *Die Erziehung des Menschengeschlechts* (The Education of the Human Race, 1780), in which Lessing had argued that human history's relationship to God was driven by a sequence of divine "primers" made available to mankind, each at exactly the right time to illuminate a "new" and important truth about the nature of God and the immortal destiny of mankind. The possibility put forward by Lessing at the end of the *Erziehung* that every human being might benefit in the attainment of moral perfection by being reborn over and over until that pinnacle is reached (metempsychosis), was categorically denied by the speakers in Herder's *Über die Seelenwanderung. Drei Gespräche* (On Transmigration of Souls: Three Dialogues) of 1782.[24] Five years later, Herder was moved to formulate his own position in the Spinoza and pantheism controversy that had been unleashed by Goethe's friend Friedrich Heinrich Jacobi (1743–1819) when he published his account and interpretation of conversations with Lessing in 1780, shortly before the latter's death in 1781. Jacobi had made Lessing out to be a Spinozist and therefore a rationalistic atheist.[25] Herder, for his contribution to the debate, set out to reconcile his understanding of Spinoza's thought with Leibnizian monadological philosophy in *Gott: Einige Gespräche* (God: Some Dialogues, 1787), attempting in so doing both to pull Lessing out of danger and to salvage Spinoza for polite philosophical company.[26] The view of God and Nature elaborated in these dialogues is similar to what he had already put forward in the first two parts of the *Ideen*.

As a modern thinker who, although admiring Martin Luther for his achievement in reforming the Church in Northern Europe and supposedly liberating religious thought from the Roman yoke,[27] no longer identified with strict Lutheran orthodoxy, Herder distanced himself from the Neologians, the theological innovators of the middle and later eighteenth century. Herder's major work on theological correctness, *Briefe, das Studium der Theologie betreffend* (Letters On the Study of Theology), first published in 1780, with a second revised edition published in 1784, was contemporaneous with intensive work on the *Ideen*. In the letters, addressed to a beginning theology student, Herder stresses that the student should learn first things first and worry about more complicated or controversial things later. For now he should concentrate on the basics and not waste his time with learned commentaries (aside from dictionaries and other philological helps) or abstruse subjects, such as the investigation of the canon. Most of the books recommended fall in the mainstream of eighteenth-century German Lutheran theology and Church history and include many that Herder himself must have read during his studies in Königsberg. Neologians receive little attention. Not surprisingly, Luther is a favorite source of wisdom (serving the function of an arbiter), for example with regard to the doctrine of justification by faith: "Die Lehre der *Rechtfertigung* ist mit jener vom *Glauben* so nahe verwandt, daß Eine mit der andern stehn und fallen muß; auch bei ihr, dem Eckstein des Luthertums, halten Sie sich vorzüglich an Luthers Schriften"[28] (The doctrine of *justification* is so closely related to that of *belief* that the one must stand and fall with the other; here too, with this cornerstone of Lutheranism, you must orient yourself above all according to Luther's writings). Herder has little sympathy for Pietism and what he calls its "Methodismus," or for enthusiasm (*Schwärmerei*) in general. He abhors the skeptic David Hume (1711–76) and is highly critical of Rousseau, but can find things to praise in Shaftesbury (1621–83) and some of the English deists and Bible scholars. He is no friend of Wolffian theology, which he blames for hopelessly and completely subverting Lutheran dogmatics. By encouraging the student to look to Luther and the Bible itself for his understanding of doctrine, Herder manages to sidestep, or at least to downplay the controversy between orthodox and Enlightenment theologians that so stultified eighteenth-century Lutheran intellectual life.[29]

Before proceeding to discussion of the *Ideen* and *Humanitätsbriefe*, it should be stressed that Herder was not advocating any religious or philosophical program of his own; he was, in fact, quite tolerant, that is, open and receptive to other religions and variant religious practices. In the *Ideen*, he in fact argues a largely secularist point of view; he does not insist on Genesis, for example, as an orthodox Lutheran would have both then and now, as the only credible or true account of the Creation or seek to locate a Middle Eastern Garden of Eden in which mankind might have been innocent before the Fall; in treating the books of Moses as (the most ancient extant) works of inspiration and poetry, he assumes the possible existence of other, equally valid documents of early "history." He is able to note both the good and the not so good in ancient and pre-modern religions and cultures, since he sees them all contributing in one way or another to the establishment and growth of *Humanität*. There is one partial exception to this tolerance, of course: Herder's attitude toward Roman Catholicism was of necessity quite ambivalent because it was not only a historical religion, but also in fact still the majority religion of Europe and the largest Christian confession world-wide. As a Church official in a non-monolithic religious landscape, he had to be accustomed to dealing with counter-parties to a certain extent, both officially and privately. His traveling companion in Italy, Johann Friedrich Hugo von Dalberg (1752–1812), was a canon of the Trier cathedral, while his older brother, Karl Theodor von Dalberg (1744–1817), coadjutor of the Archbishop-Elector of Mainz and governor of Erfurt, was a political and intellectual ally and favorite of the Weimar government and court. In Italy, Herder had the diplomatic status of a bishop and as such was an adornment of Anna Amalia's retinue (he fretted considerably about procuring the attire appropriate to his status and his social obligations). Yet he could be very testy about the "unenlightened" nature of Catholic tradition and practice, as in his remarks about Bamberg and other Catholic territories on his way to Italy.[30] In the *Ideen*, he had to sort through multiple layers of meaning and stances toward the Roman Church in history: appreciative of its indispensable role in nurturing and spreading Christianity, hypercritical of its hegemony of superstition that had led to spiritual tyranny and to the Reformation; appreciative of its role in restoring and preserving order and culture during the turbulent Middle Ages, and bitterly denouncing the Roman hierarchy for usurping wealth and power and subjecting European rulers and societies, including empires and emperors, to its dictates and whims.[31] It was in fact precisely at the point where Humanism, the Renaissance, and the Reformation should have begun, that is, where the Roman church had to become the central topic of the work for a while again in the early modern age, that Herder ultimately broke off the *Ideen*.

Ideen and *Humanitätsbriefe*

Of all Herder's works, it is the *Ideen zur Philosophie der Geschichte der Menschheit* and the *Briefe zu Beförderung der Humanität* that are best remembered and most often studied by those who deal with German literature (including history and philosophy of history) and Weimar

Classicism. Many of the other works, important as they may be or may have been, are the province of specialists (scholars of Oriental scholarship, for example) or of those with axes to grind. The *Ideen* (especially the first two parts, because of their subject matter) garnered Goethe's full interest and sympathy and rekindled the warm friendship between the two one last time. The work was published in four parts, of five books each, in 1784, 1785, 1787, and 1791. Originally meant to be an expanded and more "scientific" (also more calmly presented) revision of the earlier *Auch eine Philosophie der Geschichte zur Bildung der Menschheit*, the work never quite measured up to its intention or ambition. The first part is a compilation of the science of the material and physical world relevant to the development of the human race; the second part deals with the various geographical and climatic conditions and the human beings who adapted to them, concluding in book 10 with a series of deliberations regarding the location of the beginnings of culture and traditions of the Creation. Part 3 is a survey of ancient cultures starting with Asia (China and India), moving through the Middle East to the Greek and Roman worlds, and concluding in book 15 with a series of thesis chapters drawing the religio-philosophical conclusions from the preceding history. Part 4 is devoted to the peoples of Northern Europe, the rise of Christianity, the fall of the Roman Empire, the Germanic migrations, and medieval history, including the growth of the influence and power of the Roman church hierarchy, the rise of Islam, and the Arab conquests in Spain and the Middle East. Book 20 contains a serious of concluding chapters devoted to commerce, chivalry, the Crusades (including crusades against heresy within Europe itself and the beginnings of the Inquisition), the culture of reason, and geographical discoveries. There was to have been a fifth part devoted to the Reformation, the rise of modern thought and science, and the Enlightenment, but Herder's plans for this last part were thwarted by the unfavorable political currents of the French revolutionary age. (The repressive atmosphere of political conservatism and censorship in the wake of the outbreak of war with France, in which Carl August played the role of a Prussian general and had to be careful to keep his own subjects under control, was no small factor.) In Herder's original conception, the *Humanitätsbriefe* were meant to be the continuation of the *Ideen* in another form, but they too failed in large part to fill in the historical gap and developmental argument left by the failure to complete the *Ideen*.

Especially in the first two parts of the *Ideen*, Herder is participating in contemporary debates about nature, the place of man on earth and in the universe, the beginnings of the human race, the destiny of man, and so on. The content is unavoidably a mixture of natural science, history, and speculation. For all the effort to keep the discussion on a natural-scientific plane, the subject matter also impinges constantly on religious and theological "certainties" that have to be taken account of in one way or another in the course of the work. There is constant difficulty, for example, in keeping God and nature separate, already in the preface:

> Niemand irre sich . . . daran, daß ich zuweilen den Namen der Natur personifiziert gebrauche. Die Natur ist kein selbstständiges Wesen; *sondern Gott ist Alles in seinen Werken*: indessen wollte ich diesen hochheiligen Namen . . . durch einen öftern Gebrauch, bei dem ich ihm nicht immer Heiligkeit gnug verschaffen konnte, wenigstens nicht mißbrauchen. Wem der Name 'Natur' durch manche Schriften unsres Zeitalters sinnlos und niedrig geworden ist, der denke sich statt dessen *jene allmächtige Kraft, Güte und Weisheit,* und nenne in seiner Seele das unsichtbare Wesen, das keine Erdensprache zu nennen vermag.[32]

> [Let no one be misled by the fact that I sometimes use the name of Nature as though it were a person. Nature is not any kind of independent being, but rather *God is everything in his works*; but I did not want to misuse his most holy name . . . by invoking it so frequently without always being able to give it all the devout respect it deserves. Whoever feels that the name "Nature" has become cheap and meaningless by being used in so many modern-day publications should imagine to himself, instead of "Nature," *that all-powerful might, goodness, and wisdom,* and recognize in his heart the invisible Being that can be properly named in no earthly language.]

Here Herder may recommend a way of dealing with the two concepts, nature and God, but their intermixing causes recurrent difficulties. To be objective and scientific, one would have to explain things solely in terms of natural laws without appealing to the will of God, yet Herder cannot avoid insisting that God is not only present in nature, but also in history as well, as evinced in the argument of book 15, which opens with a rhetorical movement into despair over the evils of the moral-historical world (quite common among those like Rousseau, Moritz, and others who paint the moral world black in order seemingly to deny that there is a divine order in it), a despair which, once evoked, is rhetorically overcome by faith that there is a *telos* in Nature and that God's providence rules all:

> Ist indessen ein Gott in der Natur: so ist er auch in der Geschichte: denn auch der Mensch ist ein Teil der Schöpfung und muß in seinen wildesten Ausschweifungen und Leidenschaften Gesetze befolgen, die nicht minder schön und vortrefflich sind, als jene, nach welchen sich alle Himmels- und Erdkörper bewegen. Da ich nun überzeugt bin, daß was der Mensch wissen muß, er auch wissen könne und dürfe: so gehe ich aus dem Gewühl der Szenen, die wir bisher durchwandert haben, zuversichtlich und frei den hohen und schönen Naturgesetzen entgegen, denen auch sie folgen.[33]

> [If, meanwhile, there is a God in Nature: then he is also in History: for man too is part of the Creation and must, even in his wildest actions and passions, follow laws which are no less beautiful and excellent than those which

all heavenly and earthly bodies obey. Since I am convinced that man can and must know what it is he has to know, I proceed confidently and willingly from the chaos of the scenes through which we have passed up to now towards the sublime and beautiful laws of Nature which they too obey.]

Law of nature, law of God, law of history — which actually has the power to explain what the work needs to explain?

Not a natural scientist himself, Herder was largely dependent on Goethe's knowledge and insights and the work of scientist-philosophers such as Bonnet, Haller (1708–77), Linnaeus (1707–78), ethnographers and writers on exploration like Johann Reinhold Forster, and the like. Regarding the place of man and the earth in the system, he actually reverts to ideas put forward by, among others, Immanuel Kant as early as 1755 in his *Allgemeine Naturgeschichte und Theorie des Himmels* (General History of Nature and Theory of the Heavens). In debates about man it was always necessary to emphasize on the one hand that he was the apex of Creation on earth, but to concede on the other hand that he occupied only a middling position in the universe as a whole, so as to make room for creatures both beneath and above him in the great chain of being who might be flourishing or approaching perfection on other planets or in other parts of the universe. Already in the dialogues *Über die Seelenwanderung* Herder had developed an argument about the place of man as a *Mittelgeschöpf* (middling creature) on a middling planet in the solar system situated between Saturn and the Sun.

In much of the first two parts of the *Ideen*, Herder is, in fact, not up to date at all in his science and scholarship, but rather synthesizes the state of knowledge and debate from earlier in the century.[34] His discussion of the place of man in the solar system plays into a common theme of eighteenth-century popular philosophy, inspired as it was by the thought that there were countless other worlds where rational creatures could either be inferior to humans or increase in perfection and surpass humans on their earth. Often it was assumed that humans proceeded to these other worlds to continue the progress of their perfection after their sojourn on earth — death did not necessarily lead straight to Heaven or Hell but to another stage in the transformation or a transposition of the individual. Covering most of the available viewpoints in the debate on immortality and perfectibility, Lessing argued in *Die Erziehung des Menschengeschlechts* for increasing perfection of the individual through metempsychosis; Herder argued vaguely for increasing perfection of the individual first during life and through transformation after death; and Kant, criticizing Herder sharply on this point in his blistering review of part 1 of the *Ideen*, argued that it was not the individual, but the species that nature had destined for progress, not through spiritual perfection, but through the development of reason, gifts, and talents sharpened in the egoistic competition of individuals and societies among themselves.[35]

Although personal perfection and immortality may be the transcendent goal of the individual, Herder posits also a developmental goal in history for individuals and societies alike: all history, all culture, all human interactions contribute to furthering *Humanität*, which as an ideal can perhaps best be rendered as "the true nature of humanity and the human race." This has nothing (at least not primarily) to do with religion or religious values alone, although for Herder, of course, Jesus was the most humane person in the history of the world. He devotes considerable space at the end of the third part of the *Ideen* (book 15, after the jeremiad about moral evil in the world) to explaining what he means by it. *Humanität* is the all-encompassing ideal for humans, he claims, because even if we imagine to ourselves angels or gods, we imagine them as ideal humans. The approach to *Humanität* is not continual or without interruption in history; in fact, societies and cultures can remain for centuries on end in their original primitive state without progressing at all, or they can even regress. But in all ages one principal law of nature remains constant: "Der Mensch sei Mensch! er bilde sich seinen Zustand nach dem, was er für das Beste erkennet" (632; Let man be man! may he create his condition according to his best lights). God/Nature created man as a "God on earth," responsible to and for himself, and through the ages people and societies have struggled to be free and to enjoy their freedom according to the "great and beneficent law of human fate":

> . . . daß was ein Volk oder ein gesamtes Menschengeschlecht zu seinem eignen Besten mit Überlegung wolle und mit Kraft ausführe, das sei ihm auch von der Natur vergönnet, die weder Despoten noch Traditionen sondern die beste Form der Humanität ihnen zum Ziel setzte. (634)

> [. . . that whatever a people or a whole race wants for itself after due consideration, and turns its strength to carrying out, that is granted it by Nature, who sets neither despots nor traditions as their goal, but rather the best form of *Humanität*.]

Humanität, a matter of self-determination and self-fulfillment, cannot depend on the other, nor can the failure to strive and achieve one's share of *Humanität* be blamed on the other:

> Mit nichten gründete sich z. B. der lange Gehorsam unter dem Despotismus auf die Übermacht des Despoten; die gutwillige, zutrauende Schwachheit der Unterjochten, späterhin ihre duldende Trägheit war seine einzige und größeste Stütze. Denn Dulden ist freilich leichter, als mit Nachdruck bessern; daher brauchten so viele Völker des Rechts nicht, das ihnen Gott durch die Göttergabe ihrer Vernunft gegeben. (635)

> [In no way, for example, was the long obedience under despotism based on the superiority of the despot; the good-natured trusting weakness of the subjugated, and afterward their forbearing patience was its sole and greatest possible support. For forbearance is easier than emphatic

improvement; that's the reason so many peoples didn't make use of the right that God gave them through the divine gift of their reason.]

Those were words not only about the medieval age that was the subject of the last part of the *Ideen*, they were words for the age in which Herder was writing. For his own age Herder began the project of the *Briefe zu Beförderung der Humanität*. They took a different form than the *Ideen*. Whereas the *Ideen* was a treatise in twenty books, the *Briefe* were conceived as a correspondence among several participants. The different participants remain anonymous, and in fact, the individual letters are not attributed to specific authors, for, as the editor asks in a note at the end of the first letter, what could initials indicate that the letters themselves don't tell us. Whereas at the outset there is a pretense of variant points of view, the letters very quickly lose the appearance of difference. The work contains a total of 124 letters in ten *Sammlungen* (collections) published in the years from 1793 to 1797.

The years when Herder was publishing the *Humanitätsbriefe* were likewise the years when the French Revolution was having its strongest impact on Germany: the beginning of the wars that were to consume Germany and Europe until the defeat of Napoleon in 1814, the execution of Louis XVI on 21 January 1793, the Reign of Terror, the occupation of much German territory. Herder did not live long enough to experience the worst. He was not free to express his opinion in all respects because of recently sharpened censorship in Prussia and other territories of the Holy Roman Empire, and because Saxe-Weimar was firmly aligned with the Prussian cause against France. Herder's own sentiments were several degrees too liberal for his master, Carl August, for Goethe, and for his Weimar surroundings. The original version of several of the letters in the second collection, in which Herder's correspondents aired their thoughts frankly about the situation in France and the undesirability of intervention by the German powers (Prussia and Austria) to save the throne of Louis XVI, was withdrawn and never published during Herder's lifetime.[36] The most direct effect of this political-intellectual situation was that instead of presenting a frank and freewheeling (and perhaps also thoroughly cohesive and connected) discourse in the letters, Herder resorted to illustrating much of the progress of *Humanität* in various ages, from Greek antiquity to modern times, by excerpting the works of others. In the first three collections alone he excerpts from Benjamin Franklin's (1706–90) autobiography, which had just been translated into German, from recently published (posthumous) works of Frederick II of Prussia (1712–86), materials dealing with Emperor Joseph II (1741–90), poems by Klopstock and others, passages from Martin Luther, part of a dialogue by Lessing, and so on. The writer who in younger years had had nothing good to say about Frederick or Joseph was now able to relate their reigns to some progress in *Humanität* after all — especially when compared to France, which, until the Revolution, had been exceedingly backward.

Both the *Ideen* and the *Humanitätsbriefe* were major works by a writer who was intensely engaged in the social and political issues of his time, who lacked nothing to be a significant political writer but the opportunity to express his opinions without fear of censorship or threat of intimidation. He was of course not free to give up or lose his post and his parsonage back of the city church without fear of harm to himself and his family. Consequently, it was not possible for either work to fulfill its original promise. It was for the younger generation to shine as political writers and critics of the affairs of the age in which Herder found himself, in the end, marooned.

Notes

[1] In one attempt to better his situation, Herder proposed to take over a vacated chair of theology at the University of Jena while continuing to fulfill his official duties as court preacher; since the court so seldom took communion, it would be no problem for him to commute from Jena to Weimar for the purpose when necessary!

[2] In his early years, he dreamed of reforming Russia, or at least Riga and the Baltic provinces, where he had begun his career; and late in life, when he had given up on the chances of reform in Weimar, he idealized his recollections of the "republican" city government of Riga.

[3] The small scale of the supervisory function is to be noted: the Saxe-Eisenach portion of Carl August's domain had its own Church/school hierarchy and consistory.

[4] This had the effect of an unofficially large scope for freedom of the press (eventually embodied officially, albeit briefly, in the post-Napoleonic constitution of the Grand Duchy).

[5] See Christoph Fasel, *Herder und das klassische Weimar: Kultur und Gesellschaft 1789–1803* (New York: Peter Lang, 1988), 57–58: "Noch 1792 gab es mehrere Lehrerstellen, die jährlich weniger als 15 Taler (!) eintrugen, sehr viele, die kaum 50 Taler einbrachten." (As late as 1792 there were some teaching posts that brought in less than 15 talers per annum, and many that barely brought in 50 talers). Fasel's work is highly informative with regard to conditions and circumstances in Weimar during the period.

[6] For a succinct treatment of Goethe's relations with the Herders, see Günter Arnold's article on Herder in *Goethe Handbuch* (Stuttgart, Weimar: Verlag J. B. Metzler, 1998), 4.1:481–86.

[7] See Fasel, 163: "Hauptgrund für die finanzielle Misere bis zu den neunziger Jahren ist nicht primär die Gastfreundschaft und Größe des Herderschen Haushaltes oder gar ein in ihm betriebener Luxus, sondern die Tatsache, daß die ursprünglich auf 2000 Taler veranschlagte Stelle, die sich ja aus den Einkommen der verschiedensten Ämter zusammensetzte, im Mittel nur 1200 Taler einbrachte." (The main reason for the financial difficulties up until the nineties was not primarily the affability or the size of the Herder's household,

much less any luxuries they indulged in, but rather the fact that the originally-promised 2000 taler position, which was put together out of the incomes of the different posts, yielded on average only 1200 talers).

[8] Fasel, 77.

[9] This was the second time Herder had negotiated with Göttingen. Because of opposition from other professors Heyne had not been able to get through a favorable appointment in the 1770s before Herder went to Weimar.

[10] See Herder's *Italienische Reise. Briefe und Tagebuchaufzeichnungen 1788–1789*. Edited and with commentary and afterword by Albert Meier und Heide Hollmer (Munich: Deutscher Taschenbuch Verlag, 1988). This collection of documents, hereinafter referred to simply as *Italienische Reise*, is remarkably short on insightful comments by Herder on his actual experiences during his Italian trip; but it is fascinating to read because of the constantly changing, ambivalent attitudes of Caroline and Herder both toward each other and toward their mutual friends and acquaintances, and their attempts to agree on their situation and the decisions to be taken (the Göttingen offer) at such long distance.

[11] Not only did the Herders finally decide he was not really cut out to be a professor of theology, who would have to endure the jealousy and criticism of his more senior and orthodox colleagues, teach several hours each day, and still write a lot as well; they were definitely apprehensive about the influence of student life in a university town on their still impressionable young sons (the nearby bad example of Jena could not be overlooked).

[12] Fasel points out, however, that it was not only Herder who was isolated in Weimar; everyone was isolated from everyone else: "Allgemein ist nicht nur die Isolation, verbreitet sind auch die Klagen in Weimar, die in der Forschung häufig als das Monopol Herders erscheinen" (152; Not only was there a general feeling of isolation, complaints were also widespread which are often treated in the scholarly literature as Herder's monopoly).

[13] On this whole matter see Wulf Koepke, "Herder and the Sturm und Drang," in *Literature of the Sturm und Drang* (vol. 6 of the Camden House History of German Literature), ed. David Hill (Rochester, NY: Camden House, 2003), 69–93.

[14] While appreciative also of the classical Greek dramatic models, for example in his famous Shakespeare essay.

[15] This is, it seems to me, actually a rather perceptive view of Greek society. Most contemporary interpretations of Greek culture emphasized "classical" beauty and totally ignored the cruel and unjust foundations of the society that produced such beauty. At the turn of the century Johann Gottfried Seume (1763–1810), like Herder a man of the people, launched a more thoroughgoing critique of ancient slavery.

[16] Herder, *Schriften zu Philosophie, Literatur, Kunst und Altertum 1774–1787*, ed. Jürgen Brummack & Martin Bollacher (Frankfurt am Main: Deutscher Klassiker Verlag, 1994), 74.

[17] In which Herder, taking a broader view of antiquity and the spread of culture from Asia to Europe in his major works (not just in *Auch eine Geschichte der Philosophie. . .*), was thankfully much less implicated.

[18] Johann Friedrich Hugo von Dalberg and his lady friend, Sophie von Seckendorff. See frequent mention of the problem posed by the presence of Frau von Seckendorff in Herder's letters to Caroline in the Meier/Hollmer edition of *Italienische Reise*, as well as extensive discussion in their "Nachwort," 623–45.

[19] Published in Meier/Hollmer's *Italienische Reise*.

[20] Herder to Trippel from Milan, 15 June 1789, on his way back to Weimar: "Zuerst wünschte ich, daß die Schultern nicht so breit ausfielen: der Kopf bekommt dadurch etwas kolossalisches u. Gigantisches, welches in einer großen Höhe zwar Wirkung machte, aber in einer Höhe, wie unsre Busten meistens gesetzt werden, scheint es mir drückend u. schwer zu werden. Ich weiß nicht, ob Göthe seine Buste kolossal bestellt hat; meine ist aber selbst größer geworden, als die seine . . . Zweitens auf der Stirn wünschte ich *etwas mehr Haar* . . . Mich dünkt, der Kontrast zwischen mir u. Göthe sei etwas zu stark: er sieht wie ein junger Alexander oder Apollo aus, u. ich gegen ihn wie ein kahler, trockner Alter" (First of all I wish that the shoulders wouldn't turn out so broad: the head gains something colossal and gigantic as a result, which at a great height would, to be sure, have quite an effect, but in the height in which our busts are usually displayed it seems to me to become oppressive and heavy. I don't know whether Goethe ordered his bust colossal, mine however has become even larger than his . . . Second I would wish for more hair on the brow . . . It seems to me the contrast between Goethe and me is somewhat too stark: he looks like a young Alexander or Apollo, and I look like a bald dry old man in comparison; *Italienische Reise*, 501–2).

[21] Herder to Caroline, 21 February 1789 (*Italienische Reise*, 350). The passage is often quoted. Herder displays great ambivalence towards Goethe in his Italian correspondence with Caroline, not only here.

[22] This title will be referred to as *Humanitätsbriefe*. It is quite impossible to translate *Humanität* as Herder uses it: it could be "Humaneness" as well as "Humanness." It does not mean "Mankind" or simply "Humanity" in any case, although perhaps it could be rendered "Humanity" in the sense of what ideally makes humankind human or humane.

[23] His involvement in church affairs was serious and never *pro forma*, as can be seen in the volume edited long ago by Eva Schmidt, *Herder im geistlichen Amt: Untersuchungen/Quellen/Dokumente* (Leipzig: Koehler & Amelang, 1956). The volume deserves to be vastly expanded and re-issued.

[24] Herder was motivated not just by Lessing's text, which was a kind of culmination of a discussion that had been going on since mid-century beginning with popular works like Johann Joachim Spalding's *Bestimmung des Menschen* of 1748 and Moses Mendelssohn's *Phädon* of 1767 (both works were reprinted and discussed many times over the years). See the editor's introduction to Herder's *Seelenwanderung* in *Schriften zu Philosophie* . . . (cited above), 1172–78.

[25] *Über die Lehre des Spinoza, in Briefen an Herrn Moses Mendelssohn*, 1785. The complete Jacobi-Mendelssohn controversy was published in *Die Hauptschriften zum Pantheismusstreit zwischen Jacobi und Mendelssohn*, ed. Heinrich Scholz (Berlin: Reuther & Reichard, 1916).

[26] Goethe, who received a copy of the work while in Italy, was enthusiastic in his praise.

[27] See Karl Aner, *Die Theologie der Lessingzeit* (Halle/Saale: Niemeyer, 1929); with respect to Herder, especially, Michael Embach, *Das Lutherbild Johann Gottfried Herders*, Trierer Studien zur Literatur, 14 (Frankfurt am Main: Verlag Peter Lang, 1987).

[28] Herder, *Theologische Schriften*, ed. Christoph Bultmann and Thomas Zippert (Frankfurt am Main: Deutscher Klassiker Verlag, 1994), 450.

[29] Controversies which, one must add, are still carried on with zest and righteousness by American Lutheran fundamentalists today. There is no space to consider here Herder's actual understanding of the Bible as a book of history whose veracity can be assumed in all important respects. The Old Testament, for example, including all the reports therein of God's direct intercourse with his chosen people, can safely be read as an authentic history of the Jewish people; similarly, Herder views the Gospels' account of the life, career, and death of Jesus, including the reports of his miracles, his resurrection and ascent into Heaven, as truthful relations of fact. In this he rejects, without explicitly saying so, Reimarus's critique and Lessing's refusal in *Über den Beweis des Geistes und der Kraft* (On the Proof of the Spirit and the Power) to accept the Gospel events as credible history.

[30] See the close of his letter to Caroline from Bamberg, 10 August 1788: "Der Katholizism ist ein abscheulich Ding, so fett, wohlbeleibt, etabliert, rund, behäglich, daß einem angst u. bange wird. Bloß hübsche fromme Weiber gibts in ihm. Gestern sah ich eine, die den Augenblick eine Madonna sein konnte. O mir Armen! wie wird mirs das Jahr hin ergehen! Ich glaube, ich sterbe vor Gemälden, Pfaffen u. Katholizismus" (Catholicism is a monstrous thing, so fat, plump, round, self-indulgent, that it is scary. There are only pretty, pious women in it. Yesterday I saw one who could instantly have become a Madonna. O poor me! what kind of a year am I going to have! I believe I'll die of paintings, priests, and Catholicism; *Italienische Reise*).

[31] In the *Ideen*, Herder displays no ambivalence at all regarding the Byzantine Empire and the Greek Church; he levels the same criticisms as at the Roman Church hierarchy but without any countervailing positive comments.

[32] *Ideen zur Philosophie der Geschichte der Menschheit*, ed. Martin Bollacher (Frankfurt am Main: Deutscher Klassiker Verlag, 1989), 17. I quote from the Frankfurt edition because it is the most recent and most accessible edition with commentary; but I would like to praise the two-volume edition edited by Heinz Stolpe (Berlin and Weimar: Aufbau Verlag, 1965 [*Ausgewählte Werke in Einzelausgaben*]) for its massive commentary and its role in furthering understanding of the work. The same must be said also of Stolpe's later edition of the *Humanitätsbriefe* (Aufbau Verlag, 1971).

[33] *Ideen*, 630.

[34] In his review of the second part of the *Ideen*, Kant noted that much had been excerpted from other authors.

[35] Kant's other main criticism of Herder's effort had to do with Herder's use of analogical argument: if this is true here in the mineral world, and in the plant and animal worlds, then it must hold for man as well, etc. Kant missed a certain philosophical-logical rigor in Herder's work.

[36] Interestingly enough, in the suppressed version of the second collection the various correspondents were in fact identified by initials.

Georg Melchior Kraus, Iphigenie, *1802. Corona Schröter as Iphigenie and Goethe as Orest in Goethe's* Iphigenie auf Tauris. *Oil on canvas, Goethe-Nationalmuseum, Weimar. Courtesy of Stiftung Weimarer Klassik, Kunstsammlungen.*

Drama and Theatrical Practice in Weimar Classicism

Jane K. Brown

FOR MOST OF THE NINETEENTH and twentieth centuries the dramas of "Goetheundschiller" stood for Weimar Classicism. The major plays of this touching amalgam of Germany's greatest playwrights were understood to embody the bourgeois ideology of *Humanität* and *Bildung*, which married Schiller's Kantianism to the new classicism brought by Goethe from Italy. The resulting modified neoclassicism, synthesized from the French and English (particularly Shakespearean) dramatic traditions, undergirds modern German literature and identity. The assertions implicit in this summary are largely true. Nevertheless, the common view overlooks a crucial point: Goethe and Schiller sought to educate the German public not through drama, but through the theater. As official director of the Weimar Court Theater from 1789 until 1817, Goethe hired and trained the company, oversaw the repertory, adapted important texts (the less important ones were usually adapted by his eventual brother-in-law Christian August Vulpius [1762–1827]), and personally directed numerous plays. After 1797 Schiller shared in many of these duties. In order to read the drama of German Classicism as a specifically historical rather than ideological phenomenon, this chapter begins with the Weimar stage and its repertory under Goethe's direction; against this background a more nuanced understanding of the ambition and achievement of German classical drama, first as a whole and then as the work of individuals, emerges.

The Weimar Stage

In the eighteenth century Germany alone in Western Europe lacked a deeply rooted theater — national or otherwise. Court drama with lavish spectacle had spread from sixteenth-century Italy to England, France, and Spain; in the course of the seventeenth century all developed flourishing commercial theaters for both spoken drama and opera. Well into the eighteenth century most of Germany, however, had only occasional school drama and itinerant troupes. Vienna had the richest theatrical life of any

German-speaking city. When, at the very end of the seventeenth century, the Jesuits ceased their lavish school performances, the emperor established an Italian court opera as well as a public theater to be leased to an enterprising troupe. Its performances, the direct ancestors of Vienna's comic light opera, were also much frequented by members of the court.[1] Some German courts, particularly Dresden and Prague, had superb Italian opera for much of the century. Less affluent courts maintained a tradition of amateur and semi-amateur court masque for special occasions (Wieland and then Goethe wrote masques for the Weimar court until 1828); otherwise their theatrical needs were served either by amateurs or strolling actors temporarily domiciled in their castles, as Goethe described in book 3 of *Wilhelm Meisters Lehrjahre* (1795–96). The common people made do with repeat performances in some public space in the town, or with troupes not good or fortunate enough to enjoy the patronage of a court. After abortive attempts to establish a commercial national theater in Hamburg, the outstanding Seyler-Ekhof troupe found reasonable stability only at the Weimar court in 1771. The destruction of the theater by fire in 1774 drove them to neighboring Gotha, where they became the first permanent court theater in Germany, supported partly by royal subsidy, partly by earned income, and were open not only to the court, but also to citizens of the town. On the death of Conrad Ekhof (1720–78) most of the company's actors moved to Mannheim, the most stable and influential court theater of the 1780s. By the end of the century court theaters on Gotha's compromise model existed all over Germany.[2]

The repertoire consisted of translations and adaptations of Italian, French, Spanish, Dutch and English plays and operas of the preceding century whose authorship was often no longer recognized.[3] In the eighteenth century the more archaic part of the repertoire was considered plebeian, and both aristocratic and bourgeois circles sporadically attempted to purify taste and create a respectable German drama. Johann Christoph Gottsched (1700–66), whose *Versuch einer critischen Dichtkunst* (Essay on Critical Poetics, 1730) was the most influential transmitter of neoclassicism in eighteenth-century Germany, also published *Die deutsche Schaubühne* (German Theater, 1741–45), an anthology of model original and translated neoclassical texts in German. But only with Gotthold Ephraim Lessing (1729–81) did any German playwright achieve durable German, much less European eminence. In the wake of these reformers a tradition of bourgeois comedy and serious drama (*Schauspiel*) flourished, of which the most important representatives were Friedrich Ludwig Schröder (1744–1816), August Wilhelm Iffland (1759–1814), and August Friedrich Ferdinand Kotzebue (1761–1819).

Germany's theatrical backwardness probably resulted as much from the religious divisions of the Thirty Years' War as from economic devastation. Protestantism has traditionally been hostile to theater as to other images, while

Catholicism fostered it for religious education. The Lutheran establishment in Hamburg opposed both the early opera there and the establishment of a serious national theater in the 1760s, while Catholic Vienna fared much better. The powerful centralized monarchies of western Europe tended to protect the stage against religious radicals, particularly in England, where the high church Protestantism of the Tudors and Stuarts had more in common with Catholicism than with the Puritanism of the urban bourgeoisie. Germany looks rather less backward when compared to the United States in the later eighteenth century, where the stage lost the protection of the British crown against radical Protestant colonists, particularly in Puritan New England and Quaker Pennsylvania. In 1774 the Congress recommended suspending all public amusements, and again in 1778 specifically banning theater: Pennsylvania's prohibition of all theater lasted until 1789. In 1802 a commentator noted that the Lutherans in Pennsylvania were about fifty years behind their brethren in Germany in their attitudes toward the stage.[4] In the U.S. a heterogeneous population and the lack of an established church rapidly overcame such objections; in Germany the alliance between the Enlightenment and the stage embodied in a figure like Lessing had taken half a century to overcome the trammels to theatrical development.

Germany's anomalous political structure was also a problem. From the late Middle Ages until the nineteenth century, the stage was one of the most effective public media in Europe, and the centralizing regimes of Europe took it rapidly under control. Theater was famously both representation and instrument of court power all over Europe from the Renaissance through the eighteenth century, except in England, where a vigorous commercial theater in London represented the emergent gentry and bourgeoisie starting in the mid-sixteenth century. But in Germany, unlike the rest of Europe including Austria, power remained fragmented among numerous, often tiny, courts, while the bourgeoisie lived equally fragmented in small cities, with no single large capital to set taste. To fill even the modest theaters in such principalities (199 seats in Gotha, a mere 100 in Weimar) or form an amateur group large enough to act, the aristocracy had to join forces with local citizens, as was already the case in Weimar under Anna Amalia before the arrival of Ekhof's troupe. The experiment with the national theater in Hamburg showed that even in the larger cities the bourgeoisie could not go it alone. The necessary synthesis resulted in the state-subsidized repertory theater still prevalent in Europe today. The older repertoire of the courts and itinerant players — political and heroic tragedy, court masque, opera, comedy — combined with the sentimental family drama, didactic comedy and light opera (*Singspiel*) preferred by the bourgeoisie. The drama of German Classicism is the remarkable result of this synthesis.[5]

The bourgeois takeover of the German stage was accompanied by a professionalization of actors. German actors had proverbially low status in

Germany until the second half of the eighteenth century, when Ekhof, Schröder, and Iffland were noted for their social respectability as well as their superlative acting. In Gotha, Ekhof's actors were employed by the court rather than by himself, and he tried to establish a pension system for them. After an unsatisfactory experience with an old-style resident troupe, Duke Carl August requested Goethe to establish a court theater in Weimar in 1791; he followed Ekhof's new system, which was becoming the norm, and raised it to new heights. To be sure, the Duke pursued an older model of court theater by publicly keeping the lead actress of the company, Caroline Jagemann, as his mistress; but he eventually ennobled her and had her received at court. Goethe's literary status showed the respect in which theater was to be held in Weimar. More important in the long run, Goethe trained his actors in ways previously unknown in Germany in declamation, movement, and stage manners. Before his work in Weimar, blank-verse classics like Lessing's *Nathan der Weise* (1779) and Schiller's *Don Carlos* (1787) could only be performed in prose versions, because no actors could recite the verse properly. Furthermore, Goethe held rehearsals and informal performances in his home, where the actors were welcome as talented professionals. No longer the occasional tools of aristocratic display, they now could claim bourgeois acceptability, even respectability, and the theater became the showcase of bourgeois values.

Except for Goethe and Schiller's publisher, Johann Friedrich Cotta, the Weimar theater was the most important organ of German Classicism. Although Goethe sometimes left the management to his second-in-command, Franz Kirms (1750–1826), during the founding period and at various times thereafter he shaped the company and its philosophy through hiring, training, selection of repertoire, and directing. During their friendship Schiller assisted. In theatrical terms, Goethe's achievement was to assemble and realize several new trends to create the first unified productions conceived and guided by a single individual — in effect he was the first modern director.[6] In addition to the new recitation skills and the discipline he made his actors bring to their work, his most important contribution was a conception of ensemble acting that made each scene a composed picture on the stage. Without Goethe, according to Michael Patterson, "the pursuit of aural and visual beauty on stage might have been confined almost exclusively to opera and the dance."[7]

It is generally said that Goethe financed his experiments in modernization and education by generous doses of popular comedy, sentimental family drama, and opera, none of which he considered significant. The perception rests on Wilhelm's hostility to opera in *Wilhelm Meisters Lehrjahre*, a position which should not, I believe, be taken for Goethe's, and on the obvious fact that while Kotzebue was the most performed dramatist on the Weimar stage, Goethe avoided him personally.[8] A closer analysis of the published listing of the repertoire in Weimar night for night, which includes 185 authors and composers (marked in the tables below with an asterisk), some 605 dramas, and twenty-six ballets, allows a more nuanced interpretation.[9] As Figure 1 shows, Kotzebue was the most popular author on the Weimar stage, with 641 performances of ninety-six different titles, Iffland a distant second, and Goethe, Schiller, and Schröder much farther behind. Different patterns emerge if we consider the number of evenings in the theater devoted to a particular author rather than titles performed, as in Figure 2, which takes account of double-bills with two different authors. This list, too, contains several unfamiliar names. Kotzebue, himself from Weimar, was the most prolific playwright of the era. His sentimental comedies, family and historical dramas swamped the European and American stage, especially from about 1795 to 1810. No one then or since thought him a great dramatist, but he rapidly turned out workmanlike plays on a dependable model with easy-to-learn type roles. Stageable with minimal rehearsal time and recycled sets, they efficiently met the public's demand for novelty. In Weimar the average Kotzebue play was staged only seven times over Goethe's directorship, a run that does not qualify Kotzebue as one of the top twenty long-running authors (see Figure 3), but in this case their ephemeral quality was an advantage. To a large extent, the same holds for the numerous plays by Iffland, Schröder, Johanna Franul von Weissenthurn (1772–1847), and many of the others in Figure 1. These predictable family comedies and dramas tend to be less colorful and lively than Kotzebue's, less witty, and less salacious; they were often written by leading actors (Iffland, Schroeder, Weissenthurn) to showcase their own talents and their companies, as Iffland's many guest performances in his own plays in Weimar testify. All of them gave Goethe the time and resources to prepare for his less familiar and more challenging demands.

Figure 1. Titles

	Author	Titles	Totals	Run
1	Kotzebue	96	641	7
2	Iffland	32	371	12
3	Goethe	19	226	12
4	Schiller	15	313	21
5	Schroeder	14	139	10
6	Shakespeare	13	79	6
7	Anon	11	19	2
8	Weissenthurn	10	54	5
9	Weigl*	10	51	5
10	Ziegler	9	56	6
11	Körner	9	48	5

Figure 1 (continued) Titles

	Author	Titles	Totals	Run
12	Jünger	9	89	10
13	Vogel	8	70	9
14	Paer*	8	73	9
15	Gotter	8	49	6
16	Dittersdorf*	8	142	18
17	Steigentesch	7	41	6
18	d'Allayrac*	7	76	11
19	Mozart*	7	304	43
20	Schall	7	19	3

Figure 2. Evenings

	Author	Nights
1	Kotzebue	606
2	Iffland	370
3	Mozart*	304
4	Schiller	283.5
5	Goethe	179.5
6	Dittersdorf*	142
7	Schroeder	136.5
8	Jünger	85
9	Shakespeare	79
10	Vogel	79
11	Paer*	72.5
12	Lessing	63
13	Mehul*	61
14	Cimarosa*	59
15	Paisiello*	58.5
16	Beck	53
17	Weissenthurn	51.5
18	Weigl*	49
19	Ziegler	48
20	d'Allayrac*	43

Figure 3. Average Run

	Author	Titles	Totals	Run
1	Mozart*	7	304	43
2	Martin*	1	35	35
3	Wranitzky*	1	27	27
4	Beck	2	49	25
5	Schenk*?	1	23	23
6	Marivaux	1	22	22
7	v Bouilly	1	22	22
8	Gluck*	1	21	21
9	Schiller	15	313	21
10	Stegmeyer	1	18	18
11	Dittersdorf*	8	142	18
12	Mehul*	5	83	17
13	Bourgogne	1	16	16
14	Lessing	4	63	16
15	Solie*	1	15	15
16	della Maria	1	15	15
17	Cherubini*	3	42	14
18	Wall	2	28	14
19	Regnard	2	28	14
20	Wiesenthal	1	14	14

Figure 4. >7 Titles by Average Run

	Author	Titles	Totals	Run
1	Mozart*	7	304	43
2	Schiller	15	313	21
3	Dittersdorf*	8	142	18
4	Goethe	19	226	12
5	Iffland	32	371	12
6	d'Allayrac*	7	76	11
7	Schroeder	14	139	10
8	Jünger	9	89	10

Figure 4 (continued) >7 Titles by Average Run

	Author	Titles	Totals	Run
9	Paer*	8	73	9
10	Vogel	8	70	9
11	Kotzebue	96	641	7
12	Ziegler	9	56	6
13	Gotter	8	49	6
14	Shakespeare	13	79	6
15	Steigentesch	7	41	6
16	Weissenthurn	10	54	5
17	Körner	9	48	5
18	Sonnleithner	7	37	5
19	Weigl*	10	51	5
20	Schall	7	19	3

Several of the challenges appear, interestingly, in Figure 1: Goethe (3), Schiller (4), Shakespeare (6), and Mozart (19). Goethe and Schiller were in charge, so of course their plays were performed. But the category "run" in Figures 1, 3, and 4 refers to the average number of performances that plays by each author received between 1791 and 1817, and Goethe kept only reasonably well-received plays in the repertoire.[10] By this measure he seems, on average, to have been as good for business as Iffland, and better than Kotzebue, while Schiller plays, which required much more elaborate staging, also drew larger audiences. Most challenging, and much the longest runner, was Mozart. The success of Mozart, whose music was technically difficult, testifies to the competence of Goethe's theater. This is not the kind of opera Wilhelm Meister condemned. Shakespeare, by contrast, also difficult to stage, lasted only about as well as Kotzebue. His relative unpopularity is perhaps surprising for audiences accustomed to his absolute priority on the German as well as the Anglo-American stage. Many of the productions were in early, problematic translations and adaptations, but more important was Shakespeare's unfamiliarity to German audiences. Goethe appears on this list, despite the common perception that his plays were unpopular in his time, and is represented by nineteen plays. Most readers today would be hard put even to name so many. Goethe's most performed plays in Weimar were "Die Geschwister" (The Siblings, 1776), "Die Mitschuldigen" (Partners in Crime, 1769, rev. 1780–83) and "Jery und Bätely" (1779) — two comedies and a short *Singspiel*. Despite bizarre twists that only Goethe could have conceived, all operate within the conventions of sentimental bourgeois comedy cultivated by Kotzebue, Iffland, and Schröder. The audience, in sum, was not anti-intellectual but still preferred the sentimentalism popularized in Germany by Klopstock and

Goethe's *Leiden des jungen Werther* (The Sorrows of Young Werther, 1774), which persisted through the Biedermeier into the 1860s.[11] German classical drama thus had to define itself within and against the taste for sentimental family drama. On the whole, however, the numbers suggest that much of what Goethe and Schiller brought to their audience did not require sweetening by the popular repertoire.

Finally, the mix of canonical and forgotten authors at the heads of these tables requires comment. Goethe, Schiller, and Mozart were trying to create a repertoire for the German theater, but so too, in their fashion, were Kotzebue, Iffland, Schroeder, and Karl Ditters von Dittersdorf (the most popular composer after Mozart, 1739–99). In the late 1790s the plays of Lessing, Iffland, Schröder, early Goethe, the young Schiller, and early Kotzebue constituted the only canon Germans had. Good theater does not depend only on good drama; as Goethe told Eckermann, "ein Stück zweiten, dritten Ranges kann durch Besetzung mit Kräften ersten Ranges unglaublich gehoben und wirklich zu etwas Gutem werden" (14 April 1825; a play of second or third rank can be incredibly elevated by casting with first-rank actors and become truly good). The differences in quality so evident to us were not necessarily clear except to the best minds in the audience at the time, and did not necessarily interfere with the project of educating a German audience. Although Germans still perceived themselves subject to the cultural hegemony of France, and although Weimar famously added English (Shakespeare), Greek (tragedy), Latin (comedy), and Spanish (Calderón) works to the repertoire, only twenty-three percent of the plays performed are identifiably translations or adaptations of non-German texts. Goethe sought to locate a German repertoire, not just create one, and it was not a hopeless task.

The figures for average number of performances per author in Figures 3 and 4 bear out this assertion. Figure 3 takes account of the occasional hit by an author not otherwise staged in Weimar, while Figure 4 represents authors apparently considered dependable by the theater administration. Very few authors — fewer than five percent — averaged ten or more performances, and three of the first four names are still considered the outstanding dramatic presences of the period in Germany. As Figure 5 shows, the five most performed plays in Weimar were by Mozart or Schiller. However much popular drama was performed on it, the Weimar stage was genuinely important for its classical repertoire.

Under Goethe's leadership the repertoire became both more serious and more musical. Figure 6 shows it divided evenly among comedy, serious drama, and musical events. By comparison (Figure 7), Ekhof's company in Gotha from 1775 to 1779, also a leading company led by a reformer and located at one of the most intellectual courts in Germany, devoted two thirds of its performances to comedies, one quarter to operas, and only one tenth to serious dramas.[12] The only comedies by canonical

Figure 5. Most Performed Plays

	Author	Title	Perf
1	Mozart*	*Die Zauberflöte*	82
2	Mozart*	*Don Juan*	68
3	Schiller	*Wallensteins Lager*	52
4	Mozart*	*Die Entführung aus dem Serail*	49
5	Schiller	*Don Karlos*	43
6	Dittersdorf*	*Das rote Käppchen*	41
7	Iffland	*Die Hagestolzen*	40
8	Schiller	*Wallenstein*	38
9	Beck	*Die Schachmaschine*	36
10	Schiller	*Maria Stuart*	36

Figure 6. Weighted Performances by Genre

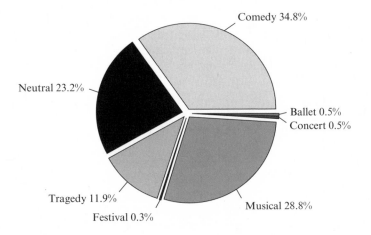

authors among the fifty most-performed plays in Weimar are Goethe's "Die Mitschuldigen" and Lessing's "Minna von Barnhelm" (1767), both conceptions of the 1760s — evidence that comedy, like sentimentality, was a holdover from the taste of the previous generation. Nevertheless, comedy held a more important place in Weimar Classicism than is usually acknowledged, because in fact much of the musical drama was comic in the same sense that the works labeled "Lustspiel," "Posse," and "Vaudeville" were: type comedies set in folksy or middle-class German circumstances (unless they were translated) that required few sets and little preparation.

Figure 7. Performances in Gotha 1755–1779

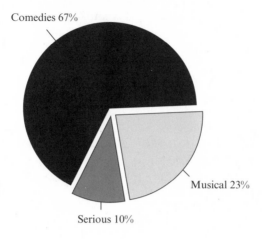

Figure 8. Performance in translations 1791–1817

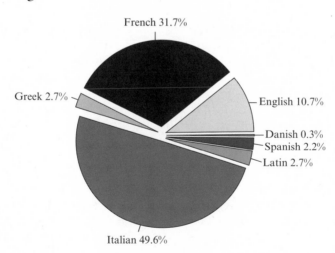

All the musical works designated "Singspiel" and most of those designated "Oper" had comic plots. In effect then, the repertoire has shifted balance not so much away from comedy as toward musical comedy.

But musical drama, like *Schauspiel*, is not exclusively comedy, even when it ends happily. First, it includes the then newly fashionable serious genres of monodrama and duodrama, in which the actors did not actually sing, but declaimed to full musical accompaniment. Second, not all opera was comic; Mozart's *La clemenza di Tito* and Gluck's *Iphigénie en Tauride*, a production in which Goethe understandably took extreme interest, were both substantial successes in Weimar.[13] Third, comic musical dramas like *Die Zauberflöte* and *Don Giovanni* were also widely understood to address serious themes. Three Mozart operas were among the four most performed works in Weimar not just because Mozart was popular, but also because the management thought they were important. Goethe and Mozart shared the aspiration of raising the German *Singspiel* to the level of genuine opera, the label used for *Die Zauberflöte* both by Mozart and in Weimar.[14] It is well known that Goethe began a sequel to *Die Zauberflöte*, but less well known that several of his libretti were set by numerous composers;[15] he desisted from his efforts to reform the *Singspiel* only after Mozart's *Entführung aus dem Serail* showed the goal had already been achieved. The importance of musical drama is also reflected in the provenance of translated works. Discussions of the Weimar stage tend to focus on the introduction of Shakespeare, Calderón, and classical plays, but Figure 8 shows that fully half the foreign texts were Italian in origin, mostly because of the volume of musical drama. And Goethe was, in fact, very interested in the comic operas he saw in Rome. Just under a third of the translations were from French, which also includes a good number of operas. Evidently musical drama was central to Goethe's concept of the modern German stage.

Musical drama embodies classical harmony both aurally and visually. Because musical harmony can be heard, it makes the harmony and balance so central to the ideology of German Classicism objectively present to the senses on the Weimar stage in the 1790s; the insight became central to the prominent discussions of music in the Romantic generation from Tieck and Wackenroder on. Musical drama also offered visual embodiment of harmony through dance, frequent enactments of musical performance on stage, elaborate sets, and emblematic stage spectacle that operated in harmony and occasionally in counterpoint with the text. Such spectacle had developed in the late sixteenth century first in the spheres of masque, opera, and ballet, and was carried over to spoken drama only gradually. In 1816 Goethe asserted that spectacle was central: "Genau aber genommen, so ist nichts theatralisch, als was für die Augen zugleich symbolisch ist"[16] (To speak precisely, nothing is theatrical that is not simultaneously symbolic for the eyes). Goethe's focus on tableau and ensemble acting constituted a final step in this development by integrating the actors into the stage picture instead of having them play individually before it. Opera and ballet are usually perceived as categorically different genres from drama on the European stage, but, for German Classicism, musical theater and spoken theater were continuous categories. Music and operatic structures pervaded Goethe's and Schiller's dramatic activity at all levels — conception, writing, performance.[17] The dominance of music on the stage in Weimar corresponded not to an audience preference for something unintellectual, but to Goethe's most serious aspirations for the German theater.

Most of the serious popular dramas are *Schauspiele*, in which the heroine survives and usually marries her lover; their themes are familiar in German drama from Lessing through Weimar Classicism. Even the most trivial involve ethical issues, quite simple to be sure and enacted by villains and by good characters with only a fault or two. Their Rousseauist Sturm und Drang heritage appears in the paranoid situations of protagonists robbed of their good name (Schröder's *Das Porträt der Mutter* [The Mother's Portrait, 1786], for example, or Iffland's *Die Jäger* [The Huntsmen, 1785]) or even of their identity (Weissenthurn's *Der Wald bei Hermannstadt* [The Forest at Hermannstadt, 1807], Zschokke's *Abällino* [novel 1793, but popular in later dramatic form]). More than their predecessors, popular late-century plays muffle class issues and confine themselves to a bourgeois atmosphere of family and work managed from the home (regardless of their ostensible class in historical dramas); the villains can be stepmothers, competitors, or superiors, but not irresponsible rulers. Although the family tensions turn on love, the seduction theme favored through the 1770s is often replaced by the threat of unwanted marriage. The hero triumphs through specifically "German" honesty and plain-speaking, in historical as well as explicitly bourgeois drama. Kotzebue's Inca warriors, Zschokke's Italian Renaissance nobles, Weissenthurn's medieval kings, and Matthäus von Collin's Roman nobles (*Regulus*, 1802) all suffer from the same difficulties and practice the same sentimental family relations.

They also speak the same language, the sober, relatively neutral prose with occasional flights of intense emotion popularized by Lessing. Like his, these plays are talky; long paragraphs are common, and speeches of two pages not a rarity. Even the exotic historical dramas with large, picturesque casts involve virtually no physical actions on stage; the few stage directions refer to expressions of the emotions obvious from the content of the speeches or from plot elements about to be revealed. The plays have single plots, clear expositions, logical connections between scenes, and, normally, a small cast of characters drawn from the standard types of Enlightenment comedy. So circumstantial are the speeches and so carefully do the plays avoid gaps in the action that the effect is more narrative than dramatic. In *Die Sonnenjungfrau* (The Sun Maiden, 1789) and *Die Spanier in Peru* (The Spaniards in Peru, 1795), two of his most popular plays everywhere, Kotzebue allows himself the occasional "meanwhile back at the ranch" situation, in which two scenes cover the same time period in different places. These are the legitimate ancestors of nineteenth-century melodrama and of the Hollywood western.

The Weimar Style

Against this background it becomes possible to characterize the drama of Weimar Classicism more precisely, for there are important continuities as well as differences between the popular theater and classical canon. Goethe's and Schiller's concerns with humanity, with ethics, with national identity, with the individual in society, the natural self, and sentiment are not unique derivations from Lessing and the Sturm und Drang but are shared by their immediate popular contemporaries. Both groups stake self-consciously bourgeois claims to previously aristocratic spheres of activity, even when the setting is historical. The popular dramatists tend to work with petty officials and the mercantile classes, while Goethe, Schiller, and after them Heinrich von Kleist (1777–1811) and Zacharias Werner (1768–1823) return to the monarchs and high nobles demanded by Aristotle's *Poetics*. Nevertheless, after the assassination of Gessler in *Wilhelm Tell* (1804), the greatest honor conceivable for the aristocrats Berta and Rudenz is assimilation to the Swiss bourgeoisie. Almost all drama of the period makes the same compromise between bourgeois autonomy and cooperation with a legitimate ruling class, whether it is a matter of driving out the evil Gessler, coming to terms with King Thoas in *Iphigenie auf Tauris* (1787), or preventing a dishonest official from ruining the lives of the honest forester in Iffland's *Die Jäger*.

Like the popular drama, the canonical texts center on family dynamics. Schiller's Marquis Posa wishes that Don Carlos cared as much about politics as about whether his father loves him; his Wallenstein stands between his daughter and his sister; the rival queens in *Maria Stuart* (1800) have both been loved by the faithless Leicester, and so it goes. Even in *Wilhelm Tell* Berta von Bruneck is threatened with a forced marriage to an unwelcome suitor by Gessler, who is for all practical purposes her foster father. Goethe departs further from the sentimental rhetoric of bourgeois drama than Schiller does, but bourgeois plot structures dominate. Egmont's beloved Klärchen is the typical girl from modest circumstances seduced by an attractive but slightly weak-willed aristocrat who will not marry her, and she dies by her own act, like Sara Sampson, Emilia Galotti, or Luise Millerin. Even Egmont's enemy Alba is preoccupied with his relation to his own son. Iphigenie is more bound to her father than any Lessing heroine; after she learns of Agamemnon's death, Thoas becomes her "second father" (l. 2004) whom she will not abandon without permission to run off with Orestes. The political ramifications of the conflict in Goethe's *Die natürliche Tochter* (The Natural Daughter, 1804) remain vague and general, while the action and motivations turn on relationships within the family; in a wonderful reversal, the result of the heroine's abduction is not death but marriage to an unwanted but good bourgeois husband.[18] In the next generation Kleist's Käthchen von Heilbronn still has a devoted father chasing after her. Even the three popular Mozart works in Weimar, *Die Zauberflöte*, *Don Giovanni*, and *Die Entführung aus dem Serail* all centrally involve an abducted heroine and a loving father figure.

A clear trajectory connects the bourgeois form of *Die Geschwister*, Goethe's most popular play in Weimar, and of *Stella* (1776, second version staged 1806, publ. 1816) to the radically classical *Iphigenie*. The first two, from the mid-seventies, are sentimental dramas. *Stella* elaborates the last two acts of a Lessing tragedy: the confrontation between the younger current beloved and the older, abandoned mistress (with child, as in *Miß Sara Sampson*). *Die Geschwister* deals with an erotic bond between an older brother/foster-father, William (also the name of Sara Sampson's father), and his daughter Marianne. The improbable endings of both plays are in accord with the romance endings so popular in Kotzebue and Iffland. In *Stella* all agree happily to a *ménage à trois* brokered by Cäcilie, the older of the two beloveds, and in *Die Geschwister* Marianne turns out to be not Wilhelm's sister, but his promised bride, entrusted to Wilhelm by her mother Charlotte on her deathbed in lieu of the relationship she and Wilhelm never realized.[19] In both plays the happy ending depends on an older woman who has suffered. *Iphigenie*, first written (in prose, the bourgeois medium) only three years later, also has the improbable happy ending of romance. Like Marianne, Iphigenie is too preoccupied with her father to consider the proposal of a highly respectable suitor. When her brother arrives, he concurs, like Wilhelm, with this rejection, albeit for different reasons. The eroticism appropriate to the recognition scene in *Die Geschwister*, where we learn that Wilhelm has always known he was not Marianne's brother, carries over to *Iphigenie*, where it frightens the true brother Orestes. Like the dead Charlotte (Iphigenie considers herself figuratively dead in Tauris) and the sad Cäcilie, Iphigenie mediates between the conflicting imperatives embodied in Thoas and Orestes. Phrases from *Stella* like "Du Gute, Duldende, Hoffende" (617; you good one, suffering one, hoping one) and "Immer dem freundlichen, vermittelnden Wort widerstrebend" (617; always resisting the kindly, mediating word) anticipate the characteristic substantivized adjectives and participial language of *Iphigenie* as well as its content. Goethe has translated bourgeois drama into the foreign medium of Greek tragedy, or, in terms of his own language of the 1790s, elevated the reality of bourgeois circumstances into the ideal of Greece.

The popular dramas also offer some insight into the improbable conclusions of these plays. Typical endings in popular *Schauspiele* and tragedies include patriotic sacrificial deaths, noble renunciation of love in favor of a best friend, general reconciliations as fathers see the light of reason, and melodramatic proofs of identity at the last moment (the latter two are also found in comedies of the period). Even Schiller, the most popular and active proponent of tragedy in the period, wrote two extremely popular and important "Schauspiele": *Wilhelm Tell* and *Wallensteins Lager*, the most performed of all Schiller's plays in Weimar. Tragicomedy is not a problem for the dramatists in the period, despite the fussing of neoclassicist theorists. Between the mid-seventeenth and the later eighteenth century it was rare for tragedies or operas anywhere in Europe, however serious their subject matter, to end unhappily.[20] Erich Heller's famous title, "Goethe and the Avoidance of Tragedy" accuses Goethe of avoiding tragedy when in fact his endings reflect the eighteenth-century norm.[21] It makes more sense to focus on how Weimar Classicism recovered tragedy in such circumstances.

Much debate in the last fifty years has centered on just how conciliatory the endings of Goethe's classical dramas, including *Faust*, actually are, with positions ranging from the perfectibilist (the conciliatory ending embodies classical faith in harmony) to the nihilist (any appearance of harmony is simply ironic), to borrow terms once common in the *Faust* scholarship. Awareness that the normal ending in the period was happy will not settle it, by any means, but it suggests that nihilism arising out of irony would have been barely perceptible to most of Goethe's audience. What can be learned from the debate is that Goethe avoided not so much tragedy as clarity in his endings. Schiller's conclusions are less ambiguous than simply double. His protagonists find certainty, but to embrace it usually means death, so that the end is at once both happy and unhappy. Goethe's penchant for ambiguous endings is connected to the fascination with disguise, masking, secrecy, transformation, and revelation that pervades his work. But it is also specifically rooted in the Schillerian notion of freedom as play so central to the ideology of German Classicism. Ambiguity is Goethe's form of play; doubleness Schiller's. For both — and the Romantic generation followed them in this — an ending remains open to further reflection. The impossibility of full closure corresponds to the Idealist inaccessibility of truth: in this fashion Goethe and Schiller reinvented a form for tragedy that questions Enlightenment optimism without denying its faith in the importance of reason.

As a reinvention of tragedy, the dramas claim a new seriousness, indeed classical status, both as successors in the continuous line of classicizing art begun in the Renaissance, and as the basis of a national canon. And in ways besides their endings the dramas stood out already in their own day as alien, high art, poetic, indeed "classical." The plays are poetic in ways that those of the popular contemporaries, despite strong emotions, are not. They are in the verse that Goethe's training efforts made practicable on the German stage. Although he and Schiller did not write the first verse dramas in German (Baroque and serious Enlightenment dramas were in alexandrines) or even the first in blank verse (Lessing's *Nathan der Weise*), they made it obvious to the generation of Kleist, Zacharias Werner, and above all, August Wilhelm Schlegel as translator of Shakespeare, that serious German drama was in blank verse.[22] In contrast to the contemporary plain style, they cultivate an elevated language based on classical linguistic and rhetorical models and a much richer array of similes, metaphors, symbols, and verbal motifs that also appear visually. Like Shakespeare, but unlike their more popular contemporaries, both Goethe and Schiller came to drama from lyric poetry. Schiller's, and especially Goethe's, plays were difficult for their audiences, as they are today, because they introduced a specifically lyrical dramatic verse to a stage on which everyone else spoke the language of rationalism.

In addition, the plays are more complex than those of their contemporaries, who still employed the unitary linear plots prescribed by Enlightenment neoclassicism. While Weimar Classicism lacks the separate, secondary plots of Shakespearean comedy, it adopts the double pairs of figures common in comic opera, as in *Die Zauberflöte*, where Papageno and Papagena echo Tamino and Pamina. The emergence of complexity is easiest to trace in Schiller, because he attached the pairs to contrasted ideas and because he mastered the technique only gradually.[23] The famously complicated plot of *Don Carlos* (1787) makes it debatable whether the tragedy is that of the title figure or of his friend, the Marquis Posa. In the Wallenstein trilogy the tragedies of the equivalent figures fall into two separate plays: that of the trusting young hero in *Die Piccolomini* (1799) and that of the older leader in *Wallensteins Tod* (1799). *Maria Stuart*'s two queens experience symmetrical tragedies — sensual Maria loses the world, rational Elizabeth loses her beloved Leicester — that both pivot around their confrontation in the third act. In *Die Jungfrau von Orleans* (1801) the central figure, Johanna, hovers between the oppositions embodied in France and England and in her various lovers (Dunois versus LaHire at the French court, the two Frenchmen versus Lionel on the English side), while in *Die Braut von Messina* (1803) symmetry pervades all levels of the text and cast, with the two brother/lovers struggling for the love of the mother/sister reflected in the double chorus. *Wilhelm Tell* floats so effortlessly among the different strands of its triple set of characters (the conspirators; Tell; Berta and Rudenz), different classes, and, finally, operatic and spoken drama that the problems of *Don Carlos* are entirely forgotten.

The dramas Goethe revised or wrote after the mid-1780s already combine the easy flow of scenes in *Urfaust* (ca. 1775) and *Götz von Berlichingen* (1773) with tightly closed structures. The title figure in *Egmont* (1788, but begun 1775) roams among three separate worlds (street, bourgeois dwelling, halls of power) with three separate casts that do not interact, yet the play proceeds with an inexorable logic.[24] Although *Iphigenie* maintains the neoclassical unities of plot, time, and place, its language evokes the absent Greece and the absent tragic past so consistently that it engages shifting dichotomies more complex than any Schiller play before *Die Jungfrau von Orleans*.[25] While *Torquato Tasso* (1790) operates with more stringent symmetries (Virgil/Ariosto, two Leonoras, Tasso/Antonio) that all represent the dichotomy ideal/real, the play offers various models for their relationship to one another that range from easy co-existence to animosity. The most extreme example is *Faust I* (1808), in this respect Goethe's most profoundly classical play. Its characters and concepts appear in constantly shifting pairs and trios, such as the debates in the prologues on the stage and in heaven, the constant arguing of Faust and Mephistopheles, the two souls in Faust's own breast (1112). At different times the devil appears as the opposing counterpart of the Lord, Faust, and Margarete, yet it would be problematic to equate the three. Similarly, Mephistopheles is both the devil and a spirit of negation, who functions only as part of a larger, virtually Hegelian system of eternally repeated negation and sublation. The resulting web of symmetries and contrasts is propelled forward by its own instability and can end only in the opposing claims of Mephistopheles and the Voice from Above that Margarete is damned or saved — or in Part 2 almost three decades later, in Faust's eternal pursuit of the eternally receding Eternal Feminine.

Tragedy, as a recovered classical form, is by definition cosmopolitan, and German classical drama, like most earlier Renaissance and post-Renaissance tragedy, tends to be set somewhere other than home. To be sure, the popular dramatists also wrote occasional historical dramas, and Kotzebue strays farther from the bounds of Europe than Goethe or Schiller (although Schiller's *Turandot* would have been an exception, had he completed it). But more than their contemporaries, Goethe and Schiller gravitated to the large myths of Europe, not just those of classical antiquity, as in *Iphigenie*, but also of modern Europe, like Maria Stuart and Joan of Arc. The mature Schiller drew his subjects from Spain, England, France, Sicily, and Switzerland. Only the Wallenstein trilogy is set on then German soil (in Bohemia, a cultural borderland), and it emphasizes the internationalism of the imperial troops and their indifference to national boundaries. Indeed, their allegiance is not to any state, but to Wallenstein personally; ultimately the Italian Octavio Piccolomini preserves the army for the Austrian Habsburgs. Of Goethe's classical plays, only *Die natürliche Tochter* is not explicitly set outside of Germany; nevertheless the repeated references to king and major court, the French source,[26] and the title, which is a transparent mutation of Diderot's *Le fils naturel*, all suggest a French rather than German context. Only in Kleist and Zacharias Werner, both promoted in Weimar by Goethe, does a specifically German milieu become self-evident in German tragic drama. The first part of *Faust*, to be sure, is set in Germany. But it also proves the rule by parodying and building on creative figures, texts, and images from the greater European tradition, such as the Bible, Homer, Virgil, Greek tragedy, the history of classical sculpture, medieval lyric, Shakespeare, Calderón, Raphael, eighteenth-century opera, bourgeois tragedy, Byron, Renaissance frescos, Baroque painting.[27] For Weimar Classicism, to be German is to be European.

In a characteristic blurring of political and aesthetic categories, Weimar cosmopolitanism was formal as well as thematic, and historical as well as geographical. Act 3 of *Faust II*, Goethe's reflection on his place in literary history from the perspective of 1827, traces European drama from Greek tragedy to contemporary opera, and opera as the defining genre of modern drama subsumes within itself the entire history of European literature. Weimar Classicism was as much Greek as French. *Iphigenie* takes Euripides rather than Racine for its model and creates a language that reads like translations from Greek; this German equivalent of Greek became the standard rhetoric of Goethe's and Schiller's dramas. *Die Braut von Messina* reintroduced the Greek chorus that was generally avoided by dramatists who otherwise cultivated classical forms in the sixteenth through eighteenth centuries. When Schiller asserts in his foreword, "Über den Gebrauch des Chors in der Tragödie" (On the Use of the Chorus in Tragedy), that the chorus forms a wall around the play, he points to the influence of Greek tragedy or at least its legitimating presence in the general insistence on the autonomy of art in Weimar Classicism. By implication he claims the same function for the chorus in opera, which Goethe was to designate as the successor to the Greek chorus in *Faust II*. Seen in conjunction with the simultaneous stagings of classical tragedies and comedies, these Greek elements were readily acknowledged at the time as an essential strand of the Weimar style.

Another strand was Pedro Calderón de la Barca (1600–1681), the great Spanish Golden Age dramatist. Goethe's assertions that he ranked Calderón with Shakespeare should be taken seriously, even though Goethe later returned to Shakespeare as the more important figure.[28] Calderón's importance has been documented for *Faust*, but numerous elements of his famous play, *La vida es sueño* (Life is a Dream), find their way into *Die natürliche Tochter*: the fall on horseback from a cliff, the child raised in seclusion and ignorance of high parentage, the cautious father engaged in power struggles, unexpected dream-like magnificence barely tasted then snatched away.[29] *Die Braut von Messina*, set in Spanish-ruled Sicily, also shows strong Calderonian influence: the love competition, the preoccupation with secrecy, the importance of coincidence are all hallmarks of Calderonian drama, while the abduction from the convent figures largely in *La devoción de la cruz* (Devotion to the Cross), translated by August Wilhelm Schlegel in 1802. In his review of Calderón's *La hija del aire* (Daughter of the Air) of 1822 Goethe particularly admires the regularity and symmetry of Calderón's dramatic practice, values central to his and Schiller's own dramas, particularly to those written after 1800. Goethe seems also to have responded intuitively to Calderón's Baroque manner of matching verbal to visual imagery. Although the frequent images of sleepwalking and dangerous driving in *Egmont* never translate into literal teetering on the stage, *Die natürliche Tochter* symbolically foreshadows the fall of the heroine and her possible resurrection to high social standing by her literal fall from a horse in the first act, where she is carried onto the stage apparently dead, then miraculously recovers. This technique becomes the norm in *Faust II:* "Mitternacht," in which the personifications of Want, Need, Debt, and Care appear on stage, was in fact first drafted around 1801. Examples of emblematic dramaturgy in *Wilhelm Tell* are the on-stage demolition of the fortress and the rainbow that presides over the swearing of the oath on the Rütli, to which Goethe returned for the emblematic introductory scene to *Faust II,* "Anmutige Gegend" (Charming Landscape), in 1827. Goethe's sponsorship of a complete translation comparable to the Schlegel-Tieck translation of Shakespeare, together with his stagings in Weimar,[30] created a standing for Calderón in Germany that he has never been accorded in Anglo-American theater.

Opera, particularly Italian, but also French and German, is the last major aspect of Weimar cosmopolitanism. The affinity of *Faust I* for opera has been well documented;[31] indeed, the plot is better known internationally in the operatic versions, particularly that of Gounod, than in Goethe's own. Margarete — pure in her fallen state, devoted, passionate — became the paradigmatic opera heroine of the nineteenth century. More important is *Faust*'s emphasis on elaborate stage spectacle and musical performances, like singing and dancing peasants, choruses of soldiers, angels, and demonic spirits. On his first trip to Italy Goethe was particularly struck by Italian comic opera, and not only revised his two successful *Singspiele, Erwin und Elmire* and *Jery und Bätely*, into verse, but also created for the second a fully musical and elaborated finale such as he was encountering in Italy. At precisely this time he shifted from prose to verse drama, even for *Faust*, which he later recast almost entirely into verse. The two scenes of *Faust* composed in Italy, "Wald und Höhle" (Forest and Cave) and "Hexenküche" (Witch's Kitchen), signal his new interest in opera. The first ends with Faust's impassioned speech, "Was ist die Himmelsfreud' in ihren Armen" (3345–65; What joy of heaven in her arms), which is structured like an opera aria, and its image of the self as flooding river (3350–51) evokes a common image in Pietro Metastasio, the dominant librettist of opera seria. "Hexenküche" contains several set pieces more designed for chanting than recitation and some of the liveliest stage spectacle in all of *Faust*: the play of the apes, the fire in the chimney, the magic mirror, the witch's magic potion. Goethe's sense of common endeavor with Mozart can only have been reinforced by the appearance of *Die Zauberflöte* in 1791, just three years after he wrote his own magical scene. Clearly, sculpture and architecture were by no means the only Italian influences on Goethe's classicism.

Schiller's work also became increasingly operatic, a quality doubtless learned from Goethe. The crowd scene in *Wallensteins Lager* is his first great success in this genre. Instead of the concise narrative exposition so typical of Shakespeare, Schiller imitates the first scene of *Egmont:* the exposition emerges from the seemingly irrelevant activities of the loafing soldiers in the camp, and the piece is a series of lively stage pictures with inserted music. Schiller is at his most operatic in his last plays. *Die Jungfrau von Orleans* calls repeatedly for musical accompaniment, not just for supporting realistic effects like Shakespearean flourishes for military events, but as an active part of the play.[32] Johanna's miraculous escape from prison in act 5, scene 11, for example, takes place to the music of the French army's battle march. When Johanna first hears it she cries that her soul will escape its prison "auf den Flügeln eures Kriegsgesangs" (3415; on the wings of your battle-hymn); after she leaps free (anticipating Puccini's Tosca by a century) a guard asks whether she has wings. She has literally escaped her prison, and the play has escaped the bonds of reality on the wings of song: Schiller could not identify the genre more clearly. *Wilhelm Tell* is full of elaborate stage spectacle, choruses, and songs all through. It is not surprising that his plays also were mined for operas in the succeeding century, with versions by Rossini (*Guillaume Tell*), Donizetti (*Maria Stuarda*), and Verdi (*Luisa Millerin, Don Carlos*) still performed today. The prominence of opera in the Weimar repertoire was thus not as a popular alternative to its serious educational works, but the two are continuous with one another.

The common view of the drama of Weimar classicism as a form of French neoclassicism with a healthy leavening of Shakespeare follows Goethe's analysis of the situation in Germany in the 1760s and 1770s in *Wilhelm Meisters theatralische Sendung* (Wilhelm Meister's Theatrical Mission).[33] The blending begins already in Lessing, continues in the experiments of the Sturm und Drang, and is fully developed by the end of the 1780s, both in canonical works like *Don Carlos* and the well-organized but indecorous works of the popular dramatists. It had already taken place much earlier in England, in the heroic tragedy of the age of Dryden, Otway, and Rowe. There can be no question that Weimar Classicism draws heavily on neoclassical forms and conventions, nor that the dramatists admired Shakespeare profoundly and learned from him. But Goethe ultimately concluded that Shakespeare was unstageable without adaptation.[34] The specific mode of adaptation Goethe and Schiller practiced points to the richer cosmopolitanism of their dramaturgy. Schiller replaces the porter scene in *Macbeth* with a hymn to the dawn, and Goethe transforms *Romeo and Juliet* virtually into a *Singspiel:* musical drama and its emblematic stage spectacle are crucial for their conception of what made something stageable in their own time. To consider, with Stendhal, dramatic form only under the rubric "Shakespeare vs. Racine," misses the point. Weimar Classicism is more catholic in its tastes — that is, well on the way to *Gesamtkunstwerk.*

Goethe and Schiller were confident about their extension of drama, but they did reflect about crossing the line into narrative in a joint discussion summarized in Goethe's essay "Über epische und dramatische Dichtung" (On Epic and Dramatic Poetry, 1797).[35] However, Schiller's occasional experimentation with narrative forms in his dramas suggests that the essay is best understood as an exploration of how epic can be used, as lyric was more obviously, to enrich drama.[36] The greatest impact was in characterization. The epistolary novel of the eighteenth century brought to the modern interior subject newly emerged from neoclassical drama a capacity to reflect at length on its feelings, including, for the first time, those not fully conscious. In *Werther* Goethe created the ultimate self-reflective sentimental hero; furthermore he added to the subject's reflection on itself an additional layer of reflection by a narrator descended (though much toned down) from the satiric novels of Henry Fielding and other Enlightenment narrators. Popular dramas on the Weimar stage teem with sentimental heroes and Werther's self-reflective rhetoric. Goethe and Schiller, however, created a dramatic idiom to encompass the narrative layer of reflection as well; in their dramas feelings are expressed, reflected upon by the characters, and then probed, analyzed, and reanalyzed so that the same analytic process must be repeated by the spectator or reader.[37]

These plays stage the self-consciousness that became the central psychological and epistemological problem of German Idealism. Characters worry less about the morality of their actions than about their motivation, and about whether they can know their motivation. Their murky depths of self became the enablers of nineteenth-century psychology and of Freud. Iphigenie, for example, tells of her ancestors' crimes, and refers several times to the culminating one, the sacrifice of herself by her father. But only in the last act does she manage to articulate how she felt at that moment (1850), and thereby seem finally to purge her preoccupation with the sins of her fathers and allow the play to move away from Tauris, the prison of her past. Schiller's Johanna loses her power when she is attacked from within by a feeling she cannot understand. Only when she recognizes that it is love for Lionel, her enemy, and with great effort renounces both it and her physical existence can she return to lead the French to victory. In Kleist's idiosyncratic response to this play, *Das Käthchen von Heilbronn* (1808), the hero spends the entire play trying to discover the heroine's motivation for loving him so blindly, which she herself is unable to explain, and then to discover his true feelings. The aesthetic alienation of these plays has now become epistemological and psychological as well.

Deepened psychology results, finally, in new moral problems. While the popular dramatists of the time remained trapped in the rationalist struggle between humanity and evil, Weimar Classicism adopted the Kantian recognition that individuality is tied to the striving for universality, and that the struggle for humanity is therefore internal. The moral ideals remain those of the Enlightenment and the Sturm und Drang, but because they are based on a more internalized notion of identity, they become harder to name and realize. Thus, the central question of Goethe's *Egmont*, "who is Egmont?" is paradigmatic.[38] Although everyone talks about him, he does not appear on stage until the middle of the second act, and then he repeatedly claims neither to know nor to want to know his own inner self. Is he good or evil, Flemish or Spanish, a private or a public figure? When, at the end of the third act, he throws open his cloak to reveal the true, the private Egmont, as he claims, but in full Spanish court regalia, he hardly clarifies the situation. Is he part of the problem or the solution to it? The play ends noncommittally: the plot suggests he dies in vain, while the allegorical spectacle of Klärchen as Freedom, the famous "leap into opera" that so irritated Schiller, suggests the opposite.[39] Schiller's protagonists are more like Iphigenie; they earnestly seek to know who they really are and how to act in accordance with that knowledge. Unlike Goethe, Schiller tends not to leave his endings open; his characters act — usually they die — and thereby affirm the possibility of willed moral action, freedom. In this respect Goethe and after him Kleist raise the moral problems that follow from the new psychology more boldly; this is probably why they were less popular than Schiller. In Goethe, self-knowledge is so deeply buried and achieving it so strenuous that little time or energy remains for moral action. The paradigmatic example, of course, is *Faust*, where Goethe invokes the whole panoply of Baroque morality theater to set an essentially interior stage. The "Prolog im Himmel" (Prologue in Heaven) makes God the spokesman for natural right, which demands striving for salvation and explicitly acknowledges that striving in the world entails error. It remains the function of the devil to call repeatedly to Faust's and to our attention that we live not in nature but in society, and that nature's error is society's evil. Thus the spontaneous, natural love between Faust and Gretchen can only destroy her and her family. Morality rooted in human nature and in an ethic of self-development is not compatible with social organization. Had Goethe reversed the roles of God and Devil, the play would have been less shocking: as it stands, he has identified the uniquely modern moral dilemma that the choice between good and evil in a post-Kantian self shatters the unity on which its very existence is premised.

The Weimar Texts

In conclusion let us briefly survey the canonical dramas of Weimar Classicism, the full-length verse dramas of Goethe and Schiller, and also Goethe's *Egmont*, which is generally considered the first drama of Weimar Classicism (even though it is in prose) and even regarded as the single most influential play of the movement.[40] *Egmont* was begun in 1775, the last two acts were completed in 1787 while Goethe was in Italy, and it was first successfully produced in Schiller's adaptation debuted in Weimar by Iffland only in 1796. The difference between the Schillerian version and Goethe's text marks the true innovations of the Weimar style, for the adaptation reveals the limited definition of serious drama at the beginning of the period; Schiller's *Egmont* is a historical drama of character with striking moments of Shakespearean influence, but not too many. Egmont appears first in his public role, as the war hero loved and admired by the citizens of Brussels, and then as the kindly but harried ruler of his people threatened by the religious intolerance of its new Spanish masters. As the Duke of Alba enters Brussels to pacify it and ensnare its Flemish leaders, Egmont and William of Orange, Egmont dallies in the private space of his bourgeois beloved, Klärchen, until, against better advice, he accepts Alba's invitation to meet and is arrested. In the last act Klärchen takes poison when she learns that Egmont will be executed; then the imprisoned Egmont triumphs over Alba by winning the affection of his son Ferdinand, accepts his fate, and goes to his death triumphantly as a martyr to freedom. The exposition among the citizens of Brussels is modeled on *Julius Caesar*, and the sentimental family situation built around Klärchen is in the familiar tradition of bourgeois drama, but heightened by the necessity for the hero to decide not between aristocratic rank and love, but between public responsibility and love.

Although Schiller added little to Goethe's text, the rearrangements and cuts are telling. Goethe's text is an elaborately symmetrical arrangement of scenes that move constantly between different social realms and between indoor and outdoor spaces. Schiller rearranged and consolidated this material to minimize set changes and to show the alternatives between public action and private love unambiguously. But in Goethe's text, there are many more options; Egmont plays different roles to different audiences, sometimes the Spanish gentleman, sometimes the simple Fleming, but always an enigma. Rather than show how he develops, the play poses the problem: who is this Egmont, and by extension, what is a real self? It is also evident that Goethe's Shakespearean tendency to let the action wander all over was too difficult to stage and too difficult to follow in a theater where more or less realistic sets were the norm. Finally, Schiller also deleted two songs sung by Klärchen on stage and a staged dream, in which Klärchen dressed as Freedom appears to Egmont sleeping in prison.[41] By eliminating the elements that made *Egmont* more operatic, both in terms of music and of stage spectacle, as well as by simplifying the concept of subjectivity, Schiller adapted out of the play precisely those elements that were to be unique to Weimar Classicism. The play continued to be popular in a slightly adjusted version of Schiller's adaptation until late in the nineteenth century, when the desire to use Beethoven's occasional music brought Goethe's own text back onto the stage. And yet, under Goethe's influence in the 1790s, Schiller adapted his own dramaturgy to Goethe's, often according to the model of *Egmont*.

Goethe's *Iphigenie auf Tauris* is commonly taken as the paradigmatic drama of Weimar Classicism. Its first version was performed, with Goethe in the role of Orestes, in 1779, the same year in which Gluck's reform opera *Iphigénie en Tauride* premiered. After repeated revisions that wavered between prose and verse, Goethe finished the final, blank-verse version in Italy and published it in 1787. The plot follows that of Euripides' *Iphigenia in Tauris* in its representation of how Orestes, sent to Tauris to steal the statue of Artemis and thereby end the curse on himself and his family, unexpectedly finds the sister he thought sacrificed years before in Aulis. But Goethe made three significant modernizations: he transformed the Furies that torment Orestes into internalized visions of them; he made Thoas, king of the Taurians, a suitor for the hand of Iphigenie; and he made Iphigenie insist upon telling the truth to Thoas so that he allows them to leave for Greece without the intervention of a *deus ex machina*. The adherence to Euripides was a modern element for its time. The French neoclassical tradition — which this play is often considered to resemble because of its rigorous unity, symmetry, dignified diction, and small cast — allowed characters to express their feelings almost exclusively to confidants, but Goethe begins with a long monologue, a Shakespearean device. In act 4 he has Iphigenie switch from blank verse to hymnic free verse in the "Parzenlied" for her moment of darkest recognition about human fate; with this move Goethe makes the first step toward restoring the Greek chorus to spoken drama in Europe. Although elevated, the diction is not that of neoclassical alexandrines, nor is it that of Shakespeare, despite the blank verse; instead it is modeled on the diction created by Klopstock for his odes and his epic, *Der Messias*, which has functioned as the German equivalent of Greek diction. The play foregrounds a sentimental but distanced form of love, the idealizing love of truth and humanity. Audiences and readers have often shared Goethe's apparent frustration with the play's idealism (Goethe called it "ganz verteufelt human") and lack of action, but it powerfully naturalizes the supernatural elements of the original and makes them represent phenomena recognizable as modern psychological structures — Orestes freed from the Furies by the intervention of his humane sister becomes a mythological representation of emotional healing. Male-centered and tradition-centered readings of the play often stop here, but Iphigenie is also freed by the action of the play from her deathlike state of separation from society and reintegrated into the world of time and action when she sets off to sea. Her recovery proceeds by her constant retelling of the curse on her family and of her own sacrifice. The play is not only psychologized, but presages the modern talking cure of psychoanalysis; the action of this play is talking, some of the most beautiful in the German language.

Torquato Tasso (1791) and *Die natürliche Tochter* (1804) are increasingly rarified versions of the formal and thematic model established by *Iphigenie*. Set at the Renaissance court of Alfonso d'Este, *Tasso* explores not the cure *from*, but the poet-hero's descent *into* madness as he fails to resolve the conflict between his pursuit of the ideal and the reality that surrounds him. His dissolution is signaled by outbreaks of physical and sexual violence, drawing a sword and kissing the Princess Leonore. The characters represent less individuals than drives toward the idealizing mental capacity or the literalizing physical self; Tasso and the Princess embody the first, Antonio and Leonore Sanvitale the second. Such plot as the long play contains exists largely in the paranoid mind of the hero; the fact that the two female protagonists share the same name makes them at one level opposing aspects of the same figure. The intensity and beauty of the language combined with the gentle, almost ritualized pageantry of what passes on stage reveal that important action is what takes place within the self, which can represent itself only in language, if then. *Die natürliche Tochter* takes this radically internalized psychology yet further. Neither locale nor character names are specified (although its source, the *Mémoires* of Stéphanie Bourbon-Conti [1798], deals with the French Revolution), all of the action except the highly symbolic opening of a trunk takes place off stage, and the details of the intrigues that surround the heroine remain largely unclarified. At the same time, some crucial relationship between individual conduct and social order is felt, rather than shown, to be at work. The play is often considered a torso because Goethe never completed the different continuations he had worked on, but this attitude is tantamount to considering *Faust I* incomplete without Part II, or a single Greek tragedy incomplete without the remainder of its trilogy.[42] Goethe's intention that the play be part of a trilogy suggests to what extent he conceived the drama in terms of Greek tragedy rather than the French neoclassical tragedy it only superficially resembles. Both *Tasso* and *Die natürliche Tochter* focus explicitly on the fate of the protagonist in the same sense that Greek tragedy does, but naturalized and psychologized as it is, fate becomes something much more in the individual's control. Even so, the love across class boundaries typical of bourgeois tragedy is central to both plays (Tasso loves the Princess; Eugenie, illegitimate daughter of a prince, marries a bourgeois official to save herself from exile), and scenes of symbolic stage spectacle in both evoke the dramaturgy of opera.[43] It remains unclear in both plays whether the protagonist ends with hope or in despair; the ambiguity registers the extent to which *Bildung* remains an ideal impossible of achievement rather than a naive hope.

It is hard to see how *Faust I*, Goethe's most substantial and sustained dramatic project, fits the patterns of his other Weimar dramas, especially since Goethe himself never staged it.[44] Far from the dignity of classical myth or history, it joins the popular plot of a scholar's pact with the devil to the typical seduction plot of bourgeois tragedy. It involves a large cast of often supernatural beings, it is mostly in rhymed madrigal verse, its language is often anything but restrained or decorous, its tone more cynical than humane. Its structure resembles less the tight, five-act, symmetrical organization of the other classical dramas, and more that of an epic, to which it is often compared. It comes closest to the other plays, perhaps, in the Lord's language in the "Prologue in Heaven," when he says the good man is always conscious of the right path, even in his darkest urges (328–29). Faust is drawn between the poles of this idealizing humanity and the destructive realism embodied in the devil Mephistopheles, just as Tasso is between the Princess and Antonio. By the end of Faust's Easter walk, these drives have been internalized into two souls that dwell within his breast (1112). *Faust*, too, represents a battle within the subject between the urge to play out one's innate natural drive, one's fate, on the one hand, and the demands imposed by living in a real social world on the other. Following his natural urges, Faust loves Margarete in what seems to both a fashion that is naturally good and necessary, and yet their love creates an intolerable situation, for it is unthinkable that they could settle down to a happy *ménage à trois* with Mephistopheles, to whom Faust is bound for the term of his earthly existence. The fact that Goethe could treat this same problem in such apparently different terms forces us to locate the essentials of his classical dramatic form in aspects the plays have in common, as we have done above.

Schiller's transition to a classical dramatic style followed in the wake of Goethe's. Schiller had arrived independently at blank verse drama with *Don Carlos* (1787), but its extreme length and sprawling plot made it less successful than his two Sturm und Drang plays, *Die Räuber* and *Kabale und Liebe*, and he kept shortening it — by as much as fifteen percent in the final version of 1805. Nevertheless, when he returned to drama again in the later 1790s, he took a new approach. *Don Carlos* had two plots, one dealing with Carlos's rivalry with his father and love for his stepmother, and one dealing with Marquis Posa and the freedom of the Netherlands. When *Wallenstein* threatened to grow similarly out of hand, Schiller divided it, in as yet only loose analogy with Greek tragedy, into a trilogy of two five-act tragedies, *Die Piccolomini* (1799) and *Wallensteins Tod* (1799), and *Wallensteins Lager* (1798). *Die Piccolomini* deals with family: Max Piccolomini is torn between the opposing shaping forces of his own father and Wallenstein, his admired leader and proposed father-in-law. *Wallensteins Tod* deals with politics: Wallenstein hesitates to betray his emperor and take definitive action. Typically Schiller's dramas are more explicitly ethical and political than Goethe's, and thus involve more confrontation between characters on the stage. The central concern, however, is still the same: the impossibility of realizing authentic selfhood in a less than ideal world. Iphigenie may talk about the curse on her family, Tasso about his artistry, Faust about knowledge, and Wallenstein about his stars, but they all mean the same thing: an identity that can be known only by dint of great effort and usually cannot be fully developed in a society not organized around individual identity. Even so, while Schiller's dramas increasingly approach the tightness and spareness of Goethe's, they remain set on the stage of the world, not that of the mind; hence they are less ambiguous and more Shakespearean than Goethe's. But in *Wallensteins Lager*, at first glance an extended Shakespearean mob scene, Schiller follows Goethe's technique from *Egmont* more closely. Large numbers of soldiers, mostly with very small roles, speak for their various masters who will appear in the following two plays. Schiller also adopted from *Egmont* the moving tableau and the use of music, both solo and chorus. The three parts of the trilogy thus represent the most important dramatic forms found at the time on the Weimar stage.

Maria Stuart (1800) and *Die Braut von Messina* (1803) adapt the style of *Iphigenie* and *Tasso* to Schiller's more realistic dramaturgy. Like them they have tightly structured, symmetrical plots that confront two modes of being associated with mind and body, or ideal and real. In the first play the poles are embodied in rival queens, Mary and Elizabeth, who come to represent a series of not quite congruent oppositions such as Catholic/Protestant, art/reality, sensuality/law. Unlike Goethe, Schiller always provides a third character who must choose between the alternatives; in this case, it is Leicester, who loves both queens. Partly perhaps because of its English subject matter, *Maria Stuart* is still reminiscent of English blank verse drama, but *Die Braut von Messina* is stylized in two more exotic traditions. The subject and rich imagery of the language evoke the awakening interest in Spanish culture among the Romantics, especially in the dramas of Calderón. Even more obvious is the play's evocation of Greek tragedy in the chorus of cavaliers, which for the first time on the German stage recreates the ancient Greek chorus by participating in and commenting upon the action. Indeed, the plot borrows heavily from Sophocles' *Oedipus Rex*, with the queen's efforts to escape the destruction of her house unwittingly bringing it about. Donna Isabella, the unfortunate ruler of Messina, is torn between her twin sons, who fight over everything, especially power, precedence, and love — their mother's and that of the mysterious beauty who turns out to be their sister. This long-hidden daughter, Beatrice, functions as the buried alter ego of Isabella, brought to light only to destroy the two princes, who, like the queens of *Maria Stuart*, embody the opposed poles of the Schillerian personality. The extreme stylization and dependence on coincidence bring the drama close to an opera libretto, and indeed the chorus's shifts from unrhymed to rhymed forms underscore the play's tendency to waver between Greek tragedy and operatic romance.

Schiller's other two classical dramas, his Joan of Arc play *Die Jungfrau von Orleans* (1801) and *Wilhelm Tell* (1804), resemble *Faust* more than *Iphigenie*. Both are epic in scope, use large casts in a variety of spaces, and engage in large amounts of stage spectacle and song. Although love across the boundaries of class continues to be present — peers of France and England fight for Johanna's love, for example — it becomes increasingly marginal to the plot. In *Wilhelm Tell* the motif appears only in a sub-plot, as the nobles Rudenz and Bertha von Bruneck, finally joined as a couple, request admission to the bourgeoisie. Bourgeois tragedy and even Greek tragedy largely yield to Shakespearean style and especially opera. Johanna and Wilhelm Tell face the same kinds of moral choices as their predecessors in other plays, but they tend to be expressed more symbolically than discursively. When Johanna is attracted to the English knight Lionel and loses her moral compass, she is driven from the French court; she recovers her own identity in a storm straight out of *King Lear;* exposure to nature's violence reduces the self to its innermost core. In *Wilhelm Tell* the symbolism extends to scenes with no human actors, reminiscent of the guttering candle and music on an empty stage that signify the death of Klärchen in *Egmont*. In the second act of *Wilhelm Tell*, after the representatives of the cantons have sworn their oath to resist Austrian tyranny and departed, the curtain remains open while music accompanies the sunrise. Goethe returned to this technique in the first scene of *Faust II*, where music accompanies the sunrise with only a sleeping Faust on stage.

Schiller subtitled *Die Jungfrau von Orleans* "Ein romantisches Schauspiel." He could have done the same for *Wilhelm Tell*. It is crucial to recognize that the full flowering of Weimar Classicism was in fact Romantic drama. Indeed, one might well add to the discussion the plays of Kleist — at least the three that were staged in Goethe's lifetime (*Der zerbrochene Krug* [The Broken Jug, 1808], *Das Käthchen von Heilbronn* [1810], *Prinz Friedrich von Homburg* [1821]) — since Kleist was first staged in Weimar and was clearly so Schillerian. One might also add the plays of Zacharias Werner that were staged in Weimar — *Wanda, Königin der Sarmaten* (1809) and *Der vierundzwanzigste Februar* (The 24th of February, 1810) — because at the time Werner was considered the obvious successor to Schiller.[45] Since the latter two figures are addressed in the Romanticism volume of this series, they will not be discussed in detail here, but their importance for the varying perception of the canon of classical drama in the nineteenth and twentieth centuries should not be overlooked.

The theatrical practice of Weimar Classicism is sui generis. It marries bourgeois and aristocratic values in a new professionalism of both actors and writers. For the first time in German culture the theater had a substantial repertoire of original German plays for performance and even, in the case at least of Kotzebue, Schiller, Goethe, and Mozart, for export. The backbone of this new dramatic culture was the sentimental bourgeois family drama with the conciliatory ending typical of the eighteenth century. In text and performance Goethe and Schiller shaped this material simultaneously toward greater seriousness and toward musical drama. They made drama poetic, complex and cosmopolitan in both thematic and formal terms. They pushed German drama beyond the amalgam of French neoclassicism and Shakespeare already inherited from the Sturm und Drang to absorb elements of ancient Greek, Calderonian, and above all operatic form. The expanded form enables the representation of the paradoxical moral situation of a profoundly interiorized post-Kantian self accessible only to the reflecting consciousness of characters and spectators. As in the narrative and lyric, Goethe, Schiller, and Mozart created the language and forms that enabled the younger generation of German Romantics to pursue the psychological and moral implications of the new subjectivity. Their immediate great dramatic inheritors were Kleist and Werner, both staged in Weimar, and in their wake the drama and opera of all nineteenth and twentieth-century Europe.

Notes

[1] I follow here the definitive history of the Viennese stage in the eighteenth century, Otto Rommel's *Die Alt-Wiener Volkskomödie; ihre Geschichte vom barocken Welt-Theater bis zum Tode Nestroys* (Vienna: A. Schroll, 1952).

[2] For effective summaries of the state of the German theater in Goethe's day, see Simon Williams, *German Actors of the Eighteenth and Nineteenth Centuries: Idealism, Romanticism, and Realism* (Westport, CT: Greenwood, 1985) and Lesley Sharpe, "Goethe and the Weimar Theatre," in *The Cambridge Companion to Goethe*, ed. Lesley Sharpe (Cambridge: Cambridge UP, 2002), 116–28.

[3] The oldest plays were Elizabethan, including several by Shakespeare, brought by the *englische Komödianten*, English troupes who came to the continent during periods of theatrical closure in England (because of plague or a period of royal mourning). German Protestant intellectuals of the seventeenth century tended to study in Holland, and from there to travel to Italy. Spanish drama reached the German-speaking countries through two routes: via Amsterdam, whence it traveled eastward, and via the Habsburg court in Vienna, which provided an additional direct conduit from the Habsburg court in Spain to the eastern end of the area.

[4] I follow here Charles Brede's *The German Drama in English on the Philadelphia Stage from 1794 to 1830* (Philadelphia: Americana Germanica Press, 1918), a detailed reporting of the repertoire of the Philadelphia stages in a comparable period to that analyzed below for the Weimar stage. The first thirty pages offer a general account of the theater in Philadelphia and the American colonies in the eighteenth century.

[5] I follow here the substance of Sharpe's argument in "Goethe and the Weimar Theatre."

[6] Marvin Carlson, *Goethe and the Weimar Theatre* (Ithaca: Cornell UP, 1978), 303.

[7] Michael Patterson, *The First German Theatre: Schiller, Goethe, Kleist and Büchner in Performance* (New York: Routledge, 1990), 83.

[8] I have argued at length that Wilhelm's position must be distinguished from Goethe's in "The Theatrical Mission of the *Lehrjahre*," *Goethe's Narrative Fiction: The Irvine Goethe Symposium* (Berlin: de Gruyter, 1983), 66–84; reprinted in *Reflection and Action: Essays on the Bildungsroman*, ed. James N. Hardin (Columbia, SC: U of South Carolina P, 1991), 142–62.

[9] The list of performances night by night was collected and cross-referenced in 1891 by C. A. Burkhardt under the title *Das Repertoire des Weimarischen Theaters unter Goethes Leitung, 1791–1817* (Nendeln/Liechtenstein: Kraus Reprint, 1977 [Hamburg: L. Voss, 1891]).

[10] The exception was *Iphigenie*, which was poorly received initially, but was successful after Goethe took Jagemann out of the lead role.

[11] Friedrich Sengle, *Biedermeierzeit: Deutsche Literatur im Spannungsfeld zwischen Restauration und Revolution, 1815–1848*, vol. 1 (Stuttgart: Metzler, 1971), esp. 110–17.

[12] The figures, from Elisabeth Dobritzsch, *Barocker Bühnenzauber: Das Ekhof-Theater in Gotha* (Munich: Bayerische Vereinsbank, 1995), 52, are not weighted to account for one-act plays, but the maximum shift caused by accounting for them in Weimar was to decrease the proportion of comedies by three percent.

[13] For a thorough survey in English of Goethe's engagement with the Weimar theater and audience reactions, see Carlson, *Goethe and the Weimar Theater*.

[14] *Hermann und Dorothea*, *Was wir bringen*, and the unfinished sequel to *Die Zauberflöte* demonstrate how seriously Goethe took the themes of the latter opera. Emil Staiger analyzes the affinity in "Goethe und Mozart," *Musik und Dichtung* (Zurich: Atlantis, 1966), 45–66, while Robert Spaethling surveys it more extensively in *Music and Mozart in the Life of Goethe* (Columbia, SC: Camden House, 1987); on *Hermann und Dorothea* and *Die Zauberflöte*, see Jane K. Brown, "Schiller und die Ironie von *Hermann und Dorothea*," in *Goethezeit: Studien zur Erkenntnis und Rezeption Goethes und seiner Zeitgenossen. Festschrift für Stuart Atkins* (Bern: Francke, 1981), 203–26.

[15] A thorough survey of Goethe's *Singspiele* and their settings may be found in Markus Waldura, "Die Singspiele," *Goethe Handbuch*, ed. Theo Buck (Stuttgart: Metzler, 1997) 2:173–94.

[16] "Shakespeare und kein Ende" (1826, Shakespeare yet Again), HA 12:296.

[17] For an extended discussion of this topic see Jane K. Brown, "Der Drang zum Gesang: On Goethe's Dramatic Form," *Goethe Yearbook* 10 (2001): 115–24.

[18] Comparable bourgeois milieu and structure also organize Goethe's earlier plays about the French Revolution, *Der Gross-Cophta* (1792), *Der Bürgergeneral* (1793), and the unfinished *Die Aufgeregten* (1817).

[19] The overlap of characters' names in *Die Geschwister* with those in *Werther* and in *Wilhelm Meister* suggests further that the play represents a stage in working through problems that occupied Goethe for many years and that the endings are

not simply to be dismissed. In any case, his audience in Weimar quite liked them; it only rebelled when he rewrote the ending of *Stella* to make it end more like a Lessing tragedy in 1805.

[20] Even in England beginning in the later seventeenth century Shakespeare tragedies were performed in adaptations that ended happily: Nahum Tate's adaptation of *King Lear*, which ends with Edgar marrying Cordelia, held the stage from 1681 until 1823.

[21] See Erich Heller, "Goethe and the Avoidance of Tragedy," in *The Disinherited Mind: Essays in Modern German Literature and Thought* (Harmondsworth: Penguin, 1961), 33–55. Stuart Atkins eloquently dismantles readings of *Tasso* as idiosyncratic or problematic tragedy in highly specific generic terms, but with the same sense for eighteenth-century sensibilities about endings, in "Observations on Goethe's *Torquato Tasso*," in *Husbanding the Golden Grain: Studies in Honor of Henry W. Nordmeyer*, ed. Luanne T. Frank and Emery E. George (Ann Arbor: Department of Germanic Languages and Literatures U of Michigan, 1973), 5–23 (cf. also *Carleton Germanic Papers* 2 [1973]: 41–59).

[22] Goethe's and Schiller's achievement is all the more significant in light of Peter Demetz's argument that Lessing originally introduced blank verse not only to make his drama more poetic, but also to camouflage unusually casual language (*Lessing: Nathan der Weise. Dichtung und Wirklichkeit* [Frankfurt am Main: Ullstein, 1966], 129–32).

[23] For an excellent discussion of Schiller's dramatic development in relation to the treatment of duality, see Ilse Graham, *Schiller's Drama: Talent and Integrity* (New York: Barnes and Noble, 1974).

[24] This structure has been plotted with great effectiveness by Benjamin Bennett in "Egmont and the Maelstrom of the Self," in *Modern Drama and German Classicism: Renaissance from Lessing to Brecht* (Ithaca: Cornell UP, 1979), 121–50.

[25] Iphigenie clearly stands between Orestes and Thoas, each of whom is accompanied by a trusted companion (Pylades, Arkas). Yet Orestes and Pylades also mirror one another in ways that Thoas and Arkas do not; Iphigenie and Orestes also mirror one another and are both "healed," brought into a living relation with their world.

[26] Goethe's source, the memoirs of Stéphanie de Bourbon-Conti (1798), is readily available in German in Bernhard Böschenstein, *Johann Wolfgang Goethe: Die natürliche Tochter. Trauerspiel. Mit den Memoiren der Stéphanie-Louise de Bourbon-Conti und drei Studien von Bernhard Böschenstein* (Frankfurt am Main: Insel, 1990), 117–303.

[27] Goethe's allusions are identified and analyzed at length in Jane K. Brown, *Goethe's Faust: The German Tragedy* (Ithaca: Cornell UP, 1986).

[28] Goethe's initial reaction to Schlegel's translation of *La Devoción de la cruz* was that Calderón was perhaps even greater than Shakespeare (reported by Schelling, October 13, 1802); otherwise he mostly referred to him as an equivalent figure. Only after his tenure as theater director did he revert to ranking Shakespeare higher.

[29] See Stuart Atkins, "Goethe, Calderón, and *Faust: Der Tragödie zweiter Teil*," in *Essays on Goethe*, ed. Jane K. Brown and Thomas P. Saine (Columbia, SC: Camden House, 1995), 259–76; his *Goethe's Faust: A Literary Analysis* (Cambridge, MA: Harvard UP, 1964, *passim*); and Jane K. Brown, *Goethe's Faust, passim.* Although Goethe's explicit reflections on Calderón began with his enthusiastic reaction to August Wilhelm Schlegel's translations beginning in 1802 and there is no documentary evidence that he knew *La vida es sueño* when he wrote *Die natürliche Tochter*, the drama of Golden Age Spain had already had enormous, often concealed impact all over Europe. Its spread in its own day, often in anonymous adaptations, is documented by Henry W. Sullivan, *Calderón in the German Lands and the Low Countries: His Reception and Influence, 1654–1980* (Cambridge: Cambridge UP, 1983). Lessing was well aware of the importance of Spanish drama, which he discussed at length in his *Hamburgische Dramaturgie* (chapters 60–69); he also sketched an adaptation of Calderón's *El alcalde de Zalamea* and began a translation of *La vida es sueño.* Calderón's plays were further, again usually anonymously, the sources of vast numbers of drama and opera plots in the seventeenth and eighteenth centuries; where they were not the specific sources they nevertheless determined the normal form, cast structure, and specific gestures and jokes (see, for example, John Loftis, *The Spanish Plays of Neoclassical England* [New Haven: Yale UP, 1973]). Because Spanish drama of the period did not distinguish between tragedy and comedy — both were *comedias* — and was mostly what we would call tragicomedy today, it was an important influence on the tendency of all plays to have happy endings until the late eighteenth century. Calderón also wrote some of the earliest opera libretti in Spanish, as well as religious dramas and court spectacles that used a great deal of music. In effect, much of his Baroque dramaturgy was still alive and well in opera in Goethe's day, particularly the comic operatic tradition of Vienna, of which Mozart was then the latest avatar. See Jane K. Brown, "The Queen of the Night and the Crisis of Allegory in *The Magic Flute*," *Goethe Yearbook* 8 (1996): 142–56.

[30] *El principe constante* (The Constant Prince), 1811; *La vida es sueño*, 1812; *La gran Zenobia*, 1815.

[31] See most recently Dieter Borchmeyer, "Goethes *Faust* musikalisch betrachtet," *Eine Art Symbolik fürs Ohr: Johann Wolfgang Goethe. Lyrik und Musik*, ed. Hermann Jung (Frankfurt am Main: Peter Lang, 2002), 87–100.

[32] The end of act 3, scene 5 calls for music to accompany a scene change and support the pantomime at the beginning of the following scene; in act 4, scene 1 the festive off-stage music changes mood so that Johanna can express her own shift of mood; the procession for the coronation in act 4, scene 6 involves no text at all, only music and stage spectacle, like the royal entries that were de rigueur in opera seria.

[33] A thoughtful analysis in this vein is that of T. J. Reed, *The Classical Centre: Goethe and Weimar, 1775–1832* (New York: Barnes and Noble, 1980). The distinction between Goethe's classicism and neoclassicism has been drawn most accurately and sensitively by Stuart Atkins in "On Goethe's Classicism," in *Goethe Proceedings: Essays Commemorating the Goethe Sesquicentennial at the University of California, Davis*, ed. Clifford A. Bernd, Timothy J. Lulofs, H. Günther Nerjes, Fritz R. Sammern-Frankenegg, and Peter Schäffer (Columbia, SC: Camden House, 1984), 1–21.

[34] He explicates the historical reasons for the position at length in section three of the essay "Shakespeare und kein Ende."

[35] The stages of development of this essay from Goethe's initial reflections in *Wilhelm Meisters Lehrjahre* are well laid out in Eric A. Blackall, *Goethe and the Novel* (Ithaca: Cornell UP, 1976), 76–110.

[36] Compare Blackall's conclusion that the discussion didn't bring substantial results, 108. Examples of epic experiments in Schiller are the *in medias res* beginning of *Maria Stuart* with Paulet angrily searching Maria's desk (in contrast to the traditional conversational exposition of *Maria Stuarda* by Jost Vondel, the great Dutch Baroque dramatist); the extensive allusions in *Die Jungfrau von Orleans* to *Hermann und Dorothea*, where Johanna is transparently modeled on Dorothea, and the crucial climactic scene includes a Homeric *teichoscopia* (act 5, scene 11, 3420–78).

[37] In this description of the newly mediated psychology of the dramas of Weimar Classicism, I follow Bennett's compelling study, *Modern Drama and German Classicism*.

[38] Bennett establishes that *Egmont* is the paradigmatic drama for German Classicism and the tradition that builds upon it (*Modern Drama and German Classicism*, 151–87); the question thus becomes the central one of nineteenth-century drama.

[39] The expression "leap" (*salto mortale*) comes from Schiller's review of *Egmont*, published in 1788. SW 5:942.

[40] Cf. SW 3:987: "Für Weimar begann mit dieser Aufführung die eigentliche klassische Theaterepoche." On *Egmont* as paradigm, see Bennett (note 38).

[41] Cf. above, note 38.

[42] The material treated in *Die natürliche Tochter* was to be the first two acts in Goethe's original outline of the play; as he finished it he planned first two more plays, then one, to complete his treatment of the theme.

[43] Cf. Brown, "Der Drang zu Gesang," 120–22.

[44] Goethe brought a manuscript of the tragedy of Margarete with him to Weimar (discovered and published only in 1887 as *Urfaust*), added two scenes in Italy, and published most of the material, except the final scene in 1790 as *Faust. Ein Fragment*. This is the version in which it had its primary influence on the early nineteenth century. At considerable urging from Schiller he added three prologues and filled in the great gap between Faust's long opening monologue and the tragedy of Margarete between 1797 and 1806. *Faust I* appeared in 1808.

[45] *Wanda* was performed eleven times between 1808 and 1813, *Der vierundzwandigste Februar*, written at Goethe's suggestion, eleven times between 1810 and 1817. The idea that Werner would be Schiller's successor derives from Iffland; see Paul Kluckhohn's introduction to *Dramen von Zacharias Werner*, Deutsche Literatur in Entwicklungsreihen, Reihe Romantik 20 (Leipzig: Reclam, 1937), 15.

Goethe's Gartenhaus. Photo by Simon Richter.

German Classical Poetry[1]

Cyrus Hamlin

THE CONCEPT OF THE "CLASSICAL" is always retrospective in its attribu-
tions. This is the lesson conveyed by a remarkable special exhibition
devoted to the artworks of ancient Greece, primarily sculpture, which was
organized at the Martin-Gropius-Bau in Berlin during the spring of 2002.[2]
We have become accustomed, at least since the studies by Johann Joachim
Winckelmann in the mid-eighteenth century,[3] to regard the artworks of
antiquity under the concept of the classical, above all with reference to the
highpoint of this tradition in Athens during the fifth century B.C. The
norm of the classical in art, whether in reference to sculptures by Phidias
or Praxiteles, to such an architectural triumph as the Parthenon, or to the
tragedies of Aeschylus and Sophocles, has served for centuries as an ideal
against which all other artworks may be measured. This was as true for
Goethe, the Schlegels, and Hegel as it had been for Winckelmann. Yet the
artists, architects, or playwrights of the classical era in ancient Athens
would not have regarded their work in any sense as "classical." Such a normative value judgment was made only much later, in retrospect, as for
instance in the Hellenistic era or in imperial Rome, when so many imitations of "classical" art were attempted, not to mention more distant views
of the artworks of antiquity as developed in the Italian Renaissance or in
German aesthetics following Winckelmann. The concept of the classical in
art invariably defines a norm regarded as having been achieved in the past
and unavoidably lost to the present. The concept of the classical thus
inevitably includes this sense of an ideal that has been lost and cannot be
retrieved. Something of this may also contribute to the fact that the concept of German Classicism has received its strongest interest in times of
trouble, conflict, and crisis. The classical thus always includes nostalgia or
a longing for what once was, but is no more.

Critical judgment concerning the concept of the classical in German
literary history is fraught with paradox. As shown definitively by such historians of criticism as René Wellek,[4] the concept of classicism was introduced to German literary history only at the very end of the nineteenth
century, referring invariably to the work of Goethe and, in part, Schiller
at the height of their careers around 1800. The opposition between
Classicism and Romanticism, furthermore, borrowed from a distinction

introduced by the Schlegels[5] in order to contrast the artworks of the Christian Middle Ages with those of antiquity, always implied a normative as well as a historical opposition, as in the famous saying by Goethe that the classical is healthy and the Romantic sick.[6] Such a sense of norm or ideal invariably pertains in any definition of German Classicism. The central paradox in studies published in the early decades of the twentieth century by such scholars as Fritz Strich[7] and H. A. Korff[8] concerning the opposition between German *Klassik* and *Romantik* resides in the fact that these two so-called movements or schools of literature occurred essentially at the same time — around 1800 — and essentially in the same place, in Weimar and Jena, two rural communities in central Germany, located only a few miles from each other. The concept of the classical in German literature thus also includes an implicit value judgment, usually in opposition to whatever is understood to constitute German Romanticism.

It should also be noted that, in recent years, when the kinds of monumental literary history undertaken earlier in the twentieth century have been replaced by more focused and often tendentious thematic studies, the concept of the classical in German literature has usually been applied exclusively to what is termed *Weimarer Klassik*. The two-volume catalogue of the newly renovated Goethe Museum in Weimar, for instance, which uses this phrase as title,[9] comes readily to mind as an example, as does the congenial overview provided by Dieter Borchmeyer in his study of the same phenomenon.[10] And what is designated by this rubric? For the most part, as always, it is the work of Goethe and Schiller — the latter often with some reservations — during the years following Goethe's return from Italy in 1788 until Schiller's death in 1805. *Klassik* thus includes less than two decades in the lengthy career of Germany's most famous and productive writer and the final phase of the much shorter career of the leading dramatist of the time.

And what of the specific production of poetry during the so-called *Weimarer Klassik*, which constitutes the subject of the present essay? Poetry was not the most significant genre for either of the two writers in question during those years, even though Goethe remained the leading poet of his age and Schiller wrote a number of programmatic, if not particularly lyrical poems. But what precisely would qualify the poetry written during this brief period to be called "classical"? The answer is quickly given and will surprise no one who is familiar with the material. Precisely during this period in German literary history, the conscious imitation of "classical" poetic forms and genres played a dominant and in many ways highly distinctive role. *Klassik* would thus include by this definition those poetic works that imitate the models and forms of antiquity, which were universally acknowledged to constitute *klassische Kunst* (classical art). Above all, the meter of the classical elegy — the so-called distichon of dactylic hexameter and pentameter lines — was a central concern for these poets. Evidence for this is found in various texts, ranging from brief epigrammatic satirical lyrics, as in Goethe's *Venetianische Epigramme* (Venetian Epigrams, 1790) and the polemical collection of so-called *Xenien* produced by Goethe and Schiller together for the latter's *Musenalmanach* of 1797, to much longer programmatic elegies, both in the ancient Roman mode, as in Goethe's *Römische Elegien*, and in the modern "sentimental" mode (as Schiller defined it), for instance in his poem "Der Spaziergang" (The Excursion), originally titled simply "Elegie."

There is, of course, a much broader diversity to the lyrical production of Goethe and even Schiller during these years of Weimar Classicism, but I do not consider the other kinds or forms of their poetry to deserve the title "classical," especially since in many ways they represent paradigmatic instances of what may be called the Romantic lyric poem. A few words of explanation on this point may be in order before turning to consider the German Classical elegy itself (to use the generic designation employed by Theodore Ziolkowski in his important study of that title[11]).

Goethe's supreme achievement as a poet resides in the simplicity and seeming spontaneity and authenticity of his songs (*Lieder*). These constituted the basis for an entire tradition that developed subsequently during the nineteenth century in response to the most familiar of such effusions, largely from his earlier years, beginning with the so-called *Sesenheimer Lieder* and continuing through the first decade of his residence in Weimar (from 1775 on). Songs such as "Willkommen und Abschied" (Welcome and Farewell), "Auf dem See" (On the Lake), "Wandrers Nachtlied" (Wanderer's Night Song; both songs with this title), "An den Mond" (To the Moon; both versions), and even the seemingly childlike lyric "Heidenröslein" (Rosebud in the Heather; composed on the model of an earlier, anonymous folksong), established a norm for the simple lyric as the central mode of Romantic poetry. This was affirmed above all by the musical compositions for these songs provided by various composers, including Goethe's friend Carl Friedrich Zelter (1758–1832), but ultimately reaching the inspired level of what came to be called the *Kunstlied* (art song) in the work of Franz Schubert (1797–1828).

Goethe's lyrical gift was fully sustained throughout what is now labeled his Classical period, as indicated above all by the songs of Mignon and the Harper in the novel *Wilhelm Meisters Lehrjahre*. These effusions of an infinite longing (*Sehnsucht*) in simplest verbal form, both in the childlike lyrics of the mysterious naïve spirit Mignon, who sings what came to be perhaps the most famous lyric of German literature, "Kennst du das Land, wo die Zitronen blühn?" (Do you know the land where the lemon trees blossom?), and in the sentimental musings of a suffering and broken sensibility in the songs by the Harper, constitute a supreme achievement in European literature for what came to be called the Romantic lyric. Imitations and variations by the poets who followed Goethe and who were all profoundly influenced by him — from Ludwig Tieck (1773–1853) and Clemens Brentano (1778–1842) to Wilhelm Müller (1794–1827), Josef Freiherr von Eichendorff (1788–1857), Heinrich Heine (1797–1856), and even Eduard Mörike (1804–1875), to name only a few of the best remembered poets of *Lieder* — bear witness to the profound and lasting achievement of the master.

Schiller never claimed a genuine lyrical gift, and his representative poems, even from his early years, are marked by a powerful sense of dramatic voice, where the force of rhetoric often overwhelms any sense of spontaneity or authenticity. The most characteristic poetic productions of the years immediately following the epoch-making encounter between Goethe and Schiller in 1794 are found in the ballads they wrote for joint publication in Schiller's *Musenalmanach* for 1798. These ballads adapt and develop another strain of the popular tradition that became the focus of antiquarian collectors and celebrants of the primitive during the later eighteenth century, as in Herder's *Volkslieder* (1778). Goethe above all demonstrated early on — in ways that Schiller could never imitate — an authenticity of voice and tone in his popular ballads, such as "Der König in Thule" (The King of Thule, c.1775; sung by Gretchen in *Faust*) or the "Erlkönig" (from his *Singspiel* [drama with music] *Die Fischerin* [The Fishermaid], 1782), which is unequalled by any other poet of the era. The later ballads composed by both poets during the so-called *Balladenjahr* (year of the ballad, 1797) — consisting of tales of the supernatural in Goethe's case, such as "Der Gott und die Bajadere" (The God and the Temple Dancer) and "Die Braut von Korinth" (The Bride of Corinth), and heroic evocations of high moral conflict and struggle in Schiller's case, such as "Die Kraniche des Ibykus" (The Cranes of Ibycus), "Die Bürgschaft" (The Surety), or "Der Taucher" (The Diver) — constitute a corpus of "Romantic" tales that deserve to stand side by side with the most famous products of English Romanticism, the *Lyrical Ballads* (1798) of Wordsworth and Coleridge, composed for the most part within a year following the appearance of the German *Musenalmanach*. It would be a contradiction in generic and historical terms to assign these ballads to German Classicism, when they so clearly belong to the central tendencies of European Romanticism. A detailed comparison of the supernatural component in Coleridge's ballads, such as "The Rhyme of the Ancient Mariner," with those by Goethe, as also of the ethical content of Wordsworth's ballads with those by Schiller — all of them distinctly in what Schiller would have called the "sentimental" mode — has yet to be attempted.

Schiller also developed a form of didactic philosophical poetry that might appear to constitute a significant component of the German

Classical lyric, were it not for the larger intellectual context that motivated their composition. Through his philosophical essays and poems, Schiller became the leading respondent to Kant's critical philosophy, as also to more general theoretical concerns of the time with cultural history and the proper functions of art. Such poems as "Die Götter Griechenlands" (The Gods of Greece, 1788), "Die Künstler" (The Artists, 1789), and, most remarkable of all, "Das Ideal und das Leben" (The Ideal and Life, original title "Das Reich der Schatten" [The Realm of the Shadows], 1795) established a mode of poetological discourse — subsequently developed even farther by Hölderlin — that belongs within the larger context of Romantic literary and cultural theory, to which Schiller's major philosophical essays also contributed in significant ways. The distinction between Classical and Romantic in these instances makes no sense whatsoever.

German Classical poetry within the more narrow sense of a poetic imitation of models from classical antiquity may be said to commence with Goethe's *Römische Elegien* (composed in 1789–90; published in 1795), the group of poems in the meter of the classical distichon that he composed soon after returning to Weimar from Rome.

> Saget, Steine, mir an, o spricht, ihr hohen Paläste!
>   Straßen, redet ein Wort! Genius, regst du dich nicht?
> Ja, es ist alles beseelt in deinen heiligen Mauern,
>   Ewige Roma; nur mir schweiget noch alles so still.
> O wer flüstert mir zu, an welchem Fenster erblick ich
>   Einst das holde Geschöpf, das mich versengend erquickt?
> Ahn ich die Wege noch nicht, durch die ich immer und immer
>   Zu ihr und von ihr zu gehn, opfre die köstliche Zeit?
>
>   (Elegy 1, lines 1–8)

> [Speak to me, stones, oh, tell me, you lofty palaces!
>   Streets, will you say but a word! Genius, do you not stir?
> Yes, everything lives in spirit within your sacred walls,
>   Roma eternal; but only for me is it all so silent.
> So who will whisper to me, at which window revealed
>   At last the graceful creature, whose glance will stir me and scorch?
> As yet I know not the ways, which ever and ever again
>   Will lead me to her and back, spending my precious time?]

Readers of this remarkable cycle have often regarded the love relationship depicted there to serve as a quasi-autobiographical document. Insofar as this may hold true, the basis for the poet's love affair would be his sexual liaison with Christiane Vulpius, the young woman who approached Goethe in the park of Weimar soon after his return in 1788. The location of the affair in Rome as depicted in the cycle of elegies would thus involve a fictional projection and displacement. Far more important for an assessment of these elegies as imitations of the classical model, however, is the use of Rome as setting, not primarily for the poet's erotic experience but for the act of imitating the elegiac poets of ancient Rome. The god Amor as patron of love initiates the poet into the mysteries of love through the example of the triumvirate of elegiac poets who had once served him in Rome: Ovid, Tibullus, and above all, Propertius.

> Froh empfind ich mich nun auf klassischem Boden begeistert;
>   Vor- und Mitwelt spricht lauter und reizender mir.
> Hier befolg ich den Rat, durchblättre die Werke der Alten
>   Mit geschäftiger Hand, täglich mit neuem Genuß.
> Aber die Nächte hindurch hält Amor mich anders beschäftigt;
>   Werd ich auch halb nur gelehrt, bin ich doch doppelt beglückt.
> Und belehr ich mich nicht, indem ich des lieblichen Busens
>   Formen spahe, die Hand leite die Hüften hinab?
> Dann versteh ich den Marmor erst recht; ich denk und vergleiche,
>   Sehe mit fühlendem Aug, fühle mit sehender Hand.
> Raubt die Liebste denn gleich mir einige Stunden des Tages,
>   Gibt sie Stunden der Nacht mir zur Entschädigung hin.
> Wird doch nicht immer geküßt, es wird vernünftig gesprochen;
>   Überfällt sie der Schlaf, lieg ich und denke mir viel.
> Oftmals hab ich auch schon in ihren Armen gedichtet
>   Und des Hexameters Maß leise mit fingernder Hand
> Ihr auf den Rücken gezählt. Sie atmet in lieblichem Schlummer,
>   Und es durchglühet ihr Hauch mir bis ins Tiefste die Brust.
> Amor schüret die Lamp indes und denket der Zeiten,
>   Da er den nämlichen Dienst seinen Triumvirn getan.
>
> (Elegy 5)

> [Joyous now I can feel how this classical soil inspires me;
>   Ancient and modern worlds speak clearly and charming to me.
> Here I follow advice from the works I read of antiquity
>   With industrious care, daily with pleasure renewed.
> But through the nights I am held to other business by Amor;
>   If I learn only but half, still I have twice the delight.
> And do I not learn a lot, as I observe the form of her lovely
>   Breasts, slide my hands down her hips and thighs?
> Then I understand truly the marble statues; I think and compare,
>   See with a feeling eye, feel with a seeing hand.
> If my loved one steals from me several hours of the daytime,
>   She gives back hours of the night, making amends for my loss.
> Not all the time is spent by kissing, sometimes we talk quite sensibly;
>   And when she falls asleep, I lie there and think about much.

Often I also have written poems while lying in her arms,
   Counting hexameter lines silent with fingering hand
Across her naked back. She breathes so lovely in slumber,
   Warmly her breath glows through me into the depths of my heart.
Amor then lowers the lamplight, thinking about the time when
   Long ago for his triumvirs he performed identical service.]

The role of Amor becomes closely identified with the poetic inspiration received by the poet of the *Römische Elegien* from his ancient Roman models. It is in the act of imitation and appropriation that the singular achievement of Goethe's cycle is to be found, in which the alien German visitor from the north adapts his voice and his manner to the form and the style of the classical tradition.

A further dimension of Goethe's poetic achievement in the elegies is found in the implicit role of memory in the evocation of his fictional Roman experiences. Goethe's cycle does not serve as a poetic document for his actual experience of living in Rome. Quite on the contrary, the act of poetic re-creation, like the performance of a drama in the theater, thematizes the process of recollection as the imaginative filter through which the world of Rome is represented and realized. This process of recollection coincides closely with the act of imitation itself, through which the medium and the poetic form of the ancient elegy is revived and given new life in the idiom of the modern German poet. On the one hand, an ironic conflation occurs between the ancient and the modern, as though the German poet were writing in the company of the ancients, united with them through the power of Amor. Yet, on the other, the attentive reader will be aware that this conflation occurs only through the power of the poet's language to bridge the enormous historical gap between the classical world of ancient elegy and the modern world of these poems as it is recreated and recollected through the medium of this poetic event. The significance of Goethe's classicism thus resides in this process of imitation and re-creation, where the evocation of Rome with the experience it provides is necessarily accompanied by a sense of difference and cultural distance, so that the seeming immediacy of the activities described is offset by a corresponding sense of artifice and poetic fiction. What abides in the mind of the reader is the motive for such a poetic re-creation, where the norm or ideal of classical poetry resides in the source texts of antiquity and the goal to be achieved is intuitively understood to reside in the attempt to equal the ancient model of elegy, both in its metrical form and in its narrative style.

At a more practical level of craftsmanship, it should be emphasized that the effort by Goethe's friend Karl Ludwig von Knebel (1744–1834) to translate the Latin elegies of Propertius into German provided a vivid example close at hand of the challenge of poetic imitation that Goethe was attempting in his *Römische Elegien*. From various biographical sources it appears that Goethe encouraged his friend to attempt revisions of his initial prose versions into the classical meter of elegy and that, conversely, Knebel provided Goethe with metrical advice and guidance in composing his elegies in the same classical meter. It is all the more appropriate, therefore, that Knebel's metrical versions of Propertius in German should have been published in Schiller's journal *Die Horen* (1795) in close proximity to the appearance there of Goethe's *Elegien*. Goethe's poems caused a minor scandal because of their vivid erotic subject matter. Readers failed to recognize that this eroticism, similar to the metrical form of the elegies, had been borrowed and adapted in large part from the poet's Latin sources. The singular poetic power of these poems resides in the subtle combination of desire, or longing, for the distant world of the classical ideal and the irony of that distance, which makes the act of imitation always an exercise in reconstruction or fictional semblance. The classical gesture is thus sustained by what should best be termed Romantic longing and Romantic irony.

Only belatedly has it become clear to critics of Schiller's poetry that his status within German Classicism depends almost entirely on his philosophical poems, and that his supreme achievement in this regard is found in the long elegy "Der Spaziergang." Many of the earlier poems are characterized by rhetorical excess and dramatic posing to the point of bombast, especially in the juvenilia collected in the *Anthologie auf das Jahr 1782* and in the several hymns composed in the years just following, notably in "An die Freude" (Ode to Joy, 1785), subsequently made famous by Beethoven in the final choral movement of his *Ninth Symphony* (1824). The various ballads, in particular those composed in conjunction with Goethe for the *Musenalmanach* of 1798 (as mentioned earlier), strike a modern reader as pompous and sententious, although many German schoolboys during the nineteenth century were obliged to learn them by heart as examples of moral rectitude. Schiller's appropriation of the elegiac meter, however, influenced as it certainly was by the example of Goethe's *Elegien*, reveals little if any concern for the imitation of classical models. Schiller's poem is defined by its programmatic content, very much resembling an essay in universal history filtered through the individual poetic self as it moves through an imagined landscape toward a privileged perspective at the summit of a high mountain.

Ziolkowski persuasively chooses Schiller's "Spaziergang" as the paradigm for the German Classical elegy,[12] even though he also acknowledges the validity of M. H. Abrams's assertion, in his monumental study of Romanticism, *Natural Supernaturalism* (1971), that "this remarkable poem . . . can serve as a résumé of . . . [the] design, imagery, and ideas in works of the Romantic imagination."[13] I would single out two aspects of Schiller's poem that demonstrate this confluence of the Classical and the

Romantic in paradigmatic manner: the structure of its discourse, which is outlined diagrammatically by Ziolkowski (9), and the dynamics of its central metaphorical conceit as journey through a landscape. In both respects, Schiller borrows from traditions in literature that are familiar from earlier sources, as has been widely recognized, with particular reference to the poet as mental traveler, from the example of Francesco Petrarch's ascent of Mont Ventoux in 1336 to the more immediate example of Jean-Jacques Rousseau's *Rêveries du promeneur solitaire* (Reveries of the Solitary Walker, 1782).[14] The model thus established for the elegy became — especially in the hands of Germany's greatest elegiac poet, Friedrich Hölderlin, who was himself directly influenced by Schiller's example — the basis for a highly sophisticated conceptual sense of the poet's place and the purpose of poetry within the broader context of Romanticism in its classical mode.

"Der Spaziergang" consists of 100 elegiac couplets, or distichs. No subdivision occurs within the text, neither into stanzas nor into verse paragraphs. The impact of reading the text can thus initially lead to a sense of confusion or even bewilderment. A preliminary sense of structure, however, emerges in the representation of landscape as the panorama of human history. Ziolkowski (4–9) argues for four discrete stages in the poet's meditation on this history: 1) Natural Man (lines 29–54); 2) Heroic Culture (lines 59–86); 3) Diversified Civilization (lines 101–38); and 4) Decline of Civilization (lines 143–56). The vision of Natural Man, for instance, is conveyed as follows:

> Glückliches Volk der Gefilde! Noch nicht zur Freiheit erwachet,
> Theilst du mit deiner Flur fröhlich das enge Gesetz.
> Deine Wünsche beschränkt der Ernten ruhiger Kreislauf,
> Wie dein Tagewerk, gleich, windet dein Leben sich ab!
>
> (55–58)

> [Fortunate country dwellers! Not yet awakened to freedom,
> You share with your pastures joyously limited laws.
> Your desires are narrow within the peaceful harvest cycle,
> Like your day labor, so also your lives are enclosed!]

The opening of the poem (lines 1–10) and its conclusion (lines 173–84) provide what Ziolkowski calls "Scenic Description." Such a progression by stages establishes a sense of design, but the symmetry of composition only emerges when the several apostrophes or direct invocations by the poet are recognized as transition passages throughout the poem. What results is a perfect balance of six units that correlate with each other in a pattern of mirrored relations, each of equal length to its corresponding unit.[15] This schema suggests a carefully crafted structure, although the discourse of the poem is so continuous that few among its many critics have noticed such symmetry.

More important for an assessment of "Der Spaziergang" as classical
elegy is the role of the poet as rhetorical agent and reflective consciousness
throughout the entire text. Schiller's poem fulfills by design the central
quality of what he termed the "sentimental" in his essay "Über naïve und
sentimentalische Dichtung" (On Naive and Sentimental Poetry), composed in the months just following the writing of this poem and published,
like the poem, in his journal *Die Horen*. The sentimental poet, he argues,
in contrast to the naïve poet, who simply represents nature without conscious mediation, always writes from an awareness of the ideal in its conflicted relation to reality. The language of the sentimental is thus the
language of reflectivity and self-consciousness. To quote his most famous
definition:

> [Der sentimentalische Dichter] reflektiert über den Eindruck, den die
> Gegenstände auf ihn machen, und nur auf jene Reflexion ist die Rührung
> gegründet, in die er selbst versetzt wird und uns versetzt. Der Gegenstand
> wird hier auf eine Idee bezogen, und nur auf dieser Beziehung beruht
> seine dichterische Kraft. Der sentimentalische Dichter hat es daher immer
> mit zwei streitenden Vorstellungen und Empfindungen, mit der
> Wirklichkeit als Grenze und mit seiner Idee als dem Unendlichen zu tun,
> und das gemischte Gefühl, das er erregt, wird immer von dieser doppelten
> Quelle zeugen. (SW 5:720–21)

> [The sentimental poet reflects on the impression which the object makes
> on him and solely upon this reflection is the emotional state grounded to
> which he is transported and to which he transports us. The object is thus
> set in relation to an idea, and only upon this relation does his poetic power
> reside. The sentimental poet thus is always concerned with two conflicting
> concepts and emotions, with reality as a limit and with his idea as the infi-
> nite, and the mixed feeling that he evokes will always bear witness to this
> double source.]

This is not the appropriate place to consider Schiller's poetic theory in
detail, but the fact that his poem, initially given the generic title "Elegie,"
purposefully demonstrates the sub-category of sentimental poetry that he
defines in his essay as "elegy" is significant. He distinguishes the genres of
the sentimental with regard to what he terms "modes of feeling"
(*Empfindungsweisen*), where a tension or conflict always pertains between
the real and the ideal, between the object and the idea. If the gap or contradiction between actuality and the ideal dominates, then the poem will
be "satire"; if the poem depicts a correspondence or a harmony between
the real and the ideal, the result is "pastoral." If, however, as he argues in
a lengthy footnote, the poem conveys a dynamic movement between
these two modes, varying between conflict and harmony, the result is
"elegy" (SW 5:744–46). Precisely such a variation from the original state
of harmony in nature through division and conflict in society toward an
ultimate vision of at least the possibility of reconciliation constitutes the

story of human development surveyed in "Der Spaziergang." The ultimate utopian goal of human history in a state of freedom is cited in the following passage:

> Seine Fesseln zerbricht der Mensch. Der Beglückte! Zerriss' er
>   Mit den Fesseln der Furcht nur nicht den Zügel der Scham!
> Freiheit ruft die Vernunft, Freiheit die wilde Begierde,
>   Von der heil'gen Natur ringen sie lüstern sich los.
>
> (139–42)

> [Man now breaks loose from his chains. The fortunate one! But never,
>   When he rips off the chains of fear, may he break the bridle of
>   shame!
> "Freedom!" is reason's call, "Freedom!" calls wild desire,
>   They eagerly strain for release from sacred Nature's bonds.]

This story, furthermore, is mediated through the emotional and reflective response of the poet, who seems to witness the entire process before his eyes as a panorama of landscape. The entire drama of history unfolds as the vista through which the poet as traveler makes his way.

Precisely here in the central thematic metaphor of the journey resides the second fundamental feature of Schiller's classical elegy. His poem begins as a liberating movement of the self from its confinement indoors out into the landscape of springtime. Its advance is presented as an ascent up toward the summit of a mountain, which is eventually reached as vantage point for a comprehensive vision of history, represented as a panorama spread out before the experiencing mind.

> Aber wo bin ich? Es birgt sich der Pfad. Abschüssige Gründe
>   Hemmen mit gähnender Kluft hinter mir, vor mir den Schritt.
> Hinter mir blieb der Gärten, der Hecken vertraute Begleitung,
>   Hinter mir jegliche Spur menschlicher Hände zurück.
> Nur die Stoffe seh' ich gethürmt, aus welchen das Leben
>   Keimet, der rohe Basalt hofft auf die bildende Hand.
> Brausend stürzt der Gießbach herab durch die Rinne des Felsen,
>   Unter den Wurzeln des Baums bricht er entrüstet sich Bahn.
> Wild ist es hier und schauerlich öd'. Im einsamen Luftraum
>   Hängt nur der Adler und knüpft an das Gewölke der Welt.
>
> (173–82)

> [But where am I? The pathway is hidden. Abysses drop sheer away
>   With yawning cliffs behind and ahead they hinder my steps,
> Left behind the familiar escort of gardens and hedgerows,
>   Left behind is every trace of human hands.
> Only raw matter do I see piled up, from which life may be
>   Formed, raw basalt awaits expectant a fashioning hand.

Torrents roaring plunge downward through splits in the rock,
      Beneath the roots of the trees their course breaks free.
Wild and frighteningly desolate is it here. In the lonely spaces of air
      Hovers an eagle and connects the clouds to the world.]

The final assertion of the poem unites the origin of cultural history in
Homeric epic with the present time.

Aber jugendlich immer, in immer veränderter Schöne
      Ehrst du, fromme Natur, züchtig das alte Gesetz!
Immer dieselbe, bewahrst du in treuen Händen dem Manne,
      Was dir das gaukelnde Kind, was dir der Jüngling vertraut,
Nährest an gleicher Brust die vielfach wechselnden Alter;
      Unter demselben Blau, über dem nämlichen Grün
Wandeln die nahen und wandeln vereint die fernen Geschlechter
      Und die Sonne Homers, siehe! Sie lächelt auch uns.

(193–200)

[Yet forever youthful, in an ever changing Beauty,
      Pious Nature, you honor strictly the ancient law!
Ever the same, you preserve and sustain a man in faithful hands,
      What a playful infant, what a youth once revealed to you,
Nourish at your selfsame breast the constantly changing ages,
      Beneath the selfsame blue, above the constant green
Travel united the races of men, both near and distant,
      And, behold! the sun that shone on Homer also smiles on us.]

It is the movement from the realm of the beautiful in nature toward the
sublime as the extreme limit to what may be known and comprehended.
The idea of poetry as the dynamic movement of thought and experience,
constituting what might best be called an imaginary journey, assumes the
status of an archetype for Romanticism generally. In this regard "Der
Spaziergang" resembles any number of other poems, not only in German
literature, where the poet moves through a landscape in a complex interaction between subjective sensibility and objective setting. Parallel instances
in poems by Goethe come quickly to mind, such as "Wanderers Sturmlied"
(Wanderer's Storm-Song), "Der Wandrer" (The Wanderer) or "Harzreise
im Winter" (A Winter Journey in the Harz), and, with an even more
explicit program for his poetry, "Zueignung" (Dedication), which Goethe
subsequently placed at the head of his collected works. Corresponding
examples from Wordsworth also may be cited, such as "Lines Composed a
Few Miles Above Tintern Abbey," or the opening of his autobiographical
epic *The Prelude,* to cite only obvious instances. The theme of the sentimental journey is also central to the other arts in this period, as in
Beethoven's *Pastoral Symphony* or Schubert's song cycle (to poems by
Wilhelm Müller) *Winterreise,* to paintings by Caspar David Friedrich,

where a figure is located within a symbolic landscape, thematizing the relationship of the self and external nature.

Most of the mature poetry by Hölderlin, to which I shall turn shortly, may be located within this archetypal myth of the poet as mental traveler. Ultimately, what stands behind this image is the central concern of post-Kantian idealist philosophy with the experiential processes of the mind, as in Fichte's *Wissenschaftslehre* (Science of Knowledge, 1794–95) in its concern for the "gegenseitige Wechselbestimmung des Ich und des Nicht-Ich"[16] (the reciprocal opposing determination of the self and the not-self), to which Schiller was responding, and, a decade later, Hegel's monumental exploration of the *Phänomenologie des Geistes* (Phenomenology of Spirit, 1807), originally titled *Wissenschaft der Erfahrung des Bewußtseins*[17] (Science of the Experience of Consciousness).

The German Classical elegy was thus created conjointly, if independently, by Goethe and Schiller. To refer to this poetic form as a separate genre and to attempt to trace its history may imply a greater stability and continuity than the evidence justifies. At the same time, the significance of such elegies is found within the larger intellectual and cultural context of what is still best termed European Romanticism. Schiller did not repeat his triumphant success with "Der Spaziergang," even though he composed several other shorter and minor poems in elegiac meter. None of them would merit consideration under the heading of Classical elegy. Goethe, by contrast, writing no doubt under the direct influence of Schiller's theory of sentimental poetry, composed several elegies during the later 1790s that merit further discussion. They are greatly varied in subject matter: "Alexis und Dora" qualifies as quasi-pastoral, and "Hermann und Dorothea" reflects on the paradox of the modern poet writing a mini-epic in Homeric hexameter about refugees from the wars of the French Revolution ("Doch Homeride zu sein, auch nur als letzter, ist schön" [30; And yet to be one of the Homeridae, even if the last one, is beautiful]), while "Die Metamorphose der Pflanzen" (The Metamorphosis of Plants) offers an elegant and ironic poetic survey of Goethe's theory on the pattern of growth in plants, based on his botanical studies.

Only one of these poems, "Euphrosyne," written during the poet's trip into the Swiss Alps in 1797 and in direct response to news of the early death of a young actress who studied under him in the Weimar theater, Christiane Neumann-Becker (1778–97), deserves serious consideration as a classical elegy. Presumably under direct influence from Schiller's example, Goethe's poem begins high in the mountains at sunset:

Auch von des höchsten Gebirgs beeisten zackigen Gipfeln
    Schwindet Purpur und Glanz scheidender Sonne hinweg.
Lange verhüllt schon Nacht das Tal und die Pfade des Wandrers,
    Der, am tosenden Strom, auf zu der Hütte sich sehnt,

Zu dem Ziele des Tags, der stillen hirtlichen Wohnung;
    Und der göttliche Schlaf eilet gefällig voraus,
Dieser holde Geselle des Reisenden. Daß er auch heute
    Segnend kränze das Haupt mir mit dem heiligen Mohn!

                                                (1–8)

[Even the jagged, icy peaks of the highest mountains
    As the sun departs now lose their shine of purple and gold.
Long have the valley and path of the traveler been concealed in night,
    Aside this roaring stream, as he seeks to reach the lodge,
Goal of his day's excursion, the quiet abode of the herdsman;
    And a desire hastens enticing ahead for heavenly sleep,
Congenial companion of every traveler. May it also today
    Place its crown with a blessing upon my head like a sacred opiate!]

Of particular interest is the fact that Goethe first published this poem in Schiller's *Musenalmanach* for 1799 using, as had Schiller before him, the generic title "Elegie." The poem consists of a spiritual encounter high in the Alps between the poet and the shade of the dead actress.

Welche Göttin nahet sich mir? Und welche der Musen
    Suchet den treuen Freund, selbst in dem grauen Geklüft?
Schöne Göttin! enthülle dich mir, und täusche, verschwindend,
    Nicht den begeisterten Sinn, nicht das gerührte Gemüt.
Nenne, wenn du es darfst vor einem Sterblichen, deinen
    Göttlichen Namen; wo nicht: rege bedeutend mich auf,
Daß ich fühle, welche du seist von den ewigen Töchtern
    Zeus', und der Dichter sogleich preise dich würdig im Lied.

                                           (15–22)

[Which goddess approaches me? And which of the muses
    Seeks out her loyal friend, even in this hostile chasm?
Beauteous Goddess! reveal yourself, and do not, by vanishing,
    Trick my inspired mind or thwart the feelings you touch.
Tell me your sacred name, if you may speak to a mortal,
    How you are called; and if not, move me to feel
And intuit which you may be of the daughters eternal of
    Zeus, and praise for you the poet will offer at once in song.]

Most of the text consists of a monologue by her spirit, recalling her brief career and her limited triumphs on the stage — especially her performance as the young Arthur in Shakespeare's *King John*, where she acted her death scene so realistically that Goethe as director was momentarily concerned — ironically suitable to recollection in an elegy! — that she might truly have died. Her appeal to the poet as she departs forever into the underworld, led by the god Hermes, is that he might memorialize her in his verses, so that she would join the company of other immortal women in the realm of myth, such as Penelope, Evadne, Antigone, and Polyxena.

> "Bildete doch ein Dichter auch mich; und seine Gesänge,
>   Ja, sie vollenden an mir, was mir das Leben versagt." —
> Also sprach sie, und noch bewegte der liebliche Mund sich,
>   Weiter zu reden; allein schwirrend versagte der Ton.
> Denn aus dem Purpurgewölk, dem schwebenden, immer bewegten,
>   Trat der herrliche Gott Hermes gelassen hervor;
> Mild erhob er den Stab und deutete; wallend verschlangen
>   Wachsende Wolken, im Zug, beide Gestalten vor mir.
> Tiefer liegt die Nacht um mich her; die stürzenden Wasser
>   Brausen gewaltiger nun neben dem schlüpfrigen Pfad.
> Unbezwingliche Trauer befällt mich, entkräftender Jammer,
>   Und ein moosiger Fels stützet den Sinkenden nur.
> Wehmut reißt durch die Saiten der Brust, die nächtlichen Tränen
>   Fließen; und über dem Wald kündet der Morgen sich an.
>
> (129–42)

> ["My poet educated me as well, and his songs,
>   Yes, they complete for me what was denied by my life." —
> Thus she spoke, and still her lovely mouth continued to move,
>   As if to say more; but the sound with a whirring fell silent.
> For out of the purplish cloud, which floated ever in motion,
>   The splendid god appeared, Hermes the silent companion;
> Gently he lifted his staff and pointed the way; billowing mists
>   Rolled in more densely to conceal both figures from me.
> Deeply the night surrounds me here; the plunging waters
>   Roar more powerfully now alongside the slippery path.
> Unbearable mourning oppresses me, disconsolate despair,
>   And with a sinking spirit I lean against moss covered rock.
> Misery tears at the strings of my heart, nocturnal tears
>   Flow forth; and over the trees comes the first glimpse of dawn.]

The poignant, though ironic point of Goethe's elegy is of course the successful achievement of just such a memorial, documenting, as it were, the farewell address by the dead spirit, preserved in the elegiac couplets of the poem. To give the poem, and by implication the dead actress, the name Euphrosyne, one of the Graces in classical mythology, thematizes what I argue to be the central concern of the Romantic elegy in general: the re-creation of the lost ideal of art within the form and idiom of modern poetry. In this regard, however different in focus and method, Goethe's poem stands beside Schiller's elegy as the fulfillment of such a complex and paradoxical poetic program. Were it not for the even greater achievement of Hölderlin's elegies, these two poems by Schiller and Goethe, "Der Spaziergang" and "Euphrosyne," could be celebrated as the highest achievement of the German Classical elegy in the Romantic mode.

The case of Hölderlin for any survey of the poetry of German Classicism is complicated by the fact that his mature work was relatively unknown during his lifetime and that much of his best poetry was not published until the twentieth century. His work proves the point with which I began, however, that the concept of the classical is always a retrospective judgment. Just as he modeled his best work on the example of ancient Greece, so we may judge his work within the broader context of efforts to imitate and recreate that model in modern German literature. Hölderlin sets the norm against which all other examples must be measured, even the best work by Goethe and Schiller. At the same time, he demonstrates the essential difference and the limit between the classical model and the modern re-creation, as he also thematizes this difference as a central issue within his own poetry. In a literary survey such as this, there is only time for the briefest glance at his achievement in general terms, but a few more detailed remarks concerning the greatest of his elegies, "Brod und Wein" (Bread and Wine), will conclude this essay.[18]

The earlier work of Hölderlin, modeled in large measure on Friedrich Gottlieb Klopstock (1724–1803) and Schiller, already looks to ancient Greece as source and ideal of its inspiration. At the same time, however, Hölderlin recognized even then the degree to which the culture of ancient Greece was irretrievably lost, for which he established a fundamentally elegiac, even tragic tone for much of what he came to write. The most representative work embodying both the longing to renew the culture of Greece and the recognition of its impossibility is found in Hölderlin's novel *Hyperion, oder der Eremit in Griechenland* (Hyperion, or the Hermit in Greece, 1797/99). The central figure of this epistolary narrative, who recounts retrospectively the history of his life and hopes following his ultimate failure, serves as a model for the modern poet, trying to make sense of the ruins of Greece in order to prepare for a future return of the glorious culture of antiquity, which now lies beyond access. Many of Hölderlin's mature poems, composed during the few short years following publication of *Hyperion* until his final mental breakdown in 1806, bear witness to this cultural project and to its inevitable failure. Hölderlin wrote odes on the model of Horace, and he later attempted to imitate choral lyric modeled on the victory songs of Pindar. In immediate response to the classical elegies of both Schiller and Goethe, however, he also composed several major elegies that explore in various ways the attempt to revive and renew the spirit and the form of ancient Greece, making use above all of the central theme of the mental journey on a circular path, leading back to antiquity and returning again into the present situation within which he lived and wrote. The titles of the elegies reveal this tendency: "Der Wanderer,"

"Menons Klagen um Diotima" (originally given, as had been the case with Schiller and Goethe, the generic title "Elegie"), "Stutgard" (possibly also titled "Herbstfeier" in a later manuscript now lost), "Heimkunft," and "Brod und Wein."

"Der Wanderer" is the earliest of Hölderlin's elegies (first version 1796) and shows the influence of Schiller's didactic manner most clearly. The imaginary journey of the poem is presented in schematic fashion through a series of stanzas, starting with the heat of the African desert, then moving to the frozen ice of the North Pole, and finally shifting to a celebration of the moderate and welcoming landscape of his homeland: "Aber jetzt kehr' ich zurück an den Rhein, in die glückliche Heimat" (37; But now I turn back to the Rhine, to my happy homeland). "Menons Klagen" shows the influence of Schiller's theory of elegy in its complex structure but also appears to be a response to Goethe's "Euphrosyne," since it concerns compensation for the loss of the beloved woman, presumably the figure of Diotima from the novel *Hyperion*, who dies in the latter section of that narrative.[19] Both "Stutgard" and "Heimkunft" document actual locations in Hölderlin's life after his return to Swabia from Homburg in the summer of 1800: the former celebrates the festival of autumn within the landscape of his beloved homeland, where he goes out to meet his friend Siegfried Schmid (1774–1860), to whom the poem is dedicated; the latter describes his return from Switzerland in the spring of 1801 after his aborted stay in Hauptwyl, where he had been offered a job as private tutor, his descent from the Alps to Lake Constance, and his journey on foot north into the Neckar Valley, where his relations ("Die Verwandten," to whom the elegy is dedicated) await him to receive his oracular pronouncement that a new age of peace is at hand. The agenda of these elegies reveals the scope and flavor of Hölderlin's mythical landscape and the fundamental issues of history and culture that his poetry seeks to proclaim and celebrate. The specific program of his poetry, however, in the context of his preoccupation with ancient Greece is fully presented in the elegy "Brod und Wein."

Originally entitled "Der Weingott" (The Wine God) in an early manuscript, the elegy describes an evening scene, where the poet apparently sits drinking wine in a tavern with his friend Wilhelm Heinse (1745–1803), the older writer whom Hölderlin had met during a trip to Kassel from Frankfurt in the summer of 1796 and to whom the poem is dedicated. Relatively little attention is paid to the particulars of this scene, neither to the connubial pleasure of the wine as it intoxicates and inspires them nor to the exchange of views between the two friends, "Meister und Knaben" (38; master and apprentice). They are particularly concerned with the nature and function of poetry in the present cultural darkness in which they live. Initially, the elegy focuses more on the night itself as a condition of absence or deprivation with regard to a divine power, like a goddess,

who ascends over the scene in seeming indifference to the humans
(15–18). The night provides an appropriate setting and condition for the
visionary journey that commences in the central section of the poem (stanzas 4 to 6), a journey that leads through imaginary displacement back to
the realm of Greece and that conjures up an image of its ancient culture.
All this may seem confusing and obscure at first reading, since the initial
description of the night in stanza 1 — "die Schwärmerische," "die
Erstaunende," "die Fremdlingin unter den Menschen" (the fantastic, the
astonisher, the stranger among mankind) — leads to the singular challenge
of the poet's transport — "So komm! daß wir das Offene schauen, / Daß
ein Eigenes wir suchen, so weit es auch ist" (41–42; So come! So that we
may witness the open, seeking what is our own, ever so far though it be).
This visionary transport leads away from the present situation toward the
unknown realm of light and spirit in the distant past, toward the festive
land of the Greeks. What the reader needs is some sense of motive or purpose to the discourse of the poem. Such a sense of focus is only provided
gradually as the elegy advances and finally emerges as a program for the
poet's own poem and for modern poetry in general. As with so many representative works of European Romanticism, "Brod und Wein" ultimately
proves to be a highly sophisticated and complex inquiry into the nature
and function of poetry in the modern world.

"Brod und Wein," however convoluted and often bewildering its
formulation, is carefully crafted and structured from beginning to end. As
critics have noted, the entire poem is built around patterns of three, starting at the level of the individual distichon and extending to the
macrostructure of the elegy as a whole. The poem is divided into nine
stanzas, each of which (excepting only the seventh, apparently by mistake)
contains nine elegiac couplets. The action of the poem with its imaginary
journey to Greece and back fills the nine stanzas with a perfect symmetry:
the first three stanzas constitute the scene of drinking and conversation;
the middle three stanzas conjure the visionary image of ancient Greece;
and the final three stanzas, after an abrupt return to poetic self consciousness, struggle to interpret the lesson of the journey and to apply it
to the present situation. In addition, at the micro level, with some variations, each stanza divides into three units consisting of three disticha
each. The entire elegy is thus a fabric of overlapping and interwoven units
of three. To a degree this triadic structure may be described as dialectical
in the Hegelian sense: the poem does not move forward in a linear fashion as if it were a narrative, but constantly turns and circles about, moving from assertion to reaction and a final resolution. The poem is thus
delineated through its structure as a performative cognitive event.
Precisely in this technique reside that ironic self-distancing and imaginative questing and inquiring that correspond to what Schiller, under the
heading of the sentimental, would define as the reflective self-awareness

of the poem. This programmatic reflectivity is achieved most eloquently at the end of stanza 8 (139–42), where the actual function of Hölderlin's elegy is defined as a remembrance, as a celebration, and as a giving thanks.

The motive or purpose of the poet's imaginary journey to Greece is not made fully clear in the opening section of the poem, although the determining factor is clearly a sense of divine power that is attributed to the night as such. In the final lines of stanza 2, it is asserted that the night provides several distinctive gifts specifically to the poets in response to their service to her: ". . . die Vergessenheit und das Heiligtrunkene . . ., das strömende Wort . . . und vollern Pokal und kühneres Leben, / Heilig Gedächtnis auch, wachend zu bleiben bei Nacht" (33–36; . . . forgetfulness and sacred drunkenness . . ., flowing words . . . and a fuller cup and a bolder life, sacred memory also, to stay awake through the night). All these attributes pertain directly to the process of poetic production and relate directly to the power of inspiration, which, akin to drunkenness and even madness, causes the mind ultimately to break loose, like lightning, the divine fire, and to seek what is "Open" (*das Offene*). The poet invokes this power as the means to his transport toward Greece, toward the sacred setting of Dionysus, the wine god, above the city of Thebes on the slopes of Mt. Kithairon, where at the end of stanza 3 the god is revealed as looking backward and also forward as the divinity that is to come: "Dorther kommt und zurück deutet der kommende Gott" (54; From there he comes and backwards signals the coming God). What precisely does the poet seek in Greece, insofar as he is at all in control of his inspiration?

The answer to this question of motive is only provided implicitly from evidence in the central stanzas of the poem. Initially, the vision of Hellas includes a sense of divine presence, where the landscape itself constitutes the feast hall of the gods: "Festlicher Saal! der Boden ist Meer! und Tische die Berge" (57; Festive hall! whose floor is the sea! and tables the mountains). But the poet remains equally aware — as the questions in stanza 4 and again in stanza 6 make clear — that all is empty and fragmented. The realm of Greece is now bereft of divine presence, ruined and abandoned; yet once it was otherwise. In three measured statements, extending across these three middle stanzas, through the poetic power of memory, that ancient event of epiphany and presence is recalled and recreated, whereby the human and the divine were united and the reality of the gods was affirmed. In each case this occurred, as the poem represents it, through a collective poetic act, by means of which the unique culture of ancient Greece was established and the ideal norm of classical art achieved.

In the first instance (stanza 4), the power of the divine broke loose like lightning out of a clear sky, and the response was a collective cry by a thousand tongues: "Vater Aether!" (Father Aether, 65), repeated and slightly varied phonetically four lines later: "Vater! Heiter!" (69).[20] This event of divine epiphany may have been the cause of communal celebration, but its immediate effect among humans is signaled by the apostrophic call of the people as "uralt Zeichen" (69–70; primal sign), which proclaims the day of divinity as event, unmediated and present to all. In the second instance (stanza 5), the process of assimilation and comprehension is described as a heroic conflict, where the power of the divine threatens to overwhelm the human, but gradually, through struggle and suffering, is gathered into the mind as a gift or a kind of grace. The outcome again is signaled by language, indeed by the giving of names to the divine powers in words that grow forth and blossom like flowers: "Nun, nun müssen dafür Worte, wie Blumen, entstehn" (90; Now, now the words must come, grow forth and blossom, like flowers). Emphasis is placed upon the organic process of this growth, where language emerges essentially as flowers do through the agency of a natural semiotics that is presumably also unaware of itself. Finally, in the third instance (stanza 6), the outcome of this productive encounter is celebrated as cultural artifact, as the construction of temples and cities along with their appropriate rituals of festival celebration, involving commerce and government, but also defined by games of competing skills with weapons and chariots at Olympia and by festival performances presumably in the theater of Dionysus in Athens. This final instance above all serves as the symbol of ancient Greek art and culture: the tragedies of Sophocles and Euripides, where the immediacy of the divine was openly revealed, as in the blinding of Oedipus — the god inscribes his stamp upon the brow of the hero (105–6)[21] — and the appearance of the god Dionysus in the guise of a human in the final work of the ancient theater, the *Bacchae*: "Oder er kam auch selbst und nahm des Menschen Gestalt an / Und vollendet' und schloß tröstend das himmlische Fest" (107–8; Else he appeared himself, assuming the guise of human, / And completed and closed gently the heavenly feast).

These allusions remain oblique and even obscure, but there can be no question that Hölderlin is celebrating not only the meaning of ancient Greece as festive union of the human and the divine, but also the medium through which this occurred, namely the art and poetry, the cultural constructs and the dramatic performances, which from our modern perspective constitute what is termed the classical. More than anywhere else in the literature of European Romanticism, Hölderlin here evokes the ideal of ancient art as the ultimate model to which this work of the modern poet is dedicated. Yet such tribute also inevitably includes the consciousness that this ideal is lost and remains inaccessible to the modern artist, whose work must necessarily be very different. In this regard, the celebration of the naïve ideal (in Schiller's sense), where art and nature are one, where the divine and the human are united, is offset by the ironic consciousness of the sentimental as the vehicle of a mediated and artificial vision.

The return to self-consciousness in the final three stanzas, which also includes the return to the scene of conversation established at the outset of the poem, provides the occasion of an inquiry into the possibility of poetry for the modern age. Significantly, this occurs through dialogue, through an implicit exchange between the poet and his companion, the older Heinse. In stanza 7, the condition of modernity is outlined both with reference to the gods, who are now absent, inaccessible, and unknowable (109–12), and with regard to the situation of the poet, who must sustain the memory of the departed powers in the manner of a dream and through a vigil of isolation in the night (recall the end of stanza 3, 31–36). We may hear the urgency of Hölderlin's own voice in the central question of the entire elegy, formulated in these now-famous lines of stanza 7:

> . . . Indessen dünket mir öfters
> Besser zu schlafen, wie so ohne Genossen zu sein,
> So zu harren und was zu tun indes und zu sagen
> Weiß ich nicht und wozu Dichter in dürftiger Zeit?
> (119–22)

> [But meanwhile to me it seems often
> Better to sleep than to be so without comrades, alone,
> Always waiting, and what to do and to say in the meanwhile,
> I do not know, and why poets in a time of such need?]

The answer to his question is provided, surprisingly, by his companion, who asserts in the final couplet of the stanza: "Aber sie sind, sagst du [i.e., Heinse is quoted as he speaks to Hölderlin], wie des Weingotts heilige Priester, / Welche von Lande zu Land zogen in heiliger Nacht" (123–124; But they [the poets] are, you say, like the sacred priests of the Wine God, / They who from land to land traveled through sacred night).

One may well ask just who these priests might be who are to serve as model for the modern poet. The answer is found when we recognize that a subtle shift of reference has occurred in the poem from classical mythology to the Christian tradition. Dionysus as wine god has been conflated with Christ, a conjunction that had a long tradition in medieval thought, as Hölderlin well knew. Suddenly, the revised title of the elegy assumes central significance for the poetological import of the poem. The status of the sign in modern, sentimental (or Romantic) poetry corresponds precisely to the gifts left behind by the choir of divinity when it ascended into its heavenly retreat (131–36): the bread and the wine of the Holy Eucharist that serve in the act of worship as symbols for the body and blood of Christ. The poet's assertion near the end of stanza

8 that these gifts provide a consolation and a reassurance concerning divinity in its absence includes an implicit theological perspective on the doctrine of consubstantiation. The bread and the wine for Hölderlin do not actually become the body and blood of Christ during the service of Communion; they merely signify as signs that which is absent, so that they may communicate to the mind the memory or the thought of what they signify. Bread is said to be the fruit of the earth, but it is also blessed by the light of heaven. Wine, as the experience of the poet and his friend throughout the elegy has demonstrated, provides a joy that derives from the "thundering god."

> Brod ist der Erde Frucht, doch ists vom Lichte geseegnet,
>> Und vom donnernden Gott kommet die Freude des Weins.
>
> (137–38)

> [Bread is the fruit of the earth, yet is blessed by the warmth of
> the sun,
>> And from the thundering God down comes the joy of the wine.]

Both these signs may be contrasted with those celebrated in antiquity, which were described in the central stanzas of the poem — the thousand-fold cry of Father Aether (the primordial sign), the names for the gods that grew and blossomed like flowers, and the festival celebrations that united the human and the divine, even in the catastrophes of tragic drama. Such discontinuity between the sign and what it signifies, specifically in the Holy Eucharist, provides implicitly the example of reflective self-consciousness that constitutes modern poetry. Precisely such a view of language and its function for the modern poet is expressed, I submit, in the final lines of the stanza.

> Darum denken wir auch dabei der Himmlischen, die sonst
>> Da gewesen und die kehren in richtiger Zeit,
> Darum singen sie auch mit Ernst die Sänger den Weingott
>> Und nicht eitel erdacht tönet dem Alten das Lob.
>
> (139–42)

> [Therefore we also think thereby of the heavenly ones, who
>> once were here and will come back again all in good time,
> Therefore the singers also in earnest sing of the Wine God,
>> And, not idly conceived, praise for the old one resounds.]

The function of poetry is to foster thought about divinity and to convey this to its recipients in the form of praise. It thus serves as an act of thanksgiving — "es lebt stille noch einiger Dank" (136; yet lives silently some kind of thanks) — as it is also a medium of self-conscious recognition. In effect, the modern poet bears witness to what is absent through the power of his poem to evoke and recollect, to celebrate and to commemorate, but *not* to embody or to reveal directly that which can no longer be experienced as present and immediate. In this regard Hölderlin's elegy constitutes the highest example of the German Classical lyric in its Romantic mode, recognizing what it cannot be at the same time that it affirms what it may do and mean. To quote from the final stanza of "Menons Klagen um Diotima": "Komm! Es war wie ein Traum! Die blutenden Fittige sind ja / Schon genesen, verjüngt leben die Hoffnungen all" (115–16; Come! It was all like a dream! The bleeding wings are all healed, our hopes rejuvenated all live).

One last point needs to be mentioned concerning the challenge of reading Hölderlin's "Brod und Wein": how do we view the unity of this poem across all the diversity of its various formal and structural strategies? Where do we stand at the end? And how may we refer that final position of poetic self-consciousness to the opening stanza, seemingly naïve and immediate in its descriptive and realistic strategies? The best and most direct answer to these questions can be provided by comparing the final stanza of the poem with the opening stanza. That there is a fundamental contrast in language, style, tone, and formulation between the two is beyond question. But the possibility that these two statements, placed at the opposite extremes of the elegy, the one as beginning and the other as ending, should be juxtaposed and compared has rarely been recognized.

The opening stanza consists of pure description, seemingly naturalistic at first and without any thematic intrusion of a consciousness, whether attributed to the poet as speaker and observer or to the reader as recipient of his discourse. The stanza divides with a perfect symmetry into three equal parts, the first three disticha delineating the process of repose that pervades the city as the evening comes on. The threefold use of the verb *ruhen* makes this focus clear. Then in the second section of the stanza attention is turned toward sounds that are heard originating from human sources (with the single exception perhaps of the flowing fountains), beginning with the lutesong (or whatever stringed instrument may be intended by *Saitenspiel*, 7) from distant gardens and proceeding to the ringing churchbells and the night watchman calling out the hour. Such sounds delineate more than a human order within the setting of nocturnal repose; they also establish a pattern of consciousness or reflective thought in a time of seeming inactivity, a pattern of cognition for the poem that is strongest with reference to the sound of music, which the poet interprets, however hypothetically, as either an affair of love (*ein Liebendes*, 8) or as a lonely man, thinking about distant friends or the days of his youth. It does not require much effort on the part of an attentive reader to surmise that this figure of a lonely man, whose song may also constitute a mode of thought and remembrance about some beloved object or experience now absent to him, may stand as a legitimate emblem for the poet of this poem as he begins to compose it. Perhaps only from a retrospective wisdom, achieved at the end of the poem, are we in a position to recognize such implications of implied self-reference at the beginning. Finally, the concluding portion of the stanza with its seemingly naturalistic references defines a threefold natural activity of approach and arrival (the verb *kommen* is used three times): for the breeze, for the moon as it rises, and for the night. But the last of these referents assumes a privileged status through threefold emphasis as personified divinity, assuming qualities of emotional power in relation to the poet as implied respondent to her, even if the full implications of such responses to the night can only be comprehended from the vantage point achieved at the end of the poem. This power is described as fantastic (*die Schwärmerische,* 15), as astonishing (*die Erstaunende,* 17), and as alien (*die Fremdlingin,* 17), all attributes in the form of adjectival nouns (two of which are derived from verbs), which serve to thematize qualities of the night as persona in the purview of the human realm. What we learn above all is that this power, even in its presence as here and now, is also remote, above our heads, and supremely indifferent to the life of mankind: *wohl wenig bekümmert um uns* (16). Given what we as readers of the entire poem have come to understand, including the poetics of the sign as signifying the absence of divinity developed in the eighth stanza, how should we respond to this evocation of the night as divine presence, however remote and indifferent?

The answer to this question about the night is provided only by the final stanza of the elegy. Yet to give this answer we need first to consider the fundamental difference in style and mode between the two, a difference that defines an essential basis in common between them, perhaps even to the point where they might be said to share a common ground-tone (*Grundton,* a term from music theory that Hölderlin himself uses in his theoretical essays) across the dialectical difference of hermeneutical consciousness that the poem as a whole imposes upon its reader. How may this point be best clarified? Consider the use of mythological imagery in the final stanza as a purposeful analogue, however different, to the naturalistic and realistic imagery of the opening stanza. Instead of the naïve depiction of the city at rest when night comes on, we confront at the end an extremely sophisticated and complex allusion to mythological associations that apply not to the city and the figure of night but to prophecies about the end of history from both classical antiquity and the Bible. The figures of both Dionysus and Christ are conflated with the spirit of wine (cf. "Weingott," 141) as a legitimate *sign* of divinity in its absence within the darkness and isolation of the poet's actual historical situation, which is referred to figuratively in accord with the traditional concept of the underworld in mythology, whether Hades or Hell (though neither name is used; cf. 148, 153, and 156). The central assertion of this concluding stanza, which would seem to contrast with the image of night in stanza 1, yet is strictly correlated to it and follows from it, is that the spirit of wine has the capacity to bring the trace (*Spur*, 147) of absent divinity downwards among the godless. This capacity of the sacramental sign to illuminate vicariously the darkness in which we dwell may also be referred to the vehicle of Hölderlin's poem, which legitimately claims for itself a corresponding status for the verbal sign. In this sense, I suggest, the assertion by the poet, repeated emphatically in several contexts during the central portion of the final stanza, that we — that is, *we* who constitute a hypothetical community of readers within a common hermeneutical consciousness achieved through the experience of reading the poem — we, precisely and wonderfully ("wunderbar und genau," 151), are the fulfillment of ancient prophecies concerning the children of god and the fruit of Hesperia (149–50) as symbols for the fulfillment of historical time. Such a figurative affirmation for the fulfillment of time alone can serve as the vehicle for the second coming, that is, for the return of the gods to earth, which occurs only within the consciousness of the human community, in a mediated analogy to the ancient call of "Father Aether!" (65–70), mediated through the verbal medium of the poem as the semiotic representation of the promise in its totality and in its truth. Such fulfillment can only be realized *in us,* specifically in our hermeneutical consciousness as readers of the poem, solely through our capacity to understand and affirm the validity of the promise conveyed to us by the poem. Nor will this fulfillment be complete, as the poem goes on to assert, until the prophecy is acknowledged as fulfilled with complete faith by one and all: "until our / Father Aether is known, each one to each and to all" (153–54).

Of interest also in comparing the last with the first stanza is the apparent gender shift that has taken place between the night as goddess, always referred to in the feminine, and the aether as father god. Perhaps within the mythological strategy of the poem as a whole this shift is not inappropriate to the final naming of the spiritual power that descends into the darkness to us and brings with it the trace of the departed gods as "Son of the Highest" (155–56). An implicit theogony may thus be established between the heavenly father, the aether, and the mother, associated with the earth but also called night, who are conjoined, as in the sacramental signs of bread and wine, products of the nourishing power of the earth and the heavenly power of the sunlight, to produce an offspring that fulfills the definition of halfgod, as was also the case mythologically for both Dionysus and Christ. The end of the poem thus achieves a crucial revision of the naturalism of the beginning in terms of this theogony as the affirmation of a mediated theophany in the minds of those who have achieved an adequate hermeneutical consciousness for the proper function of those sacramental signs still available to us as the gifts of the absent gods, the bread and the wine, but including also the poem itself.

The task of the reader is to measure his or her hermeneutical response to the message of the elegy as a whole against the response attributed at the end to those "blessed wise ones" ("seelige Weise," 157) who see this event of visitation and respond with a smile and with tears (157 and 158). We may thus affirm the adequacy of our understanding by acknowledging the essential identity between the opening realistic image of repose in the description of the city (in stanza 1) and the concluding couplet of the elegy, which describes how the Titan is embraced by the Earth, in whose arms he dreams and sleeps, and how the watchdog of Hades from the classical myth, Cerberus, also partakes of this same power of the spirit mediated through the wine — an inspired variant on the drugged cakes given to this same watchdog by the Sybil in Vergil's *Aeneid!* — so that after drinking he falls asleep (159–60). The resonances of this splendid cadence, which conclude the poem in mythological images of repose even in the midst of the darkness, extend all the way back to the opening line of the elegy, which — we may well recall — began "Rings um ruhet die Stadt."

Hölderlin's late poems demonstrate the limit, and perhaps ultimately the futility, of classicism as descriptive category. No other poet in the European tradition exhibits such a deep and sustained concern with the re-creation of forms and modes of classical poetry in modern guise, and no other poet reveals so persuasively the limits of its possibility. Hölderlin's greatest poetic achievement is without question the imitation of the Pindaric victory odes during the final productive, if brief phase of his career. These few poems constitute a level of sophistication and eloquence that has never been equaled before or since in German literature. Readers are still struggling with the task of interpreting the texts, and philological controversies about their literary status continue unabated. Much good work has also been done on the question of Pindar as source, as also on the technique of composition by which Hölderlin succeeded in creating an adequate idiom and structure for what he himself termed "vaterländische Gesänge"[22] (Songs of the Fatherland). Representative of these Pindaric poems are "Die Wanderung," which addresses explicitly the challenge of adapting and transferring to German the poetic techniques of ancient song, and "Der Rhein," perhaps the supreme achievement in this Pindaric mode, where the river is celebrated as a symbol for the destiny of the German, or Western, spirit, in its convoluted course from an origin high in the Alps to its mature path through German lands to the sea. These hymns deserve detailed discussion with regard to the question of the classical in European Romanticism, but such consideration would also strain the legitimacy of the classical as concept beyond the limits of literary history. Among the other completed hymns, "Germanien" (Germania), "Friedensfeier" (Festival of Peace; only discovered in fair copy in 1954), and "Patmos" demonstrate the unique perambulations of the poet's mythical vision in ways that might finally best be termed "anti-Classical" or "post-Romantic." Hölderlin must remain an isolated figure in the context of his time, where his final phase of poetic composition leaves every convention and thematic consideration, even within the larger concerns of European Romanticism, far behind. His work defeats all available notions of the classical in ways that are best described as *sui generis*.

In conclusion, let me reiterate the basic premise stated at the outset of this essay. I do not accept the concept of Classicism as a distinct period in German literary history. What is considered to be classical art always indicates a normative category, referring as it did for all who used the term in Germany, from Winckelmann to Hegel, exclusively to the artwork of antiquity, specifically in ancient Greece. Classical art was regarded consistently as the embodiment of a unique ideal, where the divine and the human are commingled and fused — as in the sculptures of the gods in human form — and where beauty is revealed in its highest form as, to cite Hegel's definition, "das sinnliche Scheinen der Idee"[23] (the sensuous manifestation of the idea). Yet inherent also to the concept of the classical, as emphasized at the outset, is the cognitive distance of historical change and cultural decline. The classical is that which once existed but is now lost and beyond recovery. The concept itself includes a degree of sentimental nostalgia, so that each work in the period of German poetry considered here looks to the classical as a model to which it aspires, but which it acknowledges to be beyond access. The "classical" is for the Romantic spirit always that which is lost and absent, so that it functions essentially as a negative ideal. Yet the attempt to re-create this ideal, even if acknowledged always to be artificial and futile, nonetheless enabled the leading poets of the age — Goethe, Schiller (always with reservations), and Hölderlin above all — to create some of the most remarkable literary works of the time.

Schiller is finally more interesting as a theorist of the classical, in contradistinction to what he termed the sentimental, than as a poet putting his theories into practice. Even "Der Spaziergang" commands interest primarily as an elegy committed to an idea of its own art. Goethe, by contrast, mastered the form of the ancient elegy with an ease equaled by no other modern poet, and the *Römische Elegien* enjoy a unique status within the tradition of classical imitations, above all for their irony and their playfulness, but also for the implicit sense of a cognitive distance and artifice that sustains them from first to last. The true example of classical elegy in Goethe's work is found in "Euphrosyne," where the theory of this mode — derived essentially from Schiller — is put into practice with consummate artistry and a genuine poignancy in tribute to the young actress whose death is commemorated and whose art is memorialized. Hölderlin, however, sets the norm for what is possible in this imitative and sentimental mode. He staked everything on the challenge of the classical and in a real sense suffered a tragic defeat in the attempt to re-create it. Yet that defeat included unique triumphs of reflective eloquence and poetic power. As argued from the example of "Brod und Wein," Hölderlin succeeded in delineating a poetics of difference and absence, which his poem also demonstrates in practice, a poetics that finally accepts the dichotomy of the classical and the Romantic as inevitable and unavoidable, but also affirms the classical as the ideal norm against which its own difference must be measured.

With regard to this achievement and in tribute to the unique eloquence of this troubled poet, let me conclude by quoting the final stanza of Hölderlin's Pindaric hymn "Die Wanderung":

> Wenn milder athmen die Lüfte,
> Und liebende Pfeile der Morgen
> Uns Allzugedultigen schikt,
> Und leichte Gewölke blühn
> Uns über den schüchternen Augen,
> Dann werden wir sagen, wie kommt
> Ihr, Charitinnen, zu Wilden?
> Die Dienerinnen des Himmels
> Sind aber wunderbar,
> Wie alles Göttlichgeborne.
> Zum Traume wirds ihm, will es Einer
> Beschleichen und straft den, der
> Ihm gleichen will mit Gewalt;
> Oft überraschet es einen,
> Der eben kaum es gedacht hat.

[When the breezes breathe more mildly and the morning sends up loving arrows (=*Homer's rosy-fingered dawn*) for us who are all too patient, and the light clouds blossom above our timid eyes, then we will say, 'how is it, you Graces, that you come to (us) wild ones?' The handmaidens of heaven however are wonderful, like everything divinely born. Yet it turns into a dream for those who try to stalk it and punishes with violence those who try to be equal to it; but often it surprises someone who has just begun to think about it.]

Notes

1 Passages quoted from the elegies discussed from Goethe and Schiller are accompanied by non-metrical translation. The version of Hölderlin's "Brod und Wein" in the appendix is an attempt to approximate the metrical form of the original.

2 *Die griechische Klassik: Idee oder Wirklichkeit* (Mainz am Rhein: Zabern, 2002).

[3] Johann Joachim Winckelmann, *Gedanken über die Nachahmung der griechischen Werke in der Malerei und Bildhauerkunst* (1755) and *Geschichte der Kunst des Altertums*, 2 vols. (1764).

[4] René Wellek, "The Term and Concept of Classicism in Literary History," *Discriminations: Further Concepts of Criticism* (New Haven & London: Yale UP, 1970), 55–90. Wellek also refers to his earlier discussions concerning the polarity of Classicism and Romanticism in German literary theory: "The Concept of Romanticism," *Concepts of Criticism* (New Haven: Yale UP, 1963), 128–98, and *A History of Modern Criticism, II: The Romantic Age* (New Haven: Yale UP, 1955), 12–14, 57–60, 110–11, 226.

[5] The origin of this opposition has often been discussed with reference to the early writings of Friedrich Schlegel, especially in his various fragments, published and unpublished, during the later 1790s. It was his older brother, however, August Wilhelm, who established this polarity as a commonplace in European literary history, above all through his lectures in Vienna: *Über dramatische Kunst und Literatur*, 2 vols. (Heidelberg: Mohr & Zimmer, 1809–11). Directly influenced by Schlegel (if not indeed dictated by him) is the famous brief chapter by Mme. de Staël (1766–1817) on the subject of Classical and Romantic literature in the second section of her book *De l'Allemagne,* 3 vols. (London: 1813).

[6] "Das Klassische nenne ich das Gesunde, und das Romantische das Kranke," in his conversations with Eckermann for 2 April 1829.

[7] Fritz Strich, *Deutsche Klassik und Romantik, oder Vollendung und Unendlichkeit: Ein Vergleich* (Munich: Meyer & Jessen, 1922). Strich attempts to outline a comprehensive typology for the opposition of these opposing literary modes or styles under the direct influence of Heinrich Wölfflin's *Kunstgeschichtliche Grundbegriffe* (1915).

[8] Hermann August Korff, *Geist der Goethezeit: Versuch einer ideellen Entwicklung der klassisch-romantischen Literaturgeschichte*, 5 vols. (Leipzig: J. J. Weber, 1923–57). This monumental attempt to survey the age of Goethe in accord with the tenets of "Geistesgeschichte" divides the period into four stages: *Sturm und Drang, Klassik, Frühromantik*, and *Hochromantik*. The second volume, as one would expect, is devoted almost exclusively to the works of Goethe and Schiller.

[9] *Weimarer Klassik: 1759–1832. Wiederholte Spiegelungen: Ständige Ausstellung des Goethe-Nationalmuseums*, ed. Gerhard Schuster and Caroline Gille, 2 vols. (Munich: Hanser, 1999).

[10] Dieter Borchmeyer, *Weimarer Klassik: Porträt einer Epoche* (Weinheim: Beltz Athenäum, 1994).

[11] Theodore Ziolkowski, *The Classical German Elegy: 1795–1950* (Princeton UP, 1980).

[12] Ziolkowski, *Elegy*, ch. 1, "The Model: Schiller's Meditative Mountainclimb," 3–26.

[13] M. H. Abrams, *Natural Supernaturalism: Tradition and Revolution in Romantic Literature* (New York: Norton, 1971), 453, cited in Ziolkowski, 25–26.

[14] This background in European literature is surveyed by Ziolkowski, ch. 2, "The Sources: The Mountain as Image and Locus," 27–54. See also Thomas M. Greene, *Calling from Diffusion: Hermeneutics of the Promenade* (Smith College: Northampton, MA, 2002).

[15] The opening and closing sections are each twenty-eight lines long, followed by the first and last meditations plus apostrophes, each thirty lines long. The two central sections, each forty-two lines long, also exactly correspond with each other, each meditation accompanied by an apostrophe.

[16] Fichte, *Grundlage der gesammten Wissenschaftslehre* (1794–95), esp. §5 (*Gesamtausgabe der Bayrischen Akademie der Wissenschaften*, ed. Reinhard Lauth and Hans Jacob [Fromann-Holzboog: Stuttgart-Bad Canstatt, 1965], 1.2:385–416). The phrase cited in German here is not a direct quotation from Fichte's text but uses the terms that recur continuously throughout his argument, particularly with regard to the reflectivity of the self.

[17] Hegel, *Phänomenologie des Geistes*, 6th ed., ed. Johannes Hoffmeister (Meiner: Hamburg, 1952), 577.

[18] The text of "Brod und Wein" is contained, along with a verse translation into English by the author, in an Appendix to this essay. All references to this poem in what follows will be indicated by stanza and line number within parentheses.

[19] I discuss this elegy in detail in another essay: Cyrus Hamlin, "The Philosophy of Poetic Form: Hölderlin's Theory of Poetry and the Classical German Elegy," *The Solid Letter: Readings of Friedrich Hölderlin*, ed. Aris Fioretos (Stanford: Stanford UP, 1999), 291–320, 466–68.

[20] Hölderlin establishes an ingenious phonetic pun on the pronunciation of the Greek term αιθήρ with a peculiar abstract substantive (*Heiter!*) formed from the adjective *heiter* (bright, cheerful), which occurs only here in his poetic work.

[21] I take this peculiar image of the god striking the brow of the hero to be an allusion to the passage in Sophocles' *Oedipus tyrannus*, lines 1327–34, where, after Oedipus appears blinded with blood streaming down his face, the chorus asks who has done this to him. He replies that it was the god Apollo who thus struck him, even though the hand that did the deed was his own.

[22] This phrase, which has been generally adopted by editors and scholars with reference to Hölderlin's Pindaric hymns (above all by Friedrich Beißner in the Stuttgart edition), derives from a letter he wrote to his publisher Friedrich Wilmans, dated 8 December 1803, apparently referring to precisely these poems: "Einzelne lyrische größere Gedichte 3 oder 4 Bogen, so daß jedes besonders gedrukt wird weil der Inhalt unmittelbar das Vaterland angehn soll oder die Zeit, will ich Ihnen auch noch diesen Winter zuschiken" (I will send you still this winter single lyrical larger poems 3 or 4 sheets, so that each be printed separately because the content should be of immediate concern to the fatherland or the times). Nr. 242, *Grosse Stuttgarter Ausgabe*, vol. 6.1: *Briefe. Text*, ed. Adolf Beck (Kohlhammer: Stuttgart, 1954), 435.

[23] This definition of Beauty as the ideal of art appears famously in the edited text of Hegel's *Aesthetics*, the lecture course he delivered several times in Berlin during the 1820s. "Das *Schöne* bestimmt sich dadurch als das sinnliche *Scheinen* der Idee."

Hegel, *Ästhetik*, ed. Friedrich Bassenge, vol. 1 (Frankfurt am Main: Europäische Verlagsanstalt, [n.d.]; from the 2nd ed. of Hotho, 1842), 117. As his subsequent argument concerning "classical art" (*klassische Kunst*) makes clear, the ideal of beauty is made perfectly manifest only in the artworks of ancient Greece. In this regard Hegel and his close friend from earlier years, the poet Hölderlin, were in full agreement.

Appendix

Brod und Wein.
An Heinze.

1.

Rings um ruhet die Stadt; still wird die erleuchtete Gasse,
    Und, mit Fakeln geschmükt, rauschen die Wagen hinweg.
Satt gehn heim von Freuden des Tags zu ruhen die Menschen,
    Und Gewinn und Verlust wäget ein sinniges Haupt
5   Wohlzufrieden zu Haus; leer steht von Trauben und Blumen,
    Und von Werken der Hand ruht der geschäfftige Markt.
Aber das Saitenspiel tönt fern aus Gärten; vieleicht, daß
    Dort ein Liebendes spielt oder ein einsamer Mann
Ferner Freunde gedenkt und der Jugendzeit; und die
               Brunnen,
10   Immerquillend und frisch rauschen an duftendem Beet.
Still in dämmriger Luft ertönen geläutete Gloken,
    Und der Stunden gedenk rufet ein Wächter die Zahl.
Jezt auch kommet ein Wehn und regt die Gipfel des Hains auf,
    Sieh! und das Schattenbild unserer Erde, der Mond
15   Kommet geheim nun auch; die Schwärmerische, die Nacht kommt,
    Voll mit Sternen und wohl wenig bekümmert um uns,
Glänzt die Erstaunende dort, die Fremdlingin unter den Menschen
    Uber Gebirgeshöhn traurig und prächtig herauf.

2.

Wunderbar ist die Gunst der Hocherhabnen und niemand
20   Weiß von wannen und was einem geschiehet von ihr.
So bewegt sie die Welt und die hoffende Seele der Menschen,
    Selbst kein Weiser versteht, was sie bereitet, denn so
Will es der oberste Gott, der sehr dich liebet, und darum

Bread and Wine
To Heinse.

1.

Round us the town is at rest; the lighted streets are grown silent,
    And, with torches adorned, carriages rumble away.
Filled with the joys of day, the people to rest have gone homeward,
    And a reckoning mind measures out profit and loss,
Well contented at home; the busy market place stands now   5
    Empty of flowers and grapes, resting from labors of men.
But string music resounds from a garden far off; it may be some
    Song of love is at play there, or a man all alone
Thinks about distant friends and the time of his youth, while
                the fountains,
    Ever flowing and fresh, splash upon flowering beds.   10
Silently in the twilight air the church bells are ringing,
    And to keep track of the time, watchmen call out every hour.
Now a breeze comes as well, and the crests of the grove are in motion,
    Look!, the moon rises too, shadowy image of earth,
Comes up also in secret; the night comes on, the fantastic,   15
    Filled with stars and in truth little concerned with ourselves,
There the stranger among mankind, the astonisher shines forth
    Over the mountaintops, sadly and proudly on high.

2.

Wonderful is the grace of the high sublime one, and no one
    Knows how it is and why she can affect people so.   20
Thus does she move the world and the hopeful spirit of humans,
    Even a wise man knows not what she counsels, for thus
Wills it the highest god, who very much loves you, and therefore

Ist noch lieber, wie sie, dir der besonnene Tag.
25 Aber zuweilen liebt auch klares Auge den Schatten
Und versuchet zu Lust, eh' es die Noth ist, den Schlaf,
Oder es blikt auch gern ein treuer Mann in die Nacht hin,
Ja, es ziemet sich ihr Kränze zu weihn und Gesang,
Weil den Irrenden sie geheiliget ist und den Todten,
30   Selber aber besteht, ewig, in freiestem Geist.
Aber sie muß uns auch, daß in der zaudernden Weile,
Daß im Finstern für uns einiges Haltbare sei,
Uns die Vergessenheit und das Heiligtrunkene gönnen,
Gönnen das strömende Wort, das, wie die Liebenden, sei,
35 Schlummerlos und vollern Pokal und kühneres Leben,
Heilig Gedächtniß auch, wachend zu bleiben bei Nacht.

3.

Auch verbergen umsonst das Herz im Busen, umsonst nur
Halten den Muth noch wir, Meister und Knaben, denn wer
Möcht' es hindern und wer möcht' uns die Freude verbieten?
40   Göttliches Feuer auch treibet, bei Tag und bei Nacht,
Aufzubrechen, So komm! daß wir das Offene schauen,
Daß ein Eigenes wir suchen, so weit es auch ist.
Fest bleibt Eins; es sei um Mittag oder es gehe
Bis in die Mitternacht, immer bestehet ein Maas,
45 Allen gemein, doch jeglichem auch ist eignes beschieden,
Dahin gehet und kommt jeder, wohin er es kann,
Drum! und spotten des Spotts mag gern frohlokkender Wahnsinn,
Wenn er in heiliger Nacht plözlich die Sänger ergreift.
Drum an den Isthmos komm! dorthin, wo das offene Meer rauscht
50   Am Parnaß und der Schnee delphische Felsen umglänzt,
Dort ins Land des Olymps, dort auf die Höhe Cithärons,
Unter die Fichten dort, unter die Trauben von wo
Thebe drunten und Ismenos rauscht im Lande des Kadmos,
Dorther kommt und zurük deutet der kommende Gott.

4.

55 Seeliges Griechenland! du Haus der Himmlischen alle,
Also ist wahr, was einst wir in der Jugend gehört?
Festlicher Saal! der Boden ist Meer! und Tische die Berge
Wahrlich zu einzigem Brauche vor Alters gebaut!
Aber die Thronen, wo? die Tempel, und wo die Gefäße,

Dearer to you than she is the enlightening day.
But on occasion even a lucid eye loves the shadows   25
    And, before there is need, samples for pleasure repose,
Also a faithful man gazes gladly into the darkness,
    Yes, it is good to grant wreathes to the night, and to sing,
For, to those who are lost, she is sacred, and to the dead,
    But she herself abides, ever a spirit that's free.   30
But in the hesitations of time she must grant to us, so that
    In the darkness for us, something is there that endures,
Grant us forgetfulness and sacred drunkenness also,
    Grant us the flowing words, which, like the lovers, can be
Slumberless, and a fuller cup and a life that is bolder,   35
    Sacred memory too, staying awake through the night.

3.

Also in vain we conceal the heart in our breasts, and in vain we
    Still keep control of our mood, master and youth, for who might
Wish to hinder it, who could wish to forbid us our pleasure?
    Also the fire divine struggles, by day and by night,   40
Breaking forth. So come! So that we may witness the Open
    Seeking what is our own, ever so far though it be.
One thing is sure; it can last till noontime or keep going onward
    Even till late in the night, always a limit applies,
Common to all, yet to each one also his own is allotted,   45
    Each one goes and returns, there to wherever he can.
Therefore! and gladly it makes a mockery, madness triumphant,
    When in the sacred night swiftly it seizes our song.
Therefore come to the Isthmos! The place where the wide open ocean
    Roars at Parnassos and snow flashes on Delphian cliffs,   50
There in the land of Olympos, there on the heights of Kithairon,
    Under the fir trees there, under the vineyards, from where
Thebes below and the Ismenos roars in the country of Kadmos,
    There he comes forward and back signals his coming, the God.

4.

Blessed land of the Greeks! you house of the heavenly all, so   55
    Is it then true, what once we in our youth had been told?
Festive hall! whose floor is the sea! and tables the mountains,
    Truly for singular use built up long ages ago!
But the thrones and the temples, where? and where are the vessels,

60   Wo mit Nectar gefüllt, Göttern zu Lust der Gesang?
       Wo, wo leuchten sie denn, die fernhintreffenden Sprüche?
          Delphi schlummert und wo tönet das große Geschik?
       Wo ist das schnelle? wo brichts, allgegenwärtigen Glüks voll
          Donnernd aus heiterer Luft über die Augen herein?
65   Vater Aether! so riefs und flog von Zunge zu Zunge
       Tausendfach, es ertrug keiner das Leben allein;
       Ausgetheilet erfreut solch Gut und getauschet, mit Fremden,
          Wirds ein Jubel, es wächst schlafend des Wortes Gewalt
       Vater! heiter! und hallt, so weit es gehet, das uralt
70   Zeichen, von Eltern geerbt, treffend und schaffend hinab.
       Denn so kehren die Himmlischen ein, tiefschütternd gelangt so
          Aus den Schatten herab unter die Menschen ihr Tag.

5.

       Unempfunden kommen sie erst, es streben entgegen
          Ihnen die Kinder, zu hell kommet, zu blendend das Glük,
75   Und es scheut sie der Mensch, kaum weiß zu sagen ein Halbgott,
          Wer mit Nahmen sie sind, die mit den Gaaben ihm nahn.
       Aber der Muth von ihnen ist groß, es füllen das Herz ihm
          Ihre Freuden und kaum weiß er zu brauchen das Gut,
       Schafft, verschwendet und fast ward ihm Unheiliges heilig,
80   Das er mit seegnender Hand thörig und gütig berührt.
       Möglichst dulden die Himmlischen diß; dann aber in Wahrheit
          Kommen sie selbst und gewohnt werden die Menschen des Glüks
       Und des Tags und zu schaun die Offenbaren, das Antliz
          Derer, welche, schon längst Eines und Alles genannt,
85   Tief die verschwiegene Brust mit freier Genüge gefüllet,
          Und zuerst und allein alles Verlangen beglükt;
       So ist der Mensch; wenn da ist das Gut, und es sorget mit Gaaben
          Selber ein Gott für ihn, kennet und sieht er es nicht.
       Tragen muß er, zuvor; nun aber nennt er sein Liebstes,
90   Nun, nun müssen dafür Worte, wie Blumen,
             entstehn.

6.

       Und nun denkt er zu ehren in Ernst die seeligen Götter,
          Wirklich und wahrhaft muß alles verkünden ihr Lob.
       Nichts darf schauen das Licht, was nicht den Hohen gefället,
          Von den Aether gebührt müßigversuchendes nicht.

Where, with nectar divine, pleasing the gods, is the song?   60
Where, oh, where do they shine, the oracles striking afar?
    Delphi slumbers, and where echoes that fatal sublime?
Where is the swift? Where breaks forth, filled with such joy all
    Present, thundering down from a clear sky on our eyes?
Father Aether! the cry, and the sound flew from tongue to tongue,   65
    Thousandfold, and for life, no one could bear it alone;
Such wealth brings joy when divided up and bartered, with strangers, a
    Jubilation expands, sleeping, the power of the word:
Father! Brighter! and hails, so far as can be, the primordial
    Sign, a parental decree, striking, creating below.   70
Thus do the heavenly enter, and quaking deeply it reaches,
    Out of the shadows below, down among humans their day.

5.

Unperceived at the first they come, and only the children
    Reach out to greet them; too bright comes, and too blinding their bliss,
Humans avoid them, and what to say, a halfgod can hardly   75
    Know who they are by name, they who approach him with gifts.
Great is the courage received from them, and his heart overflows with
    All their joys, and he scarce knows how to use so much wealth,
Brings forth, squanders, and almost makes holy what is unholy,
    Which he with blessing hands foolish and kindly has touched.   80
Far as can be the heavenly tolerate this; until then they
    Truly appear themselves, people get used to the joy
And the day, to behold them revealed, to see their true faces,
    Those who always were called One-and-All, and who filled
Ever so deeply the heart concealed by their generous excess,   85
    And at first and alone every desire is fulfilled;
Thus is a man; when the goods are there and even a god takes
    Care of him with his gifts, knows not nor can he perceive.
First he must bear it; but now he finds names for those who are dearest,
    Now, now the words must come, grow forth and blossom,
        like flowers   90

6.

Now though he means to honor the blessed gods in full earnest,
    Truly and really must now all of them signal their praise.
Nothing may see the light but that which pleases these high ones,
    There in the aether's realm idle endeavor is wrong.

95 Drum in der Gegenwart der Himmlischen würdig zu stehen,
 Richten in herrlichen Ordnungen Völker sich auf
Untereinander und baun die schönen Tempel und Städte
 Vest und edel, sie gehn über Gestaden empor —
Aber wo sind sie? wo blühn die Bekannten, die Kronen des
 Festes?
100 Thebe welkt und Athen; rauschen die Waffen nicht mehr
In Olympia, nicht die goldnen Wagen des Kampfspiels,
 Und bekränzen sich denn nimmer die Schiffe Korinths?
Warum schweigen auch sie, die alten heilgen Theater?
 Warum freuet sich denn nicht der geweihete Tanz?
105 Warum zeichnet, wie sonst, die Stirne des Mannes ein Gott nicht,
 Drükt den Stempel, wie sonst, nicht dem Getroffenen auf?
Oder er kam auch selbst und nahm des Menschen Gestalt an
 Und vollendet' und schloß tröstend das himmlische Fest.

7.

Aber Freund! wir kommen zu spät. Zwar leben die Götter
110 Aber über dem Haupt droben in anderer Welt.
Endlos wirken sie da und scheinens wenig zu achten,
 Ob wir leben, so sehr schonen die Himmlischen uns.
Denn nicht immer vermag ein schwaches Gefäß sie zu fassen,
 Nur zu Zeiten erträgt göttliche Fülle der Mensch.
115 Traum von ihnen ist drauf das Leben. Aber das Irrsaal
 Hilft, wie Schlummer und stark machet die Noth und die
 Nacht,
Biß daß Helden genug in der ehernen Wiege gewachsen,
 Herzen an Kraft, wie sonst, ähnlich den Himmlischen sind.
Donnernd kommen sie drauf. Indessen dünket mir öfters
120 Besser zu schlafen, wie so ohne Genossen zu seyn,
So zu harren und was zu thun indeß und zu sagen,
 Weiß ich nicht und wozu Dichter in dürftiger Zeit?
Aber sie sind, sagst du, wie des Weingotts heilige Priester,
 Welche von Lande zu Land zogen in heiliger Nacht.

8.

125 Nemlich, als vor einiger Zeit, uns dünket sie lange,
 Aufwärts stiegen sie all, welche das Leben beglükt,
Als der Vater gewandt sein Angesicht von den Menschen,

Therefore to stand before the heavenly ones in full honor,   95
    Peoples assemble themselves always in glorious ranks,
One with another, and build the beautiful temples and cities,
    Firm and noble, they rise up at the edge of the shore —
But where are they? Where blossom, well known, the festival's
      garlands?
    Athens is withered and Thebes; weapons no longer resound   100
There in Olympia, no golden chariots race in the games there?
    Are the ships of Corinth decked out no longer with flowers?
Why are they also silent, the ancient festival theaters?
    Why no longer to take joy in the sacrosanct dance?
Why does a god not inscribe, as once, the brow of the hero,   105
    Why no longer, as once, stamp on the victim his seal?
Else he appeared himself, assuming the guise of a human,
    And completed and closed gently the heavenly feast.

7.

But, my friend!, we have come too late. True, the gods are still living,
    But they're above our heads, up in a different world.   110
Endlessly they are active there and seem to care little
    Whether we live, so much spare us the heavenly ones.
For not always a fragile vessel can manage to bear them,
    Only at times can a man carry the force of the gods.
Dreaming about them afterwards is our life. But the errors   115
    Help, like slumber, and need gives us the strength, and the
      night,
Till there are those who grow in the brazen cradle, the heroes,
    Hearts as once in their strength, just like the heavenly ones.
Thundering then they come. But meanwhile to me it seems often
    Better to sleep than to be so without comrades, alone,   120
Always waiting, and what to do and to say in the meanwhile,
    I do not know, and why poets in a time of such need?
But they are, you say, like the sacred priests of the Wine God,
    They who from land to land traveled through sacred night.

8.

Namely, when some time ago, to us it appears such a long time,   125
    Upwards ascended all those who had brought joy into life,
When from humankind the father averted his visage,

Und das Trauern mit Recht über der Erde begann,
  Als erschienen zu lezt ein stiller Genius, himmlisch
130   Tröstend, welcher des Tags Ende verkündet' und schwand,
  Ließ zum Zeichen, daß einst er da gewesen und wieder
    Käme, der himmlische Chor einige Gaaben zurük,
  Derer menschlich, wie sonst, wir uns zu freuen vermöchten,
    Denn zur Freude, mit Geist, wurde das Größre zu groß
135 Unter den Menschen und noch, noch fehlen die Starken
    zu höchsten
    Freuden, aber es lebt stille noch einiger Dank.
  Brod ist der Erde Frucht, doch ists vom Lichte geseegnet,
    Und vom donnernden Gott kommet die Freude des Weins.
  Darum denken wir auch dabei der Himmlischen, die sonst
140   Da gewesen und die kehren in richtiger Zeit,
  Darum singen sie auch mit Ernst die Sänger den Weingott
    Und nicht eitel erdacht tönet dem Alten das Lob.

9.

Ja! sie sagen mit Recht, er söhne den Tag mit der Nacht aus,
    Führe des Himmels Gestirn ewig hinunter, hinauf,
145 Allzeit froh, wie das Laub der immergrünenden Fichte,
    Das er liebt, und der Kranz, den er von Epheu gewählt,
  Weil er bleibet und selbst die Spur der entflohenen Götter
    Götterlosen hinab unter das Finstere bringt.
  Was der Alten Gesang von Kindern Gottes geweissagt,
150   Siehe! wir sind es, wir; Frucht von Hesperien ists!
  Wunderbar und genau ists als an Menschen erfüllet,
    Glaube, wer es geprüft! aber so vieles geschieht,
  Keines wirket, denn wir sind herzlos, Schatten, bis unser
    Vater Aether erkannt jeden und allen gehört.
155 Aber indessen kommt als Fakelschwinger des Höchsten
    Sohn, der Syrier, unter die Schatten herab.
  Seelige Weise sehns; ein Lächeln aus der gefangnen
    Seele leuchtet, dem Licht thauet ihr Auge noch auf.
  Sanfter träumet und schläft in Armen der Erde der Titan,
160   Selbst der neidische, selbst Cerberus trinket und schläft.

Then all across the earth mourning correctly began,
 When at the last a silent genius appeared, and providing
  Heavenly solace, proclaimed day's end and then disappeared,   130
Left as a sign that once it was here and would at some time come
  Back, the heavenly choir left us some tokens behind,
Which to enjoy in a human way, as once, we are able,
  Since for such spirited joy, great things became much too great
Here among humans and still, still we lack the strong who   135
   can carry
  Highest joys, but yet lives silently some kind of thanks.
Bread is the fruit of the earth, yet is blessed by the warmth of the sunlight,
  And from the thundering God down comes the joy of the wine.
Therefore we also think thereby of the heavenly ones, who
  Once were here and will come back again all in good time,   140
Therefore the singers also in earnest sing of the Wine God,
  And, not idly conceived, praise for the old one resounds.

9.

Yes! they are right to say he reconciles daytime with nighttime,
  Guides all the heavenly stars downward and upward for us,
Always with joy, like the boughs of the living, evergreen fir tree,   145
  Which he loves, and the wreath, woven of ivy, he chose,
Since he endures, and himself a trace of the gods who are absent
  Brings down into the dark, there where the godless abide.
What was foretold by the songs of old about God's own true children,
  See! it is we, we ourselves: fruit of Hesperia, too!   150
Wonderful and exact, it's fulfilled, as if upon humans,
  Know it, if put to the test!, so many things though are done,
Nothing works, for we all are heartless, shadows, until our
  Father Aether is known, each one to each and to all.
Meanwhile though, as a torchbearer, comes the Son of the Highest,   155
  He, the Syrian, comes downward to visit the shades.
Blessed wise ones can see it; and smiles from their captive
  Souls shine forth, and the light moistens their eyes as with dew.
Gently dreaming sleeps in the Earth's embraces the Titan,
  Even the envious one, Cerberus drinks and he sleeps.   160

* — Translated by Cyrus Hamlin*

The Novel in Weimar Classicism: Symbolic Form and Symbolic Pregnance[1]

R. H. Stephenson

A WARENESS OF STYLISTIC TECHNIQUE is necessary to aesthetic apprecia-tion; but formal analysis is not sufficient for criticism. In the case of the novel, which, as Henry James (1843–1916) insisted, is an "ado about something,"[2] the "formalistic fallacy" is peculiarly inappropriate. Unless we appreciate the status of the material deployed — unless we have some idea of what is being related to what — we are in no position to grasp the mean-ing of the resultant structure. It is, therefore, part of the scholarly business of literary history to provide an adequate sense of the significance of a writer's subject matter, by placing it in historical perspective. In the flood of novels published in German in the eighteenth and nineteenth centuries, joining the ranks of translations of English, French, and Spanish novels,[3] this subject matter is astonishingly homogeneous. Whether we consider the epistolary novel, modeled on the work of Samuel Richardson (1689–1761) and Jean-Jacques Rousseau, or the Bildungsroman, or the novel of enter-tainment, of adventure, of travel, we are presented with the same set of themes, with only marginal variations.[4] Otherwise helpful periodizations of literary history tend to obscure the fact that works as superficially different as Christoph Martin Wieland's *Die Geschichte des Agathon* (The Story of Agathon, 1766) and Johann Wolfgang von Goethe's *Die Leiden des jungen Werther* (Sorrows of Young Werther, 1774) made their appearance within only a decade of each other. Undue reliance on established periodization also tends to obscure the fact that, throughout the length of the eighteenth century and into our own time, novelists treat themes that are the staple commonplaces, not just of their chosen genre, but of other modes of discourse as well, including philosophy. In Germany as in England, the novel continued to be regarded by many "as a typical example of the debased kind of writing by which the booksellers pandered to the reading public."[5] Like Proust much later, the eighteenth and nineteenth-century German novelist, operating on whatever level in whatever sub-genre, "res-urrects the insignificant [elements of experience], conjures them up with their full setting, and discovers for them their real meaning."[6] In terms recently borrowed from Ernst Cassirer (1874–1945) — who himself bor-rowed them from eighteenth-century German literary theory — and enlighteningly re-applied to Goethe's fiction, we may say that a novelist invariably works, as raw material, with any or all of those "symbolic forms" by which we habitually, and as often as not unconsciously, lend significance to ordinary, daily life — in order to shape a novel structure of renewed significance, of "symbolische Prägnanz" (symbolic pregnance).[7]

The assertion by Christian Friedrich von Blanckenburg (1714–96), in his pathbreaking *Versuch über den Roman* (Essay on the Novel, 1774), that a novelist should clarify the interrelationship between "character" and "world,"[8] is an accurate theoretical description of the central preoccupation to which I refer above, at least since the appearance of the novels of Christoph Martin Wieland, whose evocations of the contrast between reality and subjectivity generate that elegant irony that first inspired Blanckenburg to make his insightful contributions to aesthetics. Until at least the final version of Goethe's *Wilhelm Meisters Wanderjahre* (Wilhelm Meister's Journeymanship, 1821; final version 1829), the division of human experience into that of body and spirit, body and mind, along with the metaphysical, socio-cultural, and political corollaries of such a dichotomy — fate and freedom, nature and culture, fantasy and reality, faith and knowledge, world and individual — constitutes common thematic property for the group of novels discussed here. Largely displacing the organizing theme in Baroque novels of a dialectic between the sublime and the ordinary, the depiction of everyday life, feeling, and thought became a *topos* inherited from the Enlightenment novel, exemplified by the *Lebensläufe* (Life Stories, 1778–81) by Theodor Gottlieb Hippel (1741–96), in which a world of disorder offered only a retreat into egocentric reflection — the novel begins with the word "ich" (I). Rousseau's *Nouvelle Héloïse* (1761) had already powerfully portrayed the rights of feeling as an irresistible force of nature, reflected with yet greater intensity in Goethe's tragic hero Werther, a complex figure of alienation, expressing division at every level of consciousness, with whom almost all German novelists of the period came to terms. The eponymous hero in the novel *Anton Reiser* (1785–90) by Karl Philipp Moritz is pulled between sober reality and euphoric fantasy — today we should diagnose him as manic-depressive.[9] Wilhelm Meister's working out of the apparent polarity between fate and individual freedom, like his uneasy shifting between the fantasy life of the theater and the bourgeois philistinism of his home background, as represented in the *Lehrjahre* (Apprenticeship Years, 1795–96), is entirely typical of the problematic presented in novel after novel. In *Die unsichtbare Loge* (1792) by Jean Paul — which, like Goethe's *Lehrjahre* and *Wanderjahre*, draws on the mumbo-jumbo and paraphernalia of the secret societies of the day — we find perhaps the most brilliant treatment of the motif, often taken up by other novelists, right down to Thomas Mann, of the climactic and all-subsuming tension between life and death. When Friedrich Hölderlin, in the 1794 preface planned for his *Hyperion*

(1797/99), came to discuss the reconciliation of the polarity of "self" and "world" as "das Ziel all unseres Strebens"[10] (the goal of all our strivings), he was summarizing the central concern of his age. Likewise, in drawing on a typology from Schiller's 1794 essay, *Über naïve und sentimentalische Dichtung*, to develop the type of the idealist (Hyperion, who strives for a "new church") and of the realist (Alabanda, who seeks a "new state"), Hölderlin is also employing a technique characteristic of Jean Paul, derived from Cervantes's *Don Quixote*, and a stock-in-trade of the Romantic novel to come: the embodiment of the dichotomy of human experience in two contrasting, yet complementary, main characters.

Tension implies reconciliation, and attempts to resolve thematic dichotomies are as commonplace as the problems presented. Like Wilhelm in the Ur-Meister, *Wilhelm Meisters Theatralische Sendung* (Wilhelm Meister's Theatrical Calling, composed between 1776 and 1785, but never published by Goethe), Anton Reiser considers the theater a resolution to the ideal/real tension, a solution that turns out to be as unconvincing then as it is in the later *Lehrjahre*. The fragmentary nature of *Woldemar* (1779–1796), in which Friedrich Heinrich Jacobi explored the psychology of his sensitive and emotional Werther-like hero pulled between two contrasting women, suggests, too, that a compromise synthesis of the defining dichotomies of the Zeitgeist proved difficult to effect. The same inference can be drawn from Schiller's failure to complete his novelistic critique of fashionable superstition, *Der Geisterseher* (The Spirit-Seer, 1787–89): Schiller's hallucinating German prince, locked into his fantasy world, alienated from reality, is a disturbing embodiment of a desire for irrational integration (with "higher powers") that became a cultural epidemic in Europe after the trauma of the 1789 French Revolution. Other novelists followed Wieland's example in *Agathon*, mirroring the tendency in autobiography before the psychological acumen of Rousseau's *Confessions* (1781), to see the development of personality in intellectual terms: Agathon is open to feeling, but it is feeling mediated, and checked, by "mind," as the cult of *Empfindsamkeit* (sentimentalism) advocated. Friedrich Maximilian Klinger (1752–1831) proposed a rationalistic, ethical solution in the preface to his cycle of nine philosophical novels, beginning in 1791 with *Fausts Leben, Taten und Höllenfahrt* (Faust's Life, Deeds, and Journey to Hell) and ending in 1803 with *Der Weltmann und der Dichter* (The Man-of-the-World and the Poet, begun 1798). Influenced by his reading of Rousseau and Immanuel Kant, especially the latter's *Kritik der praktischen Vernunft* (Critique of Practical Reason, 1788), Klinger's resolution of feeling and reason amounted to a firm subordination of inclination to duty (though only after many years of titillating, sensuous adventure!). But such stern moralizing was a minority voice; most followed the example of Henry Fielding in portraying the happy adaptation of the individual to society.[11] Hölderlin's promise, in his 1797 preface to *Hyperion*, of an "Auflösung der Dissonanzen in einem gewissen Charakter"[12] (the resolution of dissonances in a certain character), while perhaps unfulfilled in his own novel, accurately sums up much of the appeal of the contemporary popular novel. The success of the widely-read family novels of Heinrich Lafontaine (1758–1831), especially of his *Gemälde des menschlichen Herzens* (Portrait of the Human Heart, 1797), derived from a seductively simple presentation of the innate balance of feeling and reason as a cure for vice: the *Naturmensch* (natural man) was inclined toward harmony once the complicating pretensions of civilization were cast off. Indeed, the popularity of the *Frauenroman (Women's Novel)*, including the immensely successful *Geschichte des Fräuleins von Sternheim* (1771) by Sophie von La Roche, is due in part to the location of the cultural values inherent in imagination and feeling — the despised "lower faculties" of rationalistic Enlighteners — in woman qua *Naturmensch*. The "schöne Seele" (beautiful soul) harmonizes just those opposing qualities, clustering around the body-mind antithesis, which had become common motifs of the novel. But such essentialism, in which virtue flows from nature and culture from character, only restates on a psychological level the problems of division and alienation. The dilettante heroine of *Florentin* (1801) by Dorothea Schlegel is typical of the fashionable reliance on character: she is so full of contradictions that the recourse to inborn goodness of heart wears thin, and the novel remains a sentimental fragment.

As if to compensate for the limitations of positing a naturally harmonious human nature — ruthlessly exposed as self-deluding in the sixth chapter of Goethe's *Lehrjahre*, "Die Bekenntnisse einer schönen Seele" (The Confessions of a Beautiful Soul) — novelists of the period commonly introduce the theme of *Entsagung* (renunciation), thus giving simplistic solutions an air of moral dignity. Possession of a "beautiful soul" involves, after all, renunciation of worldly sophistication and complexity: it is only by enthusiastically embracing otherworldly values that Julie in Rousseau's *Nouvelle Héloïse* remains a *belle âme*. Apparently, wherever one looks, renunciation is being advocated. Renunciation, the common property of every higher religion, was given special emphasis in German eighteenth-century Pietism. And its age-old pedigree, reaching back at least as far as Pindar, remaining central to the Stoic tradition since its foundation by Zeno in ca. 310 B.C., and given classical formulation by Plato, St. Augustine, and Blaise Pascal (1623–62),[13] gives it, as a moral imperative, the authority of "second nature." We find Hippel's main character in the *Lebensläufe* following the example of Michel Montaigne (1533–92) and Voltaire, renouncing the chaotic world and retreating to an idyll of reflection. Just as Klinger's abiding theme is renunciation of all Faustian and Promethean revolt against the order of the universe, so Jacobi's Woldemar seeks the kind of selfless affection associated with the doctrines of Benedict Spinoza. Equally, in reverent acceptance of the intrinsic polarity and fundamental unity of nature's cycles, Hölderlin's *Hyperion* consciously renounces intellectual analysis of its workings. Goethe, in subtitling his *Wanderjahre* "oder die Entsagenden" (or the renunciants), is not being original; nor is he diverging from the common agenda of the novel by showing, in the novellas he interpolates into the *Wanderjahre*, that passion is containable only by *Entsagung*. For there is renunciation, too — of a kind that overlaps with Goethe's this-worldliness — in the love of the little things of this earth, which animates both Viktor, the central figure of Jean Paul's first truly successful novel, *Hesperus* (1792–94), and the eponymous hero of his *Quintus Fixlein* (1794–95); and renunciation is likewise essential to the success of Albano — in contrast to the unrestrained, titanic revolt of the other characters — in Jean Paul's *Titan* (1800–1803).

Most of the novels produced during the period of Weimar Classicism are narratologically poorly organized, and their thematic content is rarely given much intensity, precision, suggestiveness, or fullness of implication. And yet, as Goethe points out,[14] such works have value in treating important subject matter because they participate in issues which the novel as genre tackles in offering "a model of coming to know the world."[15] In, say, the hugely successful *Trivialroman Rinaldo Rinaldini* (1798) by Goethe's brother-in-law Christian August Vulpius history may be a mere stage setting, but like the much more accurate historiography in the novels of Benedikte Naubert (1756–1819), the work provided orientation at a time of fundamental ideological and political change, one that found satisfaction in *Ahnung und Gegenwart* (Presentiment and Presence, 1815) by Joseph Eichendorff. In moving rapidly from a God- and Bible-centered culture to a secular one, readers felt the need for reassurance, which an everyday presentation of apparently viable lifeforms, offered as alternatives to what seemed in the general culture to be either an overly rationalistic or an unduly emotional approach to experience, seemed to give. Goethe's position is not that the trivial has no value. He had, after all, used all the motifs of what Germans call the "trivial novel" — divorce, abduction, incest, suicide — in the eighth chapter of his *Lehrjahre*, in much the same way as E. T. A. Hoffmann (1776–1822) was to do in *Die Elixiere des Teufels* (1815–16). Rather, what Goethe maintains (like Schiller and Jean Paul in commending Dorothea Schlegel's *Florentin*) is that such value can be enhanced by formal development.

Marshall McLuhan's view of the function of the novel in modern culture as "a homogenized body of common experience"[16] is borne out, then, by the development of the German novel in the eighteenth and nineteenth centuries. The experiential importance of the thematic matrix clustered about the problematic relation of "self" and "world" is underlined by its continuing to be drawn upon by the Romantic novelists. *William Lovell* (1793–95) by Ludwig Tieck presents the isolation of

Lovell's solipsistic egoism, anticipating the terms in which the idealist philosopher Johann Gottlieb Fichte was to deal with the problem of the ego's relation to the world. In disillusionment at being taken in by the hocus-pocus of magic, reminiscent of Schiller's *Geisterseher*, Lovell spends such time as is left to him before his untimely, violent death reverting to Enlightenment values and cultivating his garden in the way Voltaire had recommended in his philosophical tale *Candide* (1759). Fantastic enthusiasm and sober reflection alternate in the mind of Tieck's main character, just as in *Lucinde* (1799) by Friedrich Schlegel, significantly subtitled "Bekenntnisse eines Ungeschickten" (Confessions of a Clumsy Man); it is inner tension issuing in ineptitude in action that is treated — a theme fully realized by Hoffmann in the paradigmatically self-divided, alienated figure of Johannes Kreisler in *Die Lebensansichten des Katers Murr* (The Views on Life of the Tomcat Murr, 1819–21).

The fact that *Hamlet* was the most frequently performed Shakespeare play of the eighteenth century indicates the contemporary interest in the problem of the alienated individual.[17] And the ambition to conciliate the "ideal" and the "real" is the stock preoccupation, too, of the contemporary philosophical debate. The notion of an unbridgeable epistemological gap between "mind" and "world" had, since the impact of the philosophy of René Descartes (1596–1650), become almost a cliché. Its corollary, that common sense is incompatible with the higher problems of existence, was for the eighteenth and nineteenth centuries both an equally familiar notion and a constituent of everyday experience.[18] Partly as a result of the scientific revolution of the seventeenth century, and partly as a result of the social reality of an emergent middle class keen to have its workaday experience given theoretical clarification, the impulse to resolve the divergence between the philosopher's and the ordinary individual's common-sense experience of the world had, since the publication of the *Treatise of Human Nature* (1739–40) by David Hume, become the central concern of philosophical discourse. Moreover, even before Hume, the *Essay Concerning Human Understanding* (1690) by John Locke (1632–1704) had been decisive in undermining those who based their ethics on religious faith by insisting on the necessity of a rational basis of morality. Among philosophers in Germany, the desire to reconcile "mind" and "world" took the form of an ambition to create an "empirical rationalism," of which the best example is Kant's critical philosophy. The problem of relating ordinary empirical perception and the rigor proper to philosophy was tackled before Kant's *Kritik der reinen Vernunft* (Critique of Pure Reason, 1781) by trying to accommodate and assimilate sensation to the supposedly higher faculty of representation, which was upheld by traditions as diverse as Leibnizian rationalism and inspirational Pietism.[19] If the eighteenth-century yearning to overcome the feeling-reason dichotomy (a dubious, regressive symptom of which was the widespread desire to be reborn culturally as a Greek [Goody, 7]) was to be taken seriously after Kant attacked the idea of the easy fusion of ethics and aesthetics in the fashionable notion of "moral beauty" in his *Grundlegung zur Metaphysik der Sitten* (Foundation of the Metaphysics of Morals, 1785), the notion of the "beautiful soul" would need to be reconsidered. Taken for granted until the 1780s as a valid conception of reality by laymen and learned alike, it furnished the Enlightenment with its ethical ideal, promising the "good life" and happiness.[20] In the novel, ever since Wieland's introduction in 1758 of the term *kalokagathia* to cover the somewhat vague phenomenon of the beautiful human being personified in his Agathon, the opaque idea of an innately harmonious personality had seemed to underwrite the sketchy outlines offered as a resolution to the experience of alienation. The Richardsonian sentimentalist ethic, in which, as in *Clarissa* (1748), conviction is derived from moral feeling alone, needed to be revised in light of the new philosophy's enhanced grasp of the complexity of the concepts involved. The Enlightenment novel tradition, commended by Blanckenburg (*Versuch*, 8), of holding up to critical scrutiny what passes for reality, which was built into its rhetoric of ironic skepticism on the part of narrator (and character), made avoidance of the new philosophy in any case well-nigh impossible; and Klinger's novel cycle of 1791–1803, beginning with *Fausts Leben, Taten und Höllenfahrt*, is entirely typical in being open to ongoing philosophical developments.

The intellectual divorce effected by Kant's critical philosophy between ethics and aesthetics — dramatically symbolized by his devoting separate *Critiques* to each: his second critique, *Die Kritik der praktischen Vernunft* (The Critique of Practical Reason), to moral issues and his third, *Die Kritik der Urteilskraft* (The Critique of Judgment, 1790), to the question of beauty — intensified the trend in the German novel, already underway, toward depicting the process rather than the product of experience. The career and above all the education of the major characters, as already set out in Wieland's *Agathon*, shifted emphatically to the center of attention. For if — as Wieland's playful skepticism had tirelessly insinuated — one could not be whole simply by throwing off the distorting burdens of culture and regressing to one's essential "good-beautiful" self, it was yet possible to envisage becoming whole through time, by successively developing different facets of one's personality and in that way overcoming, by rhythmic alternation of aesthetic and ethical response, the evils of division. That faith motivated the German transmutation in the late eighteenth and early nineteenth century of the novel of travel and adventure into the novel of education or Bildungsroman (a term coined in 1803 to characterize *Wilhelm Meister*).[21]

Insisting, very much in the spirit of Fichte's philosophy, on *Bildung* as self-education to a socially useful purpose, the influential educational theorist Johann Heinrich Pestalozzi (1746–1827) also stressed the crucial importance of exposing oneself to a variety of cultural influences through close, personal contact[22] — a programmatic statement of the kind of career upon which the self-cultivating hero of the German novel of development embarked. "The relationship of the humanistic cultivation of the whole personality to the world of bourgeois society" was not just the central theme of Goethe's *Lehrjahre*;[23] it was, as the philosopher Georg Wilhelm Friedrich Hegel observed, one of the most familiar and most appropriate tasks of the novel, to tackle "den Konflikt zwischen der Poesie des Herzens und der entgegenstehenden Prosa der Verhältnisse" (the conflict between the poetry of the heart and the opposing prose of circumstance) — indeed, in his *Phänomenologie des Geistes* (1806), what Hegel "proposed to write really was the *Bildungsroman* of the human spirit," as Walter Kaufmann insists.[24] Reflecting the gentlemanly passive education of the Grand Tour, the theme of education was part of that "introduction to life" that Samuel Johnson (1709–84) held to be one of the main functions of the novel, making it "a form of Wisdom Literature" (Goody, 277, 473). For all the emphasis he placed on the novel's ability to present human life as "being," Blanckenburg was well aware of the necessity to present it as also in process: "Jeder Mensch hat seine Geschichte" (*Versuch*, 388; every person has a history). And for a simple, though profound (metaphysical) reason: "alles ist *werdend* in der Natur" (379; everything *becomes* in nature,). Thus in *Anton Reiser* Moritz blends self-observation with a pedagogic intent, though it is perhaps difficult (Robertson, xxii–xxiv) to discern a significant pattern in the stages of Anton's wanderings. And Goethe's shift in the *Theatralische Sendung* from Wilhelm's achievement of being in the theater to his becoming in his travels (Borchmeyer, 330) is the leading idea of the whole novel, sustained in the *Lehrjahre* and *Wanderjahre* by the intimate, face-to-face contact with various fundamental cultural ("symbolic") forms of life. The novel of development retains the multi-perspectival quality of the Richardsonian epistolary novel, drawing to the same effect on dialogue, letters, and diaries, to give expression to an array of educative influences. In Jean Paul's novels, in which the static idyll as utopian locus of reconciliation of division looms large, considerable effort is expended on portraying, as in *Unsichtbare Loge* and *Titan*, the educative process of rubbing up against a multi-faceted world. Hölderlin's *Hyperion* is divided into four books, each of which deals with a distinct phase of Hyperion's interactive education: his formative childhood experience in the first book; in the second, his transformation through love; active experimentation in the third; and, in the fourth, reflective coming-to-terms with death. Even the journey within in *Heinrich von Ofterdingen* (1799–1801), by Novalis, the pseudonym of Friedrich von Hardenberg (1772–1801), follows a discernible pattern, that of the traditional mystical "threefold birth" of "illumination," the "dark night of the soul," and finally "enlightenment"; and Eichendorff's Friedrich discernibly progresses from "presentiment" to "presence."

It is indicative of Goethe's peculiar "classical" attitude to the stock themes of the novel that, on return from Italy in 1788, he was appalled by *Ardinghello* (1787) by Wilhelm Heinse. At first sight, Heinse's subsequently highly influential novel might well seem wholly consonant with that "geistig-sinnliche Überzeugung" (intellectual-sensuous conviction) that Goethe claims to have enjoyed in Italy in the presence of beauty.[25] The novel's proclamation of an old-new Dionysian outlook, reminiscent of the eroticism of the Greek and Roman novel and anticipating the erotic focus of such Romantic novels as *Godwi* (1801) by Clemens Brentano, might appear to chime with Goethe's newly-found enthusiasm for the life of the body. "Jede Form ist individuell, und es gibt keine abstrakte"[26] (Every form is individual, and there is no such thing as an abstract one) declares Ardinghello, setting the tone at the opening of a novel in which unification of the self with beauty is hailed as "der edelste Trieb unseres Geistes" (106; the noblest impulse of our spirit), transcending time and elevating one to the level of divinity: "Genuß jedes Augenblickes, fern von Vergangenheit und Zukunft, versetzt uns unter die Götter" (135; Enjoyment of every moment, far from past and future, places us amongst the gods). But in fact, for all the novel's championing of art and the tradition of the European cultural ideal of the *uomo universal* — and despite Heinse's exquisite sensitivity, above all to color, written in descriptive prose of the highest order — what Heinse has in mind is very different indeed from what Goethe, restating Schiller's central theoretical doctrine, meant by sensitivity to the particulars of sensuous beauty.[27] Ardinghello may dismiss his (and Heinse's) aesthetic attitude as *Mückenwahrheit* (small-minded truth; Heinse, 135) whenever adventurous exploits call him to action, but art remains throughout "the vehicle of the enjoyment of love, and eroticism pervades the vivid sensuous descriptions [of paintings and statues]" (Heinse, 684), on occasion employing "pornographic images" (694), as Baeumer points out. What Goethe has in mind, by contrast, is an aesthetic experience that coordinates raw empirical experience with clear intellectual reflection to yield intuitive knowledge of individual objects: aesthetic insight arises when, however fleetingly, our sense impressions are coordinated with our conceptual thought (rather than subordinated to purposive thinking as in practical action). Beauty for Goethe, as for Schiller, is more than mere sensuous enjoyment; it is also intellectual (the principle that informs Schiller's critique of *Ardinghello* in *Über naïve und sentimentalische Dichtung*).

This is more than "the usual neoclassical bias towards the general and the universal" (Watt, 272); for it is not a case of mere taste, of the strong "preference" that underpins "neoclassical orthodoxy" (16–17), but a recognition of the necessary co-implication of universal and particular. Because aesthetic experience, like all human perception, is in part mental; and because, in the view taken by the Weimar Classicists, perception of reality is fundamentally aesthetic, we need to employ ideas not only to obtain an intellectual grasp of reality, but also to perceive truly. In particular, intellect is required in order to grasp and represent development: "die Vernunft ist auf das Werdende . . . angewiesen" (Reason is concerned with becoming).[28] It is, therefore, not difficult to see why Goethe should have been dismayed by the reduction of thought to feeling animating Heinse's novel, to which the philosopher Demetri gives explicit articulation in identifying reason with "ursprüngliche Empfindung" (Heinse, 284; original emotion). Comparison of *Ardinghello* with Goethe's *Lehrjahre* uncovers, too, important implications of this fundamental difference between their respective authors' conceptions of *Bildung*. Heinse's Ardinghello is a static creature of many-splendored perfection, needing only to unfold against the backdrop of an idealized Renaissance, and reaching full perfection in the elitist utopianism of the idyll of "the happy isles" announced in the novel's subtitle. There is no development discernible in Ardinghello as a character; indeed, Heinse's brilliantly impressionistic style seems to inhibit any overall structure at all. Goethe's Wilhelm Meister, by contrast, is an inadequate human being who, through a process of interactions with a not always supportive, often utterly philistine world, nonetheless becomes eventually both tolerably self-possessed and socially useful. The world of *Wilhelm Meister* is an unambiguously post-revolutionary world, not an aristocratic one of static hierarchy, that is, of "being"; it is rather a workaday, cooperative, insecure world of "doing" — and "becoming."[29] The aristocracy may suggest standards by virtue of its tradition-bearing function, but it is the active individual who is finally decisive.

All this is "part of the historicity of the *Lehrjahre*," and realistically reflects late eighteenth-century social and cultural life.[30] At the same time, it expresses a view of development that has become a cultural commonplace of modernity as a whole. If the kind of model of human psychological development set up by Erik Erikson in his *Identity — Youth and Crisis*[31] is applied to Wilhelm's career in the *Lehrjahre*, a schema emerges that may be outlined as follows: (a) Wilhelm's rejection of his family ties; (b) the childish solipsism of his love affair with Mariane; (c) his enthusiasm for the theatrical life and especially his identification with Hamlet, "the morbid young intellectual" (Erikson, 237–38), as the eighteenth century saw him; (d) his subsequent disillusionment and disgust with this period of his life; and (e) his identity crisis proper: his entrance into the responsible adult world of the Society of the Tower. Although this notion of the "ages of man" was as much a commonplace for the age of Goethe as it is for our own, the discrepancy between how Wilhelm conceives of his own development — "mich selbst, ganz wie ich bin, auszubilden, das war von Jugend an mein Wunsch und meine Absicht" (290; to unfold myself just as I am was from youth onwards my desire and my intent) — and how the narrator records, and the reader interprets, Wilhelm's career is one of the constituent ironies of the novel. Moreover, it precisely mirrors the preformation-versus-epigenesis controversy that marked the height of the modern phase of the novel in the 1750s. Wilhelm (unwittingly) embraces preformation, "growth without differentiation, all the complexity of the finished form being supposed to be present initially" (Needham, 183), while the narrator — like Erikson (92) — describes the gradual emergence and organization of aspects of Wilhelm's personality in epigenetic interaction with the world of chance and circumstance. Seen in this perspective Wilhelm's fatalistic passivity which punctuates the *Lehrjahre* is no more, and no less, than "that greedy blind bliss of youth, when the world appears to be arranged by our impulses and full of convenient omens, of encouraging signs," as John Updike characterizes the same stage of life in his 1986 novel *Roger's Version*.[32] Ardinghello's titanic self-unfolding, seen in this same perspective, transcends Wilhelm's amusing self-conceit; it borders on the unintentionally comic.

The peculiarity of Goethe's classical handling of the *topoi* of the novel is thrown into even sharper relief by comparison with Jean Paul. Like Wilhelm Meister, Jean Paul's heroes have to struggle in and against a refractory world. Goethe has his character Aurelie use the phrase "Paradiesvogel" (bird of paradise) of Wilhelm, indicating precisely what Jean Paul had in mind in his many uses of the term (in *Hesperus, Quintus Fixlein, Siebenkäs* [1796–97], and *Titan*):[33] like the bird of paradise, both Wilhelm and Jean Paul's heroes "hätten keine Füße, sie schwebten nur in der Luft und nährten sich vom Äther" (HA 7:318; reportedly had no feet, just hovered in the air and fed off the ether). Unlike Ardinghello's immediate mastery of the external world, most of the time they evince an incapacity for coming to terms with life easily and quickly, and finally do so somewhat precariously, after protracted, labyrinthine searching. In *Titan* as in *Wilhelm Meister*, the main theme is the achievement of one's true profession and the fulfillment of one's true self, eventually attained by (Albano's) hard-won self-discipline and gradual understanding of renunciation. Even in Jean Paul's *Flegeljahre* (1804) the apparently sublime hero, Peter Gottwalt, to whom quotidian matters are of little concern, is presented in a humorous light, as a kind of visibly idealized version of the eccentric *Quintus Fixlein*. The implicit contrast between high-minded ideal and the frustrating particulars of everyday life is as much a source of irony in Jean-Paul's *Komet* (1820–22) as in *Wilhelm Meister*.[34] Both Jean Paul and Goethe represent experience as Saul Bellow in his 1990 short story, "A Half Life," defines it: "a process of revision, of the correcting of errors."[35] Moreover, in dubbing the *Wanderjahre* an *Aggregat* (an assemblage) in conversation with Friedrich von Müller (18 February 1830), Goethe points to a tradition, reaching back at least as far as the *Encyclopédie* (1751–76), of organizing data by "assembling" a mental map (*mappemonde*) — a tradition in which both his *Lehrjahre* and *Die Wahlverwandtschaften* (Elective Affinities, 1809), by virtue of their extensive interpolations, also participate. Jean Paul's conglomerates of almost every

available form of fiction also stand in this tradition — just as both his and
Goethe's novels, especially in respect of their similar employment of diffuse,
open rhetorical frameworks, owe a great deal to *Tristram Shandy* (1760–67)
by Laurence Sterne (1713–68), itself in the tradition of "learned wit" coming down to Sterne from François Rabelais (1494?–1553) and from *The
Anatomy of Melancholy* (1621) by Robert Burton (1577–1640).[36] Both
authors take advantage of the seemingly limitless site for the play of imagination and ideas that Friedrich Schlegel (1772–1829) extolled as one of
the defining qualities of the modern novel, its status as *Kompendium*:[37] "the
impression of amplitude, of allowing room for our desires to play in,"
which has been a feature of the genre since antiquity (Goody, 10). The
open-endedness of Jean Paul's novels is matched by Goethe's rounding-off
his final, 1829 version of the *Wanderjahre* with the words "Ist fortzusetzen"
(To be continued) — as if reflecting the universal biological law that "the
end of the lineal sequence sets up conditions for a future repetition," as
Gregory Bateson has it.[38] The narrator's deeply ambivalent gesture toward
an afterlife in the final paragraph of *Die Wahlverwandtschaften* is as unsettling as Jean Paul's constantly shifting narratorial perspectives. The rather
borné, middle-brow, worldly wisdom of the narrators of the *Lehrjahre* and
Die Wahlverwandtschaften, like the equally unreliable, aged, and mystically-
minded narrator of the *Wanderjahre*, is, as Ehrhard Bahr puts it, part of that
"revolution against the given artistic code" that puts paid to any easy assimilation of Goethe to orthodox neoclassicism.[39]

Goethe is as aware as Jean Paul that "the recognition of imperfection,
of the mixed nature of experience, lies at the very heart of the Novel, and
is part of its appeal" (Goody, 478). They both write in accordance with
Blanckenburg's observation (*Versuch*, 515) that the mixing of genres is itself
a genre constraint of the novel, though neither of them was willing to go
as far as Friedrich Schlegel's advocacy in his 116th *Fragment* of a complete
Verschmelzung (fusion) to produce "das Wesentliche im Roman . . . die
chaotische Form" (the essential in a novel . . . chaotic form).[40] Certainly,
Jean Paul's *Unsichtbare Loge* could be described as deploying every available
kind of novel form, from the dramatic antithetical structures of Schiller's
Geisterseher to Sterne's ludic deployment of erudition, from Werther-like
epistolary effusions to the acute psychological analyses of *Anton Reiser*.
Goethe's designation (to Schiller, 10 June 1795) of *Hesperus* as a first-rate
Tragelaph (half deer, half goat) highlights the novel's mixed modes. The
compositional principle of repetition-with-variation in Jean Paul's works
also underpins the order Goethe achieved in his own by means of "wiederholte Spiegelung" (repeated reflection), thus avoiding the kind of confused
chaos that Schlegel advocated.[41] Perhaps because of these similarities —
perhaps, too, because both authors lend to their narratologically imperfect
novels, by means of rhetorical virtuosity, a powerful sense of human significance — it is hardly surprising that Jean Paul felt on occasion that he had

some sort of affinity with Weimar Classicism, or that Goethe should pay such handsome tribute to him as the German writer closest to the oriental *Geist* (wit) Goethe held in such high esteem.[42]

It is easy to establish, by comparing Goethe's fiction with that of the German Romantics, the obvious antithesis of Classical finitude versus Romantic infinity. Novalis's *Heinrich von Ofterdingen*, in which perfection is posited as being reached only after death and the aim of *Bildung* as mastery of one's transcendent self, revealed in the afterlife, is strikingly at variance with the temper of Goethe's *Wilhelm Meister*. Goethe, for whom life itself was the highest value,[43] could never subscribe to Novalis's assertion that "der Tod ist eine Selbstbesiegung, — die, wie alle Selbstüberwindung, eine neue, leichtere Existenz verschafft"[44] (death is a self-conquest — which like all self-overcoming, produces a new, lighter existence). Ludwig Tieck's unfinished novel *Franz Sternbalds Wanderungen* (1789), with its central theme of the external world as a dream, contrasts with Goethe's robust realism, just as Schlegel's *Lucinde* (1799), in which the union of Julius and Lucinde is mystical in nature, is a far cry from the deplorable loss of identity such oneness entails in *Die Wahlverwandtschaften*. But because the differences between Jean Paul and Goethe's novels are more subtle, they are more revealing. In *Titan*, Schoppe's search for an "absolute" beyond earthly life is revealed by the narrator's sardonic satire as a solipsistic delusion, as much an insubstantial dream as the naïveté of the eponymous hero's would-be idyllic existence in *Leben des Schulmeisterleins Maria Wuz in Auenthal* (1793) or Nikolaus Marggraf's inability to accommodate the "objective" world of his little German country town called "Rore" in *Komet*. Nonetheless, from *Unsichtbare Loge* on, happiness in Jean Paul's novels can be experienced only by those who lift themselves sufficiently high above the triviality of earthly life to glimpse at least something of the life beyond. Experience of death, if not Novalis's yearning for release from this vale of tears, is yet a primal, formative experience for Jean Paul's chief characters, inspiring them to develop themselves in this world with a view to coming ever closer to the ideal beauty of perfection that beckons from the beyond; a human being is, in Jean Paul's much repeated formula, "ein wunderbares Mittelgeschöpf"[45] (a wondrous amphibian of two worlds). In *Wilhelm Meister*, by contrast, the idyll (whether of the theater in the *Lehrjahre* or of the "paradise" of Lake Maggiore in the *Wanderjahre*, HA 8:226–40) is, as in Schiller's aesthetic state, an actuality, albeit not one translucent with eternity, but threatened with transience.[46] Since, on the aesthetic theory of Weimar Classicism, art — indeed all aesthetic experience, including gracious, idyllic living — expresses "das Innere" (the inner life), the phrase "Kunst des Ideals," as Goethe and Schiller employ it, means not "perfect art" or "intellectual art," but art replete with significant import ("idea" in its broadest contrastive sense with "reality"). This affective content of art (*Gehalt*) is both more than intellectual and less than mystical, even if its material (*Inhalt*) is wholly or partly conceptual or religious. This stance distinguishes Goethe and Schiller's classicism from the Romanticism of Hölderlin, Friedrich Schlegel, and Novalis (and from the post-Kantian idealism of Fichte, Schelling, and Hegel), all of whom subordinate art to philosophy and/or religion. To the extent that Jean Paul, in his definition of "das Romantische" in his *Vorschule der Ästhetik* (Pre-School of Aesthetics, 1804) as "das Unentbehrlichste am Roman"[47] (the most indispensable aspect of a novel), had in mind "romance," the freer conception of the novel's form, Goethe could agree; but in as far as the longing for transcendence was meant, Goethe could only demur. Whereas Heinse saw degrees of sublimity as differentiating types of art (Heinse, 705), it is essential to Weimar Classicism's strategy of uncovering the inadequacy of the traditional conception of the Beautiful Soul, mercilessly pilloried in Schiller's *Der Geisterseher*, that the moral category of the sublime be kept quite distinct from that of beauty. In his *Ästhetische Erziehung des Menschen*, Schiller strenuously argues, it is true, for the aesthetic as the necessary, though not sufficient, condition of both the birth and the continuance of ethical behavior. But ethics and aesthetics are not identical for him (or for Goethe); since the grace of a truly Beautiful Soul presupposes the moral integrity it helps to sustain, it is, according to Schiller, impossible to feign, by virtue of the fact that aesthetic behavior is an "aufrichtiger Schein" (*Ästhetische Erziehung*, 26; honest semblance): it consists in appearing to be aesthetically what ethically one in fact is. If in many respects Jean Paul comes close to Weimar Classicism, his insistent gesturing (as the foundation of his proto-Romantic irony) toward a higher world, which, ultimately, lends significance to this lower world, is much closer to Hölderlin's mysticism than to Goethe and Schiller's devotion to this world (as essentially an aesthetic, expressive phenomenon). In the *Wanderjahre*, Makarie's cosmic consciousness is an intuitive sympathy with the fundamental laws of the universe, not with any transcendental entity; and in *Die Wahlverwandtschaften*, Ottilie's hard-won and protracted renunciation is a matter of rational will.[48]

In contrast to Jean Paul's educational treatise *Levana* (1807), with its exhortations to moral and religious uplift, Goethe's tendency, like Pestalozzi's, is to ground religious sentiment in humanity. When, in the Pedagogic Province in the *Wanderjahre*, the wise elders outline the three kinds of reverence appropriate to the three fundamental forms of religion, there arises from the three a fourth reverence more profound than all the others: "die Ehrfurcht vor sich selbst"[49] (reverence for oneself). Thomas Mann makes the same humanistic point in much the same inherited terms in the concluding sentence of his foreword (1939) to *Der Zauberberg* (The Magic Mountain, 1929): "Alle Humanität beruht auf Ehrfurcht vor dem Geheimnis des Menschen"[50] (All humane values rest on reverence for the mystery of humankind). The real nature of Ottilie's triumph in *Die Wahlverwandtschaften* is obscured if we follow the narrator in conflating her development with an orthodox Christian striving for God. Admittedly, Ottilie's ascetic, moral struggle "to keep to her way" may well remind the reader of the injunction in *De Imitatione Christi* by Thomas à Kempis (1380–1471): "Control the appetite and you will more easily control all bodily desires."[51] But there is one crucial difference: if the saint's supreme wisdom is to "despise the world and draw daily nearer the Kingdom of heaven" (*Imitatione*, 49), Ottilie is emphatically no saint. When she writes of the "inner light" by which traditionally Christians are to make their way to God, she characteristically speculates on turning the light out into the world. As poorly understood by the people around her as by the narrator, she is driven to desperate measures to try to assert and sustain her independent identity as a person, as a moral agent — measures that happen to kill her. But life, not death, is her orientation, as her dying plea to Eduard makes clear: "Versprich mir zu leben" (Promise me you'll live). The underlying implication of Hölderlin's *Hyperion*, that the love of beauty *is* religion, is as antithetical to Goethe the novelist's secular presentation of the modern human predicament as is Novalis's emphasis on the Inner Way or Friedrich Schlegel's definition of the novel as "ein mystisches Kunstwerk" (a mystical work of art).[52]

Goethe reported that he found Jean Paul's wit ultimately uncongenial because of the way its sudden syntheses degenerate into melancholy and ill-humor (in a letter to Karl Friedrich Zelter, 30 October 1808).[53] Jean Paul's humor and his occasional nihilism have been described as placing before us the problem of the infinite by calling forth the contrast between the finite and the infinite.[54] As in the so-called "Romantic irony" of those novelists whom Jean Paul influenced, everything is seen *sub specie aeternitatis*, from the superior viewpoint that quotidian reality is only a reflection of the eternal. Goethe's irony is of a different kind. Nature's incredibly complex processes are, in Goethe's view, utterly unlike the comparatively simple, logical structure of ideas; if they are like anything, it is the complex processes at work within human beings, but at a much more primitive level than abstract rationality. Goethe's injunction is "nichts hinter den Phänomenen suchen" (to seek nothing behind phenomena).[55] Although his acceptance of theory is wholehearted, he is insistent that all thinking must be done "mit Ironie" (with irony).[56] Goethe's irony is directed toward the inadequacy of the intellect in the face of reality, rather than to the aspects of reality which the mind finds wanting.[57] Just as Schiller argues that the concepts of the "naïve" and the "sentimental" are merely aspects of an undivided reality, so Goethe insists on the dynamic, interactive balance of apparent opposites characterizing Weimar Classicism at every level, from theoretical formulation to stylistic detail. This polar structure is at work in his novels, without any fixed point other than the ironic gesture toward experience.[58]

Setting his novels in their immediate socio-cultural context reveals Goethe's sophisticated analysis of the central political polarities at work in modern Western society, of, on the one side, a conservatism born of commitment to real, individual entities, and, on the other, of a progressivism derived from the moral conviction that human conditions ought to be improved. Neither is shown to be wholly convincing, but both are shown to constitute at base the problems with which his characters have to contend. Ottilie's recognition (noted in her journal)[59] of the constraining necessity of responding to society's demand that we present ourselves in socially acceptable ways alerts the reader to the dialectic of individual-and-society, played out in a world that is also ours: a society largely devoid of aesthetic values in its ever-increasing, philistine dependence on pure instrumentalism. Equally, the society presented in *Wilhelm Meister* is recognizably our own in all essentials, defined as it is by the channeling and shaping of human development and growth by modernity's insistence on productive performance and efficiency.[60] Throughout the *Wanderjahre* Wilhelm practices a renunciatory asceticism whose aim is vocational, an activity of economic as well as personal value. The realism of *Wilhelm Meister* is undoubtedly the precipitate of Goethe's own experience of, and reflection on, such events as the French Revolution, the economic crisis of the 1820s, European colonialism, and the Industrial Revolution (reflected respectively in the relations of bourgeois and aristocracy, the financial cooperative set up by the Society of the Tower, the very dubious colonialist ambitions of its members, and the threats and opportunities of the Machine Age).[61] Goethe's coolly ironic presentation of the dualistic historical forces that drive modern society links him as a novelist both with the novels of the Enlightenment and those of late Romanticism, since both Blanckenburg's insistence that the novel reflect the society in which it is written (*Versuch*, 8) and Friedrich Schlegel's insistence on its intrinsic historicity (*Literary Notebooks*, 95) are accommodated. But Goethe also remains true to the traditional requirement, reaching back to antiquity and forward to our own day, that the novel descend to the daily, unpoetic level and focus our interest on the perennially less than heroic aspects of human life (Goody, 10, 476).

One of the principal sources of irony in *Wilhelm Meister* and *Die Wahlverwandtschaften* derives from the polarity between historical realism and a mythological framework.[62] In both parts of *Wilhelm Meister*, the characters are caught up in a tension between two worlds: the contingent one of chance and the mythological one of fate. As an integral part of the novel of antiquity, with which eighteenth-century writers were very familiar (Goody, xix), mythology was drawn on by writers as diverse as Wieland, Heinse, and many a Romantic novelist, for whom, as for Goethe, the picaresque tradition was an important channel of transmission in this living continuity with Greek and Roman fiction. In Goethe's case the two elements are blended to produce a sense of the abiding presence of the past, an amalgam transcending the expectations fostered by nineteenth-century bourgeois realism, one which many commentators have identified in other contexts as the "New Classicism" of a post-modern era.[63] The *Wanderjahre*, which seemed to Emil Staiger a feeble product of old age, open to any — and therefore no significant — interpretation,[64] appears today, given the possibilities revealed by postmodernism, to be an anticipation of the self-reflexive characteristics of "experimental" novels, a feature of the genre which has in fact a long history (Goody, 298). The narrative framework of Goethe's classical novels — the *Wanderjahre* in particular is presented as if all its constituent parts had been sorted and assembled by one or more cautious narrator-editors — and the presence of blatantly unintegrated "stowaways"[65] (the *Novellen*, aphorisms, poems) show that the novel form taken up by Goethe is the collage, mounted in such a way, like the array of images in the Pedagogic Province, that the reader is invited to adopt that same open, interpretive attitude of mind that Wilhelm, like Ottilie, learns to cultivate.

It is only when mythology is knowingly played with, as in the Western novel tradition (Goody, 155) — as what Schelling in his 1802 to 1803 Jena lectures called "partielle Mythologie"[66] (partial mythology) — that its essentially "symbolic form" is uncovered, argues Cassirer. Without such "philosophical freedom" myths "are not regarded as symbols but as realities."[67] In *Die Wahlverwandtschaften*, as in *Wilhelm Meister*, "society is shown to function as a system of elaborate semiotics" (Swales, 59, 100), in which the particular serves the general allegorically as a typical instance (producing, amongst other things, types rather than rounded characters). While the infinite deferral of meaning entailed by entrance into semiosis is interpreted as an allegory of a higher reality by the high-minded souls in Jean Paul's *Hesperus*, in Goethe's case reading symbols as mere signs is only half the story. He developed a highly differentiated theory of symbolism, which, while embracing the notion of symbol-as-self-referential-sign, also embraces symbol as sturdy, concrete percept. While acknowledging the advantages of intellect, Goethe insists that a concrete, aesthetic response is the superior response: art, aesthetic play (as distinct from the merely intellectual play of semiotic undecidability) is the "true symbolism."[68] This double structure, theorized by Goethe in his analyses of the symbol as both abstract and concrete, absent and present, is at work within the bewildering density of the self-reflexive signification of his classical novels.

For the expressive, aesthetic kind of Goethean symbol, Cassirer offered the useful term "symbolische Prägnanz" (Krois, 5–9; symbolic pregnance). It is an apt designation because it captures precisely the abnormal "musical" vigor of poetry, to draw on Ezra Pound's definition of aesthetic intensity in language as "music just forcing itself into articulate speech."[69] Such intense passages of heightened diction are distributed throughout Goethe's novels, providing patches of stable meaning within the shimmering undecidability of the rest of the text. In both *Wilhelm Meister* and *Die Wahlverwandtschaften*, the apparently interpolated aphorisms constitute instances of sudden precipitates of clear meaning emerging out of the delicately suspended solution of semiotic interplay. In *Die Wahlverwandtschaften*, it is the aesthetic language of Ottilie's diary entries that offers an arresting point of interpretative orientation; in *Wilhelm Meister*, such aesthetic stylization is perhaps at its most evident in the interpolated poems in the *Wanderjahre*.[70]

But, whereas often mystical "dream poems" are to be found in Jean Paul's fiction (as in the Romantics' novels), we look in vain in Goethe's novels for the brilliant metaphorical flights of fancy and wit with which Jean Paul set the standard for the poetic prose of the Romantic novelists who followed him. The following passage, from the "Clavis Fichteana" (Key to Fichte) of the Comic Appendix to *Titan*, taking up the great Renaissance theme of self-realization, illustrates Jean Paul's rhetorical mastery in giving free play to his combinatory wit. The essential source of the humor here is Leibgeber's apparent lack of awareness of the fact that he implicitly denies the greatness which he claims for himself; far from being the beggar who awakes as a king, as he professes, he reveals himself to be the self-styled god who in reality is mired in the mud:

> Es frappiert mich selber (sagt' ich, als ich mein System während eines Fußbades flüchtig überblickte, und sah bedeutend auf die Fußzehen, deren Nägel man mir beschnitt), daß ich das All und Universum bin; mehr kann man nicht werden in der Welt als die Welt selber (§.8) und Gott (§.3) und die Geisterwelt (§.8) dazu. Nur so lange Zeit (die wieder mein Werk ist) hätt' ich nicht versitzen sollen, ohne darauf zu kommen, nach 10 Visthnu's Verwandlungen, daß ich die *natura naturans* und der Demiurgos und der Bewindheber des Universums bin. Mir ist jetzt wie jenem Bettler, der, aus dem Schlaftrunk erwachend, sich auf einmal als König findet. Welch ein Wesen, das, sich ausgenommen (denn es *wird* nur, und *ist* nie), alles macht, mein absolutes, alles gebärendes, fohlendes, lammendes, heckendes, brechendes, werfendes, setzendes Ich★★![71]

> [I am myself astonished (said I, casting a cursory eye over my System, while bathing my feet, and looking meaningfully at my toes while the nails were being cut), that I am everything and the universe; you can't really get on much more in the world than become the world itself (§ 8) and God (§ 3) and the realm of the spirit (§ 8) on top of that. But I should not have whiled away so much time (another of my handiworks) before I cottoned on to the fact, after 10 Vishnu avatars, that I am *natura naturans*, the demiurge, and the winder-up of the universe. I feel like the beggar who awakes from a sleeping-draught and finds himself King suddenly. What a being that, himself excepted (for it only *becomes* and never *is*), makes everything, my absolute Ego, all-birthing, -foaling, -lambing, -hatching, -breeding, -dropping, -setting!]

The grotesque contrast drawn between the solemnity of the mystical idea of man-becoming-God and the seemingly philistine conceit of Leibgeber's inflated idea of himself is articulated by sustained juxtaposition on the rhetorical and conceptual levels. The opening vignette, of Leibgeber taking a footbath and having his toenails clipped while suddenly realizing his pantheistic divinity, sets the surrealistic tone from the outset. The syllepsis, yoking together the two verbs of vision to cover two quite disparate objects (his toes and his metaphysical "System," which in any case can scarcely be cursorily perused), like the punning on "das All" and "die Welt," meaning both "everything in this life" in the colloquial sense suggested by the German idiom used and being synonyms of "universe" and "cosmos" — like, too, the exotic, recondite comparison of whiling away one's time bathing one's feet with ten Vishnu avatars — contributes to a build-up of tension. This, in turn, is intensified by the quasi-periodic syntax and the superabundant accumulations: "and God and the realm of spirit"; (the Latin) *natura naturans* and (the Greek) *demiurge* and the mock-German loan-translation *Bewindheber* (winder-up), which, in its farcical combination of *Urheber* (originator) and *Bewandtnis* (explanation), attempts a would-be, strikingly novel and elegant, though difficult to translate articulation of God's self-grounding and creative nature, only to evoke unfortunate connotations of wind-baggery. The contradiction running through the whole passage — between the axiomatic statement that his ego has no being, only becoming, on the one hand and, on the other, the emphatic assertion of self-existence in the repeated use of "I am" — is given climactic metaphorical formulation in the shockingly zoological associations of the seven participial synonyms of giving birth in respect to different species of animals, the last three of which, we are told in a ridiculously gratuitous and misleading footnote, have to do with hunting — whereas, in truth, the last is an allusion to Fichtean "positing" of the ego, here brought, by association, down to earth with a bump.

Such extended metaphor (or "allegory," as Jean Paul called it in his *Vorschule*) is what the Romantics meant by *Poesie* in the novel.[72] As Novalis perspicaciously observed with reference to the *Lehrjahre*, Goethe's fictional prose is not poetically pregnant in the sense in which Heinse's style is said to be aphoristically pregnant, that is, full of rich association and far-reaching metaphor, like Jean Paul's. "Die Melodie des Stils" (the melody of style) that Novalis praised so highly in Goethe's "Magie des Vortrags" (magical discourse) has, in his view, the effect of "einer glatten, gefälligen, einfachen und doch mannigfaltigen Sprache"[73] (a smooth, agreeable, simple, and yet varied language; *Fragmente*, no. 1975).

The precision of Novalis's analysis of Goethe's classical style may be confirmed by comparing with Jean Paul's lyrical rhetoric the following short passage on the same theme of self-realization, taken from the indenture Wilhelm is given by the Society of the Tower toward the end of the

Lehrjahre. A series of familiar propositions is assembled, beginning with perhaps the best known:

> Die Kunst ist lang, das Leben kurz, das Urteil schwierig, die Gelegenheit flüchtig. Handeln ist leicht, Denken schwer; nach demGedanken handeln unbequem. (HA 7:496)

> [Art is long, life short, judgment difficult, opportunity fleeting. Action is easy, thinking difficult; action according to one's thoughts uncomfortable.]

The conceptual antitheses in these opening lines, taken from Hippocrates, ascribe all the prestige of what is difficult to the artificial pole of "art" — to conscious judgment and thought — while the natural pole of life — action and opportunity — is said to be ephemeral and easy. (Later in the text this evaluation switches.) What is of particular interest here is how, by means of the aesthetic deployment of language, what is otherwise the hard-won result of a process of reasoning is presented in a palpable, plastic form. In the very opening lines, a cluster of sound-look touches links what is conceptually antithetical: *schwierig* by homeoteleuton to *flüchtig*, *Denken* to *Leben*; alliterations link *Kunst* with *kurz* and *Gelegenheit* with *Gedanken*; most significant is that the key terms of the binary opposition *handeln-denken* are interwoven by means of a visual and aural chiasmus. Thus, the central burden of the *Lehrjahre* is presented, not this time discursively elaborated, but *in nuce* to our feeling: (inherited) thought and (spontaneous) action are felt as fundamentally and inextricably one. Goethe's "symbolic pregnance," in Cassirer's sense — inhering in the classical restraint on the infinite regress of rhetoric exercised by internal textual relations — raises significant patches of his fictional prose to the level of aesthetic symbol, the aim of which is not the stimulating effect of rhetoric, but rather the satisfying resolution of the reader's felt-thought projected onto the text (HA 12:340): "der Roman fühlt uns vor"[74] (the novel anticipates our feelings).

In presenting "a whole panorama of the relations between life and art, the aesthetic and the novel, between semblance, true, false, and misplaced,"[75] Goethe in his novels, like Schiller in his theoretical writings, has provided a complex and compelling response to the challenge of the Romantics' description of the modern novel as seeking to reclaim for poetry her lost rights in the modern prosaic world (Swales, 85). For the totality that Schiller aimed at in his *Ästhetische Erziehung* is not the totality that is so routinely attacked in much contemporary cultural theory. Wholeness for Weimar Classicism is neither perfection nor the universality promoted by the Romantics and systematically codified by Hegel. Whatever term may be used, totality for Goethe and Schiller means the imperfect but unique integrity of a particular. The human mind, Goethe argues, while enjoying the elevation of high abstraction, longs for the particular, without losing a universal perspective. It is the office of the classical artist to provide this stereoscopic perspective by epitomizing human significance in a specific form. The novel offered Goethe an appropriately imperfect form[76] in which he could not only present discursively the tenets of his postmodern classicism, but also enact in its very style what he saw as the true function of art: the symbolic, pregnant embodiment of the inner life of human beings.

Notes

[1] I am grateful to the Arts and Humanities Research Board for the award of a Large Research Grant for a four-year project (2002 to 2007) on "Conceptions of Cultural Studies in Cassirer's Theory of Symbolic Forms," which enabled me to undertake research in this area.

[2] Preface to *The Portrait of a Lady* (1881; Harmondsworth: Penguin, 1983), xi.

[3] Albert Ward, *Book Production, Fiction, and the German Reading Public, 1740–1800* (Oxford: Clarendon, 1974).

[4] Martin Greiner, *Die Entstehung der modernen Unterhaltungsliteratur: Studien zum Trivialroman des 18. Jahrhunderts* (Hamburg: Rowohlt, 1964), especially 80–82 and 87–88; Dieter Borchmeyer, *Weimarer Klassik: Porträt einer Epoche* (Weinheim: Beltz Athenäum, 1994), 327–50 and 363–72.

[5] Ian Watt, *The Rise of the Novel: Studies in Defoe, Richardson, and Fielding* (Harmondsworth: Penguin, 1963), 56. See also Borchmeyer, *Weimarer Ästhetik*, 344.

[6] Wallace Fowlie, *A Reading of Proust* (London: Dobson Books, 1967), 4.

[7] See the section "*Wilhelm Meisters Wanderjahre* als Roman der symbolischen Formen," in Barbara Naumann, *Philosophie und Poetik: Cassirer und Goethe* (Munich: Fink, 1998), 107–92, where she employs this key concept of Ernst Cassirer's.

[8] Christian F. Blanckenburg, *Versuch über den Roman*, Faksimiledruck der Originalausgabe von 1774, with an afterword by E. Lämmert (Stuttgart: Metzler, 1965), 313–14 and 388. Subsequent references to this work will occur parenthetically in the text as *Versuch* and page number.

[9] See Ritchie Robertson's helpful introduction to his English translation of Karl Philipp Moritz, *Anton Reiser* (Harmondsworth: Penguin, 2000). Henceforth referred to in text as Robertson and page number.

[10] Friedrich Hölderlin, "Vorrede zum Thalia-Fragment," *Sämtliche Werke*, vol. 3, ed. Friedrich Beissner (Stuttgart: Cotta, 1946–85), 163.

[11] See Watt, *Rise of the Novel*, 282.

[12] See Beissner's edition of Hölderlin, *Sämtliche Werke*, 3:5.

[13] Arthur Henkel, *Entsagung: Eine Studie zu Goethes Altersroman* (Tübingen: Niemeyer, 1964), 111, 131, and 165–68.

[14] *Maximen und Reflexionen*, HA 12:498.

[15] Margaret Anne Goody, *The True Story of the Novel* (London: Harper Collins, 1997), 475. Subsequently referred to parenthetically in text as Goody and page number.

[16] Marshall McLuhan, *The Gutenberg Galaxy: The Making of Typographic Man* (London: Routledge & Kegan Paul, 1967), 273.

[17] Jane K. Brown, "The Theatrical Mission of the *Lehrjahre*," in *Goethe's Narrative Fiction: The Irvine Goethe Symposium*, ed. William G. Lillyman (Berlin: de Gruyter, 1983), 69–84 (75, 80).

[18] Stephen Toulmin, *The Uses of Argument* (Cambridge: Cambridge UP, 1958), 10.

[19] Manfred Kuehn, *Scottish Common Sense in Germany, 1768–1800: A Contribution to the History of Critical Philosophy* (Kingston & Montreal: McGill-Queen's UP, 1987), 3–12.

[20] Robert E. Norton, *The Beautiful Soul: Aesthetic Morality in the Eighteenth Century* (Ithaca, NY: Cornell UP, 1995), 157, 217, and 221.

[21] For the historical provenance of the term, see Hartmut Steinecke, "The Novel and the Individual: The Significance of Goethe's *Wilhelm Meister* in the Debate about the Bildungsroman," in *Reflection and Action: Essays on the Bildungsroman*, ed. James Hardin (Columbia, SC: U of South Carolina P, 1991), 69–96. See also Borchmeyer, *Weimarer Klassik*, 330.

[22] J. H. Pestalozzi, *Ideen* (1826), ed. Marine Hürlimann (Zurich: Insel, 1927), 2:187.

[23] Georg Lukács, *Goethe and His Age* (London: Martin Press, 1968), 50.

[24] G. W. F. Hegel, *Sämtliche Werke*, ed. H. Glockner (Stuttgart: Fromann, 1927–30), 14:396; Walter Kaufmann, *Discovering the Mind* (New York: McGraw-Hill, 1980), 1:231, 225, 227, 261.

[25] *Italienische Reise*, HA 11:456.

[26] Wilhelm Heinse, *Ardinghello und die glücklichen Inseln*, ed. with an afterword by Max L. Baeumer (Stuttgart: Reclam, 1985), 12. Henceforth referred to in text as Heinse and page number.

[27] "Ruysdael als Dichter," 1816, HA 12:142.

[28] *Maximen und Reflexionen*, HA 12:438. See R. H. Stephenson, "The Cultural Theory of Weimar Classicism in the Light of Coleridge's Doctrine of Aesthetic Knowledge," in *Goethe 2000: Intercultural Readings of his Work*, ed. Paul Bishop and R. H. Stephenson (Leeds: Northern UP, 2000), 150–69; and *Goethe's Conception of Knowledge and Science* (Edinburgh: Edinburgh UP, 1995), 7–10, 12, 14–15.

[29] See Elizabeth M. Wilkinson and L. A. Willoughby, "'Having and Being,' or Bourgeois versus Nobility," in Elizabeth M. Wilkinson and L. A. Willoughby, *Models of Wholeness: Some Attitudes to Language, Art and Life in the Age of Goethe*, eds. Jeremy Adler, Martin Swales, and Ann Weaver (Oxford: Peter Lang, 2002), 227–32.

[30] Martin Swales and Erika Swales, *Reading Goethe: A Critical Introduction to the Literary Work* (Rochester, NY: Camden House, 2002), 80 and 82.

[31] Erik H. Erikson, *Identity – Youth and Crisis* (London: Faber, 1968), 23, 41–42, 50, 53–54, 71, 92, and 237–38, in his influential psychological theory of ego development; Joseph Needham, *The History of Embryology* (Cambridge: Cambridge UP, 1959), 139–40, 168, 183, and 220–21 for the seventeenth- and eighteenth-century debate on the general conceptions of "development."

[32] John Updike, *Roger's Version* (London: André Deutsch, 1986), 52.

[33] Hans Heinrich Borcherdt, *Der Roman der Goethezeit* (Stuttgart: Post Verlag, 1949), 280.

[34] Patricia Zecevic, *The Speaking Divine Woman: Lópa de Úbeda's 'La Picara Justina' and Goethe's Wilhelm Meister* (Oxford: Peter Lang, 2001), 120–49; Henriette Herwig, *Wilhelm Meisters Wanderjahre: Geschlechterdifferenz, Sozialer Wandel, Historische Anthropologie* (Tübingen: Francke, 2002).

[35] Saul Bellow, *It All Adds Up* (Harmondsworth: Penguin, 1995), 101.

[36] Jean le Rond d'Alembert, "Discours Préliminaire de l'*Encyclopédie*" (1751), *Œuvres de d'Alembert* (Paris: 1853), vol.1; Christopher Ricks's introduction to Laurence Sterne, *The Life and Opinions of Tristram Shandy* (Harmondsworth: Penguin, 1974), 11–12; P. Michelsen, *Laurence Sterne und der deutsche Roman des 18. Jahrhunderts* (Gottingen: Vandenhoeck & Ruprecht, 1962).

[37] Friedrich Schlegel, *Kritische Ausgabe*, eds. Ernst Behler, Jean-Jacques Anstett, and Hans Eichner (Munich: F. Schöningh, 1958–), 2:156.

[38] Gregory Bateson, *Mind and Nature: A Necessary Unity* (Glasgow: Collins, 1980), 113.

[39] Ehrhard Bahr, "Revolutionary Realism in Goethe's *Wanderjahre*," in Lillyman, 161–75 (175); See also Jane K. Brown, *Goethe's Cyclical Narratives: "Die Unterhaltungen deutscher Ausgewanderten" and "Wilhelm Meisters Wanderjahre"* (Chapel Hill: U of North Carolina P, 1975).

[40] R. H. Stephenson, "Goethe's Prose Style: Making Sense of Sense," *Publications of the English Goethe Society*, NS 66 (1996): 33–41 (38); Friedrich Schlegel, *Literary Notebooks 1797–1801*, ed. Hans Eichner (London: Athlone Press, 1957), 180. Henceforth referred to in text as *Literary Notebooks*. For Jean Paul's reservations with regard to Friedrich Schlegel, see, for example, the footnote on Schlegel's "parziale Verfinsterung" (partial obfuscation) in the Appendix to the First Appendix of *Titan* (*Jean Pauls Sämtliche Werke*, ed. Eduard Berend [Weimar: Böhlau, 1927–], 3:476).

[41] Manfred Karnick, *Wilhelm Meisters Wanderjahre oder die Kunst des Mittelbaren* (Munich: Fink, 1969); Ehrhard Bahr, "*Wilhelm Meisters Wanderjahre oder die Entsagenden* (1821–1829): From Bildungsroman to Archival Novel," in *Reflection and Action: Essays on the Bildungsroman*, 163–94; Lucie Stern, "*Wilhelm Meisters Lehrjahre* und Jean Paul's *Titan*," *Zeitschrift für Ästhetik und allgemeine Kulturwissenschaft* 16 (1992), 35–68.

[42] *Noten und Abhandlungen zu Besserem Verständnis Des West-Östlichen Divans*, 1819, HA 2:184.

[43] "Cäsars Triumphzug, gemalt von Mantegna," 1823, HA 12:196.

[44] Friedrich von Hardenberg (Novalis), *Gesammelte Wekke,* vol. 2, ed. Carl Seelig (Herrliberg-Zurid Buehl-Verlag, 1945), 39.

[45] "Etwas über den Menschen," 1781. *Jean Pauls Sämtliche Werke,* ed. Eduard Berend (Weimar: Böhlau, 1927–), 2.1:189; see also 182 and 273.

[46] Günter Sasse, "'Der Abschied aus diesem Paradies': die Überwindung der Sehnsucht durch die Kunst in der Lago Maggiore-Episode in Goethes *Wanderjahren,*" *Jahrbuch der Deutschen Schiller Gesellschaft* 42 (1998): 95–119.

[47] *Jean Pauls Sämtliche Werke,* ed. Berend, 1:11, 234.

[48] Barbara Hunfeld, "Das sprachliche All und der Kosmos der Sprache: zur Sternwartsszene in Goethes *Wanderjahre,*" in *Über Grenzen: Limitation und Transgression in Literatur und Ästhetik,* ed. Claudia Benthien and Imela Marie Krüger-Fürhoff (Stuttgart: Metzler, 1999), 38–60.

[49] *Wilhelm Meisters Wanderjahre,* HA 8:155–57.

[50] Thomas Mann, "Vorrede," *Der Zauberberg* (Stockholm: Fischer, 1950), xxix.

[51] Thomas à Kempis, *Imitatio Christi* (Harmondsworth: Penguin, 1978), 28; see Astrid Orle Tantillo, *Goethe's "Elective Affinities" and the Critics* (Rochester, NY: Camden House, 2001).

[52] Friedrich Schlegel, *Fragmente I, 1797* in *Literary Notebooks,* ed. Eichner, 71.

[53] *Goethes Briefe,* Hamburger Ausgabe, 4 vols., ed. Bodo Morawe (Hamburg: Wegner Verlag, 1968), 3:92.

[54] Paul Böckmann, "Die humoristische Darstellungsweise Jean Pauls," in *Festschrift für Eduard Berend,* ed. H. W. Seiffert and B. Zeller (Weimar: Böhlau, 1959), 38–53 (53).

[55] *Maximen und Reflexionen,* HA 12:432.

[56] "Vorwort zur Farbenlehre," 1808, HA 13:317.

[57] Stephenson, *Goethe's Conception of Knowledge and Science,* 3, 58.

[58] See Ehrhard Bahr, *Die Ironie im Spätwerk Goethes ". . . Diese sehr ernsten Scherze . . .," Studien zum Westöstlichen Divan, zu den Wanderjahren und zu Faust II* (Berlin: Erich Schmidt, 1972); Catriona MacLeod, *Embodying Ambiguity: Androgyny and Aesthetics from Winckelmann to Keller* (Detroit: Wayne State UP, 1993), ch. 2; Eric A. Blackall, *Goethe and the Novel* (Ithaca, NY: Cornell UP, 1976), 136.

[59] *Die Wahlverwandtschaften,* HA 6:396.

[60] R. H. Stephenson and Patricia Zecevic, "'Das Was bedenke . . .' On the Content, Structure, and Form of Goethe's *Wilhelm Meister,*" *London German Studies* 5 (1993), 79–94.

[61] Stefan Blessin, *Goethes Romane: Aufbruch in die Moderne* (Munich: Schöningh, 1996), 11.

[62] See Heinz Schlaffer, *Der Bürger als Held: Sozialgeschichtliche Auflösungen literarischer Widersprüche* (Frankfurt am Main: Suhrkamp, 1976); Hannelore Schlaffer, *Wilhelm Meister: Das Ende der Kunst und die Wiederkehr des Mythos* (Stuttgart: Metzler, 1980); Walter Benjamin, "Goethes *Wahlverwandtschaften,*" in *Illuminationen: Ausgewählte Schriften,* ed. Siegfried Unseld (Frankfurt am Main: Suhrkamp, 1961), vol. 1.

[63] See Charles Jencks, *Postmodernism* (New York: Academy Editions, 1987), 329–35; Joan Wright, "'Eine zarte Empirie' — The Novel Poetics of Goethe's *Wilhelm Meisters Wanderjahre*," unpublished Ph.D. thesis, National University of Ireland, 1999.

[64] Emil Staiger, *Goethe* (Zurich: Atlantis Verlag, 1959), 3:134–37.

[65] George C. Buck, "The Pattern of the Stowaway in Goethe's Works," *PMLA* 71 (1956), 451–64; see also Ehrhard Bahr, *The Novel as Archive: The Genesis, Reception and Criticism of Goethe's "Wilhelm Meisters Wanderjahre"* (Columbia, SC: Camden House, 1998).

[66] F. W. J. Schelling, *Philosophie der Kunst, Vorlesungen, gehalten im Winter-Semester 1802/03 in Jena*, in *Sämtliche Werke*, ed. K. F. A. Schelling (Stuttgart: Cotta, 1856–61), 5:675.

[67] Ernst Cassirer, *The Myth of the State* (New Haven: Yale UP, 1946), 47. Cf. J. M. Krois, *Cassirer: Symbolic Forms and History* (New Haven: Yale UP, 1987), 60 and 91. Henceforth referred to in text as Krois.

[68] *Maximen und Reflexionen*, HA 12:367, 471.

[69] Ezra Pound, "The Later Years" (1914), in *Literary Essays of Ezra Pound*, ed. with an introduction by T.S. Eliot (London: Faber, 1954), 380.

[70] R. H. Stephenson, "'Man nimmt in der Welt jeden, wofür er sich gibt': The Presentation of Self in Goethe's *Die Wahlverwandtschaften*," *German Life and Letters* 47 (1994),400–407; "Theorizing to Some Purpose: 'Deconstruction' in the Light of Goethe and Schiller's Aesthetics — the Case of *Die Wahlverwandtschaften*," *Modern Language Review* 84 (1989), 381–92.

[71] *Jean Pauls Sämtliche Werke*, ed. Berend, 1.9:483.

[72] Eric A. Blackall, *The Novels of the German Romantics* (Ithaca, NY: Cornell UP, 1983), 264.

[73] Novalis, *Gesammelte Werke*, vol. 4, ed. Carl Seelig (Herrliberg-Zurich: Buehl-Verlag, 1946), 261–62.

[74] Goethe's review of the anonymous "Der deutsche *Gil Blas*" (1824), JA 37:204.

[75] Elizabeth M. Wilkinson and L. A. Willoughby, "Introduction," in Friedrich Schiller, *On the Aesthetic Education of Man: In a Series of Letters*, ed. and trans. E. M. W. and L. A. W. (Oxford: Clarendon, 1982), cxcvi.

[76] Terence Wright, "The Imperfect World of the Novel," *Modern Languages Review* (1978), 73:1–16.

German Women Writers and Classicism

Elisabeth Krimmer

T HE CLASSIFICATION OF TEXTS by women writers of the late eighteenth
and early nineteenth centuries is notoriously difficult.[1] Often considered trivial, the works of women writers of this period have remained
below the radar screen of many literary histories. Efforts to remedy the
omission and add these stray texts to the existing canon are often thwarted
by the nature of the works themselves and by the precarious situation of
their female authors. Female authorship constituted a transgression against
contemporary gender norms. Consequently, women writers strove to
downplay or hide their literary activities.[2] They did not formulate literary
programs, rarely shared their aesthetic reflection explicitly, and, for the
most part, did not belong to established literary groups. Many shrank from
defining themselves as writers. The uneven nature of their works also defies
easy categorization. Attempts to pinpoint aesthetic and ideological affinities are complicated by the fact that many of these works were conceived
not in emulation of, but in conscious or unconscious deviation from male
models. Many women writers found themselves poised between admiration for the literary and philosophical achievements of their male contemporaries — evidenced by the frequency with which women writers quoted
Goethe, Schiller, and other writers[3] — and repulsion at the misogyny of
their gender politics.

It is not surprising, in light of these predicaments, that some scholars
have argued for alternative categories. Christa Bürger, for example, claims
that women writers can be assigned neither to Enlightenment nor to
German Classicism and suggests instead the term "middle sphere." Many
recent publications on women writers of this period favor the phrase
"around 1800."[4] When scholars do choose to attribute the works of a
woman writer to an existing literary period, their efforts are often inconsistent and vague. Christine Touaillon, for example, lists Caroline von
Wolzogen (1763–1847) as a classicist author, but asserts repeatedly that
her works oscillate between Enlightenment and Romanticism. Sophie
Mereau (1770–1806) has been claimed for Romanticism and German
Classicism alike. Friederike Helene Unger (1741 or 1751–1811 or 1813),

on the other hand, is not usually grouped with Classicism, although her works engage in an explicit and direct dialogue with Goethe's aesthetic ideals. This confusion is partly fueled by the temptation to base decisions on the female writer's biographical and geographic affinities to male luminaries. Although this is understandable — after all, a woman's access to the public sphere was usually mediated through her male friends and relatives — it is necessary to consider the texts themselves in addition to social contexts.

The works discussed in this article are chosen primarily for their stylistic and ideological proximity to German Classicism. In most cases, biographical and aesthetic affinities are congruent. Grouping Caroline von Wolzogen with Weimar Classicism, for example, is justified by her aesthetics and her collaboration with her brother-in-law Friedrich Schiller. Similarly, the writings of Charlotte von Stein (1742–1827) and Johanna Schopenhauer (1766–1838), as well as their association with Goethe and Weimar, provide sufficient evidence for their close alliance with Weimar Classicism. Friederike Helene Unger, the wife of one of Goethe's publishers, is geographically removed from Weimar, but her novel *Bekenntnisse einer schönen Seele von ihr selbst geschrieben* (Confessions of a Beautiful Soul: Related by Herself,1806) deserves mention in this context, since it is most directly engaged in a dialogue with both Goethe's novel *Wilhelm Meisters Lehrjahre* (1795–96) and Schiller's theoretical works. Both conceptually and biographically, Sophie Mereau, the wife of Clemens Brentano and protégée of Schiller, occupies a place between Classicism and Romanticism. Of course, this list is not exhaustive. A more extensive study of women writers and classicism might have included several other texts, such as Charlotte von Kalb's novel *Cornelia* (1851), Amalie von Imhoff's epic poem *Die Schwestern von Lesbos* (The Sisters of Lesbos, 1790), and Caroline von Wolzogen's drama fragment *Der Leukadische Fels* (Leucadia's Rock, 1792).

Body Bildung

Although equally disenfranchised with respect to politics and law, women writers of the late eighteenth and early nineteenth centuries did not form a homogenous group. One of the most visible divisions is along class lines. Aside from rare exceptions, most notably Anna Luisa Karsch (1722–1791), the lower classes were excluded from literary production. Aristocratic women were more likely to enjoy the privileged access to culture that had defined their class for centuries. The cultural resources of bourgeois women depended very much on the inclinations and competency of the men in their lives.[5] Women whose husbands or fathers were professors, writers, or publishers, such as Therese Huber, Friederike Helene Unger, Sophie Mereau, and Dorothea Schlegel often found the means to engage in literary activities themselves. However, if such domestic resources did not counterbalance women's exclusion from all institutions of higher learning, they were likely to receive a rudimentary education, limited to etiquette, religion, French, and calligraphy.[6]

The restricted access to an education fit to equip women with the skills necessary for a career as a writer is linked to a shift in gender ideology that took place in the late eighteenth century. The last third of the eighteenth century saw the emergence of a new model of gender in which the female body and female "nature" became inseparably intertwined. According to Barbara Becker-Cantarino, this new model of *Geschlechtscharakter* is based on the claim that woman's psychological and moral constitution is determined by her biological disposition.[7] In other words, the body prescribes how social and moral tasks are to be distributed between the genders.[8] Women were assigned to the private sphere and the realm of emotions, men the public sphere and rational thought.[9]

The effects of this model on the conceptualization of women's education are evidenced by the following quote from Friedrich Schiller's essay *Über naive und sentimentalische Dichtung*:

> Dem andern Geschlecht hat die Natur in dem naiven Charakter seine höchste Vollkommenheit angewiesen . . . die größte Macht des Geschlechts [beruhet] auf dieser Eigenschaft. Weil aber die herrschenden Grundsätze bei der weiblichen Erziehung mit diesem Charakter in ewigem Streit liegen, so ist es dem Weibe im moralischen eben so schwer als dem Mann im intellektuellen mit den Vortheilen der guten Erziehung jenes herrliche Geschenk der Natur unverloren zu behalten. (NA 20:425)

> [Nature has assigned the highest perfection to the other sex in the form of the naïve character . . . the greatest power of the sex (is based) on this quality. However, because the reigning principles of female education are in an eternal state of war with this character, it is as difficult for a woman in the moral realm, as it is for a man in the intellectual realm, to preserve this splendid gift of nature untouched by the benefits of a good education.]

Curiously, although education was hailed as an ideal for an entire epoch, Schiller, and many with him, believed that education for women is more likely to do harm than good.[10] Any form of instruction that is not designed to help women fulfill their triple roles as wives, mothers, and housekeepers is likely to be greeted with suspicion and ridicule.

What Schiller claims for the Enlightenment ideal of education also holds true for *Bildung* (education, cultivation), the holy grail of the Weimar Classicists. Whereas men must undergo a development to achieve the harmonious maturity of *Bildung*, women as *schöne Seelen* (beautiful souls) embody it from the start.[11] Paradoxically, it is woman's supposed natural

perfection that precludes all maturation. Thus, for women, *Bildung* —
defined as a process of maturation and identity formation through interaction with the world — is even more elusive than education, insofar as
the latter refers to all formal and informal kinds of instruction.[12] With
respect to education, women are socially disadvantaged; with respect to
Bildung, they are conceptually non-existent.[13] Rather than subjects of
Bildung in their own right, women function as catalysts on men's path
toward maturation.[14]

In narrative terms (as in women's lives), this much-lauded state of natural perfection, and hence of complete stasis, poses a problem. Women
writers tended to favor the genre of the novel, which did not gain in prestige until the emergence of Goethe. After the publication of *Wilhelm
Meisters Lehrjahre*, the sub-genre of the novel that simultaneously attracted
and troubled women writers the most was the *Bildungsroman*.[15] But how
is it possible to conceive of a female novel of *Bildung*, that is, of a
Bildungsroman centered on a female protagonist, when the heroine's
departure from nature's original gift of perfectly harmonious naiveté is
defined, at least by Schiller, as deterioration? Given the assumption that
women are innately passive and domestic, how can a hero be female and
yet actively engage with the world around her? Since *Bildung* implies
change brought about by an interaction between individual and world,
female *Bildung* represents a contradiction in terms. Consider, for example,
the following list of plot elements typical of the *Bildungsroman*: confrontation with one's parents; the influence of mentors and institutions of
education; exposure to art; erotic adventures; initiation into a profession;
and engagement in public and political life.[16] For a female hero, almost all
of these activities constitute transgressive acts. Clearly, given all these pro-
hibitions, the chances that a Wilhelmine Meister might be able to drive the
plot forward are slim indeed.

It should be evident by now that writing a female novel of *Bildung*
presupposes an exercise in subversion. In order to portray an active female
protagonist, a woman writer needed to disguise action as reaction, to
couch her heroine's adventures in defensive terms.[17] Wilhelmine Meister
does not strive toward her goal or fight evil opponents; rather, she resists
the lure of temptation and seduction and withstands all corrupting influences. However, while Wilhelmine's rectitude should satisfy the guardians
of proper gender roles, it will not please the arbiters of literary accomplishment. For within this framework, the female *Bildungsroman* is in
constant danger of reverting to the older model of the *Prüfungsroman*
(novel of virtue), whose most famous example is Samuel Richardson's
Clarissa (1747–48). Moreover, a second reduction is likely to take
place. Just as female *Bildung* is defined as the lack thereof, female self-
determination is likely to be trimmed down to the heroine's safeguarding
her chastity. Sexual innocence is Wilhelmine Meister's most valuable

asset, and marriage represents the supremely desirable goal that crowns her path.

It is obvious that such a focus on the preservation of sexual purity imposes distinct limitations on the development of the plot. It is less obvious that it exposes women writers to a treacherous double bind. On the one hand, narratives by and about women are inextricably linked with the body, since female status hinges on sexual purity; on the other hand, such narratives are locked in conflict with the body, since in the late eighteenth century *Bildung* and the female body are set up as irreconcilable opposites.[18] After all, it is woman's physiology that provides the excuse for her social and political disenfranchisement. Consequently, every female writer of the late eighteenth century was forced to grapple with the fact that the conceptualization (and realization) of female *Bildung* and self-determination were impeded by the contemporary construction of the female body. To women writers, the female body was a danger zone. In the plot of marriageability, it was a potential site of corruption. If her sexual purity was at all questionable, the heroine turned into a social outcast. In the plot of maturation, the body is defined as an ontological obstacle that bars woman's access to rationality and self-determination, and hence to *Bildung*.

As is to be expected, different women writers negotiated this perilous terrain in different ways. Some celebrated virginity and chastity as ways to preserve female autonomy. Others relied on cross-dressing as a playful veiling of the female body. Some texts portray adultery as a form of insurrection against the ownership of the female body by the husband.[19] Others imagine the death of the protagonist as the only possible form of relief from the female body. This last (and very common) option demonstrates most drastically the price one has to pay if one is to rid oneself of the burden of the female body. It also serves to illustrate that, more often than not, the strategies of protest and resistance that these writers chose functioned in collusion with the dominant norms and ultimately reproduced what they had set out to defeat.

All the works discussed in the following are concerned with the interrelation between female identity formation, self-determination, and the body. The first four texts, by Wolzogen, Unger, Mereau, and Schopenhauer, are novels and thus speak directly to the connection between female identity, *Bildung*, and the *Bildungsroman*. The following two texts by Charlotte von Stein replay questions of female autonomy, identity, and the body in the genre of drama. In spite of the genre disparity and although the texts span the period from 1794 to 1819, a solution to the problems that mark them is as absent in Schopenhauer's *Gabriele*, as it was in von Stein's *Dido*. In the late eighteenth century, any reconciliation of the female body and female gender identity with the wish for autonomy and the ideal of *Bildung* remains a precarious endeavor.

Caroline von Wolzogen's
Agnes von Lilien (1798)

Caroline von Wolzogen is best known as the sister Schiller did not marry. Born in 1763, Caroline, an avid reader of Greek drama and philosophy, is often considered the more intellectual of the Lengefeld daughters. Financial necessity prompted her to accept the offer of marriage of von Beulwitz in 1784. She divorced her husband in 1793 and married Wilhelm von Wolzogen in 1794. In addition to *Agnes von Lilien*, Wolzogen also wrote a biography of Schiller (1830) and a second novel entitled *Cordelia* (1840). She died in 1847.

Beginning in October 1796, parts of *Agnes von Lilien* were published anonymously in the journal *Die Horen*, edited by Wolzogen's brother-in-law Friedrich Schiller. The entire novel then appeared in book format in 1798. Its anonymity gave rise to many an inspired guess. Several astute readers, among them the brothers Schlegel, believed that Goethe had authored this work. Caroline Schlegel-Schelling is even reported to have praised Goethe for creating his first truly "reinen und vollkommenen weiblichen Charakter"[20] (pure and perfect female character).

Peter Boerner, editor of the recent edition of Wolzogen's novel, calls *Agnes von Lilien* a *Bildungsroman* because it portrays the internal process of maturation of its female protagonist.[21] Indeed, *Agnes von Lilien's* preface would seem to invite such a classification. Its opening pages identify *Bildung* and female identity as the main themes of the novel: "Was ich bin, oder was ich zu seyn wähne, und unter welchem freundlichen Einfluß des Schicksals ich es wurde — sollen Euch diese Blätter zeigen"[22] (What I am, or what I think I am, and under what friendly influence of destiny I became what I am — these pages will show you). However, although it purports to portray a narrative of development, the novel in fact enacts a stasis. The first one-hundred pages depict how the heroine, Agnes von Lilien, meets and falls in love with Baron Nordheim, whom she is clearly destined to marry. The remaining 700 pages are concerned with numerous impediments, most notably Agnes von Lilien's mysterious descent, that prevent her union with the desired partner. The marriage between Agnes's biological father, Hohenfels, later known as the painter Charles, and her mother, the princess, was kept secret because the princess's father, the duke, was opposed to the match. When the duke learns that his scheme to prevent the union of his daughter with a member of the lower nobility has failed and that the princess has given birth, he takes the child, Agnes, away from its mother and places it with strangers. Through a lucky twist of fate, Hohenfels happens on his own child by accident and places her in the trusted care of a country parson. It is in the parson's home that Agnes first encounters Baron Nordheim, and it is also in his home that the young couple is eventually married.

Agnes von Lilien, whose natural sense of propriety manifests itself in her resistance to corrupting influences, might be said to exemplify Schiller's ideal of female perfection. Wolzogen's heroine, who hopes to remain as she always was and is determined never to be at the mercy of external circumstances (1:108 and 1:113), is caught in the paradox of female *Bildung*. "Deine ganze Tugend ist, das zu bleiben, wozu die Natur dich machte" (1:112; Your entire virtue consists in remaining that which nature made you). Simultaneously, and paradoxically, the author's celebration of her heroine's nature is accompanied by a deep commitment to female education. Thus, *Agnes von Lilien*, like many women's novels of the late eighteenth century, clandestinely subverts the gender norms of her age. Much as Agnes professes her determination to remain the same, she nonetheless undertakes to develop all her talents. Since *Bildung*, insofar as it implies maturation through interaction with the world outside the domestic realm, is off limits for a female protagonist, education must fill the breach. Agnes reports proudly that her father improved her mind through thorough and extensive instruction in geography, French, Latin, and Greek (1:12). At court, Agnes studies painting, so as to be able to support herself independently. Education is Agnes's path toward an ideal of self-improvement and self-determination from which her gender excludes her. The benefits of this training would not appear to be lessened by the fact that Agnes learns quite "naturally," that is, without being aware of doing so.

Wolzogen minimizes the potentially transgressive aspects of her heroine's education by pointing out that, although Agnes is the recipient of this educational effort, she is not meant to be its main beneficiary. In the context of female marriageability, a woman's education is justified as an ancillary measure that contributes to the well being of husband and family. Notwithstanding earlier assurances that Agnes need only remain what she always was, Wolzogen now claims that the innate riches of female nature are not in themselves sufficient guarantors of a woman's moral character. Readers are informed that entire families have been ruined because of the weakness of the female sex (1:231) and that, in order to avoid such grave misfortunes, women must be educated properly. Undoubtedly, Wolzogen means to encourage education for women, but her argumentation is a double-edged sword. In locating the purpose of Agnes's education outside of Agnes herself, Wolzogen effectively denies the female autonomy and self-actualization that she is trying to promote.

Moreover, even if we chose to ignore the fact that Agnes's *Bildung* should more appropriately be called education, and that even this education is ultimately not undertaken for her sake, we could still not be sure of this diminished form of female *Bildung*. In order to guarantee a smooth process of maturation one has yet to tame female desire. In *Agnes von Lilien*, wishes must be made to harmonize with reality so that "das stille Geschäft einer höheren *Bildung* nimmt seinen ununterbrochnen Fortgang, ohne von den beunruhigenden Träumen eines ungestillten Verlangens gestöhrt zu werden" (iv–v; the quiet business of higher *Bildung* continues on its uninterrupted course without being disturbed by the unsettling dreams of unfulfilled desire). Obviously, female desire and "higher *Bildung*" cannot coexist. Or rather, female desire and "higher *Bildung*" could not coexist if *Agnes von Lilien* did not posit an a priori harmony between the two. In Wolzogen's novel, any conflict between sexual desire, rational deliberation, and moral necessity is simply impossible: obligation (*Pflicht*) and inclination (*Neigung*) are always coterminous.[23] This harmony is achieved not because Agnes's inclination bends itself gracefully to the iron law of necessity — Schiller's concept of the female "beautiful soul" — but because her obligations happen to conform to her inclinations. Conveniently, Nordheim is not only ethically, intellectually, and financially superior to any other man in the novel, he is also radiantly handsome (1:21) and the object of Agnes's undivided desire and love. Agnes and Nordheim's relationship is suffused with images of physical fulfillment. Their initial encounter strikes every key on the register of bodily pleasure. Agnes experiences "einen noch nie empfundenen süßen Schauer" (1:38; a sweet shudder as I had never felt it before). The mere memory of Nordheim's touch excites her (1:67). Later on, there are hugs and kisses, dances and dizziness (1:272), and shivers and tearful exultation (1:78). The imaginative license of the author allows Wolzogen to have her cake and eat it too. While her introduction warns us that we must learn to perceive necessity as benevolence if we are to experience happiness (viii), while Agnes's father instructs us that we will become slaves if we desire what we should not desire (1:28), the storyline itself erases any such difference between want and should. Since there is no conflict between mind and body, desire need not be suppressed to make "das stille Geschäft einer höheren *Bildung*" possible. If we accept Wolzogen's mislabeling of education as *Bildung* and of sexuality as rational, we might indeed agree that *Agnes von Lilien* is a *Bildungsroman*.

Although Wolzogen's introduction promises a story of female identity formation, Agnes's initial striving for independence gradually vanishes behind the overwhelming importance given to the marriage plot. The story of the preservation of chastity replaces that of maturation. *Agnes von Lilien* does not depart from the established paradigm in which marriage is conceived of as the ultimate goal of a woman's life. But the novel stresses equally that it is the heroine herself who must consent to this union. For Agnes, autonomy and self-determination are defined as the right to reject unwelcome suitors. In fact, the obstacles that stand in the way of the desired union appear to be introduced by the author solely to provide a foil for the only acts of self-determination open to the heroine.

The need to prove that Agnes's marriage is undertaken of her own free will also accounts for the novel's peculiar narrative structure. Agnes's love for Nordheim and his love for her are established in the very beginning. When Nordheim asks her foster father for her hand immediately after their first encounter, the story is in danger of reaching its end point when it has barely begun. Tellingly, the narrator does not reveal why Nordheim's proposal is not accepted at this point. The reply that Nordheim and the reader are left with is the foster father's assertion that "sie kann sich nur selbst geben" (1:104; only she can give herself). The fact that Agnes cannot give her consent at this point, even though she is madly in love with Nordheim, is indicative of the oxymoronic nature of female self-determination. Since the female "yes" is invariably perceived as obedient compliance, it cannot appear credible unless it is contrasted with a series of refusals that constitute the female subject as autonomous. Consequently, Agnes von Lilien has to fend off not only a small army of prospective marriage candidates, but also a host of characters who act as advocates of their respective favorite suitors. Agnes's struggle to marry the partner of her choice ultimately represents not only her endeavor to retain control over her body and her sexuality, but also the only means of self-determination available to Wolzogen's protagonist. In her portrayal of Agnes's joyful and sensual union with Nordheim, Wolzogen attempted to square the circle by promoting female autonomy and *Bildung* without erasing the body. But her concept of autonomy exhausts itself in the selection of the proper husband, and Agnes's journey towards *Bildung* turns into a pursuit of education interrupted by her flight from numerous unwanted suitors.

Friederike Helene Unger's *Bekenntnisse einer schönen Seele von ihr selbst geschrieben* (1806)

As wife of the Berlin publisher Johann Friedrich Unger (1753–1804), Friederike Helene Unger had immediate access to the literary market of her time. She translated numerous works, including Rousseau's *Confessions*, and wrote many essays and novels, such as *Julchen Grünthal* (1784), *Karoline von Lichtfeld* (1787), *Gräfin Pauline* (1800), *Melanie oder das Findelkind* (1804), and *Die Franzosen in Berlin* (The French in Berlin, 1809). She also managed the Unger publishing house after the death of her husband in 1804.

Although Unger's works were popular with her contemporaries and even received some critical attention — Goethe, for example, wrote a review of Unger's *Bekenntnisse*[24] — they fell out of favor soon after the author's death. Unger's novels remained obscure until feminist critics rediscovered her in the 1980s, but scholarly works on Unger are still few and far between.[25]

Unger's *Bekenntnisse einer schönen Seele: von ihr selbst geschrieben* (Confessions of a Beautiful Soul: Related by Herself) is framed as a female *Bildungsroman*.[26] In keeping with Unger's characteristic style, *Bekenntnisse* contains numerous allusions to and discussions of various artists (Haller, Goethe, Michelangelo, and others) and is filled with humorous asides and comic exaggerations. Mirabella, the first-person narrator, relates the story of her maturation to her friend Caesar. Although there is mention of the Seven Years' War and Frederick II, journeys to Switzerland and Italy, all references to German locations remain vague. Separated from her biological parents, whose identity remains a mystery, Mirabella is raised by a French pastor and his sister. Her idyllic childhood in the country ends when she is sent to the capital to make her debut in court society. Here, Mirabella befriends the young Adelaide and her brother Moritz, but her blossoming relationship with Moritz breaks off when the latter leaves his family and friends to serve in the army of Frederick II in the Seven Years' War. After Moritz's death in combat, Mirabella vows to remain unmarried. She becomes the companion of the young princess Caroline, for whom she develops a passionate liking. Princess Caroline, whose marriage with Prince Carl is exceedingly unhappy, removes herself from the court, and she and Mirabella travel through Europe. Their companionship ends when Caroline dies. Mirabella subsequently makes the acquaintance of Eugenie, a rich widow. After several adventures in Vienna, Eugenie buys a country estate where the two women continue to live in harmony.

Unger's novel aims to explore the connection between a woman's social identity and her body quite programmatically. "Wie ich mit den körperlichen und geistigen Eigenschaften, in deren Besitz ich gewesen und allenfalls auch noch bin, eine Jungfrau habe bleiben können? In Wahrheit, dies ist das Hauptproblem, das gelöset werden muß, wenn man mich in meiner Individualität begreifen will"[27] (How I was able to remain a virgin with the physical and spiritual qualities in whose possession I have been and still am? In truth, this is the main problem that must be solved if one wants to comprehend me in my individuality). According to Unger's heroine, virginity is the *sine qua non* of female individuality in a society intent on discouraging female independence. Consequently, the first part of Mirabella's story focuses all its narrative energy on the dissociation of woman and body. But Unger does not stop at creating a virginal heroine. Rather, all actual and metaphorical ties between the female protagonist and her bodily existence need to be cut, and Mirabella is given the benefit of an immaculate conception. Since there is no trace of her biological parents, Mirabella enters the story as the spiritual brainchild of her foster father who, in turn, is not married but lives in chaste union with his sister. Indeed, their home is so devoid of any form of sexuality that Mirabella, who is taught never to take off her clothes in the presence of another person, panics at the sight of a young man who adjusts his stockings and is compelled to flee his presence immediately. A violation of her sense of modesty by her dance instructor is portrayed in a similarly dramatic manner. Aghast at the impropriety of her instructor, who forcefully bent her knees with his own, Mirabella slaps him in the face and leaves the room in righteous indignation. In her aversion to dancing and in her disassociation from the body, Mirabella would seem to follow in the footsteps of Goethe's "beautiful soul," who proclaims that "meine Seele ohne Gesellschaft des Körpers dächte; sie sah den Körper selbst als ein ihr fremdes Wesen an, wie man ein Kleid ansieht"[28] (My soul would think without the company of my body; it regarded the body itself as a being foreign to it, just as one regards clothing). But Unger's humorous exaggerations indicate that she is not paying homage to, but rather making fun of the literary model for her female protagonist.

While Mirabella's autonomy is grounded in her virginity, that is, the absence of a sexual body, her story is predicated on another form of absence. Mirabella states explicitly that she would not have addressed her story to Caesar if her companion, Eugenie, had been present. Readers may glean from this a clue that Mirabella's renunciation is a cheating game. Just as Eugenie's absence is a temporary one, the absence of Mirabella's sexuality is a topical one: it concerns heterosexual relationships only.[29] Mirabella's alleged love for Moritz and his conveniently timed death on the field of honor are but feeble excuses for the heroine's aversion to the holy state of matrimony. Mirabella's devotion to her dead beloved functions as a smokescreen designed to ward off any future proposals of marriage. Although Mirabella encourages her readers to imagine "mit welchem Feuer . . . wir uns umfaßt haben [würden], hätte es keinen Friedrich den Zweiten gegeben" (103–4; with what fire we would have embraced each other if there had been no Frederick the Great;), she also asks whether she "hatte . . . durch seinen Tod das Mindeste an ihm verloren" (117; had I suffered the smallest loss through his death,) and suggests that "es sehr problematisch war, ob das Verhältnis, worin ich mit ihm stand, so modifiziert werden konnte, daß aus dem Bräutigam ein Gemahl wurde" (117; it was very problematic whether the relationship in which I was with him could be modified in such a way that the bridegroom could have become a husband).

The bloodless nature of Mirabella and Moritz's love is particularly evident when compared with her relationship with the princess. When Moritz asks his beloved for a kiss before he leaves to join the army, Mirabella responds that she is "nicht berechtigt, dieses Zeichen weiblichen Wohlwollens . . . vorzuenthalten" (106; not authorized to withhold this sign of female benevolence). In contrast, when Caroline and Mirabella share a passionate moment while reading Tasso's *Jerusalem Delivered*, Mirabella throws herself at Caroline's feet and declares that she is all hers (197) while the princess vows that she could be happy only with Mirabella (209). Together they go to a summer residence (*Lustschloss*) which they leave occasionally so as to avoid any appearance of impropriety (207).[30] This constellation allows for a surprising twist. Since chastity is defined in heterosexual terms, Mirabella's particular brand of virginity does not require the renunciation of her sexuality. Mirabella seems to be a heroine who has it all: individuality, bodily bliss, and *Bildung*.

Or does she? Sigrid Lange maintains that Unger's novel is built on a paradox: the heroine must undergo a male process of socialization in order to be constituted as a female self.[31] One might object that the paradox in question is even more basic. Although Mirabella promises to regale her readers with the story of her development, she often finds herself compelled to defend her unusual situation and character by invoking the authority of nature. But again, attributing one's *Bildung* to nature precludes the very idea of development. Thus, when Mirabella informs us that nature herself had ordained that a being such as herself should exist, that her maturity was bestowed on her when she was born, she undoes the premises of her project. Even Mirabella, sprung from her father's head like Athena, is frozen in a posture of natural femininity.

Sophie Mereau's *Amanda und Eduard: Ein Roman in Briefen* (1803)

Sophie Schubart was born in Altenburg in 1770. She married Friedrich Karl Mereau, a professor of law, in 1793. Unhappy in her marriage, Mereau received a divorce in 1801, married Clemens Brentano in 1803, and died in childbirth in 1806. Mereau authored numerous stories, poems, two novels, and the literary journal *Kalathiskos*.[32] During her early career as a writer she was supported literarily by Schiller, who published her poetry in his journals *Thalia* and *Die Horen*. The first version of her epistolary novel *Amanda und Eduard: Ein Roman in Briefen* (Amanda and Eduard: A Novel in Letters, 1797) appeared in three installments in Schiller's *Die Horen*. Mereau later expanded on the initial eight letters. This longer and substantially revised version was published in 1803.[33]

Amanda und Eduard met with Schiller's — albeit somewhat condescending — approval: "Für die Horen hat mir unsere Dichterin Mereau jetzt ein sehr angenehmes Geschenk gemacht. . . . Es ist der Anfang eines Romans in Briefen, die mit weit mehr Klarheit Leichtigkeit und Simplicität geschrieben sind, als ich es je von ihr erwartet hätte. Sie fängt darinn an, sich von Fehlern frey zu machen, die ich an ihr für ganz unheilbar hielt. . . . Ich muß mich doch wirklich darüber wundern, wie unsere Weiber jetzt, auf bloß dilettantischem Wege, eine gewiße Schreibgeschicklichkeit sich zu verschaffen wißen, die der Kunst nahe kommt" (Schiller to Goethe, 30 June 1797; The poetess Mereau has made me a very pleasant present for the Horen. . . . It is the beginning of a novel in letters that are written with far more clarity, ease, and simplicity than I would ever have expected of her. In this, she is starting to rid herself of mistakes that I considered utterly incurable in her. . . . I am really astonished how our women manage to acquire a certain skill of composition in a purely dilettante manner that approximates art). Although Mereau's works were popular with her contemporaries — Mereau even succeeded in making a living as a writer — they were forgotten soon after the author's death and remained obscure until the late twentieth century.

With the exception of a few concluding lines by a fictitious editor, *Amanda and Eduard* consists entirely of letters penned by the two protagonists. Through this juxtaposition, Mereau encourages her readers to view the same events from both a female and a male perspective. The epistolary style also facilitates Mereau's preference for emotional nuances over social context. Amanda, the female protagonist, is unhappily married to Albret, who shows neither love nor respect for her. She falls in love with Eduard, but the couple's happiness is short-lived. On his deathbed, Albret demands that she not have any contact with Eduard for a period of four months. Because of several miscommunications and misunderstandings, this seemingly innocuous sacrifice alienates the lovers from each other. Separated from Eduard, Amanda makes the acquaintance of the painter Antonio and falls in love with him. Eduard is considering marriage to another partner as well. But just as Amanda makes up her mind to marry Antonio, Eduard reenters her life. Her tender feelings for him are reawakened and they marry. Shortly after the wedding, Amanda contracts a fever and dies.

Mereau's novel opens with a letter by Amanda that expatiates on her matrimonial misery, thus conveying a strong indictment of marriages of convenience.[34] Prodded by her impecunious father, Amanda had accepted Albret for purely financial reasons. Readers are informed that she might have been able to support herself and avoid marriage to a hated suitor if she had received a proper education: "Die Umstände vergönnten mir nicht, dir eine Erziehung zu geben, welche die in dir vielleicht schlummernden Talente hätte gehörig entwickeln können, damit du jetzt in ihrer Ausbildung Mittel zu einem leichten und anständigen Unterhalt finden möchtest"[35] (Circumstances did not permit an education for you that might have developed properly talents that perhaps lie dormant in you so that you might now find in their progress means to support yourself easily and honestly). As it is, however, Amanda's marriage to Albret is little more than a socially sanctioned form of prostitution. She cannot love her husband and experiences their union as degradation.

Interestingly, Mereau's novel appropriates and reinterprets Kantian philosophy to further women's rights. Albret's treatment of his wife is morally repugnant because it constitutes a violation of Amanda's human rights. In using Amanda as a tool to achieve his own sinister aims, Albret transgresses the Kantian dictum that every human being carries its own purpose within itself and must never be used as a means to an end. Thus, Mereau employs Kant to expose Albret's justifications of his iniquitous actions as ethically flawed, misogynistic platitudes.

In addition to its appropriation of Kantian philosophy, *Amanda and Eduard* also discusses the concept of *Bildung*. Because of the dual perspective of her novel, Mereau is able to contrast a female version of *Bildung* with a male one. To Amanda, *Bildung* is not maturation resulting from the interaction of individual and society, but is synonymous with the freedom to preserve one's own individuality intact. Amanda further believes that individuality resides in one's emotions, which are sacred in every shape and form and can never lead us astray: "Wer sein natürlich reines Gefühl bewahrt hat, kann sich die undankbare Mühe ersparen, seine Neigungen bekämpfen zu wollen; sie führen ihn recht; er darf sich ihnen überlassen" (119; He who has preserved his natural pure feelings can save himself the thankless effort of fighting his inclinations; they guide him on the right path; he may surrender to them). Amanda's emphasis on the sacred nature of feelings must be read within the context of the marriage of convenience and the paradox that it engenders. On the one hand, men like Albret insist that women are creatures of emotion. On the other, women like Amanda must ignore their emotions if they are to marry men they cannot love. Seen in this light, Amanda's celebration of authentic feelings is an emancipatory act. In the context of *Bildung*, however, its liberating impact is lost. Conservation replaces maturation, and *Bildung* collapses into resistance to, rather than transformation through, an encounter with the world.

Amanda's reliance on authentic feelings is combined with a problematic reluctance to impose her will on the world. Interestingly, such resigned acceptance of one's fate meets with the disapproval of the author. Amanda may be a true student of Schiller's gender philosophy, but Mereau most definitely is not. Her decision to juxtapose Amanda and Eduard's notions of *Bildung* effects a subtle critique of the passivity inherent in Amanda's worldview. Unlike Amanda's, Eduard's version of *Bildung* combines a strong sense of personal identity with self-determination and active transformation of the world. Conversely, Amanda's refusal to have an active hand in changing the course of her life — "Nein! Nur dem Mann, dem Machtvollen, kommt es zu, die Begebenheiten zu schaffen, alles Äußere nach seinem Gefallen zu lenken" (160; No: it is the right of men only, of the powerful ones, to create opportunities, to steer everything external according to their own liking) — is presented as the main cause of her misery. *Amanda and Eduard* invites its readers to ponder what might have happened if Amanda had not considered action the prerogative of the other sex.

In *Amanda and Eduard*, marriage is the antithesis of female *Bildung* and self-realization. Consequently, Amanda's adulterous relationship with Eduard constitutes an attempt to regain control over her life and body and thus to reclaim her personal dignity.[36] But if Amanda's love for Eduard is portrayed in a positive light, why then does the novel not end with the happy reunion of the lovers? Is Amanda's death a narrative shortcut introduced by a feckless author to rid herself of the dilemma of the love triangle? Certainly, portraying a *ménage a trois* would have been too grave a transgression even for a free-spirited author such as Mereau. Conversely, an ending that denied the authenticity of Amanda's feelings would have been equally impossible, given the novel's emphasis on emotion as the only true and reliable guide to happiness. But if Amanda is torn between two men, why then does her last letter, which reports the reunion and wedding, not contain any trace of remorse or even remembrance of Antonio? Perhaps it is not the love triangle, but a much more fundamental contradiction that occasions this "hasty wrapping-up?"[37]

For a woman writer of the late eighteenth century, the truly unthinkable ending is one in which sensual fulfillment, female self-determination, and integration into society coexist in peaceful harmony. Shortly before her death, Amanda visits a hermit. In their conversation, the impossibility of satisfying both the need for freedom and the desires of the body is singled out as the root cause of earthly unhappiness (216–17). Similarly, Amanda's narrative of her reunion with Eduard precedes fantasies of disembodiment: "entkörpert tauche ich mich in das unendliche Meer der Liebe" (220; disembodied I dive into the endless ocean of love). In *Amanda and Eduard*, death as disembodiment offers the only escape route from an ideology that defined autonomy and the female body as incompatible. It is Mereau's intellectual honesty and unwillingness to compromise the clarity of her insights that make the tragic ending of her heroine inevitable.

Johanna Schopenhauer's *Gabriele* (1819)

If we circumscribe the period of German Classicism as lasting roughly from 1787 to 1805, Johanna Schopenhauer is most decidedly a latecomer. Her first novel, *Gabriele*, was published in 1819. In spite of this chronological gap, Schopenhauer's work is written in direct response to Classicist aesthetics and is best understood in this context.[38]

Johanna Henriette Trosiener was the daughter of a well-to-do Danzig merchant. She received a thorough education, including English, history, and geography, but her desire to become a painter was ridiculed by her father.[39] She married Floris Schopenhauer in 1788 and the couple traveled to England and France, eventually settling in Hamburg. After the death of her husband, Schopenhauer moved to Weimar where she held a weekly salon in her house.[40] Her oeuvre consists of no less than twenty-four volumes, including numerous travelogues and the novels *Sidonia* (1928), *Die*

Tante (The Aunt, 1823), and *Richard Wood* (1837). During her lifetime, Johanna Schopenhauer's works far outsold those of her famous
son Arthur.

Gabriele tells the story of Gabriele von Aarheim, the daughter of the
misanthropic Count von Aarheim in a vaguely contemporary setting.
Aarheim, consumed by his passion for alchemistic experiments, sends
Gabriele to stay with her aunt, Countess Rosenberg. In her aunt's house,
Gabriele falls in love with the young and dashing Ottokar, who is engaged
to Countess Rosenberg's daughter Aurelia. Unfortunately, Gabriele does
not muster the courage to confess her feelings to Ottokar until the latter's
engagement to Aurelia is made public. Although Ottokar now realizes that
he reciprocates her love, Gabriele convinces him that it is his duty to abide
by his father's wishes and marry Aurelia. Weakened by the enormity of her
sacrifice, Gabriele almost succumbs to a grave illness. When she recovers,
her motherly friend Frau von Willnangen takes her to Karlsbad, where
Gabriele makes the acquaintance of her cousin Moritz von Aarheim, the
future owner of Aarheim castle. Moritz's extraordinarily ridiculous character marks him as wholly unsuitable for matrimony with the novel's heroine, but Gabriele's father insists on her marrying this most ludicrous of
men, and she obeys his wishes. Comforted by the thought that his daughter will be taken care of, her father commits suicide. As expected, Gabriele
bears the humiliations of her marriage with dignity. Several years into her
marriage, she makes the acquaintance of the young Hippolit, a Hungarian
count who is as handsome as Apollo, immensely rich, and madly in love
with Gabriele. Tortured by his unrequited passion, Hippolit decides to
travel to Italy, where Gabriele's fatherly friend Ernesto devotes himself to
perfecting Hippolit's education. In the flower of his manhood, Hippolit
returns to Gabriele, who now discovers that she too is in love with him.
The struggle to resist her feelings for Hippolit weakens her delicate constitution, and she dies. Immediately after her death, Ottokar arrives from
Italy bearing the news that Gabriele's husband Moritz is dead.

Schopenhauer's novel depicts Gabriele's development from a shy and
clumsy young maiden to a radiantly beautiful lady much admired in elegant society. Gabriele's maturation evokes the term *Bildung*, but it is cut
short by her premature death.[41] Furthermore, in spite of her impressive
development, and although she exercises some control over trifles,
Schopenhauer's heroine never achieves even the smallest degree of self-
determination in matters of true import for her life and happiness. In fact,
one might wonder whether the union between the exemplary Gabriele and
the "lächerlichsten und lästigsten aller Karikaturen"[42] (most annoying and
ridiculous of all caricatures) is meant to draw attention to the immense gap
between female strength on the one hand and the inability to exercise control over one's life on the other. In any case, Gabriele's sad fate certainly
conveys Schopenhauer's strong opposition to arranged marriages.[43]

Although often referred to as a novel of renunciation, *Gabriele* might more appropriately be characterized as "an Anti-*Entsagungsroman*, a novel that denounces both female resignation and the abuse of paternal authority."[44] To be sure, Gabriele's life consists of an uninterrupted chain of acts of self-sacrifice, though these acts are not extolled, but instead portrayed as pointless, unnecessary, and even physically harmful. When Gabriele and Ottokar discover their love for each other, Ottokar counters Gabriele's objections with an urgent plea that it is not too late. After all, he is not married yet, and an engagement is easily dissolved. Consequently, Gabriele's willingness to sacrifice both herself and Ottokar on the altar of duty must appear as rather gratuitous. In addition, Gabriele's renunciation leads to the unhappy coupling of two incompatible characters, causing great misery for all three parties. The futility of Gabriele's propensity for self-sacrifice is even more pronounced when she obeys her father's wishes and consents to marry Moritz.[45] Firstly, Moritz himself does not want a wife who marries him against her will. Secondly, Gabriele has the means to escape, since her fatherly friend Ernesto, who is violently opposed to the union, urges Gabriele to reconsider and offers his assistance. But Gabriele is resolved to place her father's happiness above her own. Ironically, her act of renunciation buys her father less than a few minutes of happiness. He commits suicide on her wedding day. Moreover, the narrator insinuates that she is indirectly responsible for her father's suicide, since her consent prompted him to sever all ties. By marrying Moritz, Gabriele pronounced her father's death sentence. We are led to conclude that both she and her father would have been far better off if she had resisted his unjust demands.

Because Gabriele's acts of renunciation are described as futile and destructive, her mother's teachings of quiet suffering are subjected to critical scrutiny. Gabriele's mother, Auguste, advised her daughter that happiness is to be found in loving others, not in being loved. She taught her daughter to love without hope of being loved and to wish and hope for nothing. Tellingly, Gabriele's affection for Ottokar finds expression in her desire to suffer for him. However, as Gabriele matures, she gradually becomes unable to repress her own feelings and finds it increasingly difficult to follow her mother's philosophy: "Wie fern stand ihr jetzt jener kindliche Glaube, daß Liebe in sich beglücke" (370; How far from her now was that childish belief that loving in itself conveys happiness). The pinnacle of Gabriele's maturation is her declaration of love for Hippolit. But if Schopenhauer's novel depicts female *Bildung* as a process of learning to accept one's desires, it also shows that accepting one's desires makes life unlivable. In affirming her sexuality, the heroine precipitates her tragic death. Like Mereau, Schopenhauer takes the concept of female *Bildung* to its logical conclusion. Since woman's identity is defined as a function of her body, as is evident in the concept of *Geschlechtscharakter*, and since it is the body that prevents her from gaining *Bildung*, she must transcend her earthly existence in order to become a truly free agent. It is by following the rules of female *Bildung* to the letter that Schopenhauer effects their most drastic critique.

Charlotte von Stein's *Dido* (1794) and *Ein neues Freiheitssystem oder Verschwörungen gegen die Liebe* (1798)

Charlotte von Stein, best known for her role as Goethe's friend, muse, and possibly lover, was a lady-in-waiting to the mother of the future Duke Carl August, Duchess Anna Amalia. She was married to Josias von Stein (1735–1793), the master of the stables at the court of Weimar. Von Stein gave birth to seven children, three of whom survived, and wrote several dramas, including *Rino* (1776) and *Dido* (1794). Her drama *Die Zwey Emilien*, based on the British woman writer Sophia Lee's (1750–1824) novel *The Two Emilies*, is the only work that was published during her lifetime.

Von Stein's tragedy *Dido*, written in 1794, has often been compared to Goethe's *Iphigenie auf Tauris* (1787).[46] Queen Dido, who rules over the prosperous and culturally refined empire of Carthage, is presented as a mature and competent leader. Paradoxically, however, Dido, who might be said to exemplify the ideal of *Bildung*, has no control over her personal fate. This becomes evident when the barbarian King Jarbes desires to marry her and threatens to wage war if she refuses his hand. Jarbes finds allies in Dido's court intellectuals Ogon, Dodus, and Aratus, who resent being ruled by a woman and conspire against their own queen. Dido, widowed and unwilling to remarry, plans to abdicate and spend the rest of her life in solitude in a secret location. She makes her escape only to find that her friends and advisers have been held captive in her stead. Her people are in uproar and the priest Albicerio, the only one who knows where Dido is hiding, is to be executed because he refuses to betray his queen. When Dido returns to Carthage to save her friends, she finds that the only way to avoid marriage to Jarbes is to stab herself.

Von Stein locates the heart of the tragic conflict in a woman's refusal to relinquish control over her body. It is tragically ironic that not only King Jarbes, but every citizen of Carthage should feel entitled to dispose of the queen's body ("Das Volk giebt deine Hand dem König Jarbes"[47]). The only person with no say in the matter is Dido herself. Von Stein underscores Dido's agonizing lack of autonomy by painting her suitor Jarbes as an utterly despicable person. In contrast, the portrayal of Dido's impressive achievements as a sovereign, especially when compared with Jarbes's lack of qualifications, highlights the irrationality of the intellectuals' objection to being ruled by a woman. To Dodus, Orgon, and Aratus, the fact that Dido must be credited with laying the foundation for Carthage's cultural and economic efflorescence is of little consequence. Blinded by prejudice, they consider the gender of their sovereign infinitely more important than his or her personal suitability for the task.

Von Stein leaves no room for doubt that a union with Jarbes is tantamount to utter humiliation. The barbarian potentate is not only morally revolting but also feels not the slightest degree of affection or respect for his wife-to-be. His design in marrying her is to make her his slave and take all her riches. To call Jarbes constitutionally incapable of love is an understatement: "Dieses glüklich gepriesene Gefühl des Herzens haben mir die Götter versagt, Sklavinnen sind alles, was ich begehre, und in der Liebe sind meine schönen afrikanischen Pferde mir die nächsten am Herzen" (497; The gods have denied me this happy lauded feeling of the heart, all I desire is female slaves, and when it comes to love my beautiful African horses are closest to my heart).

Dido's unwillingness to surrender her body to her male suitor causes public anarchy. The radical thrust of von Stein's text is revealed in the fact that the only remedy for Dido's dilemma is her physical self-destruction. Tellingly, dying is not enough. After stabbing herself, Dido jumps onto a sacrificial pyre whose flames will consume her body entirely. Her suicide springs from her conviction that no happiness is possible within the confines of bodily existence, a belief echoed by a hermit whom she visits before her death:

> Ich [war] in einer an Wahnsinn gränzenden Ungewißheit . . ., welche von beiden Erscheinungen, Körper oder Geist, ich für die wahre halten sollte. Dadurch wurde ich wie verwaißt unter den Menschen, aber ich genoß eine Seeligkeit, die selten ein Erdenbewohner begreift, und da ich vom körperlichen immer getrennt blieb, so gehe ich weiter in andere Sphären und werde nie eine Bildung dieser Erde wieder erfassen. (514–15)

> [I felt an uncertainty bordering on madness as to which of the two phenomena, body or spirit, I should take for real. Because of this I was estranged from human beings, but I enjoyed a bliss hardly understood by people who dwell on this earth, and because I always remained separated from all things physical, I move on to different spheres and will never again grasp a form of this earth.]

Again, the desire for autonomy results in the complete destruction of the female body. But whereas *Dido* re-enacts the same predicaments that plagued Mereau and Schopenhauer, von Stein's comedy *Neues Freiheitssystem oder die Verschwörung gegen die Liebe* (New System of Freedom or the Conspiracy Against Love, 1798) offers a playful solution.

Neues Freiheitssystem oder die Verschwörung gegen die Liebe was written in 1798 and first published in 1867 by von Stein's great grandson, who changed the original text considerably.[48] Depicting eighteenth-century society as von Stein knew it, *Freiheitssystem* is a play of intrigues and misunderstandings that contains enchantingly humorous portrayals of foolish aristocrats and smart-alecky servants. Avelos and Daval are old friends who have not seen each other in years. When Avelos spends some time in a spa to recover from wounds received in combat, Daval happens upon his name on the list of guests and invites his friend to his country estate. Daval for his part is a philosopher who believes that romantic love inevitably leads to slavery and tyranny. He has devoted his life to freeing people from their misguided pursuit of romance, and now engages Avelos to kidnap two actresses whom he hopes to save from the aberrations of love. However, since Daval's instructions lack precision — the ladies are to be identified by their white veils — Avelos kidnaps the wrong women, Menonda and Theodora, the nieces of Major Herbert from Warsaw. When Officer Montrose, the cousin of the ladies, learns of the abduction, he immediately calls for his weapons. Susette, Menonda and Theodora's servant, is worried about Montrose's martial behavior and decides to anticipate him and rescue her mistresses herself. She dresses as an officer and makes her way to Daval's castle. Meanwhile, Menonda is revealed to be Daval's long-lost sister who was once engaged to marry his friend Avelos. Their relationship ended because Daval, once again bent on the eradication of romance, forged his sister's handwriting to produce a letter in which he rejected Avelos in his sister's name. Finally, the forgery is uncovered, the former lovers are reunited, Theodora is engaged to marry Montrose, and even Daval is to marry Luitgarde.

In von Stein's comedy, misogynistic gender stereotypes are the results of ludicrous misinterpretations of female behavior. Throughout the play, Menonda and Theodora's every move is misconstrued and taken as proof of the deceitfulness of women. The guileless innocence with which they respond to their kidnapping, for example, cannot shake Avelos's conviction that the ladies have consented to a staged abduction. Far from doubting the wisdom and propriety of his own actions, he feels confirmed in his belief that women are masters of deception (28). By emphasizing women's lack of agency, von Stein strengthens the impression that misogynistic notions are male phantasmagorias, wholly disconnected from the actual character of the women in question.

Von Stein's comedy not only pokes fun at the hollowness of misogynistic gender stereotypes, but also effects a humorous deconstruction of the concept of gendered character. Repeatedly, the play undermines the notion that there is a causal connection between body, character, and social position. In von Stein's comedy, one's gender is determined not by the body, but by one's clothing. Personal identity is not inscribed in the body, but is constituted through performance. Thus, the cross-dressed maid

Susette succeeds effortlessly in passing as Montrose, while Montrose himself is dependent on his uniform if he wants to pass as an officer:

MAJOR: Überdies, Junker, du siehst selbst noch wie ein
Frauenzimmer aus.
MONTROSE: Aber meine Uniform straft mein Gesicht Lügen. (24)

[MAJOR: Moreover, squire, you yourself still look like a woman.
MONTROSE: But my uniform gives the lie to my face.]

It would appear that the lightness of the genre of comedy freed von Stein from the weight of the female body. To gain agency and autonomy for her female protagonists, the author of comedies need not erase the female body, but only disguise it.

If one were to summarize the results of this survey, one might say that where one expects to find the female *Bildungsroman*, one encounters the fairy tale of romantic love, the parody of male-authored gender norms, and the tragedy of the destruction of the female body. There is a direct correlation between the earnestness of the pursuit of *Bildung* and autonomy and the catastrophic ending of the respective text. If we remember that Goethe once interpreted Wilhelm Meister's progress to mean that "der Mensch, trotz aller Dummheiten und Verwirrungen, von einer höheren Hand geleitet, doch zum glücklichen Ziele gelange"[49] (a human being, who is guided by a higher hand, despite all stupid acts and confusions still reaches the happy goal), the contrast with Wilhelmine Meister is evident. In spite of her perfect conduct, Wilhelmine Meister — if she does not choose to surrender her autonomy to an ideal husband as in *Agnes von Lilien*, or thumb her nose at the conventions of Weimar Classicism as in Unger's *Confessions* — is most likely to die prematurely. Since *Bildung* precludes the realm of the female body, the female *Bildungsroman* in the period of Weimar Classicism remained a precarious endeavor.

Notes

[1] For recent studies of women's literature of this period see Barbara Becker-Cantarino, *Der lange Weg zur Mündigkeit: Frau und Literatur 1500–1800* (Munich: Deutscher Taschenbuch Verlag, 1989); Barbara Becker-Cantarino, *Schriftstellerinnen der Romantik: Epoche Werk Wirkung* (Munich: Beck, 2000); *Bitter Healing: German Women Writers From 1700 to 1880: An Anthology*, ed. Jeannine Blackwell and Susanne Zantop (Lincoln: U of Nebraska P, 1990); Sylvia Bovenschen, *Die imaginierte Weiblichkeit: Exemplarische Untersuchungen zu kulturgeschichtlichen und literarischen Präsentationsformen des Weiblichen* (Frankfurt am Main: Suhrkamp, 1979); *Deutsche Literatur von Frauen: Vom Mittelalter bis zum Ende des 18. Jahrhunderts*, ed. Gisela Brinker-Gabler, vol. 1 (Munich: Beck, 1988); Christa Bürger, *Leben Schreiben: Die Klassik, die Romantik und der Ort der Frauen* (Stuttgart: Metzler, 1990); *Untersuchungen zum Roman von Frauen um 1800*,

ed. Helga Gallas and Magdalene Heuser (Tübingen: Max Niemeyer Verlag, 1990); *In the Shadow of Olympus: German Women Writers Around 1800*, ed. Katherine R. Goodman and Edith Waldstein (Albany: State U of New York P, 1992); Dagmar von Hoff, *Dramen des Weiblichen: Deutsche Dramatikerinnen um 1800* (Opladen: Westdeutscher Verlag, 1989); Eva Kammler, *Zwischen Professionalisierung und Dilettantismus: Romane und ihre Autorinnen um 1800* (Opladen: Westdeutscher Verlag, 1992); Susanne Kord, *Ein Blick hinter die Kulissen: Deutschsprachige Dramatikerinnen im 18. und 19. Jahrhundert* (Stuttgart: Metzler, 1992); Kord, *Sich einen Namen machen: Anonymität und weibliche Autorschaft 1700–1900* (Stuttgart: Metzler, 1996); Sigrid Lange, *Spiegelgeschichten: Geschlechter und Poetiken in der Frauenliteratur um 1800* (Frankfurt am Main: Ulrike Helmer Verlag, 1995); Helga Meise, *Die Unschuld und die Schrift: Deutsche Frauenromane im 18. Jahrhundert* (Berlin: Guttandin & Hoppe, 1983); Lydia Schieth, *Die Entwicklung des deutschen Frauenromans im ausgehenden 18. Jahrhundert: Ein Beitrag zur Gattungsgeschichte* (Frankfurt am Main: Peter Lang, 1987); Antonie Schweitzer and Simone Sitte, "Tugend — Opfer — Rebellion: Zum Bild der Frau im weiblichen Erziehungs- und Bildungsroman," in *Frauen Literatur Geschichte: Schreibende Frauen vom Mittelalter bis zur Gegenwart*, ed. Hiltrud Gnüg and Renate Möhrmann (Frankfurt am Main: Suhrkamp, 1989), 144–65; *Beruf Schriftstellerin: Schreibende Frauen im 18. und 19. Jahrhundert*, ed. Karin Tebben (Göttingen: Vandenhoeck and Ruprecht, 1998); Christine Touaillon, *Der deutsche Frauenroman des 18. Jahrhunderts* (Bern: Peter Lang, 1979); Birgit Wägenbaur, *Die Pathologie der Liebe: Literarische Weiblichkeitsentwürfe um 1800* (Berlin: Schmidt, 1996).

[2] See Kord, *Sich einen Namen machen*, 102–5.

[3] See Kammler, *Professionalisierung*, 31–32. According to Kammler, the authors most frequently quoted by women writers are Goethe, Schiller, Klopstock, Wieland, and Gellert.

[4] In her excellent study *Schriftstellerinnen der Romantik*, Becker-Cantarino claims that it is unproductive to attempt to add women writers to the existing canon and instead prefers to focus on women "who wrote during the era of German Romanticism" (11, see also 13). However, her choice of authors is informed by a clear preference for women writers traditionally associated with German Romanticism, such as Bettina Brentano-von Arnim, while she omits others whose texts conform to a different aesthetics, such as Friederike Helene Unger.

[5] The situation of the bourgeois woman was riddled with contradictions. On the one hand, the dissolution of the whole household and the concomitant division into private and public spheres provided bourgeois women with more free time. On the other hand, bourgeois ideology, evidenced for example by the debate on the pernicious effect of reading on the female mind, prevented women from using it for their pleasure and education.

[6] On female education in the eighteenth century, see Becker-Cantarino, *Der lange Weg zur Mündigkeit*, 167–89.

[7] Barbara Becker-Cantarino, "(Sozial)geschichte der Frau in Deutschland 1500–1800: Ein Forschungsbericht," in *Die Frau von der Reformation zur Romantik: Die Situation der Frau vor dem Hintergrund der Literatur- und Sozialgeschichte*, ed. Barbara Becker-Cantarino (Bonn: Bouvier, 1980), 247.

[8] For more information on the relation between body and character see Thomas Laqueur, *Making Sex: Body and Gender from the Greeks to Freud* (Cambridge: Harvard UP, 1990) and Londa Schiebinger, *The Mind Has No Sex: Women in the Origins of Modern Science* (Cambridge: Harvard UP, 1989). For information on the background and genesis of the model of *Geschlechtscharakter* see Claudia Honegger's work *Die Ordnung der Geschlechter: Die Wissenschaften vom Menschen und das Weib 1750–1850* (Munich: Deutscher Taschenbuch Verlag, 1996) and Barbara Duden, *The Woman Beneath the Skin: A Doctor's Patients in Eighteenth-Century Germany*, trans. Thomas Dunlap (Cambridge: Harvard UP, 1991). According to Duden, "the historical conditions that shaped our modern body perception did not emerge until the second half of the eighteenth century" (1).

[9] See Karin Hausen, "Die Polarisierung der Geschlechtscharaktere: Eine Spiegelung der Dissoziation von Erwerbs- und Familienleben," *Sozialgeschichte der Familie in der Neuzeit Europas: Neue Forschungen*, ed. Werner Conze (Stuttgart: Klett, 1976), 363–93.

[10] Kord argues that early Enlightenment thinkers viewed "learned" women favorably whereas toward the end of century learning was defined as transgression against woman's nature. Relevant texts in this context are Kant's "Anthropologie in pragmatischer Hinsicht," Schiller's "Über Anmut und Würde," Humboldt's "Über männliche und weibliche Form," and Fichte's "Erster Anhang des Naturrechts: Grundriß des Familienrechts" (Kord, *Sich einen Namen machen*, 39–40).

[11] See Bovenschen, *Die imaginierte Weiblichkeit*, 33, 251.

[12] See Mechthilde Vahsen, *Die Politisierung des weiblichen Subjekts: Deutsche Romanautorinnen und die Französische Revolution 1790–1820* (Berlin: Erich Schmidt, 2000), 37–39.

[13] See Volker Hoffmann, "Elisa und Robert oder das Weib und der Mann, wie sie sein sollten: Anmerkungen zur Geschlechtercharakteristik der Goethezeit," in *Klassik und Moderne: Die Weimarer Klassik als historisches Ereignis und Herausforderung im kulturgeschichtlichen Prozeß*, ed. Karl Richter and Jörg Schönert (Stuttgart: Metzler, 1983), 89.

[14] See Catriona MacLeod, *Embodying Ambiguity: Androgyny and Aesthetics from Winckelmann to Keller* (Detroit: Wayne State UP, 1998), 138–39.

[15] For more information on the *Bildungsroman* see Jürgen Jacobs, *Wilhelm Meister und seine Brüder: Untersuchungen zum deutschen Bildungsroman* (Munich: Fink, 1972); Jürgen Jacobs and Markus Krause, *Der deutsche Bildungsroman: Gattungsgeschichte vom 18. bis zum 20. Jahrhundert* (Munich: Beck, 1989); Thomas Kahlcke, *Lebensgeschichte als Körpergeschichte: Studien zum Bildungsroman im 18. Jahrhundert* (Würzburg: Königshausen & Neumann, 1997); Todd Kontje, *Private Lives in the Public Sphere: The German Bildungsroman as Metafiction* (University Park: Pennsylvania State UP, 1992); Gerhard Mayer, *Der deutsche Bildungsroman: Von der Aufklärung bis zur Gegenwart* (Stuttgart: Metzler, 1992); Michael Minden, *The German Bildungsroman: Incest and Inheritance* (Cambridge: Cambridge UP, 1997); Rolf Selbmann, *Der deutsche Bildungsroman* (Stuttgart: Metzler, 1984); Martin Swales, *The German Bildungsroman from Wieland to Hesse* (Princeton: Princeton UP, 1978).

[16] Jacobs, *Bildungsroman*, 37; some recent research considers the *Bildungsroman* a phantom genre and draws attention to the lack of maturation in *Wilhelm Meister's* eponymous protagonist. However, in analyzing how late eighteenth-century women writers tried to adapt the male project of *Bildung* to the female realm, it is helpful to depart from a traditional understanding of *Bildung* as the "shaping of the individual self from its innate potentialities through acculturation and social experience to the threshold of maturity," quoted from Jeffrey L. Sammons, "The *Bildungsroman* for Nonspecialists: An Attempt at a Clarification," in *Reflection and Action: Essays on the Bildungsroman*, ed. by James Hardin (Columbia: U of South Carolina P, 1991), 41. Wilhelm Meister may not achieve the desired level of maturity, but the fact that he can leave the parental home all by himself and join a theater group already implies a degree of freedom that is wholly out of reach for the female protagonists of the novels discussed here. Rejecting the term *Bildungsroman* on the basis of its subtle subversion in works such as *Wilhelm Meister* fails to do justice to the much more fundamental lack of agency and autonomy expressed in works by women writers.

[17] See Lange, *Spiegelgeschichten*, 46.

[18] See Susanne Zantop, "Eignes Selbst und fremde Formen: Goethes *Bekenntnisse einer schönen Seele*," *Goethe Yearbook* 3 (1986): 78–79.

[19] See Anke Gilleir, "On the Presentation of the Body in the Works of Therese Huber and Johanna Schopenhauer," in *Harmony in Discord: German Women Writers in the Eighteenth and Nineteenth Centuries*, ed. Laura Martin (Oxford: Peter Lang, 2001), 218.

[20] Schiller to Goethe, 6 December 1796, quoted from NA 29:22. For an excellent survey of the gossip surrounding the authorship of *Agnes von Lilien* see Schieth, *Entwicklung*, 83–86.

[21] Peter Boerner, "Afterword," Caroline von Wolzogen's *Agnes von Lilien*, ed. Peter Boerner (Hildesheim: Georg Olms, 1988), 400.

[22] Quoted from Caroline von Wolzogen, *Agnes von Lilien*, ed. Peter Boerner (Hildesheim: Georg Olms, 1988), iv.

[23] See Touaillon, *Der deutsche Frauenroman*, 470.

[24] "Bekenntnisse einer schönen Seele. Melanie das Findelkind. Wilhelm Dumont." MA 6.2:626–36.

[25] For recent studies of Unger's works see Susanne Zantop, "Aus der Not eine Tugend . . . Tugendgebot und Öffentlichkeit bei Friederike Helene Unger," in *Untersuchungen zum Roman von Frauen um 1800*, ed. Heuser and Gallas, 132–47; Susanne Zantop, "The Beautiful Soul Writes Herself: Friederike Helene Unger and The Große Göthe," *In the Shadow of Olympus: German Women Writers Around 1800*, ed. Goodman and Waldstein, 29–51; Magdalene Heuser, "Spuren trauriger Selbstvergessenheit: Möglichkeiten eines weiblichen *Bildungsromans* um 1800: Friederike Helene Unger," *Frauensprache — Frauenliteratur: Für und wider eine Psychoanalyse literarischer Werke. Kontroversen, alte und neue: Akten des VII. Internationalen Germanisten-Kongresses, Göttingen 1985*, ed. Inge Stephan and Carl Pietzcker (Tübingen: Niemeyer, 1985), 30–42; Marianne Henn and Britta Hufeisen, "Bekenntnisse einer schönen Seele aus weiblicher Sicht: Friederike

Helene Ungers Roman," in *Frauen: MitSprechen, MitSchreiben. Beiträge zur literatur- und sprachwissenschaftlichen Frauenforschung*, ed. Marianne Henn and Britta Hufeisen (Stuttgart: Heinz, 1997), 48–68. The first monograph on Unger appeared in 2003 (Birte Giesler, *Literatursprünge: Das erzählerische Werk von Friederike Helene Unger* [Göttingen: Wallstein, 2003]).

[26] *Bekenntnisse einer schönen Seele* has also been attributed to Paul Friedrich Buchholz. However, it is not only the style of the novel, with its many humorous asides and comical exaggerations, typical of Unger's works, that makes this attribution highly unlikely. While we know of numerous works by women attributed to men, there are practically no examples of texts by men falsely attributed to women. There is a recent edition of this novel in the series *Frühe Frauenliteratur in Deutschland* by Olms (*Bekenntnisse einer schönen Seele von ihr selbst geschrieben*, ed. Susanne Zantop [Hildesheim: Olms, 1991].

[27] Quoted from Friederike Helene Unger, *Bekenntnisse einer schönen Seele: Von ihr selbst geschrieben* (Berlin: Unger, 1806), 5.

[28] *Wilhelm Meisters Lehrjahre*, MA 5:417.

[29] For analysis of the representation of lesbian desire in Unger's works see Angela Steidele, *Als wenn du mein Geliebter wärest: Liebe und Begehren zwischen Frauen in der deutschsprachigen Literatur 1750–1850* (Stuttgart: Metzler, 2003).

[30] When Caroline's marriage finally breaks apart, her relationship with Mirabella is named as the reason for the failure and the two women are accused of "Lastern, die uns selbst dem Namen nach unbekannt waren" (vices not even whose names we know" (230).

[31] See Lange, *Spiegelgeschichten*, 85.

[32] For biographical information see Dagmar von Gersdorff, *Dich zu lieben kann ich nicht verlernen: Das Leben der Sophie Brentano-Mereau* (Frankfurt am Main: Insel, 1984). For recent studies of Mereau's works see Beatrice Guenther, "Letters Exchanged Across Borders: Mme de Stael's *Delphine* and the Epistolary Novels of Juliane von Krüdener & Sophie Mereau," in *The Comparatist: Journal of the Southern Comparative Literature Association* 22 (1998): 78–90; Katharina von Hammerstein, "Eine Erndte will ich haben. . .: Schreiben als Beruf(ung): Sophie Mereau-Brentano (1770–1806)," in *Beruf Schriftstellerin: Schreibende Frauen im 18. und 19. Jahrhundert*, ed. Tebben, 132–59; Sigrid Weigel, "Sophie Mereau (1770–1806)," in *Frauen: Porträts aus zwei Jahrhunderten*, ed. Hans Jürgen Schultz (Stuttgart: Kreuz Verlag, 1990), 20–32; Jacqueline Vansant, "Liebe und Patriarchat in der Romantik: Sophie Mereaus Briefroman *Amanda und Eduard*," in *Der Widerspenstigen Zähmung: Studien zur bezwungenen Weiblichkeit in der Literatur vom Mittelalter bis zur Gegenwart*, ed. Sylvia Wallinger and Monika Jonas (Innsbruck: Institut für Germanistik, Universität Innsbruck, 1986), 185–200.

[33] Some passages of the novel are taken from letters that Mereau wrote to the student Johann Heinrich Kipp, with whom she had an affair while married to Mereau.

[34] In her chapter on Mereau in *Die weibliche Muse: Sechs Essays über künstlerisch schaffende Frauen der Goethezeit* (Columbia: Camden House, 1986), Helene M.

Kastinger Riley points out that the first version began with a different letter. Mereau's decision to open the novel with a description of Amanda's domestic misery highlights the importance of this theme (72).

[35] Quoted from Sophie Mereau-Brentano, *Das Blütenalter der Empfindung. Amanda und Eduard*, ed. Katharina von Hammerstein (Munich: Deutscher Taschenbuch Verlag, 1997), 79.

[36] Critics disagree as to whether Eduard and Amanda's relationship is consummated. Fleischmann believes it is; see Uta Fleischmann, *Zwischen Aufbruch und Anpassung: Untersuchungen zu Werk und Leben der Sophie Mereau* (Frankfurt am Main: Peter Lang, 1989), 116; Todd Kontje claims that "the most striking feature of the work is the sympathetic depiction of marital infidelity"; see "Reassessing Sophie Mereau: The Case for Amanda und Eduard," in *Colloquia Germanica* 24 (1991), 316.

[37] Kontje, "Reassessing," 320.

[38] Gilleir claims that after the French occupation of 1806 Schopenhauer's salon became a site for the "resurrection and even continuity of classical aesthetics," quoted from Anke Gilleir, *Johanna Schopenhauer und die Weimarer Klassik: Betrachtungen über die Selbstpositionierung weiblichen Schreibens* (Hildesheim: Olms, 2000), 107. According to Diethe, Schopenhauer was "a more central figure to Weimar classicism than her nervously charged fiction might suggest," quoted from Carol Diethe, *Towards Emancipation: German Women Writers of the Nineteenth Century* (New York: Berghahn Books, 1998), 50.

[39] For more information on Schopenhauer's childhood and education see her autobiography, *Ihr glücklichen Augen: Jugenderinnerungen, Tagebücher, Briefe*. Ed. Rolf Weber (Berlin: Verlag der Nationen, 1978). For her father's opposition to her desire to paint see 124–25.

[40] See Astrid Köhler, *Salonkultur im klassischen Weimar: Geselligkeit als Lebensform und literarisches Konzept* (Stuttgart: M &P, 1996), 11–28.

[41] Although *Gabriele's* plot is consistent with that of a novel of *Bildung*, it has come to be identified with the designation "novel of renunciation," first introduced by Wolfgang Menzel, and has often been compared to Goethe's *Elective Affinities*. Goethe himself wrote a review of *Gabriele* (MA 13.1:466–69). Unfortunately, Goethe's review is so vague that one wonders whether he read the book or merely obliged a female friend.

[42] Quoted from Johanna Schopenhauer, *Gabriele: Ein Roman* (Munich: Deutscher Taschenbuch Verlag, 1985), 289.

[43] See Katherine R. Goodman, "Johanna Schopenhauer (1766–1838), or Pride and Resignation," in *Amsterdamer Beiträge zur neueren Germanistik* 28 (1989), 205.

[44] Todd Kontje, *Women, the Novel, and the German Nation 1771–1871: Domestic Fiction in the Fatherland* (Cambridge: Cambridge UP, 1998), 129.

[45] Friederike Fetting, *Ich fand in mir eine Welt: Eine sozial- und literaturgeschichtliche Untersuchung zur deutschen Romanschriftstellerin um 1800: Charlotte von Kalb, Caroline von Wolzogen, Sophie Mereau-Brentano, Johanna Schopenhauer* (Munich: Wilhelm Fink, 1992), 131.

[46] See Arnd Bohm, "Charlotte von Stein's *Dido, Ein Trauerspiel*" in *Colloquia Germanica* 22 (1989), 46; and Sigrid Lange, "Über epische und dramatische Dichtung Weimarer Autorinnen: Überlegungen zu Geschlechterspezifika in der Poetologie," in *Zeitschrift für Germanistik* 2 (1991), 343. For a discussion of Stein's sources see Bohm 45–46. For recent interpretations of von Stein's works see Susan L. Cocalis, "Acts of Omission: The Classical Dramas of Caroline von Wolzogen and Charlotte von Stein," in *Thalia's Daughters: German Women Dramatists From the Eighteenth Century to the Present*, ed. Susan L. Cocalis and Ferrel Rose (Tübingen: Francke, 1996), 77–98; Susanne Kord, "Not in Goethe's Image: The Playwright Charlotte von Stein," in *Thalia's Daughters*, ed. Cocalis and Rose, 53–75; and Katherine R. Goodman, "The Sign Speaks: Charlotte von Stein's Matinees," in *In the Shadow of Olympus: German Women Writers Around 1800*, ed. Goodman and Waldstein, 71–93.

[47] Quoted from Charlotte von Stein, *Dramen: Gesamtausgabe*, ed. Susanne Kord (Hildesheim: Georg Olms, 1998), 531.

[48] Von Stein's original is lost and it is therefore impossible to determine the exact nature and extent of the changes made by Felix von Stein. In her introduction to von Stein's works, Kord summarizes von Stein's changes: "Felix von Stein faßte die ursprünglichen fünf Akte in vier zusammen, strich "manches für unsere Zeit 'zopfige'" und nahm andere Änderungen vor, behauptete jedoch, Handlung und Charaktere des Originals beibehalten zu haben" (condensed the five acts into four, eliminated "much that is considered 'dated' in our time," made other changes, but nevertheless claimed to have kept situations and characters true to the original; Susanne Kord, introduction, *Charlotte von Stein, Dramen: Gesamtausgabe* [Hildesheim: Georg Olms, 1998], xiii).

[49] *Gespräche mit Eckermann*, 18 January 1825.

The Büstenzimmer (room of busts) in Goethe's house.
Among the statues the Ilioneus, cast after the original (4th century,
Glyptothek, Munich). Also busts of Herder (original in marble by
Alexander Trippel) and Schiller (by Johann Heinrich Dannecker).
Courtesy of Stiftung Weimarer Klassik, Kunstsammlungen.

Weimar Classicism as Visual Culture

Helmut Pfotenhauer

IN JUNE 1796, Jean Paul, who had only just become a successful writer with his novel *Hesperus* (published 1795), visited Weimar. Goethe and Schiller were intrigued at the prospect of meeting him and read his novel in anticipation. Their impression was mixed. The author of the book, wrote Schiller in a letter to Goethe dated 28 June 1796, is "fremd wie einer, der aus dem Mond gefallen ist, voll guten Willens und herzlich geneigt, die Dinge außer sich zu sehen, nur nicht mit dem Organ, mit dem man sieht" (alien, like one who has come from the moon, full of good will and well disposed to see the things besides himself, just not with the organ with which one sees). Jean Paul had no eye for appearances, for perception and visualization; an aptitude for mental reflection predominated. This judgment, which would eventually lead to intense polemical debate,[1] is characteristic of the standard and ideal of art and literature propagated by the two intellectual giants of Weimar. Not that Schiller, the philosopher-poet, who also suffered from a surplus of mental reflection, would apply the same standard to himself. But with Goethe as his example, this evidentiary ideal, this sensuous, sensate configuration of what is comprehensible to the eye, was set as the measure for all aesthetic efforts. Two years earlier, shortly after their first personal acquaintance, Schiller had written to Goethe in an effort to clarify for himself the peculiar nature of Goethe's creative talent. His conclusion: Goethe's perceiving gaze rested so quietly and peacefully on things that he was never in danger of "going astray," of succumbing to speculation or to arbitrary and willful imagination (23 August 1794).

Later, in 1804, Jean Paul himself would speak of poetic nihilism, the arbitrariness of egotism, and the wasteland of excessive fantasy in order to warn of the tendencies and dangers of his own Romantic age.[2] For Jean Paul, this was a Christian epoch bent on destroying the world of the senses, with all its charms, and replacing it with a new spiritual world.[3] In the poetry of his time, he wrote, the realm of the infinite blossoms on the funeral site of the finite. The anti-sensualist Christian "beyond" is in the process of driving out the sensuous plenitude and optical pleasure of Greek culture.[4]

Schiller modified this insight along philosophico-historical lines: Christianity was a primary cause of this turn away from the senses; other

culprits included the philosophical interests of the age and the empower-
ment of the subject to think for himself. It was an age in the thrall of intellect and of a basic longing for what was absent. It was not a time that
favored what was immediately apprehensible by the senses.

One may therefore rightly speak of a crisis of perception at the end of
the eighteenth century. Nature, as Schiller never tired of repeating, was
viewed as something governed by abstract laws. The gods, who had earlier
been credited with causing things to happen, whom people had readily
imagined in anthropomorphic form, had disappeared, as Schiller wrote in
the first version of his poem "Die Götter Griechenlands": "Gleich dem
toten Schlag der Pendeluhr, / Dient sie knechtisch dem Gesetz der
Schwere, / Die entgötterte Natur"[5] (Like the dead chiming of the clock,
godless nature slavishly serves the law of gravity). The gods, according to
Schiller, returned home, "Und alles Schöne, / Alles Hohe nahmen sie mit
fort, / Alle Farben, alle Lebenstöne, / Und uns blieb nur das entseelte
Wort"[6] (And all that is beautiful, all that is sublime they took with them, all
colors, all the sounds of life, and for us remained only the soulless word).

We do notice a decline in the eighteenth century of the traditional cultural techniques of perception: the rhetorical traditions of figuration, of
emblematics, of allegory, and of the ability to understand the images and
stories of not only the ancient gods, but also of the Christian saints.[7] In the
midst of this decline, a new cult of perception presented itself. Goethe,
blessed with a gaze that rested so quietly and purely on the objects of the
world, and that in so doing compensated for any costs of reflection, instinc-
tively made the earlier Greek culture of the visually perceptible his own —
it was Goethe who for Schiller stood at the center of the new cult of per-
ceptibility. It was he who would cause the totality, the essence, the aesthetic
law to appear in the particular and sensuously present. It was he who would
reactivate the cultural traditions in which this had happened earlier. As we
shall see, his mastery extended over literature and the visual arts, optics,
morphology and semiotics, theater and garden, architecture and interior
design. In a word, Goethe determined the cultural politics of Weimar.

In his August 1794 letter, Schiller emphasized that the culture of perception was not simply a given, but required a high degree of mediation,
indeed passage through the modern culture of reflexivity. As such, it bore
the signature of longing in an age of loss; this culture was a construct, a
form of compensation for the burdens of aesthetic modernization. With
help from its rational faculty, according to Schiller, the imagination must
attempt to replace what reality withholds. The naïveté of this mode of sensuous perception was thoroughly sentimental, to use an expression from
elsewhere in Schiller's oeuvre.[8]

An idealizing art and nature under certain circumstances, Schiller
continued in the same letter, constituted the chief terrain for this perception. By idealizing art Schiller meant art of the ancient Greeks, especially

sculpture, to the extent that it transformed human nature in its sensuous appearance into divine substance. And by nature he meant a set of conditions such as were to be found in Greece and Italy, where Greek art enjoyed its Renaissance, and that were favorable to the human body in terms of climate, light, and the harmony of the landscape. Such conditions allowed the body to appear as beautiful and superior to everything that mere accident and the everyday can offer.

As we see, the cult of the perceptible, which contributed immeasurably toward Weimar later being perceived as classical, was classicistically oriented. Its compass was its own ideal of an ideal art and of the nature of Greek antiquity and the Renaissance. But we must not lose sight of the fact that the cult of the perceptible was an effect of modernity just as much as Romanticism, and for that reason it was in principle not distinguishable from the latter, but rather parallel to it in many respects — searching, as did the Romantics, for model images in a generally imageless age, even if with different results. Weimar Classicism and Romanticism were not as different as they have sometimes seemed. Because of Turkish occupation, Greece was not easily accessible at this time. Therefore, Italy was the only space in which the longing for the perceptible ideal could become real experience. For that reason, Italy, or rather, the Germans in Italy, stand at the beginning of our overview of Weimar as a culture of the perceptible.

The Prerequisite: Goethe and Moritz in Italy (1786–88)

Goethe

"Denn es geht, man darf wohl sagen, ein neues Leben an, wenn man das Ganze mit Augen sieht"[9] (A new life, one might say, is in the process of beginning, if one looks at the whole with one's eyes). With this aesthetic variation on the Pietistic notion of rebirth and new life, Goethe begins the account of his first sojourn in Rome, November 1786 to February 1787. Birth, new life — this is the language of a beginning, the beginning of a new existence, entirely under the sign of beautiful appearance. Yet one also hears in these words, as with all sentimental discourse about the originary, an awareness of fictionality, of the artificially composed. The dreams of youth, writes Goethe, have come to life. But it is a present that is as beautiful as a dream.

From this dream only a few characteristic episodes will be selected. The first shows how emphatically Goethe broke with the conventions of visual interpretation and established a new, autonomous kind of visual comprehension as a prerequisite for the perception of the authentically beautiful. On All-Saints, shortly after his arrival in Rome, Goethe saw a painting by Giovanni Francesco Guercino (1591–1666) in the Quirinal Palace, depicting St. Petronilla.[10] The picture showed how the body of the saint was lifted out of the grave and, at the same time, ascended into heaven to be greeted by an angelic youth. Goethe was irritated by this double action (3 November; BA 14:289), which superseded earthly existence by pointing to the beyond. He rejected this iconographical tradition, the transgression of the visible for the sake of the invisible, and marveled only over the artistry of the representation, what appears to the eyes: "Das Bild ist unschätzbar" (The picture is invaluable). This pattern was repeated when he viewed a Titian next door.[11] Goethe had no patience with the surrounding figures, among them St. Sebastian, and their conventional iconic meaning. He admired the Madonna with child and the beauty of the composition in which they appeared:

> Wir sagen uns: hier muß ein heiliges altes Überliefertes zum Grunde liegen, daß diese verschiedenen unpassenden Personen so kunstreich und bedeutungsvoll zusammengestellt werden konnten. Wir fragen nicht nach wie und warum, wir lassen es geschehen und bewundern die unschätzbare Kunst. (BA 14:290)

> [We say to ourselves: something holy, transmitted over generations, must explain the fact that these various inappropriate persons are so artfully and meaningfully assembled. We do not ask how or why, we just let it happen and admire the priceless artistry.]

Here, image conventions are dismissed; a new unburdened autonomous kind of visual comprehension takes their place. Art, even the meaning-saturated art of the Christian tradition, must be perceived as a coherent and complete structure. Only then does what comes to appearance also have immediate meaning, without needing first to refer to a transcendent meaning.

Such a forceful rejection of traditional visual language for the sake of a pure seeing was, according to Goethe, not necessary with respect to other Roman icons, namely those of antiquity. Winckelmann had already laid down their new understanding for Goethe's generation. In his *Geschichte der Kunst des Altertums* (History of the Art of Antiquity, 1764), he had above all described the Belvedere Apollo as the epitome of a human shape elevated to the level of the divine, thus ennobling sensuous nature, the sensuously present, by means of a new classicistic mythology.[12] Goethe continued in the same vein, gushing about the "höchsten Hauch des lebendigen, jünglingsfreien, ewig jungen Wesens" (25 December 1786; BA 14:314; the most sublime whisper of vital, youthfully free, eternally young essence). Winckelmann had actually ascribed cryptic meanings to the divine image, bolstered by reference to Homer. Goethe needed to see past them in order to see at all: only what the eye grasps is valid, and only the eye is capable of perceiving the divine in the human body. The appearance becomes the essence, the particular becomes the whole. When we come to Goethe's friend Karl Philipp Moritz, it will become clear what kind of critical engagement is required, also with respect to earlier classicism, in order to assert such an absolute immanence of beauty and art.

Goethe turned to the so-called Juno Ludovisi, that colossal bust from the first century A.D., for the female counterpart to Apollo. A gigantic plaster cast of the Juno would later take up residence in Goethe's house on the Frauenplan. The classicism of the time saw in her the earthly woman elevated to the level of the divine.[13]

The so-called Medusa Rondanini offers a further example of Goethe's Roman perception. According to Goethe, she expresses the "ängstliches Starren des Todes . . . in einer hohen und schönen Gesichtsform . . . unsäglich trefflich" (25 December; BA 14:314; captures unspeakably well the anxious rigidity of death in a sublime and beautiful facial form). That even death can be beautiful is the farthest-reaching assertion of Classicism.[14] This Medusa tells us that the face of death need not remind us of a consoling beyond, as is the case in the Christian tradition, but that death itself should be represented euphemistically and beautifully, and that all that is ugly and painful in our nature can be transformed into something noble. The ancients left us an example of how this work of art is to be accomplished. "Wie die Alten den Tod gebildet" (How the Ancients Represented Death) was therefore the name of a longstanding debate, initiated by Lessing and Herder, and resumed by Goethe, regarding the ancient figure of the genius with an overturned torch as a sign of expiring life. But, as the horrifyingly beautiful snakes of Medusa suggest, even what is disgusting in sensuous nature can be the occasion for visual pleasure.

In February 1787, Goethe made his way to Naples and Sicily. In Palermo, confronted by the abundant, lush, and partially unfamiliar world of plants, Goethe returned to an idea he had already entertained in the botanical garden of Padua (27 September 1786), namely to focus the multiplicity of appearances on a *single principle* of the creation of plants in order to make them more comprehensible. Goethe was not interested in an abstract principle. On the contrary, and this is what really sets Goethe apart, the principle should be visible in the plants themselves. In the leaf itself,[15] Goethe maintained, one can perceive the potential for every shape, from the seed to the fruit. Goethe's theory of metamorphosis, the basis for his morphology, is presented here.[16] Everything proceeds from the eye; the eye desires to order the world of appearances into a perceptible coherence. A further discovery of this selected realm of nature that Goethe undertook, as he turned his back on Rome and its idealizing art, was that of light and color. In Sicily, colors could be perceived with particular intensity.[17] Already during the boat journey from Naples to Palermo, Goethe observed in the contrast of the bright sky and dark water, as well as in the mist between, the origin of colors: not as spectral colors, but rather as the reflection of a contest between light and darkness.[18] Goethe's theory of color, his optics, thus began here. And, once again, it was a matter of a law of nature disclosing itself to the eye. Italy, with its multiplicity of phenomena, became a visual paradigm for the later works completed in Weimar.

Through the shading of colors, the watery mists, and the purity and simultaneous gentleness of the contours of the coasts, Goethe discovered yet another aspect of this beautiful, perceptible nature: landscape and landscape painting. Goethe had already been schooled in landscape by studying the paintings of the seventeenth-century French painter, Claude Lorrain. Lorrain was the master of light, of spaces that drift off into sheer endlessness, and of a depth of perception accomplished through color.[19] Through his lens, the Sicilian landscape, and indeed landscape in general, became an aesthetic event for Goethe. The particular became perceptible as a part of the whole; a harmony of sky, sea, and earth prevailed, as Goethe writes (3 April 1787; BA 14:403).

All this visual pleasure, however — and we should not overlook this — is wrested from brute experiential reality. The signs of decay are omnipresent: the wild temple ruins, the traces of earthquakes, the cultic sites of death. The decision to oppose this decay of the world of the perceptible, of the corporeally sensuous, was not taken without nagging doubts.

Moritz

Goethe thought of Moritz as his younger brother, one furthermore prone to misfortune. Goethe first encountered and began supporting him in the late fall of 1786. But Goethe was also in his debt: Moritz advised him on prosody and thus helped Goethe in his versification of *Iphigenie* and *Tasso;* he sharpened Goethe's aesthetic judgment. His essay *Über die bildende Nachahmung des Schönen* (On the Artistic Imitation of the Beautiful), which he developed in Rome and published in the late fall of 1788 while staying in Weimar, was discussed at length with Goethe.[20] It contained an intensification of the rule of immanence in art: art should be complete in itself; meaning should inhere in that which art presents to the eyes — art is useless for any reference to transcendent meaning. Goethe's emphatic concept of art, intended to counter the preponderance of reflection and thought, found its radical formulation in Moritz. Of course, Moritz's Italy was not as bright as Goethe's. Moritz was incapable of seeing beauty in all things, but was obsessively struck by ugliness: poverty, social injustice, and the macabre aspects of the death cults. And, above all, he was incapable of drawing his own existence into that splendor. This did not prevent him from all the more emphatically postulating that, in regard to the realm of the beautiful, meaning should be perceptible to the senses, and the essential must be expressed in outer appearance. This view is important to understand the specificity of the beautiful and its anomalous, pictorially visual perception, especially as it relates to Weimar.

Moritz's account of his stay in Italy was published in 1792–93, under the title *Reisen eines Deutschen in Italien* (Travels of a German in Italy). It contained not only the details of his travels and experiences, but also basic discussions of aesthetic questions in connection with these experiences. At first glance, they appear to contradict what we have just averred, for Moritz constantly speaks of the beautiful in connection with its quality as sign. Discussing the famous Belvedere Apollo statue in the Vatican, Moritz argues in a seemingly Platonic sense that the particular work of art, as well as appearances in nature, are signatures of a higher beauty, which reveals itself in them.[21] What Moritz means is the beauty of creation — everything can be read as its trace. The beautiful, therefore, is essentially connected with metaphysics. On the other hand, Moritz also writes of the Apollo statue that it is a complete whole, resting in itself,[22] and that one's spirit need not, as Winckelmann claimed, depart from its corporeal presence into the realm of non-corporeal beauty in order to understand its meaning. It is corporeal beauty itself, beauty that one can perceive with the eye, that constitutes the higher charm. The grand totality of the cosmos reveals itself in corporeal beauty as a creation in miniature.[23] Winckelmann's transcendent allegorizing is thus rejected. It was no accident that the most important essay Moritz wrote before leaving for Italy was entitled "Der Begriff des in sich selbst Vollendeten" (The Concept of the Complete in Itself, 1785).[24] In this work, conventional metaphysical perspectives and radical notions of aesthetic immanence and autonomy came together. This tension in Moritz's concept of art can also be described as a tension between objectivism and formalism. On the one hand, it is a matter of making the potential for creation visible in the most exquisite objects. None are more exquisite than mankind and his apotheosis, his representation as a god, as the Greek artists had already made visible. That is why Moritz speaks of "imitation," that is, of a re-presentation of what is given in nature. On the other hand, the point is to emphasize the shaping power that assures that each artistic configuration is complete in itself. *Bildung* is the key word in this connection and means the way in which the parts come together in a whole, analogous to the formation of an organism as understood by biology of the same period.[25] Not representation, but rather a rigorous separation from all given nature is the motto. Moritz was thinking in particular of the ornament as an object that bears no meaning, but is beautiful in itself and expresses the free shaping power of the artist. Antiquity offers examples for this as well. Classicism, or the appeal to the ancients, can lead to entirely different image conceptions. Without these tensions or contradictions, Moritz's theory of beauty cannot be grasped.[26] We will see that the Weimar semiotics that Goethe and the art historian Heinrich Meyer developed in the 1790s is unthinkable without Moritz.

Moritz explored his interest in the decorative arts in his *Vorbegriffe zu einer Theorie der Ornamente* (Preliminary Attempt at a Theory of

Ornaments, 1793).[27] His interest was initially piqued by the sensational excavations of Pompeii, Herculaneum, and Portici — and the ancient wall decorations discovered there. In Rome, the baths of Titus, or the *domus aurea*, also presented him with useful examples of ornamentation, as did the wall tapestries of Raphael (1483–1520) in the Vatican or in the Villa Madama in Rome. In all of these, one saw arabesques, botanical ornaments, grotesques, fabulous creatures, even suspended dancers. For Moritz, they count as signs of an unrestrained imagination, not bound to anything in nature, nor committed to any principle of imitation, but merely refreshing and elevating the everyday. For Moritz, this playfulness denotes the noble impulse towards the beautiful and the perfect, which distinguishes humans from animals.[28]

At this point we should recall that eighteenth-century classicism began as a critique of ornament, especially that of the rococo; the suspicion was strong that decorative playfulness amounted to an unacceptable arbitrariness contrary to the actual goal of art, namely the idealization of nature. The "classical" ornamentation of the newly excavated ancient towns of Pompeii and Herculaneum posed a dilemma for Moritz and Goethe. Yet the pleasure of the eyes asserted itself, as did the interest in an art that was not primarily mimetic, but rather complete and purposeless. By favoring this sense of aesthetic autonomy and turning away from the grand objects and ancient examples of their representation, Weimar Classicism as formulated by Moritz strangely overlapped with the early Romantic preference for the ornamental.[29]

In the early months of 1789, after his return from Rome and a brief stay in Weimar, Moritz was appointed professor of art and mythology at the Akademie der schönen Künste in Berlin. There he worked intensely for the propagation of a neo-classicistic ornamentalism, which, according to him, should beautify even a vase or the buckle of a shoe.[30] Goethe did not go quite as far. From Rome, he wrote an essay entitled "Von Arabesken" (Of Arabesques) and insisted that they be understood as and limited to "subordinate art" (BA 19:85). But he, too, was aware of their seductive power over the eyes, of the way they could confuse classicistic orthodoxy and transform even Weimar Classicism into a multifaceted phenomenon. In Goethe's home, one can still see the Juno Ludovisi posed before a frieze shaped with arabesques.[31]

Goethe and Heinrich Meyer: The Objects of the Visual Arts or Weimar Semiotics

The concept of art as complete in itself contains a tendency toward deobjectification, but also a contrary obligation to search for particularly appropriate subjects, and this in two senses: on the one hand, one must reflect on the structure of the work of art and ask oneself which objects, as Goethe says, determine themselves through their sensuous existence;[32] in what objects, in other words, does the sign, that is, the sensately visible, coincide with the signified, that is, the intended meaning. Thus, the question about the beautiful becomes a semiotic question and is answered with the concept of the symbol. On the other hand, Goethe organized art contests for contemporary artists and prescribed appropriate subjects. We will begin our look at Weimar semiotics with reference to the visual arts, although art in general is implied.

"Die vorteilhaftesten Gegenstände sind die, welche sich durch ihr sinnliches Dasein selbst bestimmen" (the most advantageous subjects are those which determine themselves through their sensuous existence) writes Goethe in his essay "Über die Gegenstände der bildenden Kunst" (On the Subjects of the Visual Arts, 1797). These subjects should "[sich]beim ersten Anschauen sowohl im ganzen als in ihren Teilen selbst erklären" (should explain themselves in their totality, as well as in their parts on first glance). This is not the case with allegories, since they refer to a meaning that lies beyond what is concretely present. Goethe is primarily thinking about representations in Christian art, all of which point to something beyond the sensory realm. He calls such works "mystical." Those works that satisfy his definition, by contrast, he calls "symbolic." In a letter to Schiller a few weeks before writing the essay, he had spoken of such subjects as

> eminenten Fällen . . . die in einer charakteristischen Mannigfaltigkeit, als Repräsentanten von vielen andern dastehen, eine gewisse Totalität in sich schließen, eine gewisse Reihe fordern, Ähnliches und Fremdes in meinem Geiste aufregen und so von außen wie von innen an eine gewisse Einheit und Allheit Anspruch machen. (16 August 1797)

> [eminent cases that stand there in a characteristic multiplicity, as representatives of many others, which enclose a certain totality in themselves, demand a certain sequence, stimulate like and unlike in my mind, and thus from within and without lay claim to a certain unity and allness.]

Schiller, for his part, speaks in a responding letter of the "pregnant moment" as the temporal mode in which this sort of subject comes into appearance (15 September 1797). It is the sort of moment that readily allows one to see with what subsequent moments it is literally pregnant.

It remained for Johann Heinrich Meyer, Goethe's friend since the first Italian journey[33] and advisor in matters of art, to further develop the topic in Goethe's journal, *Die Propyläen*.[34] He did not limit himself to general principles, but actually listed the subjects he considered appropriate or inappropriate. His contribution thus also revealed the doctrinaire tendencies of Weimar Classicism. Like Goethe and Moritz, he too desired that one be able to make out "ein Ganzes für sich" (a whole in itself) in a work of art, that the artwork "sich selbst ganz ausspreche" (express itself entirely). Allegories exceed the limits of art.[35] Only in symbolic figures does art treat its highest subjects.[36] Once again we have this crucial semiotic opposition between symbol and allegory. And now Meyer distinguishes between "advantageous" and "objectionable" subjects and indicates what is and is not allowed. Human actions, in which the historical, mythological, or sacred grandeur shimmers through, are recommended, as are symbolical figures of the gods or their attributes. The Virgin Mary as mother and mother of God simultaneously is mentioned as an example. "Widerstrebend und unstatthaft für die bildende Kunst sind alle diejenigen Gegenstände, welche nicht sich selbst aussprechen, nicht im ganzen Umfange, nicht in völliger Bedeutung, vor den Sinn des Auges gebracht werden können"[37] (Contrary and unsuitable for the visual arts are all those subjects that do not enunciate themselves, that cannot be presented to the eye in their entirety, in their full meaning). Everything that is ugly and cruel, scenes of death and torture — Meyer mentions the "Flaying of Marsyas" by Raphael — that expose the vulnerability of our bodies and thus empty the visible of meaning and sense, should be banished from art. It is clear, too, whom Meyer has in mind: besides the Christian artists since the Renaissance, he above all means those who in his own time have opposed Weimar Classicism by propagating Christianity in art: the Romantics.

The Art Contests of the Weimar Friends of Art

It was in this spirit that the guidelines for contemporary artists were drafted by the "Weimar Friends of Art" (above all Goethe and Meyer) and became the basis for a series of contests from 1799 to 1805. In this manner, a classicistic war of culture was waged on the upstart Romantics.

Acceptable or "bequeme" subjects were selected and assigned to the artists, subjects that speak for themselves.[38] In line with Winckelmann's new interpretation of ancient art in reliance on the Homeric myths, Goethe and Meyer began with scenes from the *Iliad*.[39] For Winckelmann, ancient tradition claimed that painting was mute poetry; that is what the poet Simonides (556–648 B.C.) had said. According to Pausanias (2nd century A.D.) statues were the embodiment of Homer's "doctrine of fables"; and the poetics of Horace (65–68 B.C.) included the prescription: better to take a subject from the *Iliad* than to invent a new one. Of course, in *Laokoon: oder über die Grenzen der Malerei und der Poesie* Lessing had famously pointed to the stark differences between literature and the visual arts. One cannot simply translate a literary representation into the medium of sculpture or painting. Literature, according to Lessing, is a temporal art, while painting and sculpture are spatial. Goethe was in full in agreement with Lessing.[40] The artist must first find the moment in the story that visibly and "pregnantly" contains everything else. But even if the freedom of the artist in the face of slavish imitation and the laws of the autonomy of the arts and artworks are to be observed, art will nonetheless find its best models in Homer, for he had already shaped everything so plastically that it was simply a matter of continuing his work in the other medium.[41]

"Die Szene am Ende des dritten Buches der Ilias, wo Aphrodite (Venus) dem *Alexandros* (Paris) die *Helena* zuführt, vereinigt in sich alle erforderlichen Eigenschaften"[42] (The scene at the end of the third book of the *Iliad*, where Aphrodite [Venus] presents Helena to Alexandros [Paris], combines all necessary characteristics). The scene can be understood as a mythological story, but also as something purely human with regard to the lovers, which discloses itself immediately. The first artists to win the annual contest were Heinrich Kolbe and Ferdinand Hartmann. Goethe and Meyer judged them according to content and invention first and foremost, and only secondarily in terms of painterly execution. Most submissions were modest and came from mediocre artists. The subjects for the following year included Hector taking leave of Andromache and the death of Rhesus. We will return to this shortly when we discuss Schiller. In 1802, no theme was specified and artists were at liberty to select their own. In 1803, subjects from the *Odyssey* were chosen, and in 1804, universal, human subjects, not from Homer, were desired, for example, "people threatened by the element of water."

Soon it became clear that artists from the younger generation were also participating, artists who would later be counted among the Romantics: the Riepenhausen brothers, Franz (1786–1831) and Johannes (1787–1860), who later devoted themselves entirely to religious art, were represented by a reconstruction of Polygnotus's painting in the Lesche of Delphia according to Pausanias's description; Schnorr von Carolsfeld (1794–1872) submitted his works, as did Philipp Otto Runge (1777–1810) and Peter Cornelius (1783–1867) — all of whom would go onto become significant Romantic painters. One of the last contestants was Caspar David Friedrich (1784–1840) in 1805 with entirely unclassicistic subjects: a procession at sunrise and a fisherman's cabin at sea. It was in 1805, the year of Schiller's death, that the contests were discontinued. Classicistic doctrine could not be imposed. "Das Entgegengesetzte von unsern Wünschen und Bestrebungen tut sich hervor; die Weimarischen Kunstfreunde, da sie Schiller verlassen hat, sehen einer großen Einsamkeit entgegen" (BA 19:456; The contrary of what we hoped and aimed for has occurred; the Weimar Friends of Art, bereft of Schiller, peer into the face of a great loneliness). The soul "with a tendency toward religion" had recently gained the upper hand over art. Only the morally high-minded counted, no longer the height of sensate art in which all content must first be embodied.

Schiller and Classical or Classicistic Art

Schiller was not an artist of the eye, however much he praised Goethe for being so. In the jointly composed essay "Der Sammler und die Seinigen" (The Collector and His Friends, 1798–99), Schiller is represented as a philosopher who lacks an eye in the domain of the visual arts (BA 19:239). Schiller rarely spoke about paintings and the visual arts. But when he did, he did so emphatically. As we shall see shortly, he also expressed strong opinions about the art contests of the Weimar Friends of the Arts.

In 1785, Schiller offered an account of his first classicistic art experiences in "Brief eines reisenden Dänen"[43] (Letter from a Traveling Dane). His fictive Dane reports about a visit to the Hall of Antiquities in Mannheim. He sees the plaster casts there of the Belvedere Apollo, the Laocoön, and of other icons of classicism. But he is content with the casts that were to be seen in Mannheim. He deems a trip to Italy to see the objects themselves unnecessary.[44]

In 1800, Schiller wrote a letter to the editors of the *Propyläen* (that is, Goethe and Meyer), in which he discussed both prizewinning artworks of that year: "Hector Taking Leave from Andromache" by Johann August Nahl and "The Death of Rhesus" by Joseph Hoffmann. In connection with the second subject, Schiller emphasized the precariousness of the theme, which required a clever choice of the pregnant moment, lest Ulysses and Diomedes, who have attacked a sleeping enemy, appear as Rhesus's assassins. It must be the moment after the deed and not the deed itself. The repulsiveness of the murder must be covered with shadows so that the beholder is able to savor the success of the flight (SW 5:892–93). The goddess Athena is required in order to elevate the event above its mean and scandalous nature. Schiller stressed that the merely visible is not sufficient for representing the beautiful; the prosaic quality of reality is the ghost of time — to transcend it, the understanding must turn to a higher level of meaning (SW 5:896–97). Classicistic handling of the topic is therefore precarious: it requires reflection, must surpass the visible and point to the invisible so as not to fall victim to the ugliness of the world of experience. Schiller's observations gave the lie to the classicistic doctrine of self-evidence.

The other painting — Hector's leave-taking — exemplifies another danger of pursuing the classicistic in modern times, according to Schiller. It is the danger of becoming sentimental, excessively moved, while beholding a representation of the sorrow of parting. What arouses pathos must therefore find a dignified form of expression. Nahl succeeded by depicting Hector and Andromache without any distorting expression of pain and only showing the child's nurse, overcome by pain, fallen to her knees. It is not easy to spare the beautiful from the ugliness of modernity in this sentimental classicism.

Schiller speaks of beauty and the artwork of antiquity not only where he exclusively treats the visual arts, but also more emphatically in his philosophico-aesthetic writings of the 1790s. One could argue that the culture of the image is the secret center of these important writings. In the letters that constitute *Über die ästhetische Erziehung des Menschen*, it is an ancient marble image that enables the mediation of opposites that otherwise remains locked in eternal tension. The Juno Ludovisi, the *passé partout* of Weimar Classicism, is what embodies the law of nature and morality, inclination and will, sensuousness and reason, and thus simultaneously reconciles what lies separated for reflection into an aesthetic utopia for perception.

> Es ist weder Anmut noch ist es Würde, was aus dem herrlichen Antlitz *der Juno Ludovisi* zu uns spricht; es ist keines von beiden, weil es beides zugleich ist. Indem der weibliche Gott unsere Anbetung heischt, entzündet das gottgleiche Weib unsere Liebe; aber indem wir uns der himmlischen Holdseligkeit aufgelöst hingeben, schreckt die himmlische Selbstgenügsamkeit uns zurück. In sich selbst ruhet und wohnt das ganze Gestalt, eine völlig geschlossene Schöpfung. (SW 5:618–19)

> [Neither grace nor dignity speaks from the wonderful visage of the Juno Ludovisi; it is not one of the two, because it is both at the same time. While the female god demands our reverence, the divine woman ignites our love; but while we submit ourselves to heavenly beauty, heavenly self-contentment scares us back. The entire gestalt rests and lives within itself, a completely self-contained creation.]

And for this phenomenon, Schiller adds, reason has no concept, no language, no name. Only in the perception itself, in the model of antiquity, can such a triumph achieve presence. The philosophical artist, for whom the eye is not the superior organ, must at a decisive point simply give up on finding a logical formulation for the magic of the image.

Already in Schiller's essay *Über Anmut und Würde* (On Grace and Dignity, 1793), we encounter this mediating function of the visual arts and their perception in philosophical discourse. Grace and dignity, the sensuous and nonsensuous, which are so remote from the crude world, are present in a single form in these works of art:

> Mit gemilderten Glanze steigt in dem Lächeln des Mundes, in dem sanftbelebten Blick, in der heitern Stirne die *Vernunftfreiheit* auf, und mit erhabenem Abschied geht die *Naturnotwendigkeit* in der edeln Majestät des Angesichts unter. Nach diesem Ideal menschlicher Schönheit sind die Antiken gebildet, und man erkennt es in der göttlichen Gestalt einer Niobe, im belvederischen Apoll, in dem borghesisschen geflügelten Genius und in der Muse des Barbarinischen Palastes. (SW 5:481)

> [With restrained brilliance, the freedom of reason rises in the smile of the mouth, in the gently animated glance, in the cheerful brow, and with sublime adieu the necessity of nature in the noble majesty of the face

descends. The antiquities were formed according to this ideal of human beauty, and one recognizes it in the divine shape of a Niobe, in the Belvedere Apollo, in the Borghesian winged genius, and in the muse of the Barbarini Palace.]

Schiller cites here straight from Winckelmann's history of art. In other words, the perception is not his own; it is borrowed from Winckelmann.

Goethe, Meyer, and Fernow on *Winckelmann und sein Jahrhundert*

The demise of the Weimar art contests, Schiller's death, and the publication of *Winckelmann und sein Jahrhundert* (Winckelmann and His Century) — a compilation of essays edited by Goethe and the last significant manifesto of Classicism — all occurred in 1805. Winckelmann was the founder of the classicizing culture of the visible that would a generation later become constitutive for Weimar. His perceptions were visions. Through what was sensuously, immediately present he saw what is higher, noble, and worthy. In his description of the Apollo, he challenges the reader to gaze upward with a higher, more spiritual eye into the realm of noncorporeal beauty.[45] In the description of the Belvedere Torso, the reader is urged to complete what is missing through an imaginative, indeed almost hallucinatory gaze:

> Der erste Anblick wird dir vielleicht nichts, als einen ungeformten Stein sehen lassen: vermagst du aber in die Geheimniße der Kunst einzudringen, so wirst du ein Wunder derselben erblicken, wenn du dieses Werk mit einem ruhigen Auge betrachtest. Alsdenn wird dir *Herkules* wie mitten in allen seinen Unternehmungen erscheinen.[46]

> [The first glance will perhaps permit you to see nothing other than an unformed stone: but if you are capable of penetrating into the secrets of art, you will perceive a miracle of the same, if you behold this work with a peaceful eye. Then Hercules will appear to you as though in the midst of all his labors.]

Still, it is the eye that sees here. Winckelmann never dispensed with the claims of the eye.

Now, in 1805, the hymn of this manner of seeing was sung and, indirectly, also its swan song. Winckelmann was mythologized, his place in an historical discourse assured, and his writings became the object of editorial philology. All of these measures amount to cautious postures of distance.

The occasion for the Winckelmann book was a series of letters Winckelmann wrote to his friend Hieronymos Berendis Dietrich (1719–82), a Weimar official; Goethe had received them from the Duchess Anna Amalia for the purpose of publication. Surrounding these letters were the contributions of Goethe, Meyer, the art theorist Carl Ludwig Fernow (1763–1808), and the philologist Friedrich August Wolf (1759–1824).

In his "Skizzen zu einer Schilderung Winckelmanns" (Sketches toward a Depiction of Winckelmann), the opening essay of *Winckelmann und sein Jahrhundert*, Goethe provided a biographical summary. This work must be seen in the context of other important biographical writings of the time — on Philipp Hackert (1811); on Cellini, whose *Vita* Goethe translated (1803); and Fernow's monograph on Carstens (1806). From the beginning, Goethe emphasizes that the commemoration of remarkable people must basically be "ein Anschauen ihres besondern Ganzen" (the perception of their peculiar wholeness) and not a matter of "Reflexion und Wort" (BA 19:480). Goethe programmatically develops an *image* of Winckelmann — an aestheticizing myth, as we shall see. Like the ancients, Winckelmann did not strive for the infinite, but arranged himself "innerhalb der lieblichen Grenzen der schönen Welt" (BA 19:482; within the charming borders of the beautiful world). Goethe stresses the pagan nature of Winckelmann — despite his conversion to Catholicism, a conversion he carried out for the sole purpose of gaining entry into the Church bureaucracy in Rome, so as to have access to his beloved antiquities, which were largely housed in the Vatican. He emphasizes that Winckelmann's life was dedicated to the enjoyment of art "von aller Bedürftigkeit entfernt" (BA 19:493; removed from all want). Winckelmann wrote about art in a poetic, indeed artistic manner (BA 19:506–7). According to Goethe, his words, like his life, not only pointed to beauty, but were themselves beautiful. This aestheticizing peaks in aesthetic myth. The last chapter deals with Winckelmann's *Hingang* (passing). His horrifying death at the hands of a sailor in Trieste in June 1768, a shock for the cultured world of all Europe, is transformed into a gracious gesture on the part of the gods to spare him the failings of old age and the diminution of his faculties. The erection of a monument is the intention of such a biographical mode; but monuments are set for things that have passed.

Heinrich Meyer contributed an "Entwurf einer Kunstgeschichte des achtzehnten Jahrhunderts" (Draft of an Art History of the Eighteenth Century) to the Winckelmann volume. Like Winckelmann in his *Geschichte der Kunst des Altertums*, Meyer attempts to combine a historical relativization of individual epochs with a normativity based on the ancients and the classicistic imitation of antiquity. He names the contemporary artists of his choice — especially Asmus Jakob Carstens (1754–98), the prematurely crushed hope of German-Roman Classicism.[47] And he praises Winckelmann, with a sober glance at the present state of classical studies. As with Winckelmann himself, the recommendation to imitate the ancients cannot blithely forget the fact of history. Here, too, one has the distinct impression that an epoch is passing.

Spliced into Meyer's contribution are "Bemerkungen eines Freundes" (Observations of a Friend), by Carl Ludwig Fernow, art philosopher in Weimar from 1804 on. Fernow argues that the prevailing religious spirit of the times is driving out plasticity and sensuousness of art and encouraging an art form consisting of riddles, allegory, and transcendence.[48] The opponent, namely the Romantics, against whom all of this is written, is implied without ever being named.

In Fernow's 1806 monograph on Carstens, published the year after the Winckelmann book edited by Goethe, we once again encounter that other classicizing tendency of de-objectification and formalization, which we had already noted in connection with Moritz, and which comes close to Romantic views. Carstens's drawings are characterized by a sketchiness that particularly distinguishes his talent, his genius, the freedom of his spirit, and his artistic aspiration, and not by virtue of any precision in imitation, whether of nature or ancient models. The tendency of Weimar Classicism to avoid imitation in art once again asserts itself against the command to imitate. Here, too, we see that Classicism is too multifaceted to be distinguished from Romanticism on a doctrinaire basis. Classicism merely draws the line at Christian piety.

At the conclusion of the Winckelmann volume, Friedrich August Wolf calls for the publication of the collected works of the master. Fernow assumed the task, and two volumes appeared before his death.[49] Meyer and others continued the project. Fernow conceived the edition as a way to celebrate the classicist as classic and to erect a philological monument to him.[50] Winckelmann and his followers were thus in the process of becoming historical.

Classicistic Theater: The Weimar Style of Staging Theater

From 1791 to 1817, Goethe was director of the Weimar Court Theater. He performed the duties not only of author, but also of director, actor, and producer. His Weimar aesthetics of the visible found its practical application here.

Classicistic stagecraft was idealizing, aestheticizing, and imagistic; to that extent, it was decidedly anti-naturalistic, and therefore also somewhat difficult for spectators and actors alike. Goethe constantly had to justify his efforts. In 1797, he went a step further and mounted a radical conceptual experiment recorded in his essay "Über Wahrheit und Wahrscheinlichkeit der Kunstwerke" (On Truth and Verisimilitude in Art). He imagined not only the stage, but the entire theater as a picture, including the spectators: "Auf einem deutschen Theater ward ein ovales, gewissermaßen amphitheatralisches Gebäude vorgestellt, in dessen Logen viele Zuschauer gemalt sind, als wenn sie an dem, was unten vorgeht, teilnähmen"[51] (An oval, so to speak, amphitheatrical building was introduced to a German theater, in whose boxes many spectators were painted, as if they participated in what transpired below). The "real spectators" were not pleased and complained about how untrue and improbable the production was.

Now, it requires considerable explanation to convince anyone that the improbable, precisely because it is distinguished from the everyday and because it transforms life into a painting, can be true in a higher, artistic sense. It devolves in Goethe's essay to a dispute between an advocate of art and a spectator, with the advocate explaining that in all theatrical presentations, it is beautiful appearance (*schöner Schein*), and not faithfulness to nature, that occasions aesthetic satisfaction. His most convincing example is the pleasure of the opera. Here, as in every other theatrical event, the performance must cohere and constitute a little world in itself, without regard for the world outside (BA 17:14). The latter would amount to copying nature in the manner of an ape. By contrast, the cultivated spectator prefers the hyper-natural, "das in sich Vollendete" (BA 17:16; the complete in itself). The spectator in the dialogue does not want to appear to be a cultural Philistine and finally gives in.

But what does this higher, artistic truth actually look like in practice? In 1803, Goethe wrote *Regeln für Schauspieler*[52] (Rules for Actors) for two of his actors.

Zunächst bedenke der Schauspieler, daß er nicht allein die Natur nachahme, sondern sie auch idealisch vorstellen solle, und er also in seiner Darstellung das Wahre mit dem Schönen zu vereinigen habe.

Jeder Teil des Körpers stehe daher ganz in seiner Gewalt, so daß er jedes Glied gemäß dem zu erzielenden Ausdruck frei, harmonisch und mit Grazie gebrauchen könne.

Die Haltung des Körpers sei gerade, die Brust herausgekehrt, die obere Hälfte der Arme bis an die Ellbogen etwas an den Leib geschlossen, der Kopf ein wenig gegen den gewendet, mit dem man spricht, jedoch nur so wenig, daß immer dreiviertel vom Gesicht gegen die Zuschauer gewendet sind. (BA 17:93)

[The actor should first of all keep in mind that he is not only imitating nature, but should also represent nature in an idealized manner, and that he must therefore combine the true with the beautiful in his representation. He must therefore control every part of his body so that he can use every limb according to the desired expression with all freedom, harmony, and grace.

The posture of the body should be erect, with extended breast; the upper part of the arm to the elbow should be held somewhat against the body, the head inclined slightly toward the person with whom he speaks, yet so little, that three-quarters of the face is always turned toward the audience.]

Goethe's intention was to combat the predominant naturalistic style that depended on exaggerating the mundane.[53] He opposed this style with an art of representation that in its mime, gesture, and posture should recall the visual arts, particularly the statues and reliefs of antiquity.[54] This required decorative poses on the part of individual actors and their arrangement in groups on the stage in the manner of paintings or bas-reliefs. Goethe himself attempted to present a model of this classicizing style. Georg Melchior Strauss depicted him in the role of Orestes from *Iphigenie* (see illustration on 132):[55] Angelika Kauffmann, a friend from the stay in Rome, did the same in a drawing of the insanity scene.[56]

Goethe also provided for fitting stage decorations: a set that resembled the frame of a painting, a tableau. He wrote plays that, in contrast to *Iphigenie*, had their sole purpose in the sort of theatrical effects they were to achieve: *Paläophron und Neoterpe* (1803), for example, a festival production in masks that was intended to remind spectators of the ancient visual arts, while at the same time presenting a vibrant and lively work for their eyes,[57] or the melodrama *Proserpina*, a series of scenes with musical accompaniment that approached opera, and whose set resembled a landscape by the classicistic painter Nicolas Poussin (1594–1665).[58]

Goethe also mounted works by other authors, especially Schiller. Goethe staged an exemplary production of the latter's *Braut von Messina* in 1803. It was a perfect fit. As Schiller had written in the preface, it was his intention "dem Naturalism in der Kunst offen und ehrlich den Krieg zu erklären" (to openly and honestly declare war on naturalism in the arts).[59] From this attitude emerges, as Schiller claimed, an art of the ideal that turns its back on the contingencies of appearance and dedicates itself to the essence of nature. This art is "wahrer als alle Wirklichkeit und realer als alle Erfahrung" (SW 2:818; truer than all reality and more real than all experience). Such art depends on an exclusively metrical language and the reintroduction of the ancient chorus, which reflects on and comments on the plot. The chorus is a living wall that the tragedy wraps around itself in order to cut itself off from the prosaic world of the everyday and to open up to the ideal, poetically free world. The chorus is like "die faltige Fülle der Gewänder" (SW 2:820; the folded abundance of robes) that the visual artist drapes over his figures. It is once again the visual arts of antiquity and classicism that provide the model. The goal is to present the passions, in this case love between siblings, and at the same time to moderate them through distancing effects. This corresponds to what Winckelmann had seen in the Laocoön statue group: emotion and its containment through art.

Schiller and his director, Goethe, set their actors "auf den Kothurn" (SW 2:822; on the cothurn [the tall boots worn by actors in Greek and Roman tragic drama]), so to speak. They were forced to declaim complex verse rhythms while striking statuesque poses in accordance with the *Regeln für Schaupieler*. Together with the chorus, they had to form a symmetrical group, as in a painting. They created a *tableau vivant*.[60] A painting by Johann Friedrich Matthei from 1812 recalls the effort.[61]

The *Augenblick* in Goethe's Novels and Novellas

This is not the place for a detailed discussion of Goethe's prose literature. Yet, it is apropos to call attention to the fact that in his prose, in which nothing is directly summoned before the eyes, the *Augenblick* (the moment in time, literally the "glance of an eye") nonetheless plays a structural role — even if it is not precisely an *Augenblick* of classicistic visibility.[62] In other words, the predominance of visuality during the period of Classical Weimar even extends to works of narrative.

Since the middle of the eighteenth century, the novel had increasingly evolved into a story of a character's inner development[63] in deliberate contrast to a merely external story describing a chain of adventures. A story of development as an evolution to something higher, a process of maturation, or, as one was inclined to say by the end of the century, as *Bildung* — this was the goal of the novel. On his return from Italy, Goethe rewrote his *Meister* novel along these lines — the result, *Wilhelm Meisters Lehrjahre*, was written from 1791–96. In 1794–95, he interrupted his work on the novel to provide Schiller with several short novelistic stories in the style of Boccaccio for the *Horen*.[64] These stories became the *Unterhaltungen deutscher Ausgewanderten* (Tales of German Exiles, 1795). In marked contrast to the novel, they were oriented around moments of discontinuity and abruptness, the stark moment that sets itself off, that cannot be explained or predicted on the basis of the temporal sequence leading up to it. This phenomenon, too, is part of the culture of the visible. The moment, or *Augenblick,* lays claim to the imagination, spatializing the event into an image. It should be noted that this sudden assertion of visuality interrupting the narrative is not marked by idealization; in other words, it is not consistent with the classical project in that respect. The emphasis on visuality for its own sake, however, is.

In the frame narrative, the poetics of these stories is discussed: what is new is important because it arouses wonder without context and sets the imagination in motion for a moment, an *Augenblick* (BA 12:299). The hidden interiority of human nature reveals itself in such a momentary image. And then stories are told of inexplicable sounds and sudden frightening sights, such as the one of the two naked bodies on a table in front of burning straw whose flickering shadows eerily suggest erotic encounter in the story "Das Erlebnis des Marschalls von Bassompierre." Who or what these signs are, what the real story is, is not explained. What counts is the sensational image that captivates the eye.

The novel, too, is familiar with images that interrupt the plot and, in freeze-frame, without regard for the maturation process, unfold their effects as surprising, beautiful, or emotional. They can be images from the visual arts that occasion pause, such as the frequently mentioned portrait of the king's sick son from the collection of Wilhelm's grandfather in *Wilhelm Meister*, as well as images like the appearance of the mysterious female who so captivates Wilhelm, and whom he terms the beautiful Amazon after the ambush (book 4, ch. 6), or people who do not submit to a process of development, especially the androgynous Mignon, whose corpse is laid out like the image of an angel at the novel's conclusion. The linear narrative needs disruptive moments to achieve a quality of complexity, poetic freedom, and an openness to the dysfunctional.

Goethe planned further novellas, among them one with the title "Wahlverwandtschaften." Out of this evolved a novel, *Die Wahlverwandtschaften* (Elective Affinities, 1808), which included a novella — "Die wunderlichen Nachbarskinder" (The Remarkable Neighbor Children) — in addition to many other novella-like moments: the framed garden arrangements at the beginning, the series of *tableaux vivants* that form part of the entertainment at a party, the disastrous scene of a child's drowning, which is almost visually frozen as if chiseled in marble, to the laying out in state of Ottilie as if an image behind glass.

Weimar Culture of the Visible as Experiential Spaces of Daily Life

Even the daily culture of Weimar around 1800 was constructed for the eye. Daily life, too, was under the sign of Weimar Classicism. A few examples should make this evident.

Interior Spaces: Goethe's House on the Frauenplan and the Residential Palace

Goethe had already occupied the Haus am Frauenplan (see illustration on 90), built 1709, as a tenant from 1782–86. In 1792, he moved in again, this time as owner, and, while he participated in the campaign in France with Duke Carl August in the summer and fall of that year, he had the building renovated in a classicistic style.[65] Heinrich Meyer, who moved into the upper story, directed the project and the interior design. The Renaissance architect Andrea Palladio (1508–80), whom Goethe admired and often mentioned in the *Italienische Reise*, served as the "godfather," so to speak, of the entrance hall staircase. Goethe arranged his house as a display space for his many art treasures; the house was in effect a museum. He thus staged his life and his life experience; he monumentalized himself.

Whatever was accidental or ugly was erased by the new classicistic splendor. It was no accident that the beautiful house in Weimar was created as an alternative to the dirt and death of the French war. Distance from life and idealization were the mottos. Visitors could not miss it. Jean Paul, whom we met at the outset as a Weimar outsider, wrote his friend Christian Otto in 1796, after his first visit: "Sein Haus (Pallast) frappiert, es ist das einzige in Weimar in italienischem Geschmack, mit solchen Treppen, ein Pantheon voll Bilder und Statuen, eine Kühle der Angst presset die Brust"[66] (His house is striking. It is the only one in Weimar in Italian taste, with such stairs, a pantheon full of paintings and statues, an anxious coldness weighs on one's breast).

The oval ceiling painting showed the divine messenger, Iris, by Johann Heinrich Meyer; it picked up the Pompeian motif of floating and associated it through the rainbow with Goethe's theory of color. Below it one finds the Ildefonso group, the copy of a late ancient marble sculpture that represented sleep and death and whose downturned torch symbolized the extinguishing of passions. In the wall niches, there are bronze copies of the Belvedere Apollo and the Borghese Ares.[67]

The *Büstenzimmer* (room of busts; see illustration on 264), to name just one of the many spaces of this extraordinary house, displayed, in addition to a copy of an ancient torso of a youth, an array of portrait busts in antique mode, among them Herder and Schiller.[68] The present and recent past were in the process of being wrenched from time and classicistically stylized in marble or plaster.

We should also call attention to Goethe's extensive collections and how they were displayed at that time in the small dining room; particularly notable was Goethe's incredible collection of engravings, with pictures not only from the sixteenth and seventeenth centuries, but also representative prints from his own classicistic and Romantic time: Carstens, Hackert, and Angelika Kauffmann, but also Runge and Caspar David Friedrich, among others.[69] Finally, we should also mention the Juno room. For the longest time, Goethe had to do without this icon of classical aesthetics and beauty in original scale, until in 1823 a Berlin admirer gave him a cast as a gift.

The residential palace was rebuilt in 1789, after having been demolished by a fire in 1774. The east wing was rebuilt in the Palladian style[70] according to a plan by Johann August Arens, while the interior design was carried out with the assistance of some of the most important classicistic artists of the period: the staircase was designed by Heinrich Gentz, and a good portion of the eclectic, Pompeian-style decoration, modeled after the style of the Villa Hadriana in Tivoli, was executed by Nicolaus Friedrich Thouret, successor to Arens as the reconstruction project manager. Painters such as Johann Heinrich Meyer and sculptors such as Christian Friedrich Tieck also helped.[71]

The Park

Another essential element of the Weimar culture of perceptible beauty was the English landscape garden, which idealized nature in a manner that could be experienced by walking through it. It arose in the early eighteenth century as the result of a European trend toward an open, seemingly unplanned park in contrast to the French, highly ornamental park that was typical of the absolutistic regimes of the seventeenth century. The park on the Ilm was designed on the model of the famous Wörlitz Park. The small landscape garden in nearby Tiefurt should also be considered. Writers and philosophers such as Pope and Shaftesbury, the former with the practical example of the garden in Twickenham south of London, played a crucial role.[72] William Kent (1685–1748), the first landscape architect, created a park for Lord Burlington in Chiswick by London, and then in Stowe, Rousham, and Claremont, to give more examples. In these gardens, one could see nature artfully and artificially coming into its own, so to speak: there were picturesque views, botanical frames, views of Greek temples, Gothic churches, artificial ruins, an apparently infinite breadth of landscape, winding paths, and serpentine walks that constantly offered new views — all of this transformed gardening into landscape painting. With Henry Hoare's — still existing — Stourhead Garden in Stourton, in all likelihood designed after a painting by Claude Lorrain,[73] this trend reached its peak.

Ever since Chiswick, the neo-Palladian villa was often an important component of scenic arrangement. A new "naturalism" and sensibility (*Empfindsamkeit*) in the face of this elevated nature entered into a close alliance with neoclassicism. In the next generation, Lancelot Brown and William Chambers adapted Kent's garden concept — Brown moved in the direction of a less picturesque, now merely "gardenesque" sort of nature, with undulating grounds and clumps of trees, while Chambers, by contrast, tended toward the integration of even more artificial elements, such as chinoiserie.

In Wörlitz, Prince Leopold II of Anhalt-Dessau created Germany's first large landscape park after the English model in the 1760s and 70s. The architect Erdmannsdorff added a Palladian castle in 1768–73. Goethe visited the grounds for the first time in 1778 and compared them to the Elysian Fields.[74] He derived many impulses for the design of Weimar's Ilm Park from this visit.

In 1776, Goethe had already moved into the garden house on the Ilm, which Duke Carl August had presented to him. Starting in 1778, he and the Duke proceeded to shape the flow of the river toward the southeast, starting from the old formal French castle park and redirecting it into a meadow landscape. Besides Wörlitz, they also had the Seiersdorf Valley in Dresden in mind.[75] Several locations for contemplation or emotion

(*Empfindung*) were created, such as the Dessau Stone, reminiscent of Wörlitz, or the *Schlangenstein* (Snake Rock), a Roman temple fragment or sphinx grotto. Columns and statues, many by the court sculptor Martin Klauer (1742–1801), were intended to produce various states of mind.[76] It is true that Goethe generally rejected exaggerated sentimentalism (*Empfindelei*) and had already written a parody of precisely such behavior in his 1777 *Triumph der Empfindsamkeit* (Triumph of Sensibility); still, a certain measure of elevated emotion, contained by reference to classical models, was considered desirable in relation to these scenic arrangements. After his return from Italy, during the period that particularly interests us, Goethe continued to redesign the garden landscape. He removed some of the scenic views and contemplative sites and in their stead created larger prospects, with meadows and clumps of trees. The "Römisches Haus" (Roman House; see illustration on 346), Karl August's classicistic summer home, which was built by Johann August Arens from 1792 to 1797 at Goethe's instigation, now served as the primary eye-catcher. Georg Melchior Krauss, director of the Weimar School of Drawing, captured its appearance on an aquatint etching.

Just a few miles from Weimar lies Tiefurt, a princely residence that was remodeled after the Weimar palace fire of 1774 to house the duke's younger brother, Constantin, and his tutor, Karl Ludwig von Knebel (1744–1834). The former rental property was redesigned as a small castle and the garden as a small English park according to Knebel's plans.[77] Here, too, one could find the serpentine paths and memorial sites with sculptures by Klauer. Amateur theater was performed here, and copy for the so-called *Tiefurter Journal* was written by residents and guests over a period of many years. In 1781, Anna Amalia shifted her summer residence to Tiefurt, and the Weimar writers and artists, as well as their guests, regularly gathered there until 1806, when the place was plundered by French soldiers during the Napoleonic wars.

Future Perspectives: Image Worlds after 1805. The Other Antiquity and the Romantic Discoveries

Around 1800 Winckelmann's interpretation of classical art and his predilections in classical antiquities dominated Weimar. The taste of the time was schooled on late Hellenistic art, the smooth marble copies of original Greek bronzes of earlier epochs, such as the Belvedere Apollo. These artworks matched the notion of playful grace or sublime but pleasing dignity, or provided the basis for these concepts. What we now know to be the high classical period of the fifth century B.C., especially that of the Parthenon sculptures of Phidias, was at that time hardly known. It was not until Lord Elgin, the English ambassador in Constantinople from 1803–13, purchased a great many of the Acropolis sculptures, particularly those of the Parthenon, and shipped them to London, that the prevailing views changed. In 1816, the British Museum bought the art treasures, and for the first time Europe was in a position to become acquainted with a different, in some respects perhaps less pleasing and less beautified antiquity.

It is characteristic for the sovereignty of Goethe's aesthetic judgment that he greeted these new and certainly at first irritating sculptures with enthusiasm. In 1816–17, he was already busy trying to secure reproductions[78] and recommended Phidias as the supreme example for German sculptors.[79] Goethe was clearly not doctrinaire, but on the contrary extremely adaptable. He rejected the unfavorable comparison of the newly discovered art with the Belvedere Apollo as "albern" (silly): like Herder, he believed that every epoch has its place and should be judged according to its own accomplishments (BA 20:94). In connection with Phidias, Goethe wrote in the *Tag- und Jahresheften* (journals) of the "äußersten Grenzen menschlicher Kunsttätigkeit" (outermost limits of human artistic activity) and his own good luck at having been able to see Phidias's work (BA 16:302). In 1819 in Jena, Goethe saw a cast of the head of one of the horses of the Selene and wrote about it.[80] In a letter, he wrote that he no longer had any desire to travel to Italy, but did feel a pull to London in order to see the Elgin marbles.[81] An artistic paradigm that was based on the obligatory journey to Italy thus bids farewell.

In these later years, Goethe faced and met one other challenge, that of old German and Netherlandic art. Already in the compilation of essays and a short story, the *Herzensergießungen eines kunstliebenden Klosterbruders* (Outpourings of an Art-Loving Monk, 1796), Wackenroder and Tieck had set these artistic forces in opposition to the art of antiquity and the enthusiasm of the Renaissance for classicistic art. Goethe now became further acquainted with this "northern" art through the collection of the Boisserée brothers in Heidelberg. Sulpiz (1783–1854) and Melchior (1786–1851) Boisserée had already collected paintings by von Memling, van der Weyden, and van Eyck, among others, in Cologne in the first decade of the nineteenth century and had moved to Heidelberg in 1810.

Goethe had been acquainted with the brothers since then, and visited them during his travels in 1814–15. With all due reserve in the face of these conceptual paradigms of Romantic art, Goethe was nonetheless impressed. This is evident in his essay "Über Kunst und Altertum in den Rhein- und Main-Gegenden" (Of Art and Antiquity in the Rhine and Main River Regions) of 1816.[82] Goethe attempted to do the paintings justice without accepting Romantic art doctrine wholesale.[83] In his descriptions — such as that of the portrait of the Holy Veronica — he releases the paintings from their religious context and perceives them structurally according to composition, drawing, and expression. He categorizes them historically to gain distance. But he does not deny himself aesthetic pleasure in viewing and analyzing these works. The pleasure of the eyes has precedence over any prior opinion. And that was the real character of the Weimar culture of the perceptible, even beyond the narrow — and narrowly understood — parameters of the classicistic period. Classicism and Romanticism stood in renewed opposition to each other; but they also, as they did before 1800, entered into a tense and productive association.

Notes

[1] Cf. Peter Sprengel, *Jean Paul im Urteil seiner Kritiker: Dokumente zur Wirkungsgeschichte Jean Pauls in Deutschland* (Munich: C. H. Beck, 1980), xxviii–xxxii.

[2] Jean Paul Richter, *Vorschule der Ästhetik, Sämtliche Werke* 10 vols., ed. Norbert Miller (Munich: Hanser, 1960–85), 5:31. Hereafter cited as Jean Paul.

[3] Jean Paul, 5:93.

[4] Cf. the consecutive chapters "Über die griechische oder plastische Dichtkunst" and "Über die romantische Dichtkunst," Jean Paul, 5:67–101.

[5] "Die Götter Griechenlands," first version, 1788. SW 1:168.

[6] Second version, 1800. SW 1:173.

[7] For an art-historical analysis of this process and of the crisis of the language of iconographic images, see Werner Busch, *Das sentimentalische Bild: Die Krise der Kunst im achtzehnten Jahrhundert und die Geburt der Moderne* (Munich: C. H. Beck, 1993).

[8] I refer, of course, to the title of his theoretical essay, *Über naive und sentimentalische Dichtung* (1795–96).

[9] BA 14:287. Written in 1813–15, the work appeared in 1816 under the title *Aus meinem Leben: Dichtung und Wahrheit*. It was 1829 before it was first called *Italienische Reise* (Teil I, II) in the *Ausgabe letzter Hand* (the last edition of Goethe's works completed in his lifetime).

[10] Today in the Pinacoteca of the Palazzo dei Conservatori on the Campidoglio.

[11] Madonna of San Niccolò de'Frari ("Madonna in gloria con il bambino e sei santi"), Pinacoteca Vaticana, originated perhaps in the mid-1540s.

[12] Various versions of this famous description of the Apollo along with commentary may be found in Helmut Pfotenhauer, Markus Bernauer, Norbert Miller, eds., *Frühklassizismus: Position und Opposition: Winckelmann, Mengs, Heinse*, Bibliothek der Kunstliteratur, vol. 2 (Frankfurt am Main: Deutscher Klassiker Verlag, 1995), 149–66 and 486–91. This volume contains seminal essays by Winckelmann, Anton Raphael Mengs, and Wilhelm Heinse.

[13] See the sections on Schiller and on Goethe's residence below.

[14] Cf. my article: "Der schöne Tod: Über einige Schatten in Goethes Italienbild," in H. P., *Um 1800: Konfigurationen der Literatur, der Kunstliteratur und Ästhetik* (Tübingen: Niemeyer, 1991), 113–36.

[15] *Zweiter Römischer Aufenthalt*, report of 17 May 1787, BA 14:503.

[16] Cf. Palermo, 17 April 1787 and Naples, 17 May 1787. See Peter Sprengel, "Die 'Urpflanze': Zur Entwicklung von Goethes Morphologie in Italien," Albert Meier, ed., *Ein unsäglich schönes Land: Goethes "Italienische Reise" und der Mythos Siziliens* (Palermo: Sellerio, 1987), 122–37.

[17] Cf. Helmut Pfotenhauer, "Farbe: Goethes sizilianische Ästhetik," in H. P., *Um 1800*, 103–12.

[18] Cf. the notes from 1–3 April 1787; also, see the unreleased edition of his *Italienische Reise* in WA 1.31:333.

[19] Cf. Marcel Roethlisberger, ed., *Im Licht von Claude Lorrain: Landschaftsmalerei aus drei Jahrhunderten* (Munich: Hirmer, 1983).

[20] *Zweiter römischer Aufenthalt*, March 1788, BA 14:730–39.

[21] Cf. the section entitled: "Signatur des Schönen. (Bei der Betrachtung des Apollo von Belvedere)" from Part 3 of *Reise eines Deutschen in Italien*, quoted here from Karl Philipp Moritz, *Werke in zwei Bänden*, ed. Heide Hollmer and Albert Meier, Vol. 2 (Frankfurt am Main: Deutscher Klassiker Verlag, 1997), 745.

[22] Moritz, *Werke* 2:753–54.

[23] Cf. also *Über die bildende Nachahmung des Schönen*.

[24] Moritz, *Werke* 2:943–9.

[25] Cf. Johann Friedrich Blumenbach, *Über den Bildungstrieb und das Zeugungsgeschäfte* (Göttingen, 1781) and Sabine Schneider, *Die schwierige Sprache des Schönen: Moritz und Schillers Semiotik der Sinnlichkeit* (Würzburg: Königshaussen und Neumann, 1998), 237–44, as well as Helmut Pfotenhauer, "Apoll und Armpolyp: Die Nachbarschaft klassizistischer Kreationsmodelle zur Biologie," ed. Christian Begemann and David Wellbery, *Kunst — Zeugung — Geburt: Theorien und Metaphern ästhetischer Produktion in der Neuzeit* (Freiburg im Breisgau: Rombach, 2002), 203–24.

[26] Cf. Schneider, *Die schwierige Sprache*.

[27] Full text plus commentary in Helmut Pfotenhauer and Peter Sprengel, eds., *Klassik und Klassizismus*, Bibliothek der Kunstliteratur, vol. 3 (Frankfurt am Main: Deutscher Klassiker Verlag, 1995), 384–450 and 758–801. This volume includes seminal texts by Johann Gottfried Herder, Goethe, Heinrich Meyer, Karl Philipp Moritz, Schiller, and Carl Ludwig Fernow.

[28] Pfotenhauer and Sprengel, eds., *Klassik und Klassizismus*, 385–86.

[29] Cf. Friedrich Schlegel's *Gespräch über die Poesie* of 1800, in which arabesques are depicted as the prototype of human fantasy; *Kritische Friedrich-Schlegel-Ausgabe*, vol. 2: *Kritische Schriften und Fragmente. 1798–1801*, ed. Ernst Behler and Hans Eichner (Paderborn: Schöningh, 1988), 204.

[30] Pfotenhauer and Sprengel, eds., *Klassik und Klassizismus*, 400, 448.

[31] Jochen Klauss, *Goethes Wohnhaus in Weimar: Ein Rundgang in Geschichten* (Weimar: Verlag der Klassikerstätten, 1991), 30.

[32] *Über die Gegenstände der bildenden Kunst* (1798), BA 19:164–67.

[33] Cf. *Italienische Reise,* 3 November 1786; for a later appreciation of Meyer: *Zweiter römischer Aufenthalt,* 25 December 1787; cf. also the corresponding article on Meyer by Ines Boettcher and Harald Tausch, *Goethe-Handbuch,* vol. 4.2, ed. Hans-Dietrich Dahnke and Regine Otto (Stuttgart, Weimar: Metzler, 1998), 702–6.

[34] *Über die Gegenstände der bildenden Kunst,* in this instance quoted from the full text in Pfotenhauer and Sprengel, eds., *Klassik und Klassizismus,* 162–207.

[35] Pfotenhauer and Sprengel, eds., *Klassik und Klassizismus,* 174.

[36] Pfotenhauer and Sprengel, eds., *Klassik und Klassizismus,* 180.

[37] Pfotenhauer and Sprengel, eds., *Klassik und Klassizismus,* 193.

[38] Meyer, Goethe, "Nachricht an Künstler und Preisaufgabe" (1799), in Pfotenhauer and Sprengel, eds., *Klassik und Klassizismus,* 270–81. Cf. also Walter Scheidig, *Goethes Preisaufgaben für bildende Künstler 1799–1805,* Schriften der Goethe-Gesellschaft, vol. 57 (Weimar: Hermann Böhlaus Nachfolger, 1958).

[39] Cf. Ernst Osterkamp, "Aus dem Gesichtspunkt reiner Menschlichkeit': Goethes Preisaufgaben für bildende Künstler 1799–1805," in Sabine Schulze, ed., *Goethe und die Kunst,* Ausstellung Frankfurt 1994 (Ostfildern: Hatje, 1994), 310–22.

[40] "Anzeige der Propyläen" (1799), BA 19:293.

[41] Pfotenhauer and Sprengel, eds., *Klassik und* Klassizismus, 280.

[42] Pfotenhauer and Sprengel, eds., *Klassik und Klassizismus,* 280–81.

[43] Schiller, SW 5:879.

[44] Cf. my essay "Würdige Anmut: Schillers ästhetische Verlegenheiten und philosophische Emphasen im Kontext bildender Kunst," in *Um 1800,* 157–78. On the topic of Schiller and the visual arts, see also Wolfgang Riedel, "Schriften zum Theater, zur bildenden Kunst und zur Philosophie vor 1790," *Schiller-Handbuch,* ed. Helmut Koopmann (Stuttgart: Kröner, 1998), 560–74.

[45] *Geschichte der Kunst des Altertums,* in Pfotenhauer, Bernauer, Miller, eds., *Frühklassizismus* (see n. 13), 165.

[46] "Torso-Beschreibung," *Bibliothek der Schönen Wissenschaften und der freien Künste* (1762); in Pfotenhauer, Bernauer, Miller, eds., *Frühklassizismus,* 175.

[47] *Winckelmann und sein Jahrhundert in Briefen und Aufsätzen,* ed. Goethe, Tübingen 1805, new edition edited by Helmut Holtzhauer (Leipzig: Seemann, 1969), 181–82.

[48] Text and commentary in Pfotenhauer, ed., *Klassik und Klassizismus,* 475–80, 824–30. On Fernow, see Harald Tausch, *Entfernung der Antike: Carl Ludwig Fernow im Kontext der Kunsttheorie um 1800* (Tübingen: Niemeyer, 2000).

[49] Cf. Helmut Pfotenhauer, "Fernow als Kunsttheoretiker in Kontinuität und Abgrenzung von Winckelmanns Klassizismus," in Michael Knoche, Harald Tausch,

eds., *Von Rom nach Weimar — Carl Ludwig Fernow* (Tübingen: Niemeyer, 2000), 38–51.

[50] Cf. the plan for the edition in Tausch, *Entfernung der Antike*, 271–72.

[51] "Über Wahrheit und Wahrscheinlichkeit der Kunstwerke," BA 17:10.

[52] From the *Nachlaß* released in the *Ausgabe letzter Hand* (1832); quoted here from BA 17:82–105.

[53] Cf. Heinz Kindermann, *Theatergeschichte der Goethezeit* (Vienna: Bauer, 1948), 578–626; Valerian Tornius, "Goethes Theaterleitung und die bildende Kunst," *Jahrbuch des freien deutschen Hochstifts* 1912, 192–211, as well as a newer interpretation: Friedmar Apel, "'Man lache nicht': Caroline Jagemann spielt eine Rolle," in Gerhard Schuster and Caroline Gille, eds., *Wiederholte Spiegelungen: Weimarer Klassik 1759–1832*. Ständige Ausstellung des Goethe-Nationalmuseums, vol. 2 (Munich: Hanser, 1999), 695–703.

[54] Sebastian Trifft, "Zwei Theaterszenen," in *Wiederholte Spiegelungen,* vol. 2, 705. Cf. also Ulrike Müller-Harang, *Das Weimarer Theater zur Zeit Goethes* (Weimar: Verlag der Klassikerstätten, 1991), 12.

[55] This depiction refers of course to the performance of the 1779 prose version of *Iphigenie*; Corona Schröter played the part of Iphigenie. The picture, however, was not painted until 1801–2. It complies with the *Regeln für Schauspieler* even concerning the correct way to hold one's fingers: "Die zwei mittlern Finger sollen immer zusammenbleiben, der Daumen, Zeige- und kleine Finger etwas gebogen hängen. Auf diese Art ist die Hand in ihrer gehörigen Haltung und zu allen Bewegungen in ihrer richtigen Form" (BA 17:96; The two middle-most fingers should always stay together, the thumb, index, and little finger should hang bent ever so slightly. In this way, the hand is properly positioned and in the correct form for any movement;).

[56] This refers to the original production of the 1802 version; cf. Kindermann, *Theatergeschichte*, Fig. 48.

[57] BA 6:259.

[58] Written in 1778, furnished with commentary and performed with music by Eberwein in May 1815; cf. BA 17:142.

[59] "Über den Gebrauch des Chors in der Tragödie," preface to *Die Braut von Messina oder Die feindlichen Brüder. Ein Trauerspiel mit Chören,* SW 2:819.

[60] Cf. August Langen, "Attitude und Tableau in der Goethezeit," in *Gesammelte Studien zur neueren deutschen Sprache und Literatur*, Festschrift for August Langen, ed. Karl Richter et al. (Berlin: E. Schmidt, 1978), 292–353.

[61] It shows the fourth act; cf. Kindermann, *Theatergeschichte*, Fig. 50.

[62] See my extensive survey of representativeness in Goethe's novels: "Bild versus Geschichte: Zur Funktion des novellistischen Augenblicks in Goethes Romanen," in H. P., *Sprachbilder: Untersuchungen zur Literatur seit dem achtzehnten Jahrhundert* (Würzburg: Königshausen und Neumann, 2000), 45–66.

[63] This had already been theorized by Wieland's contemporary Friedrich von Blanckenburg in *Versuch über den Roman* (Leipzig: 1774).

[64] Cf. the letter of 27 November 1794.

[65] Cf. Klauss, *Goethes Wohnhaus*, 11–15.

[66] Jean Paul, *Sämtliche Werke. Historisch-kritische Ausgabe*, ed. Eduard Berend, 3rd section, vol. 2: *Briefe* 1794–97 (Berlin: Akademie-Verlag, 1958), 212–13.

[67] Klauss, *Goethes Wohnhaus*, 12.

[68] Ilioneus, cast from the Greek original from the fourth century B.C., Munich, Glyptothek; Portrait busts of Herder (right, the marble original by Alexander Trippel) and of Schiller (left, by Johann Heinrich Dannecker).

[69] Cf. *Kostbarkeiten aus Goethes Kunstsammlung:* Ausstellung der Nationalen Forschungs- und Gedenkstätten der klassischen Literatur, Goethe-Nationalmuseum Weimar (Duisburg: 1987), as well as *Der Sammler und die Seinigen: Handzeichnungen aus Goethes Besitz*, ed. Gerhard Schuster (Munich: Hanser, 1999).

[70] Cf. Rolf Bothe, *Dichter, Fürst und Architekten: Das Weimarer Residenzschloß vom Mittelalter bis zum Anfang des 19. Jahrhunderts* (Ostfildern-Ruit: Hatje Cantz, 2000), 43–46.

[71] The so-called poets' rooms were created in the west wing of the palace shortly after Goethe's death — memorial places for the Weimar authors who by 1800 were recognized as "classical": Goethe, Schiller, Wieland, Herder. See Christian Hecht, *Dichtergedächtnis und fürstliche Repräsentation: Der Westflügel des Weimarer Residenzschlosses. Architektur und Ausstattung* (Ostfildern-Ruit: Hatje Cantz, 2000).

[72] Frank Maier-Solgk and Andreas Greuter present a good summary of the development in *Landschaftsgärten in Deutschland* (Frechen: Komet, 2000), 10–15.

[73] *Aeneas in Delos*, London, National Gallery.

[74] To Charlotte von Stein, 14 May 1778.

[75] Cf. Adrian von Buttlar, *Der Landschaftsgarten: Gartenkunst des Klassizismus und der Romantik* (Cologne: Du Mont, 1989), 158.

[76] Cf. Ulrich Müller, "Georg Melchior Klaus fixiert Durchblicke," 271–80. In *Wiederholte Spiegelungen*, vol. 1.

[77] Cf. Johannes Saltzwedel, "Karl Ludwig von Knebel erfindet Tiefurt," 199–208. In *Wiederholte Spiegelungen*, vol. 1.

[78] "Elginische Marmore," BA 20:94, 106.

[79] "Verein der Deutschen Bildhauer," BA 20:106–10.

[80] Cf. commentary in BA 20:588.

[81] To Georg Sartorius, 20 July 1787.

[82] BA 20:44–55.

[83] Cf. especially Ernst Osterkamp, *Im Buchstabenbilde: Studien zum Verfahren Goethescher Bildbeschreibungen* (Stuttgart: Metzler, 1991), 224–318.

The Irrelevance of Aesthetics and the De-Theorizing of the Self in "Classical" Weimar

Benjamin Bennett

IN 1750, IN THE FIRST PARAGRAPH of his *Aesthetica*, Frankfurt professor Alexander Gottlieb Baumgarten (1714–62) defines this brand-new intellectual discipline as "scientia cognitionis sensitivae" (the science of sensate knowledge). But unfortunately — at least for those who value neatness in history — most of the major thinkers who follow (Kant being the notable exception) either forget or neglect or simply discard this definition, concentrating instead on a pair of important, but subordinate concepts in Baumgarten's system — *art* and *beauty* — which are understood henceforward as the true content of "aesthetics." Once this de-etymologizing move has been made *(aistheta,* in Greek, are simply things perceived by the physical senses), the historical situation is also muddied, and the brand-new discipline is henceforth regarded as an age-old discipline, traceable at least as far back as Plato and Aristotle.

Needless to say, there are possibilities for confusion here, as well as for development; but the one possibility that is definitely excluded is that "aesthetics" should cohere as a single scientific discipline with a well-defined scope. (Do art and beauty even really belong together as objects of study?) This essay will, in fact, suggest that aesthetics is best understood not as an area of inquiry in the first place, but as a specific cultural *project* in eighteenth- and nineteenth-century Europe. For the time being, however, we can get a feel for what aesthetics does by considering the various issues it raises.

With respect to art, the opposition between imitative and expressive theories (traced back to the supposed founding instances of Aristotle and pseudo-Longinus) becomes increasingly important toward the end of the eighteenth century. M. H. Abrams's critical classic *The Mirror and the Lamp* (1953) treats this opposition mainly with reference to British literature. Imitative doctrine tends to struggle with the question of exactly what art imitates, which receives answers ranging from the highly specific (Winckelmann) to the uncomfortably hedged (Batteux's [1713–80] "beautiful nature") to the semiotically cagey (Lessing). Expressive doctrine, in some instances, encourages a modern secular hermeneutics, while in others (Shaftesbury, Herder) it flirts with the analogy between artistic creativity and God's own world-creation.

With respect to beauty, the first problem is whether there is such a thing to begin with, and if so, in what sense. Can beauty be recognized by objective characteristics, or only by way of a particular kind of feeling or judgment on the part of the recipient? Answers of the latter type are more frequent — although the issue is still contested today by some behavioral experimenters and a few neo-Pythagorean theorists — but also tend to be vague and inapplicable; and a principal achievement of Kant's *Critique of Judgment* is to have systematized this matter in a relatively lucid and durable form.

Of all the questions posed by aesthetics, however, the one with perhaps the greatest historical weight is that of the *function* of art, or of beauty, in society or in the development of cultures. In late eighteenth-century Germany, in particular, it is asked whether aesthetic experience or artistic production may be regarded as an *instrument* for the establishment of rational or moral truth, or for the attainment of specific social benefits. And the supposedly modern or forward-looking answer to this question, attributed mainly to Kant and novelist and essayist Karl Philipp Moritz, is that the aesthetic domain may not properly be instrumentalized in any sense, that art is radically autonomous, conforming to the concept of "that which is complete in itself."

But no sooner is aesthetic autonomy accepted as a principle than precisely that autonomy, precisely the *separateness* of the aesthetic from society and politics, is found to have a social and political function of fundamental importance. This is the position adopted by Schiller in his aesthetic writings — if one takes them at face value, which I do not. And such is the seductive power of this position that we ourselves — if, say, Theodor W. Adorno's *Ästhetische Theorie* (Aesthetic Theory, 1970) (which I do take at face value) is any measure — do not seem to have got much beyond.

If there is any reason for saying "German Classicism" — rather than simply saying what these words (in my view) really refer to, namely the works of Goethe and Schiller produced during the period of their association and collaboration — if there is any coherent spirit in those works that justifies the value-laden notion of the "classical" otherwise than by mere nationalistic convenience[1] — then in view of the high level of abstraction that characterizes our authors' conversations about poetry and art in general, we shall expect to find that spirit reflected in the form of aesthetic theory. And in the late eighteenth century, "aesthetics" means something distinctly more specific than just "the philosophical study of art," which could refer to any number of intellectual initiatives from Plato on down. We can begin by identifying what we might call an "aesthetic movement" in European, and especially German thought of the eighteenth century. On the one hand, the term "aesthetic," which Baumgarten coined in 1735 as not much more than an afterthought in his *Meditationes* on poetry, is adopted and employed with extraordinary alacrity by an extraordinary variety of thinkers, including Johann Georg Hamann (1730–88), Mendelssohn, Kant, and Schiller; on the other hand, even where the term itself is not prominent, the practice of bringing questions of beauty and art, of artistic judgment and artistic production, into what would earlier have been the preserve of metaphysics, becomes ever more common, in thinkers like Nicolai, Lessing, Herder, Moritz, and Goethe. And the question we must ask is: what is at stake in the general intellectual tendency that we associate with the emergence of aesthetics as a discipline?

This question has already been asked, and in fact is asked in exactly these terms, and answered, by Andrew Bowie, when he writes:

> Baumgarten's *Aesthetica*, part one 1750, part two 1758, and Hamann's *Aesthetica in nuce*, of 1762, already begin to suggest what is at stake in the emergence of aesthetics as an independent branch of philosophy. Despite their obvious differences, Baumgarten and Hamann share a concern with the failure of the Rationalist traditions of the eighteenth century to do justice to the immediacy of the individual's sensuous relationship to the world which is part of aesthetic pleasure.[2]

Bowie is right, as far as he goes, and he succeeds, a bit further on, in putting his finger on what becomes a crucial question for Goethe and Schiller: "Revaluing the sensuous particular and giving it primacy in one branch of philosophy poses problems: how does one abstractly grasp the particular without abolishing its value as particular?" (5). But his formulation is still itself too abstract, too deeply invested in the conventions of philosophy as an institution, in relation to which "the particular," problematic as it may be, is not problematic enough, for it still supposedly stands exposed as a possible object of investigation. In truth, the particular is never really exposed, but is radically and irrevocably *hidden* from philosophy. *Individuum est ineffabile* (the individual is inexpressible) is a truth not only for Herder, Goethe, and the philosopher Wilhelm Dilthey (1833–1911).

A more exact and complete statement of what is at stake in the growth of aesthetics is given by Schiller in letter 4 of *Über die ästhetische Erziehung des Menschen* (On the Aesthetic Education of Man, cited below as *Aesthetic Letters*), the summary and culmination of his struggle with aesthetic questions in the 1790s.

> Aber eben deswegen, weil der Staat eine Organisation sein soll, die sich durch sich selbst und für sich selbst bildet, so kann er auch nur insoferne wirklich werden, als sich die Teile zur Idee des Ganzen hinaufgestimmt haben. Weil der Staat der reinen und objektiven Menschheit in der Brust seiner Bürger zum Repräsentanten dient, so wird er gegen seine Bürger dasselbe Verhältnis zu beobachten haben, in welchem sie zu sich selber

stehen, und ihre subjektive Menschheit auch nur in *dem* Grade ehren können, als sie zur objektiven veredelt ist. Ist der innere Mensch mit sich einig, so wird er auch bei der höchsten Universalisierung seines Betragens seine Eigentümlichkeit retten, und der Staat wird bloß der Ausleger seines schönen Instinkts, die deutlichere Formel seiner inneren Gesetzgebung sein. (SW 5:578)

[But just because the state is to be an organization formed by itself and for itself, it can only become a reality inasmuch as its parts have been tuned up to the idea of the whole. Because the state serves to represent that ideal and objective humanity that exists in the heart of each of its citizens, it will have to observe toward those citizens the same relationship as each has to himself, and will be able to honor their subjective humanity only *to the extent* that this has been ennobled in the direction of objective humanity. Once man is inwardly at one with himself, he will be able to preserve his individuality however much he may universalize his conduct, and the state will be merely the interpreter of his own finest instinct, a clearer formulation of his own sense of what is right.[3]]

The question, in other words, is not merely whether philosophical systematics succeeds in doing justice to a human "particularity" or "immediacy" understood as pre-existing. What is at stake, rather, is whether — in a practical and therefore *political* sense — we human beings shall be able *to have in the first place,* each of us, his or her own relatively unfettered, personal, particular, individual being. The very condition of the self is in question. In letter 6, in his discussion of the difference between ancient Hellenic civilization and its modern European descendants, Schiller insists that the self, by which he means our experience of our own being, is not historically constant, but historically and culturally contingent, that it is in fact possible for "the individual concrete life" to be "destroyed," that a mode of individual experience can be annihilated ("so wird denn allmählich das einzelne konkrete Leben vertilgt" [SW 5:585]) by developments in the cultural and political sphere. And the task of aesthetics, accordingly, is to restore the self, to restore a condition in which our strict *Eigentümlichkeit,* the unrepeatable particularity of our being as ourselves, can be preserved even in the face of universal moral and social claims on us, to restore us to a condition in which we, like the Greeks, will be "at once individual and genus," namely *"representatives* of the human genus" (W/W 177), *"Repräsentanten* der Gattung" (SW 5:668).

Of course it will be objected that Schiller presents this restoration of our human selfhood as the task of beauty itself, not that of aesthetics. But if the effect that Schiller hopes for can be expected from the simple operation of artistic beauty upon contemporary sensibilities, then why does he write his treatise in the first place? Does the very existence of the *Aesthetic Letters* not imply that beauty alone, or the practice of art alone, is insufficient?

Is it not implied that an advance in the study or understanding of beauty, an advance, that is, in aesthetics, will also be needed?[4] Indeed, does it not follow logically that aesthetics must pave the way for beauty's effects? For if the corruption of our modern experience of the individual self, the destruction of our "concrete life," is the result of a process of abstraction, a submission to the power of "das Abstrakt des Ganzen" (SW 5:585; the abstract idea of the whole, W/W 101), then it follows that we can be led back to a more fully human condition only by a process that begins where we after all are, on a high level of abstraction, and proceeds toward the particular and immediate. Which is exactly what aesthetics, as represented by Schiller's *Letters*, seems to be doing. The actual logical argument of the *Letters* begins in letter 11 with the words:

> Wenn die Abstraktion so hoch, als sie immer kann, hinaufsteigt, so gelangt sie zu zwei letzten Begriffen, bei denen sie stille stehen und ihre Grenzen bekennen muß. Sie unterscheidet in dem Menschen etwas, das bleibt, und etwas, das sich unaufhörlich verändert. Das Bleibende nennt sie seine *Person*, das Wechselnde seinen *Zustand*. (SW 5:601)

> [When abstraction rises to the highest it can possibly attain, it arrives at two ultimate concepts before which it must halt and recognize that here it has reached its limits. It distinguishes in man something that endures and something that constantly changes. That which endures it calls his *person*, that which changes, his *condition*. (W/W 115)]

We are offered not merely an abstraction, but the highest possible abstraction. It simply cannot happen, therefore, that an individual (the reader) might be too thoroughly corrupted by an abstract self-relation to be engaged by this argument. And only five letters later, at the end of letter 15, we have arrived — by a process Schiller presents as the strictly logical development of his initial abstraction — at the idea of a state of utter emotional immediacy, an aesthetically aroused state in which we find ourselves "zugleich in dem Zustand der höchsten Ruhe und der höchsten Bewegung, und es entsteht jene wunderbare Rührung, für welche der Verstand keinen Begriff und die Sprache keinen Namen hat" (SW 5:619; at one and the same time in a state of utter repose and extreme agitation, and there results that wondrous stirring of the heart for which mind has no concept nor speech any name; W/W 132). *Individuum est ineffabile,* and yet aesthetics claims to open through logic an avenue by which such an ineffable condition might be somehow communicated and shared after all. It is significant, in addition, that the abstract notions from which Schiller starts out are obviously related to Cartesian dualism, for in this way a historical summary of the progress of aesthetics is also suggested. The intellectual corruption of the experiencing self, we infer, reaches a kind of climax in Descartes — who in a sense actually *derives* the self logically and so exposes it utterly to the universal — whereupon the way is opened for an opposed philosophical movement, the development of aesthetics, that is aimed at restoring our immediate humanity.

An earlier parallel with Schiller's view emerges, unexpectedly, in Lessing's famous essay *Laokoon, oder Über die Grenzen der Malerei und Poesie* (1766) — unexpectedly, because Lessing studiously avoids the term "aesthetic" and attacks Baumgarten's *Aesthetica* in his introduction. It is further unexpected because Lessing's retention of the terminology of artistic "imitation" serves as an excuse for most historians to place him outside the development of aesthetics proper, as representing the "instrumental" view of art that is superseded by that development. In reality, the self is as much at stake in Lessing as in Schiller, perhaps more consistently so. For in Lessing's view of the individual's reception of a work of art, the interaction between what the work contributes and what is supplied by our imagination constitutes an exact model of the wholeness of immediate experience that the Greeks possessed but we lack. In addition, since at least in the case of poetry that interaction contains an inherently theoretical component, the idea that an aesthetic treatise like *Laokoon* might play a role in the renewal of our mode of experiencing is not nearly so far-fetched as it may appear in Schiller. These points follow from: (1) Lessing's argument that the Greeks somehow experienced life more fully than we "barbarians" do; and (2) his insistence that the task of at least epic poetry is to make directly available to us the sensory experience of its fiction.[5]

The parallel between Schiller and Lessing, because of the theoretical distance that separates them, carries considerable weight. But before we can claim to locate Goethe and Schiller with respect to aesthetics as a whole, we must deal with at least one other view of what is at stake here, the view — associated most often with Kant and with Karl Philipp Moritz — that what matters most about art in the new age of aesthetics is its "autonomy," its liberation from its traditional role as an "instrument" in the furtherance of social, political, or religious ends. In fact, however, Kant, in the *Critique of Judgment,* is concerned centrally not with the domain of art, but with the faculty of judging as such, including especially judgments of taste, which are made "durch ein Wohlgefallen oder Mißfallen *ohne alles Interesse*" (§5; by way of an *entirely disinterested* pleasure or displeasure), and which, in the case of pleasure, designate their object as "schön" (beautiful). And if we ask what is at stake in his project, we are brought back, by a somewhat different path, to the idea of the wholeness of the self, the idea of judgment as making possible a transition between the otherwise radically separate cognitive faculties of "Verstand" and "Vernunft" (Einleitung, III; understanding and reason).

The text that is usually the center of attention in discussions of an emerging artistic autonomy in the eighteenth century is Moritz's 1785 essay, "Versuch einer Vereinigung aller schönen Künste und Wissenschaften unter dem Begriff des *in sich selbst Vollendeten*" (Attempt to Unify All

Beaux Arts and Belles Lettres under the Concept of *That Which Is Complete in Itself*), where we read, for instance:

> Wir bedürfen des Schönen nicht so sehr, um dadurch ergötzt zu werden, als das Schöne unsrer bedarf, um erkannt zu werden. Wir können sehr gut ohne die Betrachtung schöner Kunstwerke bestehen, diese aber können, als solche, nicht wohl ohne unsre Betrachtung bestehen. Jemehr wir sie also entbehren können, desto mehr betrachten wir sie um ihrer selbst willen, um ihnen durch unsre Betrachtung gleichsam erst ihr wahres volles Dasein zu geben. Denn durch unsre zunehmende Anerkennung des Schönen in einem schönen Kunstwerke, vergrößern wir gleichsam seine Schönheit selber, und legen immer mehr Werth hinein. Daher das ungeduldige Verlangen, daß alles dem Schönen huldigen soll, welches wir einmal dafür erkannt haben: je allgemeiner es als schön erkannt und bewundert wird, desto mehr Werth erhält es auch in unsern Augen.[6]

> [It is not so much that we need the beautiful for our pleasure, as that the beautiful needs us, in order to be recognized. We can exist perfectly well without observing beautiful works of art, but these works cannot exist, as such, without our observing them. The more we can thus do without them, by so much more do we observe them for their own sake, in order as it were to endow them, for the first time, with their own full existence by our contemplation. For by means of our increasing recognition of the beautiful in a beautiful work of art, we increase, so to speak, its own beauty and endow it with more and more value. Hence our impatient desire that everyone should pay homage to beauty where we have recognized it; the more generally it is recognized and admired as beautiful, the more value it acquires in our eyes.]

The relation of the last sentences here to Kant's argument that an aesthetic judgment includes automatically the attribution of the same judgment to every human being (*Critique of Judgment*, §6) is obvious. But more interesting, for our purposes, and more fundamental than the idea of artistic autonomy, is the bridge Moritz creates between the Kantian argument and the idea that the work of art is somehow constituted, brought into full existence, only in the process of its reception.

This idea is central in the development of aesthetics from the very beginning. One of the least remarked innovations in Baumgarten's *Meditationes philosophicae de nonnullis ad poema pertinentibus* (Philosophical Meditations on Several Things Having to Do with Poems, 1735), for instance, is the assertion that an "oratio sensitiva perfecta" (perfect sensory discourse, §VII) is even possible. This assertion implies that immediate sense experience, sensory "representations," can be adequately incorporated into discourse and fully reconstituted by a reader. Baumgarten himself does not develop this thought much further; and in fact, at one point, he seems worried by its implications, when he acknowledges that a particular representation may be more nearly "distinct" for one reader than for another

(§XII). But the decisive aesthetic move is evident nonetheless, the idea that the work of art is not contained in the material of which it is made, but is first fully constituted, first comes into existence, in the mind of a sensitive recipient. For Baumgarten, again, the very nature of the "poetic" includes "affectus movere" (§XXV), the exciting of affects in the reader.

This idea in its more general form is not new in Baumgarten and can be related in an obvious way to the development of social and economic conditions in Europe in the seventeenth and eighteenth centuries. As various elements of the middle class gained standing, leisure, and cultural importance, and as the value of works of art therefore had to be justified increasingly from the point of view of a purchaser or a paying audience, it was inevitable that the study of art would orient itself more and more toward the work's reception — rather than, for example, toward its production. Indeed, the increasing primacy of the concept of "beauty" in artistic studies already shows this orientation. But such socio-economic considerations by no means imply that the focus of aesthetics upon reception lacks a philosophical dimension — at least not unless we are willing to believe that Lessing's and Schiller's meticulous analyses of the process of reception, as well as Moritz's in *Über die bildende Nachahmung des Schönen* (On the Plastic Imitation of the Beautiful, 1788), are motivated solely by a need to accommodate the conditions of precisely that contemporary society against which much of their argument is directed.

Even on this elementary level, therefore, the question of what is at stake in aesthetics arises; but to understand exactly how it operates here, we must refine our concepts a bit. When Schiller speaks of the "destruction" of the concrete experiencing self, he is speaking of a condition that in the terminology of the next century would come to be known as "alienation." The sensate self has ceased to exist not literally, but rather in the sense that it lacks any guarantee or confirmation of its existence. It exists in a kind of strict isolation, cut off entirely from its Cartesian counterpart *quod cogitat ergo est* (which thinks and therefore is), from the ego that is constituted by logical thinking; and it is therefore exiled especially from the common human world-girdling network of discourse, in which it might conceivably have found itself reflected and confirmed. Baumgarten, again, appears to understand the basic situation here, when he notes in his *Metaphysica* (§512) that in respect to the lower cognitive faculties — those faculties engaged by the work of art — a person is limited absolutely by the position of his or her body in the world. But again, he does not carry out in detail the aesthetic implications of this thought. For if the strictly limited sensate self not only perceives the beautiful in art, but is the place where the work of art, or the perfect sensory discourse of poetry, *first achieves its full being* — or even if we merely have reason to form this impression (which is what Moritz actually suggests) — then the alienation of that sensate self has been overcome, its existence is in effect confirmed and reintegrated into the world of communicable representations, hence reconnected with the rational self in a newly whole person. (Curiously enough, since Baumgarten does not go into these ramifications of his subject matter, it follows that his treatment of it does not yet qualify as "aesthetics" in Schiller's or Moritz's sense — where the rehabilitation or reintegration of the self is at stake — but remains a theory of sensate cognition in general.)

Again, therefore, I contend that Schiller's view of what is at stake in aesthetics reflects a clear understanding of the general historical situation. But if we assume (heuristically) that it is precisely this historical situation, that it is the question *of* aesthetics that interests Schiller, rather than any particular aesthetic questions, then we are tempted to conclude that the *Letters* arrive finally at a *reductio ad absurdum* of the whole aesthetic project. For what is at stake in aesthetics is the reintegration of the self, which means the rescue or rehabilitation of the particular sensate self in the course of a needful de-theorizing of the ego as a whole. But aesthetics itself is a theoretical discipline. Therefore, it must assign the task of accomplishing its anti-theoretical project to art alone, or to beauty. And yet, what reason is there for confidence that art, or beauty, is in the least suited to this task? The historical evidence, as Schiller points out, tends in exactly the opposite direction:

> In der Tat muß es Nachdenken erregen, daß man beinahe in jeder Epoche der Geschichte, wo die Künste blühen und der Geschmack regiert, die Menschheit gesunken findet und auch nicht ein einziges Beispiel aufweisen kann, daß ein hoher Grad und eine große Allgemeinheit ästhetischer Kultur bei einem Volke mit politischer Freiheit und bürgerlicher Tugend, daß schöne Sitten mit guten Sitten, und Politur des Betragens mit Wahrheit desselben Hand in Hand gegangen wäre. (SW 5:598–99)

> [And indeed it must give pause for reflection that in almost every historical epoch in which the arts flourish, and taste prevails, we find humanity at a low ebb, and cannot point to a single instance of a high degree and wide diffusion of aesthetic culture going hand in hand with political freedom and civic virtue, fine manners with good morals, refinement of conduct with truth of conduct. (W/W 113)]

Even our judgment of the Greeks is poisoned by this reflection upon history:

> Solange Athen und Sparta ihre Unabhängigkeit behaupteten und Achtung für die Gesetze ihrer Verfassung zur Grundlage diente, war der Geschmack noch unreif, die Kunst noch in ihrer Kindheit, und es fehlte noch viel, daß die Schönheit die Gemüter beherrschte. . . . Als unter dem Perikles und Alexander das goldne Alter der Künste herbeikam und die Herrschaft des Geschmacks sich allgemeiner verbreitete, findet man

Griechenlands Kraft und Freiheit nicht mehr, die Beredsamkeit verfälschte die Wahrheit, die Weisheit beleidigte in dem Mund eines Sokrates, und die Tugend in dem Leben eines Phocion. (SW 5:599)

[As long as Athens and Sparta maintained their independence, and respect for the laws served as the basis for their constitution, taste was as yet immature, art still in its infancy, and beauty far from ruling over the hearts of men. . . . When, under Pericles and Alexander, the golden age of the arts arrived, and the rule of taste extended its sway, the strength and freedom of Greece are no longer to be found. Rhetoric falsified truth, wisdom gave offence in the mouth of a Socrates, and virtue in the life of a Phocion. (W/W 113–14)]

And even without these historical worries, as we have seen, the very existence of aesthetics calls its own project into question. If beauty alone were sufficient to improve the human condition, why would aesthetics be necessary?

Is Schiller really suggesting a *reductio ad absurdum* of aesthetics in this sense? This question contains two parts: (1) Can we adduce further interpretive evidence in support of such a negative reading of the *Letters*?; and (2) Can one form a plausible conjecture about why Schiller should want to develop that negative position, about what end he has in mind? In response to (1) I will offer a reading of the *Letters* alongside *Wallenstein* and *Maria Stuart*. And question (2) will lead us to *Wilhelm Tell*, as well as to both the person and the work of Goethe.

The thought of the aesthetic *Letters* is complicated, and at some points at least pretends to a high degree of technical philosophical refinement.[7] For this reason, some simple interpretive questions about this text are hardly ever asked. The whole historical dimension of the argument, for instance, provokes such a question: why does Schiller insist so strongly upon his historical scheme, upon the assertions that (1) the Greeks represented a clear maximum of aesthetic culture (SW 5:586), (2) the further development of civilization in Europe necessarily entailed a disintegration of that human wholeness, and (3) the disintegration can be repaired, our wholeness restored, only by way of an ennobling of character in the present age (SW 5:592)? Why does he suggest in letters 11 through 15 (as noted above) that the development of aesthetics represents a reversal of the whole historical unfolding of philosophy that culminates in Descartes? He himself points out, in another passage we have looked at, that perfect Greek humanity is something that never actually happened in history; and in the very midst of his historical presentation, he reminds us that we are not bound by our historical circumstances:

Kann aber wohl der Mensch dazu bestimmt sein, über irgend einem Zwecke sich selbst zu versäumen? Sollte uns die Natur durch ihre Zwecke eine Vollkommenheit rauben können, welche uns die Vernunft durch die ihrigen vorschreibt? Es muß also falsch sein, daß die Ausbildung der einzelnen Kräfte das Opfer ihrer Totalität notwendig macht; oder wenn auch das Gesetz der Natur noch so sehr dahin strebte, so muß es bei uns stehen, diese Totalität in unsrer Natur, welche die Kunst zerstört hat, durch eine höhere Kunst wiederherzustellen. (SW 5:588)

[But can man really be destined to miss himself for the sake of any purpose whatsoever? Should nature, for the sake of her own purposes, be able to rob us of a completeness that reason, for the sake of hers, enjoins upon us? It must, therefore, be wrong if [sic: correct trans. = "that"] the cultivation of individual powers involves the sacrifice of wholeness. Or rather, however much the law of nature tends in that direction, it must be open to us to restore by a higher art the totality of our nature that the arts themselves have destroyed. (W/W 104)]

When Schiller later speaks of the need for an "ennobling of character," he is invoking a concept (expressed in the German "Charakter") that can refer either to individuals themselves or to a general level of individual development. But the context, especially the comparison with the Greeks, makes clear that "Individuen" themselves (SW 5:583) are at issue; and the passage just quoted implies that precisely *as* individuals we are not subject to the historical forces that have supposedly corrupted our "character."

There is perhaps not an actual inconsistency here, but there is enough vagueness, ambiguity, and conceptual slippage to cause us concern about the integrity of the whole edifice. Why does Schiller raise the question of history in the first place? Why not simply set forth the abstract idea of beauty, and that of the "ästhetischer Zustand" (SW 5:633–36; aesthetic state) in which perfect freedom is restored to us, and then show how these ideas suggest possibilities for dealing with the corrupt political and cultural situation of Europe in the 1790s? Or to look at it the other way around, why does he mention "aesthetic education" in his title, and then not say anything about ways in which people might actually be educated, about practical possibilities for propagating aesthetic culture? As the text stands, the idea of "education" in the title serves no real purpose except to call attention to the bind we get into when we ask whether the educative task is assigned to beauty alone, or to aesthetics. There is, to be sure, at the end of letter number 9, a long exhortation to enthusiastic young readers about how they are to keep themselves pure in the present age; but no practical educative advice is offered (SW 5:595).

It appears, then, that either the thought of the *Letters* is disordered, or there is something going on beneath the surface that unifies the endeavor.[8] I think there is some measure of truth in both of these possibilities. But obviously the subsurface unifying tendency will be the more interesting object of inquiry; and in fact, once we have seen how tricky the logical and rhetorical situation really is, we will also understand why Schiller can be forgiven some confusion in his argument.

In the very last letter, number 27, Schiller turns away from the mainly psychological discussion of the "aesthetic state [of mind]," or aesthetic "Bestimmbarkeit" (SW 5:632–36; determinability), which had occupied him in letters 20 through 25, and comes back to the question of politics and history. Now he defines three types of polity.

> Wenn in dem *dynamischen* Staat der Rechte der Mensch dem Menschen als Kraft begegnet und sein Wirken beschränkt — wenn er sich ihm in dem *ethischen* Staat der Pflichten mit der Majestät des Gesetzes entgegenstellt und sein Wollen fesselt, so darf er im Kreise des schönen Umgangs, in dem *ästhetischen* Staat, nur als Gestalt erscheinen, nur als Objekt des freien Spiels gegenüberstehen. *Freiheit zu geben durch Freiheit* ist das Grundgesetz dieses Reichs. (SW 5:667)

> [If in the *dynamic* state of rights it is as force that one man encounters another, and imposes limits upon his activities; if in the *ethical* state of duties man sets himself over against man with all the majesty of the law, and puts a curb upon his desires; in those circles where conduct is governed by beauty, in the *aesthetic* state, none may appear to the other except as form, or confront him except as an object of free play. *To bestow freedom by means of freedom* is the fundamental law of this kingdom. (W/W 176)]

The task of history, obviously, is to realize the third, "aesthetic" political type. But in the immediately preceding letter, number 26, Schiller has already poisoned this historical suggestion at its root:

> Bei welchem einzelnen Menschen oder ganzen Volk man den aufrichtigen und selbständigen Schein findet, da darf man auf Geist und Geschmack und jede damit verwandte Trefflichkeit schließen — da wird man das Ideal, das wirkliche Leben regieren, die Ehre über den Besitz, den Gedanken über den Genuß, den Traum der Unsterblichkeit über die Existenz triumphieren sehen. Da wird die öffentliche Stimme das einzig Furchtbare sein, und ein Olivenkranz höher als ein Purpurkleid ehren. (SW 5:659)

> [In whatever individual or whole people we find this honest and autonomous kind of semblance, we may assume both understanding and taste, and every kindred excellence. There we shall see actual life governed by the ideal, honor triumphant over possessions, thought over enjoyment, dreams of immortality over existence. There public opinion will be the only thing to be feared, and an olive wreath bestow greater honor than a purple robe. (W/W 169)]

This passage obviously contradicts the empirical historical discussion of the Greeks in number 10, and so calls attention to the manner in which historical fact makes nonsense of the idea of an "aesthetic" polity. Why does Schiller return to historical argument in the first place — and then why in so transparently unconvincing a fashion?

There can be only one possible answer, provided we concede that the question exists. The last two letters, numbers 26 and 27, are a *gesture,* suggesting that it is somehow important to *pass beyond* the psychological argument that is, after all, the work's logical culmination. Indeed, assuming we are in agreement about what is at stake in the emergence of aesthetics, it follows that Schiller's idea of a psychological state of "aesthetic determinability" marks the culmination of *aesthetics as a whole,* the idea of a mental state in which "eine wirkliche *Vereinigung* und Auswechslung der Materie mit der Form und des Leidens mit der Tätigkeit vor sich geht," so that "die *Vereinbarkeit* beider Naturen, die Ausführbarkeit des Unendlichen in der Endlichkeit, mithin die Möglichkeit der erhabensten Menschheit bewiesen [ist]" (SW 5:654; an actual *union* and interchange between matter and form, passivity and activity, momentarily takes place, so that the *compatibility* of our two natures . . . hence the possibility of sublimest humanity, is thereby actually proven, W/W 164–65). Surely, once this "proof" is established, the goal of all aesthetics, the reintegration of the self, has been achieved. Why does Schiller now distract us by reopening the treacherous question of history?

The trouble with the conception of the aesthetic state of mind is that while it *is* in a sense the culmination of aesthetics, it cannot legitimately be *thought of* as a goal or culmination. For if, in the aesthetic state of mind, "die Selbsttätigkeit der Vernunft schon auf dem Felde der Sinnlichkeit eröffnet [wird]" (the autonomy of reason is already opened up within the domain of sense itself), then that "Selbsttätigkeit," meaning "autonomy" in the sense of an *active* faculty, cannot establish itself except *by acting,* by taking "[den] Schritt von dem ästhetischen Zustand zu dem logischen und moralischen" (SW 5:642; the step from the aesthetic to the logical and moral state, W/W 153), which means that the ultimate proof of aesthetic determinability is furnished only by the act of self-determination that proceeds from it. When determinability, or freedom from determination, is desired for its own sake, then a perversion of its very nature occurs. This argument is not made in the *Letters* themselves, but it emerges clearly from Schiller's treatment of the figure of Wallenstein, and of the figure of Leicester in *Maria Stuart:*

> Wärs möglich? Könnt ich nicht mehr, wie ich wollte?
> Nicht mehr zurück, wie mirs beliebt? Ich müßte
> Die Tat *vollbringen,* weil ich sie *gedacht,*
> Nicht die Versuchung von mir wies — das Herz
> Genährt mit diesem Traum, auf ungewisse
> Erfüllung hin die Mittel mir gespart,
> Die Wege bloß mir offen hab gehalten? —
> . . .
>
> Wars unrecht, an dem Gaukelbilde mich
> Der königlichen Hoffnung zu ergötzen?
> (*Wallensteins Tod,* 139–51)

[Is it possible? That I can no longer do as I wish, can no longer go back if I feel like it? I have to *carry out* the deed just because I *thought* of it, didn't banish temptation, nourished my heart with this dream, stored up the wherewithal just in case, just because I kept my paths open? — . . . Was it wrong to enjoy the delusive image of royal hope?]

And like Wallenstein, Leicester also suggests a travesty of the aesthetic state of mind, in that his intentness on keeping his options open — his taking of free determinability as a goal — only plunges him all the more helplessly into a determination over which he has no control.

Again, the true aesthetic state of mind (if it exists) can never be a goal, only the way toward a goal.[9] Hence the last two historical numbers of the *Letters,* which make the gesture of superseding the concept of the aesthetic state of mind, but also, in their contradictoriness, reveal that such superseding cannot possibly occur *in a work of aesthetic theory,* where that concept is the culmination of the whole discipline. Thus, the possibility of a *reductio ad absurdum* of aesthetics as a whole arises, a showing that, in its quality as theory, aesthetics cannot help taking as a goal or culmination precisely the concept whose very nature is thereby utterly perverted. In fact, given that what is at stake in aesthetics is the rescue of the human self from the disruptive powers of theoretical abstraction, the indictment suggested by the *Letters* cuts even deeper. For of all the possible types of philosophical anthropology, disciplines of abstract thought that have humanity as their object, aesthetics now turns out to be the most pernicious, because it subjects to abstraction the most complete and integrated idea of humanity that can be imagined. Aesthetics, in this view, is thus a symptom, or indeed a principal *cause* of exactly those problems in history against which it is supposedly erected.

And yet, a clear critical exposé of this theoretical situation, showing how aesthetics, by being theory, contradicts itself and compromises its own glorified vision of a reintegrated humanity, would still itself inevitably *be* a work of aesthetics. By showing the fault of aesthetics in the disintegration of the self, it would still be advocating aesthetically an integration of that self; and by thus advocating what it is itself unable to take the responsibility for achieving, it would simply be repeating the hypocritical procedure of the aesthetics it criticizes. Therefore, the only possible method of dealing with the problem of aesthetics is the one that appears to be employed in the *Letters*: not to attack aesthetics, but to affirm it, to *develop* it to a level of conceptual completeness at which it cannot help but destroy itself by way of its own contradictions — including the two utterly incompatible views of human history that are required in its unfolding. The *Letters,* in this interpretation, would be an *unreadable* text, in the sense that one cannot possibly gain anything or learn anything by reading them. They are unreadable because they bring about the self-overthrow of exactly the generic or disciplinary presuppositions that make their specific statements intelligible. And if this conclusion seems outlandish, we need only recall that a similar idea is profiled in the *Letters* themselves, by the entirely gratuitous mention of "education" in the title. Only when we ask about the educative content or message of the *Letters* are we faced with the absence of any such content or message, and thus nudged toward the understanding that in the end this text is nothing but a kind of pantomime, an essentially mute performance of the emptiness or irrelevance of aesthetics as a whole. This, of course, does not mean that the *Letters* are a useless work, or that the reintegration of the self is a worthless project. By undermining aesthetics as a theoretical discipline, the *Letters* can in fact be said to *liberate* that project, the renewal of the self, from its theoretical shackles, thus perhaps to make it a real possibility after all.

In any event, the fact that an unmasking of the absurdity of aesthetics was certainly *not* part of Schiller's original project does not invalidate this interpretation. It is entirely possible that Schiller wrote practically all of the *Letters* without having a clear idea of where he was actually headed. After all, the difference between a positive reading of that text, as if it were a simple contribution to aesthetics, and the radically negative reading outlined above, is very small; the negative reading, again, asserts that the *Letters* undermine aesthetics precisely by developing its concepts to the last possible degree. In fact, the difference between these two possible readings boils down, basically, to how we visualize *the mind of the reader*. And fortunately, we have a very good idea of how Schiller himself visualizes his reader from about 1794 on. His principal and model reader is Goethe; and in a sense, in letters we will look at, he specifically appoints Goethe as his principal reader for the *Letters*.

The *Letters* are not discussed in great detail in the two men's correspondence, but the discussion that exists is interesting. It is clear, above all, that Schiller has great difficulty in justifying to himself and to Goethe precisely the quality of the *Letters* as theory. In his letter of 7 January 1795, he complains:

> Ich kann Ihnen nicht ausdrücken, wie peinlich mir das Gefühl oft ist, von einem Produkt dieser Art [*Wilhelm Meisters Lehrjahre*] in das philosophische Wesen hinein zu sehen. Dort ist alles so heiter, so lebendig, so harmonisch aufgelöst und so menschlich wahr, hier alles so strenge, so rigid und abstrakt und so höchst unnatürlich, weil alle Natur nur Synthesis und alle Philosophie Antithesis ist. Zwar darf ich mir das Zeugnis geben, in meinen Spekulationen der Natur so treu geblieben zu sein, als sich mit dem Begriff der Analysis verträgt. . . . Aber dennoch fühle ich nicht weniger lebhaft den unendlichen Abstand zwischen dem Leben und dem Räsonnement —

> [I cannot express how much it pains me to turn away from (your novel) and look back at philosophical matters. There everything is so cheerful, so

alive, so harmoniously relaxed and humanly true, while here everything is so strict, rigid and abstract, so extremely inhuman, since all nature is synthesis and all philosophy antithesis. True, I can claim to have been as true to nature in my speculations as the concept of analysis permits . . . but still I feel no less vividly the infinite distance between life and reasoning.]

And then, a short while later, in the letter of 27 February, he pulls himself together and asserts:

Ich bemächtige mich meines Stoffes immer mehr und entdecke mit jedem Schritt, den ich vorwärts tue, wie fest und sicher der Grund ist, auf welchem ich baute. Einen Einwurf, der das Ganze umstürzen könnte, habe ich von nun an nicht mehr zu fürchten. . . .

[I am getting more and more in control of my material, and I discover, with every forward step that I take, how solid and certain the ground is on which I have built. From now on I shall no longer fear any objection that might overturn my structure of thought.]

But precisely this vacillation shows how deeply the questions of system and abstraction concern him — as well they might in his relations with Goethe, whom he regards as a prime example of the strictly nonabstract mentality of "Genie" (23 August 1794; genius), which, without benefit of philosophical labor, knows more and knows it better than any philosopher.

The one thing genius supposedly cannot know about, however, is *itself.* Schiller, with a curious kind of adolescent tactlessness, cannot resist making this point directly to Goethe, first in the letter of 23 August 1794 where he says, "und nur weil es als ein Ganzes in Ihnen liegt, ist Ihnen Ihr eigener Reichtum verborgen . . . (weil das Genie sich immer selbst das größte Geheimnis ist)" (and only because it resides in you as a totality, is your own wealth of knowledge hidden from you . . . for genius is always, from its own point of view, the greatest mystery). And it then feels like a redoubling of this insensitive forwardness when he sends to Goethe, with a request that he read it and respond, the manuscript of the *Letters*, precisely that type of systematic, abstract work which the genius cannot be expected to profit from. Indeed, Schiller goes even further, in his letter of 20 October 1794, where he says to Goethe:

So verschieden die Werkzeuge auch sind, mit denen Sie und ich die Welt anfassen, und so verschieden die offensiven und defensiven Waffen, die wir führen, so glaube ich doch, daß wir auf Einen Hauptpunkt zielen. Sie werden in diesen Briefen Ihr Porträt finden, worunter ich gern Ihren Namen geschrieben hätte, wenn ich es nicht haßte, dem Gefühl denkender Leser vorzugreifen.

[As different as the tools may be with which you and I take hold of the world, as different the offensive and defensive weapons that we employ, still I believe that we aim for the same principal point. In these letters you will find your own portrait, under which I would gladly have written your name if I did not hate to anticipate the feeling of thoughtful readers.]

The concept of ambivalence does not begin to cover what is expressed here. Schiller insists that his thought is radically different from Goethe's, except perhaps in its ultimate goal, but then claims that he has observed, understood, and *recognizably* portrayed Goethe in (of all things) his work of systematic aesthetic philosophy — he means presumably that Goethe is an example of aesthetically whole mankind — and would Goethe now please respond to this claim. In fact, Goethe does respond, politely, on 26 October:

> Das mir übersandte Manuskript habe sogleich mit großem Vergnügen gelesen, ich schlurfte es auf Einen Zug hinunter. Wie uns ein köstlicher, unsrer Natur analoger Trank willig hinunter schleicht und auf der Zunge schon durch gute Stimmung des Nervensystems seine heilsame Wirkung zeigt, so waren mir diese Briefe angenehm und wohltätig, und wie sollte es anders sein? da ich das, was ich für recht seit langer Zeit erkannte, was ich teils lebte, teils zu leben wünschte, auf eine so zusammenhängende und edle Weise vorgetragen fand.

> [I have read the manuscript you sent me with great pleasure, I drank it all down in one draft. Just as a delicious drink, one that is analogous to our nature, slips easily down our throat and on our tongue already shows its wholesome effect by harmonizing our nervous system, thus these letters were pleasant and beneficial to me; and how could they have been otherwise? since I found what I have long recognized as right, and what I have in part lived and in part wished to live, set forth in such a cohesive and noble manner.]

It is clear, from this, that Goethe did very carefully read Schiller's letter — he talks about the *personal* resonance that Schiller had suggested — but it is not at all clear that he had read any of the *Letters* themselves. And the suggestion I wish to advance, as a complement to my negative reading of the *Letters,* is that Schiller eventually *accepted* this form of non-reading as the correct response to his text. If the reader is not seduced into the text's procedure of abstract speculation, if, like Goethe, the reader seems in fact not even to notice the work's rigid systematicity and forbidding abstractness, then precisely by this instinctive resistance to abstraction (but without being irrational), the reader demonstrates exactly that wholeness of humanity which is "portrayed" in the text as the goal it can never truly be. For this reader, moreover, that human wholeness is *not* a goal, but is simply the ever-repeated precondition of reading (or observing) and understanding.

To look at it differently, the *Letters* engage the reader's abstract reasoning power, but employ that engagement only to exhibit their own unreadability and so, at the same time, abandon the reader to his or her own strict immediate particularity. The text thus offers itself, as Schiller offered it, to an audience of Goethes, and in the process also does as much as is humanly possible toward the inherently aesthetic end of encouraging and perhaps even producing such an audience. There are many things in the story of Wilhelm Tell that attracted Schiller, but not least among them, I think, was the image of Tell as a non-speculative spirit, a kind of Goethe, who neither has nor needs an abstract grasp of the idea of freedom, but simply by being who he is, becomes the place where freedom *happens as a fact*. This seems to me a fairly clear allegory of the situation of Goethe as reader with respect to the idea of free human wholeness that is always aimed at, but can never be achieved, by aesthetics as an intellectual discipline. That human wholeness can *happen as a fact* only in something like Goethe's non-reading of the *Letters*. And Tell of course also shares with Goethe the virtue of analytic blindness; he can accept Parricida man to man ("Ihr seid ein Mensch — Ich bin es auch" [*Wilhelm Tell*, 3224]), but his fundamentally healthy being is utterly unreceptive to any conception of the depth to which Parricida reflects him and in effect indicts him. Tell is thus a development of the figure of Goethe as he is portrayed (and now identified by name after all) in the essay *Über naive und sentimentalische Dichtung*: Goethe, the naïve poetic spirit who in *Werther* achieves representational mastery over a sentimental story that by rights ought to lie beyond his ability to conceive of it (SW 5:738). And my point is that this figure, this Goethe, who accomplishes the paradox of unsentimentally imagining the sentimental, is already present — but behind the scenes — in the aesthetic *Letters,* as the reader of the unreadable, the reader who somehow manages to understand the book by a route that is entirely incommensurate with the book's own aesthetic systematics, a reader for whom aesthetics can therefore perhaps retain a certain validity in the very process of being reduced to the absurd.

What Schiller eventually recognizes, in other words, is that the loss or corruption of the self — to the extent that such a thing ever actually happens — must be thought of as a result of the process of *reading,* at least as we normally conceive of this process. It is in reading, more than anywhere else, that we attempt to leave behind our immediate, particular self for the sake of opening our mind to what we hope will be a thoroughly unfamiliar meaning, a meaning by which, once we have understood it, our mental horizon will be significantly changed. Hence, once again, the fundamental self-contradictoriness of aesthetics. For in reading a work of aesthetics, we not only undergo, but we positively embrace precisely that move of alienation against which aesthetics is supposedly erected. Or at least we do this if we read as we normally assume we are expected to. Goethe — even without reading the aesthetic *Letters* in detail — understands this problem perfectly, which is why he responds to Schiller by suggesting (with the metaphor of a drink's effect on the nervous system) not that the work had broadened his mind, but that it had nourished him almost corporeally, by suggesting, thus, that an entirely different form of reading is required in order to rescue the work from its contradictions. And Schiller eventually understands and accepts this suggestion, perhaps even before finishing the *Letters* in June 1795 (which would explain the change of subject in the last two numbers), and certainly before finishing the more freely and affirmatively paradoxical essay on naïve and sentimental poetry.

But where does this leave our argument as a whole? Schiller, in the *Aesthetic Letters,* creates an unreadable text, a text that does not so much assert as *perform* a reduction to absurdity of the whole aesthetic project as he had received it, especially from Kant. He does not, however, appear to be aware of his own accomplishment until fairly late in the game, when Goethe calls it to his attention, obliquely, by intimating that the only adequate reader of those *Letters* is the reader who does not need aesthetics in the first place, the utterly non-alienated reader for whom reading is nothing but an assimilation of the text to his own immediate personal requirements. Thus we are faced with two widely differing ideas of aesthetics. Either aesthetics (as practiced by Schiller) is at once both necessary and futile, humanity's tragic protest against a radically alienated condition from which there is no escape, since the protest itself only exacerbates it; or aesthetics (as, in effect, dismissed by Goethe) is a hypochondriac dramatizing of humanity's alienated condition, which in fact only creates the problems it pretends to respond to.

But if we look back at the path by which we have arrived at this point, we recognize that there is really no disagreement after all, for the negative or tragic reading of the *Letters* is established only by Schiller's *ceding authority,* in aesthetic matters, to Goethe, the (supposedly) alienationless reader. Thus, in the final analysis, the *Letters* are revealed as an even more paradoxical document than we had imagined: a systematic and detailed aesthetic argument by which not merely the contradictoriness, but the irrelevance or pointlessness of aesthetics is established — to the extent that an aesthetic argument, on this view, could "establish" anything at all. In any case, Schiller's ceding of authority in aesthetics is evident from the fact that he never again wrote a systematic treatise on the subject, even though there are plenty of loose ends to be tied up in the *Letters,* especially the idea of "education." And the one major essay that he did still write, on naïve and sentimental poetry, is not really aesthetic at all, but more an extended elaboration of his struggle, again, with the figure of Goethe, which Goethe himself acknowledges in his letter of 29 November 1795. Indeed, in view of the critical and paradoxical, rather than systematic quality of this essay, one perhaps even fancies that Schiller has here ceded to Goethe not only authority, but authorship itself.[10] It is true that later on, from time to time (for instance, in his letter of 9 July 1796), Schiller continues to insist on the

Letters as marking his own methodological position vis-à-vis Goethe. But in the end, such passages only remind us of how difficult and painful — while nevertheless genuine — that ceding of authority to Goethe, that acceptance of the irrelevance of aesthetics, really was for Schiller.

Only one question remains: is Goethe's position, as Schiller accepts it, really Goethe's position? And if so, is it really a "position" to begin with, not merely an involuntary manifestation of Goethe's "genius"? These questions can be answered, and answered in the affirmative, without our needing to treat a great deal of textual material, especially if we keep in mind, as a guide, Goethe's later, clearer pronouncements in the little essay "Nachlese zu Aristoteles Poetik" (Another Look at Aristotle's *Poetics)* from 1827. If the poet does his duty, says Goethe, if the work of poetry (in general, not only tragedy) is constructed and rounded off as a complete object, then the reader or spectator *will not be changed by it,* will not experience the slightest long-term effect upon his character, behavior, or perceptions (WA 41.2:251). The educative effect of poetry, and the whole aesthetic notion of a rehabilitation of the self, are thus simply denied.

And in order to understand how these ideas operate in poetic practice, we do not need to look much beyond one key passage in a text that critical tradition has long considered one of Goethe's most obviously educative endeavors, *Iphigenie auf Tauris.* In act 2, scene 1, Pylades apparently succeeds in dispelling for a moment Orest's deadly despair by reminding him of their friendship, and of how they had once dreamt together of great deeds (662–79). But curiously enough, he does not further encourage this reminiscence. He now admonishes Orest:

> Unendlich ist das Werk, das zu vollführen
> Die Seele dringt. Wir möchten jede That
> So groß gleich thun, als wie sie wächs't und wird,
> Wenn Jahre lang durch Länder und Geschlechter
> Der Mund der Dichter sie vermehrend wälzt.
> Es klingt so schön was unsre Väter thaten,
> Wenn es in stillen Abendschatten ruhend
> Der Jüngling mit dem Ton der Harfe schlürft;
> Und was wir thun, ist, wie es ihnen war,
> Voll Müh' und eitel Stückwerk!
> So laufen wir nach dem, was vor uns flieht,
> Und achten nicht des Weges den wir treten,
> Und sehen neben uns der Ahnherrn Tritte
> Und ihres Erdelebens Spuren kaum. (680–93)

[The work that our soul strives to complete is infinite. We would like to do each deed right now on as large a scale as it assumes over time when the song of poets has long propelled and magnified it through various lands and peoples. It sounds so beautiful, what our fathers did, when, resting in the quiet evening, a young man drinks it in with the sound of a harp; and what *we* do is, as their deeds were to them (our fathers), full of effort and mere patchwork. Thus we run after what flees from us, and pay no attention to the road we are traveling, and barely see *next to us* the footsteps of our ancestors and the traces of their earthly lives.]

In itself, the idea here is easy enough. The deeds from the past that we celebrate were, while they were actually being done, as effortful, clumsy, and fragmentary, and in fact as *insignificant* (lacking the completed form of achievements), as our own actions appear to us. The significance and exemplary quality of our forefathers' deeds are solely a result of their having been magnified and perfected in poetic representation. And yet, precisely this exemplary quality has a damaging effect, since it teaches us to expect our own deeds to appear to us in a poetically monumental form, which is of course impossible and keeps us from undertaking anything at all. "Ich halte nichts von dem, der von sich denkt / Wie ihn das Volk vielleicht erheben möchte" (697–98; I have no respect for the person who thinks of himself in the form in which his people might one day exalt him), says Pylades a bit further on.

But problems arise when we consider this passage in relation to our reading, here and now, of the poetic work *Iphigenie auf Tauris*, for Pylades appears to be arguing *in general* against the poetic magnification of existence, against the tendency of poetry to endow events with monumental significance, so that we may be edified and educated by them. Or more precisely, he is arguing against our habit of *reading* poetic works in this manner. Thus, unless we dismiss his words as nothing but an expression of his particular character, with no inherent truth-value, we are faced with a considerable dilemma. If we agree with both of his basic assertions, that poetry inevitably universalizes its content, and that such universalizing is morally damaging for the reader, then Goethe's text, *Iphigenie*, has become "unreadable" in exactly the same way as Schiller's *Aesthetic Letters* do, in their reduction to absurdity of their own procedure. The meaning of *Iphigenie* reduces the reading of *Iphigenie* to a moral absurdity. And the only hope we have of avoiding this dilemma is by finding a way to read *Iphigenie* without buying into its universalizing educative quality as poetry, just as Goethe suggests the possibility of reading the *Aesthetic Letters* without buying into their procedure as systematic philosophical aesthetics.

Indeed, the relation here between *Iphigenie* and the *Aesthetic Letters* may be more than one of mere analogy. For surely the aesthetically rehabilitated and reintegrated self is one of those delusive poetic magnifications of existence that Pylades is talking about, by which we are induced not to strive, but merely to despair over our own actual condition. And when Goethe responds to the *Letters* by saying he has received them not as a systematic challenge, but as a soothing drink, surely he is not merely preening himself on possessing the natural "genius" Schiller has credited him with. On the contrary, he is saying, as Pylades would say, that the idea that mankind once possessed a more perfect self than ours is a poetic delusion, that our mode of individual being is not substantially either more or less disintegrated than the Greeks', and that we need only read as the people we *are* — without looking for universal truths or lessons or edification that might change us — in order to leave the specter of aesthetics, the aesthetic Furies who torment us with our supposed degeneracy, behind us.

The ultimate lesson of *Iphigenie,* therefore, is that we must not seek any lesson in *Iphigenie.* In fact, the speech of Pylades on which we have based this inference merely underscores a quality of the play that is already fairly clear from the general disposition of motifs and incidents. If the play is really about an eighteenth-century notion of "humanity" — as many of the speeches in it suggest — then why was this particular work of Euripides chosen for adaptation, in which the whole plot rests on a supernatural premise, a divine action that cannot, by any stretch of reasoning, be reduced to the "human"? This incongruity operates not only in general, but also more pointedly in act 3, scene 1, where Orest has perfectly good reason to think the priestess has gone mad (1188–89), which interferes with the motif of his own supposedly irrational despair. And why does Goethe handle the riddling oracle as he does? Why not let the riddle be solved, the true "sister" be identified, *before* Iphigenie's climactic plea for reconciliation (2064–94)? As the scene stands, Iphigenie's humane pleading fails to solve the plot's problems, and a verbal gimmick is needed to take up the slack. And what about Thoas? The play's politically experienced audience has a very good idea of what happens to lame-duck rulers, kings for whom no clear line of succession exists. Their courts break down into factions, intriguing against one another with a view to producing the next king, and the present king is lucky if he does not get assassinated in the process. For all her humane sentiments (2152–74), this is the situation in which Iphigenie is leaving her royal benefactor.

The more one looks at this work, the more one recognizes that it is practically made of incongruities, and what purpose can this kind of structure have if not to thwart the reader's or spectator's universalizing appetite, to deny us anything that might be regarded as a general lesson? Many, if not most, Goethe scholars would counter this suggestion by referring not to the text of the play itself, but to a poem of Goethe's from 1827, addressed to the actor Krüger and sent with a copy of *Iphigenie.*

> Was der Dichter diesem Bande
> Glaubend, hoffend anvertraut,
> Werd' im Kreise deutscher Lande
> Durch des Künstlers Wirken laut.
> So im Handeln, so im Sprechen
> Liebevoll verkünd' es weit:

> Alle menschliche Gebrechen
> Sühnet reine Menschlichkeit. (WA 4:277)

[What the poet, in faith and hope, has entrusted to this volume, let it become public in the circle of German lands through the artist's agency. Thus in acting, thus in speaking, lovingly proclaim it abroad. . . .]

The last lines (not yet translated above) are normally read as Goethe's idea of the lesson to be learned from the play *Iphigenie*. But in my opinion those lines are normally not "read" at all, but merely garbled. Do they really state that "all human weaknesses" are atoned for, or made good, or excused, or cancelled out, by "pure humanity"?

First of all, there is a word play here. A much more expectable object than *Gebrechen* (faults, lacks, afflictions), for the verb *sühnen* (assuming it really means "atone for"), would be *Verbrechen* (crimes). In order to atone for something, one must first be responsible for it, and *Gebrechen* are, pretty unambiguously, faults that one is *not* responsible for. Does *sühnen*, then, really mean "atone for"? This question turns out to be trickier than one might expect, since in the whole huge corpus of Goethe's utterances (including letters and conversations), the present poem is the *only* place where Goethe uses that verb.[11] The verb he normally uses to denote atonement, or the making good of a wrong, the expiation or cleansing of guilt, is *entsühnen* — which appears four times in *Iphigenie* itself (1617, 1702, 1969, 2138). Moreover, if a two-syllable verb is needed, a trochee, with roughly the meaning of *entsühnen*, why does Goethe not use *heilet* or *tilget* (heals or cancels), or if the meaning tends more toward "alleviate," why not *mildert* or *lindert?* At least one of these suggestions has a parallel elsewhere in Goethe, in the *Maskenzug* of 1818 where we read:

> O, warum schaut er nicht, in diesen Tagen,
> Durch Menschlichkeit geheilt die schwersten Plagen!
> (WA 16:271)

[Oh why does he not see, these days, that the greatest ills are healed by humanity.]

But what Goethe does in the poem on *Iphigenie* is choose a strange verb, a verb he has never used before and will never use again. Surely he has a special purpose in mind.

The verb *sühnen*, as I have said, denotes responsibility with respect to its object, and, unlike *entsühnen*, includes the idea of *paying*, or making reparation for a wrong.[12] But *Gebrechen*, unlike *Verbrechen*, are faults for which one is normally not responsible. What the last lines of the poem say, therefore, is that "pure humanity" *assumes* responsibility for "alle menschliche Gebrechen." But while some *Gebrechen* or failings may be common to all humans, it is certainly true that *all* such failings include an infinite number of peculiar traits that characterize only this or that particular individual at particular times. Therefore, if pure humanity assumes responsibility as the source of "*all* human failings," then it follows that "pure humanity" *is not something that all humans have in common*. It is certainly not a "perfected humanity," not a humanity purified of faults, not a kind of universal virtue that wipes away, or cancels out, human afflictions. It follows, in fact, that "pure humanity" is not even the same thing in different circumstances; or at least it cannot be known to be the same thing. It is a quality that can only be known "locally," in immediate experience, and cannot be abstracted from those individual peculiarities of experience for which it assumes responsibility. What is "lovingly proclaimed," in the poem as in the play *Iphigenie,* is thus in effect immediate experience itself, the utter particularity of what we actually are, except that even to make *this* statement is to abstract illegitimately from the immediacy it means. To make any general statement at all, even if that statement affirms the strictly particular, is to take the first useless step toward "aesthetics," which, as an abstract discipline, simply cannot engage the immediate local particularity of human life without seeking to incorporate it into an ideal, supposedly reconstituted human nature. "Humanity," in other words, does not by any means transcend temporary human failings, but is indissolubly bound to them, an idea which is also reflected in Goethe's playing (WA 5.1:230, 279) on *Menschlichkeit* ("humanity," singular) and *Menschlichkeiten* ("human failings," plural).

Like the spectator of tragedy, therefore, in Goethe's reading of Aristotle, we must learn to dispense with the expectation of being edified or in any sense changed by what we read. Or rather, we must *have* dispensed with that expectation, since even this last step of "learning," as an act, would violate its own content. For the same reason, it would be incorrect to say that Schiller is confirmed by Goethe in an understanding of the *contradictoriness* of aesthetics, an understanding he had been groping toward in the *Aesthetic Letters* without fully knowing it. For aesthetics does not *become* contradictory until after one has committed oneself to precisely the method of abstraction that brings about its contradictions. With respect to the domain and content of poetry, rather, with respect to the strict immediacy and particularity of life as it is actually lived — with respect, in other words, to its own avowed object — aesthetics must be recognized as *irrelevant*.

And finally, if the paradox seems overstrained when we speak of a work whose ultimate lesson is that it has no lesson, let us recall that *Iphigenie* is only a first step toward realizing this idea. The most important and obvious instance is the book Goethe was actually working on when he claimed to have imbibed Schiller's *Letters* as a soothing drink, *Wilhelm Meisters Lehrjahre.* Any lesson learned from this novel becomes significant only to the extent that we apply it to our own lives; and what

Wilhelm's experience demonstrates is precisely that such generalizing from experience is inevitably misleading.[13] Again, the problem we are presented with is one of learning how to read, of reading without taking the aesthetic step of attempting to appropriate from the text some human essence, some radical liberation, some cure for our supposedly damaged existential integrity. As Goethe says later of Laurence Sterne:

> So sehr uns der Anblick einer freien Seele dieser Art ergötzt, eben so sehr werden wir gerade in diesem Fall erinnert, daß wir von allem dem, wenigstens von dem meisten, was uns entzückt, nichts in uns aufnehmen dürfen. (WA 42.2: 204)

> [As much as we enjoy the sight of this kind of free soul, to the same extent, precisely in this case, we are reminded that of everything that delights us here, or at least of most of it, we may absorb no part into ourselves.]

Notes

[1] If it was ever excusable to be blind to the nationalistic dimension of the concept of German "classicism" (*Klassik*), which implies undying value and is strictly distinguished from *Klassizismus*, which does not — then it stopped being so with the publication of *Die Klassik-Legende*, ed. Reinhold Grimm and Jost Hermand (Frankfurt am Main: Athenäum, 1971). Three of the book's essays are important in this regard. Wilfried Malsch, "Die geistesgeschichtliche Legende der deutschen Klassik" (108–40), suggests fundamental intellectual oppositions between the thinking of authors in the "classical" period itself and the image of that period in later writing. Max L. Baeumer, "Der Begriff 'klassisch' bei Goethe und Schiller" (17–49), summarizes lucidly eighteenth-century usage of the notion of the "classical," including its decidedly non-nationalistic use by Goethe. And above all, Klaus L. Berghahn, "Von Weimar nach Versailles: Zur Entstehung der Klassik-Legende im 19. Jahrhundert" (50–78), shows how the development of German nationalism co-opts the idea of the "classical" and in the process distorts and obscures the actual history of writing in Germany. Other important early works in the demystifying of German *Klassik* include René Wellek, "Das Wort und der Begriff 'Klassizismus' in der Literaturgeschichte," *Schweizer Monatshefte*, 45 (1969), 154–73, and Eva D. Becker, "'Klassiker' in der deutschen Literaturgeschichtsschreibung zwischen 1780 und 1860," in *Zur Literatur der Restaurationsepoche 1815–1848*, ed. Jost Hermand and Manfred Windfuhr (Stuttgart: Metzler, 1970), 349–70. But why, then, does the idea of a German *Klassik* persist even today? If we worry about this question enough, we begin to get a feel for the central concept in W. Daniel Wilson, *Das Goethe-Tabu: Protest und Menschenrechte im klassischen Weimar* (Munich: DTV, 1999). There are certain things people simply don't want to think about Goethe. And while Wilson's specific concern is human rights, his arguments also highlight, more generally, Goethe's complete *lack of principle*, a trait which, even in his own time, people (like Schiller) euphemized by speaking of his "natural genius." Part of what I hope to show in the present essay is that with respect to aesthetics, precisely this character

trait supports an historically significant move on Goethe's part, and Schiller's along with him.

[2] Andrew Bowie, *Aesthetics and Subjectivity: from Kant to Nietzsche* (Manchester: Manchester UP, 1990), 4.

[3] The translation of Wilkinson and Willoughby, in Friedrich Schiller, *Essays*, ed. Walter Hinderer and Daniel O. Dahlstrom (New York: Continuum, 1995), 94–95. Henceforth cited as "W/W."

[4] Compare Terry Eagleton, *The Ideology of the Aesthetic* (Oxford: Oxford UP, 1990), 2–3: "With the birth of the aesthetic, then, the sphere of art itself begins to suffer something of the abstraction and formalization characteristic of modern theory in general; yet the aesthetic is nevertheless thought to retain a charge of irreducible particularity, providing us with a kind of paradigm of what a non-alienated mode of cognition might look like. Aesthetics is thus always a contradictory, self-undoing sort of project, which in promoting the theoretical value of its object risks emptying it of exactly that specificity or ineffability which was thought to rank among its most precious features."

[5] See my *Beyond Theory: Eighteenth-Century German Literature and the Poetics of Irony* (Ithaca: Cornell UP, 1993), Ch. 3, "Lessing's *Laokoon*: The Poetics of Experience," 116–61. The comparison between Hellenic and later European modes of experiencing is found mainly in chapter 1 of *Laokoon*: see Gotthold Ephraim Lessing, *Werke*, 8 vols., edited by Herbert G. Göpfert (Munich: Hanser, 1970–79), 6:12–15. The idea that epic poetry must make us forget its words and undergo directly "die wahren sinnlichen Eindrücke [der] Gegenstände" occurs in chapter 17, 6:110.

[6] Karl Philipp Moritz, *Beiträge zur Ästhetik*, ed. Hans Joachim Schrimpf and Hans Adler (Mainz: Dieterich, 1989), 9–10. Martha Woodmansee, *The Author, Art, and the Market: Rereading the History of Aesthetics* (New York: Columbia UP, 1994), and Jonathan M. Hess, *Reconstituting the Body Politic: Enlightenment, Public Culture and the Invention of Aesthetic Autonomy* (Detroit: Wayne State UP, 1999), both attribute *originary* significance to this text. Aesthetics, in their view, does not come into its own, does not really begin, until it is de-instrumentalized by Moritz, an event that Woodmansee describes as a "radical departure" (12), while Hess sees Kant's version of Moritz's supposed innovation as marking a "paradigm shift" (159), which idea he claims to borrow (265) from Manfred Frank, *Einführung in die frühromantische Ästhetik* (Frankfurt am Main: Suhrkamp, 1989), 38. (In fact, Frank is much more circumspect. He first suggests the idea of a *Paradigmenwechsel* in discussing Novalis's debt to Kant [30]; but in the passage Hess refers to [38], he is still only *asking* whether this idea is justified, and continues to suggest doubts even later [50]. His decision seems to be, finally, that there is after all a radical change in the idea of art from the eighteenth to the nineteenth century, but that this change takes considerable time to develop, in the works of Schiller and the post-Kantian idealists [103], not that it is suddenly all there in Kant and Moritz.) But is Moritz's thinking really unprecedented — his idea of a perfectly self-contained artistic realm that requires no justification in the form of social or individual usefulness? Again the example of Lessing is instructive; for surely the basic argument of *Laokoon*, that the artistic medium radically determines a work's fictional or representational content,

asserts artistic autonomy (art's giving itself its own laws, regardless of anyone's inclinations or needs) in much more specific terms than Moritz ever arrives at. In any case, the assertion that an idea on the scale of aesthetic autonomy is invented, or originates, in one particular text, is always ill-advised; for it presupposes a reliable interpretive knowledge of all other contemporary texts in which the idea might conceivably be found. Klopstock's essay "Von dem Range der schönen Künste und der schönen Wissenschaften" (1758), for instance, is full of obviously "instrumentalist" statements about art. But when the arrival of *Tanzkunst* at the end overthrows the essay's whole order of concepts, how deep does the irony cut? Perhaps to the very idea of art as instrument?

[7] Consider, for example, in letter 19, the paragraph beginning, "Hier müssen wir uns nun erinnern . . ." (SW 5:629), which states that the "transcendental philosopher," unlike the "metaphysician," does not have to worry about contradictions that occur in his conceptual edifices: ". . . so stellt er beide [sich scheinbar widersprechenden] Begriffe mit vollkommner Befugnis als gleich notwendige Bedingungen der Erfahrung auf, ohne sich weiter um ihre Vereinbarkeit zu bekümmern." It almost seems that Schiller is parodying himself here, or even parodying Kant. And curiously enough, this whole passage is found, copied down, in Kant's own posthumous papers. See *Schillers Sämtliche Werke: Säkular-Ausgabe*, 16 vols. (Stuttgart and Berlin: 1904), 12:372. In fact, in the balance of this paragraph, where he insists on a strict distinction between "the mind itself" and the two drives that after all constitute that mind (a textbook example of *petitio principii*), I think Schiller had to be aware of the logical skullduggery he is engaged in.

[8] Woodmansee argues in her chapter on Schiller (57–86) that the *Letters* show a kind of hypocrisy, that the "expressly political" aim asserted at the beginning turns out only to mask "the very material existential considerations of a professional writer in Germany at the end of the eighteenth century" (58–59). Wolfdietrich Rasch, in "Schein, Spiel und Kunst in der Anschauung Schillers," *Wirkendes Wort*, 10 (1960), 2–13, advances the radical suggestion that Schiller is seeking to create an "aesthetic" effect with the *Letters* themselves.

[9] For much of this same argument, but oriented in a different direction, see my "Trinitarische Humanität: Dichtung und Geschichte bei Schiller," in *Friedrich Schiller: Kunst, Humanität und Politik in der späten Aufklärung*, ed. Wolfgang Wittkowski (Tübingen: Niemeyer, 1982), 164–77.

[10] On Goethe as in a sense the true author of *Über naive und sentimentalische Dichtung*, see my *Goethe as Woman: The Undoing of Literature* (Detroit: Wayne State UP, 2001), 217–19.

[11] At least this is true if the search function for the on-line WA can be trusted.

[12] Especially the phrase "zur Sühne," as Goethe uses it, suggests reparation for a wrong committed. See, for example, book six of *Reineke Fuchs*, 186, and 388–413, where the phrase occurs a number of times. Also, in letters, see WA 4. 27:241, 50:90.

[13] See my *Beyond Theory*, 41–44.

Goethe's "Classical" Science

Astrida Orle Tantillo

MANY CONSIDER THE birth of Weimar Classicism to have occurred because of a scientific debate: the friendship of the two greats of German classicism, Schiller and Goethe, began in 1794 over a heated, but ultimately friendly, discussion about the metamorphosis of plants. Although Goethe had known Schiller since 1788, they were not friends. Goethe had moved beyond his Sturm und Drang period and was repelled by the strong, emotional tone of Schiller's *Die Räuber* (The Robbers, 1781) and *Don Carlos* (1787). He believed that his aesthetic and philosophical differences with Schiller were too great ever to permit friendship or collaboration. The two men were, in Goethe's view, intellectual antipodes of each other. Goethe avoided Schiller, and Goethe's aloof manner rightly offended Schiller. Then, one day in July of 1794, the two men happened to leave a scientific meeting together. The meeting that they had attended was one of the regular, monthly meetings of a scientific society, the *Naturforschende Gesellschaft in Jena*, a society organized by the botanist, August Johann Georg Karl Batsch (1761–1802). This society met between the years 1793 and 1805. Schiller was an honorary member of the group; Goethe often participated in its meetings and was elected president in 1804. Thus, Goethe's conversation with Schiller about plants did not occur in a vacuum, but was a part of the lively intellectual atmosphere in Weimar. The topics of this society were often closely related to those of another society in Weimar, the *Freitagsgesellschaft*, a group that met from 1791–97. The members of this society were charged to present their current research to the others. Thus, the doctor/chemist/apothecary Wilhelm Heinrich Sebastian Buchholz (1734–98) discussed his latest chemical findings, the doctor Christoph Wilhelm Hufeland (1762–1836) discussed his work *Makrobiotik oder die Kunst, das menschliche Leben zu verlängern* (Macrobiotics, or the Art of Prolonging Human Life, 1797), and Goethe presented his theory of colors.

Goethe and Schiller's conversation about plants in July of 1794 (recounted by Goethe in his 1817 essay "Glückliches Ereignis" [Fortunate Encounter]), was quite intense. Schiller quite pointedly questioned Goethe's theories. Goethe believed that a symbolic plant could explain the growth and development of all plants. After Goethe had sketched such a plant, Schiller shook his head and said: "Das ist keine Erfahrung, das ist eine Idee"[1] (that is not an experience — that is an idea). For Schiller, a symbolic plant could not exist in the real world of experience, but only in an ideal one. The mind could create categories outside of the realm of experience. For Goethe, ideas were inextricably linked to direct experiences and indeed arose from them. He was annoyed at Schiller's comment and realized that it epitomized the crux of their differences. He replied: "Das kann mir aber sehr lieb sein, daß ich Ideen habe ohne es zu wissen, und sie sogar mit Augen sehe" (FA 24:437; Then I may rejoice that I have ideas without knowing it, and can even see them with my own eyes, 12:20[2]). Schiller, however, managed in the end to pacify Goethe: they agreed to disagree, and the great period of their collaboration began.

Goethe's account, however, not only solidified the view of the two men's lives and works in terms of polar, albeit complementary, characteristics. It has also served to color the way in which Goethe's scientific works have been interpreted. The fact that he sketched "eine symbolische Pflanze" (a symbolic plant) has led generations of scholars to view Goethe's science during his "classical" period in terms of Platonic forms — as forms that are generally understood to be universal and constant. Scholars viewed this account as a clear indication that Goethe was an idealist who believed in static and universal concepts. Moreover, many further argued that the only way in which these forms could be put into motion was through Aristotelian, teleological striving — a striving that is generally considered to tend toward particular, constant, and hierarchical goals. Goethe's most famous scientific essay, "Versuch, die Metamorphose der Pflanzen zu erklären" (Essay on the Metamorphosis of Plants, 1790), thus became the account of how an ideal form (the leaf) could, through an Aristotelian, teleological drive, achieve the pinnacle of nature: reproduction. In a similar vein, scholars have generally viewed Goethe's use of such terms as *Typus* (type) or *Budget* in his essays on comparative anatomy as clear indications of his allegiance to idealized and regular forms. In other words, scholars viewed Goethe's science as classical in the sense that it closely followed models that were based on Platonic and Aristotelian interpretations. This essay takes issue with viewing Goethe's scientific works as "classical" in this way and argues instead that his works are classical in a broader sense.

Classical Categorization

Of course, it is difficult to classify any group of works according to one category, and the term "Weimar Classicism" is a particularly complicated one in reference to Goethe's science for several reasons. First, if one defines the period based on Goethe's collaboration with Schiller, then one must exclude Goethe's important scientific work, the aforementioned "Versuch, die Metamorphose der Pflanzen zu erklären," which he wrote four years before their friendship. Although Schiller clearly influenced Goethe's scientific works (especially his essays on comparative anatomy), Goethe never departed from his early conviction that scientific ideas, even seemingly mystical ones, were based on empirical observations. Second, if one instead turns to Goethe's Italian journey as the crystallizing event in establishing a period of classical activity, then one forces an arbitrary break between his earlier works on the intermaxillary bone (1784–86) and granite (1784) and his later works on plants and comparative anatomy. Despite their differences in style and intended audiences and topics, all these works have central themes in common, including the following: the continuity of nature, the close relationship between human beings and nature, and nature's ability to take one simple principle or object and vary it in infinite ways.

A further difficulty in using the term "Weimar Classicism" in connection with Goethe's scientific views is that it implies that his scientific works were somehow created if not in a vacuum, than at least in a very particular petri dish in Weimar. This is not to imply that Goethe was not heavily influenced by his collaborations with many individuals from the Weimar and Jena areas. He worked closely with local scientific societies, scientists, industrialists, and professors. He studied botany with Batsch and anatomy with Justus Christian Loder (1753–1832). He had chemical consultations with Johann Friedrich August Göttling (1753–1809), as well as with Johann Wolfgang Döbereiner (1780–1849), and he was quite pleased that the Jena physicist, Thomas Johann Seebeck (1770–1831), accepted the principles of his *Farbenlehre* (Theory of Colors, 1810).[3] However much Goethe relied on and was stimulated by the local talent, the influences on his scientific works were far reaching. He actively corresponded with prominent European scientists and closely followed the scientific advances and debates of the day. He had studied the works of George-Louis Leclerc, Comte de Buffon (1707–88) as a student in Leipzig and was familiar with the works of the most prominent eighteenth-century scientists, including the renowned botanist Carl von Linnaeus (1707–1778), the doctor and preformationist Albrecht von Haller (1708–1778), the epigenesist Caspar Friedrich Wolff (1734–94), the Swiss naturalist Charles Bonnet (1720–1793), and even the botanical writings of the philosopher Jean-Jacques Rousseau (1712–1778). He also had direct contact with several scientific luminaries of his day: he visited with comparative anatomist Johann Friedrich Blumenbach (1752–1840) in Göttingen, had numerous discussions with the anatomist Samuel Thomas Sömmerring (1755–1830), corresponded with the Dutch anatomist Peter Camper (1722–89), and met four times and corresponded for years with the explorer Georg Forster (1754–94). He also had extensive personal contact with both Humboldt brothers: the linguist and philosopher Wilhelm (1767–1835) interacted with Goethe more on literary issues, while the explorer and scientist Alexander (1769–1859), who was to become one of the most famous men of Europe of his day, influenced his scientific works in significant ways.

Similarly, Goethe also followed the philosophical developments of the day. In a short essay of 1820, "Einwirkung der neueren Philosophie" (The Influence of Modern Philosophy), he describes the process that he underwent in his attempts to understand Kantian philosophy (FA 24:442–46). He discusses his difficulties in understanding Kant's *Kritik der reinen Vernunft* (Critique of Pure Reason, 1781) and how Herder's disagreements with Kant as well as his own long conversations with Schiller shaped his reading of Kant. Within this essay, he also further credits the great philosophers around him at the time — Johann Gottlieb Fichte, Friedrich Wilhelm Joseph Schelling, Georg Wilhelm Friedrich Hegel — with helping him understand the "sage" from Königsberg, Kant. And although Goethe states that he eventually made progress with the *Kritik der reinen Vernunft,* he ultimately found the *Kritik der Urteilskraft* (Critique of Judgment, 1790) much more comprehensible and amenable to his own natural studies. Specifically, he approved of the way in which Kant discussed the relationship between art and nature and was very pleased to see Kant's rejection of certain strands of teleology. Indeed, it is noteworthy that many of these same themes are developed in Goethe's *Metamorphose der Pflanzen,* which was published the same year as Kant's *Kritik der Urteilskraft.*

Despite the artificial nature of categorizing periods or works in an author's life, the term classicism is central to a discussion of Goethe's life and works. After all, Goethe's contemporaries spoke of his classicism and the classical influences on his works. Indeed, Goethe credits himself and Schiller with creating the literary categories of German Classicism and Romanticism. In a conversation with Eckermann (21 March 1830), he then somewhat grumpily reports that the terms were soon taken up by the Schlegel brothers and spread about so that now "everybody" uses them. Often, especially in the case of Goethe's literary supporters, "classicism" became a catchall term of praise. It connoted elevation, restraint, resignation, harmony, and high culture. For example, in the debates that raged after his publication of the highly controversial novel, *Die Wahlverwandtschaften,* those who wished to defend it against charges of immorality pointed to its "classical elements": its sense of tragedy, economy, and its portrayal of the mind triumphing over matter.[4] In other words, the term "classical" had become part of the cultural dialog of the time and was central in the earliest reception and, I would argue, misconceptions, of Goethe's work.

Relying on narrow definitions of classicism, many commentators have thus argued that Goethe's "classical" and primarily rule-based natural philosophy reflects the religious and mystical bent of a pious, if "pagan" or "heathen" man. Such an interpretation of his scientific corpus further reinforces an image of a highly conservative Goethe whose philosophy may be easily divided into strict categories, whether those of polar hierarchies (masculine over feminine, mind over body, etc.), goal-driven striving, or orderly, step-by-step progressions. In other words, some view Goethe's science as classical because it mirrors an understanding of classicism that emphasizes the orderliness, restraint, and regularity of Greek art and philosophy.

This essay challenges such views of Goethe's classicism. By turning to his scientific works, it argues that a re-examination of Goethe's own understanding of classicism broadens the term to mean very different things. It is quite clear that he actively sought traditional, classical models throughout his works, whether scientific or literary. His *Italienische Reise* (1816–17) is all about his attempts to rediscover and re-invent classicism for the modern age. But it is important to realize that, although Goethe emulated certain aspects of classical art and thought in his works, he was quite critical of others. Moreover, Goethe did not limit his classical models to those defined by Winckelmann's famous characterization of antiquity as "eine edle Einfalt und eine stille Größe" (a noble simplicity and quiet grandeur). Rather, Goethe also embraced those classical models that displayed chaos, passion, disruption, and disorder. Homer, Lucretius, Catullus, and Aristophanes were as much a part of the classical tradition for Goethe as were Plato, Aristotle, and the Greek tragedians. It is, I believe, no coincidence that his thoughts in Sicily kept turning to the archetypal plant while working on a play inspired by Homer, *Nausikaa* (17 April 1787): both the plant (as I will argue) and Homer represent concepts that can be disruptive and characterized by change. In the past, however, scholars have emphasized only the regular and more contained aspects of Goethe's science, and consequently, have created a skewed version of its ultimate message.

A close study of Goethe's scientific texts presents a view of nature that is much more unwieldy and disruptive than commonly accepted under the traditional classical model. This essay thus revisits the accepted notion that Goethe viewed nature as primarily regular, peaceful, and linear. Instead, it argues that Goethean nature, at its heart, is also irregular, competitive, and unpredictable. His natural philosophy thus rejects the classical tradition that emphasizes orderliness and stability. However, rather than completely rejecting classical models as sources of Goethe's natural philosophy, this essay argues that Goethe's science is classical in a broader sense. His scientific works illustrate the influences of the ancients who stressed disorder and creativity: Homer, the pre-Socratics, and Lucretius. Goethean science is thus not solely or even primarily modeled on the traditional understanding of Platonic forms or Aristotelian teleology, but also on the more dynamic and unpredictable figure of Proteus, a figure that can change its shape and essence at will.

In the classical tradition, Proteus is a minor sea-god, who in the *Odyssey* is characterized as much by his ability to take on any shape or form as by his reputation for being knowledgeable and truthful (but only when subdued by force and cunning). In the story, Menelaus is able to subdue this god by first imitating nature and then by using force. He disguises himself as a seal to approach Proteus and then captures him by holding him fast as he changes into a variety of forms — whether living (a tree, various animals) or inanimate (water). Because Menelaus is able to hold onto these ever-changing forms, he is able to receive the answers from Proteus that he seeks. In a conversation with Friedrich Wilhelm Riemer (1 March 1805), Goethe remarks that this Homeric scene would be an apt motto for a society of chemists. Proteus would represent nature while Menelaus would be a symbol of the chemist who forces nature's hand.

One can further see the relevance of the Protean image in Goethe's most mature work, *Faust, Part II*. Proteus is similarly depicted here, as in Homer, as a creature of knowledge and one who is able to change forms. His knowledge in this work, however, is of a more profound nature: his ability to change forms is linked with the creation of life itself. Homunculus, a manufactured and formless being, is to go to Proteus to ask: "Wie man entstehn und sich verwandeln kann" (8153; How man originates and how he can transform himself). This time, however, Proteus is not subdued by force, but by cunning. Thales manipulates the situation so that Proteus gives in to his own acute sense of curiosity and thus answers the question of how one can come into being. The answer is a somewhat violent one. Homunculus can only gain life by consuming other lives:

> Im weiten Meere mußt du anbeginnen!
> Da fängt man erst im kleinen an
> Und freut sich, Kleinste zu verschlingen,
> Man wächst so nach und nach heran
> Und bildet sich zu höherem Vollbringen. (8260–64)

[You must begin out in the open sea. / That's where you start on a small scale / glad to ingest the smallest creatures; / little by little you'll increase in size / and put yourself in shape for loftier achievements. (2:210)]

Goethe's depiction of Proteus within *Faust* is similar to his use of the term Protean in his scientific works, and indeed this figure symbolizes many of the central aspects of Goethe's philosophy of nature, namely: (1) scientists must find a way to hold nature fast if they are to understand its malleability; and (2) nature itself is not a placid, orderly entity, but one that is brutal, demanding that organisms be fiercely competitive to survive and thrive.

"Versuch die Metamorphose der Pflanzen zu Erklären"

Goethe's essay on plant metamorphosis is his best known scientific work from the Weimar Classical period. We know a great deal about its composition and reception because Goethe himself wrote for decades about these aspects of the essay. His *Italienische Reise* recounts his search for an archetypal plant, while several short essays[5] retell minute details of its history, whether of the difficult search for a publisher, its poor reception among scientists and laymen (including lists of those scientists who cited the essay[6]), or its relationship to his other scientific works. One of the main claims of the essay is that every part of a flowering plant (calyx, petals, stamens, etc.) is a modified version of the leaf. The leaf, moreover, achieves these more and more specialized/intensified forms of itself through six alternating polar phases of expansion and contraction. Thus, the calyx is formed during a period of contraction, the petals during a period of expansion, and so on.

That Goethe throughout the essay emphasizes the single and simple form of the leaf as the unifying element of development has led many scholars to equate this form with Platonic idealism. In the words of Ernst Mayr, the prominent zoologist and historian of science, Goethe's study of the leaf was "a fusion of Plato's essentialism with aesthetic principles."[7] According to this view, the leaf becomes a kind of Platonic and static form that one recognizes under its varied manifestations. A close look at both Goethe's essay and his numerous supplementary essays on it, however, point to a different scientific and philosophical perspective. The most important aspect of the leaf in this essay is not its static qualities, but its malleable ones. What is remarkable about the plant's development is not that a stable form is at the root, so to speak, of every organ, but that a simple form may change and transform into a myriad of forms. In other words, Goethe emphasizes movement and change over stasis. Envisioning a form, whether an actual leaf or the symbolic plant discussed with Schiller, is thus useful not for finding what is universal (as in the case of Plato), but for tracking the changing particulars. The central aspect of the theory of the leaf is that one organ can be *transformed* into myriad and even irregular forms.

Throughout his scientific corpus, Goethe speaks of the economy of nature and how it can through small variations and limited principles take the most basic of elements and create the most infinite and varied forms.[8] In the case of plant metamorphosis, he stresses repeatedly the malleable and changeable aspects of this process. Nearly thirty years after Goethe first published his essay, he republished it in 1817 in his morphological journal, *Zur Morphologie,* and prefaced it with several shorter essays. In one of these essays, "Die Absicht eingeleitet" (The Purpose Set Forth), he is highly critical of the German concept of *Gestalt*. In discussing this term, which, roughly translated, means "form," Goethe dismisses the term's ability to express what lies at the heart of nature — its power to change and transform: "[Der Deutsche] abstrahiert bei diesem Ausdruck von dem Beweglichen, er nimmt an, daß ein Zusammengehöriges festgestellt, abgeschlossen und in seinem Charakter fixiert sei" (FA 24:392; With this expression the Germans abstract from what is mutable and assume that an interrelated whole is identified, defined, and fixed in its character). He rejects the term *Gestalt* because it focuses too much on what is fixed instead of on that which constantly changes. Instead, he turns to the word *Bildung* (in this case, formation) because it includes the all important concept of malleability within it, since it may be used to describe the process of formation, as well as its end product.

In many ways, scholars treated Goethe's leaf in terms of *Gestalt* and thus viewed nature precisely in the way Goethe warns against: they emphasized its abstract form instead of its ability to transform from one organ into another. They thus focused upon the fixed aspects of nature, its form, rather than on its power to change and transform, its *Bildung*. In the quotation above, Goethe rejects such codification of organic forms, because a close examination of nature and its forms reveals "daß nirgend ein Bestehendes, nirgend ein Ruhendes, ein Abgeschlossenes vorkommt, sondern daß vielmehr alles in einer steten Bewegung schwanke" (FA 24:392; that nowhere does one encounter something at rest, something self-contained and complete, rather everything fluctuates in constant motion). He further suggests that his own concept of morphology is a more appropriate means of studying nature, because it allows one to focus on the changing and transforming. Here, it is noteworthy to see how Goethe uses variations of the term *Bildung* to emphasize this change:

> Das Gebildete wird sogleich wieder umgebildet, und wir haben uns, wenn wir einigermaßen zum lebendigen Anschaun der Natur gelangen wollen, selbst so beweglich und bildsam zu erhalten, nach dem Beispiele mit dem sie uns vorgeht. (FA 24:392)

> [When something has acquired a form it metamorphoses immediately into a new one. If we wish to arrive at some living perception of nature we must remain as quick and flexible as nature and follow the examples it gives. (12:64)]

Scientists not only have to be aware of this natural dynamism, but they must, accordingly, be willing to use dynamic models of nature themselves. Goethe's morphological approach encourages one to seek that which is changing and not that which is stable. His discussion of the plant's leaf illustrates such a methodology. The leaf is primarily of use to see how the plant changes throughout its growth and development and not how it remains the same.

Thus, nature is not viewed primarily as a stable force, but according to its ability to change and transform. While it may be difficult to see the importance of this distinction within his botanical writings, it becomes a central factor in Goethe's understanding of evolution, as I will argue below. Even in the case of plants, however, some plants break Aristotle's rules of teleology: they do not strive to reproduce, but toward beauty.

Goethe's essay on plant metamorphosis has been the subject of a great deal of discussion. The essay at times takes on an almost mystical tone because Goethe speaks of the leaf ascending a spiritual ladder, discusses the changing quality of the sap as a process of inner purification, and likens the moment of reproduction to a spiritual anastomosis.[9] However, to focus on the mystical qualities of the essay is to miss some of its more central points, whether botanical or philosophical. The structure of the entire essay is self-reflexive and highly complex. During the course of the essay, the stages of the plant's development become an analog to the scientific method itself. For example, Goethe discusses the "Blätter" (§9; leaves/pages) of his own work and presents his essay in "Schritten" (§9; steps) that echo the step-by-step growth of a regular plant.[10] Most importantly, however, the essay is modeled not on a plant with a regular, teleological pattern of growth, but on one that is irregular and retrogressive. Such a plant fails to follow a regular pattern of development and is characterized by its ability to break teleological patterns. A retrogressive plant does not move forward toward "dem großen Zwecke" (the great goal) of reproduction, but often takes backward or irregular steps that lead to more beautiful (albeit at times sterile) plants (§7). Goethe tells us to study these plants because they "enthüllen" (unveil/uncover) that which the regular plant keeps "verheimlicht" (hidden). If one is to understand nature, one must therefore study its irregular forms.

Goethean natural studies, unlike Aristotelian ones, thus take their cue not from what is regular or normal, but what is irregular and abnormal. After Goethe has chronicled the steps of the regular, progressive plant, he turns back to examine earlier phases of development. He does so by turning to types of plants that were considered monstrous or abnormal: composite flowers (the perfoliate rose and carnation). These plants grow flower on flower at the expense of their ability to form fertile sexual organs. In other words, these retrogressive types of plants illustrate nature's protean qualities. They have the ability suddenly to change from regular to irregular patterns of growth. And just as the essay presents one complete plant cycle, from seed to seed, so too does the structure of the essay present a cycle. It concludes by returning to the beginning and repeating the main points of the whole. By going back to rephrase his main points, Goethe imitates the method of observation that he advocates: studying the progression and retrogression of the leaf (§120).

Throughout Goethe's later botanical writings, he emphasizes repeatedly how regular patterns are disrupted and new forms arise. He speaks of plants and trees in which entelechy or teleological growth patterns are abandoned, as when, for example, a tree grows in the shape of a crook rather than in an upright pattern. He further returns several times to his early example of the perfoliate rose. Within these discussions, Goethe rejects pejorative uses of the term "abnormal" (das Abnorme) or "monstrous" (das Monstrose) to describe these plants. First, these plants are as much a part of nature as its more regular manifestations; and second, nature, in these various transformations, shows itself to be creative and somewhat free of strict rules: "Die Natur überschreitet die Grenze, die sie sich selbst gesetzt hat, aber sie erreicht dadurch eine andere Vollkommenheit, deswegen wir wohltun uns hier so spät als möglich negativer Ausdrücke zu bedienen"[11] (Nature oversteps the boundary it has set for itself, but it attains thereby a different kind of perfection; therefore we would do well to defer the use of negative terminology as long as possible). Nature thus is not limited to linear striving. Nor is it bound to follow regular rules, because it may suddenly change those rules at any time. The perfoliate rose therefore may be considered irregular, though it is precisely its irregularity that makes it both more beautiful and more fragrant than a rose that has followed more "regular" patterns of development.

Comparative Anatomy

Just as Goethe's *Metamorphose* has been viewed as evidence of his Platonic and Aristotelian tendencies, so too have his essays on comparative anatomy been viewed in this way. Goethe's use of the term "type" within these essays, however, functions in a similar manner as his "leaf": the focus is on movement and transformation and not upon an idealized form. Both the leaf and the type represent for Goethe nature's versatility. He urges scientists to create a type as a comparative tool to enable the study of nature's disparate forms. The type therefore offers a means by which to track an ever-changing and developing nature.

That scholars have tended to emphasize the stable rather than the changing in Goethe's science has led to several serious misconceptions about his scientific corpus, as well as his philosophy in general. On the one hand, the belief that Goethe was an idealist has been used as an argument that he could never have endorsed evolution in its modern sense.[12] On the other, the belief that he saw stability in nature has been used to argue that he sought particular types of political and social stability as well.[13] In his essays on comparative anatomy, he specifically emphasizes that the type is a construct to enable the study of the *fluidity* of nature. In other words, the type does not demonstrate that Goethe's ideas could not be evolutionary because he focused on unchanging forms. Rather, the type emphasizes Goethe's belief in the variability of nature, and thus at the very least, leaves the door open to the question of Goethe's evolutionary beliefs.

Goethe's essays on comparative anatomy[14] (written in 1795–96) clearly reflect Schiller's influence and are directly linked with their philosophical discussions. Shortly after the beginning of their friendship, they began corresponding on aesthetic issues, which for Goethe during this period were closely linked to an understanding of organic forms. At this time (1794), Goethe sent Schiller his sketch on freedom and organic forms, "In wiefern die Idee: Schönheit sei Vollkommenheit mit Freiheit, auf organische Naturen angewendet werden könne" (The Extent to which the Idea "Beauty is Perfection in Combination with Freedom" May be Applied to Living Organisms). Schiller was delighted that they could agree on the centrality of freedom within an understanding of aesthetics, even though they approached the topic from diametrically opposed points of view. Both men agreed that freedom was a central component in anything that could be termed beautiful. Whereas Schiller in his works focuses on the term in its moral and human sense, Goethe applies it more broadly to include the organic realm. Within this essay, Goethe postulates that human beings as well as animals are most beautiful when they seem to be in control of their bodies, have the ability to conduct a myriad of functions, and most importantly, have the ability to initiate voluntary actions that are without purpose:

> Damit also ein Tier nur die notwendigen beschränkten Bedürfnisse ungehindert befriedigen könne, muß es schon vollkommen organisiert sein; allein wenn ihm neben der Befriedigung des Bedürfnisses noch so viel Kraft und Fähigkeit bleibt, willkürliche gewissermaßen zwecklose Handlungen zu unternehmen; so wird es uns auch äußerlich den Begriff von Schönheit geben.
>
> Wenn ich also sage dies Tier ist schön, so würde ich mich vergebens bemühen diese Behauptung durch irgend eine Proportion von Zahl oder Maß beweisen zu wollen. Ich sage vielmehr nur so viel damit: an diesem Tiere stehen die Glieder alle in einem solchen Verhältnis, daß keins das andere an seiner Wirkung hindert, ja daß vielmehr durch ein vollkommenes Gleichgewicht derselbigen Notwendigkeit und Bedürfnis versteckt, vor meinen Augen gänzlich verborgen worden, so daß das Tier nur nach freier Willkür zu handeln und zu wirken scheint. Man erinnere sich eines Pferdes das man in Freiheit seiner Glieder gebrauchen sehen. (FA 24:220).

[Therefore, if an animal is to satisfy even its most limited basic needs without difficulty, it must be perfectly organized. After satisfying its needs, however, it may have enough strength and power left to initiate voluntary actions which are somewhat without purpose; in this case its exterior will also yield an impression of beauty.

> Thus if I say this animal is beautiful I am unable to prove my asser-
> tion by using some proportion of number or measure. Instead I am stat-
> ing only: in this animal all the members are so related that none hinders
> the action of another; compulsion and need are entirely hidden from my
> sight by a perfect balance so that the animal seems free to act and work
> just as it chooses. We may recall the sight of a horse using its limbs in free-
> dom. (12:22)]

In discussing what contributes to an animal's beautiful appearance, the
short piece focuses mainly on the outward appearances and movements of
the animals. Goethe considers animals that have limbs that enable the most
disparate and capricious of movements to be the most free and beautiful.
Although the essay does address the limitations of particular features of
particular animals, it does not seek to explain the causes that brought
about different animals or their various features. At the end of the piece,
however, Goethe explains that if one truly were to understand exterior
principles of beauty and aesthetics, one would have to delve into the realm
of anatomy and physiology. In other words, if one is to understand how an
animal carves out a beautiful form and existence for itself, the quest should
begin with its physical form, to discover how its various parts came into
existence. His subsequent essays on comparative anatomy take on this task,
and strikingly, he concludes that an animal's capriciousness, sense of freedom, and force of will are not confined to bodily movements, but extend
to the very formation of that body.

Goethe's essays on comparative anatomy were influenced by many of
his contemporaries. Herder's *Ideen zur Philosophie der Geschichte der
Menschheit* (Ideas Concerning the Philosophy of the History of Mankind,
1784–91) with its hint at the idea of a descent of the species, conversations
with the Jena anatomist Loder, and the works of Sömmerring,
Blumenbach, and Camper all played important parts in the development of
Goethe's theories. In many ways, Goethe's anatomical essays were an out-
growth of his earlier work on the intermaxillary bone (1784). Goethe had
consulted these men in person or in writing while he was working to solve
the question of whether the human skull contained this bone.[15] (Goethe
was one of the first to argue that it existed in the human skull.) The "non-
existence" of this bone in humans had long been used to support the argument that human beings were physically different from animals. Goethe
complained that prejudice was impeding scientific progress. People did not
look for the bone because they were not inclined to find it; only if scientists had an open mind would they discover the similarities between
humans and animals.

Goethe's methods in his research on the intermaxillary bone carried
into his studies on comparative anatomy. Accordingly, if one wanted to
understand human beings, one had to compare them to animals. Goethe's
collaboration with Schiller also influenced his work. After Goethe had

informally presented his ideas on comparative anatomy to Schiller, as well as to the Humboldt brothers, who happened to be in Jena at the time (1795), they all encouraged him to develop his ideas further and to write them down. The results were two related essays on comparative anatomy that flesh out both Goethe's notion of the "type," as well as his theory of compensation.

Goethe's concept of the type and his theory of compensation are closely related. In general, he advocates creating and using a general type (*Typus*) as a standard or model of measurement. Whereas most comparative studies focused on the particular features of particular animals, Goethe argued that more progress would be made if these comparisons were made against a generalized model that was not based on any particular animal. The general type was to be created so that the particulars of various organisms could be better studied. He argued that one reason why comparative anatomy had not made larger scientific strides is that no standards existed by which to compare different animal types. He further noted that each discipline or trade (anatomists, butchers, horsemen, and so on) has its own language for talking about animal anatomy, and more progress could be made in understanding the various parts of animals and their functions if reference were made to the same model or type. The type thus functions as a *Vergleichungskanon* (comparative canon), because it acts as a stable unit of measure against which one may compare both similarities and differences among animals or changes within one species.

Historically, Goethe's discussion here has been linked to Platonic forms, not only because types are used as a kind of standard, but also because Goethe uses the word "Idee" while discussing the type.[16] Goethe, however, is using the term differently than in the universalized sense of forms, or ideas, in Plato's *Republic*. Goethe's goal here is not to discover a universal truth, but to create a model through which one may study different and changing forms. Of course, this kind of language is reminiscent of Platonic ideals, but as in the case of the leaf, here too, the type or form is being used for quite different purposes. The main issue, ultimately, is how one views the stability of truth and the ability of nature to create. Whereas Plato urges the study of particulars to find the universal, Goethe creates a general concept to study the particulars. In addition, whereas Plato's forms emphasize unchanging aspects, Goethe's type focuses on the evolving and changing forms of nature. Goethe's type is designed to find uniqueness and measure change; Plato's forms seek to uncover universality and stability. For Plato, truth rests in what is stable; for Goethe, what is stable is used as a tool to measure what is dynamic.

The very essence of Goethe's type is change and process. First, he argues that scholars must be willing to change their conception of the type, because they may gain new information that would necessitate the change. The type in this sense is therefore provisional.[17] Second, and perhaps most important, they must be willing to change their notion of the type, because nature itself is subject to change. Because natural forms are constantly changing, scientists by necessity over time will have to adapt the models that they create. Goethe speaks in several of his works of changing animal features or of one animal evolving into another (e.g., a whale evolving into a sloth, evolving into an ape).[18] The type would therefore have to be subject to change, because nature changes all the time. And although Goethe eventually hopes to arrive at a type that as a whole is consistent enough for general comparisons, he nevertheless simultaneously emphasizes the need for flexibility. Goethean science, thus, at its heart includes categories that constantly undergo change. Truth, even scientific truth, is subject to flux. In this context, Goethe likens his type to Proteus, that is, a being that is able to change its shape at will:

> Nun aber müssen wir, indem wir bei und mit dem Beharrlichen beharren, auch zugleich mit und neben dem Veränderlichen unsere Ansichten zu verändern und mannigfaltige Beweglichkeit lernen, damit wir den Typus in aller seiner Versatilität zu verfolgen gewandt seien und uns dieser Proteus nirgend hin entschlüpfe. (FA 24:234)

> [But now that we have endured in the realm of what is enduring, we must also learn to change our views along with ever-changing nature. We must learn many different movements so that we grow deft enough to follow the archetype in all its versatility, and so that this Proteus never slips from our grasp. (12:121)]

The language here is reminiscent of Goethe's preference for the concept of *Bildung* versus that of *Gestalt*. The focus of the observer should be on change and not on a static concept. Goethe admonishes scientists to be versatile, even in the creation of types, if they are to grasp nature in all its complexity.

Goethe's notion of the type is perhaps best understood within his discussion of his theory of compensation. Indeed, in many instances, he appears to use the two concepts interchangeably. In explaining how we are to compare animals to one another, he advises us to think of each animal as having a particular budget, a metaphor that becomes a means against which one can compare all animals and their features. This budget, or theory of compensation, works according to a theory of balance. Each animal is given a "budget." The more an animal "expends" on one feature, the less it has to "spend" on another. For example, the snake gains in length what it loses in appendages, whereas the lizard loses in body length what it gains by having feet. And although this theory has its roots in Aristotle,[19] one can again see within Goethe's works how he ultimately views nature as being freer and more creative. Throughout the essays, Goethe uses economic language (*Etats, Budget, haushälterisches Geben und Nehmen*, etc.)

to emphasize that while all animals are alike in having a budget, each species has a great deal of freedom to "spend" those funds:

> Hier sind die Schranken der tierischen Natur, in welchen sich die bildende Kraft auf die wunderbarste und beinahe auf die willkürlichste Weise zu bewegen scheint, ohne daß sie im mindesten fähig wäre den Kreis zu durchbrechen oder ihn zu überspringen. Der Bildungstrieb ist hier in einem zwar beschränkten, aber doch wohl eingerichteten Reiche zum Beherrscher gesetzt. Die Rubriken seines Etats, in welche sein Aufwand zu verteilen ist, sind ihm vorgeschrieben, was er auf jedes wenden will, steht ihm, bis auf einen gewissen Grad, frei. Will er der einen mehr zuwenden, so ist er nicht ganz gehindert, allein er ist genötigt an einer andern sogleich etwas fehlen zu lassen; und so kann die Natur sich niemals verschulden, oder wohl gar bankrott werden. ("Erster Entwurf," FA 24:233–34)

> [These are the bounds of animal nature; within these bounds the formative force seems to act in the most wonderful, almost capricious way, but is never able to break out of the circle or leap over it. The formative impulse is given hegemony over a limited but well-supplied kingdom. Governing principles have been laid down for the realm where this impulse will distribute its riches, but to a certain extent it is free to give to each what it will. If it wants to let one have more, it may do so, but not without taking from another. Thus nature can never fall into debt, much less go bankrupt. (12:121)]

In what sense can an organism exhibit a capricious power to change or influence its own form? For Goethe, this question has several answers. First, he is speaking of nature's powers generally. Nature is able to take one general principle, in this case compensation, and create a myriad of animal forms. Throughout his scientific corpus, Goethe writes of nature's ability to take a small number of principles (including polarity and intensification) and then use them to vary forms ad infinitum. Second, Goethe believes that organisms have the ability to vary their forms according to their given environment. Within these early essays, he discusses how certain animals react to their environments by fashioning particular forms for themselves. A fish, for example, will be more bloated and fleshy than a light, feathery bird because of its heavier, watery environment (FA 24:236). The agency for the creature's form is significantly not a teleological one: "Man wird nicht behaupten, einem Stier seien die Hörner gegeben daß er stoße, sondern man wird untersuchen, wie er Hörner haben können um zu stoßen" (FA 24:234; We will not claim that a bull has been given horns so that he can butt; instead, we will try to discover how he might have developed the horns he uses for butting, (12:121).

Third, and most strikingly, Goethe uses his principle of compensation to develop a theory closely related to a modern understanding of evolution.[20] For example, in a later (1822) review essay on d'Alton's work on sloths and pachyderms ("Die Faultiere und die Dickhäutigen," FA 24:545–51), Goethe postulates how animal life began in the water, then evolved into large and cumbersome land creatures, until finally developing into freer and more sophisticated ape-like creatures. Significantly, at each evolutionary stage, Goethe gives agency to the animals themselves. In this case, it is not even the environment that determines their forms, because the organisms in question select their own environments. A whale in the ocean "decides" to try to live on land and "throws itself" on the shore. Goethean creatures do not vary spontaneously as in Darwin's theories, but play active roles in their development. The exertion of will is Goethe's analog to the spontaneous change that brings about Darwinian evolution. The type or budget, then, comes to demonstrate how radically animal forms change over time and how much influence the organisms themselves exert on those changes. Species change over time because they in some way will their change. In another review essay, "Die Skelette der Nagetiere" (FA 24:632–37), Goethe even speculates that many different animals share with human beings the desire for upright posture. In Goethe's mind, the squirrel who delicately holds a nut in its "hands" while standing on two feet differs from human beings only in degree.

Such a discussion of a creative will undoubtedly seems somewhat mystical. In the longer passage above, Goethe uses the term *Bildungstrieb* (formative drive) to explain how nature can create new forms. *Bildungstrieb* was a term coined by Blumenbach and then adapted (and in the process, significantly changed) by many contemporaries, including Kant, Schelling, A. von Humboldt, and Goethe.[21] It was a highly charged term for the eighteenth century. In general, it represented an attempt to counter the tendency to explain organic growth primarily according to mechanical and material principles. As Goethe explains, Blumenbach rejected an earlier explanation (Wolff's) of development through *vis essentialis*, a generative power, as being untenable because it offers a primarily mechanical explanation for organic development. The problem, according to Goethe, was that such explanations do not address the first cause of development. How could matter, on its own, organize itself? Organic forms, accordingly, had to have some ability to influence their actions, whether in adapting to sudden obstacles presented to them or in healing themselves — or in the more radical sense — to transform their forms over time. Goethe praises Blumenbach's concept because it looks beyond material causes to explain organic development:

> Betrachten wir das alles genauer, so hätten wir es kürzer, bequemer und vielleicht gründlicher, wenn wir eingestünden, daß wir, um das Vorhandene zu betrachten, eine vorhergegangene Tätigkeit zugeben müssen und daß, wenn wir uns eine Tätigkeit denken wollen, wir derselben ein schicklich Element unterlegen, worauf sie wirken könnte, und daß wir zuletzt diese Tätigkeit mit dieser Unterlage als immerfort zusammen

bestehend und ewig gleichzeitig vorhanden denken müssen. Dieses Ungeheure personifiziert tritt uns als ein Gott entgegen, als Schöpfer und Erhalter, welchen anzubeten, zu verehren und zu preisen wir auf all Weise aufgefordert sind. ("Bildungstrieb," FA 24:451–52)

[We can examine this assertion more quickly, easily, and perhaps more thoroughly, if we recognize that in considering a present object we must suppose an action prior to it, and in forming a concept of an action we must presume a suitable material for it to act on. Finally, we must think of this action as always coexisting with the underlying material, the two forever present at one and the same time. Personified, this prodigy confronts us as a god, as a creator and sustainer, whom we are constrained to worship, honor, and praise. (12:35)]

Although Goethe's statement about the relationship of form and matter resembles Aristotle's treatment of causes, Goethe emphasizes a different aspect of this relationship. He argues that the relationship primarily concerns the ability of the formative drive to create and to bring about change. That he goes so far as to equate this force with a god demonstrates how central this force is to organic formations and new creations of all kinds. But Goethe also distinguishes between Blumenbach's approach and his own. He writes that one needs to add his own concept of metamorphosis into the discussion in order to emphasize nature's freedom to create and transform. He postulates that one cannot see the freedom of the *Bildungstrieb* without the concept of metamorphosis. Here, we once again see the influence of his discussions with Schiller. Organic nature, like human beings, reaches its pinnacle through free, playful, or capricious actions. The moments of transformation, as witnessed through a process of change, best illustrate nature's freedom to change and progress.

Goethe's science thus departs from the more narrowly understood "classical" notions of human uniqueness and a stable and universalized understanding of nature. For Goethe, the pinnacle of non-human natural creativity was not, as it was for Aristotle, relegated simply to procreation. Rather, in Goethe's view, plants and animals, and even parts of plants and animals, could participate in creation through the fashioning of their physical bodies.

Within his two comparative anatomy essays, Goethe claims that his type and budget theories demonstrate the unity of nature and the place of human beings within it. Human beings and animals are subject to the same laws and operate according to the same principles. This is not to say that he believed all animals were equal. According to his schema, human beings were more advanced. The "animal" in us is transformed for higher purposes (FA 24:228; "Im Menschen ist das Tierische zu höhern Zwecken gesteigert"). In order to understand ourselves and how we have advanced, he tells us to begin with lower animals and then ascend toward human beings from these more simple beings. He implies a kind of evolutionary development, especially when he argues that his readers will be better able to understand certain aspects of the human form and structure once they have studied lower animal forms.[22] He further notes in this context that the denial of the existence of the intermaxillary bone (by Camper and Blumenbach, among others) hindered the development of comparative anatomy because this trait "sollte das Unterscheidungszeichen zwischen uns und dem Affen sein" (FA 24:239; was to distinguish us from the apes, 12:124). In other words, the inability to see our relationship to apes and other animals prevented scientists from seeing important connections between the two.

Protean Nature

In his scientific works, Goethe sought to break away from the scientific traditions that impeded an understanding of nature's creativity. He thus rejected many of the views commonly associated with classicism, including teleology, the separation of human beings from the rest of nature, and stable, universalized forms. Thus, to view Goethe's science as "classical" in a traditional sense is to misconstrue many aspects of his philosophy, which in turn masks the radical and creative aspects of his approach. However, the principles of malleability and capriciousness found within Goethe's science reveal that it is classical in a different sense. His natural philosophy is also closely related to the Dionysian aspect of ancient thought: the wilder, more capricious, and unpredictable obverse of the more ordered and principled world of Plato and Aristotle. It therefore at times is influenced more by the examples of Homer's Proteus and Lucretius's explanation of random motion and free will than by the works of Plato and Aristotle. I have argued above that within Goethe's "classical" period, one can see the seeds of a natural philosophy that emphasizes change and malleability. By briefly turning to some of Goethe's works after 1805, where these statements are made more explicit, we can better see the anti-static and dynamic elements of his earlier scientific works.

What is perhaps most striking about Goethe's characterization of nature in his later works is not so much his description of its protean abilities to change patterns or create new forms, but the violence with which it is willing to do so. A prime example of this violence is found in Goethe's short essay "Die Lepaden" (The Barnacles) written in 1824. Here, as in his earlier "Metamorphose" essay, he speaks of both regular and irregular patterns of growth. He quickly rejects the more regularly growing barnacle as uninteresting and turns his attention instead to the irregular ones. The focus is on the fierce desire of each disparate barnacle part to come into being. The outer skin of this barnacle is rough and covered with countless tiny round spots that Goethe characterizes as sublime (*erhaben*).

Each of these spots represents a potential shell that competitively struggles to exist. The description of this struggle is rather violent, where each shell-point can exist only by consuming its smaller competitors:

> Und hier, bei genauer Betrachtung, scheint es als wenn jeder Schalpunkt sich eile, die nächsten aufzuzehren, sich auf ihre Kosten zu vergrößern, und zwar in dem Augenblick ehe sie zum Werden gelangen. Eine schon gewordene noch so kleine Schale kann von einem herankommenden Nachbar nicht aufgespeist werden, alles Gewordene setzt sich mit einander ins Gleichgewicht. Und so sieht man das in der Entenmuschel [Lepas anatifera] regelmäßig gebundene, gesetzliche Wachstum, in der andern [Lepas polliceps] zum freiern Nachrücken aufgefordert, wo mancher einzelne Punkt so viel Besitz und Raum sich anmaßt als er nur gewinnen kann. (FA 24:612)

> [And here, by more exact observation, it seems as if every shell-point rushes to consume the next one, to enlarge itself at the cost of the others, and does so in that moment before they are able to come into existence. An already formed, ever so small shell, cannot be eaten by its approaching neighbor — all things that have come into existence place themselves in an equilibrium against other existing things. And so one sees that the growth, which is regularly bound and law-like in the goose barnacle [*Lepas anatifera*], is encouraged to freer advancement in the other barnacle [*Lepas polliceps*], where many an individual point usurps as much property and space as it can gain.]

Goethe further writes that observing the competitive battles of the barnacle points through a microscope would be "eins der herrlichsten Schauspiele" (one of most wonderful spectacles) that the friend of nature could ever wish to see. He goes so far as to compare these battles, which lead to irregular growth patterns, to god-like and human nature:

> Da ich nach meiner Art zu forschen, zu wissen, und zu genießen, mich nur an Symbole halten darf, so gehören diese Geschöpfe [*Lepas polliceps*] zu den Heiligtümern welche fetischartig immer vor mir stehen und, durch ihr seltsames Gebilde, die nach dem Regellosen strebende, sich selbst immer regelnde und so im kleinsten wie im größten durchaus Gott- und menschenähnliche Natur sinnlich vergegenwärtigen. (FA 24:612–13)

> [Because according to my way of researching, knowing, and enjoying I allow myself to hold only to symbols, so these creatures (*Lepas polliceps*) belong to the sacred relics that in a fetish-like manner always stand before me. And they, through their odd structure, that striving toward the ruleless (irregular), always regulating themselves and therefore, in the small as well as large scale, make present to the senses god-like and human-like nature.]

The irregular barnacles illustrate a number of central principles within Goethe's works. First, nature is most interesting not when it is following regular patterns of behavior, but irregular ones, because these examples point to nature at its most creative. Second, although regular rules of behavior exist, irregular ones demonstrate the underlying chaos and battles of the natural world. Because rules can be broken, and because resources may be scarce, fierce competition exists on every level of existence — whether one barnacle point is struggling to come into being or one animal part attempts to gain more of the animal's overall "budget." The irregular barnacles are not governed by regular rules, but like human beings, strive to break free as much as possible from patterned behavior. In this sense, they are rather like Goethe's most famous character, Faust. They strive to expand the scope of their physical space as much as possible. They also are an embodiment of Proteus's instructions to Homunculus in *Faust II*; they must eat the smaller beings in order to grow and thrive.

Goethe's nature thus turns out to be much more interesting in its competitive and transformational moments. Organic nature has the ability to change and transform itself because of its possession of a capricious will — a will that is related to Lucretius's swerve of the atom.[23] Many centuries earlier, the atomist Lucretius had maintained in his famous poem, *De rerum Natura* (On the Nature of Things), that all motion, will-driven action and creativity found its source in the random, spontaneous swerve of an atom. In his vision of the universe, atoms could suddenly and without explanation or external cause suddenly change their course of direction. It was this spontaneous swerve on the atomic level that allowed all of nature's creatures to "wrest from the fates" their power to make choices large and small.[24] Unless the atoms had the ability to change their regular motions, how could one, Lucretius argues, explain the exertion of will in human beings and animals? If animals could exert a will, then according to an atomistic conception of the universe, so should the inanimate atoms. Like Lucretius, Goethe believed that nature's parts, whether large or small, acted in similar ways. Unlike Lucretius, however, Goethe credited nature and its parts not with random or spontaneous actions, but with more will-driven ones. The parts of the barnacle exert a will to fashion their own existence, as do the parts of a plant when they suddenly force the plant to depart from its regular course of action.

Goethe's protean understanding of nature is significant because it set him apart from traditional conceptions of nature — and with it — of truth. Traditionally, the classical understanding of truth is based on an understanding of nature. Plato and Aristotle's views of truth closely corresponded to their conceptions of nature. The truth, like nature's ideal categories, was universal and unchanging. Goethe, like his classical predecessors, also based his understanding of truth on his conception of nature. However, because he viewed nature as an eternally changing entity, truth for him was not static. For Goethe, truth is like Proteus in that it remains in one state for a moment, but when it transforms in the next, may have to be re-captured again. Nature's Protean will to create enables it to disrupt regular, teleological patterns of development unexpectedly and at any time. Scientists therefore need to create categories and study rules, while at the same time always being prepared to change those categories and to expect new rules to emerge. Species may be created, but they must then be readjusted as nature changes. This understanding of a changing nature does not mean that Goethe is completely modern, or postmodern, in his views of truth. He is not, for example, a nihilist. Although Proteus may change from one moment to the next, at any given moment one may make true statements about his condition and form. One may therefore speak of present truths even if those may be changing before our very eyes.

Notes

1 "Glückliches Ereignis" (Fortunate Encounter, 1817), FA 24:437.

2 Most English translations of Goethe's works in this essay are taken from *Goethe's Collected Works.* 12 vols. (New York: Suhrkamp, 1983–89). Translations lacking citation by volume and page number are my own.

3 Goethe mentions Seebeck's approval of the *Farbenlehre* several times over the years in the *Tag- und Jahres-Hefte* (e.g., paragraphs 578, 593, 719; FA 17:185, 189, 226).

4 For a further discussion, see my *Goethe's Elective Affinities and the Critics* (Rochester: Camden House, 2001), 11–36.

5 Such as "Das Unternehmen wird entschuldigt," "Die Absicht eingeleitet," "Der Inhalt bevorwortet" (1817) FA 24:389–95; 402–5.

6 Goethe, for example, is pleased that the French botanist Antoine Laurent de Jussieu (1748–1836) mentions the "Metamorphose" essay, but complains that he does not go into enough detail. Similarly, although the well-known Berlin botanist Karl Ludwig Willdenow (1765–1812), references Goethe's essay in an outline of botany, Goethe feels he does not give him enough recognition ("Drei günstige Rezensionen," FA 24:454–55).

7 Ernst Mayr, *The Growth of Biological Thought: Diversity, Evolution, and Inheritance* (Cambridge: Belknap Press of Harvard UP, 1982), 457.

8 "Metamorphose der Pflanzen" §102, FA 24:143.

9 Some scholars, such as Ronald Gray (*Goethe the Alchemist* [Cambridge: Cambridge UP, 1952]), have argued that the essay is not really an attempt to establish a scientific theory, but to offer a kind of coded alchemical treatise on the philosopher's stone.

10 Paragraph numbers refer to the numbers in the original and in most subsequent editions.

11"Nacharbeiten zur Metamorphose" (1820), FA 24:462.

12 See Mayr (457–58) and George A. Wells, *Goethe and the Development of Science 1750–1900* (Alphen aan den Rijn: Sijthoff & Nordhoff, 1978).

[13] For example, although Goethe himself opposed teleology and saw its political misuses, scholars still argue today that he believed in teleological systems. For a more detailed discussion, see my *The Will to Create: Goethe's Philosophy of Science* (Pittsburgh: U of Pittsburgh P, 2002), 95–103.

[14] "Erster Entwurf einer allgemeinen Einleitung in die vergleichende Anatomie, ausgehend von der Osteologie" and "Vorträge, über die drei ersten Kapitel des Entwurfs einer allgemeinen Einleitung in die vergleichende Anatomie, ausgehend von der Osteologie" (FA 24:227–81).

[15] All of these men were interested in comparing the skulls or skeletons of human beings with animals. Loder was a prominent Jena anatomist who allowed Goethe access to his anatomical collections. Goethe also attended Loder's lectures at the university and at the court at Weimar. Sömmerring was a doctor and anatomist whom Goethe first met in 1783 in Cassel. Goethe sent him a letter outlining his theory of the intermaxillary bone. Blumenbach is widely considered to be one of the main founders of physical anthropology, and his natural history was very influential at the time. Camper was the "founder" of craniology and one of the first to compare the skull measurements of apes and the different races in order to seek relationships among these groups. (For a discussion of craniology, see Londa Schiebinger, *Nature's Body: Gender in the Making of Modern Science* [Boston: Beacon Press, 1993], 149–50). Although Goethe never met Camper, he corresponded with him and sent him a copy of his treatise on the intermaxillary bone. For a discussion of the racist and sexist implications of Camper's and Blumenbach's work, see Schiebinger. For a detailed discussion of Goethe's contact with these men while he was developing his intermaxillary bone theory, see Hermann Bräunig-Oktavio, *Vom Zwischenkieferknochen zur Idee des Typus: Goethe als Naturforscher in den Jahren 1780–1786, Nova Acta Leopoldina, Neue Folge*, No. 12, vol. 18 (Leipzig: Johann Ambrosius Barth Verlag, 1956).

[16] "Erster Entwurf," FA 24:229.

[17] "Erster Entwurf," FA 24:230.

[18] See, for example, Goethe's essays, "Fossiler Stier" (FA 24:553) and "Die Faultiere und die Dickhäutigen" (FA 24:545–51).

[19] Aristotle's "Parts of Animals": 655a18–34, 657b5–35, 663a30, 664a1–14, 674a32–674b18; and his "Generation of Animals": 749b5–750a5, 750a21–35. Cited from *The Complete Works of Aristotle,* ed. Jonathan Barnes, vols. 1 and 2 (Princeton, NJ: Princeton UP, 1984).

[20] For a more detailed discussion of Goethe's evolutionary views, see my book, *The Will to Create,* 114–28.

[21] For a discussion of this term and its importance for Romantic theories of development, see Robert J. Richards, *The Romantic Conception of Life: Science and Philosophy in the Age of Goethe* (Chicago: U of Chicago P, 2002), 207–29; 255–61; 289–306. In contrast to Lenoir and others who argue that Blumenbach's term at its heart is "teleomechanical," Richards argues for a more vitalistic interpretation.

[22] "Erster Entwurf," FA 24:237; cf. "Vorträge," FA 24:265–70.

[23] Goethe was intimately familiar with Lucretius's poem. In a letter written in 1789, he claims to be an adherent — more or less — of Lucretian philosophy; he

placed excerpts of the poem in the Historical Part of his *Farbenlehre*; and at one point he planned to write his own natural philosophic poem modeled on Lucretius's poem. He paraphrases several passages from *De Rerum Natura* in several of his works, and he discussed Knebel's German translation of the poem with Knebel over a period of nearly thirty years.

[24] Lucretius, *De Rerum Natura*, Loeb edition, trans. W. H. D. Rouse, new revision by Martin Ferguson Smith (Cambridge: Harvard UP, 1975), 2:220–23; 253–60.

Ansicht des Römischen Hauses von der Wiesen Brücke.

Georg Melchior Kraus, the Roman House in the Weimar Park, 1799. Aquatint/pen and ink drawing on paper. Goethe-Nationalmuseum, Weimar. Courtesy Stiftung Weimarer Klassik, Kunstsammlungen.

The Political Context of
Weimar Classicism

W. Daniel Wilson

THE PERIOD COVERED by this volume, from the publication of some central classical works in 1787 to Schiller's death in 1805, roughly coincides with the period of the impact of the French Revolution in Germany and the dissolution of the Holy Roman Empire.[1] The events from the storming of the Bastille in 1789 to Napoleon's declaration in 1799 that the Revolution had ended were almost as cataclysmic for mentalities in Germany as they were in France. In literature the importance of this political matrix was so great that many newer histories of German literature identify the epoch of German Classicism and Romanticism by reference to the revolutionary period.[2] However, the overdue attention to the upheaval in both politics and literature caused by the French Revolution should not distract attention from the important political structures and mentalities that reveal considerable continuity from the pre-revolutionary into the revolutionary period in Germany.

Eighteenth-century "Germany" was a patchwork of hundreds of tiny to large sovereign states, held together loosely in the Holy Roman Empire, which was laid to rest by Napoleon in 1806 following a period of increasing irrelevance. Most of these territories were monarchies. The Empire exerted minimal control over sovereigns, mainly in the form of legal courts that communities or individuals could use against the power of their prince. These expedients were singularly ineffective in limiting monarchic power, and yet many Germans argued that the checks on state authority were the basis of a peculiarly German kind of freedom that went under the name of a German "constitution" — not in the modern sense of the term, but rather a conglomerate of guarantees of certain rights of traditional estates vis-à-vis the monarch.

Many Germans also felt that their peculiar brand of Enlightenment lent them the blessings of a well-ordered, benevolent polity. For the Enlightenment in Germany — in contradistinction to France, but paralleling similar patterns in Austria, Russia, Sweden, Italy, and Spain — had entered into a momentous, even fateful, alliance with the absolutist state. In the model known later as "enlightened absolutism," the ruler retained his absolute — or, more accurately, nearly absolute — power, but his attitudes were modified by enlightened thought so that he placed the good of his lands and subjects above that of his own person and dynasty.[3] Legitimacy flowed not from his divine right to rule, but from his claim to be the "first servant of the people," to use the expression of Frederick II ("the Great") of Prussia (1712–86), the most famous of these rulers. This, at least, was the theory. In reality, "enlightened absolutism" was fraught with contradictions. The princes were not seriously interested in relinquishing power or granting substantial new rights to their subjects. In the end, the feudal and absolutist system remained largely intact. However, German thinkers clung tenaciously to this model. They had little choice, because most of them were beholden to it. Since writers in eighteenth-century Germany could not live from their publications, they had to work in other occupations, and almost all of these were dependent on the state or local governments. Thus, it was next to impossible for them to develop any kind of truly oppositional — much less revolutionary — consciousness. They were also plagued by the considerable problem of communication, because unlike France or England, Germany had no single large metropolis where intellectuals could live and exchange ideas.

Potentially critical intellectuals were thus largely co-opted by the various states or cities on which they depended for their livelihood. Yet, there were audible voices of discontent; fully uncovered and appreciated again only in the 1970s, these intellectuals expressed increasingly virulent critique of the existing absolutist order.[4] One of the primary venues for expressing — but also absorbing — this critical potential was secret societies. Freemasonry was so widespread that almost all important writers were members. More political (at least potentially political) was the Order of Illuminati.[5] Numbering no more than about 1200, the members of this primarily German secret society envisioned an end to states and princes. This quasi-anarchist goal was, however, only a long-term project that was never pursued with any seriousness. It was to be achieved by slow, moral influence on rulers, and thus can be viewed as an ingenious variant of the project of "enlightened" absolutism. And yet the idealistic goal of eliminating the existing order sounded threatening enough to absolutist princes, who kept a careful eye on this secret society whenever they found out about its existence in their realms.

The 1780s were a time of increasingly critical political discourse in Germany and were also the heyday of the Illuminati. But by 1785 this secret society had been betrayed and shut down, and in 1787 — coincidentally a literary watershed year, when the first classical blank-verse plays, Schiller's *Don Carlos* and Goethe's *Iphigenie auf Tauris*, were published — the Bavarian government published a large cache of Illuminati documents that had been seized during a house search. The publication of these documents was an important political event in Germany. It caused a scandal throughout Europe and a reactionary backlash that has been seen as instrumental in the rise of political conservatism and even a police mentality in Germany, where the scandal stands at the beginning of political modernity.[6] Soon the brouhaha was exacerbated by the most pernicious and deadly conspiracy theory of modern times. In this same year, 1787, the Weimar Illuminati member Johann Christoph Bode (1730–1793) journeyed to Paris and visited Masonic lodges there. His goal and activities are still unclear, but a few of the later revolutionary leaders were members of these lodges. This coincidence — and it must, in fact, be seen as a coincidence — was sufficient evidence for the reactionaries to implicate the German Illuminati as the real instigators of the French Revolution. Soon Masons were included in the conspiracy theory, and, during the nineteenth century, Jews (who were, in reality, excluded from Freemasonry) and Communists were mixed in. By the twentieth century, this fantastic notion of a grand Masonic-Jewish-Bolshevist plot to undermine the existing order became one of the primary ideological motors of National Socialism and other fascist and conservative movements.[7]

The conspiracy theory was only one attempt at explaining a phenomenon that was incomprehensible to many Germans (who did not have anything like the urban culture of Paris, with its underclass) and challenged the interpretive prowess of others. In general, Germans saw the Revolution through the lens of their own situations.[8] There were those Germans who wanted to limit the power of their prince by some sort of constitution or other arrangement. These intellectuals generally supported the Revolution, but wished to limit it to France; they hoped that the French example would serve as a moral warning sign to German princes that they must introduce reforms if they were to avoid insurrection in their own realms. This position was probably influenced by the widespread dramatic theory of the time: French politics was something of a theater (and was often described as such in travel narratives of Germans in revolutionary France), and German princes were envisioned as the audience, which was expected to internalize a moral (and ultimately political) message after seeing the performance: avoid tyrannical behavior so that you will not end up like the French king, on a scaffold. These thinkers generally felt that "enlightened absolutism" had made and would continue to make a revolution unnecessary in Germany. They looked with approval on the events in France — which they viewed as a nation truly in need of revolutionary change — as long as this model of constitutional monarchy seemed to be the aim of the upheaval. However, they generally rejected the violent episodes in the revolutionary process and were alienated by the unwashed masses in Paris. They essentially valorized the middle-class revolutionaries, particularly the Gironde, and rejected the Jacobins. When the "second revolution" radicalized the course of events in the fall and winter of 1792–93 and led to increasing bloodshed — the overthrow of the monarchy on August 10, the September massacres, the trial and execution of Louis XVI in January, 1793 — these intellectuals almost all turned their backs on the Revolution. By the beginning of the Terror in the summer and fall of 1793, there were few supporters of the Revolution left in Germany.

Among intellectuals, there were very few champions of the Jacobin radicalization and even fewer supporters of a revolution in Germany. The few who existed were centered mainly in southwest Germany and the Rhineland, where French influence was greatest.[9] In these lands there were, indeed, revolutionary movements, most famously the republic of Mainz — the first republic on German soil.[10] It was established under French occupation in October of 1792 and ended with the reoccupation of the city by Prussian and Austrian troops in July 1793. It included other Rhenish territories besides the city of Mainz and was echoed in other short-lived republics, especially in the years after 1795. For many Germans, the Mainz revolutionaries — foremost among them the famous ethnologist Georg Forster (1754–94), who sailed around the world with Captain Cook and during the republican phase became Mainz's ambassador to Paris to request that the French annex Mainz — were the worst sort of traitors. For others, they were an important model.

The lower classes in Germany responded to the Revolution somewhat differently than the intellectuals, but they, too, saw the events in France in the light of their own experiences.[11] Peasants suffered under the crushing burden of the feudal order. Living often on the edge of subsistence, they had not only to take care of their own farming, but also had to perform unpaid or scarcely paid feudal labor duties for their landlord (who was usually a local nobleman, but often a leaseholder on land owned by the prince). They had to pay myriad taxes, from which their noble lords were exempt. In the course of the eighteenth century, the landlords attempted to expand the peasants' feudal duties, and this pressure led to sometimes violent conflicts. Peasant uprisings and unrest were a staple of public life in the eighteenth (and earlier) centuries. However, the revolution in France lent them an entirely new quality. The princes began to fear true revolt — a wholesale overthrow of the existing order, rather than just local unrest in favor of minimal changes within the status quo — and usually responded more forcefully than in the pre-revolutionary period to disturbances and even to nonviolent petitions for change. The uprisings themselves were sometimes almost revolutionary in their implications after the beginning of the French Revolution; most significant was the violence in Saxony in 1790, which involved a large-scale military response. Most of the uprisings, to be sure, continued to demand only reforms within the feudal and absolutist system, because peasants were generally illiterate and had little conception of fundamental change. However, they were well enough informed to know of the events in France and their radical character. And they began to exploit the French example to lend force to their grievances and demands. While this tactic did not make the demands themselves any more revolutionary, it did contribute to a rise in political consciousness in Germany and of course to a rise in princely fears of revolution.

Traditional depictions of the duchy of Saxe-Weimar saw it as more or less isolated from these developments, with happy subjects basking in the glow of their benevolent Duke Carl August (1757–1828, duke since 1775) under the liberal influence of his most famous minister and friend, Johann Wolfgang (von) Goethe:[12] a "glückliche Insel im erschütterten Europa"[13] (happy island in shaken Europe). But recent research has shown that the Revolution had a much broader impact there than was suspected earlier, and even in the pre-revolutionary period, Weimar had its share of peasant unrest and other political conflicts.[14] Goethe participated in suppressing protest and resistance in the lower classes as one of the four (later five) members of the Privy Council (*Geheimes Consilium*).[15] He was most involved in this political role in the nine years between the spring of 1776, when he was first appointed, and the spring of 1785. When he "fled" Weimar (to use his own expression) in 1786 to recuperate in Italy, he was not only escaping the heavy burden of administrative work, but also the political contradictions of his role as minister. While he wished to guide Carl August toward a more liberal polity, he increasingly identified with the duke's interests and rejected change when he felt those interests to be at risk.

After Goethe's return to Weimar he worked out an arrangement with the duke that he would no longer participate in the twice- or thrice-weekly sessions of the Council, but would instead focus on a few areas of interest to him, particularly relating to the arts and scholarship, including affairs relating to the University of Jena. However, attention should not be focused only on Goethe's newly restricted political arena, since the totality of political life in Classical Weimar forms the backdrop to understanding cultural and literary life there, regardless of whether Goethe was directly involved in it. And Goethe was in any case more involved in political conflicts, particularly those relating to professors and students, than earlier scholarship recognized. The difference is that, after 1791, he generally exerted influence not directly, in meetings of the Privy Council, but indirectly through constant informal consultations with the new councilor Christian Gottlob Voigt (1743–1819). Thus, Goethe's work as privy councilor in this period is documented less in regular writings for the Council than in letters to Voigt and others.[16] In the following account, however, we will not restrict ourselves to Goethe's role, but will examine the totality of response to the French Revolution in the duchy.

Peasant unrest in Saxe-Weimar continued into the revolutionary period, and was generally met with harsher treatment than before. In the towns, too, there was considerable discontent. For a few weeks in the fall of 1792, it seemed that French troops, who had advanced eastward after taking Frankfurt am Main in late October, might occupy Eisenach, at the western end of the duke's territories. This prospect frightened many inhabitants of Eisenach, but others gathered on the market square and jubilantly sang songs celebrating the expected arrival of the French: "es kommen die Franzosen, um zu prügeln die Großen!," the children chanted (the French are coming, to beat up the privileged). According to this same report, "schon war den Abend der ganze Markt voll von Bürgern, Weibern und Kindern, die laut ihre Freude über den nahen Einzug der FreyheitsBeschützer zu erkennen gaben, und laut mancherley Beschwerden recapitulirten"[17] (in the evening, the market square was full of men, women, and children, who loudly proclaimed their joy at the imminent arrival of the protectors of freedom and repeated loudly many a complaint). The privy councilors wrote to the duke — who was commanding a Prussian regiment at the front, with Goethe in tow — that there was a real danger of revolt in Eisenach. Even in the city of Weimar some citizens are reported to have worn revolutionary cocardes on their hats. After the French threat was turned back by coalition troops, the excitement subsided, but it had become clear that political dissatisfaction lurked below the surface in the duchy's less privileged classes. To be sure, the enthusiasm for the French soon grew cold among most citizens, as the invading troops sometimes exploited and plundered the occupied towns in Germany. The execution of the French king on 21 January 1793 further disabused many Germans of illusions about the Revolution: Weimar and Jena burghers now contributed voluntarily to the duke's war chest. But unrest did not die out easily, especially in the lower classes. In the summer of 1793, textile workers in the proto-industrial town of Apolda revolted, sending their employers scurrying to Weimar, where they pleaded for military intervention. Although the government redressed some of the grievances of the workers, it also dispatched troops and thus discouraged future unrest. The privy councilors interpreted these events, too, as results of the Revolution in France.

They also saw the widespread student disturbances at the University of Jena in 1792 as a product of "demokratische Schwärmerey" (democratic effusions), and made sure that the students were intimidated by the military (and Goethe, in particular, was concerned to make a show of superior force[18]). Professors who were known for their liberal politics — culminating in the famous idealist philosopher Johann Gottlieb Fichte (1762–1814) — were appointed in Jena, but only under the condition that they abstain from expressing their political views. Fichte was eventually dismissed in 1799, ostensibly on the grounds of his supposed atheism, but he and others were convinced that it was his political views that had been punished, and the Weimar government explicitly had sought only a pretense to get rid of Fichte.[19] The government used paid informants to keep track of stirrings at the university (and Goethe was involved in securing financing for them and benefited from their reports in sessions of the

Privy Council). Other intellectuals, too, were the targets of attempts at intimidation in these years, particularly the circle around Johann Gottfried Herder, including the former tutor to Carl August's brother, Carl Ludwig von Knebel (1744–1834), the writer and former tutor to Carl August, Christoph Martin Wieland (1733–1813), and the previously mentioned Illuminati chief Bode. Herder and Knebel were denounced by a government employee, and the duke ordered Voigt to muzzle them, which he did. All of these thinkers dallied with revolutionary ideology. Herder and Wieland represent a less regressive side of Weimar Classicism that should not be overlooked in any political account of this literary movement. Herder, who supported the revolution even in its darkest hours, gradually gave up these aspirations under pressure from the duke and his family — and Goethe rebuked Herder's wife when she dared to insist on the study stipend that the duke had promised their son when his loose revolutionary talk became known.[20]

Wieland was the best-informed and most influential writer in Weimar in matters of the revolution. He provided a running commentary on events in France in his prominent journal *Der Teutsche Merkur*, revealing intimate knowledge of the power struggles there and even prophesying important milestones of the revolution.[21] His attitude was close to that of the less radical Gironde, but he did not hesitate to announce his adherence to the ideals — but ultimately not the practice — of the revolutionaries. In private, he expressed opinions that were often less moderate than his published writings, and he was criticized in heated letters written by the duke and his ministers.[22]

Literary scholarship has recognized since at least the 1980s that the French Revolution and its impact in Germany formed an important context to the "high" classical literature of Goethe and Schiller. Goethe himself wrote in 1822 of "die vieljährige Richtung meines Geistes gegen die französische Revolution" (the direction of my mind for many years against the French Revolution), and admitted that "die grenzenlose Bemühung dieses schrecklichste aller Ereignisse in seinen Ursachen und Folgen dichterisch zu gewältigen" had "mein poetisches Vermögen fast unnützerweise aufgezehrt"[23] (the boundless effort to master this most horrible of all events in its causes and consequences had consumed my poetic talent almost fruitlessly). However, these writers' response was always considered to be one directed against the adherents of the French cause — and sometimes of a German revolution — in other German lands, never in Saxe-Weimar itself. We now know that at least some of the counterrevolutionary writing of Goethe and Schiller responded to political conflicts at their very doorstep.

At stake was often the fictionalized figure of the revolutionary agitator. Before the Revolution, Goethe had portrayed such a character in his tragedy *Egmont*, begun before his removal to Weimar in 1775 (and thus containing elements of Sturm und Drang), completed in Italy and published in 1788.

The revolt portrayed there was very much a pre-Bastille one: the Reformation uprising of the Netherlands against the Spanish rule of Philipp II, but seen through eighteenth-century eyes. The play sets the "altes Recht" (ancient rights) of the local nobility against the illegitimate authority of the Spanish king. After the play appeared, Goethe drew a parallel between the Dutch plot and the revolt of the Austrian Netherlands against the rule of the Austrian Emperor and King Joseph II, and this parallel is not without justification: it was a conservative revolution, favoring religion and entrenched tradition against the innovations of Enlightenment that were forced on the populace by an alien power. Goethe incorporated the true revolutionary agitator in the person of Vansen, who is grotesquely caricatured even though he champi‐ oned views that were demonstrably Goethe's own. This contradiction reveals Goethe's ambivalence toward violent revolt, even when it serves a laudable cause.[24] The play shies away from portraying the actual uprising, which occurs only after the curtain falls — a telling indicator of Goethe's ambivalence toward political revolt in the cause of conservative values that he shared.

The events beginning in 1789 gave Goethe an entirely different model for revolutionary action, though he retained his aversion to political vio‐ lence. The first of his several plays devoted to the French Revolution is rather oblique. *Der Groß-Cophta* (The Grand Cophta, 1791) treats the scandals around the notorious Affair of the Diamond Necklace in 1785 and connects it to the supposed threat from secret societies and in partic‐ ular the charlatan known as Cagliostro (pseudonym for Giuseppi Balsamo, 1743–95).[25] Thus, this play deals more with a sidelight in the prehistory of the Revolution than with the events beginning in 1789. Nevertheless, it is an effective critique of aristocratic corruption, but also of the pernicious influence of secret societies.

Goethe's next play, *Die Aufgeregten* (The Rebels), was probably writ‐ ten in 1792 and 1793, but he left it unfinished and published it as a frag‐ ment in 1816. He most likely began work on it before taking part in the coalition campaign against the French in the fall of 1792: while war is cen‐ tral in all other works of Goethe that deal with the Revolution, it plays no role in this work. The normative figure is a German countess who has just traveled to Paris, where she witnessed unspecified events of the Revolution. She is now determined to introduce reforms to avoid similar upheaval in her own realm. Thus, she is an example of the sort of "the‐ atrical" observer of the Revolution mentioned above, who has drawn a moral lesson from the drama of which she was a spectator. Both she and a middle-class administrator seek to overcome the divisions between the pro- and antirevolutionary parties in Germany of the day, who were referred to as "aristocrats" and "democrats": the administrator, though middle-class, respects the accomplishments of the nobility, and the count‐ ess, for her part, criticizes her class for narrowly insisting on its rights, exploiting the other classes whenever possible, and ignoring the ominous signs of dissatisfaction and the seeds of revolt. Goethe later called this play his "politisches Glaubensbekenntnis jener Zeit"[26] (political confession of that time), pointing to these characters' attempt to bridge the differences between the parties. But his analysis is more subtle than any pat credo. Although scholars have often asserted that the play lampoons revolutionary ideals, in actuality it names real and valid grievances that provoke the revolt — though of course they are grievances voiced by German peasantry of the day, not by French revolutionaries. Furthermore, aristocratic privilege is shown to be arbitrary and unreliable, even in the countess's family. And the play's predicament — finding a document that will reveal whether the peasant's claims are just — is resolved by a flintlock-wielding daughter of the countess, who threatens to shoot a corrupt official who has spirited off the document for his own advantage. This daughter, Friederike, loves to hunt even when it damages the peasants' crops and has no regard for their needs, so the play's ending is thoroughly ambiguous. It could almost be said to justify a revolution as much as it satirizes revolutionaries. Besides this satire, Goethe's intent was probably to warn the German nobility that it should develop a sense of responsibility to the common weal. Interestingly, the prince is barely present in the play, replaced by benevolent local nobility, so that Goethe seems to advocate something like "enlightened feudalism," the responsible rule of lords on their estates, instead of "enlightened absolutism" at the more abstract level of the state, as a political model to resolve German issues of reform and authority. In any case, the play embodies one of the most important aspects of Goethe's attitude toward the Revolution: he acknowledged on many occasions that its roots lay in the failure of privileged elites to live up to their responsibilities.

The figure of the woman who resolves the action with a gun is part of a new gender discourse in these years. Reports of radical revolutionary feminists who demanded equal rights for women and were eventually guillotined haunted the pages of German newspapers. Perhaps more influential were two images of violent women in other reports from France: the celebrated plebian women on the streets of Paris, and women who served (dressed as men) in the French armies.[27] Goethe probably had more experience of the latter than most Germans, though it was mediated. At the front in August 1792, Carl August had reported in a letter to Voigt that a French woman had shot one of the German soldiers dead; and in the next year, during the siege of Mainz, he related that women captured among the troops at Valenciennes had claimed that there were 1700 of them in the French army.[28] In both cases, the reports were written by the duke only about ten days before Goethe joined him at the front lines, so Goethe must have heard the stories, because they caused quite a sensation. Even if he did not hear of them, news of these novel events was common coin. And the impact in literature was immediate. Goethe had never portrayed an armed woman before the Revolution; in *Egmont*, Clärchen laments that she is not a man and therefore cannot liberate her lover from prison because she is not strong enough to carry a weapon. In works by other authors, too, female figures almost always resorted to poison to carry out their misdeeds, or lent a dagger to a man (as in Lessing's *Emilia Galotti*, 1772). It was apparently taboo to portray a woman strong enough to carry a weapon like a sword or flintlock, let alone actually to use it. After the beginning of the Revolution, armed women flourish in literary works: Goethe depicted them not only in *Die Aufgeregten*, but also in *Herrmann und Dorothea* (as we shall see). This discourse was also at work in Heinrich von Kleist's play about the Amazon queen *Penthesilea* (1808), and in Friedrich Schiller's Joan of Arc drama, *Die Jungfrau von Orleans* (The Maiden of Orleans, 1801).[29] This was a time of all sorts of confusion of traditional gender roles, even though they were being codified and propagated. In Goethe's novel *Wilhelm Meisters Lehrjahre*, for example, we encounter in Wilhelm's beloved Mariane an actress dressed in a man's uniform, not to mention a "beautiful Amazon" and a girl named Mignon who in the first version of the novel, *Wilhelm Meisters theatralische Sendung* (Wilhelm Meister's Theatrical Mission), is alternately referred to with female and male pronouns (MA 2.2:143–44).[30] Much of this confusion can certainly be attributed to the shock that French revolutionary women caused to gender stability.

While *Die Aufgeregten* represented a serious grappling with the issues of revolution and the feudal abuses that can lead to it, Goethe's next play, *Der Bürgergeneral* (The Middle-Class General, 1793) was little more than a burlesque. It is generally considered a failure because it deals with such a serious, deadly topic rather off-handedly. Yet this play is even closer to the political conflicts in Saxe-Weimar than its predecessor. On 27 December 1792, the duke wrote to Goethe from his regiment's winter quarters in Frankfurt: "Leider habe ich schon auß manchen Briefen erfahren, daß unser Häuflein [i.e., in Weimar] sehr zweispaltig ist; indeßen verwundert mich dieses nicht: ich hoffe aber sehr auf deine Bindekraft; deine Ankunft giebt dorten ein allgemeines Intereße und wirckt auf unsere république, wie der Krieg auf die Fränckische. Siehe zu, was du bewircken kannst, und gieb mir zuweilen Nachricht davon"[31] (I have unfortunately learned from many a letter that our little group is very disunited; I'm not surprised at this, but I'm counting very much on your powers of cohesion. Your arrival there creates a common interest and has the same effect on our republic as the war does on the French one. See what you can do and report to me once in a while on it). This was an unmistakable directive, of the type that Carl August constantly issued in letters rather offhandedly, and Goethe and the other privy councilors unfailingly carried them out. By "letters" the duke was referring to secret missives that autumn denouncing Herder, Knebel, and others.[32] In other documents, another privy councilor and a

Weimar diplomat had suggested that the duchy's best writers be mobilized to combat the effects of revolutionary newspapers that were being read there.[33] This is apparently just what Goethe did — not only in certain passages of his epic poem *Reinecke Fuchs* (Reinecke the Fox, 1794), written in the following months, but also in *Der Bürgergeneral.* After it was completed that spring, Herder and his wife Caroline saw a production of the comedy and attested that they were themselves a target of the work's satire.[34] Goethe, too, described the goal of the work as defamatory, namely, "thörige oder tückische Unpatrioten in Deutschland zu entdecken"[35] (to expose foolish or malicious non-patriots in Germany). He also indicated, when describing the origin of the work, that he personally *knew* such misguided or malevolent admirers of the Revolution.[36] He was probably referring not only to such Mainz revolutionaries as Forster, who are openly parodied in the play, but also, in Weimar itself, the likes of Herder, Knebel, Wieland and Bode — not to mention more dangerous agitators in Eisenach and elsewhere of whom Goethe had knowledge.[37] It seems, then, that the impulses for writing this play came not only from Goethe's work as director of the Weimar court theater but also from political conflicts in Saxe-Weimar and even from a directive of the duke. Although the main character in the play is actually a sham revolutionary out to profit from his disguise, he still lampoons revolutionary ideals; it is precisely his egotistical motives that Goethe repeatedly attributed to revolutionaries. "Alle Freiheits-Apostel, sie waren mir immer zuwider; / Willkür suchte doch nur jeder am Ende für sich" (All apostles of freedom, they've always been loathe to me; / Every one of them always sought arbitrary power for himself), he wrote in one of his *Venezianische Epigramme* (Venetian Epigrams, 1795; MA 3.2: 136). In *Der Bürgergeneral*, the agitator disrupts a rural idyll of happy peasants presided over by an enlightened, paternalist lord who sees his subjects as part of his own family — a social fantasy that deconstructed itself in the eyes of most of Goethe's readers. In fact, much else in these two plays was contradictory. For example, although both plays assign normativity to middle-class values, these values are ultimately abstract: the characters who are meant to embody them are portrayed without reference to their family, supposedly the locus of these norms. Thus, even in this most blatantly anti-revolutionary of Goethe's works, he undercuts his own message — a common phenomenon for a writer who seldom conveyed an unalloyed political message in his complex works.

In the year after writing *Der Bürgergeneral*, Goethe's friendship with Schiller began (June–July 1794). This relationship was not only personal and literary, but also political, an alliance against liberal and revolutionary enemies — culminating in their attacks on both their literary and political critics in their collaborative collection of distichs, *Xenien* (1796). To be sure, Schiller originally conceived of the classical project as standing above political strife. This political abstinence had a background in events in Jena, where Schiller was a professor. His early plays, from the early to mid-1780s, had such a revolutionary flavor (though not, in fact, real revolutionary import) that the French had declared him an honorary citizen of their Republic — news of which reached Weimar at a particularly inconvenient time, the fall of 1792, when not only repression had set in at the University of Jena, but when Schiller himself was being championed as a hero by student agitators using verses from his early play *Die Räuber* (1782) as their tumult song. This confluence — as well as the commonplace description of the French revolutionaries as robbers — led not only to joking reproaches from conservatives in Weimar like Charlotte von Stein, but also to the more serious annoyance of the duke and the privy councilors.[38] Schiller, then, had every reason to remain unpolitical — it is true that he had never really supported the revolution (despite what one can often read in literary histories), but now, when his reputation threatened to suggest otherwise, he was careful not to get involved in political issues at all. His 1794 project for a new journal, *Die Horen*, sought contributors who would devote their writings entirely to the fine arts. The theoretical grounding for this political abstinence appeared in the journal under the title *Über die ästhetische Erziehung des Menschen. In einer Reihe von Briefen* (1795). The work was originally conceived in letters to Schiller's patrons, Prince (and later Duke) Friedrich Christian of Schleswig-Holstein-Sonderburg-Augustenburg (1765–1814) and Count Ernst Heinrich von Schimmelmann (1747–1831), both of whom were active reformist statesmen in Denmark and warm admirers of the Revolution. In these letters, Schiller justified his attention to aesthetics in the face of the more burning political issues of the day — issues that included a belated attempt to revive the Illuminati, for which Prince Augustenburg had attempted to recruit him.[39] Schiller steered clear of politics. He bitterly criticized the revolutionaries in France, who merely proved that although the moment that brought them to power was felicitous, human nature had not yet evolved to a level of moral dignity where it could be truly free and shoulder the momentous responsibilities of political self-determination. For Schiller, the only way around this depravity was the ennoblement of humanity through art; he thus postponed political liberation to the distant future, when the project of rescuing humanity from its moral baseness would be complete. Although Goethe probably disagreed with fundamental aspects of Schiller's project as expressed in this text, it was nevertheless ultimately canonized as the central manifesto of Weimar Classicism. The impact of this project for future readers was momentous: generations of scholars and students of German literature devalued working for political progress in favor of "aesthetic education," all on the authority of Germany's most prestigious writers.

Goethe's own contribution to Schiller's journal did not conform to the editor's principle of political neutrality in all respects.[40] *Unterhaltungen deutscher Ausgewanderten* (1794) is built around a framework narrative that depicts German nobles driven from their homes on the left bank of the Rhine by French troops, and the portrayal decidedly comes down against the character Carl, who is most sympathetic to the revolutionary cause and defends it vigorously. Because of Goethe's (in this instance, anonymous) championing of the counterrevolutionary cause, Schiller's project was roundly criticized by liberals for the hypocrisy of smuggling in conservative views under the guise of political neutrality[41] — and Schiller himself pointed out the contradiction in a letter to Goethe.[42] Despite its one-sided political tenor, Goethe's portrayal in the *Unterhaltungen* was hardly as trivial as in *Der Bürgergeneral*, and his approach was at least superficially an even-handed one, regardless of his sympathetic depiction of the anti-revolutionary characters: political strife was to be avoided by the Boccaccian telling of tales. Thus, Goethe's solution to the problem of political strife was dignified and civil sociability and the key classical norm of *Bildung* (sometimes translated as "self-formation"). In other words, Goethe valorized a flight from political discourse into art. In Goethe's letters, too, we find sporadic attempts to remain above the political fray of the revolutionary years, claiming that he was not interested in the cause either of revolutionaries or of counterrevolutionaries.[43] In the end, of course, he worked both as a writer and as a privy councilor against stirrings of resistance to absolutism in Germany. In doing so, he gave the lie to the notion — persistent even to this day — that Weimar Classicism represents a "disengagement" from politics.[44] Goethe and Schiller both mobilized literature against the forces of revolution.

In 1796, after the beginning of the moderate Directory period in France, Goethe's portrayal of the effects of the Revolution in Germany was somewhat more generous than in the *Unterhaltungen* or the earlier plays. He was able to step back from the events and appreciate the revolutionaries' intentions. His verse epic *Herrmann und Dorothea* again depicted the coalition wars, this time through the lens of an idyllic provincial town in Germany through which the sad procession of (this time less privileged) refugees passes. At the beginning of canto 6, Goethe deftly gives voice to the enthusiastic fervor — which he had himself not shared — that gripped German observers at the beginning of the Revolution:

> Denn wer leugnet es wohl, daß hoch sich das Herz ihm erhoben,
> Ihm die freiere Brust mit reineren Pulsen geschlagen,
> Als sich der erste Glanz der neuen Sonne heranhob,
> Als man hörte vom Rechte der Menschen, das allen gemein sei,
> Von der begeisternden Freiheit und von der löblichen Gleichheit!
> Damals hoffte jeder, sich selbst zu leben; es schien sich
> Aufzulösen das Band, das viele Länder umstrickte,
> Das der Müßiggang und der Eigennutz in der Hand hielt.
>
> (MA 4.1: 592)

[For who will deny that his heart was lifted, / His freer breast beat
with purer pulse, / When the first glow of the new sun dawned, /
When one heard of the right of mankind, common to all, / Of
inspiring freedom and of laudable equality! / Back then, everyone
hoped to live his own life, the shackles / That bound many nations
seemed to be broken, / No longer held in place by indolence and
egotism.]

And later in the work, he gives a moving description of the revolutionary
zeal of Dorothea's first fiancé, who joined the revolutionary cause but ultimately became its victim. All of this points to a certain objectivity in treating the still-explosive topic of revolution. However, the depiction of
enthusiasm for the Revolution is only a contrasting prelude to the deep
disappointment after the beginning of war (which is implicitly blamed on
the French) and the Terror. And the man with whom Dorothea is now to
be married, Herrmann, ends the work with a frighteningly chauvinist call
to arms against the French. To be sure, since the 1970s critics have stressed
the pervasive irony in this work, emanating not least of all from the clash
of hexameters — echoing sublime Greek epics — with banal German middle-class content.[45] And the irony has a clear gender twist: Like other
female characters in this period, Dorothea is armed, cutting down maraud-
ing French soldiers and would-be rapists with a saber, and yet she is
described almost in the same breath as a demure housewifely type ("ein
häusliches Mädchen," MA 4.1: 597). Herrmann, too, comes in for more
than his share of irony. Even Goethe's spelling of his name, eschewing
the usual form "Hermann," emphasizes in its doubling of "Herr"
["gentleman," "sir," "lord"] and "Mann" ["man"] masculine traits and
thus casts even more irony on this would-be warrior who weeps in his
mother's arms. For the average reader, however, the ending of the work
erases all such irony and rings with proto-nationalist militarism: the entire
nineteenth century canonized this epic and its concluding warlike threats
as the most popular of Goethe's works after *Faust*. This was Goethe's
intent; he was explicitly writing for a wider public in *Herrmann und
Dorothea*, even "writing down" to an audience which he hoped to woo
after having lost it with his earlier, esoteric works written primarily for a
courtly audience.[46]

Schiller had a similarly popularizing design with one of his most widely
read works, *Wilhelm Tell* (1804): he stressed the "Volksmäßigkeit" (popularity) of the theme,[47] remarked that he was writing the play "für das *ganze
Publikum*"[48] (for the *entire audience*), and admitted: "Noch hoffe ich in
meinem poetischen Schreiben keinen Rückschritt gethan zu haben, einen
Seitenschritt vielleicht, indem es mir begegnet seyn kann, den materiellen
Foderungen der Welt und der Zeit etwas eingeräumt zu haben"[49] (I am still
hoping that I have not taken a step backward in my poetic writing, perhaps
a step to the side, since I might have made concessions to the material

demands of the world and of the times). The political message of this play at first seems clear, since it favorably depicts a rebellion and defends the right to resistance to illegitimate authority, even terrorism — and thus ran into problems with the censors (and with producers, in Weimar no less than in Berlin). Furthermore, echoes of the French Revolution abound: the symbol of the rising sun (used often in describing the Revolution's effect); the gathering of Swiss conspirators paralleling the National Assembly in France; and the equality of the participants in the rebellion, regardless of class. In addition, the French revolutionaries had used the Swiss national revolt as a symbol of the republic that they established in Switzerland.[50] However, these echoes only serve to heighten the marked distancing of the play from the French example. Schiller leaves no doubt that Tell's act is a solitary one, made independently of the conspiracy of his countrymen, and that it is justified as a defense of family and home, not as a political act in itself. And in contradistinction to the French forging of new human rights, Schiller's protagonists explicitly declare that they do not wish to break new ground, but rather hark back to the "old rights" of the feudal system that had been taken from them by a rationalist government:

> Abtreiben wollen wir verhaßten Zwang,
> Die alten Rechte, wie wir sie ererbt
> Von unsern Vätern, wollen wir bewahren,
> Nicht ungezügelt nach dem Neuen greifen.
> (1353–56; WuB 5:434)

[We want to destroy hated force, / We want to preserve the old rights / As we inherited them from our fathers, / And not grasp for what's new with unfettered greed.]

One critic has aptly called the work a republican but anti-Jacobean play.[51] Its parallels to the French Revolution only serve to highlight the contrasts elsewhere in the text.

At around the same time, Goethe turned away from the popularizing mode (*Die Aufgeregten, Der Bürgergeneral, Herrmann und Dorothea*) and finally aimed at treating the revolutionary theme in a high tragedy in the lofty blank-verse mold of his earlier plays for the court, *Iphigenie auf Tauris* and *Torquato Tasso*. The new play, *Die natürliche Tochter* (The Bastard Daughter, 1803) is Goethe's most serious attempt to grapple with the earth-shaking significance of the events in France — which were now, after Napoleon's rise, historically distanced enough to allow a more generous assessment. As he himself wrote later, the plan for this play was "ein Gefäß, worin ich alles, was ich so manches Jahr über die Französische Revolution und deren Folgen geschrieben und gedacht, mit geziemendem Ernste niederzulegen hoffte"[52] (a vessel in which I hoped to deposit — with the appropriate seriousness — everything that I had written and thought for many a year about the French Revolution and its consequences). The phrase "appropriate seriousness" suggests that Goethe realized the inappropriateness of his earlier comical treatments of the theme. And yet, the Revolution is not directly depicted in *Die natürliche Tochter* any more than in the earlier plays. The tragedy portrays an intrigue around the illegitimate daughter of a duke, an "Amazonen-Tochter" (Amazon daughter), who likes to hunt and ride horses. She attempts to validate her claims of parentage but is blocked by a brother jealous of his inheritance. Goethe originally intended the work as a trilogy, but completed only the first part, and so the envisioned appearance of the "Volk" on the stage never materialized. As such, the play essentially portrays the corruption and self-centeredness of the *ancien régime* nobility, on whom Goethe placed a great deal of the responsibility for the outbreak of the Revolution: in their petty insistence on ancient privileges, their arbitrariness and intriguing, they pave the way for upheaval of the masses. But the revolution itself is only on the horizon. As Georg-Michael Schulz has pointed out, the focus on an individual robs the play of its general political implications.[53] Precisely this focus, however, is part and parcel of Goethe's view of the Revolution as a force of nature that negates human concepts of freedom.[54] He often likened it to a flood, a storm or a volcano; in fact, even his championing of the "Neptunists" against the "Vulcanists" — that is, his view that the earth originated in gradual growth from the seas rather than in volcanic eruption — was influenced strongly by his antipathy to the violent forces of the revolution. (Goethe portrayed this conflict allegorically in the "Klassische Walpurgisnacht" [Classical Walpurgis Night] of *Faust*, Part Two.)

After the deaths of Herder (1803), Schiller (1805), and Wieland (1813), the political opinions and actions of the principal figures of Weimar Classicism were reduced to those of Goethe. His views lost nothing of their conservative flavor and indeed hardened somewhat. Political apologists of Classical Weimar point out that the duchy introduced the first constitution in German lands in response to the promises made at the Congress of Vienna. However, Weimar's 1816 "constitution" was in most respects not the modern, liberal kind that we associate with the term today, but rather an estate-based (*ständisch*) constitution that granted individuals few rights. One of the rights that it did grant was freedom of the press, but as soon as Weimar subjects dared to lay claim to it, they learned that it was an empty guarantee: Goethe aided in prohibiting journals that became too vocal and even in punishing editors; and in any case, the Weimar constitution can hardly be attributed to Weimar Classicism, since Goethe opposed it.[55] He also opposed a Weimar measure allowing Jews and Christians to marry — just as he had opposed granting any sort of emancipation to Jews, steadfastly refusing to come to the aid of the ghettoized Jews in his hometown of Frankfurt who sought relief from some of the most notorious repression in Europe.[56] His attitude was probably less a result of his purported anti-Semitism — an issue on which scholars are in disagreement — than of his undisputed resistance to granting any new rights to his duke's subjects. Ironically, it was the duke who sought to introduce limited reforms in these years, not Goethe.

And yet Goethe's political views were not entirely steeped in the spirit of retrenchment. His distaste for war and nationalism have rightly been stressed by his apologists.[57] Naturally, this aversion must be seen in the perspective of his wider political views. And yet, even when war was designed to rescue the order in which he believed — the monarchist state — Goethe seems to have felt that armed conflict was in any case worse than the alternative. When he learned, while accompanying the duke in the campaign against the French, that his colleagues in Weimar's Privy Council had voted to declare the conflict no longer simply a dispute between Prussia and Austria against France, but one committing the military resources of the entire Holy Roman Empire, Goethe wrote: "Wir werden also auch mit der Heerde ins Verderben rennen — Europa braucht einen 30 jährigen Krieg um einzusehen was 1792 vernünftig gewesen wäre"[58] (So we will run headlong into our ruin with the rest of the herd. Europe needs another Thirty Years' War to understand what would have been prudent in 1792). This was a far-sighted prophecy, only slightly exaggerating the more than two decades of conflict — and repression — into which Europe was plunged in 1792 by the intervention against the rise of democracy in France. Even before the revolution, Goethe had, as director of the War Commission, drastically reduced the size of the duke's beloved military (the budget was more than halved). And in *Egmont*, he had portrayed vividly the ravages of war, through the mouthpiece of the protagonist, who argues with the Duke of Orange against inciting the populace to revolt against the iron rule of Spain:

> Was wir lange mühselig gestillt haben wirst du mit Einem Winke zur schröcklichsten Verwirrung aufhetzen. Denk an die Städte, die Edlen, das Volk, an die Handlung, den Feldbau! die Gewerbe! und denke die Verwüstung, den Mord! — Ruhig sieht der Soldat wohl im Felde seinen Kameraden neben sich hinfallen — Aber den Fluß herunter werden dir die Leichen der Bürger, der Kinder, der Jungfrauen entgegen schwimmen, daß du mit Entsetzen dastehst und nicht mehr weißt wessen Sache du verteidigst, da die zu Grunde gehen für deren Freiheit du die Waffen ergriffst. Und wie wird dirs sein, wenn du dir still sagen mußt: für meine Sicherheit ergriff ich sie. (MA 3.1: 281)

> [What we have finally calmed with much effort, you will stir up to the most horrible chaos with a single stroke. Think of the cities, the nobles, the people, commerce, farming! trade! and think of the desolation, the killing! — To be sure, the soldier is unmoved when his comrade is killed in battle next to him — but the bodies of civilians, of children, of maidens will float past you on the river so that you will stand there gripped by horror und you won't know whose cause you are defending, since those for whose freedom you took up arms will be destroyed. And how will you feel if you have to say to yourself: I took up arms for my personal security.]

Here, of course, Egmont is arguing not just against war, but against revolt, and he certainly has other than lofty reasons for doing so. And *Herrmann und Dorothea*, as we saw, ends with a ringing call to arms to protect German families against the revolutionary onslaught. This position only seems at first glance to contradict Goethe's later rejection of the armed uprising against Napoleon in 1813 and especially its nationalist overtones. In both cases, his reasons were partly dictated by his predilection for small principalities, whose existence was threatened by the French in the one case, and the German nationalists in the other — and the latter were, in this early phase, inspired by liberal political thought that was anathema to Goethe. Goethe's well-known devotion to Napoleon himself remains something of a puzzle, given the poet's aversion to war; it must, however, be seen precisely in terms of Napoleon's perceived stabilization of the monarchist order against its enemies — enemies that included the radical revolutionaries and democrats at home in France. Ultimately, then, Goethe's aversion to war can generally be explained by his fear of threats to the absolutist order in which he saw the major guarantor of European stability; even in the case of the imperial war against France, which he ostensibly opposed, he expressed the hope that it would soon successfully eject "die leidigen Franzen" (the horrid Frenchies) from German lands.[59] But a moral element remains, a principled loathing of the horrors of war.

It is an unfortunate but entirely understandable aspect of Goethe's legacy that his aversion to armed conflict hardly influenced mentalities in Germany in the centuries after his death. Instead, every scrap of nationalist or apparently nationalist sentiment in German Classicism was mobilized in the cause of German unification, and then, after two disastrous world wars and again after the reunification of Germany in 1989, Goethe was transformed into a harbinger of democracy.[60]

Both tendencies do violence to the historical record. Despite the abhorrence of militarism and minor reform initiatives, the political heritage of Weimar Classicism – at least when we ignore Herder and Wieland — is deeply conservative, at times even reactionary. This uncomfortable fact can be attributed partly to the general backwardness of German politics at the time, and in particular to the impossibility of a revolution there. But the Weimar Olympians did not even stand behind the many appeals for fundamental reform of absolutist territories and limited democratization. The decisive factor in this attitude was Goethe's symbiosis with absolutism as a minister of state. Though it is difficult to separate aesthetics from politics in works of German Classicism, it is important to recognize the conservative political thrust of works that otherwise can be counted as deservedly "classical"; to do otherwise risks propagating antidemocratic values incorporated in texts of the highest aesthetic caliber.

Notes

[1] Among the many histories of Germany in this period, the best in English is James J. Sheehan, *German History, 1770–1866* (New York: Oxford UP, 1989). On the impact of the Revolution, see the essays and bibliography in *The Internalized Revolution: German Reactions to the French Revolution, 1789–1989*, ed. Ehrhard Bahr, Thomas P. Saine (New York: Garland, 1992); also Thomas P. Saine, *Black Bread — White Bread: German Intellectuals and the French Revolution* (Columbia, SC: Camden House, 1988).

[2] See Gerd Ueding, *Klassik und Romantik: Deutsche Literatur im Zeitalter der Französischen Revolution 1789–1815,* Hansers Sozialgeschichte der deutschen Literatur, vol. 4 (Munich: Hanser, 1987); *Zwischen Revolution und Restauration: Klassik, Romantik,* vol. 5 of *Deutsche Literatur: Eine Sozialgeschichte,* ed. Horst Albert Glaser (Reinbek: Rowohlt, 1980); Gerhard Schulz, *Das Zeitalter der französischen Revolution 1789–1806,* part 1 of *Die deutsche Literatur zwischen Französischer Revolution und Restauration,* vol. 7 of *Geschichte der deutschen Literatur von den Anfängen bis zur Gegenwart* (Munich: Beck, 1983).

[3] See the essays in *Enlightened Absolutism: Reform and Reformers in Later Eighteenth-Century Europe,* ed. H. M. Scott (Ann Arbor: U of Michigan P, 1990), as well as my more comprehensive treatment in volume 5 of the present literary history: W. Daniel Wilson, "Eighteenth-Century Germany in Its Historical Context," in *German Literature of the Eighteenth-Century: The Enlightenment and Sensibility,* ed. Barbara Becker-Cantarino, vol. 5 of *Camden House History of German Literature* (Rochester, NY: Camden House, 2004), 265–83.

[4] See the anthologies *Von deutscher Republik 1775–1795: Texte radikaler Demokraten,* ed. Jost Hermand (Frankfurt am Main: Suhrkamp, 1975), and, specifically for the revolutionary period, *Die Französische Revolution im Spiegel der deutschen Literatur,* ed. Claus Träger (Leipzig: Reclam, 1975), and *Die Französische Revolution in Deutschland,* ed. Friedrich Eberle and Theo Stammen (Stuttgart: Reclam, 1989).

[5] For scholarship on the Illuminati, see volume 5 of the *Camden House History of German Literature.*

[6] See Klaus Epstein, *The Genesis of German Conservatism* (Princeton: Princeton UP, 1966).

[7] See Epstein as well as Johannes Rogalla von Bieberstein, *Die These von der Verschwörung, 1776–1945: Philosophen, Freimaurer, Juden, Liberale und Sozialisten als Verschwörer gegen die Sozialordnung* (Bern: Herbert Lang, 1976).

[8] For an excellent collection of German responses to the Revolution — including those of travelers to Paris — see *Die Französische Revolution: Berichte und Deutungen deutscher Schriftsteller und Historiker,* ed. Horst Günther (Deutscher Klassiker Verlag, 1985).

[9] Among the copious scholarship on the German "Jakobiner" see the multivolume series *Deutsche revolutionäre Demokraten* (Stuttgart: Metzler, 1971–78) and the short introduction by Helmut Reinalter, *Der Jakobinismus in Mitteleuropa* (Stuttgart: Kohlhammer, 1981).

[10] See Heinrich Scheel, *Die Mainzer Republik,* 3 vols. (Berlin: Akademie, 1975–89).

[11] See Peter Blickle, *Unruhen in der ständischen Gesellschaft, 1300–1800* (Munich: Oldenbourg, 1988); Andreas Würgler, *Unruhen und Öffentlichkeit: Städtische und ländliche Protestbewegungen im 18. Jahrhundert* (Tübingen: Bibliotheca Academica, 1995).

[12] The classic depiction is Fritz Hartung, *Das Großherzogtum Sachsen unter der Regierung Carl Augusts 1775–1828* (Weimar: Böhlau, 1923), followed by the myriad works of Hans Tümmler, especially his introduction to vol. 2 of *Politischer Briefwechsel des Herzogs und Großherzogs Carl August von Weimar,* ed. Willy Andreas, Hans Tümmler (Stuttgart: Deutsche Verlags-Anstalt, 1958). On the ideological bias of the work of these scholars, especially Tümmler, see W. Daniel Wilson, "Tabuzonen um Goethe und seinen Herzog: Heutige Folgen nationalsozialistischer Absolutismuskonzeptionen," *Deutsche Vierteljahrsschrift für Literaturwissenschaft und Geistesgeschichte* 70 (1996): 394–442.

[13] Dieter Borchmeyer, *Weimarer Klassik: Portrait einer Epoche* (Weinheim: Beltz Athenäum, 1994), 248. Borchmeyer relies heavily on the work of Tümmler and others mentioned in the previous note.

[14] For the following, see W. Daniel Wilson, *Das Goethe-Tabu: Protest und Menschenrechte im klassischen Weimar* (Munich: Deutscher Taschenbuch Verlag, 1999) and *Goethes Weimar und die Französische Revolution: Dokumente der Krisenjahre* (Cologne: Böhlau Verlag, 2004).

[15] On Goethe's administrative activity, see the introductions to the first two volumes of *Goethes amtliche Schriften: Veröffentlichung des Staatsarchivs Weimar,* 4 vols. to date, ed. Willy Flach (vol. 1) and Helma Dahl (vols. 2–4) (Weimar: Böhlau, 1950–), and Wilson, *Das Goethe-Tabu.*

[16] See the corrective account in Helma Dahl's introduction to vol. 2 of the *Amtliche Schriften.*

[17] Wilson, *Goethes Weimar,* 437 (from a report by Eisenach Kammerrat Johann Carl Salomon Thon, 25 Nov. 1792). On the other events cited here, see the documents in this edition.

[18] "[E]ine Demonstration von überlegner Gewalt," in a letter from Privy Councillor Voigt to Duke Carl August citing Goethe's opinion, 14 July 1792, Wilson, *Goethes Weimar,* 220.

[19] See Karl-Heinz Fallbacher, "Fichtes Entlassung: Ein Beitrag zur Weimar-Jenaischen Institutionengeschichte," *Archiv für Kulturgeschichte* 67 (1985): 111–35.

[20] See Wilson, *Das Goethe-Tabu,* ch. 5.

[21] See the writings collected in Christoph Martin Wieland, *Meine Antworten: Aufsätze über die Französische Revolution 1789–1793,* ed. Fritz Martini (Marbach: Deutsches Literaturarchiv, 1983).

[22] See the introduction to Wilson, *Goethes Weimar,* 47–48.

[23] *Bedeutende Fördernis durch ein einziges geistreiches Wort* (1822), MA 12:308.

[24] See W. Daniel Wilson, "Hunger/Artist: Goethe's Revolutionary Agitators in *Götz, Satyros, Egmont,* and *Der Bürgergeneral,*" *Monatshefte* 86 (1994): 80–94.

[25] For the following analysis of this play, as well as *Der Bürgergeneral* and *Die Aufgeregten,* see W. Daniel Wilson, "Dramen zum Thema der Französischen

Revolution," *Goethe Handbuch,* vol. 2: *Dramen,* ed. Theo Buck (Stuttgart: Metzler, 1996), 258–87, with bibliography.

[26] Conversation with Eckermann on 4 Jan. 1824, MA 19: 493.

[27] See Claudia Opitz, "Der Bürger wird Soldat — und die Bürgerin . . . ? Die Revolution, der Krieg und die Stellung der Frauen nach 1789," *Sklavin oder Bürgerin? Französische Revolution und Neue Weiblichkeit 1760–1830,* ed. Viktoria Schmidt-Linsenhoff (Frankfurt am Main: Jonas, 1989), 38–54.

[28] To Voigt, Monfort, 17 Aug. 1792, and "Im Lager vor Maintz," 16 May 1793, Wilson, *Goethes Weimar,* 339, 595. In December 1792, too, Carl August experienced the capture of a woman in the uniform of the National Guard; see Willy Andreas, *Carl August von Weimar in und nach der Kampagne gegen Frankreich,* Sitzungsberichte der Bayerischen Akademie der Wissenschaften zu München, Philosophisch-Historische Klasse; 1954, 5 (Munich: Verlag der Bayerischen Akademie der Wissenschaften, 1955), 54.

[29] See Inge Stephan, " 'Da werden Weiber zu Hyänen . . . '— Amazonen und Amazonenmythen bei Schiller und Kleist," *Feministische Literaturwissenschaft: Dokumentation der Tagung in Hamburg vom Mai 1983,* ed. Inge Stephan and Sigrid Weigel (Berlin: Argument, 1984), 23–42, and a forthcoming dissertation by Julie Koser.

[30] See Catriona MacLeod, "Pedagogy and Androgyny in *Wilhelm Meisters Lehrjahre,*" in her *Embodying Ambiguity: Androgyny and Aesthetics from Winckelmann to Keller* (Detroit: Wayne State UP, 1998), 91–139.

[31] *Briefwechsel des Herzogs-Großherzogs Carl August mit Goethe,* ed. Hans Wahl, 3 vols. (Berlin: Mittler, 1915–1918), 1:168; Wilson, *Goethes Weimar,* 491–92.

[32] See W. Daniel Wilson, *Geheimräte gegen Geheimbünde: Ein unbekanntes Kapitel der klassisch-romantischen Geschichte Weimars* (Stuttgart: Metzler, 1991), 352–56.

[33] See Wilson, *Goethes Weimar,* 450, 466.

[34] Herders to Goethe, 2 June 1793, Wilson, *Goethes Weimar,* 599.

[35] Letter to Bertuch, 6 June 1793, WA 4.18:49.

[36] In *Campagne in Frankreich 1792* (1822), MA 14: 512.

[37] See Voigt's letter to Carl August, 17 Dec. 1792, Wilson, *Goethes Weimar,* 468–69.

[38] See Wilson, *Das Goethe-Tabu,* 217–28.

[39] See Wilson, *Geheimräte,* 163–67; Hans-Jürgen Schings, *Die Brüder des Marquis Posa: Schiller und der Geheimbund der Illuminaten* (Tübingen: Niemeyer, 1996).

[40] See Reiner Wild's commentary in MA 4.1:1040–53 and the essay by Ulrich Gaier cited there; for a contrary position, see Borchmeyer, *Weimarer Klassik,* 253.

[41] Most effectively by the famous composer — and prorevolutionary — Johann Friedrich Reichardt (1752–1814), in his journal *Deutschland* 1, 1 (1796): 59–60.

[42] Letter of 29 November 1794, MA 4.1:1056.

[43] On 18 August 1792 Goethe wrote to Friedrich Heinrich Jacobi after visiting his home town of Frankfurt that ". . . mir weder am Todte der Aristocratischen noch Democratischen Sünder im mindesten etwas gelegen ist. Meine alten Freunde und meine zunehmende Vaterstadt habe ich mit Freuden gesehen, nur kann es nicht

fehlen daß man nicht in allen Gesellschaften lange Weile habe, denn wo zwey oder drey zusammenkommen, hört man gleich das vierjährige Lied pro und contra wieder herab orgeln und nicht einmal mit Variationen sondern das crude Thema" (I do not care the slightest whether the democratic or aristocratic rascals are killed off. I was glad to see my old friends and my growing home town, but it's difficult not to be bored in any gathering, because where two or three people get together, you hear the four-year-old ditty being played again, and not even with any variations, but just the crude theme). WA 4.10:6.

[44] See Borchmeyer, 247.

[45] Instrumental in this reassessment was Frank G. Ryder and Benjamin Bennett's, "The Irony of Goethe's *Hermann und Dorothea*: Its Form and Function," *PMLA* 90 (1975): 433–46.

[46] On 3 January 1798 Goethe wrote to Schiller: "In Herrmann und Dorothea habe ich, was das Material betrifft, den Deutschen einmal ihren Willen gethan und nun sind sie äußerst zufrieden" (In *Herrmann and Dorothea*, for once, I humored the Germans [as far as the subject is concerned], and now they are extremely content; WA 4.13:5).

[47] To Iffland, 5 August 1803, and to Humboldt, 18 August 1803, WuB 5:751–52.

[48] To Iffland, 9 November 1803, WuB 5:754.

[49] To Humboldt, 2 April 1805, WuB 5:772.

[50] See Dieter Borchmeyer, "Altes Recht und Revolution: Schillers *Wilhelm Tell*," in *Friedrich Schiller: Kunst, Humanität und Politik in der späten Aufklärung*, ed. Wolfgang Wittkowski (Tübingen: Niemeyer, 1982), 69–113.

[51] See Gonthier-Louis Fink, "Schillers *Wilhelm Tell*, ein antijakobinisches republikanisches Schauspiel," *Aufklärung* 1 (1986): 57–81.

[52] *Tag- und Jahreshefte 1799*, MA 14:60.

[53] Georg-Michael Schulz, "Die natürliche Tochter," *Goethe Handbuch* 2: 288–303.

[54] See Goethe's letter to Schiller of 9 March 1802, MA 8.1:887, and Schulz, 300.

[55] See documents no. 264, 267, 274–75, 277–79, 284–86 in *Amtliche Schriften* 2.2.

[56] See W. Daniel Wilson, "'Humanitätssalbader': Goethe's Distaste for Jewish Emancipation, and Jewish Responses," in *Goethe in German-Jewish Culture*, ed. Klaus L. Berghahn and Jost Hermand (Rochester, NY: Camden House, 2001): 146–64.

[57] Foremost among these is Ekkehart Krippendorff, *"Wie die Großen mit den Menschen spielen": Versuch über Goethes Politik* (Frankfurt: Suhrkamp, 1988).

[58] Letter of 15 October 1792 to Voigt, *Amtliche Schriften* 2.1:301.

[59] Letter to the dowager duchess Anna Amalia, 22 June 1793; WA 4.10:82.

[60] On Goethe's reception in Germany, see the magisterial work by Karl Robert Mandelkow, *Goethe in Deutschland: Rezeptionsgeschichte eines Klassikers*, 2 vols. (Munich: Beck, 1980, 1989). A particularly far-fetched attempt to establish Goethe as the *spiritus rector* of the German constitution can be found in Katharina Mommsen's speech to the Goethe Society in Weimar on the occasion of the 250th anniversary of Goethe's birth: *Goethe und unsere Zeit* (Frankfurt am Main: Suhrkamp, 1999).

Bibliography

Primary Literature

Baumgarten, Alexander Gottlieb. *Meditationes philosophicae de nonnullis ad poema pertinentibus*, 1735. Translated by Karl Aschenbrenner & William B. Holther as *Reflections on Poetry*. Berkeley: U of California P, 1954.

———. *Metaphysica*, 1750. Translated into German by Ursula Niggli as *Die Vorreden zur Metaphysik*. Frankfurt am Main: Klostermann, 1999.

———. *Aesthetica I & II*, 1750/58. Selections translated into German by Hans Rudolf Schweitzer as *Texte zur Grundlegung der Ästhetik*. Hamburg: F. Meiner, 1983.

Bertuch, Friedrich Justin, ed. *Allgemeine Literatur-Zeitung*, 1785–1808.

———, ed. *Journal des Luxus und der Moden*, 1786–1827.

———, trans. *Don Quixote*, 1773.

Blanckenburg, Christian Friedrich von. *Versuch über den Roman*, 1774.

Blumenbach, Johann Friedrich. *Über den Bildungstrieb und das Zeugungsgeschäfte*, 1781.

Brentano, Clemens. *Godwi oder Das steinerne Bild der Mutter: Ein verwilderter Roman*, 1801–2. 2 vols.

Böttiger, Karl August. *Literarische Zustände und Zeitgenossen*, 1838. First complete edition by Klaus Gerlach und René Sternke, Berlin: Aufbau Verlag, 1998.

Cellini, Benvenuto. *Leben des Benvenuto Cellini Florentinischen Goldschmieds und Bildhauers von ihm selbst geschrieben: Übersetzt und mit einem Anhange*, 1803. 2 vols. Translated by Johann Wolfgang von Goethe. Translated by Julia Conaway Bondanella and Peter Bondanella as *My Life*. Oxford and New York: Oxford UP, 2002.

Collin, Heinrich Joseph von. *Regulus: eine Tragödie in fünf Aufzügen*, 1802.

Die Historia von D. Iohan Fausten, 1587. Translated anonymously as *The History of the Damnable Life, and Deserued Death of Doctor Iohn Faustus*, 1592.

De Staël-Holstein, Mme. *De l'Allemagne*, 1813. Translated and edited by Max F. Müller and O. W. Wight as *Germany*. New York: Derby & Jackson, 1859.

Eckermann, Johann Peter. *Gespräche mit Goethe in den letzten Jahren seines Lebens*, Vols. 1 &2, 1836; Vol. 3, 1848. Translated and edited by David Luke as *Conversations and Encounters*. London: O. Wolff, 1966.

Eichendorff, Joseph Freiherr von. *Ahnung und Gegenwart: Ein Roman*, 1815.

Fichte, Johann Gottlieb. *Grundlage der gesammten Wissenschaftslehre als Handschrift für seine Zuhörer*, 1794. Revised 1802. Edited and translated by Peter Heath and John Lachs as *Foundations of the Entire Science of Knowledge (Wissenschaftslehre), with the First and Second Introductions.* New York: Appleton-Century-Crofts, 1970; Cambridge: Cambridge UP, 1982.

Gluck, Christoph Willibald von. *Iphigénie en Tauride*, 1779.

Goethe, Johann Wolfgang von. *Die Mitschuldigen: Ein Schauspiel*, 1769. Revised 1780–83.

———. "Heidenröslein," 1771. Translated by John Frederick Nims as "Rosebud in the Heather," in *Johann Wolfgang von Goethe. Selected Poems.* Vol. 1. Boston: Suhrkamp/Insel, 1983.

———. *Sesenheimer Lieder*, 1771.

———. "Willkommen und Abschied," 1771/89. Translated by Christopher Middleton as "Welcome and Farewell," in *Johann Wolfgang von Goethe. Selected Poems.* Vol. 1. Boston: Suhrkamp/Insel, 1983.

———. "Der Wandrer," 1772. Translated by Edgar Alfred Bowring as "The Wanderer," in *The Poems of Goethe, translated in the original metres.* London: G. Bell & Sons, 1885.

———. "Wanderers Sturmlied," 1772. Translated by Christopher Middleton as "Wanderer's Storm-Song," in *Johann Wolfgang von Goethe. Selected Poems.* Vol. 1. Boston: Suhrkamp/Insel, 1983.

———. *Götz von Berlichingen mit der eisernen Hand: ein Schauspiel*, 1773. Translated by Cyrus Hamlin as *Goetz von Berlichingen with the Iron Hand*, in *Goethe's Collected Works.* Vol. 7, *Early Verse Drama and Prose Plays.* New York: Suhrkamp, 1988.

———. "Der König in Thule," 1774. Translated by John Frederick Nims as "The King in Thule," in *Johann Wolfgang von Goethe. Selected Poems.* Vol. 1. Boston: Suhrkamp/Insel, 1983.

———. *Die Leiden des jungen Werthers*, 1774. Translated by Victor Lange and J. Ryan as *The Sorrows of Young Werther*, in *Goethe's Collected Works.* Vol. 11. New York: Suhrkamp, 1988.

———. *Götter Helden und Wieland: Eine Farce*, 1774.

———. "Auf dem See," 1775. Translated by Christopher Middleton as "On the Lake," in *Johann Wolfgang von Goethe. Selected Poems.* Vol. 1. Boston: Suhrkamp/Insel, 1983.

———. *Egmont: Ein Trauerspiel in fünf Aufzügen*, 1775. Translated by Michael Hamburger as *Egmont*, in *Goethe's Collected Works.* Vol. 7, *Early Verse Drama and Prose Plays.* New York: Suhrkamp, 1988.

———. *Erwin und Elmire: Ein Schauspiel mit Gesang*, 1775–88.

———. *Die Geschwister: Ein Schauspiel*, 1776. Translated anonymously as *The Sisters*, in *Dramatic Pieces from the German.* Edinburgh and London: printed for William Creech and T. Cadell, 1792.

Goethe, Johann Wolfgang von. *Stella: Ein Schauspiel für Liebende in fünf Akten*, 1776. Translated by Robert M. Browning and Frank Ryder as *Stella*, in *Goethe's Collected Works*. Vol. 7, *Early Verse Drama and Prose Plays*. New York: Suhrkamp, 1988.

————. "Wandrers Nachtlied," 1776. Translated by Henry Wadsworth Longfellow as "Wanderer's Night Song," in *Johann Wolfgang von Goethe. Selected Poems*. Vol. 1. Boston: Suhrkamp/Insel, 1983.

————. *Wilhelm Meisters theatralische Sendung*, 1776/85. Translated by Gregory A. Page as *Wilhelm Meister's Theatrical Mission*. London: W. Heinemann, 1913.

————. "An den Mond," 1777/89. Translated anonymously as "To the Moon," in *Johann Wolfgang von Goethe. Selected Poems*. Vol. 1. Boston: Suhrkamp/Insel, 1983.

————. "Harzreise in Winter," 1777. Translated by Christopher Middleton as "A Winter Journey in the Harz," in *Johann Wolfgang von Goethe. Selected Poems*. Vol. 1. Boston: Suhrkamp/Insel, 1983.

————. *Triumph der Empfindsamkeit*, 1777.

————. *Proserpina: Ein Monodrama*, 1778. Translated by Cyrus Hamlin as *Prosperina*, in *Goethe's Collected Works*. Vol. 7, *Early Verse Drama and Prose Plays*. New York: Suhrkamp, 1988.

————. *Jery und Bätely: Ein Singspiel*, 1779. Translated by Frank Ryder as *Jery and Betty*, in *Goethe's Collected Works*. Vol. 7, *Early Verse Drama and Prose Plays*. New York: Suhrkamp, 1988.

————. *Elpenor*, 1781.

————. "Auf Miedings Tod," 1782.

————. "Erlkönig," 1782. Translated by Christopher Middleton as "Erlkönig," in *Johann Wolfgang von Goethe. Selected Poems*. Vol. 1. Boston: Suhrkamp/Insel, 1983.

————. "Zueignung" (prologue to *Schriften*, 1789), 1784. Translated by W. E. Aytoun, Theodore Martin, and Christopher Middleton as "Dedication," in *Johann Wolfgang von Goethe. Selected Poems*. Vol. 1. Boston: Suhrkamp/Insel, 1983.

————. *Iphigenie auf Tauris: Ein Schauspiel*, 1787. Translated by David Luke as *Iphigenia in Tauris*, in *Goethe's Collected Works*. Vol. 8, *Verse Plays and Epic*. New York: Suhrkamp, 1987.

————. *Nausikaa*, 1787–88.

————. "Einfache Nachahmung der Natur, Manier, Stil," 1789. Translated by Ellen von Nardroff and Earnest H. von Nardroff as "Simple Imitation of Nature, Manner, Style," in *Goethe's Collected Works*. Vol. 3, *Essays on Art and Literature*. New York: Suhrkamp, 1986.

————. "Römische Elegien," 1789–90. Translated by Michael Hamburger as "Roman Elegies," in *Johann Wolfgang von Goethe. Selected Poems*. Vol. 1. Boston: Suhrkamp/Insel, 1983. Translated by David Luke as *Roman Elegies*. London: Libris, 1988.

Goethe, Johann Wolfgang von. "Von Arabesken," 1789.

———. "Die Metamorphose der Pflanzen," 1790. Translated by Douglas Miller as "The Metamorphosis of Plants," in *Johann Wolfgang von Goethe*. Vol. 12, *Scientific Studies*. New York: Suhrkamp, 1988.

———. *Torquato Tasso: Ein Schauspiel*, 1790. Translated by Michael Hamburger as *Torquato Tasso*, in *Goethe's Collected Works*. Vol. 8, *Verse Plays and Epic*. New York: Suhrkamp, 1987.

———. *Der Groß-Cophta: Ein Lustspiel in fünf Aufzügen*, 1791.

———. *Die Aufgeregten*, 1791–92.

———. *Der Bürgergeneral: Ein Lustspiel in einem Aufzuge. Zweyte Fortsetzung der beyden Billets*, 1793.

———. "In wiefern die Idee: Schönheit sei Vollkommenheit mit Freiheit, auf organische Naturen angewendet werden könne," 1794. Translated by Douglas Miller as "The Extent to Which the Idea 'Beauty is Perfection in Combination with Freedom' May be Applied to Living Organisms," in *Johann Wolfgang von Goethe*. Vol. 12, *Scientific Studies*. New York: Suhrkamp, 1988.

———. *Reinecke Fuchs*, 1794. Translated by Alexander Rogers as *Reineke Fox*, in *Reineke Fox, West-Eastern Divan, and Achilleid: Translated in the Original Metres*. London: Bohn, 1890.

———. *Das Märchen*, 1795. Translated by Carol Tully as *The Fairy Tale*, in *Romantic Fairy Tales*. London: Penguin Books, 2000.

———. *Die Zauberflöte, Zweiter Teil*, 1795–98.

———. "Literarischer Sansculottismus," 1795.

———. "Der Marschall von Bassompierre," in *Unterhaltungen deutscher Ausgewanderten*, 1795.

———. *Unterhaltungen deutscher Ausgewanderten*, 1795. Translated by Jan van Heurck, in cooperation with Jane K. Brown, as *Conversations of German Refugees*, in *Goethe's Collected Works*. Vol. 10. New York: Suhrkamp, 1989.

———. *Wilhelm Meisters Lehrjahre: Ein Roman*, 1795/96. 4 vols. Translated by Eric Blackall and Victor Lange as *Wilhelm Meister's Apprenticeship*, in *Goethe's Collected Works*. Vol. 9. New York: Suhrkamp, 1989.

———. "Alexis und Dora," 1796. Translated by Edgar Alfred Bowring as "Alexis and Dora," in *The Poems of Goethe, translated in the original metres*. London: G. Bell & Sons, 1885.

———. *Epigramme: Venedig 1790*, 1796. Translated by Michael Hamburger and Christopher Middleton as "Venetian Epigrams," in *Johann Wolfgang von Goethe. Selected Poems*. Vol. 1. Boston: Suhrkamp/Insel, 1983.

———. "Xenien," 1796. Written in collaboration with Friedrich Schiller. Translated by Paul Carus as *Goethe and Schiller's Xenions*. Chicago: Open Court Publishing, 1915.

———. "Der Gott und die Bajadere," 1797. Translated by John Whaley as "The God and the Bayadere," in *Goethe: Selected Poems*. London: J. M. Dent, 1998.

Goethe, Johann Wolfgang von. "Die Braut von Korinth," 1797. Translated by W. E. Aytoun, Theodore Martin, and Christopher Middleton as "The Bride of Corinth," in *Johann Wolfgang von Goethe. Selected Poems*. Vol. 1. Boston: Suhrkamp/Insel, 1983.

———. "Euphrosyne," 1797.

———. "Über die Gegenstände der bildenden Kunst," 1797.

———. "Die Metamorphose der Pflanzen," 1798. Translated by Michael Hamburger as "The Metamorphosis of Plants," in *Johann Wolfgang von Goethe. Selected Poems*. Vol. 1. Boston: Suhrkamp/Insel, 1983.

———. "Einleitung in die Propyläen," 1798. Translated by Ellen von Nardroff and Earnest H. von Nardroff as "Introduction to the *Propylaea*," in *Goethe's Collected Works*. Vol. 3, *Essays on Art and Literature*. New York: Suhrkamp, 1986.

———. *Hermann und Dorothea*, 1798. Translated by David Luke as *Hermann and Dorothea*, in *Goethe's Collected Works*. Vol. 8, *Verse Plays and Epic*. New York: Suhrkamp, 1987.

———. "Über Laokoon," 1798. Translated by Ellen von Nardroff and Earnest H. von Nardroff as "On the *Laocoon* Group," in *Goethe's Collected Works*. Vol. 3, *Essays on Art and Literature*. New York: Suhrkamp, 1986.

———. *Über Wahrheit und Wahrscheinlichkeit der Kunstwerke*, 1798. Translated by Ellen von Nardroff and Earnest H. von Nardroff as "On Realism in Art," in *Goethe's Collected Works*. Vol. 3, *Essays on Art and Literature*. New York: Suhrkamp, 1986.

———. *Achilleid*, 1799. Translated by Alexander Rogers as *Achilleid*, in *Reineke Fox, West-Eastern Divan, and Achilleid: Translated in the Original Metres*. London: Bohn, 1890.

———. *Paläophron und Neoterpe*, 1800.

———. *Was wir bringen: Vorspiel, bey der Eröffnung des neuen Schauspielhauses zu Lauchstädt*, 1802.

———. *Regeln für Schauspieler*, 1803.

———. *Die natürliche Tochter*, 1804. Translated by Hunter Hannum as *The Natural Daughter*, in *Goethe's Collected Works*. Vol. 8, *Verse Plays and Epic*. New York: Suhrkamp, 1987.

———. *Rameaus Neffe: Ein Dialog von Diderot. Aus dem Manuskript übersetzt und mit Anmerkungen begleitet*, 1805. Translated by Goethe.

———. "Skizzen zu einer Schilderung Winckelmanns," in *Winckelmann und sein Jahrhundert*, 1805.

———. "Die Absicht eingeleitet," 1807. Translated by Douglas Miller as "The Purpose Set Forth," in *Johann Wolfgang von Goethe*. Vol. 12, *Scientific Studies*. New York: Suhrkamp, 1988.

———. *Faust: Eine Tragödie*, 1808; *Zweyter Theil in fünf Akten*, 1832. Translated and edited by Stuart Atkins as *Faust 1 & 2*, in *Goethe's Collected Works*, vol. 2. New York: Suhrkamp, 1984.

Goethe, Johann Wolfgang von. *Die Wahlverwandtschaften: Ein Roman,* 1809. 2 vols. Translated by Victor Lange and J. Ryan as *Elective Affinities,* in *Goethe's Collected Works.* Vol. 11. New York: Suhrkamp, 1988.

———. "Die wunderlichen Nachbarskinder," in *Die Wahlverwandtschaften,* 1809.

———. *Zur Farbenlehre,* 1810. 2 vols. Translated by Douglas Miller as "Theory of Color," in *Johann Wolfgang von Goethe.* Vol. 12, *Scientific Studies.* New York: Suhrkamp, 1988.

———. *Aus meinem Leben: Dichtung und Wahrheit,* 1811–13. 3 vols. Translated by Thomas Saine and R. Heitner as *My Life: Poetry and Truth,* in *Goethe's Collected Works.* Vol. 4. New York: Suhrkamp, 1987.

———. "Letzte Kunstausstellung 1805," 1812.

———. "Shakespeare und kein Ende," 1815. Translated by Ellen von Nardroff and Earnest H. von Nardroff as "Shakespeare Once Again," in *Goethe's Collected Works.* Vol. 3, *Essays on Art and Literature.* New York: Suhrkamp, 1986.

———. *Aus meinem Leben, zweyter Abtheilung erster Theil, zweyter Theil: Italienische Reise,* 1816–17. 2 vols. Translated by R. Heitner as *Italian Journey,* in *Goethe's Collected Works.* Vol. 6. New York: Suhrkamp, 1989.

———. "Elginische Marmore," 1817.

———. "Glückliches Ereignis," 1817. Translated by Douglas Miller as "Fortunate Encounter," in *Johann Wolfgang von Goethe. Scientific Studies.* Vol. 12. New York: Suhrkamp, 1988.

———. *Bey Allerhöchster Anwesenheit Ihro Majestät der Kaiserin Mutter Maria Feodorowna in Weimar Maskenzug,* 1818.

———. "Einwirkung der neueren Philosophie," 1820. Translated by Douglas Miller as "The Influence of Modern Philosophy," in *Johann Wolfgang von Goethe.* Vol. 12, *Scientific Studies.* New York: Suhrkamp, 1988.

———. "Klassiker und Romantiker in Italien, sich heftig bekämpfend," 1820.

———. "Die Faulthiere und die Dickhäutigen abgebildet, beschrieben und verglichen von Dr. E. d'Alton," 1821.

———. "Ein deutscher Gil Blas," 1821. Translated by Ellen von Nardroff and Earnest H. von Nardroff as "A German Gil Blas," in *Goethe's Collected Works.* Vol. 3, *Essays on Art and Literature.* New York: Suhrkamp, 1986.

———. "Fossiler Stier," 1821.

———. *Wilhelm Meisters Wanderjahre oder Die Entsagenden: Ein Roman. Erster Theil,* 1821. Revised and enlarged 1829. Translated by Krishna Winston as *Wilhelm Meister's Journeyman Years or The Renunciants,* in *Goethe's Collected Works.* Vol. 10. New York: Suhrkamp, 1989.

———. *Aus meinem Leben, zweyter Abtheilung fünfter Theil: Campagne in Frankreich 1792,* 1822. Translated by Thomas Saine and R. Heitner as *Campaign in France 1792,* in *Goethe's Collected Works.* Vol. 5. New York: Suhrkamp, 1987.

Goethe, Johann Wolfgang von. *Bedeutende Fördernis durch ein einziges geistreiches Wort*, 1822.

———. "Nachlese zu Aristoteles Poetik," 1827. Translated by Ellen von Nardroff and Earnest H. von Nardroff as "On Interpreting Aristotle's *Poetics*," in *Goethe's Collected Works*. Vol. 3, *Essays on Art and Literature*. New York: Suhrkamp, 1986.

———. "Über epische und dramatische Dichtung," 1827. Translated by Ellen von Nardroff and Earnest H. von Nardroff as "On Epic and Dramatic Poetry," in *Goethe's Collected Works*. Vol. 3, *Essays on Art and Literature*. New York: Suhrkamp, 1986.

———. "Novelle," 1828. Translated by Victor Lange and J. Ryan as *Novella*, in *Goethe's Collected Works*. Vol. 11. New York: Suhrkamp, 1988.

———. *Zweiter Römischer Aufenthalt*, 1829.

———. *Maximen und Reflexionen*, 1907. Translated by Elisabeth Stopp as *Maxims and Reflections*. London and New York: Penguin Books, 1998.

———. *Goethes amtliche Schriften: Veröffentlichung des Staatsarchivs Weimar*. 4 vols. Edited by Willy Flachs and Helma Dahl. Weimar: Böhlau, 1950–87.

———. *Faust in ursprünglicher Gestalt nach der Göchenhausenschen Abschrift*, 1887. Translated by Douglas M. Scott as *The Urfaust: Goethe's Faust in the Original Form*. Woodbury, NY: Barron's Educational Series, 1958.

———, ed. *Die Propyläen: Eine periodische Schrift*, 1798–1800. 3 vols.

———, ed. *Winckelmann und sein Jahrhundert: In Briefen und Aufsätzen herausgegeben*, 1805. Translated by Ellen von Nardroff and Earnest H. von Nardroff as "Winckelmann and His Age," in *Goethe's Collected Works*. Vol. 3, *Essays on Art and Literature*. New York: Suhrkamp, 1986.

———, ed. *Ueber Kunst und Alterthum*, 1816–32. 6 vols.

Gottsched, Johann Christoph. *Versuch einer critischen Dichtkunst vor die Deutschen*, 1730. Revised 1737. Enlarged 1742. Revised 1751.

———. *Die deutsche Schaubühne nach den Regeln und Exempeln der alten Griechen und Römer eingerichtet, und mit einer Vorrede herausgegeben*, 1741–45. 6 vols.

Hamann, Johann Georg. "Aesthetica in nuce," in Hamann's *Kreuzzüge des Philologen*, 1762.

Hamilton, William. "On the Worship of Priapus in the Kingdom of Naples," 1786.

Hegel, Georg Wilhelm Friedrich. *System der Wissenschaft: 1. Theil. Die Phänomenologie des Geistes*, 1807. Translated by A. V. Miller as *Phenomenology of Spirit*. Oxford and New York: Oxford UP, 1977.

———. *Vorlesungen über die Aesthetik*, 1835–38. 3 vols. Translated by T. M. Knox as *Hegel's Aesthetics: Lectures on Fine Arts*. Oxford and New York: Oxford UP, 1975.

Heinse, Johann Jakob Wilhelm. *Ardinghello und die glückseligen Inseln: Eine Italiänische Geschichte aus dem sechszehnten Jahrhundert*, 1787. 2 vols. Revised 1794.

Herder, Johann Gottfried. *Älteste Urkunde des Menschengeschlechts*, 1774–76. 2 vols.

———. *Auch eine Philosophie der Geschichte zur Bildung der Menschheit*, 1774. Translated by Eva Herzfeld as "Johann Gottfried von Herder's 'Yet Another Philosophy of History for the Education of Humanity': A Translation with a Critical Introduction and Notes." Ph.D. dissertation, Columbia University, 1968.

———. *Über die neuere Deutsche Literatur: Fragmente*, 1768. Translated by Ernest A. Menze as *Fragments on Recent German Literature*. University Park: Pennsylvania State UP, 1992.

———. *Kritische Wälder: Oder Betrachtungen, die Wissenschaft und Kunst des Schönen betreffend, nach Maasgabe neuerer Schriften*, 1769. 3 vols.

———. *Volkslieder*, 1778–79. 2 vols.

———. *Ideen zur Philosophie der Geschichte der Menschheit*, 1784–91. 4 vols. Translated by T. Churchill as *Outlines of a Philosophy of the History of Man*. London: printed for J. Johnson by L. Hansard, 1800; reprinted, Atlantic Highlands, NJ: Humanities Press, 1977.

———. *Zerstreute Blätter*, 1785–97. 6 vols.

———. *Gott: Einige Gespräche*, 1787. Revised as *Gott: Einige Gespräche über Spinozas System; nebst Shaftsburis Naturhymnus*, 1800. Translated by Frederick H. Burkhardt as *God: Some Conversations. A Translation, with a Critical Introduction and Notes*. Indianapolis: Bobbs-Merrill, 1940.

———. *Briefe zu Beförderung der Humanität*, 1793–97. 10 vols.

———. *Reise nach Italien: Briefwechsel mit seiner Gattin, vom August 1788 bis Juli 1789*, 1859. Edited by Düntzer und Herder.

Hippel, Theodor Gottlieb von. *Lebensläufe nach aufsteigender Linie nebst Beylagen A, B, C*, 1778–81. 4 vols.

Hoffmann, E. T. A. *Die Elixiere des Teufels: Nachgelassene Papiere des Bruders Medardus, eines Capuziners*, 1815–16. Translated by Ronald Taylor as *The Devil's Elixirs*. London: Calder, 1963.

———. *Lebens-Ansichten des Katers Murr nebst fragmentarischer Biographie des Kapellmeisters Johannes Kreisler in zufälligen Makulaturblättern*, 1820–22. 2 vols. Translated by Anthea Bell as *The Life and Opinions of the Tomcat Murr: Together with a Fragmentary Biography of Kapellmeister Johannes Kreisler on Random Sheets of Waste Paper*. London and New York: Penguin Book, 1999.

Hölderlin, Friedrich. "Der Wanderer," 1796/1800. Translated by Michael Hamburger as "The Traveller," in *Friedrich Hölderlin: Selected Poems and Fragments*. London: Penguin Books, 1994/98.

———. *Hyperion oder Der Eremit in Griechenland*, 1797–99. 2 vols. Translated by Willard R. Trask as *Hyperion; or, The Hermit in Greece*. New York: Ungar, 1965.

———. "Brod und Wein," 1801. Translated by Michael Hamburger as "Bread and Wine," in *Friedrich Hölderlin: Selected Poems and Fragments*. London: Penguin Books, 1994/98.

Hölderlin, Friedrich. "Der Archipelagus," 1801. Translated by Michael Hamburger as "The Archipelago," in *Friedrich Hölderlin: Selected Poems and Fragments.* London: Penguin Books, 1994/98.

——. *Empedokles,* 1801.

——. "Friedensfeier," 1801. Translated by Michael Hamburger as "Celebration of Peace," in *Friedrich Hölderlin: Selected Poems and Fragments.* London: Penguin Books, 1994/98.

——. "Germanien," 1801. Translated by Michael Hamburger as "Germania," in *Friedrich Hölderlin: Selected Poems and Fragments.* London: Penguin Books, 1994/98.

——. "Heimkunft," 1801. Translated by Michael Hamburger as "Homecoming," in *Friedrich Hölderlin: Selected Poems and Fragments.* London: Penguin Books, 1994/98.

——. "Menons Klagen um Diotima," 1801. Translated by Michael Hamburger as "Menon's Lament for Diotima," in *Friedrich Hölderlin: Selected Poems and Fragments.* London: Penguin Books, 1994/98.

——. "Die Wanderung," 1807. Translated by Michael Hamburger as "The Journey," in *Friedrich Hölderlin: Selected Poems and Fragments.* London: Penguin Books, 1994/98.

——. "Stuttgart," 1807. Translated by Michael Hamburger as "Stuttgart," in *Friedrich Hölderlin: Selected Poems and Fragments.* London: Penguin Books, 1994/98.

——. "Der Rhein," 1808. Translated by Michael Hamburger as "The Rhine," in *Friedrich Hölderlin: Selected Poems and Fragments.* London: Penguin Books, 1994/98.

——. "Patmos," 1808. Translated by Michael Hamburger as "Patmos," in *Friedrich Hölderlin: Selected Poems and Fragments.* London: Penguin Books, 1994/98.

Hufeland, Christoph Wilhelm. *Makrobiotik oder die Kunst, das menschliche Leben zu verlängern,* 1797/1800. Translated by Erasmus Wilson as *Art of Prolonging Life (1800).* Whitefish, MT: Kessinger Publishing, 2003.

Humboldt, Wilhelm von. "Über das Studium des Altertums und des Griechischen insbesondere," 1793.

——. "Über den Geschlechtsunterschied und dessen Einfluß auf die organische Natur," 1794.

——. *Ästhetische Versuche. Theil 1: Über Göthe's Hermann und Dorothea,* 1799.

——. "Geschichte des Verfalls und Unterganges der griechischen Freistaaten," 1807.

Iffland, August Wilhelm. *Die Jäger: Ein ländliches Sittengemälde in fünf Aufzügen,* 1785. Translated by Bell Plumptre as "The Foresters: A Picture of Rural Manners. A Play in Five Acts." London: Vernor and Hood, 1799.

——. *Die Künstler: Ein Schauspiel in fünf Aufzügen,* 1801.

Imhoff, Anna Amalia von. *Die Schwestern von Lesbos*, 1790/1800.

Jacobi, Friedrich Heinrich. *Woldemar: Eine Seltenheit aus der Naturgeschichte. 1. Band*, 1779. Revised as *Woldemar*, 1794. 2 vols. Revised 1796.

Jean Paul (Johann Paul Friedrich Richter). *Die Unsichtbare Loge: Eine Biographie*, 1793. 2 vols. Revised 1822. Translated by Charles T. Brooks as *The Invisible Lodge*. New York: Holt, 1883.

———. *Leben des Schulmeisterleins Maria Wuz in Auenthal*, 1793. Translated by John D. Grayson as "Life of the Cheerful Schoolmaster Maria Wutz," in *Nineteenth Century German Tales*, edited by Angel Flores, 1–37. New York: Doubleday, 1959.

———. *Hesperus, oder 45 Hundsposttage: Eine Biographie*, 1795. 3 vols. Revised and enlarged 1798. 4 vols. Translated by Brooks as *Hesperus; or, Forty-five Dog-post-days*. 2 vols. New York: Lovell, 1864; London: Trübner, 1865.

———. *Leben des Quintus Fixlein, aus fünfzehn Zettelkästen gezogen*, 1796. Revised and enlarged 1801. Translated by Thomas Carlyle as *Life of Quintus Fixlein*. Reprint, Columbia, SC: Camden House, 1991.

———. *Blumen- Frucht- und Dornenstücke oder Ehestand, Tod und Hochzeit des Armenadvokaten F. St. Siebenkäs im Reichsmarktflecken Kuhschnappel*, 1796–97. 3 vols. Revised and enlarged 1818. 4 vols. Translated by Edward Henry Noel as *Flower, Fruit, and Thorn Pieces; or, The Married Life, Death, and Wedding of the Advocate of the Poor, Firmian Stanislaus Siebenkäs*. 2 vols. London: Smith; Boston: Munroe, 1845.

———. *Titan*, 1800–1803. 4 vols. Translated by Brooks as *Titan: A Romance*. 2 vols. Boston: Ticknor and Fields, 1862; London: Trübner, 1863.

———. *Flegeljahre: Eine Biographie*, 1804–5. 4 vols. Translated by Eliza Buckminster Lee as *Walt and Vult; or, the Twins*. 2 vols. Boston: Munroe; New York: Wiley and Putnam, 1846.

———. *Vorschule der Ästhetik*, 1804. 3 vols. Revised and enlarged 1813. Translated by Margaret R. Hale as *Horn of Oberon: Jean Paul Richter's School for Aesthetics*. Detroit: Wayne State UP, 1973.

———. *Levana oder Erziehungslehre*, 1807. 2 vols. Revised and enlarged 1814. 3 vols. Translated by "A. H." as *Levana; or, the Doctrine of Education*. London: Longman, Brown, Green & Longmans, 1848; Boston: Ticknor and Fields, 1861.

———. *Der Komet oder Nikolaus Marggraf: Eine komische Geschichte*, 1820–22. 3 vols.

Kalb, Charlotte von. *Cornelia*, 1851.

Kant, Immanuel. *Allgemeine Naturgeschichte und Theorie des Himmels, oder Versuch von der Verfassung und dem mechanischen Upsprunge des ganzen Weltgebäudes, nach Newton'schen Grundsätzen abgehandet*, 1755. Translated by William Hastie as *Universal Natural History and Theory of the Heavens*. Ann Arbor: U of Michigan P, 1969.

———. *Kritik der reinen Vernunft*, 1781. Revised 1787. Translated by Norman Kemp Smith as *Immanuel Kant's Critique of Pure Reason*. London: Macmillan, 1929.

Kant, Immanuel. *Grundlegung zur Metaphysik der Sitten*, 1785. Revised 1786. Translated by H. J. Patton as *The Moral Law*. London: Hutchinson, 1948. Republished as *Groundwork of the Metaphysic of Morals*. New York: Harper, 1948.

———. *Kritik der praktischen Vernunft*, 1788. Translated by Beck as *Critique of Practical Reason*. New York: Liberal Arts Press, 1956.

———. *Kritik der Urteilskraft*, 1790. Translated by James C. Meredith as *Kant's Critique of Aesthetic Judgement* and *Kant's Critique of Teleological Judgement*. Oxford: Clarendon Press, 1911, 1928. Republished as *Critique of Judgement*. Oxford: Clarendon Press, 1957.

Kleist, Heinrich von. *Penthesilea: Ein Trauerspiel*, 1808. Translated by Joel Agee as *Penthesilea*. New York: Perennial Press, 2000.

———. *Das Käthchen von Heilbronn oder Die Feuerprobe: Ein großes historisches Ritterschauspiel*, 1810. Translated by Frederick E. Pierce as *Kaethchen of Heilbronn or The Test of Fire: Great Historic Chivalric Drama in 5 Acts*, in *Romantic Drama*, volume 2 of *Fiction and Fantasy of German Romance: Selections from the German Romantic Authors, 1790–1830 in English Translation*. New York: Oxford, 1927.

———. *Der zerbrochne Krug: Ein Lustspiel*, 1811. Translated by Carl R. Mueller as *The Broken Jug*. North Stratford, NH: Smith & Kraus, 2000.

Klinger, Friedrich Maximilian. *Fausts Leben, Thaten und Höllenfahrt in fünf Büchern*, 1791. Revised and enlarged 1794. Translated by George Borrow as *Faustus: His Life, Death, and Descent into Hell*. London: Simpkin & Marshall, 1825.

———. *Der Weltmann und der Dichter*, 1798.

Klopstock, Friedrich Gottlieb. "Von dem Range der schönen Künste und der schönen Wissenschaften," 1758.

Knight, Richard Payne. *Discourse on the Worship of Priapus*, 1786.

Kotzebue, August Ferdinand Friedrich von. *Der Freimüthige*, 1803–7.

———. *Die Sonnen-Jungfrau: Ein Schauspiel in fünf Akten*, 1791. Translated by Benjamin Thompson as *Rolla, or, The Virgin of the Sun*. London: Vernor & Hood, 1805.

———. *Die Spanier in Peru oder Rollas Tod: Ein romantisches Trauerspiel in fünf Akten*, 1796. Translated by William Dunlap as *Pizzaro in Peru; or, The Death of Rolla*. New York: printed by G. F. Hopkins for W. Dunlap, 1800.

La Roche, Sophie von. *Geschichte des Fräuleins von Sternheim*, 1771. Edited by Christoph Martin Wieland. Translated by James Lynn as *The History of Lady Sophie Sternheim*. New York: New York UP, 1992.

Lessing, Gotthold Ephraim. *Miß Sara Sampson: Ein Trauerspiel in fünf Aufzügen*, 1755. Translated by Ernest Bell as *Sara*. Bath, UK: Absolute Press, 1990.

———. *Laokoon: Oder Über die Grenzen der Mahlerey und Poesie*, 1766. Translated by Edward Allen McCormick as *Laocoön: An Essay upon the Limits of Painting and Poetry*. Baltimore: Johns Hopkins UP, 1984.

Lessing, Gotthold Ephraim. *Hamburgische Dramaturgie*, 1767–69. 2 vols. Translated by Helen Zimmern as *Hamburg Dramaturgy*. 1 vol. New York: Dover, 1962.

———. *Minna von Barnhelm*, 1767. Translated by Kenneth J. Northcott as *Minna von Barnhelm*, in *Nathan the Wise, Minna von Barnhelm, and Other Plays and Writings*, ed. Peter Demetz. New York: Continuum, 1991.

———. *Emilia Galotti: Ein Trauerspiel in fünf Aufzügen*, 1772. Translated by Anna Johanna Gode von Aesch as *Emilia Galotti*, in *Nathan the Wise, Minna von Barnhelm, and Other Plays and Writings*, ed. Peter Demetz. New York: Continuum, 1991.

———. *Über den Beweis des Geistes und der Kraft an den Herrn Direktor Schumann, zu Hannover*, 1777.

———. *Nathan der Weise: Ein dramatisches Gedicht in fünf Aufzügen*, 1779. Translated by Bayard Quincy Morgan as *Nathan the Wise*, in *Nathan the Wise, Minna von Barnhelm, and Other Plays and Writings*, ed. Peter Demetz. New York: Continuum, 1991.

———. *Die Erziehung des Menschengeschlechts*, 1780. Translated by Frederick William Robertson as *The Education of the Human Race*. London: Smith, Elder, 1858; New York: Colier, 1909.

Manso, Caspar Friedrich and Johann Gottfried Dyck. *Gegengeschenke an die Sudelköche in Jena und Weimar von einigen dankbaren Gästen*, 1797.

Mendelssohn, Moses. *Phaedon oder Über die Unsterblichkeit der Seele in drey Gesprächen*, 1767. Translated by Charles Cullen as *Phaedon; or, The Death of Socrates*. London: printed for the author by J. Cooper, 1789; reprinted, New York: Arno Press, 1973.

Mereau, Sophie. *Amanda und Eduard: Ein Roman in Briefen*, 1797/1803.

———. *Kalathiskos*, 1801–2.

———. "Ninon de Lenclos," 1802.

Meyer, Heinrich Johann. "Entwurf einer Kunstgeschichte des achtzehnten Jahrhunderts," in *Winckelmann und sein Jahrhundert*, ed. Goethe, 1805.

———. "Nachricht an Künstler und Preisaufgabe," 1799. Written in collaboration with Goethe.

Moritz, Karl Philipp. *Anton Reiser: Ein psychologischer Roman*, 1785–90. 4 vols. Translated by John R. Russell as *Anton Reiser: A Psychological Novel*. Columbia, SC: Camden House, 1996.

———. "Versuch einer Vereinigung aller schönen Künste und Wissenschaften unter dem Begriff des *in sich selbst Vollendeten*," 1785.

———. *Über die bildende Nachahmung des Schönen*, 1788. Excerpts translated by Robert Heitner as *On the Creative Imitation of Beauty*, in *Italian Journey* by Johann Wolfgang von Goethe, edited by Thomas P. Saine and Jeffrey L. Sammons, 431–36. New York: Suhrkamp, 1989.

———. *Götterlehre oder mythologische Dichtungen der Alten*, 1791. Translated by "C. F. W. J." as *Mythological Fictions of the Greeks and Romans*. New York: Carvill, 1830.

Moritz, Karl Philipp. *Reisen eines Deutschen in Italien in den Jahren 1786 bis 1788,* 1792–93. 2 vols.

———. *Vorbegriffe zu einer Theorie der Ornamente,* 1793.

Müller, Wilhelm. "Die Winterreise," in *Gedichte aus den hinterlassenen Papieren eines reisenden Waldhornisten,* 1824. Republished as *Lieder des Lebens und der Liebe,* 1824. Translated by Louise McClelland Urban as *Winterreise,* in *Schubert's Winterreise: A Winter Journey in Poetry, Image, and Song.* Madison: U of Wisconsin P, 2003.

Nestroy, Johann. *Einen Jux will er sich machen: Posse mit Gesang in vier Aufzügen,* 1844. Translated anonymously as *The Matchmaker: A Farce in Four Acts.* New York: French, 1957. Translated and adapted by Tom Stoppard as *On the Razzle,* in *Tom Stoppard Plays 4.* London: Faber & Faber, 1999.

Novalis (Friedrich von Hardenberg). *Heinrich von Ofterdingen: Ein nachgelassener Roman,* 1799/1802. Translated by Palmer Hilty as *Henry von Ofterdingen.* New York: Ungar, 1964.

Pestalozzi, Johann Heinrich. *Ideen,* 1826.

Reichardt, Johann Friedrich. *Deutschland,* 1796. 4 vols.

Schelling, Friedrich Wilhelm Joseph von. "Philosophie der Kunst," 1859. Translated by Douglas W. Scott as *The Philosophy of Art.* Minneapolis: U of Minnesota P, 1988.

Schiller, Friedrich. *Die Räuber: Ein Schauspiel,* 1781. Revised 1782 as *Die Räuber: Ein Trauerspiel. Neue für die Mannheimer Bühne verbesserte Auflage.* Revised 1782 as *Die Räuber: Ein Schauspiel in fünf Akten.* Translated by Robert David MacDonald as *The Robbers,* in *Schiller: Five Plays.* London: Oberon Books, 1998.

Schiller, Friedrich. *Anthologie auf das Jahr 1782,* 1782.

———. "Brief eines reisenden Dänen," 1785.

———. *An die Freude: Ein Rundgesang für freye Männer. Mit Musik,* 1786. Rendered in English by Henry G. Chapman as *Schiller's Ode to Joy.* New York: G. Schirmer, 1910.

———. *Don Karlos, Infant von Spanien,* 1787. Translated by Hilary Collier Sy-Quia as *Don Carlos.* London and New York: Oxford UP, 1999.

———. *Der Geisterseher: Eine interessante Geschichte aus den Papieren des Grafen von O*** herausgegeben aus Herrn Schillers Thalia,* 1788. Republished 1789 as *Der Geisterseher: Eine Geschichte aus den Memoires des Grafen von O**.* Translated by David Bryer as *The Man who Sees Ghosts: From the Memoires of the Count Von O***.* London: Pushkin Press, 2003.

———. "Die Götter Griechenlandes," 1788.

———. "Die Künstler," 1789.

———. *Geschichte des Dreißigjährigen Krieges,* 1791–93. 3 vols. Translated by Rev. A. J. W. Morrison as *The History of the Thirty Years' War in Germany.* Boston: F. A. Niccolls, 1901.

Schiller, Friedrich. *Über Anmuth und Würde: An Carl von Dalberg in Erfurth*, 1793.

———. *Über das Pathetische*, 1793. Translated by Daniel O. Dahlstrom as *On the Pathetic*. New York: Continuum, 1993.

———. "Das Ideal und das Leben," 1795.

———. "Der Spaziergang," 1795.

———. *Über die ästhetische Erziehung des Menschen in einer Reihe* von *Briefen* 1795. Translated by Elizabeth M. Wilkinson & L.A. Willoughby as *Letters on the Aesthetic Education of Man*. New York: Continuum, 1993.

———. "Über naive und sentimentalische Dichtung," 1795–96. Translated by Daniel O. Dahlstrom as *On Naïve and Sentimental Poetry*. New York: Continuum, 1993.

———. "Der Taucher," 1797.

———. "Die Kraniche des Ibycus," 1797. Translated by W. E. Frye as "The Cranes of Ibycus." London: Boosey, 1819.

———. "Der Sammler und die Seinigen," 1798–99. Written in collaboration with Goethe.

———. *Wallensteins Lager* (1798), in *Wallenstein: Ein dramatisches Gedicht*, vol. 1, 1800. Translated by F. J. Lamport as "Wallenstein's Camp," in *Wallenstein*. Harmondsworth, UK & New York: Penguin, 1979.

———. "Das Lied von der Glocke," 1799. Translated by Thomas C. Zimmerman as *The Song of the Bell, and Other Poems*. Reading, PA, 1896.

———. "Die Bürgschaft," 1799.

———. *Die Piccolomini* (1799), in *Wallenstein: Ein dramatisches Gedicht*, vol. 1, 1800. Translated by F. J. Lamport as "The Piccolomini," in *Wallenstein*. Harmondsworth, UK & New York: Penguin, 1979.

———. *Wallensteins Tod* (1799), in *Wallenstein: Ein dramatisches Gedicht*, vol. 2, 1800. Translated by F. J. Lamport as "Wallenstein's Death," in *Wallenstein*. Harmondsworth, UK & New York: Penguin, 1979.

———. *Maria Stuart: Ein Trauerspiel*, 1801. Translated by Hilary Collier Sy-Quia as *Mary Stuart*. London and New York: Oxford UP, 1999.

———. *Kalendar auf das Jahr 1802: Die Jungfrau von Orleans. Eine romantische Tragödie*, 1802. Translated by Robert David MacDonald as *Joan of Arc*, in *Schiller: Five Plays*. London: Oberon Books, 1998.

———. *Turandot, Prinzessin von China: Ein tragicomisches Mährchen nach Gozzi*, 1802. Translated by Sabilla Novello as *Turandot: the Chinese Sphinx: a dramatic oddity*. London: French, 1872.

———. *Die Braut von Messina oder Die feindlichen Brüder: Ein Trauerspiel mit Chören*, 1803. Translated by Charles E. Passage as *The Bride of Messina; or, The Enemy Brothers: A Tragedy with Choruses*. New York: Ungar, 1962.

———. "Über den Gebrauch des Chors in der Tragödie," 1803.

Schiller, Friedrich. *Wilhelm Tell: Ein Schauspiel. Zum Neujahrgeschenk auf 1805*, 1804. Translated by William F. Mainland as *William Tell*. Chicago and London: U of Chicago P, 1972.

———, ed. *Thalia*, 1786–91. 12 vols.

———, ed. *Die Horen: Eine Monatsschrift*, 1795–97. 12 vols.

———, ed. *Musen-Almanach*, 1796–1800.

Schlegel, August Wilhelm. *Die Gemälde*, 1799.

———. "Vorlesungen über Enzyklopädie der Wissenschaften," 1803.

———. "Vorlesungen über schöne Litteratur und Kunst," 1803–4/1884. 3 vols.

———. *Über dramatische Kunst und Litteratur: Vorlesungen*, 1809–11. 2 volumes in 3. Translated by John Black as *A Course of Lectures on Dramatic Art and Literature*. 2 vols. London: printed for Baldwin, Cradock & Joy, 1815; 1 vol. Philadelphia: Hogan & Thompson, 1833. Translation revised by A. J. W. Morrison. London: Bohn, 1846; reprinted, New York: AMS Press, 1973.

Schlegel, Dorothea. *Florentin: Ein Roman*, 1801. Translated by Edwina Lawler and Ruth Richardson as *Florentin: A Novel*. Lewiston, NY: Edwin Mellen Press, 1988.

Schlegel, Friedrich. "Über das Studium der griechischen Poesie," in *Die Griechen und Römer: Historische und kritische Versuche über das Klassische Alterthum*, 1795–97. Translated and edited by Stuart Barnett as *On the Study of Greek Poetry*. Albany: State U of New York P, 2001.

———. *Athenäum: Eine Zeitschrift*, 1798–1800.

———. *Lucinde: Ein Roman, Erster Theil*, 1799. Translated by Peter Firchow as *Friedrich Schlegel's Lucinde and the Fragments*. Minneapolis: U of Minnesota P, 1971.

———. "Gespräch über die Poesie," 1800. Translated by Ernst Behler & Roman Struc as "Dialogue on Poetry," in Schlegel, *Dialogue on Poetry and Literary Aphorisms*. University Park: Pennsylvania State UP, 1968.

———. "Ideen," 1800. Translated by Peter Firchow as "Ideas," in *Friedrich Schlegel: Philosophical Fragments*. Minneapolis: U of Minnesota P, 1991.

Schlosser, Johann Georg. *Über die Seelenwanderung*, 1781.

Schopenhauer, Johanna. *Gabriele: Ein Roman*, 1819–20. 3 vols.

———. *Die Tante: Ein Roman*, 1823. 2 vols.

———. *Sidonia: Ein Roman*, 1827–28. 3 vols.

———. *Richard Wood: Roman*, 1837. 2 vols.

Schröder, Friedrich Ludwig. *Das Porträt der Mutter, oder, Die Privatkomödie: ein Lustspiel in vier Aufzügen*, 1786/90.

Spaldung, Johann Joachim. *Bestimmung des Menschen*, 1748.

Stein, Charlotte von. *Rino*, 1776.

———. *Dido: Ein Trauerspiel in Fünf Akten*, 1794/95.

Stein, Charlotte von. *Neues Freiheitssystem oder die Verschwörung gegen die Liebe*, 1798/1867.

———. *Die Zwey Emilien*, 1800.

Tieck, Ludwig. *Geschichte des Herrn William Lovell*, 1795–96. 3 vols.

———. *Franz Sternbalds Wanderungen: Eine altdeutsche Geschichte*, 1798. 2 vols.

Unger, Friederike Helene. *Julchen Grünthal: Ein Pensionsgeschichte. Mit allergnädigsten Freiheiten*, 1784. Revised 1787. Revised and enlarged 1798. 2 vols.

———. *Karoline von Lichtfeld*, 1787. Original by Isabelle de Montolieu. Translated into German by Unger.

———. *Gräfin Pauline*, 1800. 2 vols.

———. *Melanie, das Findelkind*, 1804.

———. *Bekenntnisse einer schönen Seele: Von ihr selbst geschrieben*, 1806.

———. *Die Franzosen in Berlin oder Serene an Clementinen in den Jahren 1806, 7, 8: Ein Sittengemälde*, 1809.

Voß, Johann Heinrich. *Homers Odüßee übersetzt*, 1781.

———. *Ilias*, in *Homers Werke*, 1793. 4 vols. Translated by Voß.

———. *Luise: Ein laendliches Gedicht in drei Idyllen*, 1795. Translated by James Cochrane as *Louisa*. Edinburgh: Johnstone, 1852.

Voss, Julius von. *Die Griechheit*, 1807.

Vulpius, Christian August. *Rinaldo Rinaldini: Der Räuberhauptmann*, 1798.

Wackenroder, Wilhelm Heinrich. *Herzensergießungen eines kunstliebenden Klosterbruders*, 1796/97. Written in collaboration with Ludwig Tieck. Translated by Edward Mornin as *Outpourings of an Art-Loving Friar*. New York: Ungar, 1975.

Weißenthurn, Johanna Franul von. *Der Wald bei Hermannstadt: Romantisches Schauspiel in 4 Aufzügen*, 1807/33.

Wieland, Christoph Martin. *Geschichte des Agathon*, 1766–67. 2 vols. Revised and enlarged as *Agathon*, 1773. 4 vols. Revised and enlarged as *Geschichte des Agathon*, 1794. 3 vols. Translated by John Richardson as *The History of Agathon*. 4 vols. London: Cadell, 1773.

———. *Musarion, oder die Philosophie der Grazien: Ein Gedicht in drey Büchern*, 1768. Revised 1769. Translated by Thomas C. Starnes as *Musarion*. Columbia, SC: Camden House, 1991.

———. *Alceste: Ein Singspiel in fünf Aufzügen*, 1773.

———. *Die Abderiten, eine sehr wahrscheinliche Geschichte*, 1774. Revised as *Geschichte der Abderiten*, 1781. 2 vols. Translated by Max Dufner as *History of the Abderites*. Bethlehem, PA: Lehigh UP, 1993.

———. *Der neue teutsche Merkur*, 1790–96. 60 vols. Published and edited by Wieland.

Winckelmann, Johann Joachim. *Gedancken über die Nachahmung der Griechischen Wercke in der Malerey und Bildhauer-Kunst*, 1755. Enlarged

1756. Translated by Elfriede Heyer and Roger C. Norton as *Reflections on the Imitation of Greek Works in Painting and Sculpture*. La Salle, IL: Open Court, 1987.

Winckelmann, Johann Joachim. "Torso-Beschreibung," 1762.

———. *Geschichte der Kunst des Alterthums*, 1764. 2 vols. Translated by G. Henry Lodge as *The History of Ancient Art*. Boston: Osgood, 1849–73, 4 vols; London: S. Low, Marston, Searle, & Rivington, 1881, 2 vols; reprinted, New York: Ungar, 1968, 2 vols.

Wolf, F. A. *Prolegomena ad Homerum*, 1795. Translated by Anthony Grafton, Glenn W. Most, and E.G. Zetzel as *Prolegomena to Homer*. Princeton, NJ: Princeton UP, 1985.

Wolzogen, Caroline von. *Der Leukadische Fels*, 1792.

———. *Agnes von Lilien*, 1798.

———. *Cordelia*, 1840.

Zschokke, Heinrich. *Abällino der große Bandit*, 1793. Translated by Matthew Gregory Lewis as *The Bravo of Venice: A Romance*. London: printed by N. Shurry for Hughes, 1804; New York: Cassell, 1804. Reprinted with an introduction by Davendra P. Varma. New York: Arno Press, 1972.

Select Secondary Literature

Useful Handbooks and Lexicons

Goethe-Handbuch. 4 vols. Ed. Bernd Witte et al. Stuttgart and Weimar: Metzler, 1996–98.

Goethe-Lexikon. Gero von Wilpert. Stuttgart: Alfred Kröner Verlag, 1998.

Goethes Weimar: Das Lexikon der Personen und Schauplätze. Ed. Effi Biederzynski. Zurich: Artemis & Winkler, 1993.

Metzler Goethe Lexikon. Ed. Benedikt Lessing et al. Stuttgart and Weimar: Metzler, 1999.

Schiller-Handbuch. Ed. Helmut Koopmann. Stuttgart: Kröner, 1998.

General, Philosophical, Cultural, Historical, and Genre-Related Studies

Andreas, Willy. *Carl August von Weimar in und nach der Kampagne gegen Frankreich. Sitzungsberichte der Bayerischen Akademie der Wissenschaften zu München, Philosophisch-Historische Klasse 5 (1954)*. Munich: Verlag der Bayerischen Akademie der Wissenschaften, 1955.

Baeumer, Max L. "Der Begriff 'klassisch' bei Goethe und Schiller." In *Die Klassik-Legende*, ed. Reinhold Grimm and Jost Hermand, 17–49. Frankfurt am Main: Athenäum-Verlag, 1971.

Bahr, Ehrhard, and Thomas P. Saine, eds. *The Internalized Revolution: German Reactions to the French Revolution, 1789–1989.* New York: Garland, 1992.

Becker, Eva D. "'Klassiker' in der deutschen Literaturgeschichtsschreibung zwischen 1780 und 1860." In *Zur Literatur der Restaurationsepoche 1815–1848*, ed. Jost Hermand and Manfred Windfuhr, 349–70. Stuttgart: Metzler, 1970.

Becker-Cantarino, Barbara. *Der lange Weg zur Mündigkeit: Frau und Literatur 1500–1800.* Munich: Deutscher Taschenbuch Verlag, 1989.

———. *Schriftstellerinnen der Romantik: Epoche Werk Wirkung.* Munich: Beck, 2000.

Bennett, Benjamin. *Beyond Theory: Eighteenth-Century German Literature and the Poetics of Irony.* Ithaca: Cornell UP, 1993.

Berghahn, Klaus. "Weimarer Klassik + Jenaer Romantik = Europäische Romantik?" *Monatshefte* 88 (1996): 480–88.

Berghahn, Klaus. "Von Weimar nach Versailles: Zur Entstehung der Klassik-Legende im 19. Jahrhundert." In *Die Klassik-Legende*, ed. Reinhold Grimm and Jost Hermand, 50–78. Frankfurt am Main: Athenäum, 1970.

Borchmeyer, Dieter. *Weimarer Klassik.* 2nd revised edition. Weinheim: Beltz Athenäum, 1994.

Bothe, Rolf. *Dichter, Fürst und Architekten: Das Weimarer Residenzschloß vom Mittelalter bis zum Anfang des 19. Jahrhunderts.* Ostfildern-Ruit: Hatje Cantz, 2000.

Bowie, Andrew. *Aesthetics and Subjectivity: From Kant to Nietzsche.* Manchester: Manchester UP, 1990.

Brandt, Helmut. "Weimar: Wie die Deutschen zu ihrer literarischen Hauptstadt kamen." In *Stätten deutscher Literatur: Studien zur literarischen Zentrenbildung 1750–1815*, ed. Wolfgang Stellmacher, 351–91. New York: Peter Lang, 1998.

Brinker-Gabler, Gisela. *Deutsche Literatur von Frauen: Vom Mittelalter bis zum Ende des 18. Jahrhunderts*, vol. 1. Munich: Beck, 1988.

Bürger, Christa. *Leben Schreiben: Die Klassik, die Romantik und der Ort der Frauen.* Stuttgart: Metzler, 1990.

Burkhardt, C. A. *Das Repertoire des Weimarischen Theaters unter Goethes Leitung, 1791–1817.* Nendeln/Liechtenstein: Kraus Reprint, 1977 (orig. Hamburg: L. Voss, 1891).

Butler, E. M. *The Tyranny of Greece over Germany.* Boston: Beacon, 1935, rpt. 1958.

Buttlar, Adrian von. *Der Landschaftsgarten: Gartenkunst des Klassizismus und der Romantik.* Cologne: Du Mont, 1989.

Carlson, Marvin. *Goethe and the Weimar Theater.* Ithaca, NY: Cornell UP, 1978.

Cocalis, Susan, and Kay Goodman, eds. *Beyond the Eternal Feminine: Critical Essays on Women and Literature.* Stuttgarter Arbeiten zur Germanistik, volume 98. Stuttgart: H. D. Heinz, 1982.

Cocalis, Susan, and Ferrel Rose, eds. *Thalia's Daughters: German Women Dramatists from the Eighteenth Century to the Present.* Tübingen: Francke, 1996.

Eagleton, Terry. *The Ideology of the Aesthetic.* Oxford: Oxford UP, 1990.

Eberle, Friedrich, and Theo Stammen, eds. *Die Französische Revolution in Deutschland.* Stuttgart: Reclam, 1989.

Elias, Norbert. *Die höfische Gesellschaft.* Neuwied and Berlin: Luchterhand, 1969.

Fallbacher, Karl-Heinz. "Fichtes Entlassung: Ein Beitrag zur Weimar-Jenaischen Institutionengeschichte." *Archiv für Kulturgeschichte* 67 (1985): 111–35.

Fetting, Friederike. *Ich fand in mir eine Welt: Eine sozial- und literaturgeschichtliche Untersuchung zur deutschen Romanschriftstellerin um 1800: Charlotte von Kalb, Caroline von Wolzogen, Sophie Mereau-Brentano, Johanna Schopenhauer.* Munich: Wilhelm Fink, 1992.

Gallas, Helga, and Magdalene Heuser, eds. *Untersuchungen zum Roman von Frauen um 1800.* Tübingen: Niemeyer, 1990.

Gille, Caroline, and Gerhard Schuster, eds. *Weimarer Klassik, 1759–1832. Wiederholte Spiegelungen: Ständige Ausstellung des Goethe-Nationalmuseums.* 2 vols. Munich: Hanser, 1999.

Glaser, Horst Albert, ed. *Zwischen Revolution und Restauration: Klassik, Romantik.* Vol. 5 of *Deutsche Literatur: Eine Sozialgeschichte.* Reinbek: Rowohlt, 1980.

Goodman, Katherine R., and Edith Waldstein, eds. *In the Shadow of Olympus: German Women Writers Around 1800.* Albany: State U of New York P, 1992.

Greiner, Martin. *Die Entstehung der modernen Unterhaltungsliteratur: Studien zum Trivialroman des 18. Jahrhunderts.* Hamburg: Rowohlt, 1964.

Grimm, Reinhold, and Jost Hermand. *Die Klassik-Legende.* Frankfurt am Main: Athenäum-Verlag, 1971.

Günther, Horst, ed. *Die Französische Revolution: Berichte und Deutungen deutscher Schriftsteller und Historiker.* Frankfurt am Main: Deutscher Klassiker Verlag, 1985.

Gutjahr, Ortrud, and Harro Segeberg. *Klassik und Anti-Klassik: Goethe und seine Epoche.* Würzburg: Königshaus und Neumann, 2001.

Harper, Anthony J., and Margaret C. Ives, eds. *Sappho in the Shadows: Essays on the Work of German Women Poets of the Age of Goethe.* Frankfurt am Main and New York: Peter Lang, 2000.

Hartung, Fritz. *Das Großherzogtum Sachsen unter der Regierung Carl Augusts 1775–1828.* Weimar: Böhlau, 1923.

Hecht, Christian. *Dichtergedächtnis und fürstliche Repräsentation: Der Westflügel des Weimarer Residenzschlosses: Architektur und Ausstattung.* Ostfildern-Ruit: Hatje Cantz, 2000.

Henke, Burkhard, Susanne Kord, and Simon Richter. *Unwrapping Goethe's Weimar: Essays in Cultural Studies and Local Knowledge*. Rochester, NY: Camden House, 2000.

Hess, Jonathan. *Reconstituting the Body Politic: Enlightenment, Public Culture and the Invention of Aesthetic Autonomy*. Detroit: Wayne State UP, 1999.

Heuser, Magdalene. "Spuren trauriger Selbstvergessenheit: Möglichkeiten eines weiblichen *Bildungsromans* um 1800: Friederike Helene Unger." In *Frauensprache—Frauenliteratur: Für und wider eine Psychoanalyse literarischer Werke. Kontroversen, alte und neue: Akten des VII. Internationalen Germanisten-Kongresses, Göttingen 1985*, ed. Inge Stephan and Carl Pietzcker, 30–42. Tübingen: Niemeyer, 1985.

Hoff, Dagmar von. *Dramen des Weiblichen: Deutsche Dramatikerinnen um 1800*. Opladen: Westdeutscher Verlag, 1989.

Hoffmeister, Gerhart, ed. *A Reassessment of Weimar Classicism*. Lewiston, Queenston, Lampeter: Edwin Mellen, 1996.

Honegger, Claudia. *Die Ordnung der Geschlechter: Die Wissenschaften vom Menschen und das Weib 1750–1850*. Munich: dtv, 1996.

Jacobs, Jürgen. *Wilhelm Meister und seine Brüder: Untersuchungen zum deutschen Bildungsroman*. Munich: Fink, 1972.

Jauß, Hans Robert. "Deutsche Klassik — Eine Pseudo-Epoche?" In *Epochenschwelle und Epochenbewußtsein* (= Poetik und Hermeneutik 11). Ed. Reinhart Herzog and Reinhart Koselleck, 581–85. Munich: Wilhelm Fink, 1987.

Kammler, Eva. *Zwischen Professionalisierung und Dilettantismus: Romane und ihre Autorinnen um 1800*. Opladen: Westdeutscher Verlag, 1992.

Kastinger Riley, Helene M. *Die weibliche Muse: Sechs Essays über künstlerisch schaffende Frauen der Goethezeit*. Columbia, SC: Camden House, 1986.

Kindermann, Heinz. *Theatergeschichte der Goethezeit*. Vienna: Bauer, 1948.

Klauß, Jochen. *Goethes Wohnhaus in Weimar: Ein Rundgang in Geschichten*. Weimar: Klassikerstätten zu Weimar, 1991.

Köhler, Astrid. *Salonkultur im klassischen Weimar: Geselligkeit als Lebensform und literarisches Konzept*. Stuttgart: M & P, 1996.

Kontje, Todd. *Private Lives in the Public Sphere: The German Bildungsroman as Metafiction*. University Park: Pennsylvania State UP, 1992.

———. *Women, the Novel, and the German Nation 1771–1871: Domestic Fiction in the Fatherland*. Cambridge: Cambridge UP, 1998.

Kord, Susanne. *Ein Blick hinter die Kulissen: Deutschsprachige Dramatikerinnen im 18. und 19. Jahrhundert*. Stuttgart: Metzler, 1992.

———. *Sich einen Namen machen: Anonymität und weibliche Autorschaft 1700–1900*. Stuttgart: Metzler, 1996.

Korff, Hermann August. *Geist der Goethezeit: Versuch einer ideellen Entwicklung der klassisch-romantischen Literaturgeschichte*. 5 vols. Leipzig: J. J. Weber, 1923–57.

Lange, Sigrid. *Ob die Weiber Menschen sind: Geschlechterdebatten um 1800.* Leipzig: Reclam, 1992.

———. *Spiegelgeschichten: Geschlechter und Poetiken in der Frauenliteratur um 1800.* Frankfurt am Main: Ulrike Helmer Verlag, 1995.

———. "Über epische und dramatische Dichtung Weimarer Autorinnen: Überlegungen zu Geschlechterspezifika in der Poetologie." *Zeitschrift für Germanistik* 1:2 (1991): 341–51.

Langen, August. "Attitüde und Tableau in der Goethezeit." In Langen, *Gesammelte Studien zur neueren deutschen Sprache und Literatur*, 292–353. Berlin: E. Schmidt, 1978.

Lukács, Georg. *Goethe and His Age.* London: Martin Press, 1968.

MacLeod, Catriona. *Embodying Ambiguity: Androgyny and Aesthetics from Winckelmann to Keller.* Detroit: Wayne State UP, 1998.

Martin, Laura. *Harmony in Discord: German Women Writers in the Eighteenth and Nineteenth Centuries.* Oxford: Peter Lang, 2001.

Meise, Helga. *Die Unschuld und die Schrift: Deutsche Frauenromane im 18. Jahrhundert.* Berlin: Guttandin & Hoppe, 1983.

Minden, Michael. *The German Bildungsroman: Incest and Inheritance.* Cambridge: Cambridge UP, 1997.

Müller-Harang, Ulrike. *Das Weimarer Theater zur Zeit Goethes.* Weimar: Verlag der Klassikerstätten, 1991.

Norton, Robert E. *The Beautiful Soul: Aesthetic Morality in the Eighteenth Century.* Ithaca, NY: Cornell UP, 1995.

Opitz, Claudia. "Der Bürger wird Soldat — und die Bürgerin . . .? Die Revolution, der Krieg und die Stellung der Frauen nach 1789." In *Sklavin oder Bürgerin? Französische Revolution und Neue Weiblichkeit 1760–1830*, ed. Viktoria Schmidt-Linsenhoff, 38–54. Frankfurt am Main: Jonas, 1989.

Patterson, Michael. *The First German Theatre: Schiller, Goethe, Kleist and Büchner in Performance.* New York, NY: Routledge, 1990.

Pfotenhauer, Helmut. *Um 1800: Konfigurationen der Literatur, der Kunstliteratur und Ästhetik.* Tübingen: Niemeyer, 1991.

Pfotenhauer, Helmut, Markus Bernauer, and Norbert Miller, eds. *Frühklassizismus: Position und Opposition: Winckelmann, Mengs, Heinse.* Bibliothek der Kunstliteratur, vol. 2. Frankfurt am Main: Deutscher Klassiker Verlag, 1995.

Pfotenhauer, Helmut, and Peter Sprengel, eds. *Klassik und Klassizismus.* Bibliothek der Kunstliteratur, vol. 3. Frankfurt am Main: Deutscher Klassiker Verlag, 1995.

Potts, Alex. *Flesh and the Ideal: Winckelmann and the Origins of Art History.* New Haven and London: Yale UP, 1994.

Purdy, Daniel. *The Tyranny of Elegance: Consumer Cosmopolitanism in the Era of Goethe.* Baltimore: Johns Hopkins UP, 1998.

Reed, T. J. *The Classical Center: Goethe and Weimar 1775–1832.* New York: Croom Helm and Barnes & Noble, 1980.

Rehm, Walther. *Griechentum und Goethezeit.* 3rd edition. Bern: A. Francke, 1952.

Richards, Robert J. *The Romantic Conception of Life: Science and Philosophy in the Age of Goethe.* Chicago: U of Chicago P, 2002.

Richter, Karl, and Jörg Schönert, eds. *Klassik und Moderne: Die Weimarer Klassik als historisches Ereignis und Herausforderung im kulturgeschichtlichen Prozeß.* Stuttgart: Metzler, 1983.

Richter, Simon. *Laocoon's Body and the Aesthetics of Pain: Winckelmann, Lessing, Herder, Moritz, Goethe.* Detroit: Wayne State UP, 1992.

———. "Priapean Fantasies: The Sexual Politics of Weimar Classicism." In *Sexualität und Imagination: Pathologien der Einbildungskraft im medizinischen Diskurs der frühen Neuzeit,* ed. Daniela Watzke, Stefanie Zaun, and Jörn Steigerwald, 193–207. Frankfurt am Main: Vittorio Klostermann, 2004.

Saine, Thomas P. *Black Bread — White Bread: German Intellectuals and the French Revolution.* Columbia, SC: Camden House, 1988.

———. *The Problem of Being Modern or The German Pursuit of Enlightenment from Leibniz to the French Revolution.* Detroit: Wayne State UP, 1997.

Schieth, Lydia. *Die Entwicklung des deutschen Frauenromans im ausgehenden 18. Jahrhundert: Ein Beitrag zur Gattungsgeschichte.* Frankfurt am Main: Peter Lang, 1987.

Schneider, Sabine M. *Die schwierige Sprache des Schönen: Moritz' und Schillers Semiotik der Sinnlichkeit.* Würzburg: Könighausen und Neumann, 1998.

Schulz, Gerhard. *Die deutsche Literatur zwischen Französischer Revolution und Restauration, Teil 1: Das Zeitalter der französischen Revolution 1789–1806.* Geschichte der deutschen Literatur von den Anfängen bis zur Gegenwart, vol. 7.1. Munich: Beck, 1983.

Schwarzbauer, Franz. *Die Xenien: Studien zur Vorgeschichte der Weimarer Klassik.* Stuttgart: Metzler, 1992.

Sharpe, Lesley, ed. *The Cambridge Companion to Goethe.* Cambridge: Cambridge UP, 2002.

Sheehan, James J. *German History, 1770–1866.* New York: Oxford UP, 1989.

Strich, Fritz. *Deutsche Klassik und Romantik, oder Vollendung und Unendlichkeit: Ein Vergleich.* Munich: Meyer & Jessen, 1924.

Swales, Martin. *The German Bildungsroman from Wieland to Hesse.* Princeton: Princeton UP, 1978.

Tebben, Karin, ed. *Beruf: Schriftstellerin: Schreibende Frauen im 18. und 19. Jahrhundert.* Göttingen: Vandenhoeck & Ruprecht, 1998.

Touaillon, Christine. *Der deutsche Frauenroman des 18. Jahrhunderts.* Bern: Peter Lang, 1979.

Träger, Claus, ed. *Die Französische Revolution im Spiegel der deutschen Literatur.* Leipzig: Reclam, 1975.

Ueding, Gerd. *Klassik und Romantik: Deutsche Literatur im Zeitalter der Französischen Revolution 1789–1815.* Hansers Sozialgeschichte der deutschen Literatur, vol. 4. Munich: Hanser, 1987.

Vahsen, Mechthilde. *Die Politisierung des weiblichen Subjekts: Deutsche Romanautorinnen und die Französische Revolution 1790–1820.* Berlin: E. Schmidt, 2000.

Vosskamp, Wilhelm, ed. *Klassik im Vergleich: Normativität und Historizität europäischer Klassiken. DFG-Symposion 1990.* Stuttgart: Metzler, 1993.

Wägenbaur, Birgit. *Die Pathologie der Liebe: Literarische Weiblichkeitsentwürfe um 1800.* Berlin: E. Schmidt, 1996.

Ward, Albert. *Book Production, Fiction, and the German Reading Public, 1740–1800.* Oxford: Clarendon, 1974.

Weissberg, Liliane. "Weimar and Jena: Goethe and the New Philosophy." In *Goethe und das Zeitalter der Romantik,* ed. Walter Hinderer, 163–74. Würzburg: Königshaus & Neumann, 2002.

Wellek, René. *A History of Modern Criticism.* Vol. 2: *The Romantic Age.* New Haven: Yale UP, 1955.

———. "The Concept of Romanticism in Literary History." In Wellek, *Concepts of Criticism,* 128–98. New Haven and London: Yale UP, 1963.

———. "The Term and Concept of Classicism in Literary History." In Wellek, *Discriminations: Further Concepts of Criticism,* 55–90. New Haven: Yale UP, 1970.

———. "Das Wort und der Begriff 'Klassizismus' in der Literaturgeschichte." *Schweizer Monatshefte* 45 (1969): 154–73.

Wilkinson, Elizabeth M., and L. A. Willoughby. "'Having and Being,' or Bourgeois versus Nobility." In *Models of Wholeness: Some Attitudes to Language, Art and Life in the Age of Goethe,* ed. Jeremy Adler, Martin Swales, and Ann Weaver, 227–32. Oxford: Peter Lang, 2002.

———. "Missing Links or Whatever Happened to Weimar Classicism?" In *'Erfahrung und Überlieferung': Festschrift for C. P. Magill,* ed. Hinrich Siefkin and Alan Robinson, 57–74. Cardiff: U of Wales P, 1974.

Williams, Simon. *German Actors of the Eighteenth and Nineteenth Centuries: Idealism, Romanticism, and Realism.* Westport, CT: Greenwood, 1985.

Wilson, W. Daniel. *Geheimräte gegen Geheimbünde: Ein unbekanntes Kapitel der klassisch-romantischen Geschichte Weimars.* Stuttgart: Metzler, 1991.

———. *Das Goethe-Tabu: Protest und Menschenrechte im klassischen Weimar.* Munich: Deutscher Taschenbuch Verlag, 1999.

Wittkowski, Wolfgang, ed. *Verlorene Klassik? Ein Symposium.* Tübingen: Niemeyer, 1986.

Woodmansee, Martha. *The Author, Art, and the Market: Rereading the History of Aesthetics.* New York: Columbia UP, 1994.

Ziolkowski, Theodore. *The Classical German Elegy, 1795–1950.* Princeton UP, 1980.

Authors and Works

Carl Ludwig Fernow

Knoche, Michael, and Harald Tausch, eds. *Von Rom nach Weimar — Carl Ludwig Fernow.* Tübingen: Niemeyer, 2000.

Tausch, Harald. *Entfernung der Antike: Carl Ludwig Fernow im Kontext der Kunsttheorie um 1800.* Tübingen: Niemeyer, 2000.

Johann Wolfgang von Goethe

Atkins, Stuart. "Goethe, Calderón, and *Faust: Der Tragödie zweiter Teil.*" In *Essays on Goethe*, ed. Jane K. Brown and Thomas P. Saine, 259–76. Columbia, SC: Camden House, 1995.

———. *Goethe's Faust: A Literary Analysis.* Cambridge, MA: Harvard UP, 1964.

———. "Observations on Goethe's *Torquato Tasso.*" In *Husbanding the Golden Grain: Studies in Honor of Henry W. Nordmeyer*, ed. Luanne T. Frank and Emery E. George, 5–23. Ann Arbor: Department of Germanic Languages and Literatures U of Michigan, 1973.

———. "On Goethe's Classicism." In *Goethe Proceedings: Essays commemorating the Goethe Sesquicentennial at the University of California, Davis*, ed. Clifford A. Bernd, Timothy J. Lulofs, H. Günther Nerjes, Fritz R. Sammern-Frankenegg, and Peter Schäffer, 1–21. Columbia, SC: Camden House, 1984.

Bahr, Ehrhard. *Die Ironie im Spätwerk Goethes '. . . Diese sehr ernsten Scherze . . .,' Studien zum Westöstlichen Divan, zu den Wanderjahren und zu Faust II.* Berlin: E. Schmidt, 1972.

———. *The Novel as Archive: The Genesis, Reception and Criticism of Goethe's "Wilhelm Meisters Wanderjahre."* Columbia, SC: Camden House, 1998.

———. "Revolutionary Realism in Goethe's *Wanderjahre.*" In *Goethe's Narrative Fiction: The Irvine Goethe Symposium*, ed. William G. Lillyman, 161–75. Berlin: de Gruyter, 1983.

Benjamin, Walter. "Goethes *Wahlverwandtschaften.*" In Benjamin, *Illuminationen: Ausgewählte Schriften*, volume 1, ed. Siegfried Unseld, 70–147. Frankfurt am Main: Suhrkamp, 1961.

Bennett, Benjamin. "Egmont and the Maelstrom of the Self." In Bennett, *Modern Drama and German Classicism: Renaissance from Lessing to Brecht*, 121–50. Ithaca: Cornell UP, 1979.

———. *Goethe as Woman: The Undoing of Literature.* Detroit: Wayne State UP, 2001.

Bennett, Benjamin, and Frank G. Ryder. "The Irony of Goethe's *Hermann und Dorothea:* Its Form and Function." *PMLA* 90 (1975): 433–46.

Blackall, Eric A. *Goethe and the Novel.* Ithaca: Cornell UP, 1976.

Blessin, Stefan. *Goethes Romane: Aufbruch in die Moderne.* Munich: Schöningh, 1996.

Borchmeyer, Dieter. "Goethes *Faust* musikalisch betrachtet." In *Eine Art Symbolik fürs Ohr: Johann Wolfgang Goethe. Lyrik und Musik*, ed. Hermann Jung, 87–100. Frankfurt am Main: Peter Lang, 2002.

Boyle, Nicholas. *Goethe: The Poet and the Age*. Vol. 1: *The Poetry of Desire (1749–1790)* and Vol. 2: *Revolution and Renunciation (1790–1803)*. Oxford & New York: Clarendon, 1991, 2000.

Bräunig-Oktavio, Hermann. *Vom Zwischenkieferknochen zur Idee des Typus: Goethe als Naturforscher in den Jahren 1780–1786*. Nova Acta Leopoldina: new series, vol. 18, no. 126. Leipzig: Johann Ambrosius Barth Verlag, 1956.

Brown, Jane K. "Der Drang zum Gesang: On Goethe's Dramatic Form." *Goethe Yearbook* 10 (2001): 115–24.

———. *Goethe's Cyclical Narratives: 'Die Unterhaltungen deutscher Ausgewanderten' and 'Wilhelm Meisters Wanderjahre.'* Chapel Hill: U of North Carolina P, 1975.

———. *Goethe's Faust: The German Tragedy*. Ithaca: Cornell UP, 1986.

———. "Schiller und die Ironie von *Hermann und Dorothea*." In Brown, *Ironie und Objektivität: Aufsätze zu Goethe*, 164–79. Würzburg: Königshausen & Neumann, 1999.

———. "Schiller und die Ironie von *Hermann und Dorothea*." In *Goethezeit: Studien zur Erkenntnis und Rezeption Goethes und seiner Zeitgenossen. Festschrift für Stuart Atkins*, 203–26. Bern: Francke, 1981.

———. "The Theatrical Mission of the *Lehrjahre*." In *Goethe's Narrative Fiction: The Irvine Goethe Symposium*, ed. William G. Lillyman, 69–84. Berlin: de Gruyter, 1983.

Damm, Sigrid. *Christiane und Goethe*. Frankfurt am Main: Insel, 1998.

Eckardt, Dieter, and Margarete Oppel. *Kostbarkeiten aus Goethes Kunstsammlung: Ausstellung der Nationalen Forschungs- und Gedenkstätten der klassischen deutschen Literatur in Weimar, DDR, Goethe-Nationalmuseum*. Duisburg: Niederrheinisches Museum der Stadt Duisburg, 1987.

Gray, Ronald. *Goethe the Alchemist*. Cambridge: Cambridge UP, 1952.

Herwig, Henriette. *Wilhelm Meisters Wanderjahre: Geschlechterdifferenz, Sozialer Wandel, Historische Anthropologie*. Tübingen: Francke, 2002.

Hunfeld, Barbara. "Das sprachliche All und der Kosmos der Sprache; zur Sternwartsszene in Goethes *Wanderjahre*." In *Über Grenzen: Limitation and Transgression in Literatur und Ästhetik*, ed. Claudia Benthien and Imela Marie Krüger-Fürhoff, 38–60. Stuttgart: Metzler, 1999.

Karnick, Manfred. *Wilhelm Meisters Wanderjahre oder die Kunst des Mittelbaren*. Munich: Fink, 1969.

Krippendorff, Ekkehart. *"Wie die Großen mit den Menschen spielen": Versuch über Goethes Politik*. Frankfurt am Main: Suhrkamp, 1988.

Mandelkow, Karl Robert. *Goethe in Deutschland: Rezeptionsgeschichte eines Klassikers*. 2 vols. Munich: Beck, 1980/89.

Molnár, Géza von. "Hidden in Plain View: Another Look at Goethe's *Faust*." *Goethe Yearbook* 11 (2002): 33–76.

Naumann, Barbara. *Philosophie und Poetik: Cassirer und Goethe.* Munich: Fink, 1998.

Øhrgaard, Per. "Roman, Bildung, Experiment: Anmerkungen zur Erzählweise in *Wilhelm Meisters Lehrjahren* (mit einem Zusatz über *die Wanderjahre*)." *Jahrbuch des Freien Deutschen Hochstifts* (2000): 27–49.

Osterkamp, Ernst. "'Aus dem Gesichtspunkt reiner Menschlichkeit.' Goethes Preisaufgaben für bildende Künstler 1799–1805." In *Goethe und die Kunst. Ausstellung Frankfurt 1994*, ed. Sabine Schulze, 310–22. Ostfildern and Stuttgart: Hatje, 1994.

———. *Im Buchstabenbilde: Studien zum Verfahren Goethescher Bildbeschreibungen.* Stuttgart: Metzler, 1991.

Pfotenhauer, Helmut. "Bild versus Geschichte. Zur Funktion des novellistischen Augenblicks in Goethes Romanen." In Pfotenhauer, *Sprachbilder: Untersuchungen zur Literatur seit dem achtzehnten Jahrhundert*, 45–66. Würzburg: Königshausen und Neumann, 2000.

Riedl, Wolfgang. "Eros und Ethos: Goethes *Römische Elegien* und *Das Tagebuch*." *Jahrbuch der deutschen Schillergesellschaft* 40 (1996): 147–80.

Saße, Günter. "'Der Abschied aus diesem Paradies': Die Überwindung der Sehnsucht durch die Kunst in der Lago Maggiore-Episode in Goethes *Wanderjahren*." *Jahrbuch der Deutschen Schiller Gesellschaft* 42 (1998): 95–119.

Schlaffer, Hannelore. *Wilhelm Meister: Das Ende der Kunst und die Wiederkehr des Mythos.* Stuttgart: Metzler, 1980.

Schuster, Gerhard, ed. *Der Sammler und die Seinigen: Handzeichnungen aus Goethes Besitz.* Munich: Hanser, 1999.

Spaethling, Robert. *Music and Mozart in the Life of Goethe.* Columbia, SC: Camden House, 1987.

Sprengel, Peter. "Die 'Urpflanze'. Zur Entwicklung von Goethes Morphologie in Italien." In *Ein unsäglich schönes Land: Goethes "Italienische Reise" und der Mythos Siziliens*, ed. Albert Meier, 122–37. Palermo: Sellerio, 1987.

Staiger, Emil. "Goethe und Mozart." In Staiger, *Musik und Dichtung.* Zurich: Atlantis Verlag, 1966, 45–66.

Steinecke, Hartmut. "The Novel and the Individual: The Significance of Goethe's *Wilhelm Meister* in the Debate about the Bildungsroman." In *Reflection and Action: Essays on the Bildungsroman*, ed. James Hardin, 69–96. Columbia, SC: U of South Carolina P, 1991.

Stephenson, R. H. "The Cultural Theory of Weimar Classicism in the Light of Coleridge's Doctrine of Aesthetic Knowledge." In *Goethe 2000: Intercultural Readings of his Work*, ed. Paul Bishop and R. H. Stephenson, 150–69. Leeds: Northern UP, 2000.

Stephenson, R. H. *Goethe's Conception of Knowledge and Science.* Edinburgh: Edinburgh UP, 1995.

———. "Goethe's Prose Style: Making Sense of Sense." *Publications of the English Goethe Society,* new series, 66 (1996): 33–41.

———. "'Man nimmt in der Welt jeden, wofür er sich gibt': The Presentation of Self in Goethe's *Die Wahlverwandtschaften.*" *German Life and Letters* 47 (1994): 400–407.

———. "Theorizing to Some Purpose: 'Deconstruction' in the Light of Goethe and Schiller's Aesthetics — the Case of *Die Wahlverwandtschaften.*" *Modern Language Review* 84 (1989): 381–92.

Stephenson, R. H., and Patricia Zecevic. "'Das Was bedenke . . .' On the Content, Structure, and Form of Goethe's *Wilhelm Meister.*" *London German Studies* 5 (1993): 79–94.

Stern, Lucie. "*Wilhelm Meisters Lehrjahre* und Jean Paul's *Titan.*" *Zeitschrift für Ästhetik und allgemeine Kulturwissenschaft* 16 (1992): 35–68.

Swales, Martin, and Erika Swales. *Reading Goethe: A Critical Introduction to the Literary Work.* New York: Camden House, 2002.

Tantillo, Astrida Orle. *Goethe's 'Elective Affinities' and the Critics.* Rochester, NY: Camden House, 2001.

———. *The Will to Create: Goethe's Philosophy of Science.* Pittsburgh: U of Pittsburgh P, 2002.

Thadden, Elisabeth von. *Erzählen als Naturverhältnis — 'Die Wahlverwandtschaften': Zum Problem der Darstellbarkeit von Natur und Gesellschaft seit Goethes Plan eines 'Roman' über das Weltall.'* Munich: Fink, 1993.

Tornius, Valerian. "Goethes Theaterleitung und die bildende Kunst." *Jahrbuch des freien deutschen Hochstifts* (1912): 192–211.

Trevelyan, Humphry. *Goethe and the Greeks.* Cambridge: Cambridge UP, 1941.

Wells, George A. *Goethe and the Development of Science 1750–1900.* Alphen aan den Rijn: Sijthoff & Nordhoff, 1978.

Wilson, W. Daniel. "'Humanitätssalbader': Goethe's Distaste for Jewish Emancipation, and Jewish Responses." In *Goethe in German-Jewish Culture,* eds. Klaus L. Berghahn and Jost Hermand, 146–64. Rochester, NY: Camden House, 2001.

———. "Hunger/Artist: Goethe's Revolutionary Agitators in *Götz, Satyros, Egmont,* and *Der Bürgergeneral.*" *Monatshefte* 86 (1994): 80–94.

Wilson, W. Daniel. "Tabuzonen um Goethe und seinen Herzog: Heutige Folgen nationalsozialistischer Absolutismuskonzeptionen." *Deutsche Vierteljahrsschrift für Literaturwissenschaft und Geistesgeschichte* 70 (1996): 394–442.

Zapperi, Roberto. *Das Inkognito: Goethes ganz andere Existenz in Rom.* Trans. Ingeborg Walter. Munich: Beck, 1999.

Zecevic, Patricia. *The Speaking Divine Woman: Lópa de Úbeda's 'La Picara Justina' and Goethe's Wilhelm Meister.* Oxford: Peter Lang, 2001.

Johann Gottfried Herder

Fasel, Christoph. *Herder und das klassische Weimar: Kultur und Gesellschaft 1789–1803.* New York: Peter Lang, 1988.

Schmidt, Eva. *Herder im geistlichen Amt: Untersuchungen/Quellen/ Dokumente.* Leipzig: Koehler & Amelang, 1956.

Friedrich Hölderlin

Hamlin, Cyrus. "The Philosophy of Poetic Form: Hölderlin's Theory of Poetry and the Classical German Elegy." In *The Solid Letter: Readings of Friedrich Hölderlin,* ed. Aris Fioretos, 291–320. Palo Alto: Stanford UP, 1999.

Sophie Mereau

Bürger, Christa. "'Die mittlere Sphäre.' Sophie Mereau — Schriftstellerin im klassischen Weimar." In *Deutsche Literatur von Frauen,* ed. Gisela Brinker-Gabler, 366–88. Munich: Beck, 1988.

Fleischmann, Uta. *Zwischen Aufbruch und Anpassung: Untersuchungen zu Werk und Leben der Sophie Mereau.* Frankfurt am Main: Peter Lang, 1989.

Gersdorff, Dagmar von. *Dich zu lieben kann ich nicht verlernen: Das Leben der Sophie Brentano-Mereau.* Frankfurt am Main: Insel, 1984.

Hammerstein, Katharina von. "Eine Erndte will ich haben . . .: Schreiben als Beruf(ung): Sophie Mereau-Brentano (1770–1806)." In *Beruf: Schriftstellerin: Schreibende Frauen im 18. und 19. Jahrhundert,* ed. Karin Tebben, 132–59. Göttingen: Vandenhoeck & Ruprecht, 1998.

Harper, Anthony J. "Sophie Mereau (1770–1806): Living to Love and Loving to Live." In *Sappho in the Shadows: Essays on the Work of German Women Poets of the Age of Goethe (1749–1832),* ed. Anthony J. Harper and Margaret C. Ives, 113–43. Frankfurt am Main and New York: Peter Lang, 2000.

Kontje, Todd. "Reassessing Sophie Mereau: The Case for Amanda und Eduard." *Colloquia Germanica: Internationale Zeitschrift für Germanistik* 24:4 (1991): 310–27.

Richter, Simon. "Sophie Mereau (1770–1806)." In *Women Writers in German-Speaking Countries: A Bio-Bibliographical Critical Sourcebook,* ed. Elke P. Frederiksen and Elizabeth G. Ametsbichler, 333–40. Westport, CT: Greenwood, 1998.

Vansant, Jacqueline. "Liebe und Patriarchat in der Romantik: Sophie Mereaus Briefroman *Amanda und Eduard.*" In *Der Widerspenstigen Zähmung: Studien zur bezwungenen Weiblichkeit in der Literatur vom Mittelalter bis zur Gegenwart,* ed. Sylvia Wallinger and Monika Jonas, 185–200. Innsbruck: Institut für Germanistik, Universität Innsbruck, 1986.

Weigel, Sigrid. "Sophie Mereau (1770–1806)." In *Frauen: Porträts aus zwei Jahrhunderten,* ed. Hans Jürgen Schultz, 20–32. Stuttgart: Kreuz Verlag, 1990.

Karl Philipp Moritz

Boulby, Mark. *Karl Philipp Moritz: At the Fringe of Genius.* Toronto: U of Toronto P, 1979.

Saine, Thomas P. *Die ästhetische Theodizee: Karl Philipp Moritz und die Philosophie des 18. Jahrhunderts.* Munich: Wilhelm Fink, 1971.

Jean Paul (Johann Paul Friedrich Richter)

Böckmann, Paul. "Die humoristische Darstellungsweise Jean Pauls." In *Festschrift für Eduard Berend,* ed. H. W. Seiffert and B. Zeller, 38–53. Weimar: Böhlau, 1959.

Sprengel, Peter. *Jean Paul im Urteil seiner Kritiker: Dokumente zur Wirkungsgeschichte Jean Pauls in Deutschland.* Munich: Beck, 1980.

Wölfel, Kurt. "Antiklassizismus und Empfindsamkeit: Der Romancier Jean Paul und die Weimarer Kunstdoktrin." In *Deutsche Literatur zur Zeit der Klassik,* ed. Karl Otto Conrady, 362–79. Stuttgart: Reclam, 1977.

Friedrich von Schiller

Borchmeyer, Dieter. "Altes Recht und Revolution: Schillers *Wilhelm Tell.*" In *Friedrich Schiller: Kunst, Humanität und Politik in der späten Aufklärung,* ed. Wolfgang Wittkowski, 69–113. Tübingen: Niemeyer, 1982.

Fink, Gonthier-Louis. "Schillers *Wilhelm Tell,* ein antijakobinisches republikanisches Schauspiel." *Aufklärung* 1 (1986): 57–81.

Graham, Ilse. *Schiller's Drama: Talent and Integrity.* New York: Barnes & Noble, 1974.

Jones, Michael T. "Schiller Trouble: The Tottering Legacy of German Aesthetic Humanism." *Goethe Yearbook* 10 (2001): 222–45.

Schings, Hans-Jürgen. *Die Brüder des Marquis Posa: Schiller und der Geheimbund der Illuminaten.* Tübingen: Niemeyer, 1996.

Schöne, Albrecht. *Schillers Schädel.* Munich: Beck, 2000.

Wittkowski, Wolfgang. "Trinitarische Humanität: Dichtung und Geschichte bei Schiller." In *Friedrich Schiller: Kunst, Humanität und Politik in der späten Aufklärung,* ed. Wittkowski, 164–77. Tübingen: Niemeyer, 1984.

Johanna Schopenhauer

Gilleir, Anke. *Johanna Schopenhauer und die Weimarer Klassik: Betrachtungen über die Selbstpositionierung weiblichen Schreibens.* Hildesheim: Olms, 2000.

Goodman, Katherine R. "Johanna Schopenhauer (1766–1838), or Pride and Resignation." *Amsterdamer Beiträge zur neueren Germanistik* 28 (1989): 187–210.

Charlotte von Stein

Bohm, Arnd. "Charlotte von Stein's *Dido, Ein Trauerspiel.*" *Colloquia Germanica* 22 (1989): 38–52.

Dietrick, Linda. "Woman's State: Charlotte von Stein's *Dido, Ein Trauerspiel* and the Aesthetics of Weimar Classicism." In *Verleiblichungen: Literatur-*

und kulturgeschichtliche Studien über Strategien, Formen und Funktionen der Verleiblichung in Texten von der Frühzeit bis zum Cyberspace, ed. Burkhardt Krause and Ulrich Scheck, 111–31. St. Ingbert: Röhrig Universitätsverlag, 1996.

Goodman, Katherine R. "The Sign Speaks: Charlotte von Stein's Matinees." In *In the Shadow of Olympus: German Women Writers Around 1800,* ed. Katherine R. Goodman and Edith Waldstein, 71–93. New York: State U of New York P, 1992.

Kord, Susanne. "Not in Goethe's Image: The Playwright Charlotte von Stein." In *Thalia's Daughters: German Women Dramatists From the Eighteenth Century to the Present,* ed. Susan L. Cocalis and Ferrel Rose, 53–75. Tübingen: Francke, 1996.

Friederike Helene Unger

Henn, Marianne and Britta Hufeisen. "Bekenntnisse einer schönen Seele aus weiblicher Sicht: Friederike Helene Ungers Roman." In *Frauen: MitSprechen, MitSchreiben: Beiträge zur literatur- und sprachwissenschaftlichen Frauenforschung,* ed. Marianne Henn and Britta Hufeisen, 48–68. Stuttgart: Heinz, 1997.

Zantop, Susanne. "Aus der Not eine Tugend . . .: Tugendgebot und Öffentlichkeit bei Friederike Helene Unger." In *Untersuchungen zum Roman von Frauen um 1800,* ed. Magdalene Heuser and Helga Gallas, 132–47. Tübingen: Niemeyer, 1990.

———. "The Beautiful Soul Writes Herself: Friederike Helene Unger and The Große Göthe." In *In the Shadow of Olympus: German Women Writers Around 1800,* ed. Katherine R. Goodman and Edith Waldstein, 29–51. New York: State U of New York P, 1992.

Caroline von Wolzogen

Boerner, Peter. "Nachwort." *Caroline von Wolzogen's 'Agnes von Lilien,'* ed. Peter Boerner, 391–410. Hildesheim: Georg Olms, 1988.

Contributors

BENJAMIN BENNETT, Kenan Professor of German at the University of Virginia, is the author of *Modern Drama and German Classicism: Renaissance from Lessing to Brecht; Goethe's Theory of Poetry: Faust and the Regeneration of Language; Theater As Problem: Modern Drama and Its Place in Literature; Beyond Theory: Eighteenth-Century German Literature and the Poetics of Irony;* and *Goethe as Woman: The Undoing of Literature.*

DIETER BORCHMEYER, professor of German and theater at the Ruprecht-Karls-Universität Heidelberg, is the author of numerous books including *Macht und Melancholie: Schillers Wallenstein; Goethe: Der Zeitbürger; Weimarer Klassik: Portrait einer Epoche;* and *Drama and the World of Richard Wagner.* He edited three volumes of the Frankfurt Goethe edition, as well as many other editions of Goethe, Schiller, Wagner, and Nietzsche. In 2004 he became president of the Bavarian Academy of the Arts.

JANE K. BROWN, professor of German at the University of Washington, is the author of *Goethe's Cyclical Narratives: The Unterhaltungen deutscher Ausgewanderten and Wilhelm Meisters Wanderjahre; Goethe's Faust: The German Tragedy; Goethe's Faust: Theater of the World;* and *Ironie und Objektivität: Aufsätze zu Goethe.* She co-edited *Interpreting Goethe's Faust Today* and *Stuart Atkins, Essays on Goethe.*

CHARLES GRAIR is associate professor of German at Texas Tech University. He is the author of several articles on Goethe and neo-Hellenism.

CYRUS HAMLIN, professor of German and Comparative Literature at Yale University, is the editor of the Norton critical edition of Goethe's *Faust*, consulting editor of *Approaches to Teaching Goethe's Faust*, general editor of the Suhrkamp edition of Goethe in English, and author of *Hermeneutics of Form: Romantic Poetics in Theory and Practice.*

GAIL HART, professor of German at the University of California, Irvine, is author of *Tragedy in Paradise: Family and Gender Politics in German Bourgeois Tragedy 1750–1850* and *Friedrich Schiller: Crime, Aesthetics, and the Poetics of Punishment.*

ELISABETH KRIMMER, assistant professor of German at the University of California, Davis, is author of *In the Company of Men: Cross-Dressed Women*

Around 1800 and *Hollywood Divas, Indie Queens, and TV Heroines: Contemporary Screen Images of Women, 1990–2003,* co-authored with Susanne Kord.

HELMUT PFOTENHAUER, professor of German at the Julius-Maximilians-Universität Würzburg, is the author of *Um 1800: Konfigurationen der Literatur; Kunstliteratur und Ästhetik; Kunstliteratur als Italienerfahrung;* and *Sprachbilder: Untersuchung zur Literatur seit dem 18. Jahrhundert.* He is the editor of the ongoing edition of Jean-Paul's collected works, and edited *Frühklassizismus: Positionen und Oppositionen. Winckelmann, Mengs, Heinse* and *Klassik und Klassizismus.*

SIMON J. RICHTER, associate professor of German at the University of Pennsylvania, is author of *Laocoon's Body and the Aesthetics of Pain: Winckelmann, Lessing, Herder, Goethe, Moritz* and *Fantasies of the Breast: Rivaling the Phallus in Eighteenth-Century German Literature and Culture* (forthcoming). He co-edited *Unwrapping Goethe's Weimar: Essays in Cultural Studies and Local Knowledge* and is the editor of the *Goethe Yearbook.*

THOMAS P. SAINE, professor of German at the University of California, Irvine, is the author of *Die ästhetische Theodizee: Karl Philipp Moritz und die Philosophie des 18. Jahrhunderts; Georg Forster; Black Bread—White Bread: German Intellectuals and the French Revolution;* and *The Problem of Being Modern, or The German Pursuit of Enlightenment from Leibniz to the French Revolution.* He co-edited *The Internalized Revolution: German Reactions to the French Revolution, 1789–1989; Interpreting Goethe's Faust Today;* and *Stuart Atkins, Essays on Goethe.* He was the founding editor of the *Goethe Yearbook.*

R. H. STEPHENSON, William Jacks Professor of German at the University of Glasgow, is the author of *Goethe's Conception of Knowledge and Science* and *Goethe's Wisdom Literature: A Study in Aesthetic Transmutation.* He co-edited *Friedrich Nietzsche and Weimar Classicism* (with Paul Bishop), *Goethe 2000: Intercultural Readings of His Work,* and the Yearbook, *Cultural Studies and the symbolic.*

ASTRIDA ORLE TANTILLO, associate professor of Germanic Studies and History at the University of Illinois at Chicago, is the author of *The Will to Create: Goethe's Philosophy of Nature* and *Goethe's Elective Affinities and the Critics.*

W. DANIEL WILSON, professor of German at the University of California, Berkeley, is the author of *Geheimräte gegen Geheimbünde: Ein unbekanntes Kapitel der klassisch-romantischen Geschichte Weimars; Unterirdische Gänge: Goethe, Freimaurerei und Politik; Das Goethe-Tabu: Protest und Menschenrechte im klassischen Weimar;* and *Goethes Weimar und die Französische Revolution: Dokumente der Krisenjahre.*

Index